The International Handbook of
School Effectiveness Research

The International Handbook of School Effectiveness Research

Charles Teddlie and David Reynolds

London and New York

First published 2000 by Falmer Press
11 New Fetter Lane, London EC4P 4EE

Simultaneously published in the USA and Canada
by Falmer Press
19 Union Square West, New York, NY 10003

Falmer Press is an imprint of the Taylor & Francis Group

© 2000 C. Teddlie and D. Reynolds

Typeset in Sabon by RefineCatch Limited, Bungay, Suffolk
Printed and bound in Great Britain by
TJ International Ltd, Padstow, Cornwall

Cover design by Caroline Archer

British Library Cataloguing in Publication Data
A catalogue record for this book is available from the British Library

Library of Congress Cataloging in Publication Data
A catalogue record for this book has been requested

ISBN 0–750–70607–4 (pbk)

Contents

Contents

List of Figures

List of Tables

Preface

School effectiveness research, and school effectiveness researchers, are now central to the educational discourse of many societies, a situation which represents a marked change to that of 10 or 20 years ago. Then, there was an overwhelming sense of pessimism as to the capacity of the educational system to improve the life chances and achievements of children, since their home background was regarded as limiting their potential, in a quite deterministic fashion. Now, the belief that effective schools can have positive effects and the practices associated with effective schooling are in existence within most countries' educational communities of practitioners, researchers and policymakers.

In spite of the centrality of the discipline, it has long been clear to us that there had been no attempt to compile the 'normal science' of the discipline and record its knowledge base in a form that enables easy access. Perhaps because of a lingering ethnocentrism in the research community, there was also a tendency for the school effectiveness community in different countries to miss the achievements and the perspectives of those in societies other than their own.

The result of this was that people wanting to access the effectiveness knowledge base found this difficult and probably ended up at a lower level of understanding than was good for them, or for the discipline. The result was also that national perspectives on the knowledge base predominated, rather than the international ones that predominate in most intellectual traditions.

It was to eliminate these 'downsides', and to gain the 'upside' of clear disciplinary foundations, that we decided to write this Handbook. It has taken us six years to complete and has involved the addition of many friends and colleagues to the writing task in areas where we have needed specialist help. We are particularly grateful also to the following colleagues for their helpful comments on our final draft:

Bert Creemers
Peter Daly
Peter Hill
David Hopkins
Peter Mortimore
Pam Sammons
Jaap Scheerens
Louise Stoll
Sam Stringfield

Sally Thomas
Tony Townsend
Peter Tymms

We are also very grateful to Avril Silk who has typed successive versions of the book with speed and accuracy.

The discipline is now moving so rapidly, however, that we suspect that this first edition of the Handbook will need to be followed by further editions to keep pace with the volume of material. If there is new material that colleagues in the field have produced, and/or if there is any existing material that we have missed in this edition of the Handbook, please let us know at the address/numbers below.

The sooner that the Handbook becomes the useful property of the discipline as a whole, the happier we will both be.

Charles Teddlie
David Reynolds

Professor Charles Teddlie
Department of ELRC
College of Education
111 Peabody Hall
Louisiana State University
Baton Rouge, LA 70803 4721
USA

Tel: (225) 388 6840
Fax: (225) 388 6918
E-mail: edtedd@unix1.sncc.lsu.edu

Professor David Reynolds
Department of Education
University of Newcastle upon Tyne
St Thomas Street
Newcastle upon Tyne
UK

Tel: +44 (191) 2226598
Fax: +44 (191) 2225092
E-mail: Avril.Silk@ncl.ac.uk

Acknowledgments

The authors would like to thank the following for their kind permission to reprint their work:

Table 1.1 Creemers, B. P. M. and Osinga, N. (eds) (1995) *ICSEI Country Reports*, Leeuwarden, Netherlands: ICSEI Secretariat.

Tables 3.2 and 3.3 Thomas, S., Sammons, P. and Mortimore, P. (1995a) 'Determining what adds value to student achievement', *Educational Leadership International*, **58**, 6, pp.19–22.

Table 3.4 Goldstein, H. and Sammons, P. (1995) *The Influence of Secondary and Junior Schools on Sixteen Year Examination Performance: A Cross-classified Multilevel Analysis*, London: ISEIC, Institution of Education.

Table 4.1 and 5.2 Teddlie, C. and Stringfield, S. (1993) *Schools Do Make a Difference: Lessons Learned from a 10-year Study of School Effects*, New York: Teachers College Press.

Tables 4.2 and 4.3 Levine, D. U. and Lezotte, L. W. (1990) *Unusually Effective Schools: A Review and Analysis of Research and Practice*, Madison, WI: National Center for Effective Schools Research and Development; Sammons, P., Hillman, J. and Mortimore, P. (1995b) *Key Characteristics of Effective Schools: A Review of School Effectiveness Research*, London: Office for Standards in Education and Institute of Education.

Figure 7.1 and Table 7.2 Hopkins, D. and Ainscow, M. (1993) 'Making sense of school improvement: An interim account of the IQEA Project', Paper presented to the ESRC Seminar Series on School Effectiveness and School Improvement, Sheffield.

Tables 8.1, 8.3 and 8.8 Scheerens, I., Vermeulen, C. J. and Pelgrum, W. J. (1989c) 'Generalisability of school and instructional effectiveness indicators across nations', in Creemers, B. P. M. and Scheerens, J. (eds) *Developments in School Effectiveness Research*, special issue of *International Journal of Educational Research*, **13**, 7, pp.789–99.

Table 8.2 Lockheed, M. E. and Komenan, A. (1989) 'Teaching quality and student achievement in Africa: The case of Nigeria and Swaziland, *Teaching and Teacher Education*, **5**, 2, pp.93–113.

Table 8.4 Fuller, B. (1987) 'School effects in the Third World', *Review of Educational Research*, 57, 3, pp.255–92.

Tables 8.5 and 8.6 Foxman, D. (1992) *Learning Mathematics and Science (The Second International Assessment of Educational Progress in England)*, Slough: National Foundation for Educational Research.

Table 9.1 Fitz-Gibbon, C. T. (1996) *Monitoring Education: Indicators, Quality and Effectiveness*, London, New York: Cassell.

Section 1

The Historical and Intellectual Foundations of School Effectiveness Research

1 An Introduction to School Effectiveness Research

David Reynolds and Charles Teddlie,
with Bert Creemers, Jaap Scheerens
and Tony Townsend

Introduction

School effectiveness research (SER) has emerged from virtual total obscurity to a now central position in the educational discourse that is taking place within many countries. From the position 30 years ago that 'schools make no difference' that was assumed to be the conclusions of the Coleman et al. (1966) and Jencks et al. (1971) studies, there is now a widespread assumption internationally that schools affect children's development, that there are observable regularities in the schools that 'add value' and that the task of educational policies is to improve all schools in general, and the more ineffective schools in particular, by transmission of this knowledge to educational practitioners.

Overall, there have been three major strands of school effectiveness research (SER):

- School Effects Research – studies of the scientific properties of school effects evolving from input–output studies to current research utilizing multilevel models;
- Effective Schools Research – research concerned with the processes of effective schooling, evolving from case studies of outlier schools through to contemporary studies merging qualitative and quantitative methods in the simultaneous study of classrooms and schools;
- School Improvement Research – examining the processes whereby schools can be changed utilizing increasingly sophisticated models that have gone beyond simple applications of school effectiveness knowledge to sophisticated 'multiple lever' models.

In this chapter, we aim to outline the historical development of these three areas of the field over the past 30 years, looking in detail at the developments in the United States where the field originated and then moving on to look at the United Kingdom, the Netherlands and Australia, where growth in SER began later but has been particularly rapid. We then attempt to conduct an analysis of how the various phases of development of the field cross nationally are linked with the changing perceptions of the educational system that have been clearly visible within advanced industrial societies over the various historic 'epochs' that have been in evidence over these last 30 years. We conclude by attempting to conduct an 'intellectual audit' of the existing school effectiveness knowledge base and its various strengths and weaknesses within various countries, as a prelude to outlining in Chapter 2 how we have structured our task of reviewing all the world's literature by topic areas across countries.

SER in The United States

Our review of the United States is based upon numerous summaries of the literature, many of which concentrated on research done during the first 20 years of school effectiveness research (1966–85). A partial list of reviews of the voluminous literature on school effects in the USA during this period would include the following: Anderson, 1982; Austin, 1989; Averch et al., 1971; Bidwell and Kasarda, 1980; Borger et al., 1985; Bossert, 1988; Bridge et al., 1979; Clark, D., et al., 1984; Cohen, M., 1982; Cuban, 1983; Dougherty, 1981; Geske and Teddlie, 1990; Glasman and Biniaminov, 1981; Good and Brophy, 1986; Good and Weinstein, 1986; Hanushek, 1986; Levine and Lezotte, 1990; Madaus et al., 1980; Purkey and Smith, 1983; Ralph and Fennessey, 1983; Rosenholtz, 1985; Rowan et al., 1983; Sirotnik, 1985; Stringfield and Herman, 1995, 1996; Sweeney, 1982; Teddlie and Stringfield, 1993.

Figure 1.1 presents a visual representation of four overlapping stages that SER has been through in the USA:

- Stage 1, from the mid-1960s and up until the early 1970s, involved the initial input–output paradigm, which focused upon the potential impact of school human and physical resources upon outcomes;
- Stage 2, from the early to the late 1970s, saw the beginning of what were commonly called the 'effective schools' studies, which added a wide range of school processes for study and additionally looked at a much wider range of school outcomes than the input–output studies in Stage 1;
- Stage 3, from the late 1970s through the mid-1980s, saw the focus of SER shift towards the attempted incorporation of the effective schools 'correlates' into schools through the generation of various school improvement programmes;
- Stage 4, from the late 1980s to the present day, has involved the introduction of context factors and of more sophisticated methodologies, which have had an enhancing effect upon the quality of all three strands of SER (school effects research, effective schools research, school improvement research).

We now proceed to analyse these four stages in detail.

Stage 1: The Original Input–Output Paradigm

Stage 1 was the period in which economically driven input–output studies predominated. These studies (designated as Type 1A studies in Figure 1.1) focused on inputs such as school resource variables (e.g. per pupil expenditure) and student background characteristics (variants of student socio-economic status or SES) to predict school outputs. In these studies, school outcomes were limited to student achievement on standardized tests. The results of these studies in the USA (Coleman et al., 1966; Jencks et al., 1972) indicated that differences in children's achievement were more strongly associated with societally determined family SES than with potentially malleable school-based resource variables.

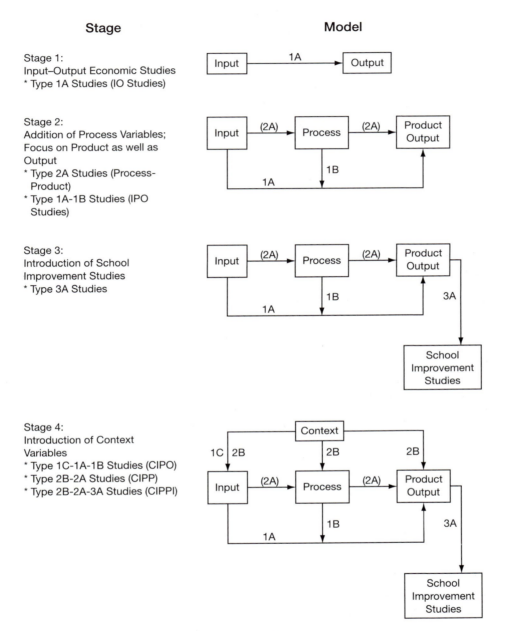

Stage	Model

Stage 1:
Input–Output Economic Studies
* Type 1A Studies (IO Studies)

Stage 2:
Addition of Process Variables;
Focus on Product as well as
Output
* Type 2A Studies (Process-
  Product)
* Type 1A-1B Studies (IPO
  Studies)

Stage 3:
Introduction of School
Improvement Studies
* Type 3A Studies

Stage 4:
Introduction of Context
Variables
* Type 1C-1A-1B Studies (CIPO)
* Type 2B-2A Studies (CIPP)
* Type 2B-2A-3A Studies (CIPPI)

Figure 1.1 Stages in the evolution of SER in the USA

The Coleman et al. (1966) study utilized regression analyses that mixed levels of data analysis (school, individual pupil) and concluded that 'schools bring little influence to bear on a child's achievement that is independent of his background and general social context' (p.325). Many of the Coleman school factors were related to school resources (e.g. per pupil expenditure, school facilities, number of books in the library), which were not very strongly related to student achievement. Nevertheless, 5–9 per cent of the total variance in individual student achievement was uniquely accounted for by school factors (Coleman et al., 1966). (See Chapter 3 for a more extensive description of the results from the Coleman Report). Daly noted:

> The Coleman et al. (1966) survey estimate of a figure of 9 per cent of variance in an achievement measure attributable to American schools has been something of a bench mark, despite the critical reaction.
>
> (Daly, 1995a, p.306)

While there were efforts to refute the Coleman results (e.g. Mayeske et al., 1972; McIntosh, 1968; Mosteller and Moynihan, 1972) and methodological flaws were found in the report, the major findings are now widely accepted by the educational research community. For example, the Mayeske et al. (1972) re-analysis indicated that 37 per cent of the variance was between schools, but they found that much of that variance was common to both student background variables and school variables. The issue of multicollinearity between school and family background variables has plagued much of the research on school effects, and is a topic we return to frequently later.

In addition to the Coleman and Jencks studies, there were several other studies conducted during this time within a sociological framework known as the 'status-attainment literature' (e.g. Hauser, 1971; Hauser et al., 1976). The Hauser studies, conducted in high schools in the USA, concluded that variance between schools was within the 15–30 per cent range and was due to mean SES differences, not to characteristics associated with effective schooling. Hauser, R., et al. (1976) estimated that schools accounted for only 1–2 per cent of the total variance in student achievement after the impact of the aggregate SES characteristics of student bodies was controlled for statistically.

As noted by many reviewers (e.g. Averch et al., 1971; Brookover et al., 1979; Miller, 1983), these early economic and sociological studies of school effects did not include adequate measures of school social psychological climate and other classroom/school process variables, and their exclusion contributed to the underestimation of the magnitude of school effects. Averch et al. (1971) reviewed many of these early studies and concluded that student SES background variables were the only factors consistently linked with student achievement. This conclusion of the Averch review was qualified, however, by the limitations of the extant literature that they noted, including: the fact that very few studies had actually measured processes (behavioural and attitudinal) within schools, that the operational definitions of those processes were very crude, and that standardized achievement was the only outcome measure (Miller, 1983).

Stage 2: The Introduction of Process Variables and Additional Outcome Variables into SER

The next stage of development in SER in the USA involved studies that were conducted to dispute the results of Coleman and Jencks. Some researchers studied schools that were doing exceptional jobs of educating students from very poor SES backgrounds and sought to describe the processes ongoing in those schools. These studies are designated as Type 2A links in Figure 1.1. In these Type 2A studies, traditional input variables are subsumed under process variables (e.g. available library resources become part of the processes associated with the library). These studies also expanded the definition of the outputs of schools to include other products, such as were measured by attitudinal and behavioural indicators.

The earlier studies in this period were focused in urban, low-SES, elementary schools because researchers believed that success stories in these environments would dispel the belief that schools made little or no difference. In a classic study from this period, Weber (1971) conducted extensive case studies of four low-SES inner-city schools characterized by high achievement at the third grade level. His research emphasized the importance of the actual processes ongoing at schools (e.g. strong leadership, high expectations, good atmosphere, and a careful evaluation of pupil progress), while the earlier studies by Coleman and Jencks had focused on only static, historical school resource characteristics.

Several methodological advances occurred in the USA literature during the decade of the 1970s, such as the inclusion of more sensitive measures of classroom input, the development of social psychological scales to measure school processes, and the utilization of more sensitive outcome measures. These advances were later incorporated in the more sophisticated SER of both the USA and of other countries in the 1990s.

The inclusion of more sensitive measures of classroom input in SER involved the association of student-level data with the specific teachers who taught the students. This methodological advance was important for two reasons: it emphasized input from the classroom (teacher) level, as well the school level; and it associated student-level output variables with student-level input variables, rather than school-level input variables.

The Bidwell and Kasarda (1980) review of school effects concluded that some positive evidence was accumulating in studies that measured 'school attributes at a level of aggregation close to the places where the work of schooling occurs' (p.403). Their review highlighted the work of Murnane (1975) and Summers and Wolfe (1977), both of which had painstakingly put together datasets in which the inputs of specific teachers were associated with the particular students that they had taught. (The Bidwell and Kasarda review also concluded that studies including information on curricular track (e.g. Alexander, K., and McDill, 1976; Alexander, K., et al., 1978; Heyns, 1974) were providing valuable information on the potential impact of schooling on achievement.)

The research of Summers and Wolfe (1977), Murnane (1975), and others (e.g. Armor et al., 1976; Winkler, 1975) demonstrated that certain characteristics of classroom teachers were significantly related to the achievement of their students. The Summers and Wolfe (1977) study utilized student-level school inputs, including characteristics of the specific teachers who taught each student. The researchers were able to explain around 25 per cent of the student level variance in gain scores using a mixture of teacher and school level inputs. Summers and Wolfe did not report the cumulative effect for school factors as opposed to SES factors, but the quality of college the teachers attended was a significant predictor of students' learning rate (as it was in Winkler, 1975).

Murnane's (1975) research indicated that information on classroom and school assignments increased the amount of predicted variance in student achievement by 15 per cent in regression models in which student background and prior achievement had been entered first. Principals' evaluations of teachers was also a significant predictor in this study (as it was in Armor et al., 1976) (see Chapter 3 for more details regarding both the Summers and Wolfe and the Murnane studies).

Later reviews by Hanushek (1981, 1986) indicated that teacher variables that are tied to school expenditures (e.g. teacher–student ratio, teacher education, teacher experience, teacher salary) demonstrated no consistent effect on student achievement. Thus, the Coleman Report and re-analyses (using school financial and physical resources as inputs) and the Hanushek reviews (assessing teacher variables associated with expenditures) produced no positive relationships with student achievement.

On the other hand, qualities associated with human resources (e.g. student sense of control of their environment, principals' evaluations of teachers, quality of teachers' education, teachers' high expectations for students) demonstrated significantly positive relationships to achievement in studies conducted during this period (e.g. Murnane, 1975; Link and Ratledge, 1979; Summers and Wolfe, 1977; Winkler, 1975). Other studies conducted in the USA during this period indicated the importance of peer groups on student achievement above and beyond the students' own SES background (e.g. Brookover et al., 1979; Hanushek, 1972; Henderson et al., 1978; Summers and Wolfe, 1977; Winkler, 1975).

These results led Murnane (1981) to conclude that:

> The primary resources that are consistently related to student achievement are teachers and other students. Other resources affect student achievement primarily through their impact on the attitudes and behaviours of teachers and students.
>
> (Murnane, 1981, p.33)

The measures of teacher behaviours and attitudes utilized in school effects studies have evolved considerably from the archived data that Summers and Wolfe (1977) and Murnane (1975) used. Current measures of teacher inputs include direct observations of effective classroom teaching behaviours which were identified through the teacher effectiveness literature (e.g. Brophy and Good, 1986; Gage and Needels, 1989; Rosenshine, 1983).

Another methodological advance from the 1970s concerned the development of social psychological scales that could better measure the educational processes ongoing at the school and class levels. These scales are more direct measures of student, teacher, and principal attitudes toward schooling than the archived data used in the Murnane (1975) and Summers and Wolfe (1977) studies.

As noted above, a major criticism of the early school effects literature was that school/classroom processes were not adequately measured, and that this contributed to school level variance being attributed to family background variables rather than educational processes. Brookover et al. (1978, 1979) addressed this criticism by using surveys designed to measure student, teacher, and principal perceptions of school climate in their study of 68 elementary schools in Michigan. Their work built upon previous attempts to measure school climate by researchers such as McDill, Rigsby, and their colleagues, who had earlier demonstrated significant relationships between climate and achievement (e.g. McDill et al., 1967, 1969; McDill and Rigsby, 1973).

These school climate measures included items from four general sources (Brookover et al., 1979; Brookover and Schneider, 1975; Miller, 1983):

1   student sense of academic futility, which had evolved from the Coleman et al. (1966) variable measuring student sense of control and the internal/external locus of control concept of Rotter (1966);
2   academic self concept, which had evolved in a series of studies conducted by Brookover and his colleagues from the more general concept of self esteem (Coopersmith, 1967; Rosenberg, 1965);
3   teacher expectations, which had evolved from the concept of the self fulfilling prophecy in the classroom (Cooper and Good, 1982; Rosenthal and Jacobsen, 1968), which had in turn evolved from Rosenthal's work on experimenter bias effects (Rosenthal, 1968, 1976; Rosenthal and Fode, 1963);
4   academic or school climate, which had roots going back to the work of McDill and Rigsby (1973) on concepts such as academic emulation and academically oriented status systems and the extensive work on organizational climate (e.g. Halpin and Croft, 1963; Dreeban, 1973; Hoy et al., 1991).

Brookover and his colleagues developed 14 social psychological climate scales based on several years of work with these different sources. The Brookover et al. (1978, 1979) study investigated the relationship among these school level climate variables, school level measures of student SES, school racial composition, and mean school achievement. Their study also clearly exemplified the thorny problems of multicollinearity among school climate and family background variables:

1   when SES and per cent white were entered into the regression model first, school climate variables accounted for only 4.1 per cent of the school level variance in achievement (the increment from 78.5 per cent to 82.6 per cent of the between schools variance);
2   when school climate variables were entered into the regression model first, SES and per cent white accounted for only 10.2 per cent of the school level variance in achievement (the increment from 72.5 per cent to 82.7 per cent of the between schools variance);
3   in the model with school climate variables entered first, student sense of academic futility (the adaptation of the Coleman Report variable measuring student sense of control) explained about half of the variance in school level reading and mathematics achievement.

Another methodological advance from the 1970s concerned the utilization of more sensitive outcome measures (i.e. outcomes more directly linked to the courses or curriculum taught at the schools under study). Two studies conducted by a group of US,

English, and Irish researchers (Brimer et al., 1978; Madaus et al., 1979) demonstrated that the choice of test can have a dramatic effect on results concerning the extent to which school characteristics affect student achievement. These two studies utilized data from England (Brimer et al., 1978) and Ireland (Madaus et al., 1979), where public examinations are geared to separate curricula. As the authors noted, such examinations do not exist at a national level in the USA, as they do throughout Europe, and there is also no uniform national curriculum in the USA.

In the Madaus study, between class variance in student level performance on curriculum specific tests (e.g. history, geography) was estimated at 40 per cent (averaged across a variety of tests). Madaus and his colleagues further reported that classroom factors explained a considerably larger proportion of the unique variance (variance attributable solely to classroom factors) on the curriculum specific tests (an average of 17 per cent) than on standardized measures (an average of 5 per cent).

Madaus et al. (1979) and others (e.g. Carver, 1975) believed that the characteristics of standardized tests make them less sensitive than curriculum specific tests to the detection of differences due to the quality of schools. These standardized tests 'cover material that the school teaches more incidentally' (Coleman et al., 1966, p.294). Madaus and his colleagues believed that 'Conclusions about the direct instructional effects of schools should not have to rely on evidence relating to skills taught incidentally' (Madaus, 1979, p.209).

Stage 3: The Equity Emphasis and the Emergence of School Improvement Studies

The foremost proponent of the equity ideal during Stage 3 of SER in the USA (the late 1970s through to the mid-1980s) was Ron Edmonds, who took the results of his own research (Edmonds, 1978, 1979a, 1979b) and that of others (e.g. Lezotte and Bancroft, 1985; Weber, 1971) to make a powerful case for the creation of 'effective schools for the urban poor'. Edmonds and his colleagues were no longer interested in just *describing* effective schools: they also wished to *create* effective schools, especially for the urban poor.

The five factor model generated through the effective schools research included the following factors: strong instructional leadership from the principal, a pervasive and broadly understood instructional focus, a safe and orderly school learning environment or 'climate', high expectations for achievement from all students, and the use of student achievement test data for evaluating programme and school success.

It was at this point that the first school improvement studies (designated as Type 3A designs in Figure 1.1) began to emerge. These studies in many respects eclipsed the study of school effectiveness in the USA for several years. These early studies (e.g. Clark, T. and McCarthy, 1983; McCormack-Larkin, 1985; McCormack-Larkin and Kritek, 1982; Taylor, B., 1990) were based for the most part on models that utilized the effective schools 'correlates' generated from the studies described above. (This early work and later increasingly more sophisticated school improvement studies are summarized in Chapter 7.)

This equity orientation, with its emphasis on school improvement and its sampling biases, led to predictable responses from the educational research community in the early to mid-1980s. The hailstorm of criticism (e.g. Cuban, 1983, 1984; Firestone and

Herriot, 1982a; Good and Brophy, 1986; Purkey and Smith, 1983; Rowan, 1984; Rowan et al., 1983; Ralph and Fennessey, 1983) aimed at the reform orientation of those pursuing the equity ideal in SER had the effect of paving the way for the more sophisticated studies of SER which used more defensible sampling and analysis strategies.

School context factors were, in general, ignored during the 'effective schools' research era in the USA, partially due to the equity orientation of the researchers and school improvers like Edmonds. This orientation generated samples of schools that *only* came from low SES areas, not from across SES contexts, a bias that attracted much of the considerable volume of criticism that swirled around SER in the mid to late 1980s. As Wimpelberg et al. note:

> Context was elevated as a critical issue because the conclusions about the nature, behaviour, and internal characteristics of the effective (urban elementary) schools either did not fit the intuitive understanding that people had about other schools or were not replicated in the findings of research on secondary and higher SES schools.
>
> (Wimpelberg et al., 1989, p.85)

Stage 4: The Introduction of Context Factors and Other Methodological Advances: Towards Normal Science

A new, more methodologically sophisticated era of SER began with the first context studies (Hallinger and Murphy, 1986; Teddlie et al., 1985, 1990) which explored the factors that were producing greater effectiveness in middle-class schools, suburban schools and secondary schools. These studies explicitly explored the differences in school effects that occur across different school contexts, instead of focusing upon one particular context. There was also a values shift from the equity ideal to the efficiency ideal that accompanied these new context studies. Wimpelberg et al. noted that:

> the value base of efficiency is a simple but important by-product of the research designs used in . . . (this) phase of the effective school research tradition.
>
> (Wimpelberg et al., 1989, p.88)

This new value base was inclusive, since it involved the study of schools serving all types of students in all types of contexts and emphasized school improvement across all of those contexts. When researchers were interested solely in determining what produces effective schools for the urban poor, their value orientation was that of equity: how can we produce better schools for the disadvantaged? When researchers began studying schools in a variety of contexts, their value orientation shifted to efficiency: how can we produce better schools for any and all students?

With regard to Figure 1.1, the introduction of context variables occurred in Stage 4 of the evolution of SER in the USA. The inclusion of context had an effect on the types of research designs being utilized in all three of the major strands of SER:

1   Within the input–output strand of SER, the introduction of context variables led to another linkage (1C) in the causal loop (1C-1A-1B-output) depicted in

Figure 1.1. Studies in this tradition may treat context variables as covariates and add them to the expanding mathematical equations that characterize their analyses (Creemers and Scheerens, 1994; Scheerens, 1992).

2   Within the process–product strand of SER, the introduction of context variables led to the 2B links depicted in Figure 1.1 and generated Type 2B-2A studies. These studies are often described in the literature as contextually sensitive studies of school effectiveness processes. This type of research design typically utilizes the case study approach to examine the processes ongoing in schools that vary both by effectiveness status and at least one context variable (e.g. Teddlie and Stringfield, 1993).

3   Within the school improvement strand of SER, the introduction of context variables led to the more sophisticated types of studies described as Type 2B-2A-3A in Figure 1.1. These studies allow for multiple approaches to school change, depending on the particular context of the school (e.g. Chrispeels, 1992; Stoll and Fink, 1992).

Other methodological advances have occurred in the past decade in the USA, leading to more sophisticated research across all three strands of SER. The foremost methodological advance in SER in the USA (and internationally) during this period was the development of multilevel mathematical models to more accurately assess the effects of all the units of analysis associated with schooling. Scholars from the USA (e.g. Alexander, K., et al., 1981; Burstein, 1980a, 1980b; Burstein and Knapp, 1975; Cronbach et al., 1976; Hannan et al., 1976; Knapp, 1977; Lau, 1979) were among the first to identify the levels of aggregation issue as an issue for educational research.

One of the first multilevel modelling computer programs was also developed in the USA (Bryk et al., 1986a, 1986b) at about the same time as similar programs were under development in the UK (e.g. Longford, 1986). Researchers from the USA continued throughout this time period to contribute to the further refinement of multilevel modelling (e.g. Bryk and Raudenbush, 1988, 1992; Lee, V., and Bryk, 1989; Raudenbush, 1986, 1989; Raudenbush and Bryk, 1986, 1987b, 1988; Raudenbush and Willms, 1991; Willms and Raudenbush, 1989). Results from this research are highlighted in Chapter 3 in the section on the estimation of the magnitude of school effects and this entire area of research is reviewed in Chapter 6 of this handbook.

Other advances have occurred during the past decade in the USA in the methodological areas addressed earlier under the description of Stage 2. For instance, several studies conducted over the past decade have related behavioural indices of teaching effectiveness (e.g. classroom management, teacher instructional style, student time on task) to school effectiveness (e.g. Crone and Teddlie, 1995; Stringfield et al., 1985; Teddlie et al., 1989a; Teddlie and Stringfield, 1993; Virgilio et al., 1991). These studies have demonstrated that more effective teaching occurs at effective as opposed to ineffective schools, using statistical techniques such as multivariate analysis of variance.

Researchers have also continued to develop survey items, often including social psychological indices, in an attempt to better measure the educational processes ongoing at the school and classroom levels. For example, Rosenholtz (1988, 1989) developed scales assessing seven different dimensions of the social organization of schools specifically orientated for use by teachers. Pallas (1988) developed three scales from the Administrator Teacher Survey of schools in the *High School and Beyond* study (Principal leadership, teacher control, and staff cooperation), and these scales have been used in recent studies of organizational effectiveness (e.g. Rowan, Raudenbush, and Kang, 1991).

In a similar vein, Teddlie and his colleagues (e.g. Teddlie et al., 1984; Teddlie and Stringfield, 1993) conducted a large scale study similar to that of Brookover et al. (1979) in 76 elementary schools during the second phase of the Louisiana School Effectiveness Study (LSES-II). These researchers utilized the Brookover school climate scales, analysed the data at the school level, and found results similar to those reported by Brookover and his colleagues. The researchers utilized second order factor analysis in an effort to deal with the problems of multicollinearity among the school climate and family background variables.

The need for more sensitive output measures in SER is still very much a problem today. Fitz-Gibbon (1991b) and Willms (1985a) have commented on the inadequate measures of school achievement used in many contemporary school effects studies. For instance, the often used *High School and Beyond* database contains a short test (only 20 items) that is supposed to measure growth in science.

The Current State of SER in the USA

Since the mid-1980s there has been much less activity in school effectiveness research in the US. In their meta-analysis of multilevel studies of school effects that had been conducted in the late 1980s and 1990s, Bosker and Witziers (1996) noted how few studies they were able to identify from the USA compared to those from the UK and the Netherlands.

There are a number of reasons for this decline in the production of school effectiveness research in the USA:

1   the scathing criticisms of effective schools research, which led many educational researchers to steer away from the more general field of school effectiveness research and fewer students to choose the area for dissertation studies after the mid-1980s (e.g. Cuban, 1993);
2   several of the researchers who had been interested in studying school effects moved towards the more applied areas of effective schools research and school improvement research (e.g. Brookover et al., 1984);
3   other researchers interested in the field moved away from it in the direction of new topics such as school restructuring and school indicator systems;
4   in the mid-1980s, there was an analytical muddle, with researchers aware of the units of analysis issue, yet not having commercially available multilevel programmes, and this situation discouraged some researchers;
5   tests of the economic input–output models failed to find significant relationships among financially driven inputs and student achievement (e.g. Geske and Teddlie, 1990; Hanushek, 1981, 1986), and research in that area subsided;
6   federal funding for educational research plummeted during Reagan/Bush (1980–92) administrations (Good, 1989), and departments of education became more involved in monitoring accountability, rather than in basic research;

7   communication amongst the SER research community broke down, with the more 'scientifically' oriented researchers becoming increasingly involved with the statistical issues associated with multilevel modelling, rather than with the educational ramifications of their research.

SER in the United Kingdom

School effectiveness research in the United Kingdom also had a somewhat difficult intellectual infancy. The hegemony of traditional British educational research, which was orientated to psychological perspectives and an emphasis upon individuals and families as determinants of educational outcomes, created a professional educational research climate somewhat unfriendly to school effectiveness research, as shown by the initially very hostile British reactions to the classic Rutter et al. (1979) study *Fifteen Thousand Hours* (e.g. Goldstein, 1980). Other factors that hindered early development were:

1   The problems of gaining access to schools for research purposes, in a situation where the educational system was customarily used to considerable autonomy from direct state control, and in a situation where individual schools had considerable autonomy from their local educational authorities (or districts), and where individual teachers had considerable autonomy within schools.
2   The absence of reliable and valid measures of school institutional climate (a marked contrast to the situation in the United States for example).
3   The arrested development of British sociology of education's understanding of the school as a determinant of adolescent careers, where pioneering work by Hargreaves (1967) and Lacey (1970), was de-emphasized by the arrival of Marxist perspectives that stressed the need to work on the relationship between school and society (e.g. Bowles and Gintis, 1976).

Early work in this field came mostly from a medical and medico-social environment, with Power (1967) and Power et al. (1972) showing differences in delinquency rates between schools and Gath (1977) showing differences in child guidance referral rates. Early work by Reynolds and associates (1976a, 1976b, 1982) into the characteristics of the learning environments of apparently differentially effective secondary schools, using group based cross sectional data on intakes and outcomes, was followed by work by Rutter et al. (1979) on differences between schools measured on the outcomes of academic achievement, delinquency, attendance and levels of behavioural problems, utilizing this time a cohort design that involved the matching of individual pupil data at intake to school and at age 16.

Subsequent work in the 1980s included:

1   'Value-added' comparisons of educational authorities on their academic outcomes (Department of Education and Science, 1983, 1984; Gray and Jesson, 1987; Gray et al., 1984; Woodhouse, G., and Goldstein, 1988; Willms, 1987).
2   Comparisons of 'selective' school systems with comprehensive or 'all ability' systems (Gray et al., 1983; Reynolds et al., 1987; Steedman, 1980, 1983).
3   Work into the scientific properties of school effects, such as size (Gray, 1981,

1982; Gray et al., 1986), the differential effectiveness of different academic sub units or departments (Fitz-Gibbon, 1985; Fitz-Gibbon et al., 1989; Willms and Cuttance, 1985c), contextual or 'balance' effects (Willms, 1985b, 1986, 1987) and the differential effectiveness of schools upon pupils of different characteristics (Aitkin and Longford, 1986; Nuttall et al., 1989).

4   Small scale studies that focused upon usually one outcome and attempted to relate this to various within-school processes. This was particularly interesting in the cases of disruptive behaviour (Galloway, 1983) and disciplinary problems (Maxwell, 1987; McLean, 1987; McManus, 1987).

Towards the end of the 1980s, two landmark studies appeared, concerning school effectiveness in primary schools (Mortimore et al., 1988) and in secondary schools (Smith and Tomlinson, 1989). The Mortimore study was notable for the wide range of outcomes on which schools were assessed (including mathematics, reading, writing, attendance, behaviour and attitudes to school), for the collection of a wide range of data upon school processes and, for the first time in British school effectiveness research, for a focus upon classroom processes.

The Smith and Tomlinson (1989) study is notable for the large differences shown in academic effectiveness between schools, with for certain groups of pupils the variation in examination results between similar individuals in different schools amounting to up to a quarter of the total variation in examination results. The study is also notable for the substantial variation that it reported on results in different school subjects, reflecting the influence of different school departments – out of 18 schools, the school that was positioned 'first' on mathematics attainment, for example, was 'fifteenth' in English achievement (after allowance had been made for intake quality). A third study by Tizard et al. (1988) also extended the research methodology into the infant school sector.

Ongoing work in the United Kingdom remains partially situated within the same intellectual traditions and at the same intellectual cutting edges as in the 1980s, notably in the areas of:

1   Stability over time of school effects (Goldstein et al., 1993; Gray et al., 1995; Thomas et al., 1997).

2   Consistency of school effects on different outcomes – for example, in terms of different subjects or different outcome domains such as cognitive/ affective (Goldstein et al., 1993; Sammons et al., 1993b; Thomas et al., 1994).

3   Differential effects of schools for different groups of students, for example, of different ethnic or socio-economic backgrounds or with different levels of prior attainment (Goldstein et al., 1993; Jesson and Gray, 1991; Sammons et al., 1993b).

4   The relative continuity of the effect of school sectors over time (Goldstein, 1995a; Sammons et al., 1995a).

5   The existence or size of school effects (Daly, 1991; Gray et al., 1990; Thomas, Sammons and Mortimore, 1997), where there are strong suggestions that the size of primary school effects may be greater than those of secondary schools (Sammons et al., 1993b, 1995a).

6   Departmental differences in educational effectiveness (Fitz-Gibbon, 1991b, 1992), researched from the ALIS (A Level Information System) method of performance

monitoring, which involves rapid feedback of pupil level data to schools. Fitz-Gibbon and her colleagues have added systems to include public examinations at age 16, a scheme known as YELLIS (Year 11 Information System), in operation since 1993, a baseline test for secondary schools (MidYIS, Middle Years Information System), and PIPS (Performance Indicators in Primary School) developed by Tymms. These systems now involve the largest datasets in school effectiveness research in the UK, with a third of UK A level results, one in four secondary schools in YELLIS and over four thousand primary schools receiving feedback each year.

Additional recent foci of interest have included:

1   Work at the school effectiveness/special educational needs interface, studying how schools vary in their definitions, labelling practices and teacher–pupil interactions with such children (Brown, S. et al., 1996).
2   Work on the potential 'context specificity' of effective schools' characteristics internationally, as in the International School Effectiveness Research Project (ISERP), a nine nation study that involved schools in the United Kingdom, the United States, the Netherlands, Canada, Taiwan, Hong Kong, Norway, Australia and the Republic of Ireland. The study involved samples of originally 7-year-old children as they passed through their primary schools within areas of different socioeconomic status, and was aimed at generating an understanding of those factors associated with effectiveness at school and class levels, with variation in these factors being utilized to generate more sensitive theoretical explanations concerning the relationship between educational processes and pupil outcomes (Reynolds et al., 1994a, 1995; Creemers et al., 1996). Useful reviews of cross national studies have also been done (Reynolds and Farrell, 1996) and indeed the entire issue of international country effects has been a particularly live one in the United Kingdom currently (see Alexander, R., 1996b for an interesting critique of the area).
3   The 'site' of ineffective schools, the exploration of their characteristics and the policy implications that flow from this (Barber, 1995; Reynolds, 1996; Stoll and Myers, 1997).
4   The possibility of routinely assessing the 'value-added' of schools using already available data (Fitz-Gibbon and Tymms, 1996), rather than by utilization of specially collected data.
5   The characteristics of 'improving' schools and those factors that are associated with successful change over time, especially important at the policy level since existing school effectiveness research gives only the characteristics of schools that have *become* effective (this work was undertaken by Gray et al. (1999)).
6   The description of the characteristics of effective departments (Harris, A. et al., 1995; Sammons et al., 1997).
7   The application of school effectiveness techniques to sectors of education where the absence of intake and outcome measures has made research difficult, as in the interesting foray into the early years of schooling of Tymms et al. (1997), in which the effects of being in the reception year prior to compulsory schooling were dramatic (an effect amounting to two standard deviations) and where the school

effects on pupils in this year were also very large (approximately 40 per cent of variation accounted for). The Department for Education and Employment funded project into pre-school provision at the Institute of Education, London, should also be noted as promising.

Further reviews of the British literature are available in Gray and Wilcox (1995), Mortimore (1991a, 1991b, 1998), Reynolds et al. (1994c), Reynolds and Cuttance (1992), Reynolds, Creemers and Peters (1989), Rutter (1983a, 1983b), Sammons et al. (1995b), and Sammons (1999).

It is also important to note the considerable volume of debate and criticism about school effectiveness now in existence in the United Kingdom (White and Barber, 1997; Slee et al., 1998; Elliott, 1996; Hamilton, 1996; Pring, 1995; Brown, S., et al., 1995) concerning its reputedly conservative values stance, its supposed managerialism, its appropriation by government and its creation of a societal view that educational failure is solely the result of poor schooling, rather than the inevitable result of the effects of social and economic structures upon schools and upon children. Given the centrality of school effectiveness research in the policy context of the United Kingdom, more of such material can be expected.

SER in the Netherlands

Although educational research has been a well established speciality area in the Netherlands since the late 1970s, SER did not begin until the mid 1980s although research on teacher effectiveness, school organization and the educational careers of students from the very varied selective educational systems of the Netherlands had all been a focus of past interest (historical reviews are available in Creemers and Knuver, 1989; Scheerens, 1992).

Several Dutch studies address the issue of consistency of effectiveness across organizational sub-units and across time (stability). Luyten (1994c) found inconsistency across grades: the difference between subjects within schools appeared to be larger than the general differences between schools. Moreover, the school effects for each subject also varied. Doolaard (1995) investigated stability over time by replicating the school effectiveness study carried out by Brandsma and Knuver (1989).

In the context of the International Educational Assessment Studies (IEA), attention was given to the development and the testing of an instrument for the measurement of opportunity to learn, which involves the overlap between the curriculum and the test (De Haan, 1992; Pelgrum, 1989). In the Netherlands, teachers included in the Second International Mathematics Study and the Second International Science Study tended to underrate the amount of subject matter presented to the students. Furthermore, for particular sub-sets of the items, teachers in the Netherlands made serious mistakes in judging whether the corresponding subject matter had been taught before the testing date (Pelgrum, 1989).

Bosker (1990) found evidence for differential effects of school characteristics on the secondary school careers of low and high SES pupils. High and low SES pupils similarly profit from the type of school that appeared to be most effective: the cohesive, goal-oriented and transparently organized school. The variance explained by school types, however, was only 1 per cent. With respect to the departmental level, some support for the theory of differential effects was found. Low SES pupils did better in departments characterized by consistency and openness, whereas high SES pupils were better off in other department types (explained variance 1 per cent).

A couple of studies have covered specific factors associated with effectiveness, including a study on grouping procedures at the classroom level (Reezigt, 1993). Reezigt found that the effects of grouping procedures on student achievement are either the same, or in some cases even negative, as compared to the effects of whole class teaching. Differential effects, (i.e. interaction effects of grouping procedures with student characteristics on achievement or attitudes), are hardly ever found in studies from the Netherlands. The effects of grouping procedures must to some extent be attributed to the classroom context and instructional characteristics. Ros (1994) found no effects of cooperation between students on student achievement. She analysed the effects of teaching behaviour during peer group work, using multilevel analysis. Monitoring, observing and controlling students and having frequent short contacts with all groups, not only promote on task behaviour but also effective student interaction.

Freibel (1994) investigated the relationship between curriculum planning and student examination results. His survey study provided little empirical support for the importance of proactive and structured planning at the school and departmental levels. In a case study including more and less effective schools, he found an indication that educational planning at the classroom level, in direct relation to instruction, may have a slightly positive effect on student results. Van de Grift developed instruments for measuring the instructional climate in educational leadership. With respect to educational leadership he found that there is a difference between his earlier results (van de Grift, 1990) and later findings. Principals in the Netherlands nowadays show more characteristics of educational leadership and these characteristics are related to student outcomes (Lam and van de Grift, 1995), whereas in his 1990 study such effects were not shown.

Several studies have been concerned with the relationship between variables and factors of effectiveness at the school and classroom levels, and even at the contextual level in relation to student outcomes. Brandsma (1993) found empirical evidence for the importance of some factors like evaluation of pupils and the classroom climate, but mostly they could not confirm factors and variables mentioned in school effectiveness studies in the UK and the USA. Hofman (1993) found empirical evidence for the importance of school boards with respect to effectiveness, since they have a contextual impact on the effectiveness of the schools they govern. It seems important that school boards look for ways of communication with the different authority levels in the school organization, so that the board's policy-making becomes a mutual act of the school board and the relevant participants in the school. Witziers (1992) found that an active role of school management in policy and planning concerning the instructional system are beneficial to student outcomes. His study also showed the effects of differences associated with teacher cooperation between departments.

In the mid-1990s attention was given to studies that are strongly related to less or more explicit models of educational effectiveness. In the studies carried out at the University of Twente, the emphasis was provided on the organizational level, focusing, for instance, on the evaluation policy of the school, in relationship to what happens at the instructional level. In Groningen, ideas about instructional effectiveness provide the main perspectives (Creemers, 1994). Here the emphasis is more on the classroom level and grouping procedures and the media for instruction, like the teacher and instructional materials and the classroom–school interface. These studies include more recently developed theories, ideas, opinions, and ideologies with respect to instruction and school organization, like the constructivist and restructuring approaches.

A cutting edge study related to both the instructional and school level carried out by the Universities of Twente and Groningen was an experimental study aimed at comparing school-level and classroom-level determinants of mathematics achievement in secondary education. It was one of the rare examples of an effectiveness study in which treatments are actively controlled by researchers. The experimental treatments consisted of training courses that teachers received and feedback to teachers and pupils. Four conditions were compared: a condition where teachers received special training in the structuring of learning tasks and providing feedback on achievement to students; a similar condition to which consultation sessions with school leaders was added; a condition where principals received feedback about student achievement; and a no-treatment condition. Stated in very general terms, the results seemed to support the predominance of the instructional level and of teacher behaviours (Brandsma et al., 1995).

Table 1.1 presents an overview of extant Dutch school effectiveness studies in primary and secondary education. In the columns the total number of significant positive and negative correlations between these conditions and educational attainment are shown. The basic information for each of these studies was presented in Scheerens and Creemers (1995). The main organizational and instructional effectiveness enhancing conditions, as known from the international literature, are shown in the left-hand column.

The total number of effectiveness studies presented in Table 1.1 in primary education is 29, while the total of studies in secondary education is 13, thus indicating that primary education is the main educational sector for effectiveness studies in the Netherlands. Primary and secondary education schools with a majority of lower SES-pupils and pupils from minority groups comprise the research sample of about 25 per cent of the studies.

The line near the bottom of the table that shows the percentage of variance that is between schools gives an indication of the importance of the factor 'school' in Dutch education. The average percentage in primary schools is 9, and in secondary schools 13.5. It should be noted that this is an average not only over studies, but also over output measures. Generally schools have a greater effect on mathematics than on language/reading, as suggested in Fitz-Gibbon (1992).

The between school variances, in most cases, have been computed after adjustment for covariables at the pupil level, so they indicate the 'net-influence' of schooling while controlling for differences in pupil intake. Since at the time these studies were conducted most primary schools had just one class per grade level, the school and classroom levels in primary schools usually coincide. A final note with respect to the measures of between school variances shown in Table 1.1 is that only in some cases have intra-class correlations been computed, which will generally be higher than the between school variances (since the intra-class correlations are computed as the ratio of the between school variance and the sum of the between school and between pupil variance).

Table 1.1 Dutch school effectiveness studies: Total number of positive and negative correlations between selected factors and educational achievement

	Primary Level		Secondary Level	
	Positive Association	*Negative Associaton*	*Positive Associaton*	*Negative Association*
Structured Teaching/Feedback	5		1	
Teacher Experience	3	1		1
Instructional Leadership		2	1	
Orderly Climate	2		3	1
Student Evaluation	5		0	
Differentiation		2	0	
Whole class Teaching	3		0	
Achievement Orientation	4		4	
Team Stability/Cooperation		3		3
Time/Homework	4		4	
Other Variables	16		8	
Average Between School Variance	9		13.5	
Number of Studies	29		13	

Note: Not all variables mentioned in the columns were measured in each and every study.

Source: Creemers and Osinga, 1995.

When considering the factors that 'work' in Dutch education, the conclusion from Table 1.1 must be that the effective schools model is not confirmed by the data. The two conditions thought to be effectiveness enhancing that are most commonly found to have a significant positive association with the effectiveness criteria in primary schools (structured teaching and evaluation practices), are found in no more than five out of 29 studies. Moreover, 'other' factors predominate both in primary and secondary education as being associated with effectiveness. It is also striking that if an effect of instructional leadership and differentiation is found, it is often negative. The set of 'other' characteristics is very heterogeneous. The most frequently found one is 'denomination', often (but not always) with an advantage for 'church schools' with a Roman Catholic or Protestant orientation over public schools. The large number of independent variables in most studies, and the fact that only several of these are statistically significant (sometimes dangerously close to the 5 per cent that could have been expected on the basis of chance), add to the feeling of uneasiness that the figures in Table 1.1 convey concerning the fruitfulness of research driven by the conventional American school effectiveness model. Some consolation can be drawn from the fact that the most positive results come from the most sophisticated study in this area (Knuver and Brandsma, 1993). In recent years, perhaps the other major contribution of Dutch SER is the generation of an 'educational effectiveness' paradigm which subsumes within it the material from both teacher/ instructional effectiveness and that on school effectiveness into a coherent, middle range set of theoretical postulates (for further examples see Scheerens and Bosker, 1997).

SER in Australia

Australians were initially reluctant to become involved in SER largely because of a concern about standardized testing procedures. The emphasis upon student performance on standardized achievement tests as the key measurement of an 'effective' school, as proposed by Edmonds (1979a and b) was met with various levels of scepticism and there were a number of Australian researchers such as Angus (1986a; 1986b), Ashenden (1987) and Banks (1988) who clearly indicated their concern that a concentration on effectiveness as it had been originally defined by Edmonds meant a diminution of concern about other equally relevant educational issues such as equality, participation and social justice. This is ample evidence that although there was no commonly agreed upon understanding of what an effective school was, the critics were sure of what it was not.

There was little early research that considered issues of school effectiveness. Mellor and Chapman (1984), Caldwell and Misko (1983), Hyde and Werner (1984), Silver and Moyle (1985) and Caldwell and Spinks (1986) all identified characteristics of school effectiveness, but it could be argued that these studies were more related to school improvement issues than to school effectiveness research. However, these studies were forerunners of many later studies that used school effectiveness as a basis for developing changed perceptions of schooling.

On the international front, Caldwell and Spinks (1988, 1992) introduced the notion of self-managing schools, which has served as a model for many of the structural changes being made by educational systems in a number of countries, including Australia, New Zealand and the UK. Chapman's work for the OECD and UNESCO has been internationally recognized for its contribution to the debate on principals and leadership (1985, 1991a), decentralization (1992) and resource allocation (1991b).

Much of the research in the area of school effectiveness has been driven by the need for governments to justify some of the changes being made towards relating education more closely to the needs of the Australian economy. Consequently, a number of large scale research projects over the past few years have been commissioned by, or are being supported by, national and state government.

In attempting to establish improvements at the school level, the Australian Education Council (AEC) initiated the *Good Schools Strategy*. The first stage of the strategy was the *Effective Schools Project*, a research activity commissioned in 1991. It was conducted by the Australian Council for Educational Research (ACER) and more than 2300 Australian schools (almost 30 per cent) responded to an open-ended questionnaire which sought advice from school communities about aspects of school effectiveness which they thought were important in determining effectiveness levels. The report of this research (McGaw et al., 1992) found the things that made schools effective were said to be staff (in 65 per cent of the responses); ethos (58 per cent); curriculum (52 per cent) and resources (48 per cent). In summarizing their findings, the researchers identified the following implications for educational policy makers:

- Accountability is a local issue, a matter of direct negotiation between schools and their communities. There is remarkably little interest in large-scale testing programmes, national profiles and other mechanisms designed to externalise the accountability of schools.

- Problems of discipline and behaviour management do not appear as major barriers to school effectiveness and school improvement. They exist, of course, but only in a minority of responses, and even there rarely as a major concern.
- School effectiveness is about a great deal more than maximising academic achievement. Learning, and the love of learning; personal development and self-esteem; life skills, problem solving and learning how to learn; the development of independent thinkers and well-rounded, confident individuals, all rank as highly or more highly in the outcomes of effective schooling as success in a narrow range of academic disciplines.
- The role of central administrators is to set broad policy guidelines and to support schools in their efforts to improve, particularly through the provision of professional support services (McGaw et al., 1992, p.174).

In addition to this large scale research, other national studies were designed to improve the impact of school for individual students. In 1992 a national study on educational provision for students with disabilities was commissioned by the AEC as part of its attempt to achieve the national goals related to equity. The study aimed to evaluate the effectiveness of the current programme and to establish a range of best practices for the 56,000 people who were identified as disabled.

The *Primary School Planning Project* (PSPP) was designed to document current practice in school-based planning in primary schools and also to gain insights into practice in specific primary schools (Logan et al., 1994). The study used qualitative techniques to develop a national picture using 2200 schools and including principals, associated administrators, teachers and parents who had been involved in school planning activities.

A number of studies which are related to improving the effectiveness of schools have occurred in the last few years. These have considered a variety of issues including the concept of school effectiveness (Banks, 1992; Hill, 1995; Townsend, 1994, 1997) and the concept of school quality (Aspin et al., 1994; Chapman and Aspin, 1997), various studies on classroom effectiveness including identifying the factors affecting student reading achievement (Rowe, 1991; Rowe and Rowe, 1992; Crévola and Hill, 1997), the characteristics of schools in which students perform well in both mathematics and reading, and in which there are positive student attitudes and high levels of parent participation (Rowe et al., 1994a), the relationship between school development planning and effectiveness (Davis and Caust, 1994), a consideration of the relationship between classroom effectiveness and school effectiveness (Hill et al., 1993; Hill, Rowe and Holmes-Smith, 1995; Rowe et al., 1994b) and the issue of standards (Hill, 1997a).

There has been a particular focus on the relationship between effectiveness and school self-management (Caldwell and Spinks, 1988, 1992, 1998; Smyth, 1993; Tickell, 1995; Townsend, 1996a, 1997), the impact of restructuring on school effectiveness (Townsend, 1996b) and a longitudinal study of the unique role of principals in the restructuring activity (Thomas et al., 1993, 1994, 1995a, 1995b, 1996, 1997). Recent areas of research include the impact of changes in education funding on families (Townsend and Walker, 1998) and on school effectiveness (Brotherhood of St Laurence, 1996; Caldwell et al., 1995; Education Committee, 1996; Education Victoria, 1996; Hind and Caldwell, 1995; Townsend, 1998a), and considerations of what the effective school of the future might look like (Caldwell and Hayward, 1998; Caldwell, 1997; Townsend, 1998b).

The Changing International Educational Discourse and SER

Our survey of different countries in this chapter shows clear trends across time, both for the individual countries surveyed and for the SER enterprise across countries. The early SER studies in the United States and the United Kingdom reflected, in their concentration upon physical and material inputs, the existence of a paradigm which saw access to the 'material', financially determined world of schooling as the key to improving both equality of educational opportunity and the overall 'excellence' of school outcomes. This 'liberal' belief in the value of education was also linked with an essentially positivistic, quantitatively orientated methodology that was utilized to generate 'truths' about education, which were then used to generate curriculum and organizational reforms that were in a 'top down' manner implemented with schools.

The failure of this liberal dream to generate much progress in both excellence and equity terms resulted in a major intellectual reaction, with the advent of school effectiveness research reinforcing a powerful belief that 'schools make no difference'. Instead of a search for quantitative positivistic truths, educational research (now doubting the validity of those truths that had failed to deliver improved outcomes and systemic reform) in the 1970s celebrated the rich, detailed, qualitatively orientated case studies of schools and classrooms. SER too, as we have noted above, increasingly involved case studies of effective schools, and school improvement in both the United States and in Europe entered a phase which gave primacy to practitioner beliefs as the levers to generate school change (this is detailed in Chapter 7).

From the late 1980s onwards, the changing economic and social contexts within advanced industrial societies such as the USA, the United Kingdom, Australia and the Netherlands all combined to shift educational reform and expansion, and the SER paradigm, to central stage. The economic pressures from emerging Pacific Rim economies, the need to again address issues of equity that had been brought into sharp focus by the emerging 'underclass' that appeared to differentiate itself out of mainstream society, and the revival of interest in educational policy matters that came with the arrival of a new generation of educational researchers who had not been intellectually and personally 'burnt' by the failure of the 1960s liberal dream, all combined to increase governmental and educational system interest in SER.

SER itself by the late 1980s and early 1990s had additionally found high levels of professional self confidence. Groups of persons who were marginal to their national educational research communities organized their own professional association, their own journal and rapidly developed the widely accepted definition of 'normal science' that is reflected in the existence of this handbook. In the United Kingdom, school effectiveness researchers advised Government, and the British Labour Government education programme reflected similar involvement. The Australian Federal Government initiated a major national enquiry on 'what makes schools effective?' in 1991, and ongoing research into teacher and school effectiveness is central to educational policies in many states (e.g. Hill, 1997b in Victoria, and Cuttance, 1994 in New South Wales). In the Netherlands, school effectiveness researchers began to directly contribute to national education policy, as in the case of the National Commission on Special

Education and the committee on the Evaluation of Primary Education. Even in the USA, where SER had intellectually, practically and politically 'boomed and busted' in the mid 1980s as we noted earlier, the growth of contextually sensitive SER and of closer links between the SER and school improvement communities, resulted in a renaissance of SER by the mid-1990s, symbolized by the meeting of the *International Congress for School Effectiveness and Improvement* in Memphis in 1997 and in San Antonio in 1999.

Conclusions

It will be obvious from the content of this chapter that SER has changed, evolved and markedly improved in both quality and quantity over the last 30 years. As it moved intellectually in the USA from the early, simplistic focus upon input–output analysis to more recent contextually specific formulations, and as it moved geographically from its original homeland in the USA to the present situation where perhaps 10 times more studies are being conducted outside the USA than inside it, it is clear that there are culturally or country specific contributions that are distinctive.

Australia shows evidence of:

- close links between school effectiveness and school improvement;
- work on the conceptual basis of school effectiveness and school quality;
- a close relationship between effectiveness/improvement and educational policy, with national policies that clearly relate to and draw on these knowledge bases.

By contrast, the Netherlands shows a flourishing, quantitatively sophisticated research base which strangely seems to be relatively unused within practice. It also shows:

- continued context specificity, with many of the most validated school effectiveness factors from outside the Netherlands failing to be replicated within;
- sophisticated theoretical formulation, and multiple level research on classrooms and schools;
- continued progress in conceptualizing and linking theoretically the instructional *and* school levels, and recognition of the need for the adoption of contingency models that might explain the failure of many school effectiveness factors to 'travel' in Dutch contexts (Scheerens and Bosker, 1997).

The United Kingdom shows:

- considerable methodological sophistication, with now axiomatic use of multilevel modelling, cohort studies and multiple intake measures including that of student achievement. Britain has also been at the forefront of the development of multilevel statistical modelling (Goldstein, 1995a);
- limited attempts to analyse instructional processes combined with sophisticated work at the school level, building upon the earlier sociology of education;
- use of multiple measures of outcomes;
- a historic 'split' between effectiveness researchers and improvement practitioners,

only recently fading with the arrival of 'blended' programmes which utilize the knowledge bases of both school effectiveness and school improvement to improve schools in carefully evaluated 'experiments of nature';

- a historic inability to investigate the possible context specificity of effective schools characteristics because of sample selection being mostly from disadvantaged communities.

Finally, the USA shows:

- contextually sensitive effectiveness research, small in quantity, but increasingly conducted within a 'mixed methods' tradition;
- considerable progress in describing and analysing both teacher and school effects together;
- an emergence of a large number of school improvement orientated programmes which incorporate rigorous evaluation of effects;
- the existence of a wide variety of fields which are school effects related.

This, then, is an overview of the knowledge base of research and practice that makes up the international body of knowledge that we will be summarizing and reviewing in Sections 2 and 3 of this handbook. Whilst clearly acknowledging the different traditions of the knowledge bases within each country as outlined above, we will from now on merge the various country contributions together as we begin to analyse the key substantive findings that the knowledge base has generated.

Before that, though, we wish to complete the foundations of the handbook by outlining in Chapter 2 how we have classified, framed, and organized the world's school effectiveness knowledge base, and what we have learnt about the school effectiveness research community across countries as we have constructed our framework.

2 Current Topics and Approaches in School Effectiveness Research: The Contemporary Field

Charles Teddlie and David Reynolds,
with Sharon Pol

Introduction

This chapter attempts to outline the contemporary field of school effectiveness. It utilizes results from an unpublished, unique survey completed before the preparation of this book (Teddlie and Roberts, 1993) as an organizational framework for Sections 2 and 3 of the book. This two-phase perceptual survey of 'experts' in SER concerned their perceptions of the current importance of certain topics (e.g. the context of school effects, the stability of school effects, the effective schools correlates) within the SER field.

The chapter includes a review of the methodology and results of this survey, followed by a description of where more detailed information on each of the topics which were identified as important is located later in the book. It also entails descriptions of three 'types' of survey respondents : the scientists, the pragmatists and the humanists. It will be argued that these groups represent three distinct traditions within SER, with each group of researchers and/or practitioners having their own values and agendas. Comparisons are then drawn with other recent surveys of the field, and the chapter concludes by outlining the research practice and conceptualizations of the 'pragmatists', who it is argued have the potential to develop the field rapidly in the next 20 years.

Topics Within SER: Why Haven't They Been Delineated?

SER as we noted in Chapter 1 initially grew out of a response to the *Coleman Report* (1966) and *Plowden Report*'s (1967) oft-stated conclusion that schools made little difference to the life chances of their students, but has proceeded to encompass a wide array of topics in the intervening 30 years. SER in this chapter includes the three major strands of research discussed in Chapter 1: *studies of school effects* that attempt to relate school inputs to school outcomes using increasingly sophisticated mathematical models; *'effective schools' studies* that describe the processes of differentially effective schools using the outlier and case study approaches; and *school improvement studies* that document the implementation (and sometimes the success) of school change efforts.

There has been no existing conventional taxonomy of SER sub-areas, although researchers often write about the *context* of school effects (e.g. Hallinger and Murphy, 1986; Teddlie and Stringfield, 1985, 1993; Wimpelberg et al., 1989), the *stability* of school effects (e.g. Mandeville and Anderson, 1987; Gray et al., 1995; Nuttall et al., 1989) and the *magnitude* of school effects (e.g. Coleman et al., 1966; Brookover et al., 1979; Reynolds, 1992a, 1992b).

There are several reasons for this lack of a conventional delineation of SER topics:

1   the fact that researchers in each of the different SER strands noted above have seldom worked together and in some cases see one another as intellectual competitors;
2   the lack of any comprehensive textbooks summarizing the SER field;
3   the dearth of school effectiveness/school improvement courses at the postgraduate level in both America and Europe, which if they existed would require professors to organize the literature into generally recognized topics for teaching purposes;
4   the severe criticism of the effective schools literature in the USA during the mid-1980s, which led to the labelling of the work as reform posing as science (Ralph and Fennessey, 1983) and of the researchers as shamans (Rowan, 1984), thus seriously retarding the field's intellectual self confidence and progress in the USA which has the largest concentration of professionals writing about educational research in the world;
5   the late development of certain important normative institutions in the field such as the American Educational Research Association's *School Effectiveness Special Interest Group* or *SIG* (formed only in 1984), the first association meeting exclusively for those interested in the field (only in 1988) and the founding of a journal devoted exclusively to the field *School Effectiveness and School Improvement (SESI)* (only in 1990). These institutions were established 18–24 years *after* the Coleman Report;
6   the intellectual and practical separation of school improvement from the other two types of school effectiveness research and practice.

There is abundant evidence that it is currently a suitable time to differentiate both topics and specific issues within each of those topical areas, in the belief that this process itself may generate studies designed to probe these issues more deeply. Evidence for the present maturity of the field includes:

1   the rapidly growing body of research subsumed under the various terms associated with SER;
2   the recent spate of articles and books that summarize different parts of the SER field (noted in Chapter 1);
3   the emergence of an international journal (*School Effectiveness and School Improvement*), as well as *the International Congress for School Effectiveness and Improvement (ICSEI)*;
4   the fact that SER is now overlapping in terms of research agendas with other, more established areas such as teacher effects (see Chapter 11 for more details);
5   the fact that researchers are now reporting replicable results in several areas such as the context, stability and magnitude of school effects.

The Survey of Expert Opinion: An Outline

There were several research questions that guided this exploratory, primarily descriptive study:

1   What major SER topics can be delineated through a literature review?
2   What importance do experts in the field assign to each of the topics derived from the literature review?
3   What other areas do experts believe should be included in a taxonomy of important topics?
4   Do different groups of respondents respond differently when rank ordering the topics in perceived importance?

   In order to answer these questions, we undertook a multistage project covering the following phases:

1   Phase 1 – Literature Review : The literature review was undertaken to develop a set of topics for the first round of the study and to identify a sample of experts (researchers and practitioners) who would serve as respondents. Sources for the literature review included an ERIC search using school effects as the keyword, the literature reviews noted above plus numerous others, all existing issues of *SESI*, the published proceedings of ICSEI and the catalogues of the 10 AERA meetings (from 1984 when the SIG was formed to 1993) using school effectiveness and school improvement as keywords. The final bibliography from these sources had over 500 references, selected as the most relevant from the much larger total list that had emerged.
2   Phase 2 – Determination of Initial Topics : Using the titles of the references and their abstracts as text, the constant comparative method was used to arrive at preliminary SER topics (Lincoln and Guba, 1985). Three separate coders were used to increase the reliability/validity of this initial categorization scheme (Patton, 1990). This process was automated using *Qualpro* (Blackman, 1991), a text database manager. A list of 17 distinct topics emerged using this procedure, such topics were then used in the first round survey which is in essential agreement with other lists of important issues or questions in the SER area. For instance, the issues that Good and Brophy identified as limitations of the extant literature in 1986 overlap considerably with the topics included in the first round survey. Also, the list of topics corresponds substantially with a list of key questions developed in 1993 by a group of British SER researchers and practitioners for a seminar series designed to review the field, funded by the UK Economic and Social Research Council (Gray et al., 1996b).
3   Phase 3 – Development of First Round Survey and Sample : The first survey consisted of two parts : a closed-ended section asking respondents to indicate the importance of the 17 topics derived from Phase 2 (on five point scales); and a series of seven open-ended questions asking participants what are the most important current issues in SER, the most important methodological issues in SER and the current strengths/weaknesses within the research area.
   From the 500+ references derived from Phase 1, a list was made of authors, and

some 150 authors were then included in the sampling frame for the first survey. Selection criteria included number of references and the perceived importance of their contribution to SER. These 150 authors were also to be included in the sampling frame for the second round survey, where our intention was to include a more broad based sample.

Our final sample for the first survey included the 40 authors who were *consensus* choices by three judges (the principal investigator and two graduate assistants) to have made the most significant contribution to SER over the past 10 years. As with many aspects of this study, this selection procedure for the first round survey was subjective, but this is the nature of exploratory work in any newly established field.

4   Phase 4 – Development of Second Round Survey and Sample : Based on results from the first round survey, a revised list of 12 topics was constructed, deleting some with low ratings and adding others suggested from the open-ended responses. The second round survey asked respondents to rank order 12 SER topics from most to least important.

The expanded sample for the second round survey included : those respondents from the first round who responded to the first survey; those authors who were designated as significant contributors to SER in phase three, but were not included in the sample for the first round survey; and a list of some 75 practitioners who had made a significant contribution to practice, sampled from two sources (AERA *SIG* list and *National Center for Effective Schools Research and Development* membership list). The final sampling frame consisted of 211 individuals.

Results from the First Survey

First round surveys were mailed to the 40 respondents identified in the previous section. A few surveys were returned as undeliverable (two surveys) or were returned by respondents who refused to reply due to the fact that they no longer considered themselves to be active in the field (two surveys). Of the 36 remaining valid members from the first survey sample, 18 returned usable completed questionnaires on the first mailout. A second mailout resulted in 10 more responses, giving a total of 28 responses. The total response rate of 78 per cent (28 of 36) was considered adequate for this survey.

Table 2.1 shows the means and standard deviations (*sds*) for the 17 response categories. Responses ranged from one (not important at all) to five (extremely important). The first notable result is the restricted range of responses to the five-point scales, since the lowest mean score was 3.5, while the highest was 4.6. Thus, these experts availed themselves of a range of only 1.1 points on five-point scale. As one respondent noted, 'They're all important'. For this reason, it was decided to use rank order scales for the second round survey.

As noted in Table 2.1, the topic with the highest average score was 'The Interaction of Teacher and School Effects', denoted as 'Teacher–School Interaction'. Those topics with the lowest mean values were 'Definitions of School Effectiveness' (denoted as 'Definitions' in Table 2.1) and 'Parental Role in School Effects' (denoted as 'Parental Role' in Table 2.1). Seven of the topics had mean scores of 3.63 or lower, while 10 of the topics had mean scores of 3.7 or higher.

Table 2.1 Respondents' ratings of importance of each topic from first round survey

Topics	Mean	Standard Deviation
1 Teacher–School Interaction	4.59	0.57
2 Context Issues	4.22	0.75
3 Role of Principal	4.22	0.80
4 Multilevel Issues	4.15	1.06
5 Methodological Issues	3.93	1.07
6 Variance Issues	3.93	1.10
7 Stability Issues	3.89	1.05
8 District Effects	3.78	1.18
9 Existence/Magnitude Issues	3.78	1.37
10 Theory	3.70	1.17
11 Consistency Issues	3.63	1.14
12 Correlates	3.63	1.14
13 Teacher Induction/Socialization	3.59	0.84
14 External School Improvement	3.59	1.42
15 Naturally Occurring Improvement	3.58	1.17
16 Parental Role	3.52	0.94
17 Definitions	3.48	1.28

Note: The data in this table are based on questionnaires returned from 28 respondents (78% of sample). Response categories for each topic range from 1 (not important at all) to 5 (very important). The names of the topics found in this table are shortened from those given on the survey.

The topic with the largest standard deviation or range was 'External School Improvement', which was also one of the items with a low overall rating (3.59). The topic with the highest overall rating (Teacher–School Interaction) also had the smallest standard deviation or range (0.57).

Revision of the Topic List Based on First Survey Results

As noted above, a major purpose of the first survey was to revise the list of topics based on expert opinion. This process was two-fold: first, those topics with low mean ratings in the survey were to be eliminated; second, the open-ended responses were to be used to generate new topics and to revise existing topics.

The following specific procedure was used to produce the list of topics to be used in the second round survey:

1   Those topics with the lowest overall mean scores were eliminated from the list. The seven topics with mean scores of 3.63 or lower were therefore dropped, although some of them were later added back to the list in different more inclusive forms, as noted below. For example, one eliminated topic was 'The Correlates of School Effectiveness', which several respondents indicated was of great historical importance but lacked current relevance.
2   The topic 'The Multilevel Nature of School Effects' was eliminated, since several respondents said it was closely related to other topics (such as 'Teacher–School Interaction' or 'District Effects upon School Effects').
3   Several respondents suggested 'The Role of Leadership in School Effects' should be substituted for the 'The Role of the Principal in School Effects', which was done.

4   Several respondents also suggested that 'The Consistency of School Effects across Measures' should be combined with 'The Stability of School Effects across Time'. These topics were combined in the second round survey.

5   Some respondents suggested that the definition of the topic 'District Effects upon School Effects' should be expanded to include 'State Effects' also. This was done and the brief description on the second survey was expanded to include 'the effects of units above the school, including school boards'.

6   While 'External School Improvement' and 'Naturally Occurring School Change' were eliminated due to low mean scores, respondents suggested that some topic should be included that addressed the issue of school change. The topic 'The Relationship of School Effects to School Change (e.g. school improvement, school restructuring, site-based management)' was included to address this issue.

7   Several respondents suggested that we add two new topics: 'School Effects and Curriculum Issues' and 'International Comparative Studies of School Effects'. While neither of these topics had showed up prominently in the earlier literature review, respondents felt that these topics would become increasingly important in the future.

As might be expected, a small number of the respondents were not satisfied with the revised list of topics, as illustrated by the following quote:

> Some of the items on the reverse side are vague or combinations of independent elements . . . I think this dooms the findings of this research to be ambiguous.
>
> (Respondent 083, second round survey)

However, it is clear that an ambiguous beginning to delineating SER topics is better than no start at all. It will be left up to future researchers to develop more refined, less ambiguous lists of topics.

The analysis of the open-ended responses from the first survey was used for two purposes:

1   to assist in the revision of the SER topic list that would be used in the second round survey;
2   to assist in the organization of the present handbook.

With regard to the second purpose, open-ended responses to the question asking 'what are the most important current issues in SER?' were utilized in the chapter organization of Sections 2 and 3 of the current book. The steps in the constant comparative analysis (Lincoln and Guba, 1985) of the responses to this question are as follows:

1   Three coders independently analysed the narrative responses to the 'current issues' question made by the 28 respondents to the first round survey.
2   Using the 'unitizing' procedure of the constant comparative method, 48 distinct units of information (UOIs) were identified from the 28 respondents.
3   Each of the three coders independently analysed the 48 units of information, assigning a 'categorical' name to each unit of information. This category

summarized the essence of the written statement (the UOI). The coders looked for similarities among the UOIs and attempted to develop the most parsimonious coding scheme.

4   After separately categorizing the UOIs, the three coders met and, by consensus, developed a final categorical schemata by comparing each of the three separate schemata that they had independently derived.

5   The final categorical schemata had six broad themes:

- methodological issues;
- process of effective schooling issues;
- context of school effects issues;
- multilevel issues;
- improvement issues;
- theoretical issues.

6   These six broad themes were further divided into some 26 specific issues. For instance, the 'methodological theme' included the issues of operational definitions, validity, reliability, generalizability and stability.

The final section of this chapter contains a more detailed summary of the results of this constant comparative analysis, which was very useful in the determination of the chapter organization for Sections 2 and 3 of this book.

Results from the Second Survey

Second round surveys were mailed to the 211 respondents identified in the phase four outlined above. Eleven surveys were returned as undeliverable or were returned by respondents who refused to reply for various professional reasons. Of the 200 remaining members on the second survey list, 144 returned usable, completed questionnaires. This response rate of 72 per cent for a one time mailout is high, indicating considerable enthusiasm for the survey, since Borg and Gall (1989) reported a synthesis of the survey literature indicating that response rates for one time mailouts averaged 48 per cent, while three mailouts were usually required to attain the greater than 70 per cent rate that was obtained on the first try with this survey. Due to this high response rate and time constraints, it was decided not to undertake a second mailout.

Table 2.2 shows the median and interquartile ranges for responses to the SER topics. The table also presents means and standard deviations for each of the 12 topics, based on an analysis that treated the data as if it were parametric. The results from the two analyses were nearly identical in that:

1   The median and mean results reported exactly the same ordering of SER topics in perceived importance, ranging from 'The Relationship of School Effects to School Change' (denoted School Change in Table 2.2), which was ranked most important, to 'International Comparative Studies of School Effects' (denoted International Studies) which was ranked least important.

2   The interquartile ranges and standard deviations revealed nearly identical scores also, ranging from 'School Change' which had the least variance in responses to

Table 2.2 Descriptive summary of respondents' rankings of topics from second round survey

Topic	Median	Mean	Interquartile Range	Standard Deviation
1 School Change	3	4.27	2–5, 4 ranks	2.89
2 Teacher–School Interactions	4	4.74	2–6, 5 ranks	2.93
3 Context Issues	5	5.51	3–7, 5 ranks	2.94
4 Role of Leadership	5	5.94	3–8, 6 ranks	3.25
5 Stability/Consistency	6	6.04	4–8, 5 ranks	2.93
6 Curriculum Issues	6	6.14	3–8, 6 ranks	3.19
7 Methodical Issues	6	6.23	3–8, 6 ranks	3.37
8 Variance Issues	6	6.61	4–8, 5 ranks	3.04
9 Theory	7	6.70	4–9, 6 ranks	3.63
10 Existence/Magnitude Issues	7	7.08	4–9, 6 ranks	3.79
11 District/State Effects	8	7.83	6–8, 4 ranks	2.96
12 International Studies	10	9.27	7–11, 4 ranks	3.27

Note: The data in this table are based on questionnaires returned from 144 respondents (72% of sample). Respondents ranked topics from 1 (most important) to 12 (least important). If a respondent did not rank order all items, the remaining items were assigned a rank that was the average of the remaining ranks. For instance, if a respondent ranked nine items, the remaining three items were ranked 11, which is the average of the remaining three ranks (10, 11, 12).

'The Existence and Magnitude of School Effects' (denoted Existence/Magnitude Issues in Table 2.2), which manifested the most variance.

Due to the high degree of similarity between the parametric and non-parametric descriptive data, it was decided to employ inferential parametric techniques when further analysing the data. As noted by Harris:

> ... we have so much strong mathematical and empirical evidence of the robustness of statistical procedures under violation of normality or homogeneity of variance assumptions that the burden of proof must be presumed to be on the shoulders of those who claim that a particular set of data can be analysed only through 'non-parametric' statistical techniques.
>
> (Harris, R., 1985, p.326)

The 'burden of proof' was not demonstrated in this dataset, which has descriptive non-parametric statistics almost identical to those generated by re-analysis of the data using descriptive parametric statistics. Thus, we used parametric statistics, such as factor analysis and multivariate analysis of variance (MANOVA) in further analyses.

Factor Analysis of Responses to Second Survey

Factor analytic work employing empirical principal components analysis, followed by a varimax rotation, resulted in a five factor solution (if the eigenvalue greater than or equal to 1.00 criteria was used) or a three factor solution (if a screen test was utilized). We decided to utilize a one factor solution for the following reasons:

1　The five factor solutions had two uninterpretable factors.
2　The three factor solution had factors which included items that were both highly positively and highly negatively loaded. Further perusal of these three factors

indicated two distinct patterns of response, one of which seemed to imply a humanistic, applied research, school change orientation, while the other suggested a more scientific, basic research, theoretical orientation. Table 2.3 contains a summary of the factor loadings from the three factor solution.

3   A one factor solution was ideal for further exploring these two orientations in a singular response pattern. The one factor solution assigns a valence to each topic, and since there is just one pattern of loadings to examine, these loadings can then be grouped into two categories (one positive, one negative). It was surmised that if the topics within each valence category grouped together based on the different orientations suggested in reason number 2 above, then there would be empirical support for the conjecture that some responders are ranking topics in one manner, while others are ranking them differently.

The data in Table 2.4 appear to confirm the existence of these two distinct response patterns. Those topics with positive valences included:

1   School Change;
2   Teacher-School Interaction;
3   The Role of Leadership;
4   Curriculum Issues (School Effects and Curriculum Issues);
5   Context Issues (The Context of School Effects); and
6   District–State Effects (District and State Effects upon School Effects).

Those topics with negative valences included:

1   Methodological Issues in SER (e.g. validity, reliability, generalizability, etc.);
2   Variance Issues (The Variance of Behaviours within Differentially Effective Schools);

Table 2.3 Topic loadings from factor analysis of responses of second round participants: three factor solution

Topic	Factor 1	Factor 2	Factor 3
1 School Change	0.05	−0.01	0.82*
2 Teacher–School Interactions	−0.58*	0.06	0.03
3 Context Issues	−0.14	−0.41*	−0.34
4 Role of Leadership	−0.11	−0.67*	0.16
5 Stability/Consistency	0.66*	0.18	−0.14
6 Curriculum Issues	−0.52	−0.13	0.18
7 Methodical Issues	0.17	0.27	−0.63*
8 Variance Issues	0.18	−0.24	−0.37*
9 Theory	0.06	0.56*	−0.04
10 Existence/Magnitude Issues	0.75*	−0.11	0.05
11 District/State Effects	−0.16	−0.34	0.52*
12 International Studies	−0.34	0.66*	−0.09

Note: These results are from a principal components factor analysis of the second round dataset, followed by a varimax rotation. Data from 144 respondents were included in this analysis. Factor loadings greater in magnitude than ±0.35 are asterisked.

Table 2.4 Topic loadings from factor analysis of responses of second round participants: one factor solution

Topic	Factor 1	Orientation
1 School Change	0.50*	Humanistic
2 Teacher–School Interactions	0.32	Humanistic
3 Context Issues	0.07	Humanistic
4 Role of Leadership	0.50*	Humanistic
5 Stability/Consistency	−0.56*	Scientific
6 Curriculum Issues	0.48*	Humanistic
7 Methodogical Issues	−0.64*	Scientific
8 Variance Issues	−0.21	Scientific
9 Theory	−0.35*	Scientific
10 Existence/Magnitude Issues	−0.34	Scientific
11 District–State Effects	0.60*	Humanistic
12 International Studies	−0.20	Scientific

Note: These results are from a principal components factor analysis of the second round dataset. Data from 144 respondents were included in this analysis. Factor loadings greater in magnitude than ±0.35 are asterisked.

3 Stability/Consistency Issues (The Stability of School Effects across Time and Consistency of School Effects across Outcome Measures);
4 Existence/Magnitude Issues;
5 Theory (the Role of Theory in SER);
6 International Studies.

Perusal of these two sets of topics confirm earlier speculation arising from the results of the three factor solution. Respondents giving high ranks to topics with positive valences are probably more interested in applied studies of school effects that have direct implications for school change processes. We might call these SER researchers 'humanists' to use the terminology of Cronbach (1982), who used this label to differentiate between the philosophical orientations of evaluators of educational and social programmes. On the other hand, those respondents who gave high ranks to topics with negative valences are more interested in theoretically driven, empirically based studies of the basic school effects processes. Cronbach (1982) called evaluators with this orientation 'scientists' and contrasted their interests with those of the 'humanists' noted above. The Cronbach differentiation between evaluation orientations seems an appropriate metaphor for the distinction between persons in school effectiveness, since the SER 'scientists' are less interested in school change processes.

A prototypical quote from a scientist in the current sample is as follows:

Theory is first, methodology is second, more specific issues third.

(Respondent number 24, second round survey)

Results of Comparisons between Humanists and Scientists and Pragmatists

The data in Table 2.5 present the results of univariate ANOVA *F* tests in which the responses of these two groups (humanists, scientists) were compared. Group assignment

Table 2.5 Average rank scores given by scientists and humanists to topics

	Humanists		Scientists		
Topic	Mean	Rank	Mean	Rank	F-Value
1 School Change	2.94	1	5.57	4	36.80****
2 Teacher–School Interactions	3.76	2	5.70	6	17.27****
3 Context Issues	5.47	5	5.54	3	0.02
4 Role of Leadership	4.74	3	7.11	9	21.56****
5 Stability/Consistency	7.37	8	4.75	2	35.28****
6 Curriculum Issues	4.89	4	7.36	10	25.00****
7 Methodogical Issues	8.11	11	4.39	1	62.23****
8 Variance Issues	6.86	7	6.36	8	0.94
9 Theory	7.77	9	5.67	5	12.96****
10 Existence/Magnitude Issues	8.10	10	6.08	7	10.73**
11 District–State Effects	6.50	6	9.13	12	41.09****
12 International Studies	9.96	12	8.61	11	6.21*

Note: One-half of the respondents were classified as humanists, while the other half were classified as scientists. Two respondents were eliminated from these analyses due to missing data, leaving a total of 142. Respondents ranked topics from 1 (most important) to 12 (least important).

* $p > 0.05$
** $p > 0.01$
*** $p > 0.001$
**** $p > 0.0001$

resulted from multiplying each respondent's ranks by the factor loading for each of the topics. Respondents' total scores were arrayed from the most positive to the most negative. A median split was performed and half of the respondents were classified as humanists, while the others were classified as scientists.

The overall multivariate *F* for the comparison between the two groups on their rankings was highly significant [F 12, 129) = 24.53, $p < .0001$], as was expected. Two of the most highly significant univariate differences between the humanists and the scientists came on the importance of 'School Change' and of 'Methodological Issues'. As indicated in Table 2.5, which also compares the order of the rankings for the two groups, the humanists gave 'School Change' an average rank of 2.94 (their highest overall rank), while the scientists gave it a rank of only 5.57. On the other hand, the scientists gave 'Methodological Issues' their highest average rank of 4.39, while the humanists gave it a much lower average rank of 8.11.

Table 2.6 compares the rankings given by the whole group, the humanists and the scientists. The rankings given by the humanists more closely parallel those given by the total group than do the rankings given by the scientists. The reason for this phenomenon lies in the variances of responses from the two groups. As indicated in Table 2.5, there is a range of about seven ranks between the humanists' highest average ranking (2.94 for 'School Change') and their lowest average ranking (9.96 for 'International Studies'). On the other hand, the range for the scientists is much smaller (4.74), going from a high rank of 4.39 for 'Methodological Issues' to 9.13 for 'District–State Effects'.

The standard deviations for the two groups' rankings confirms the differences in variations of responses, with the humanists having a standard deviation of 1.97, while

Table 2.6 Comparison of rankings for all respondents, humanistic and scientific

Topic	All Respondents	Humanists	Scientists
1 School Change	1	1	4
2 Teacher–School Interactions	2	2	6
3 Context Issues	3	5	3
4 Role of Leadership	4	3	9
5 Stability/Consistency	5	8	2
6 Curriculum Issues	6	4	10
7 Methodogical Issues	7	11	1
8 Variance Issues	8	7	8
9 Theory	9	9	5
10 Existence/Magnitude Issues	10	10	7
11 District–State Effects	11	6	12
12 International Studies	12	12	11

Note: One-half of the respondents were classified as humanists, while the other half were classified as scientists. Two respondents were eliminated from these analyses due to missing data, leaving a total of 142. Respondents ranked topics from 1 (most important) to 12 (least important). A rank of 1 on this table means the respondents' average rank for that topic was the lowest (meaning it was the most important topic for that group).

the standard deviation for the scientists was only 1.39. Scientists appear to consider many topics to be of equal importance, including some of those associated with a humanistic orientation. On the other hand, humanists definitely prefer those topics associated with 'School Change', and gave low rankings to almost all the scientific orientation topics.

Another way to look at the classification of respondents in the second round survey involves a tripartite split into three groups:

1   humanists (those individuals scoring in the upper one-third of the continuum described in the previous section);
2   pragmatists (those individuals scoring in the middle one-third of the continuum);
3   scientists – those individuals scoring the lower third of the continuum.

The inclusion of the mid-range classification has some ecological validity since there are many individuals in the field of school effectiveness who consider themselves to be both practitioners and researchers. We have decided to call these individuals 'pragmatists', to use a derivative of the term Howe (1988) employed in describing a new theoretical orientation (pragmatism) which he argues combines aspects of both positivism (the theoretical position associated with the scientific orientation) and constructivism (the theoretical position associated with the humanist orientation).

Data presented in Table 2.7 indicate significant differences between the three groups on their average rankings for 10 of the 12 topics. The overall multivariate effect was highly significant [$F(24, 254) = 28.64$, $p - 0.0001$]. On all rankings, the score of the pragmatists was intermediate between that of the scientists and the humanists and for some of the topics, the pragmatists' scores were closer to those of the humanists than to those of the scientists.

This is particularly interesting on two topics : 'School Change', and 'Existence/ Magnitude Issues'. The pragmatists believe School Change is the most important topic

Table 2.7 Average rank scores given by humanists, pragmatists and scientists to topics

Topic	Humanists		Pragmatists		Scientists		
	Mean	Rank	Mean	Rank	Mean	Rank	F-Value
1 School Change	2.83	1	3.91	1	6.06	7	19.6****
2 Teacher–School Interactions	3.98	2	4.13	2	6.08	8	8.5**
3 Context Issues	5.21	5	5.59	3	5.72	5	0.4
4 Role of Leadership	3.96	3	6.20	6	7.69	10	20.4****
5 Stability/Consistency	8.06	9	5.96	4	4.10	2	31.1****
6 Curriculum Issues	4.63	4	6.22	7	7.58	9	11.9***
7 Methodical Issues	8.69	11	6.13	5	3.88	1	37.5****
8 Variance Issues	7.52	7	6.52	8	5.77	6	4.2*
9 Theory	7.71	8	7.17	9	5.25	3	6.6**
10 Existence/Magnitude Issues	8.29	10	7.63	10	5.33	4	8.9***
11 District/State Effects	5.83	6	8.22	11	9.46	12	30.1***
12 International Studies	10.08	12	8.96	12	8.77	11	2.3

Note: One-third of the respondents were classified as humanists, one-third as pragmatists, and one-third as scientists. Two respondents were eliminated from these analyses due to missing data, leaving a total of 142. Respondents ranked topics from 1 (most important) to 12 (least important).

* $p > 0.05$
** $p > 0.01$
*** $p > 0.001$
**** $p > 0.0001$

in SER, and rank Existence/Magnitude Issues low in importance. Several of the respondents in the humanist and pragmatist groups indicated that 'Existence/ Magnitude Issues' had historical importance, but were no longer that important, since the existence of school effects was now well established. Scientists continued to believe that the study of the size of school effects was still very important.

The Importance of the Survey Findings

That large numbers of persons in the disciplines of school effectiveness and improvement participated at all in the surveys is clearly a sign of tremendous intellectual self confidence, since if researchers and practitioners were concerned about the intellectual state of the discipline, they would be unwilling to answer questions about it. Additionally, the high response rate to the surveys reported suggests a high degree of professional disciplinary commitment amongst persons in the field.

Many of the results of the survey are encouraging, when viewed in the light of knowledge of those factors which are necessary for any discipline to advance. For example, 'Definitional Issues' was dropped from the main study because of a perceived lack of importance in the pilot – in the early stages of a developing discipline there need to be things 'taken for granted' for intellectual advance to take place, which is hindered by any semi-philosophical debate or 'definitional' discussion, important though these must be in the long term. Also, the dropping of 'The School Effectiveness Correlates' from the main survey suggests a pleasing willingness of respondents to move on in the 1990s from the core concerns of the 1980s. On the other hand it may not be encouraging that 'Teacher Induction/Socialization' was not regarded as a worthy topic, since it is clear from the Louisiana School Effectiveness studies that we need to know far more about how effectiveness and ineffectiveness is maintained over time in schools of differential effectiveness levels (Teddlie and Stringfield, 1993).

In the second survey, it is perhaps encouraging that there is some interesting variance in responses among different groups. On the other hand, the low priority given to 'International Studies' by all groups (surprising given that respondents were from an international survey that did not just consist of North American respondents) must be worrying, since the discipline may need a greater range of variations in school processes and in cultural context to force the development of more sensitive theories that focus upon how factors are potentiated or hindered by their contexts.

The low priority given within the survey to 'Curriculum' issues may also be potentially damaging, since there are likely to be large differences in this area between schools in different systems within societies and in different societies in the ideological messages transmitted within curricula that are not tapped by our existing instruments, which merely measure the 'vessel' of schooling and ignore the 'contents' of the vessel. The needs of school improvement programmes also necessitate information upon curriculum matters, since practitioners may be more likely to become involved in school improvement if it reflects their focal concerns, usually deemed to be both curriculum and pedagogy (Reynolds et al., 1993).

The low priority given to 'District/State Effects' is another slightly worrying feature of the pattern of responses, since any lack of commitment to study this area of the field leads to an impoverished understanding of schools and to potentially intellectually impoverished school improvement programmes, since the District–School interaction is usually an important interface in school improvement programmes.

It is a pity that our survey did not investigate the methodological orientations of the different groups, since one further problem that is likely to continue to confront the field is the variation between the groups identified in their preferred methodological orientations and styles. Had respondents been questioned on this, results would probably have shown that the 'Humanists' prefer use of qualitative methods, and that the 'Scientists' prefer quantitative, with a significant minority of the 'Pragmatists' being attracted to mixed methodology research strategies and some of the remainder of the 'Pragmatists' belonging to either of the quantitative or the qualitative methodological groups.

The problem for the discipline generated by this state of affairs is that little routine interaction between the groups and participants within the discipline may be possible in a conventional scientific sense, if individuals and groups disavow the methodology (and therefore implicitly) the results of the 'other' groups and individuals. Even the routine sifting of valid knowledge from invalid that is needed to build normal science is impossible in these circumstances, because persons may be judging the validity/ invalidity of knowledge partially on the basis of the research methodology utilized and only regarding as valid the findings within the paradigm of which they are members. If this analysis is true, the structure of normal science in SER in terms of the existence of the professional association of the *International Congress for School Improvement (ICSEI)*, and the journal (*SESI*), both of which provide the possibilities for normal science may not be overwhelming in their positive effects because the discipline does not possess the agreed sets of procedures for assessing knowledge within that structure.

Further Findings from a Second Survey

Very similar results to those of Teddlie and Roberts (1993) were shown by Szaday (1994) in his report for the Swiss National Science Foundation. In this, a sample of 57 school effectiveness and school improvement researchers from 10 countries was determined by looking at all authors in the 1992 and 1993 volumes of the journal *School Effectiveness and School Improvement* and by selecting authors of frequently cited books and articles over the last decade. The questionnaire focused upon getting respondents to outline what they considered to be the most significant/productive research questions and lines of enquiry.

Completed questionnaires were received from 25 (44 per cent) of the sample, coming from the United States (9), the United Kingdom (5), Canada (4), Australia (3), Hong Kong (1), Macao (1) and Norway (1).

Five broad clusters were revealed, clearly depicting the views of the scientists (measurement issues) and the humanists (school change) noted above in the first survey. Of lesser importance were the clusters of the 'social, political and economic contexts of school effectiveness', 'theory development' and 'curriculum initiatives' (respondents were allowed to reply in an open-ended fashion to as many 'important' dimensions as they wished).

Detailed comments were given as follows and are given in full from the original report to give a further flavour of the 'scientific' and 'humanistic' perceptions of the important issues in the field.

Cluster 1 included respondents whose commitment to a conventional 'scientific' approach to the field was revealed in the following responses:

- how educational products and processes can be meaningfully measured (5) (the numbers after the quotes are respondent numbers);
- measurement of a broad list of pupil and school variables (4);
- the development of psychometrically reliable and intuitively valid measures of desired student outcomes (academic achievement, pro-social values and actions etc.) (20);
- the relationship between achievement on criteria and perceived achievement of official goals (9);
- what the relationship is between effective classrooms and effective schools (22);
- students' experiences in effective schools (6);
- the connections (intellectual and social) between students, parents and teachers within classrooms (5);
- the connections between good classrooms and good schools (5);
- what the relative contributions to student achievement of classroom level variables are as compared with school level variables (13);
- reconceptualization of the number and nature of the variables at school level and at level of the class–school interface (16);
- research into stability, significance with respect to outcomes, factors at the classroom, the school and the contextual level, and especially the relationship between them (7);
- the multilevel nature of educational processes looking at child, classroom, school, district and national levels (16);

- how contextual effects can be incorporated in models concerning comparative education (4);
- the possible variation in the effective schools correlates across different contexts (national, grade level, SES of catchment area, etc.) to see which factors travel (16);
- the international generalizability of school effectiveness models (also using educational indicators) (17);
- do the school effects variables explored in the USA and UK generalize to other countries (such as Switzerland)? Are there additional variables that are consistently associated with higher achievement? (20)

Cluster 2 included respondents whose 'humanistic' commitment to school improvement was revealed in the following responses:

- How do we successfully implement change? (15)
- How to improve the classroom environment and the school climate? (25)
- How to initiate school effectiveness projects under different conditions? (8)
- What factors are barriers to the effective replication of effective practices? (15)
- How to understand better the components of school culture and how they impact school improvement? (19)
- What are the relationships between processes (such as leadership, decision-making, communication, resource allocation, etc.)? (2)
- How does the *persistence* of organizational structures (e.g. the stability of institutions) affect school improvement? How can educational organizations be effectively 'backward mapped' from classrooms upward to changed administrative hierarchies? In short, how do we turn the administration of schooling 'on its head' – with kids, teachers and classrooms as 'top' priority? How can we effectively broaden the role of schooling toward a larger, integrated children's services function, in collaboration with other social service institutions? (14)
- How generalizable are the 'traditional' variables : cross-role involvement, evolutionary planning, goal consensus, transformational leadership, resources, etc. Line of enquiry: school based management, organizational learning, coordinated social services (family, community), school–university collaboration, continuous experimentation, authentic collaboration and collegiality (staff), organizational culture, teacher empowerment, role differentiation, pupil self-efficacy, focused professional development, building 'learning communities', effective instructional theory, pupil self-regulation? (11)
- To what extent do commitment building strategies in schools result in significant restructuring? Are second-order changes (changes in decision making, teacher professionalization and the like) associated with first order changes (changes in curriculum and instruction)? How can schools be structured in a way that allows for widespread participation in decision making, on the one hand, and does not overburden staff members with excessive demands on their time on the other hand? Through what processes do teachers acquire a more professionalized view of their role? How do staff members, individually and collectively, go about learning how to do their jobs more effectively? (13)
- How individualism and collectivism can co-exist in collaborative work cultures? (8)

- What is the causal nature of school and classroom effectiveness factors in planned school improvement programmes? (16)
- What are the action research projects that blend investigations of process (school improvement) with examinations of a range of outcomes (school effectiveness), taking a value added perspective on students' progress? (19)
- What are the relationships between school self-management and school effectiveness? (22)
- How is school-based management and strategic planning related to school effectiveness conceptions? (3)
- How to develop and test school self-evaluation procedures within the framework of school improvement? (17)

Humanists, Scientists and the Rise of Pragmatism

These two studies confirm the 'schizophrenic' (or with the addition of the pragmatists, multiple personality based) nature of the groups of individuals who are interested in SER. According to their survey response patterns, there are at least two types of individuals interested in SER, or more specifically in the application of SER to school improvement: those whom we have called the humanists and those denoted the scientists. Responses indicate that there may now even be a third group, who have a response pattern somewhere between the other two groups.

From a methodological perspective, it is reassuring that we have the response patterns of all three groups represented in our final sample, indicating that we have perhaps sampled the full range of those individuals interested in SER. Returning to a point from Chapter 1, where we argued that there are three distinct strands of SER (school effects, effective schools studies, school improvement studies), then our three 'types' of respondents (scientists, pragmatists, humanists) may be said to roughly align with each of those orientations:

- scientists with school effects studies, which emphasize the exploration of the scientific characteristics of school effects;
- pragmatists with effective schools studies and the implications of those studies for school improvement; and
- humanists with the more applied school improvement studies, who are committed to the improvement of practice more than the generation of research knowledge.

These results also indicate that the AERA SIG, ICSEI and the journal are aptly named (School Effectiveness *and* School Improvement) since all respondents place a heavy emphasis on 'School Change', as well as on the exploration of school effects. Even the scientists rated 'School Change' as their seventh most important area. On the other hand, the importance of 'Methodological Issues' (the number one concern of scientists) was ranked only fifth by pragmatists and eleventh by humanists. Also, apparently only the scientists were really interested in 'Theory' (ranked third by them), since the pragmatists and humanists ranked it ninth and eighth respectively.

The importance of 'Teacher–School Interaction' and of 'Context Issues' to both the pragmatists and humanists is noteworthy, since these are two areas where replicable results have been uncovered over the past five years. As one respondent noted:

Probably the most important issues are the context of school effects and the interaction of teacher and school effects . . . Both are areas in which school effects can be considered 'more scientific' since studies in these areas should continue to yield interesting and replicable findings.

(Respondent 42, first survey)

It is interesting that the scientists rated these topics (Teacher–School Interaction, Context Issues) lower than did either the pragmatists or the humanists. These are easily researchable areas which are of current vital interest to practitioners and which have generated solid, replicable findings, yet the scientists rank these two areas lower than Methodological Issues and other traditional substantive areas (e.g. the Existence, Magnitude, Stability and Consistency of School Effects). This is particularly surprising since it is the scientists whose use of multilevel statistical techniques should have alerted them to the importance of cross-level issues and 'interface between levels' issues.

The results of those two surveys reflect comments from Huberman concerning the differences between the researcher and practitioner communities in matters pertaining to school improvement. Huberman noted that:

School people often claim that much university knowledge, delivered in conventional form, is of limited utility . . . often irrelevant and framed in ways which are not assimilable to classroom life.

(Huberman, 1993, pp.1–2)

Other writers (e.g. Cuban, 1993) have also echoed these sentiments regarding the intellectual cleavage between the scientists (or those interested in school effectiveness, to use the Reynolds, Hopkins and Stoll, 1993 dichotomy) and the humanists (or those interested primarily in school improvement). Cuban rather colourfully described this separation:

If ever a continental divide existed between researchers on the one side and policymakers on the other, it is most clearly revealed over effective schools research. As researchers turned up their collective noses at this body of research, those who worked daily in improving schools embrace the findings with a relish bordering on passion . . .

(Cuban, 1993, p.ix)

Similarly, Reynolds, Hopkins and Stoll (1993) referred to 'the lack of mesh' or the 'overall lack of synchronization' between the 'enterprises' of school effectiveness and school improvement, which they attributed primarily to historic, paradigmatic and philosophical differences between the two areas. Despite this, their survey ended on a positive note in which they described three projects that interwove components of the traditional school effectiveness and school improvement paradigms (one from Canada and two from the United Kingdom). Further examples of this increasing blend of traditional 'effectiveness' and 'improvement' research and practice are outlined in Chapter 7.

The growing *rapprochement* between the scientists and the humanists is also apparent in the writings of some scholars who are beginning to seriously talk about synthesizing the two approaches. In the terms employed in this present analysis, we may call those synthesizers 'pragmatists', again utilizing the terminology of Howe (1988) who has written at a conceptual level encompassing the paradigmatic differences between positivism (which underlies the scientific or traditional school effectiveness orientation) and constructivism (which underlies the humanistic or traditional school improvement orientation). He argues that while the two paradigms have seemed to be irreconcilable on the surface, due to fundamentally different theoretical assumptions, a third paradigm called pragmatism can indeed unite components of the two approaches (see Tashakkori and Teddlie, 1998 for a further discussion of pragmatism and mixed methodology).

Essentially the same argument is made by Reynolds et al., who give:

> Examples of fruitful intellectual and practical interrelationships between the two bodies of knowledge, which represent in fact a distinctively new paradigm built on the foundations of the existing two . . .
>
> (Reynolds et al., 1993, p.38)

Pragmatists are now beginning to perform three of the four functions noted by Huberman (1993) in his description of how researchers and practitioners typically interact:

1   knowledge production – performed by both scientists and pragmatists;
2   knowledge transfer – performed by pragmatists;
3   knowledge use – performed by humanists (school improvers) and by pragmatists;
4   communication of needs – performed by humanists (school improvers).

The suggestions noted above about the intellectual desirability of a 'merger', 'synthesis' or 'synergy' between the two existing groups and the related need for a third, pragmatic orientation and epistemology are paralleled elsewhere in the field. In the United Kingdom, the Department of Education and Science project on *School Development Plans* (*SDPs*), for example, was an attempt to develop a strategy that would, among other things deal with issues of effectiveness and improvement (see Hargreaves and Hopkins, 1989, 1991). The work of Bruce Joyce and his colleagues (see Joyce et al., 1983, 1992; Joyce and Showers, 1988) has also for some time transcended both paradigms. Although located within the humanistic school improvement tradition, Joyce argues strongly for the raising of student achievement through the utilization of specific models of teaching and staff development designs and is of a scientific orientation in his own teacher effectiveness research.

Mortimore (1991b, p.223) has argued for transferring 'the energy, knowledge and skills of school effectiveness research to the study of school improvement'. Stoll and Fink additionally (1992, p.24) maintain that 'it is only when school effectiveness research is merged with what is known about school improvement, planned change and staff development, that schools and teachers can be empowered and supported in their growth towards effectiveness'. The mission statement of the journal *School Effectiveness and School Improvement* (Creemers and Reynolds, 1990) also argued for the still, small voice of empirical rationality being utilized jointly to assess the validity both of existing models of school improvement and of some existing, simplistic, factor-based theories of school effectiveness.

The Needs for Merger

The future benefits of a merged or integrated discipline become even clearer if one considers how central the two disciplines or 'paradigms' of scientific school effectiveness and humanistic school improvement are to each other. To take the practice of school improvement first, it is clear that knowledge is needed concerning the factors within schools and classrooms that should be changed to enhance processes and outcomes. Effectiveness research can provide that knowledge. Likewise, school improvement and its consequent changes to school and classroom factors can provide a testing ground for school effectiveness theories that relate processes and outcomes, and can therefore show if there are causal links involved.

What the two paradigms can contribute to each other and to enhanced educational quality is currently minimized because of a consistent lack of synchronization between the effectiveness and improvement enterprises. To take the *deficiencies in existing school effectiveness* research first:

- There are very few studies at the level of 'case studies' of effective, or even more so ineffective, schools that would show the inter-relationships between school process variables and paint a picture for improvement practitioners of the fine-grained reality of school and classroom processes. The American study by Rosenholtz (1989), and some of the 'mixed methodology' work from the 'Louisiana School Effectiveness Study' of Teddlie and Stringfield (1993), are exceptions to this trend internationally, but even they do not get particularly 'close to the action'. In the UK, for example, we still have no in-depth, qualitative portrait of the effective school equivalent to Louis and Miles's (1990) *Improving the Urban High School*, which provides excellent case studies of process variables, although the National Commission on Education's (1995) examination of 11 schools which were successful 'against the odds' has encouraged a start in this area. The absence of rich case study explanations reduces the practitioner relevance of the effectiveness research and makes the transfer of knowledge to improvement programmes difficult. Further case study evidence is in the pipeline (Gray et al., 1999).
- School effectiveness studies are very deficient at the level of the study of 'processes' rather than factors, since effectiveness researchers have considerably more experience at the level of school organizational factors. School processes defined in terms of attitudes, values, relationships and climate have been somewhat neglected, therefore, even though school improvement needs information on these factors within schools, given their centrality to the process of improvement and development that is discussed in Chapter 7.
- School effectiveness studies customarily show a 'snapshot' of a school at a point in time, not an evolutionary and moving picture of a school over time, a neglect which hinders the usefulness of the knowledge for purposes of school development. School improvement necessitates ideas about how schools came to be effective (or for that matter ineffective), in order to replicate (or for that matter

eradicate) the processes. This necessitates a dynamic, evolutionary, evolving and 'change over time' orientation within school effectiveness research.

• School effectiveness studies, with the exception of work by Rosenholtz (1989) and Coleman and Laroque (1991), have tended to neglect the importance and potential impact of other educational institutions, arrangements and layers above the level of the school. As Hopkins notes when discussing school improvement conducted within the International School Improvement Project (ISIP):

> much thought . . . was given to the way in which improvement policies are established at various levels . . . to the structured factors related to support, e.g. external support . . . Much of the effective schools literature appears to take such 'meso level' issues as unproblematic, yet the ISIP case studies suggest that this is just not so.
>
> (Hopkins, 1990, p.188)

School improvement needs to be informed by knowledge as to what conditions outside the level of the school are necessary to generate process and outcome improvement, although recent work by Stoll and Fink (1994, 1996) does begin to explore this issue.

• School effectiveness knowledge also misses the chance of satisfaction of the needs of school improvement by being dated. Improvement schemes in the 1990s need to be based on knowledge that is generated from schools that reflect the characteristics of schools in the 1990s, not the schools of the 1970s and 1980s. At the level of what makes for effective schooling, process factors such as the 'assertive principal instructional leadership' which was associated with school effectiveness in the 1980s may not be associated in the same way in the 1990s, when demands for ownership by teachers may have changed the educational cultural context. Outcomes appropriate for measurement in the 1980s, such as academic achievement or examination attainment, may not be the only outcomes appropriate to the 1990s, where new goals concerning knowledge of 'how to learn' or ability in mastering information technology may be necessary (we speculate more on this theme in Chapter 12).

• School effectiveness research has rarely been 'fine grained' enough to provide information that is needed for school improvement, since the variation in 'what works' by contexts has been a focus only of the very limited amount of North American work (Hallinger and Murphy, 1986; Wimpelberg et al., 1989). School improvement needs more than the notion of what works across context in the average school, and needs more than data on the relationships between school processes and outcomes for all schools. It needs knowledge of the factors that will generate improvement in particular schools in particular socioeconomic and cultural contexts. Since only a small amount of our school effectiveness database is analysed by context, the delineation of the precise variables that school improvement needs to target to affect outcomes is clearly impossible at present. The disaggregation of samples of schools to permit the analysis of contextual variation needs, of course, also to focus on the precise organizational and process variables that may be responsible for the differential effectiveness of schools with different groups of pupils within them (Nuttall et al., 1989), or pupils taking different subjects (Sammons et al., 1995a). Findings of differential school effects also necessitate investigations oriented towards differentiated analyses of within-school factors, rather than the present concentration upon 'common' school process factors.

Moving on from what school effectiveness research could give to school improvement programmes, it is clear that a somewhat changed school improvement enterprise could likewise perform a similar function for school effectiveness.

At the moment, *school improvement research and practice is too deficient in the following ways* to do this:

- School improvement practice/research has only rarely measured the impact of changes in improvement programmes upon the outcomes of pupils or students. Part of the explanation for this may be the historical tendency of school improvement to celebrate certain styles of professional practice, because of its association with the training needs and desires of the teaching profession within schools. Another part of the explanation may be the reluctance of many within the school improvement paradigm to be explicit about what the nature of school outcomes, or the educational goals of their programmes, really are. However, the absence of data on improvement programme effects restricts the ability of those within the school effectiveness tradition to help knowledge expand, in terms of further understanding the possible causal relationships between school processes and school outcomes.

- Those engaged in school improvement need urgently to pay attention to the implications of multilevel modelling procedures for their programmes. As noted earlier, the evidence from effectiveness research that schools can have different effects upon their pupils (Nuttall et al., 1989), and that schools effective for some groups of pupils may actually be less effective for others, has wide-ranging implication for school improvement. These results imply that improvement attempts need urgently to move away from the much vaunted 'whole-school' strategies towards more finely targeted programmes that may vary within the school in terms of their content, their focus and their target group. Above all, schools need to examine assessment data, whether these are academic results, attendance patterns, attitudes or any other measures of students' progress and development, and look for variations between different subsets of the population. By taking these differences into account, and by focusing improvement at the level of boys–girls, high ability–low ability pupils, and pupils from ethnic minorities–pupils from 'host' cultures, it would be possible to generate more appropriate school change strategies. This would in turn allow researchers to generate evidence about differentially effective school processes, as the effects of the change attempts were targeted within schools.

- School improvement research needs to refocus its activities, from placing a greater emphasis on the school level to highlighting the level of the classroom. A considerable volume of research now exists which suggests that teachers' focal concerns are with the content of their curricula and the nature of their instructional practice, rather than with the wider organization of the school. Yet many school improvement efforts have, until recently, neglected the primacy of instruction. By not focusing on instruction, school improvement runs the risk of manipulating variables only at the level of the school, which, in most research, explains much less of the variation in student outcomes than do variables at the instructional or classroom level (see for a review Creemers, 1992).

- School improvement needs to move beyond its current status as what West and Hopkins (1995) have called 'a glorified staff development activity'. Many of the growing number of networks or school improvement 'clubs' reviewed by Myers and Stoll (1993) and Stoll and Mortimore (1995) involve, when looked at closely, a traditional alliance of local authority professional developers, University Departments of Education that customarily have a strong stake in continuing professional development activities, and the senior personnel in schools. The three groups might be seen as celebrating each other's importance and status, if evaluation of the gain educational 'consumers', children or their parents, obtain from their activities is not addressed.

- School improvement may need to consider the prominence it has given to the 'voice' of the teacher. This is understandable, given that using the perceptions and language of teachers helps bring to life for teachers the improvement process, in ways that use of research perspective or language may not. As West and Hopkins (1995) note, however, it may be useful to start with the voice of the teacher as an explanatory variable but it would be an error of judgment to neglect other voices.

Pragmatism in Practice

In the four countries whose research literatures we surveyed in Chapter 1, there is now much evidence that it is precisely the interactions between the scientific and the humanistic, between effectiveness and improvement, that is generating significant 'cutting edge' advances. In the USA, the Louisiana School Effectiveness studies (Teddlie and Stringfield, 1993), have utilized multiple methods, have studied both school improvement/change and school effectiveness, and have clearly led the researchers into further intellectual development into the related 'improvement' areas of programme evaluation (Stringfield et al., 1997a) and of practical educational policy concerns about evaluation, dysfunctional schools and school development (Teddlie and Stringfield, 1993).

In the Netherlands, we will see later in Chapter 7 that school development now includes in certain instances both the school effectiveness and school improvement knowledge bases that formerly have been kept separate, with the addition of teacher effectiveness in some cases also. Creemers and Reezigt (1996) have also convincingly argued that the 'scientific' effectiveness researchers and 'humanistic' school improvement practitioners have in fact been engaged in rather similar intellectual enterprises but have labelled them in ways that both magnify differences and lead to misunderstandings.

In Australia, the school effectiveness research of Hill and associates noted in Chapter 1 has recently broadened to encompass improvement and intervention programmes that reflect both their own school effectiveness research and that of Slavin and associates from the United States (1996).

It is in the United Kingdom that perhaps the most extensive *rapprochement* of positions has taken place, with Gray et al. (1999) utilizing school effectiveness data on cohorts of children to study naturally occurring school improvement, for example (Gray et al., 1996a; Gray and Wilcox, 1995; Hopkins and Reynolds, 1999). The first nine months of 1996 saw no less than three collections of work published which have as subtitles or titles the theme of 'merger' between effectiveness and improvement (Gray et al., 1996a; Reynolds et al., 1996; Stoll and Fink, 1996) and indeed one of these (Gray et al., 1996a) was based upon a pioneering series of symposia held in 1993 and 1994 that brought together 30 of the leading British effectiveness and improvement scholars from both of the historic communities. So great has been the intellectual movement made by some individuals, that in fact there has been recent protest from some that have retained a 'classical', humanistic school improvement stance about what is seen as the betrayal of the conventional educational discourse by what is seen as a conservative, authoritarian and reactionary school effectiveness paradigm. We will return to these themes later in the handbook, and for the moment conclude with an outline of our organization of the handbook (see Elliott, 1996; Hamilton, 1996; and the reply to Elliott by Sammons and Reynolds, 1997).

Conclusions : The Organization of this Handbook

Our first survey of professional opinion in the field revealed six general topic areas:

- *methodological* issues;
- *process* of effective schooling issues;
- *context* of school effects issues;
- *multilevel* issues;
- *improvement* issues;
- *theoretical* issues.

These broad topical areas are graphically displayed in Table 2.8, which also contains the relevant issues associated with each general topic. The methodological issues are discussed in Chapter 3, in conjunction with the scientific properties of school effects with which they are associated. The process issues are discussed in Chapter 4, while context issues are delineated in Chapter 5. Chapter 6 contains a discussion of multilevel issues, while improvement issues are covered in Chapter 7. Finally, theoretical issues are explored in Chapter 10.

The remaining chapters in Sections 2 and 3 are Chapter 8 and Chapter 9. Each of these chapters concerns currently relevant SER topics that our experts did not mention in their open-ended responses to the 'current issue' question, but which seemed important to us in describing where the SER field is at this point in time.

We also wanted to be sure that each of the 12 topics from the second round survey was discussed somewhere in this book, preferably in one or two chapters only for the sake of clarity. These 12 topics had been derived primarily from the quantitative analysis of the responses to the first round survey, and their relative importance to the scientists, pragmatists and humanists was discussed above. The following outline indicates where each of the 12 topics is discussed in the book:

Table 2.8 Key topic areas in school effectiveness research

- Methodological Issues
    operational definitions of effectiveness
    validity of school effectiveness classification
    reliability of school effectiveness classification
    generalizability of school effects
    stability of school effects
    need for longitudinal studies

- Process Issues
    teacher expectations
    instructional issues
    school mission or vision
    leadership
    curricular organization

- Context Issues
    SES of parents or social class of community
    grade level configurations (elementary, middle, secondary)
    urbanicity (rural, suburban, urban)
    high support versus low support

- Multilevel Issues
    influence of the state or federal government
    influence of the district
    interaction of teacher and school effects
    'nestedness' of organizations (teacher within school within district)

- Improvement
    relationship between SER and school improvement
    characteristics of improving schools
    methods of creating improvement
        (instructional resources, curriculum changes, staff development, monitoring
            improvement)

- Theory
    relationship of SER to other areas, such as restructuring
    change theory
    learning theory
    organizational theory

- Chapter 3 – The Methodology and Scientific Properties of School Effectiveness Research
    Methodological issues in school effects research
    The existence and magnitude of school effects
    The stability of school effects across time and the consistency of school effects across measures
    The variance of behaviours within differentially effective schools
- Chapter 4 – The Processes of School Effectiveness
    The role of leadership in school
    The interaction of teacher and school effects
    District and state effects upon school effects
- Chapter 5 – Context Issues within School Effectiveness Research
    The context of school effects

- Chapter 6 – Some Methodological Issues in School Effectiveness Research
    The interaction of teacher and school effects
    District and state effects upon school effects
- Chapter 7 – Linking School Effectiveness and School Improvement
    The relationship of school effects to school change
    The role of leadership in school effects
- Chapter 8 – School Effectiveness: The International Dimension
    International comparative studies of school effects
- Chapter 10 – Theory Development in School Effectiveness Research
    The role of theory in school effects research
- Chapter 12 – The Future Agenda for School Effectiveness Research
    School effects and curriculum issues

There are only three areas in which topics overlap across chapters. The first two areas are 'The Interaction of Teaching and School Effects' and 'District and State Effects upon School Effects', both of which are discussed in terms of substantive findings in Chapter 4 (The Processes of School Effectiveness) and in terms of methodological considerations in Chapter 6 (Some Methodological Issues in School Effectiveness Research). Also, 'The Role of Leadership' is discussed in terms of substantive findings in Chapter 4 (The Processes of School Effectiveness) and in terms of improvement models in Chapter 7 (Linking School Effectiveness and School Improvement).

Further information concerning the arrangement of topics into these chapters includes the following:

1   Chapter 3 considers major methodological issues in SER and the scientific characteristics of school effects simultaneously. The determination of each of the major scientific properties of school effects involves the consideration of methodological issues; for instance, the consistency of school effectiveness classification is linked to issues regarding the validity of their measurement, while the existence and magnitude of school effects is tied to considerations of the internal validity of SER.

2   The major concerns of the *scientists* are addressed in Chapter 3 (methodological considerations and scientific properties), Chapter 6 (especially as it concerns the methodological aspects of multilevel modelling) and Chapter 10 (theory development). On the other hand, the major concerns of the *humanists* are addressed in Chapter 4 (the processes of school effects), Chapter 5 (the context of school effects) and Chapter 7 (the application of SER to school improvement). The more synergistic concerns of the *pragmatists* are found throughout these chapters.

3   We attempt to flesh out the future development of the pragmatic position in our two chapters on the interaction between SER and related cognate disciplines (Chapter 11) and our attempt to summarize the key 'cutting edge' or 'leading edge' areas in the field.

Section 2

The Knowledge Base of School Effectiveness Research

3   The Methodology and Scientific Properties of School Effectiveness Research

Charles Teddlie, David Reynolds and Pam Sammons

Introduction

The organization of this chapter presented a challenge due to the volume of studies that have accumulated over the past 30 years concerning the scientific properties of school effects. We use the term 'school effects' to describe what is known about the ability of schools (usually public) to affect the outcomes (usually achievement) of the students that they serve (Good and Brophy, 1986). This definition distinguishes 'school effects' from the two other major branches of school effectiveness research (see Chapter 1 for more details):

- effective schools research, which focuses on the processes associated with successful schools (summarized in Chapter 4); and
- school improvement research, which focuses on the processes involved in school change (summarized in Chapter 7).

The emphasis on methodological issues in this chapter is in keeping with the orientation of the 'scientists' in the field (see Chapter 2), who are responsible for generating much of the research discussed here. As noted elsewhere:

> In any study in an emerging field, the lessons learned tend to be methodological as well as substantive. This is particularly the case with school effects research, given the methodological criticisms that were levelled against studies in this area . . .
>
> (Teddlie and Stringfield, 1993, p.217)

The 'scientists' in this field have been primarily concerned that their studies be done correctly and not be vulnerable to methodological criticism, often emphasizing scientific rigour over the needs of the particular question under study. In fact, much of the school effects literature attempts to demonstrate that school based research can be executed with scientific rigour, despite criticism to the contrary (e.g. Ralph and Fennessey, 1983; Rowan, Bossert and Dwyer, 1983).

In keeping with this scientific orientation, we have elected to organize this chapter around general methodological and psychometric issues in the field of educational research (i.e. reliability, validity, generalizability, etc.). Scheerens (1993) has called studies concerned with such basic properties of school effects 'foundational studies'.

Seven scientific properties of school effects are listed in Table 3.1, together with the

Table 3.1 Scientific properties of school effects cross listed with methodological issues in educational research

Scientific Property of School Effects	Methodological Issue in Educational Research	Other Names for Issue in SER	Questions Posed by the SER Issue
Existence of School Effects	1.Psychometric and Design Issue of *Construct Validity* 2. Design Issue of *Internal Validity*	The Definition(s) of School Effects The Existence of School Effects in General	What are school effects (i.e. are we measuring what we intended to measure)? Did something actually occur as a result of schooling?
Magnitude of School Effects	*Statistical Conclusion Validity* (Have we measured the effects of schooling properly?)	Effect Sizes Variance Accounted For Gain scores	How large are school effects? (With student or school as unit of analysis)
Context Effects (between Schools)	*Generalizability* or Consistency of Effect Sizes *across School Settings* or *Contexts* (An **External Validity Issue** or EVI, also known as Ecological Validity)	Multiple Names Depending on the Context Variable Compositional Effects refer to Differences due to SES Factors. Another Type is Consistency across Phases of Schooling	Are effect sizes consistent across schools that vary by SES of students, governance structures, phases of schooling, country, etc.?
Consistency of SEIs *at One Point in Time*	Psychometric Issue of *Concurrent Validity* across Multiple Outcomes at One Point in Time	Consistency across Multiple Outcomes, Involve Cross-Sectional Studies of School Effectiveness	Do we have consistent multiple measures of school effectiveness (e.g. across Achievement, Behaviours, Attitudes)?
Stability of SEIs *across Time* (School as Unit of Analysis)	1.Psychometric Issue of *Reliability* 2.*Generalizability* of School Effects *across Time* (another EVI)	Consistency across Time Involves Longitudinal Studies of School Effectiveness	1. Are our measures reliable across time? 2. Do schools stay consistently effective (or ineffective) across time?
Differential Effects (within Schools)	*Generalizability* or Consistency of Effect Sizes *across Groups of People* within Schools and *across Academic Units* within Schools (An EVI, also known as Population Validity)	Disaggregation of Data within Schools Consistency of School Effects across Sub-groups within Schools, also Called Mean Masking of Achievement	Are schools differentially effective for groups of students within schools? Are school effects generalizable within schools? Are schools differentially effective across subject areas?
Continuity of School Effects (Student as Unit of Analysis)	1.Psychometric Issue of *Predictive Validity* 2.*Generalizability* of School Effects *across Time* with Student as Unit of Analysis	Long Term Effects of Schools on Individual Students across Phases of Schooling	Do school effects at earlier phases of schooling for students persist into later phases?

Note: SEIs refer to School Effectiveness Indices, which are indicators of a school's effectiveness status (Mandeville, 1988; Mandeville and Anderson, 1987). SES refers to socio-economic status of student body. Phases of schooling (Sammons et al., 1993a, 1996a) refer to levels, such as infant, junior, secondary, post-16 schools in the UK. Context effects also involve differences in effective schools processes, which are not discussed in Chapter 3, which is concerned solely with scientific properties of school effects. The context differences in effective schools characteristics are discussed in Chapter 5. The general methodological issues are taken from Cook and Campbell (1979) and Anastasi (1982) among other sources.

general methodological (or psychometric) issue(s) addressed by each property (e.g. Anastasi, 1982; Cook and Campbell, 1979). This chapter will be organized around the following seven topics:

- the *existence* of school effects – related to construct validity and internal validity;
- the *magnitude* of school effects – related to statistical conclusion validity;
- *context* effects – related to the generalizability of school effects across different settings or 'contexts' (e.g. differential school effects across schools with students from different socio-economic status or SES backgrounds, across schools from different countries, etc.). This is also labelled compositional effects when it relates to differences due to student body SES composition;
- the *consistency* of school effects at one point in time – related to concurrent validity;
- the *stability* of school effectiveness indices across time – related to the reliability of measures and to the generalizability of effects across time (with the school as the unit of analysis);
- *differential* effects – related to the generalizability of effects across groups of students within schools and across academic units within schools. The generalizability of effects across groups of students within schools is sometimes referred to as the 'mean masking' of achievement in the USA;
- the *continuity* of school effects – related to the issues of predictive validity and the generalizability of effects across time (with the student as the unit of analysis).

Each of these school effects topics is cross-referenced with questions posed by that issue in Table 3.1. For instance, the existence of school effects can be reconceptualized as a psychometric issue concerning the construct validity of what we call 'school effects' (i.e. what are school effects? are we measuring what we intended to measure?) and a research design issue concerning the internal validity of the SER that has been conducted (i.e. did school effects, or something else, affect student achievement or change that achievement?).

Throughout this chapter, there will be references to other summaries of the scientific research literature which have been organized differently. These reviews include the following:

- Rutter (1983a) – a review of the scientific literature from the UK and the USA at the start of the 1980s, with emphasis on methodological issues;
- Good and Brophy (1986) – a review of the USA literature (along with some classic UK studies), much of which was organized around the limitations of the extant research in the mid-1980s;
- Scheerens' (1992) and Scheerens and Bosker's (1997) reviews of the literature, which included a good mix of studies from the Netherlands, the UK and the USA through the early 1990s;
- Recent reviews of the international literature (e.g. Creemers and Osinga, 1995; Reynolds et al., 1994c) that have been organized around the research literatures from specific countries;
- Sammons et al. (1996a) – a comprehensive review of mostly UK literature (along with recent literature from the USA and the Netherlands) that was organized

around issues concerning what the authors call the 'consistency' of school effects.

Willms' (1992) and Fitz-Gibbon's (1996) books on monitoring school and educational performance are also referenced throughout this review due to their emphases on definitions, methodological issues, and the estimation of school effects. The reader should note that several of the studies discussed in this chapter will be discussed further in Chapter 5 (Context Issues within School Effectiveness Research) and Chapter 6 (Some Methodological Issues in School Effectiveness Research).

An Overview of Methodological Concerns in SER

Before discussing each of the scientific properties of school effects, a brief overview of some of the methodological concerns that have beleaguered the field will be presented. As noted above, responding to these methodological concerns has been a primary focus of many 'scientists' in the field. These concerns have been around since the field began; for example, the seminal work of Coleman and his colleagues (1966) received many criticisms, including the charge that they did not operationalize the school input variables adequately in order to properly assess the effect that schools have on student achievement. Similarly, the much referenced Rutter et al. (1979) study received numerous criticisms surrounding methodological issues such as sampling bias and appropriateness of statistical procedures (e.g. Acton, 1980; Cuttance, 1982; Goldstein, 1980; Heath and Clifford, 1980).

Methodological issues and the scientific characteristics of school effects are inseparably interwoven, as will be illustrated throughout this chapter. Different methodologies have resulted in different substantive findings both within and across countries. Thus, it is essential that this chapter begin with a discussion of the major methodological issues that have emerged in SER and with a synopsis of how to conduct a 'methodologically correct' study of school effects.

Six Methodological Concerns in SER

The remainder of this section will briefly address seven of these methodological concerns, which will be described in more detail throughout this chapter and the rest of the book (e.g. Good and Brophy, 1986; Purkey and Smith, 1983; Ralph and Fennessey, 1983; Rowan, Bossert, and Dwyer, 1983).

Inadequate Sampling

School effectiveness research studies have often been criticized for sampling problems, including the following:

- The use of narrow, skewed and relatively small samples that do not allow for much generalization of results.

This issue has been most often raised in the criticism of effective schools studies (e.g.

Edmonds, 1979a, 1979b; Weber, 1971), which typically sampled schools from one particular context: urban, poor and predominantly minority (Purkey and Smith, 1983). Studies within the school effects tradition have also been criticized for sampling issues; for example, Cuttance (1982) criticized the Rutter et al. (1979) study for the authors' attempt to generalize from a sample size of only 12 schools.

- The use of small sample sizes that do not yield sufficient units of analysis to allow proper data analysis.

Another issue concerning sample size relates to the need for a large enough number of observations to allow for data analysis with sufficient discriminative power (Scheerens, 1992) to avoid Type II errors, which involve the failure to detect true differences when they exist (Cook and Campbell, 1979).

This may especially be a problem in school effects studies in which extensive classroom observation data are collected. Classroom observation is quite expensive both in terms of time and money (Teddlie and Stringfield, 1993; Willms, 1992). If a large enough sample of schools is selected to allow proper data analysis, then the cost of conducting an adequate number of classroom observations across all of these schools may be prohibitive. In these studies, researchers must balance the value of having sufficient numbers of schools to allow adequate data analysis against the value of doing extensive classroom observations.

- Failure to include a typical school level in outlier studies.

Some authors have contended that a better comparison with effective schools would be typical or average schools rather than ineffective schools (Klitgaard and Hall, 1974; Purkey and Smith, 1983). As noted by Stringfield (1994a), some recent outlier studies have included this level for analysis.

- Another potential problem especially with large scale studies concerns the sampling and measurement error associated with the use of samples of students to represent entire schools. Willms concluded that the sampling errors associated with school effects, especially from smaller schools, may be such that 100 per cent samples are preferred:

    ... even with 50 per cent samples, the sampling errors for smaller schools may be too large for most policy purposes. It is preferable, therefore, to obtain data on whole cohorts of pupils. The costs of collecting data on entire cohorts are to some extent compensated for by saving the administrative costs of obtaining random samples within each school.

    (Willms, 1992, p.46)

The costs associated with 100 per cent samples may, however, simply be overwhelming in large studies of school effects (e.g. Stringfield, 1994a). For instance, a school effects study of 76 elementary schools conducted in the mid-1980s (Teddlie et al., 1984) had a sample of 5,400 students from around 250 classes. If 100 per cent samples had been gathered from each school, the total sample would have been over

30,000 students in over 1500 classrooms. Studies of this magnitude are very rare in educational research due to prohibitive costs.

In response to this problem, Willms (1992) demonstrated that estimates of school effects based on multilevel modelling can make adjustments for sampling and measurement error. The adjustments involve 'borrowing strength from the data set as a whole' by estimating school effects that are 'differentially "shrunk" towards the mean outcome for the entire sample' (Willms, 1992, p.46). Multilevel modelling, and this shrinkage of school effects, will be discussed in greater detail later in this chapter and in Chapter 6.

Inadequate Specification of School Level 'Process' Variables

Good and Brophy (1986) discussed the need for both behavioural and perceptual measures of the processes ongoing within the 'black box' of the school and classroom. As noted below, this criticism has been partially addressed with the advent of input–process–output (IPO) studies in the 1980s. Nevertheless, it can be concluded that process (especially in classrooms) is too often measured with perceptual indices such as surveys, rather than by direct observations of behaviours.

This issue relates to the use of archived datasets in school effectiveness studies. Such datasets (e.g. the longitudinal *High School and Beyond (HS&B)* database) are useful for exploring relationships among school inputs and outputs (e.g. Hannaway and Talbert, 1993), but they can tell us little about the processes whereby these relationships occur.

Inadequate Specification of (Multiple) Measures of School Outcomes

One of the most common criticisms of SER is that additional measures (other than achievement alone) should be used to assess school effects (e.g. Cuban, 1983; Good and Brophy, 1986; Purkey and Smith, 1983; Ralph and Fennessey, 1983; Rowan et al., 1983; Rutter, 1983a; Sammons et al., 1996a). Fortunately some researchers *have* used multiple measures of school outcomes, including behavioural indices (e.g. student and teacher attendance and retention), affective scales (e.g. self concept, locus of control) and measures of social growth. Studies using these alternative measures include: Fitz-Gibbon, 1985, 1991b; Knuver and Brandsma, 1993; Kochan et al., 1996; Mortimore et al., 1988; Reynolds, 1976a; Rutter et al., 1979.

For example, Teddlie and Stringfield (1993) used seven different outcome dimensions in their assessment of schools' effectiveness status during the second phase of a longitudinal study of school effects. These measures included achievement indices (criterion-referenced tests, norm-referenced tests), historical indices of behaviour (change in student attendance, stability of staff), observations of classroom behaviour (high-inference teaching behaviour, time-on-task), and measures of school climate (a research team completed ratings of twelve dimensions of schooling at the student, classroom and school levels).

The Overreliance on Quantitative Methods and Data

Another criticism of school effects methods reflects the general debate in education concerning the use of quantitative, qualitative and mixed methods (e.g. Brewer and

Hunter, 1989; Creswell, 1994; Lincoln and Guba, 1985; Howe, 1988; Patton, 1990; Reichardt and Rallis, 1994; Tashakkori and Teddlie, 1998). For example, many researchers using the IPO (or CIPO, context–input–process–output) approach have measured process variables using quantitative measures alone (archived data or the results of surveys), while these data sources are obviously not the best measures of the processes being studied. Scheerens (1992), as well as others, has called for direct observation of these process variables. As noted elsewhere:

> We have been discouraged by some studies that apply the most sophisticated mathematical models available to archived data that are ill suited to inform us about school processes. It is ironic, when such investigations yielded marginal results, that the investigators concluded that school effects were not found. Since the investigators did not collect the necessary data (e.g. classroom observations, faculty interviews, other proximal indicators of school effects), it should not be surprising that they were unable to explain their results.
>
> (Teddlie and Stringfield, 1993, p.229)

Issues Regarding the Proper Unit(s) of Analysis

From the scientific point of view, the methodological topic that has generated the most interest and comment concerns the use of the proper unit(s) of analysis in school effects research. An international chorus of theoreticians and researchers unleashed a veritable cacophony of criticism against the use of data aggregated to the school level in the late 1970s and throughout the 1980s (e.g. Aitkin and Longford, 1986; Burstein, 1980a, 1980b; Cronbach, 1982; Cronbach et al., 1976; Glasman and Biniaminov, 1981; Goldstein, 1986; Hannan et al., 1976; Knapp, 1977; Mason et al., 1984; Raudenbush and Bryk, 1986, 1987a, 1987b, 1988a, 1988b; Sirotnik and Burstein, 1985; Willms and Raudenbush, 1989).

Criticisms regarding the practice of aggregating data to the school level were summarized by Knapp (1977): these aggregated analyses generate biased estimates of effects because they do not take into consideration the hierarchical nature of the data; estimates of the importance of variable effects tend to be unstable and inefficient; these analyses may tend to underestimate school effects; and conclusions are subject to the risk of cross-level inference problems.

During the 1970s and into the mid-1980s, there was an analytical 'muddle' in SER regarding the aggregation issue. As noted by Glasman and Binianimov (1981), researchers either used one level of analysis (district, school, individual) or mixed the levels in a variety of potentially misleading ways. Some of the better known studies of that period used the following types of analyses (according to Glasman and Binianimov's review): district level aggregation (e.g. Bidwell and Kasarda, 1975; Katzman, 1971); school level aggregation (e.g. Hanushek, 1972); individual level aggregation (e.g. Murnane, 1975); mixed levels of aggregation, especially school and individual (e.g. Coleman et al., 1966; Mayeske et al., 1972; Summers and Wolfe, 1977; Winkler, 1975; Wolf, 1977).

Glasman and Binianimov (1981) explained the potential problems with the underestimation of school effects when mixed levels of analysis were used:

Conclusions derived from such studies using mixed data aggregation levels should be treated with caution because the effect of any input may be underestimated. Such is the case when, for instance, one school mean of years of teaching experience is correlated with different scores of several students, not all of whom are exposed to all teachers. Student assignment to particular classes . . . may be central to student achievement in those classes.

(Glasman and Binianimov, 1981, p.53)

Burstein (1980a) concluded that referring to unit of analysis issues (such as mixed data aggregation) as 'problems' is misstating the situation, because important variance is explicable at each of several levels of analysis (e.g. the district, the school, the classroom, the student). A statistical model was needed that could properly assess the impact of each of these levels of aggregation simultaneously.

As summarized by Stringfield (1994a), recently developed multilevel modelling techniques provided the answer to both the thorny unit of analysis issue *and* to issues concerning the measurement of change across time (Cronbach and Furby, 1970; Willett, 1988). The most sophisticated of these models allow for both multilevel (three, four or more) and longitudinal analyses (e.g. Rowe and Hill, 1994; Hill and Rowe, 1996; Willms, 1992).

Fitz-Gibbon (1996) defined multilevel modelling as 'analysis of data which is structured at several levels' (p.128), such as the student, the classroom, the Department, the school and the district. The value of multilevel modelling was summarized by Fitz-Gibbon (1996) as follows:

Multilevel modelling is a tool which has long been needed. There was a time when there was no solution to the problem that if you were working with the classroom as a unit of treatment you were nevertheless encouraged to use the student as the unit of analysis. The need to separate out effects at the various levels and model the data, taking account of the non-random assignment of students and classes, and of the dependence induced by this structure in the data, was acute. . . . Because the data are more realistically modelled, multilevel modelling should be able to detect differences which other methods of analysis overlook.

(Fitz-Gibbon, 1996, pp.129–30)

Fitz-Gibbon (1996) further traced the historical development of multilevel modelling to three centres of intellectual activity: Aitkin and Longford, formerly at the University of Lancaster; Bryk and Raudenbush in Chicago; and Goldstein and Rasbach at the University of London Institute of Education. Aitkin and Longford presented and then published (1986) a multilevel re-analysis of data originally gathered and analysed by Gray et al. (1983) in the mid-1980s. This re-analysis, and the rationale for it, proved influential in both Europe and North America.

By the late 1980s/early 1990s, multilevel statistical techniques were commercially available in computerized statistical packages both in Europe (Goldstein, 1987b; Longford, 1986) and North America (Bryk et al., 1986b), and extensive logical and mathematical justifications for their usage had been written (e.g. Bryk and Raudenbush, 1992; Goldstein, 1987b, 1995a, 1995b; Willms and Raudenbush, 1989). Since that time these multilevel models have become *de rigueur* for any researchers wishing to have their SER results taken seriously. More information regarding multilevel modelling is forthcoming in Chapter 6.

The Lack of Longitudinal Studies

School effects are viewed increasingly as consisting of ongoing processes, and schools are seen as falling along a continuum of development at any point in time (e.g. Reynolds, 1992a, 1992b; Scheerens and Creemers, 1989a, 1989b; Stringfield and Teddlie, 1988, 1990; Slater and Teddlie, 1992). In order to study change over time, it is necessary to study schools longitudinally (i.e. over the course of multiple years). Such longitudinal studies will inform us about many school effects properties, the most obvious of which is the stability of those effects.

Until now, longitudinal large scale studies of school effects have been rare, with the notable exceptions of the ILEA studies of secondary schools (Rutter et al., 1979) and of junior schools (Mortimore et al., 1988), the International School Effectiveness Research Programme (Creemers et al., 1996; Reynolds et al., 1994b), the Hill and Rowe (1996) study of school effects in Australia, and the ongoing Louisiana School Effectiveness Study (LSES). The LSES concluded its fifth and sixth rounds of actual on-site data gathering in school year 1995–6, and schools in this study have now been studied continuously since 1982–3 (Teddlie and Stringfield, 1993). Current longitudinal studies of school effects are also ongoing in the UK (see description and references in Chapter 1).

Growth in student achievement has been gaining acceptance from many researchers as the most appropriate criterion for assessing school effectiveness. Noting that learning implies growth and change, Willms (1992 referencing Willett, 1988) concludes that:

> A preferable indicator of a school's performance then is the distribution of the rates of growth of its pupils, rather than the distribution of pupils' scores on one occasion.
>
> (Willms, 1992, p.34)

Longitudinal studies are obviously necessary to study such growth in student learning across time, and there now exist mathematical models that can properly assess this type of data.

Designing a 'State of the Art' School Effects Study

Scheerens (1992, p.66) listed the characteristics that he believed to be necessary to carry out a 'state of the art' school effects study. The following statement of those characteristics cross lists them with the methodological issues just discussed:

- School effects studies should tap sufficient 'natural variance' in school and instructional characteristics, so that there is a fair chance that they might be shown to explain differences in achievement between schools. This relates to methodological criticism number one, inadequate sampling.
- School effects studies should have units of analysis that allow for data analysis with sufficient discriminative power. This is also a sampling issue.

- School effects studies should use adequate operationalizations and measures of the process and effect variables, preferably including direct observations of process variables, and a mixture of quantitative and qualitative measures. This relates to methodological criticism numbers two, three and four: inadequate specification of the school level 'process' variables, inadequate specification of (multiple) measures of school outcomes and overreliance on quantitative methods and data.
- School effects studies should use adequate techniques for data analysis: in many cases multilevel models will be appropriate to do justice to the fact that we usually look at classes within schools, pupils within classes and perhaps even schools within certain types of environments. This relates to methodological criticism number five: issues regarding the proper unit(s) of analysis.
- School effects studies should use longitudinal data, which was the concern of methodological criticism number six.
- School effects studies should adequately adjust effect measures for intake differences between schools (e.g. in previous achievement and SES of pupils). This methodological issue will be discussed in the section below on the internal validity of research conducted on school effects.

According to Scheerens, conducting such 'state of the art' studies is time-consuming and requires a demanding organizational effort. He lists only four large scale school effects studies which he believes to have met all these requirements:

- The Rutter et al. (1979) longitudinal (three year) study of 12 secondary schools in London. While this study has received much criticism, it also has received praise from numerous sources. Sammons et al. (1996a) summarized this mixed reaction to the study:

  > Perhaps because of the obvious political nature of this research context, studies of school effectiveness have often proved controversial . . . In the United Kingdom, publication of *Fifteen Thousand Hours* produced an avalanche of comment: highly critical and eulogistic in almost equal parts.
  >
  > (Sammons et al., 1996a, p.3)

- The Brookover et al. (1979) study of 91 elementary schools in Michigan, including a separate study of four case studies. This study is notable for the inclusion of process variables that could measure school 'climate'.
- The Mortimore et al. (1988) longitudinal study of 50 junior schools in London. Scheerens considers this to be the best example of a 'state of the art study' in SER.
- The Teddlie and Stringfield (1993) multi-phased study in Louisiana, including a cross-sectional study of 76 elementary schools (LSES-II) and a longitudinal study of 16 elementary schools (LSES-III through LSES-V).

While the scope of these four studies qualify them as methodologically correct effectiveness studies according to Scheerens, there are a number of well constructed studies from Australia, the Netherlands, the UK and the USA that meet all or most of the criteria he set forth (and, therefore, address the methodological criticisms that were described above). The results from these studies will be discussed throughout this chapter and in more detail in Chapter 4.

Six Definitions of School Effects

Before discussing the construct validity of school effects, it is necessary to consider alternative definitions of these effects, since conceptual and operational definitions play a large role in determining this type of validity. The definition(s) of school effects has changed considerably over the past 30 years as the field has become more conceptually and methodologically sophisticated.

The definitions presented in this section utilize achievement indices as the criterion measure for school effectiveness, rather than the alternative or complementary measures suggested by several authors (e.g. Rutter, 1983a, 1983b; Sammons et al., 1996a), such as classroom behaviour, student participation rates, attitudes toward learning, etc. We have defined school effects this way since the vast majority of studies examining the magnitude of school effects have utilized achievement indices exclusively. In a later section of this chapter (on general issues concerning the magnitude of school effects), we will discuss the use of alternative outcome variables as school effectiveness indices.

The following six conceptual definitions of school effects were compiled from several sources (e.g. Bosker and Witziers, 1996; Fitz-Gibbon 1996; Hill and Rowe, 1996; Raudenbush, 1989; Raudenbush and Willms, 1995; Willms, 1992). The order in which they are presented traces the evolution of the construct over the 30 year period of time from Coleman's 1966 study to today. This list is not exhaustive, but it serves as a starting point for consideration of the broad distinctions that exist between different definitions of school effects.

Definition 1: School Effects As the Absolute Effects of Schooling, Using Naturally Occurring 'Control' Groups of Students Who Receive No Schooling

In these studies (reviewed by Miller, 1983; Rutter, 1983a, 1983b; Good and Brophy, 1986), school effects are considered to be the overall effects of attending school versus not attending school. There are three types of studies of no schooling:

1 studies conducted in developing countries where education is not compulsory;
2 studies of students who have dropped out; and
3 studies in which some historical event results in 'no schooling' for some students for a period of time.

In a handful of studies examining countries where schooling is not compulsory, it has been demonstrated that the primary influence on student learning is the quality of the schools and teachers to which students are exposed, not the students' family background variables (e.g. Heynemann and Loxley, 1983; Sharp, Cole and Lave, 1979; Stevenson et al., 1978). Similarly, studies of the impact of dropping out of school on cognitive performance (e.g. Alexander, K., et al., 1985) indicate the importance of continued schooling versus no schooling.

A study of no schooling due to an historical event occurred in Prince Edward County in Virginia from 1959–63. Officials there shut down the school system in defiance of the Brown (1954) desegregation ruling. Many black students were without schooling in this county during this period of time, and researchers (Green et al., 1964) compared their performance with black students from an adjacent county. As described by Miller (1983), the differences in performance results were quite large:

> The effects on Blacks in achievement and IQ compared to Blacks in an adjacent county were devastating. Achievement levels were down from 2.5–4.0 grade levels in the group who received no formal education and IQs were depressed from 15–30 points.
>
> (Miller, 1983, p.54)

Fortunately, researchers are rarely given the opportunity of observing the effect of schooling versus no schooling. Therefore, it is important to understand that virtually all studies of school effects compare the *relative effects of schooling in countries in which schooling is compulsory* (i.e. in which all students are exposed to schools, teachers, and curriculum assignments). There are no 'control groups' in these studies of school effects. Since all students have some exposure to schools in these studies, there is necessarily an 'underestimation of the effects of school on achievement' (Good and Brophy, 1986, p.571).

Definition 2: School Effects As the Unadjusted Average Achievement of All Students in a School

Educational bureaucracies and other governmental entities in various countries have the unfortunate habit of publishing unadjusted examination results at the school level, thus allowing unfair comparisons among schools with students from very different backgrounds. Examples of these reports include the infamous 'league tables' published by the Department of Education in the UK (Fitz-Gibbon, 1996) and the School Report Cards reported annually in Louisiana (Louisiana Department of Education, 1996). While no self respecting educational researcher would consider these raw scores to be indicative of the effectiveness status of a school, lay people (such as parents), uninformed government officials, and education critics often use them for that purpose.

Definition 3: School Effects As the Impact of Schooling on the Average Achievement of All Students in a School, Adjusted for Family Background and/or Prior Achievement

In these studies, school effects are measured by the impact of input variables that are a function of school policy (e.g. class size, per pupil expenditure) or other 'manipulable' factors (e.g. school climate for learning, classroom process variables), as opposed to student family background inputs and/or prior achievement. These input–output studies typically utilize schools' average achievement scores (aggregated across all students in the school) as the output variable and employ regression analyses (Ordinary Least Squares) as the mathematical model. As noted above, Glasman and Binianimov (1981) reviewed studies of this type and concluded that some employed analyses at the school level only, while others mixed the levels of analysis (individual, school, district).

Studies using this approach were conducted in response to the conclusions of earlier input–output research (in which economic models were applied to educational data), whose results had indicated that the impact of 'manipulable' input variables was small compared to the effects of family background (e.g. Coleman et al., 1966; Jencks et al., 1972; Plowden Committee, 1967 in the UK). Willms (1992) noted that these input–output studies became more sophisticated over time (*circa* 1965–85) as researchers developed better mathematical models, used more sensitive outcome measures, and created input variables that measured school and classroom practices more precisely. These more sophisticated input–output studies demonstrated significant relationships between school inputs and achievement levels using analyses that varied with regard to the levels of analysis utilized (e.g. Brimer et al., 1978; Brookover et al., 1979; Madaus et al., 1979; Murnane, 1975; Rutter et al., 1979; Summers and Wolf, 1977; Schweitzer, 1984; Teddlie et al., 1984; Wolf, 1977). Several of these studies were discussed in Chapter 1.

Definition 4: School Effects As Measuring the Extent of 'Between Schools' Variation in the Total Variation of Their Students' Individual Test Scores

In these studies, researchers report what percentage of the total variation in their students' scores is 'between schools', as opposed to some other level within the mathematical model being used (e.g. Fitz-Gibbon, 1991b; Gray, 1989; Hill and Rowe, 1996; Sammons et al., 1993b). These studies give a general idea of the relative importance of schools to the performance of *individual students* using multilevel mathematical models, or OLS regression analysis applied to pupil-level data (e.g. Fitz-Gibbon, 1996). (More details regarding the use of regression analyses and multilevel modelling are given below.)

Studies of this nature have yielded fairly consistent results indicating that between 8–15 per cent of the variance in individual level achievement can be accounted for by school level variables (e.g. Bosker and Witziers, 1996; Reynolds and Teddlie, 1995; Scheerens, 1992). Later sections of this report will synthesize the results from several studies and reviews of studies from the past decade that have utilized this approach.

Definition 5: School Effects As Measuring the Unique Effect of Each School (in a System) on Their Students' Outcomes

Willms (1992) defined another type of school effect as:

> ... the difference between a school's average level of performance and some standard, after adjusting statistically for the intake characteristics of the school (e.g. Aitkin and Longford, 1986; Willms and Raudenbush, 1989). When the term is used this way, each school in the system is considered to have its own unique effect on pupils' outcomes. Thus, there is an 'effect' associated with attendance at a particular school.
>
> (Willms, 1992, p.39)

As was the case with Definition 4, school effects here refer to the effects of schools on individual students, and the indices are generated through the use of multilevel mathematical models. The data are reported as effect sizes for *individual schools*; hence, there is an increased interest in the separate slope(s) generated by data from individual school(s) as a measure of that particular school's effectiveness (e.g. Burstein, 1980b; Burstein and Miller, 1979; Jesson and Gray, 1991). (The 'slopes' referred to here are the 'within-groups' upward or downward sloping lines illustrating the relationship between students' performance and students' characteristics. See Chapter 6 for more information on slopes and other indices of school effectiveness associated with multilevel modelling.)

Willms (1992) (and Willms and Raudenbush, 1989) further defined Type A and Type B school effects:

1   Type A refers to how well an 'average' student would perform in School X compared with the average performance of the entire school system, and
2   Type B refers to how well an 'average' student would perform in School X compared with the performance of schools with similar composition and similar SES contexts (pp.40–1).

Bosker and Witziers (1996) differentiated between these two school effects as follows:

> Type A effects express between school differences in student achievement, controlling for student background. Type B effects are between school differences potentially attributable to different school practices by controlling for student background and context variables (e.g. characteristics of the student population, characteristics of the community). Type A effects are of interest for students and their parents in choosing the right school. Type B effects are of interest for those who want to enhance effective educational practices.
>
> (Bosker and Witziers, 1996, p.2)

Willms (1992) also uses a different measure of magnitude of school effect. Instead of variance explained, Willms prefers an effect size stated in terms of percentage of standard deviation (*sd*) units (e.g. 0.45 *sd*, 0.56 *sd*, −0.34 *sd*, −0.23 *sd*). These effect sizes can be positive or negative, meaning that the individual school is either more or less effective for an individual student compared to some standard. Other measures of effect sizes will be described below.

Definition 6: School Effects As Measuring the Impact of Schools on Student Performance over Time

As noted above, many researchers are now calling for longitudinal studies of school effects, rather than cross-sectional studies (e.g. Hill and Rowe, 1996; Raudenbush, 1989; Stringfield, 1994a; Willms, 1992). Growth in student achievement over time is now seen as the most appropriate criterion for assessing the magnitude of school effects, since some researchers believe that school effects models are better specified using longitudinal designs.

Multilevel models now allow for the measurement of change across time. One study

(Bryk and Raudenbush, 1988; Raudenbush, 1989) utilizing a longitudinal design produced some 'startling' results: over 80 per cent of the variance in student growth in mathematics achievement over three years was between-school. This study is described in more detail later. This study appears to illustrate '... powerful evidence of school effects that have gone undetected in past research' (Raudenbush, 1989, p.732).

From a psychometric point of view, the definition(s) of school effects have become technically and substantively more refined over the past 30 years. The results from an analysis of school effects can vary depending upon the particular definition that analysts choose to use. This issue is discussed in more detail in the section on construct validity.

The Existence of School Effects

Sammons, Mortimore and Thomas (1996) and others (e.g. Mortimore et al., 1988; Reynolds and Cuttance, 1992; Scheerens, 1992; Teddlie and Stringfield, 1993) have concluded that school effects do, in fact, exist. These authors have stated that:

> ... there is a common acceptance that schooling effects can be found; that they are substantial; and that – in many cases – they are differential. Although studies of variations between schools exist in both simple and more sophisticated forms, the majority tend to take account of the differences in the characteristics of the students entering and attending schools. ... the methodology for doing this has improved considerably over the last twenty years. ...
>
> (Sammons et al., 1996a, p.1)

We have maintained the separateness of these two 'properties' (existence, magnitude) solely because we wanted to review the methodological issues listed in Table 3.1 related to the 'existence of school effects': the psychometric (and design) issue of the construct validity of school effects and the research design issue of the internal validity of school effects. Each of these issues will be discussed briefly in this chapter, and then the subject of the 'existence' of school effects will be bypassed.

The Construct Validity of School Effects

When we consider the existence of school effects, we must first select our own particular *theoretical definition* (e.g. what do we believe school effects are?) and then the specific *operational definition* for those effects (e.g. how do we measure what we believe to be school effects?). As noted above and throughout the rest of this chapter, the particular definitions (theoretical and operational) that a researcher gives to school effects has a dramatic impact on whether they are found and upon their magnitude.

Choosing the theoretical definition of school effects in turn involves a set of decisions. Using just the six definitions listed earlier, researchers must determine if they are interested

- in the absolute or the relative effects of schooling;
- in the impact of schooling on the average achievement of students or the achievement of individual students;

- in the effect of a group of schools or in the effect of each individual school; and
- in achievement measured at one time or longitudinally.

The repercussions of these choices in definition will be discussed further in the section on the magnitude of school effects.

After the theoretical definition of school effects has been determined, then the specific operational definition must be selected. Construct validity, as defined by Cook and Campbell, refers to the:

> . . . approximate validity with which we can make generalisations about higher order constructs from research operations.
>
> (Cook and Campbell, 1979, p.38)

Cook and Campbell described two basic types of problems with the operational definitions of a theoretical construct:

1   construct under-representation – operations failing to incorporate all the dimensions of the construct; and
2   surplus construct irrelevancies – operations containing dimensions that are irrelevant to the target constructs.

Both of these problems have been encountered by school effects researchers.

In the earlier days of research on school effects, many studies suffered from construct underrepresentation in that adequate measures of school processes were not included in the research designs. For example, as noted above, Coleman and his colleagues (1966) were criticized for not including adequate measures of school process in their input–output model of school effects. Much of the progress in the field over the past 20 years has been in the development and inclusion of measures to adequately assess school effects, first in terms of surveys (e.g. Brookover et al., 1979) and later in terms of more proximal measures of process (e.g. classroom and school observations as in Mortimore et al., 1988 and Teddlie and Stringfield, 1993).

A common current problem with the construct validity of SER concerns the well-known 'Hawthorne effect', which involves 'surplus construct irrelevancies'. In the 'Hawthorne effect', an extraneous factor closely related to the 'treatment' has an impact on the outcome variable, and its effect is confounded with the construct itself (see Willms, 1992). For example, a school improver may introduce a restructuring programme into a school to see what impact it will have on student attitudes. His or her own personal enthusiasm may generate positive change in the school irrelevant to the programme, and the measure of success (change in student attitude) may pick up the effect of his or her enthusiastic style, as well as the restructuring effort. This would be an example of surplus construct irrelevancies, and the existence of a 'true' school restructuring effect would be in doubt.

Internal Validity Issues

This section contains a discussion of the internal validity of school effects (Campbell and Stanley, 1966; Cook and Campbell, 1979), which is the other major methodological issue concerning the existence of these effects. Cook and Campbell defined internal validity as:

> . . . the validity with which statements can be made about whether there is a causal relationship from one variable to another in the form in which the variables were manipulated or measured.
>
> (Cook and Campbell, 1979, p.38)

Some have argued that consideration of internal validity is *not* relevant to school effects research, since internal validity is related only to experimental or quasi-experimental studies, and school effects research is almost totally correlational in nature. Despite this concern about the distinction between experimental and correlational research, many school effects researchers treat conclusions from their correlational studies as if they were causal in nature. Since these scholars imply that causal relationships are demonstrated in their studies, then the internal validity of their research is relevant to their reviewers and readers.

For instance, Maughan et al. (1980) stated that the purpose of the Rutter et al. (1979) study was to determine whether school influence had any 'effect' (thus implying causation) in raising levels of student outcomes (Cuttance, 1982). Rutter (1983a, 1983b) further concluded that several school effects findings ' . . . point to the probability of a causal effect' (p.12). He discussed three sets of evidence for this conclusion:

1   the results from case studies of matched pairs of schools indicating that those that have similar inputs, but different outcomes, also differ on school climate (ethos) in a predictable manner (e.g. Brookover et al., 1979);
2   the findings that there are significant correlations between school climate and student outcomes even after the overlap with school 'composition' has been taken into account statistically (Brimer et al., 1978; Brookover et al., 1979; Madaus et al., 1979; Rutter et al., 1979); and
3   the finding that school process variables correlate more highly with pupil characteristics (i.e. behaviour and achievement) at the end of the school year than at the beginning (Maughan et al., 1980).

Rutter concluded that all three of these rather different types of results provide strong 'circumstantial evidence' of a causal effect. Researchers willing to interpret such 'circumstantial evidence' as causal should, therefore, try to eliminate from their studies (by controlling) the effect of variables not associated with school processes (e.g. the SES of the students attending the schools under study). The essence of the internal validity issue is to ensure that all other potential causes of the school outcome (typically student achievement) are entered, and thus accounted for, in the statistical model.

Much of the concern regarding threats to the internal validity of school effects research is handled with adjusted and value added outcome scores. Sammons et al. (1996a) distinguished between raw outcome measures, adjusted scores, and value added scores as follows:

- Raw outcome measures are the achievement scores reported by testing agencies, typically aggregated at the school level, such as the league tables in the UK. These scores are unadjusted for differences in the SES backgrounds of the students attending the schools; thus, higher SES schools will typically do better than lower SES schools on these raw measures.
- Adjusted scores take into consideration background characteristics of students attending schools (e.g. social class, ethnicity and gender). This technique has often been used in the USA both in research studies (e.g. Brookover et al., 1979; Teddlie and Stringfield, 1993; Witte and Walsh, 1990) and in state reports on the performance of schools.
- Value added scores also take into consideration 'prior achievement of pupils on entry to school' (Sammons et al., 1996a, p.5). By including background and prior achievement variables in models measuring the impact of school effects, researchers remove them as threats to the internal validity of their studies. This technique has often been used in the UK and the USA both in research studies and in reports on the performance of schools and departments within schools (e.g. Fitz-Gibbon, 1992; Sanders and Horn, 1995a, 1995b).

Several authors (e.g. Stringfield and Teddlie, 1990; Willms, 1992) have discussed other factors that, if not detected and properly controlled for, might also be threats to the internal validity of school effects studies: underdetected changes in SES of students attending schools (due to sudden changes in the local employment or migration of new student sub-populations); confusing administrators' efforts to boost student achievement through technical means (such as 'teaching to the test') with true school change efforts aimed at changing the 'instructional core' of the school; failure to recognize 'good' and 'bad' years of schools due to differences in cohorts of students; and other 'random fluctuations' that are hard to detect. These factors can lead to an artificial increase (or decrease) in student achievement, which can subsequently lead to the overestimation (or underestimation) of school effects.

These threats to the internal validity of school effects studies are particularly troublesome for one-point-in-time cross-sectional studies, which was the nature of much research in the area, especially through the mid-1980s. Willms concluded that longitudinal studies are necessary to avoid confusion regarding the true causal agents in research on schooling:

> To separate the effects on schooling outcomes attributable to schooling *per se* from those attributable to other factors or to random fluctuation, one requires data describing schooling inputs, processes, and outputs for successive cohorts on at least two occasions; three or more are preferable . . . . The point to be made, though, is that data for successive cohorts can be used in a longitudinal design that provides richer and more accurate information about the effects of schools.
>
> (Willms, 1992, p.36)

The Magnitude of School Effects

Statistical Conclusion Validity

General Considerations

The methodological issue associated with the magnitude of school effects in Table 3.1 is statistical conclusion validity, defined as threats to drawing valid conclusions about 'covariation' between variables based on statistical evidence (Cook and Campbell, 1979, p.37). There are several threats to statistical conclusion validity (e.g. low statistical power, violated assumptions of statistical tests, 'fishing' or the error rate problem). Two of these threats are relevant to SER:

1   The threat of low statistical power, or making incorrect 'no-difference' conclusions (Type II error), may occur when sample sizes are small. Small sample sizes has, of course, been one of the methodological difficulties frequently associated with school effects studies. In studies employing small samples, researchers run the risk of reporting erroneous results indicating that there are no school effects.

2   'Fishing' or the error rate problem occurs:

> . . . when multiple comparisons . . . are made and there is no recognition that a certain proportion of the comparisons will be significantly different by chance.
>
> (Cook and Campbell, 1979, p.42)

This 'fishing' for significant results can result in Type I errors, where it is falsely concluded that significant relationships exist when they do not. School effects studies have been subjected to this criticism. For instance, Cuttance (1982) criticized the work of Rutter and his colleagues (1979) as follows:

> Without a theory or set of hypotheses about the nature of the processes underlying the statistical models they use, there is no possibility of drawing conclusions which purport to show that the relationship in the models is causal in nature. The lack of an overall theoretical framework led the authors to embark on a fishing expedition in which the size of the holes in the net was determined by the irrelevant criterion of statistical significance. Everything that did not fall through the net was ground up into a new super fishmeal – 'school ethos'.
>
> (Cuttance, 1982, p.487)

Two points should be made with regard to this criticism of this specific study:

1   experts in the field (e.g. Good and Brophy, 1986; Scheerens, 1992) consider the Rutter study to be one of the most important and influential studies in the history of SER; and

2   the lack of a theoretical orientation is one of the primary criticisms brought against almost all SER, not just Rutter's study (see Chapter 10 for an extensive treatment of theoretical issues in SER).

Nevertheless, the comments by Cuttance illustrate the point that there have been problems with the statistical conclusion validity of even the better known SER.

Aggregated versus Disaggregated Data

The most important issue regarding statistical conclusion validity in school effects research has been the 'units of analysis' issue, discussed previously as both a methodological and a definitional problem. Specific concerns about aggregating the data to the school level include:

1   the possibility of generating biased estimates of the relationships between variables (which is a 'magnitude of effect' issue) and
2   difficulties associated with statistical conclusions that are subject to the risk of cross-level inference problems (e.g. Aitkin and Longford 1986; Alexander, K., et al., 1981; Burstein 1980a, 1980b; Cronbach et al., 1976; Hannan et al., 1976; Lau, 1979; Willms and Raudenbush, 1989).

Willms (1992) expressed the prevailing orthodox point of view regarding the preference for individual student level data, as opposed to school level data:

> School effects, as defined above, refer to the effects of schools on individual pupils, not their effect on some aggregate of pupils. . . . Aggregate data, such as school mean achievement or school mean SES, are insufficient. . . . [The] principal objection is that estimates based on aggregate data can be biased if they do not take account of the hierarchical nature of educational data. If one could assume that the relationship between pupils' outcomes and the relevant background variables were identical across schools in a system, then estimates based on aggregate data would be similar to what I refer to as Type B effects. However, this assumption does not hold in most schooling systems, and generally estimates based on aggregate data are inaccurate and misleading.
>
> (Willms, 1992, p.44)

We will return to this issue in a later section of this chapter on the importance of school as a level of analysis in SER. Results from studies utilizing the school as the unit of analysis, typically conducted before the advent of multilevel modelling, will be presented throughout this chapter. These studies have historical value in the evolution of school effects research, if nothing else.

Regression Analyses and Multilevel Modelling

The choice of the specific statistical techniques to be used in SER has again become a topic of debate over the past few years (e.g. de Leeuw and Kreft, 1995a, 1995b; Fitz-Gibbon, 1991b, 1995a; Goldstein, 1995a; Mason, 1995; Rogosa and Saner, 1995a and 1995b). While almost all contemporary, sophisticated SER utilizes multilevel modelling, there has been some concern about technical problems with its estimates and about the increasing complexity of its operations. Some researchers and statisticians (e.g. de Leeuw and Kreft, 1995a; Fitz-Gibbon, 1991b,

1995a) have concluded that regression analyses may be more appropriate for some applications.

We will return to this issue of multilevel modelling and regression analyses later in the chapter. Results from studies utilizing regression analyses, especially from the time of the Coleman Report (1966) to the Aitkin and Longford (1986) study, will be presented throughout this chapter. In a review of this type, we believe that it would be inappropriate to ignore the results from studies that constitute roughly two-thirds of the life of the study of school effects (1966–86). Such a review would be woefully inadequate in our opinion. It should be noted, however, that this point of view is not held by all researchers interested in the study of school effects. Bosker and Witziers, in a statistical meta-analysis of the magnitude of school effects, chose to not include these earlier studies, using the following logic:

> Another important aspect in meta-analysis is the quality of the research studies at hand; the validity of a meta-analysis is largely determined by the quality of the individual studies in the analysis. In this study quality was largely addressed from a statistical point of view. Studies before 1986 had to rely on – in hindsight – unsound statistical procedures (Aitkin and Longford, 1986), mainly due to the lack of appropriate statistical procedures to deal with the hierarchical nature of the data. Of course this situation has changed dramatically over the past 10 years and this implies that in this meta-analysis we have only used those studies, which . . . use the sound statistical procedures. This implies that only studies using multi-level procedures are included in our analysis . . .
>
> (Bosker and Witziers, 1996, p.6)

Results from Reviews of Research Considering the Magnitude of School Effects

Both Scheerens (1992, p.55) and Sammons et al. (1996a) have commented on how frustrating it is to summarize results concerning the magnitude of school effects. This is the case due to the broad divergence in types of school effects studies, in operational definitions of the independent variables, in choice of dependent variables, and in the statistics whereby the effects are expressed. Scheerens (1992) concluded that it was 'child's play' for the early reviews of the field to try to make conclusions based on such diverse studies and report formats. Nevertheless, he and other respected scholars have quite legitimately summarized the more recent evidence on the magnitude of school effects, and in the following section we will attempt to draw conclusions from some of the most recent of those reviews.

One point, that will become more clear below, is that the magnitude of school effects varies across several important 'contexts': by socio-economic status of student body (e.g. predominantly middle class, predominantly lower class); by phase of schooling (e.g. infant, junior, secondary in the UK); by country in which the study was conducted; etc. In fact, much of this variance seems systematic (e.g. effects at the lower grade levels are usually larger than those at the upper grade levels). This systematic variance in effect sizes will be discussed in more detail further on and in Chapter 5.

In this section of the review, we will summarize recent, comprehensive reviews of

SER, that have included extensive information on the magnitude of school effects (e.g. Bosker and Witziers, 1996; Bosker and Scheerens, 1989; Creemers and Osinga, 1995; Mortimore, 1991b; Reynolds et al., 1994a; Reynolds and Cuttance, 1992; Reynolds, Sammons, Stoll, Barber and Hillman, 1995; Sammons et al., 1993a, 1996a; Sammons, 1996; Scheerens, 1992; Scheerens and Creemers, 1994; 1995; Scheerens and Bosker, 1997; Stringfield and Herman, 1995, 1996; Teddlie and Stringfield, 1993). The next section of the chapter contains a review of the results from some selected individual studies of the magnitude of school effects.

Scheerens (1992) presented reviews of two sets of studies that included estimates of the size of school effects: twelve UK and USA studies of school effects (Brimer et al., 1978; Brookover et al., 1979; Coleman et al., 1966; Evertson et al., 1978; Gray, McPherson and Raffe, 1983 (re-analysis by Aitkin and Longford, 1986); Madaus et al., 1979; Mortimore et al., 1988; Rutter et al., 1979; Schweitzer, 1984; Spade et al., 1985; Teddlie et al., 1984; Wolf, 1977); and sixteen Dutch studies of school effects (e.g. Hoeben, 1989).

These reviews included tables that compared the studies on school type, dependent variables, analysis level, type of analysis, independent variables and effect size, between-schools variance and total variance explained by variables in the model. Scheerens (1992) concluded that:

> When we look at school effectiveness research in The Netherlands, for example, it seems that the average variance between schools amounts to 11 or 12 per cent of the total variance. This percentage hardly deviates from the results of the American and British studies discussed . . . .
>
> (Scheerens, 1992, p.70)

Bosker and Scheerens (1989) had reached similar conclusions in an earlier review of Dutch studies, concluding that the average total variance in individual student achievement due to between-school factors was 12 per cent.

Scheerens and Creemers (1995) reported basically the same results from their recent review (reported in Chapter 1) of 42 Dutch studies (29 studies in a primary setting; 13 in a secondary setting). They concluded that 9.5 per cent of the individual student variance at the primary level is due to between schools factors, while 13.5 per cent of the individual student variance at the secondary level is due to between schools effects. The following list includes some of the studies analysed in this review: Bosker, Kremers and Lugthart, 1990; Hoeben, 1989; Hofman, 1993; Hofman, 1995; Luyten, 1994a, 1994b, 1994c; Scheerens et al., 1989; Werf and Tesser, 1989.

Recent reviews of the UK literature by Reynolds, Sammons and their colleagues (e.g. Reynolds, 1992a; Reynolds et al., 1994c; Sammons, 1996) have included several studies that have examined the effect of school size (e.g. Daly, 1991; Gray, 1981, 1982; Gray, Jesson and Jones, 1986; Gray, Jesson and Sime, 1990; Jesson and Gray, 1991; Sammons et al., 1993b; Rutter et al., 1979; Smith and Tomlinson, 1989; Thomas et al., 1994; Willms and Raudenbush, 1989). These reviews have resulted in similar conclusions to those made by the Dutch reviewers:

> Early beliefs that school influence might be as large as family or community influences were misplaced. A very large number of studies in the last five years show

only 8–15 per cent of the variation in pupil outcomes as being due to differences among schools.

(Reynolds, 1992a, p.70)

Bosker and Witziers (1996) performed a statistical meta-analysis summarizing results from 103 studies that had utilized multilevel analyses in their estimation of school effects. As noted above, only studies employing multilevel analyses were included in the meta-analyses, so research from the first 20 years of SER (*circa* 1966–86) was automatically eliminated. Also, the sample was heavily weighted toward research from certain countries (e.g. 32 per cent of the total were from The Netherlands), since these studies met the criteria for inclusion.

There were two overall conclusions of interest. First, the meta-analysis indicated that over all reviewed studies, school level factors accounted for 18 per cent of the gross (unadjusted) variance in student level achievement and 8 per cent of the net (adjusted for student background) variance in student level achievement.

Secondly, the meta-analysis indicated that studies from Third World countries reported the largest school effect, followed by studies from North America, which were followed by studies from the UK, the Netherlands, and industrialized nations from the Pacific Rim. Estimates of the per cent of variance attributable to the school level would, therefore, be higher for Third World studies than the general figure reported here.

From their sample of USA studies employing multilevel modelling, Bosker and Witziers (1996) concluded that the school factors level accounted for an average of 21 per cent of the gross (unadjusted) variance in student level achievement and 10 per cent of the net (adjusted for student background) variance in student level achievement.

Some researchers and reviewers would put the USA gross unadjusted figure in the 15–30 per cent range (e.g. Bryk and Raudenbush, 1988; Miller, 1983; Murnane, 1975; Raudenbush, 1989; Teddlie and Stringfield, 1993).

Creemers, Reynolds, Stringfield and Teddlie (1996) recently reported data from the ISERP longitudinal international study of school effectiveness, which indicated that more variance in student achievement was attributable to the school level in the USA sample (16–17 per cent) than in the sample from Great Britain (8–11 per cent) or any of the other countries in the study (0–11 per cent), which were all industrialized countries (see Chapter 8 for more details regarding this study). These figures are basically in alignment with those reported by Scheerens and Bosker (1997).

Results from Selected Studies Considering the Magnitude of School Effects

The following section reviews selected studies that have examined the magnitude of school effects. These studies were selected because they present valuable information on the magnitude issue, or because they involved an important methodological or analytical breakthrough, or a combination of those two reasons. They are presented in chronological order.

Coleman et al. (1966)

The well known Coleman Report (Coleman et al., 1966) officially named the *Equality of Educational Opportunity Study,* has often been cited as the study that initiated school effectiveness research in the USA. As noted in Chapter 1, this study concluded that schools have little effect on students' achievement that is independent of their family background and social context. Madaus et al. (1980) concluded that the Coleman Report '. . . denied the efficacy of schooling as a powerful equalizer in American society' (p.28).

The federally sponsored research study that Coleman and his colleagues conducted involved 4000 elementary and secondary schools and utilized regression analyses to predict student level achievement, even though much of the input data that were utilized were not at the individual student level. Researchers who re-analysed the data came to the same basic conclusions as Coleman, although the Mayeske et al. (1972) re-analysis indicated that more of the variance was between schools.

Coleman et al. reported that 5–35 per cent of the variance in individual level achievement was attributable to between school factors, with the remaining variance attributable to within school factors. This large range in the variation attributable to between school factors (5–35 per cent) was due to differences in the between schools effect for different ethnic groups: there was more between schools variance in the scores of Puerto Ricans, American Indians, Mexican-Americans and 'Negroes' in the southern United States; there was less between schools variance in the scores of 'Negroes' in the northern United States, Whites in either the northern or southern United States, and oriental Americans. Coleman et al. (1966) called this interesting phenomenon differential 'sensitivity to variations in school quality' with the lowest achieving minority groups showing highest sensitivity.

Coleman and colleagues concluded that the between schools variation for the numerically larger groups (Whites, 'Negroes') was between 10–20 per cent of the total variation in individual student achievement. Furthermore, the proportion of that variation that was due to what Coleman considered to be true 'school factors' (e.g. teacher characteristics, material facilities and curriculum, and characteristics of the groups and classes in which pupils were placed) was even less. Since Coleman continued to report the variation accounted for separately for different ethnic groups, interpretation of the unique variation due to true school factors was somewhat obscured, but most reviewers put that variation at 5–9 per cent for the larger ethnic groups (e.g. Bosker and Witziers, 1996; Daly, 1991; Scheerens, 1992).

Interpretation of the Coleman Report results presaged much of the methodological debate in the estimation of the magnitude of school effects that persists to the present day. Three major criticisms are as follows.

1   The major criticism was that the study did not include the types of variables that would measure the true effect of the school, which was later operationalized as school climate variables by Brookover et al. (1979) and others. Coleman did include some student attitudinal variables (e.g. control of environment, interest in learning and reading, self-concept) which accounted for relatively large amounts of the between schools variation, but he concluded that these 'attitudes depend more on the home than the school' (Coleman et al., 1966, p.324). Brookover and

others later reconceptualized these variables (e.g. student sense of academic futility) as being more related to the school than the home. This issue of what really affected the variable (the home or the school) has been discussed in the literature as 'multicollinearity'. As Murnane noted, Coleman's decision to enter the home environment variables into the regression equation before the school variables biased 'the analysis against finding the school variables important' (Murnane 1975, p.9).

2   The unit of analysis issue also arose, with Coleman and his colleagues establishing the precedent that the individual student was the appropriate unit. Other researchers have chosen the school as the unit of analysis for some or all of their analyses (e.g. Brimer et al., 1978; Brookover et al., 1979; Rutter et al., 1979; Schweitzer, 1984; Teddlie and Stringfield, 1993; Teddlie et al., 1984; Wolf, 1977). This issue will be discussed more thoroughly in the next section of this chapter.

3   Coleman used verbal achievement as the outcome variable. Other researchers (e.g. Madaus et al., 1979) have argued that such standardized tests are less sensitive to differences in school characteristics than are curriculum specific tests.

The Plowden Report (1967)

The UK equivalent to the Coleman Report was the Plowden Report, officially called *Children and their Primary Schools*, produced by the Central Advisory Council for Education in England. This report concluded that 'Differences between parents will explain more of the variation in children than differences between schools' (The Plowden Report, p.35). Parental attitudinal factors, in fact, accounted for 58 per cent of the variance in student achievement in this study. Ainsworth and Batten (1974) conducted a longitudinal four year follow up study to the Plowden Report and reported very high correlations between achievement levels at the two time points and that social class was basically determinate.

Jencks et al. (1972)

These researchers re-analysed the Coleman Report data, plus data reported from several other studies. They arrived at results similar to those of Coleman, concluding that schools do not matter much with regard to either student achievement or economic success in later life. Family background characteristics of students largely determined their success in school and their future incomes.

An interesting methodological advance of the Jencks' work involved assessing the impact of home and school in terms of effect sizes, rather than per cent of variance accounted for in student achievement. Jencks et al. (1972) concluded that effect sizes for schools, controlled for student intake and prior achievement, would be no larger than 0.17 for white students and 0.20 for black students. (See discussion later in this chapter regarding various methods for estimating effect sizes.) Bosker and Witziers (1996) concluded that effect sizes of this magnitude are small using the operational definition provided by J. Cohen (1969).

Murnane (1975)

In his book entitled *The Impact of School Resources on the Learning of Inner City Children*, Murnane (1975) predicted individual level student achievement using prior achievement as a control variable, a practice not often used in USA studies until the advent of multilevel model studies. In this study, Murnane tested the hypotheses that assignment to particular classrooms and to particular schools have an impact on student achievement. Murnane concluded that both class and school assignment did have a significant effect upon student achievement, with the average amount of variance accounted for across seven separate regressions increasing 15 per cent (from 47 per cent to 62 per cent) as classroom and school assignment (dummy coded) were added to the effect of prior achievement and student background variables.

Murnane (1975, p.25) was quite prescient in his discussion of the methodological issues that he felt were important in SER, since many of his conclusions regarding these issues reflect contemporary normative practice. He argued:

- that the unit of analysis should be the individual student since intra-school variance is larger than inter-school variance;
- that longitudinal information on school inputs *applied to individual students* should be used since past school experiences can affect current performance;
- that prior achievement should be controlled for in the statistical models;
- that different 'structures' should be estimated for different types of students (e.g. different ethnicities);
- that several different outputs of the schooling process should be included; and
- that peer group influences should be separated from influences of the students' own background.

Summers and Wolfe (1977)

Their study of elementary students in Philadelphia included the following methodological advances: student-specific data were included for both inputs (where possible) and outputs; the output measure was an achievement gain score over a three year period of time; and the student-specific inputs included qualities of the teachers who taught the students. The researchers were able to explain 21–27 per cent of the student level variance in gain scores using a mixture of teacher and school level inputs; they did not report the cumulative effect for these school factors as opposed to SES factors.

The Summers and Wolfe (1977) study directly addressed the issue of the aggregation of data and of linking particular classroom/school inputs to specific students. The authors characterized previous SER as follows:

> We conclude that empirical investigations have failed to find potent school effects because the aggregative nature of the data used disguised the school's true impact. The use of school and district averages introduced so much noise as proxies for inputs into students that effective inputs were not revealed.
>
> (Summers and Wolfe, 1977, p.652)

This important issue of data aggregation is discussed in further detail later in this chapter.

Madaus et al. (1979) and Brimer et al. (1978) Studies

The major contribution of these studies was to demonstrate the need for measures of school achievement more sensitive to the school's curriculum, as opposed to the global measures of verbal ability that are often used in SER. In addition to using curriculum specific tests, Madaus and his colleagues used a technique known as symmetric variance decomposition to overcome problems with the underestimation of school effects due to multicollinearity (e.g. Beaton, 1974; Wisler, 1974).

As noted in Chapter 1, the between class variance in student performance on curriculum specific tests was estimated at 40 per cent in the Madaus et al. (1979) study. Additionally, Madaus and his colleagues concluded that classroom factors explained a larger proportion of the variance on curriculum specific tests than on standardized measures. Madaus and his colleagues concluded that their results provided evidence for the differential effectiveness of schools, even though the unit of analysis in this study was the classroom.

Madaus et al. (1979) concluded:

> Our findings provide strong evidence for the differential effectiveness of schools: differences in school characteristics do contribute to differences in achievement. . . . Examinations geared to the curricula of schools are more sensitive indicators of school performance than are conventional norm-referenced tests.
>
> (Madaus et al., 1979, p.223)

Rutter et al. (1979)

This well known longitudinal study of school effects occurred in 12 secondary schools in London and is described in greater detail in Chapter 4. The researchers utilized rank correlations and regression analyses in analysing their results, but they also reported effect sizes in terms other than 'variance accounted for in student achievement'. The rank order correlation between school inputs, as measured by a general composite process score, and examination results was 0.76. On the other hand, the regression analyses indicated that less than 2 per cent of the variance in students' examination results was due to the composite process score.

Rutter et al. (1979) discussed these results further utilizing quite different terminology:

> . . . *after adjusting for intake characteristics*, children at the most successful secondary school got four times as many exam passes on average as children at the least successful school. Or expressed another way, children in the *bottom* 25 per cent of verbal ability in the most successful school on average obtained as many exam passes as children in the *top* 25 per cent of verbal ability at the least successful school.
>
> (Rutter et al., 1979, p.19)

Rutter (1983a, 1983b) also discussed problems that he perceived in the use of 'variance' estimates, and this general issue is elaborated upon in a later section of this chapter.

Brookover et al. (1978, 1979)

This cross-sectional USA study was conducted in 68 elementary schools that represented a random sample of Michigan schools. Corollary case studies were conducted in four differentially effective low-SES schools. This study is also reviewed in Chapters 1 and 4.

The major methodological contribution of this study was the use of parallel principal, teacher, and student climate questionnaires that assessed expectation levels, academic norms, sense of academic futility, and other social psychological factors associated with the school. Brookover's definition of school academic climate was as follows:

> The school social climate encompasses a composite of variables as defined and perceived by the members of this group. These factors may be broadly conceived as the norms of the social system and expectations held for various members as perceived by the members of the group and communicated to members of the group.
>
> (Brookover and Erickson, 1975, p.364)

While beset with multicollinearity problems between SES and school climate items, the study indicated that school climate factors could be powerful predictors of student achievement: when entered first in regression models, these variables accounted for 73 per cent of the school level variance in student achievement, whereas they accounted for only 4 per cent when entered last. Student sense of academic futility explained about half of the variance in school level reading and achievement in models in which school climate factors were entered first.

This study employed the school as the unit of analysis, rather than the student, thus utilizing the third definition of school effects described earlier in this chapter. The issue of the proper unit of analysis for school effects studies was decided in the mid-1980s with the advent of multilevel models: variance in individual level student achievement is now routinely partitioned into that accountable for at the school, classroom, student, and other levels. The Brookover et al. (1979) study occurred several years before multilevel models were available. The issue of using the school as the unit of analysis, instead of the student, is revisited later in the section which contains a discussion of the utility of school level analyses when issues regarding school level policy are being examined.

Teddlie, Stringfield and Colleagues (1985, 1993)

The second phase of the multiphase Louisiana School Effectiveness Study (LSES-II) was a partial replication and extension of the Brookover study that was conducted in 76 elementary schools in 1983–4. The initial results were conducted using regression analysis with the school as the unit of analysis (Teddlie et al., 1985), while later reports (e.g. Teddlie and Stringfield, 1993) contained re-analyses using multilevel analyses. This study is also reviewed in Chapters 1 and 4.

The LSES-II researchers utilized a second-order factor analysis to address the issue of multicollinearity among the input variables (Kennedy et al., 1993; Stringfield, 1994a; Teddlie and Stringfield, 1993). Five second order factors emerged, and results from regression analyses indicated that school climate second order factors accounted for 41 per cent of the variance in school level student achievement, while family background second order factors accounted for 30 per cent of that variance. A multilevel model re-analysis using school means produced results essentially identical to the school level regressions (Kennedy, Stringfield and Teddlie, 1993).

The researchers also partitioned the variance in individual level student achievement and determined that 75 per cent of that variance was associated with the student level, 12 per cent with the classroom level, and 13 per cent with the school level. These school and classroom estimates are consistent with those often found in USA studies using multilevel analysis.

Gray (1981)

Gray utilized already existing databases that had been collected by British local education authorities, involving individual level data on various achievement tests as 'input' data and the results of public examinations at age 16 as 'output' data. The difference between the 'top' 10 per cent of schools and the 'bottom' 10 per cent of schools was of the order of 1.5 'O' level passes per student.

Aitkin and Longford (1986)

These authors re-analysed data from a study of secondary school public examination results in one English school district collected by John Gray. They reported that the unadjusted school effect in this study was 10 per cent, while the intake-adjusted figure was only 2 per cent. This study was a very influential one in the history of the study of the magnitude of school effects, since it was the first to employ multilevel modelling in the estimation of these effects.

Willms (1987)

Willms conducted a study which focused on the impact of Scottish educational authorities (districts) on the examination results for students completing their secondary education. Results from this study indicated that around 8 per cent of the adjusted variance in these students' examination results were due to school effects. Of this 8 per cent, almost half was due to school mean SES, which is a school context, or compositional, variable. This study was one of the first in the UK to use multilevel models to simultaneously assess the impact of the levels of the district, school, and student on achievement measures.

Mortimore et al. (1988) ILEA Junior School Project and Sammons,
Nuttall, and Cuttance (1993b) Re-analysis

This study is considered by several reviewers (e.g. Scheerens, 1992) to be the best example of large scale 'state of the art' SER and is described in greater detail in Chapter 4. It involved the longitudinal study of 86 classes drawn from 50 schools in London. The initial analyses of the data (Mortimore et al., 1988) yielded many estimates of school effects, including the following: at the end of the third year of the study, the adjusted variance in student level reading achievement that was accountable for by school effects was 9 per cent, while it was 11 per cent for mathematics achievement, and 13 per cent for writing achievement.

Furthermore, Mortimore and his colleagues estimated the percentage of variance accounted for in progress in student achievement between the first and third years of the study as follows: the percentage of variance in reading progress due to school effects was 24 per cent, while it was 23 per cent for mathematics progress, and 20 per cent for writing progress. Mortimore and colleagues described the results of their longitudinal analyses as follows:

> When we considered this issue of relative progress over the junior years, we found that nearly 30 per cent of the variation in children's progress was accounted for by school membership and background factors taken together. . . . But, the school has much the larger effect. School attended is responsible for nearly a quarter (24 per cent) of the variation in pupils' reading progress between the first and third year of junior education. In other words, the school was roughly four times more important in accounting for differences in pupil progress than background factors.
>
> (Mortimore et al., p.186)

The important issue of calculating school effects longitudinally, rather than cross-sectionally, will be discussed further on.

Recent multilevel re-analyses of the Mortimore et al., 1988 data (Sammons et al., 1993b) indicated that 14–15 per cent of the variance in reading and mathematics achievement at year 5 of the UK junior school was due to school effects. These estimates are somewhat higher than those reported by other UK researchers working during this time period (e.g. Daly, 1991; Gray, Jesson and Sime, 1990; Willms, 1987), but part of this difference may be that Mortimore and his colleagues were working at the primary level of schooling, while the others were working in secondary schools. A later section of this chapter on the consistency of school effects explores this issue of differential school effect sizes across grade phase of study.

Raudenbush (1989), also Reported in Bryk and Raudenbush (1988)

An even more dramatic demonstration of the potential explanatory power of school level effects across time was reported in this re-analysis of student achievement from the Sustaining Effects Study (Carter, 1984). In their re-analysis, Raudenbush and Bryk examined a sub-sample of the reading and mathematics achievement of a cohort of over 600 students in 68 elementary schools from the first through the third grade, using five different time points. Using a multilevel longitudinal model, the authors reported the following results:

> For initial status, 14.1 per cent of the variance in mathematics and 31.4 per cent of the reading variance is between schools. In general these results are consistent with reports in the school effects literature going back to *Equality of Educational Opportunity* – between 20–30 per cent of the variance in achievement is between schools. However, the results for learning rates, particularly in mathematics, are startling indeed. Over 80 per cent of the variance in mathematics learning is between schools! These results constitute powerful evidence of school effects that have gone undetected in past research. As we would expect, the between-school variance in reading rates is somewhat less, 43.9 per cent, although still substantial.
>
> (Bryk and Raudenbush, 1989b, pp.731–2)

Lee and Bryk (1989), also Reported in Bryk and Raudenbush (1988)

This study used sector effects in a multilevel model to further explore the impact of Catholic versus public school education on student achievement, thus following up on a line of research begun by Coleman and his colleagues in the early 1980s (e.g. Coleman et al., 1982a; Hoffer, Greeley and Coleman, 1985; Lee, V., 1986). This line of research had generally led to the conclusion that Catholic schools somehow weaken the relationship between social background and student achievement, thereby leading to a more equitable distribution of achievement among students. This general area of research is discussed in more detail in Chapter 5 under the context issue of differential school governance structures.

The results of this study are included in this section on the estimation of school effects because they illustrate how sector effects in multilevel models may be used to assess the impact of different school characteristics. In this study, a sub-sample of achievement from students in 160 schools from the *High School and Beyond* database were analysed using a multilevel model in which a sector effect was included: what the authors called the 'academic organization of schools', which was operationalized as Catholic or public. Results from their analyses replicated those reported by J. Coleman (Coleman and Hoffer 1987, Coleman et al., 1982a): base mathematics achievement was higher in Catholic schools than in public schools, with the greatest difference occurring in low-SES schools; the minority achievement gap was smaller in Catholic schools; and the relationship between social class and achievement was weaker in Catholic schools.

The researchers then did additional analyses that explained these student achievement results in terms of the different curricular choices, academic norms, and disciplinary environments that the academic organizations of these two types of schools presented. They concluded:

> In sum, this HLM analysis reaffirms the 'common school' hypothesis of Coleman, et al. More important from the perspective of educational theory and practice, however, is that it also provides empirical support for the contention that the academic organisation and normative environment of high schools have a

substantial impact on the social distribution of achievement within them. Sector differences appear readily explainable. There are fewer curricular choices in the Catholic sector with schools taking a more proactive stance toward the issue of what students should be taught. These schools are safe, orderly environments conducive to learning. A relatively small school size also facilitates these outcomes.

(Bryk and Raudenbush, 1988, p.183)

Willms and Raudenbush (1989)

This study is noteworthy for its investigation of Type A and Type B school effects (see Definition 5 of school effects in the section entitled 'Six Definitions of School Effects'). In this particular study, Willms and Raudenbush used data from two cohorts of students (1989) from one Scottish educational authority. The authors reported Type A effects using both regression and multilevel analyses (HLM) and Type B effects based solely on HLM. The Type A HLM results were much more stable than the regression results across the two years, as illustrated by graphs of the effect sizes presented in the article.

The authors reported significant Type A and Type B effects, but the addition of the school level variables into the model increased the explained variance in achievement only negligibly. They concluded:

> These findings emphasise a point made by Cain and Watts that an increase in R-squared is not a good measure to determine the policy relevance of variables used to explain achievement outcomes.

(Willms and Raudenbush, 1989, p.225)

Creemers and Scheerens, 1989 and Brandsma and Knuver, 1989

The increasing internationalization of SER was apparent in the publication of a special issue of the *International Journal of Educational Research* in 1989 entitled 'Developments in School Effectiveness Research' (Creemers and Scheerens, 1989). Several articles in this journal reported on original investigations of the magnitude of school effects from different countries: the Mortimore and colleagues' study from the UK previously described in this section (Mortimore et al., 1989a), the Raudenbush longitudinal study of school effects also previously described in this section (Raudenbush, 1989), a study by Brandsma and Knuver (1989) of the magnitude of school and classroom effects using a sample of schools from the Netherlands, and an international comparative study assessing the magnitude of school and teacher effects in several countries using archived data from the Second International Mathematics Study (SIMS) by Scheerens et al. (1989). Results from one of these studies concerning the magnitude of school effects will now be summarized.

The *Brandsma and Knuver (1989)* study is important for two reasons: it was one of the first studies of school effects using data gathered in the Netherlands, and it included analyses on both mathematics and language achievement. This study involved 250 primary schools, and the data were analysed using a multilevel model. The researchers concluded that school level differences accounted for 12 per cent of the variance in arithmetic achievement and 8 per cent of the variance in Dutch language achievement. This difference in the amount of variance accounted for in mathematics and language has been demonstrated in several countries and is discussed further in the section entitled 'Consistency of SEIs at One Point in Time'.

Smith and Tomlinson (1989)

In their 1989 book, *The School Effect: A Study of Multi-racial Comprehensives*, Smith and Tomlinson presented results from a study of 18 comprehensive secondary schools in the UK in which the performance of various ethnic groups was highlighted. There were four general findings from this study regarding school effects:

- the overall per cent of variance in achievement predictable at the school level was around 10 per cent across all tests, ability groups and ethnic groups;
- the effect of the school varied by the ability level of students, with the effect being greater for above or below average students and less for average students;
- the effect of the school varied depending on the subject taught, a phenomenon called the departmental effect; and
- there was also some evidence of differential school effects for students from different ethnic groups, but the effect was small.

The largest differential effect found in the study was for pupils with different patterns of prior achievement. For example, the school level accounted for about 12 per cent of the variance in the overall achievement of UK pupils with higher prior test scores, 9 per cent of the variance in the overall achievement of UK pupils with lower prior test scores, and only 2 per cent of the variance in overall achievement of UK pupils with average prior test scores.

There were also some differential department effects, leading the researchers to conclude that academic success in secondary schools should be studied by subject, or by subject groups, rather than overall. While there was evidence of differential school effectiveness by different ethnic groups, these effects were small compared to overall between-school differences. More information regarding differential effects will be presented later.

Witte and Walsh (1990) and Mandeville and Kennedy (1991)

While estimates of the variance accounted for by the school are generally higher in USA studies, these two studies reported virtually zero school effects. The Witte and Walsh (1990) study employed regression analyses and used the school as the unit of analysis, while the Mandeville and Kennedy (1991) study employed multilevel models and analysed individual student level data. The similarity between these two studies involves their use of school effectiveness factors. Both employed teacher ratings of the school effectiveness climate variables, and neither of the sets of school factors was very strongly related to student achievement. In the Witte and Walsh study, the authors reported a higher correlation between teacher ratings of school effectiveness variables and their students' family background variables than between the teacher ratings and student achievement. The general issue of the underspecification of school effectiveness factors in SER will be discussed in more detail in the next section.

Daly (1991)

This study reported secondary school effect size data from Northern Ireland. Daly concluded that between 7–11 per cent of the adjusted school variance was accountable for by the school level. This varied by type of test with mathematics having the highest variance accounted for and English the least. These results are consistent with other contemporary estimates of school effect size from the UK.

Fitz-Gibbon (1991b)

In this study, Fitz-Gibbon reported data from a performance monitoring system in the UK known as ALIS (A-level Information System), which assesses student performance at age 18. This study is important for several reasons:

- It provided another estimate of variance accounted for by school effects using a database that included subject specific tests;
- It provided theoretical arguments for the analysis of departmental effects, in addition to, or instead of, school effects at the secondary grade level;
- It compared results from multilevel and ordinary least squares (OLS) regression analyses of the same datasets;
- It provided initial information from a data monitoring system that eventually will be used to provide a national 'value added system' in the UK (Fitz-Gibbon, 1995, 1997).

Fitz-Gibbon (1991b) reported an average school effect of around 15 per cent, which was somewhat larger than the 10 per cent reported by other contemporary studies in the UK (e.g. Smith and Tomlinson, 1989). Fitz-Gibbon attributed these larger effect sizes to the tighter link between instruction and the A-level results reported, which included four subject specific results in chemistry, geography, French, and mathematics. Her argument for the use of these subject specific tests and the resultant higher school effects echoes those of Madaus et al. (1979) reported earlier.

While Fitz-Gibbon (1991b) reported data focusing on the school as the level of analysis, she indicated that department might be a more important level at the secondary level:

> From its inception in 1983, the A-level monitoring system has collected student-level data. The students may be viewed as nested within departments rather than schools because examination results for each academic subject are analysed separately. In view of pressures towards inter-school competitiveness, it is perhaps quite important that ALIS does not produce *school* indicators, but only *department* indicators.
>
> (Fitz-Gibbon, 1991b, p.71)

Fitz-Gibbon's comparisons of results from OLS regression and multilevel analyses indicated that they were similar, but that each analytic technique had advantages and disadvantages. She concluded that:

Given this kind of conflict between models, a possible solution is to provide both analyses for the all-important achievement data. . . . The solution may well be to report both OLS and multilevel analyses and to continue to warn that different questions and different assumptions lead to different answers, and this complexity in the world simply has to be borne.

(Fitz-Gibbon, 1991b, pp.80–1)

The issue of the use of multilevel and regression models is discussed in more detail further on.

Tymms (1993)

This study followed up on the earlier work of Fitz-Gibbon (1991) and Smith and Tomlinson (1989) regarding departmental effects at the secondary level in the UK. Again using the ALIS database, Tymms concluded that 7 per cent of the variance in examination performance could be attributed to the school or college.

However, when Tymms (1993) dropped school from the multilevel model and nested student within class within department, he reported proportions of variance due to class that ranged from 9–25 per cent and by department that ranged from 8–24 per cent. Tymms' results indicated that department effects in secondary schools are larger than school effects. He concluded:

In every case more variance was accounted for by the department level than the school and the proportion of variance accounted for at the class level was more than for the departmental level. . . . In accountability terms the models indicate that teachers have the greatest influence but that the influence is on a relatively small number of pupils. Schools as a whole have less influence on individual pupils but their influence is more widely spread.

(Tymms, 1993, pp.292–3)

This issue of the amount of variance in achievement attributable to each level of multilevel models is discussed in more detail at a later stage in this chapter.

Tymms, Merrell, and Henderson (1997)

This study is noteworthy for examining the effect of school on children at a very early age: the reception year in the UK, or age 4. Tymms et al. (1997) studied 1700 students' early mathematics and reading achievement scores at the start and end of their reception year as part of the Pupils Indicators in Primary Schools (PIPS) project.

Tymms and his colleagues reported a very large school effect of about 40 per cent after controlling for student background characteristics. This research project demonstrates dramatically the potential effect that school has on students of a very young age.

Hill and Rowe (1996)

This research article was based on results from the first two years of a three-year longitudinal study of elementary schools conducted in Australia.

The results from this part of the study helps to explain some of the differences in SER concerning the amount of variance attributable to the school and class levels. These researchers ran and then carefully compared the results from a series of two-level (students within schools), three-level (students within classes within schools), and four-level (students within classes within grade cohorts within schools) hierarchical analyses. The two-level analysis indicated that 18 per cent of the variance in student achievement is accounted for by between school differences; the three-level analysis indicated that 5–6 per cent of the variance in student achievement is accounted for by between school differences; and the four-level analysis indicated that a trivial amount of the variance in student achievement is accounted for by between school differences.

Hill and Rowe (1996) concluded that for a complete picture of the effect of the various levels, it would be necessary to consider all of the analyses:

> Given the sampling structure of the data, with all students assessed at each of the targeted grade levels, the 16 to 18 per cent estimate of school effects reflects real variation among schools. The three-level parameterisation, however, indicates that class effects are very large and that the unique effect of schools *over and above* that due to within-school class differences are relatively small. This does not mean that schools do not make a difference, but that they do so mainly at the level of the class.
>
> (Hill and Rowe, 1996, p.26)

The results from this study are further explored later in this chapter in the discussion of the importance of school as a level of analysis in SER and evidence for the existence of a larger school effect in longitudinal studies.

General Issues Concerning Estimation of the Magnitude of School Effects

In the previous two sections a number of influential studies and reviews regarding the magnitude of school effects were reviewed. Some general themes were recurrent across several of these studies and reviews, and they will be examined more closely in this section.

Methodological Issues that may Affect Estimates of the Magnitude of School Effects

The estimation of the magnitude of school effects has been a controversial issue from the initial Coleman Report (1966) through the most recent meta-analyses conducted by researchers from the Netherlands (Boskers and Witziers, 1996). Some would argue that had it not been for the controversy raised by the Coleman Report, and continually fuelled by studies and reviews indicating that schools have at most a modest effect, there would not have been a School Effectiveness Research area. While the field has expanded well beyond the study of the magnitude of school effects, as attested to by the wide array of topics addressed in this volume, this issue continues to intrigue researchers and others interested in the field.

Methodological concerns have always been at the heart of the magnitude of school effects issue. It is not by accident that outlier studies primarily concerned with school processes have consistently demonstrated a 'school effect', while studies emphasizing school 'products' (i.e. achievement) and utilizing representative samples of schools have *not* done so *consistently*. The specific methodologies employed in the various school effectiveness studies have either enhanced or decreased the probability of finding a meaningful school effect.

For example, we know that studies that are cross-sectional, based solely on archived data often gathered for other purposes, conducted in secondary schools, not utilizing proximal process variables for the schooling inputs, conducted in countries without much natural variance between schools due to governmental or other educational policies, and using standardized general ability tests as outcome variables are more likely to demonstrate a 'small', perhaps even negligible school effect. On the other hand, studies that are longitudinal, based on a variety of data sources gathered specifically for the purposes of the study, conducted in primary (or even pre-primary) schools, utilizing proximal process variables for the schooling inputs, conducted in countries with larger natural variance between schools due to governmental or other educational policies, and utilizing tests of specific knowledge associated with school curricula as outcome measures are more likely to demonstrate a 'large' school effect.

While almost all sophisticated contemporary studies of school effects routinely employ multilevel analyses, researchers have been less likely to attend to these other important methodological issues. Lack of attention to these issues is partially a result of the fact that studies often utilize archived data sets, which are cross-sectional in nature and do not contain valuable input and output variables. No matter how sophisticated the mathematical models used in these studies, the net impact of school (and classroom) educational factors on variance in individual student achievement will necessarily be underestimated.

In the following sections, we will consider how specific methodological decisions can influence the estimation of school effects. Since most studies have estimated the magnitude of school effects using 'variance explained in student achievement', this discussion will centre around the effect that methodological decisions have *on the amount of variation* that is explained by school level factors. The following methodological issues, related to the size of these school effects, will be discussed:

- the choice of input variables;
- the choice of outcome variables;
- the inclusion of prior indices of achievement in school effectiveness research;
- issues related to the use of the school as a level of analysis;
- the use of longitudinal as opposed to cross-sectional designs; and
- sampling decisions and the magnitude of school effects.

Other topics covered in this part of the chapter include: alternative measures of the magnitude of school effects, and data analysis issues associated with the estimation of school effects.

Continued Underspecification of School Inputs in School Effectiveness Models

This issue was discussed earlier in this chapter (Section entitled 'An Overview of Methodological Concerns in SER') and may be stated as follows: Does the study include completely and accurately specified process variables on the input side of the mathematical equations, specifically including valid indices of school level social psychological climate and measures of the school/classroom interface? While the total amount of gross (unadjusted) variance in individual student achievement attributable to school level factors appears fairly stable at 15–20 per cent (e.g. Bosker and Witziers, 1996), the amount that can be accounted for uniquely by school factors, as opposed to family background or other factors, is more variable across studies. This variability is partially due to whether SER studies include the aforementioned powerful school level variables.

The underspecification of school inputs in SER involves at least three issues, which are discussed throughout this section:

1 the specification of potential school level factors as teacher level (or some other level) factors only;
2 the failure to include certain powerful school level factors at all; and
3 having school level variables assessed by individuals (e.g. teachers) who are less sensitive to those effects, rather than by individuals who are more sensitive to those effects (e.g. students).

Addressing the issue of the impact of the overall school climate, Brookover and his colleagues concluded that:

> Although there is some variance in school climate between classrooms within the school, the within school differences are not so great as to rule out the existence of a characteristic climate for the school.
>
> (Brookover et al., 1978, p.303)

When contemporary studies of school effectiveness include school climate variables, such as teachers' perceptions of their influence on school-level decisions, they often include it as a teacher variable only, since it is measured at that level (i.e. teachers completed the surveys). While the teacher level may *technically* be the right level to enter this particular variable in multilevel models, events that occur at the school level may *actually* be the most important determinant of teachers' perceptions of their influence on school-level decisions.

For example, let us imagine an elementary school serving primarily low-SES students in a rural area at time one. Further suppose that measures of teachers' perceptions of their influence on school-level decisions were taken at time one, and they were extremely low due to the presence of an autocratic principal. Between time one and time two, a dynamic, democratically oriented new principal was hired, and she immediately began a school restructuring programme that involved getting teachers actively involved in school-level decisions regarding curriculum and governance issues. The principal's intervention worked so well that when teacher surveys were again completed at time two, the teachers' perceptions of their influence on school-level decisions both independently (measured at the teacher level) and collectively (measured at the school level by averaging all the teachers' responses) were considerably higher.

If researchers measured teachers' perceptions of their influence on school-level decisions at time two at the teacher level only, then the effect of the school level change would not be included in the model, even though it was directly responsible for the changes that occurred at the teacher level. Potential methods for including the effect of the school include:

- entering the variable 'teacher perception of participation on school-level decision making' at both the teacher and school level, as suggested by Reynolds et al., 1994c; or
- running path models in which school level factors are entered prior to teacher level factors.

The issue of using path models rather than cross-sectional multilevel models is discussed later in this chapter.

Another major issue concerns the lack of properly operationalized variables to measure processes that are known to be at work at the school level, such as selection and socialization of teachers by the principal and other administrators. For example, Crone and Teddlie (1995) conducted a mixed methods study that included teacher and principal interviews concerning teacher socialization processes (such as mentoring programmes for new teachers), instructional leadership, school wide enforcement of discipline problems, and methods for both teacher selection and dismissal. All of these variables *could* be operationalized as quantitatively scaled variables at the school level, yet such variables are seldom included in SER studies.

Instead, researchers often use inappropriate or non-powerful measures of school processes, such as teacher expectations for student learning, as school level variables. Several studies in the USA (e.g. Teddlie and Stringfield, 1993; Witte and Walsh, 1990) have found teachers' expectations for students' learning to be more highly correlated with students' socio-economic status than with students' achievement. On the other hand, both the Brookover et al. (1979) and the Teddlie and Stringfield (1993) studies concluded that student sense of academic futility (aggregated at the school level) was the best single predictor of school level student achievement. Stringfield (1994a) concluded:

> It may be the case that, as a group, teachers are unable to differentiate 'school climate' from the economic conditions from which students come. If that is true, then future large scale school effects studies should stop asking those questions directly of teachers and, instead, directly ask students about the climate of their schools.

> (Stringfield, 1994a, p.68)

Alternative Outcome Variables as SEIs

This issue was also discussed earlier in this chapter and may be stated as follows: Does the study include accurately specified outcome variables that are sensitive to school level effects? There are actually two issues at work here:

1   Are curriculum specific measures of student achievement included on the output side of the mathematical equations, rather than generic standardized tests?
2   Are alternative school outcome variables (e.g. non-achievement variables such as student participation in school, student locus of control, student self esteem, indices of student delinquency) included in the analyses that may be more sensitive to school level effects? (See the section entitled 'Consistency of SEIs at One point in Time' for further discussion of research related to this issue.)

The first issue was discussed in Chapter 1 and earlier in this chapter in the section on the Madaus et al. (1979) and Brimer et al. (1978) studies. As Hill and Rowe (1996) recently summarized:

> . . . choice of outcome measures has major implications for the conclusions that one might draw regarding the impact of student-, class- and school-level effects. With the exception of several UK studies, such as the above-mentioned study by Tymms (1993) that have made extensive use of results for secondary students in subject-based examinations, almost all studies of school effectiveness have used norm-referenced, standardised achievement tests as outcome measures. However, the majority of such tests assess skills in terms of generalised academic abilities and enduring cognitive 'traits' rather than specific learning outcomes arising from classroom instruction (Darling-Hammond, 1994; Stringfield, 1994a). To the extent that tests are not sensitive to the specifics of what has been actually taught, school and class effect sizes are likely to be smaller.
>
> (Hill and Rowe, 1996)

Also, no school effects studies have appeared thus far using authentic assessment rather than the traditional examination formats (e.g. Gifford and O'Connor, 1992; O'Connor, M., 1992; Resnick and Resnick, 1992; Shavelson, 1994; Shavelson et al., 1991), even though these assessments might be particularly sensitive to the effects of the classroom and school (Hill and Rowe, 1996). Unfortunately, at this time proponents of authentic assessment have not produced tests that can be economically administered and that are sufficiently generalizable to be used in large scale research (Stringfield, 1994a).

The second issue, the utilization of non-achievement outcomes in SER research, concerns the supposition that in some situations the school effect will be larger for these non-achievement indices than for achievement indices. Rutter (1983a, 1983b) discussed these alternative outcomes as behaviours schools should 'be aiming to effect' (p.9). His list of non-achievement variables included: classroom behaviour, absenteeism, attitudes to learning, continuation in education, employment, and social functioning. Research in this area of alternative outcome variables in SER was recently reviewed by Sammons et al. (1996a).

A contemporary example of studies using alternative outcome variables was conducted by Kochan, Tashakkori and Teddlie (1996). This study included an alternative measure of school effectiveness for use at the high school level: a composite measure of student participation that included student attendance, dropout and suspension data. Results from this study indicated a moderate sized correlation between the participation school effectiveness indicator (SEI) and a composite achievement SEI. Examination of the relationship between these SEIs and various types of demographic data indicated considerable differences in the partial correlation coefficients that were generated by the two SEIs.

The Inclusion of Prior Indices of Achievement in School Effectiveness Research

It is generally accepted that there are two types of background variables that should be included in SER models: prior achievement of students and family socio economic characteristics (e.g. Fitz-Gibbon, 1996; Sammons et al., 1996a).

Some noted researchers indicate that measures of student prior achievement are, in fact, more important as background variables than family background. For example, Willms (1992) concluded from work completed in Scotland that:

> These findings suggest that if the goal of the analysis is to estimate school effects or the effect of some intervention, then measures of prior performance are essential for statistical control. If the analysis does not include measures of prior performance, the estimate of effects will probably be biased. Measure of family background add marginally to the degree of statistical control.
>
> (Willms, 1992, p. 58)

Despite this general conclusion, however, there is some concern that the entry of certain types of prior achievement indices may have the effect of depressing the true estimate of school effects. Sammons et al. (1996a) discuss this issue as follows:

> There is now fairly general acceptance that studies of school effectiveness in cognitive areas require adequate control for prior attainment at the level of the individual pupil (McPherson, 1992; Cuttance, 1992; Reynolds, 1992a; Scheerens, 1992). Ideally such measures should be collected at the point of entry to school at the beginning of a relevant phase (infant, junior or secondary). The use of baseline attainment or ability data collected after a period of years in the same school is likely to lead to a reduction in the estimate of school effects.
>
> (Sammons et al., 1996a, p.23)

Cuttance (1985) also cautioned against the use of prior achievement, or other background variables, as controls when they are proximal to the point at which the school effects are measured. Preece (1989) commented on the potential problem of 'partialling out' school effects in such cases.

This is particularly a difficulty for elementary school studies, where it is difficult to establish a meaningful intake achievement score. What is 'prior achievement' for students when studies are conducted at the lower or middle elementary grade levels?

There typically are no prior achievement data for these students because schools do not typically administer achievement tests at the kindergarten or first grade levels, which are the true points of entry into the school. Even if they did, error variance on such achievement measures would be problematic.

Prior year achievement scores are sometimes used in SER because they are the only other student performance data available. For example, let us consider a hypothetical elementary school study that focuses on fourth grade achievement. Since there was no previous available achievement data, the researchers administered their own achievement tests at the end of the third grade. If the researchers then used as a control variable the students' achievement at third grade, it is obvious that they run the risk of not only factoring out the effect of variance due to background variables, but also variance due to school effects or the interaction between background and school variables. Therefore, for studies of elementary level school effects, family background variables may be the best control variable.

The Importance of School as a Level of Analysis in School Effects Studies

In this section, two topics will be covered: biases in the magnitude of school effects as measured by variance estimates; and the importance of the school effect from the perspective of educational policy makers.

BIASES IN THE MAGNITUDE OF SCHOOL EFFECTS AS MEASURED BY VARIANCE
ESTIMATES

Rutter (1983a, 1983b) concluded that estimates of variance accounted for in student achievement would be influenced by at least three main factors: the choice and measurement of the outcomes variables; the choice and measurement of the predictor variables; and the extent of variation (i.e. differences) on the predictor variables. Furthermore, he concluded that there was an inherent bias in the estimation of the size of the school effect due to the third factor:

> But, the last consideration – namely the extent of the variation on the predictor – is the most crucial of all. Other things being equal, a predictor with a wide range will always account for a higher proportion of the variance than a predictor with a narrow range. Because it is likely that schools tend to be more homogeneous than are families and because the differences between the 'best' and the 'worst' schools is likely to be far less than that between the 'best' and 'worst' homes, it necessarily means that (as assessed in terms of the proportion of population variance accounted for) family variables will usually have a greater 'effect' than school variables. But this does not necessarily mean that schools have a lesser influence than families on achievement.
>
> (Rutter, 1983a, 1983b, p.6)

This argument extends all the way up the multilevel model: there is more variance between students than there is between classes; there is more variance between classes than there is between grade levels or departments; there is more variance between grade levels or departments than there is between schools; there is more variance between schools than there is between school districts; etc., as demonstrated by several researchers (e.g. Hill and Rowe, 1996; Tymms, 1993). Because of this, Rutter concluded that variance attributable to schooling was an inadequate way to assess the impact of schools on students. Rutter was particularly concerned that the lack of variation in school level variables, relative to the variance at the student and classroom levels, would necessarily lead to low estimates of the school effect. He concluded:

> It is clear that the proportion of variance explained by schooling is a very poor guide to the real influence of schools in helping children gain good levels of scholastic achievement. It also follows from these (and other) considerations that the estimates of school 'effects' obtained in this way have no clear policy implications.
> (Rutter, 1983a, p.6)

Rutter gave an 'extreme hypothetical example' of this issue. Suppose that the only way to learn Sanskrit in a community was through schools, since teachers at those schools had the only books on Sanskrit and no one else in the community knew Sanskrit. Also suppose that all schools in this community were equally good at teaching Sanskrit. There would be individual student level variation in learning Sanskrit as a result of family background variables, so some children would learn Sanskrit better than others. Rutter concluded that:

> However, because all schools teach Sanskrit equally well, schooling would account for *none* of this individual variation. In short, in these terms, schools would show a *zero* effect on Sanskrit achievement in spite of the fact that *all* Sanskrit was necessarily learned only as a result of schooling!
> (Rutter, 1983a, p.6)

Rutter's point is similar to that made earlier in the chapter concerning the 'absolute effects of schooling' (Definition 1 of school effects). If students received schooling in an area of study that they could not learn elsewhere, then their achievement would be absolutely determined by the schools they attended. Yet if there was no variance between schools, the school effect would be nil.

Bosker and Scheerens came to essentially the same conclusion (1989):

> . . . *independent* variables that are closer to the output measures – like content covered and time on task will most likely explain more variance than school variables (like leadership styles and variations in organisational structure) . . . the strength of association between school characteristics and achievement will be depressed because of the smaller variance in the former characteristics.
> (Bosker and Scheerens, 1989, p.745)

Thus, studies of variance explained are inherently biased towards lower estimates of the magnitude of school effects when multilevel models are employed, yet that is the scientifically accepted method for analysing school effectiveness studies. There is later a discussion of alternative estimates of effect size (other than variance explained) which may be more appropriate for describing the true magnitude of school effects.

In spite of the sometimes disappointingly low estimates of the size of school effects, especially when variance estimates are used, there is widespread agreement that the school is an important level of analysis in educational research. There are a number of reasons for this conclusion, and they will be briefly discussed in this section. Later the implications of the importance of the school level for future studies will be discussed.

As noted in an earlier section, 'there is a common acceptance that schooling effects can be found' (Sammons et al., 1996a, p.3) and that they are important from a policy perspective, especially with regard to providing useful information for educational improvement efforts. For instance, Bosker and Scheerens concluded that:

> ... when 15 per cent of the variance in the individual level output variable is explained by the factor school – after relevant background characteristics of pupils have been controlled – school characteristics that explain 2 or 3 per cent of the individual level variance are probably meaningful.
>
> (Bosker and Scheerens, 1989, p.747)

The probability of these school characteristics being 'meaningful' to student achievement has been put into greater focus in outlier studies that examine the experiences of students in the 'best' and 'worst' schools. Estimates of large standard deviation differences between the most and least effective schools are made even more relevant when they were described in terms of the years of life that a student spends at a school (e.g. Bosker and Witziers, 1996). No one can deny that school effects that are measurable in terms of one or two lost or gained years for an average student are important both in research and practical terms.

Several researchers have written about the importance of the school as the unit of change in educational improvement work. For instance, policy-oriented research in the United States is often aimed at the school (and district) level, where improvement efforts are targeted. Glasman and Biniaminov (1981) discussed the issue of the value of student and school level data as follows:

> It might be argued that when data are aggregated on an individual student level, data loss is minimal. If the research is policy-oriented, however, the possible value of other levels of data aggregation should be considered.
>
> (Glasman and Biriaminov, 1981, p.53)

Rowan et al. (1983) agreed as indicated by the following quote:

> In our view, information about the relative effects of different school-level factors are particularly important for practitioners...
>
> (Rowan et al., 1983, p.28)

Witte and Walsh (1990) later stated the same point of view:

> ... from an operational and policy perspective, schools are the unit that can be

best evaluated and manipulated. . . . Because district change is often induced on a school-by-school basis and because schools are the organisational level at which educational activities are integrated, schools become an appropriate target of public policy.

(Witte and Walsh, 1990, p.189)

A recent example from Louisiana may make this point more clear. In the late 1980s, a new governor initiated what was called 'The Children First Act', which intended to use teacher evaluation to stimulate educational change. An elaborate system of teacher evaluation was carried out with the purpose of rewarding more effective teachers and providing remediation for less effective ones. The system ran into considerable problems with the state affiliates of national teacher unions regarding the possible loss of certification for teachers who did not reach certain performance levels after the remediation. This system eventually was abandoned for teachers as a whole and replaced by a programme evaluating beginning teachers only (Maxcy and Maxcy, 1993; Ellett et al., 1996).

The current system for educational reform in Louisiana focuses on the school level, rather than the teacher. The School and District Accountability System has recently been approved by the legislature and involves three stages all aimed at the school level:

1   calculation of residual scores (School Effectiveness Indicators or SEIs) for all schools in the state based on school level data;
2   intensive observation of schools which are earmarked for improvement, including the gathering of data at the student, class, grade or department and school levels; and
3   development of school improvement plans that join state and local resources in a combined effort.

The unit of analysis throughout this program is the school, with some specific assistance targeted to grades or departments, but with individual teacher level data being downplayed (Teddlie and Kennedy, 1997).

Policy makers in Louisiana are interested in the school as the unit of change and want researchers to target their work at that level, since integrating educational activities at the school level is very efficient and since targeting individual teachers has led to political problems in the past. Policy makers also like the clarity of the regression models that are planned to be used in this system, which report predicted, actual (called baseline performance indicators), and residual scores (called relative performance indicators) *at the school level*. Issues regarding the interpretability of the results from SER will be discussed later in this chapter, especially with regard to regression and multilevel models (e.g. Fitz-Gibbon, 1995a).

Thus, there are circumstances in which input and output variables for SER are better operationalized at the level of the school, especially when results from this research are to be used for educational improvement. In cases like the Louisiana example, it makes more sense to policy makers and researchers to focus on the school level throughout *both* the research *and* improvement phases of the integrated project. Placing emphasis on the teacher and individual student levels also (and employing the multilevel models necessary to do so) would have greatly complicated the project, especially given the difficulty of explaining multilevel level models in layperson terminology (e.g. Fitz-Gibbon, 1996). (See the coming discussion on the 'Emerging Issues Related to Multilevel Modelling' for information regarding difficulties with the Tennessee Value-Added Project, which used the teacher as the unit of analysis and employed multilevel analyses.)

Evidence for the Existence of a Larger School Effect in Longitudinal Studies

This issue was also discussed earlier in this chapter and may be stated as follows: SER is more likely to demonstrate school effects of larger magnitude if the research is longitudinal in nature. The studies of Raudenbush (1989a, 1989b) and Mortimore et al. (1988) described above are good examples of how longitudinal studies examining gain in student performance can yield much higher estimates of the magnitude of school effects.

Why is it the case that longitudinal studies conducted over several years yield larger estimates of the magnitude of school effects, whereas cross-sectional studies yield smaller school effects? Hill and Rowe (1996) answered this question as follows:

> Within cross-sectional studies, or longitudinal studies operating over a limited time-scale ... there is a risk that school effects will be unobserved, underestimated, or partialled out through the statistical adjustments used to control for differences in intake characteristics.
>
> (Hill and Rowe, 1996, pp.27–8)

Stringfield (1994a) discussed this issue in terms of the multicollinearity issues associated with cross-sectional studies:

> A problematic artefact of this multi-collinearity, at least in the United States, is that when educational researchers enter the schools and measure 'school effects' over a relatively short period in the lives of the schools and communities (six weeks to two years), they tend to attribute most of the variance which is multi-collinear to parental SES, thus underestimating the effects of schooling on students and communities.
>
> (Stringfield, 1994a, p.58)

Longitudinal designs, on the other hand, examine school effects at the point that they should make the optimal difference in a student's achievement: across the entire period of time that the student has spent at the school. At each grade level, the impact of the student's teacher(s), rather than the school, is more important to the progress that student will make for that given year. Across years, however, school effects become more important as the entire experience of attending a school for a number of years accumulates.

For instance, the cumulative effect of a school wide policy that emphasizes the generation of independent research reports, using library and other resources, will be most evident in the generation of those reports at the end of the entire school experience, rather than in any given year. Each teacher of a given student will contribute to that child's ability to generate research reports while in class, but the sum of these contributions across years can only be evaluated using a longitudinal design that examines the overall progress in report writing that the child has experienced while at the school. The entire school experience is greater than the sum of the individual classroom experiences that the child has, because the school provides a consistency of experience across classrooms that would be impossible without its organizational level. Rutter described this total school 'ethos' as follows:

> Throughout this paper, effects have been discussed in terms of 'schools,' with the implication that a whole school constitutes a meaningful entity. . . . This implies that there were school wide influences which served to make it more (or less) likely that individual teachers would conduct their classes in an effective manner or which operated outside the classroom. The former is suggested by the observation that some schools have a much higher proportion of classrooms where effective techniques are being employed. . . . This evidence, plus the rich observations stemming from the case studies of individual schools, strongly suggests that it is meaningful to speak of the ethos of the school as a whole (while still recognising marked variations between teachers and between classrooms within any single school).
>
> (Rutter, 1983a, p.33–4)

This whole school 'ethos' is best detected and its influence estimated using a longitudinal design encompassing most, if not all, of the students' years at a school.

Sampling Decisions and Size of School Effect

The general issue of sampling was discussed earlier in this chapter. With regard to the magnitude of school effects, it appears that studies in which at least part of the analyses utilize an outlier design (e.g. the upper 20 per cent and lower 20 per cent of schools) are more likely to demonstrate a school effect than are studies in which the analyses utilize exclusively a random sampling scheme in which the full range of schools are examined.

There are at least two potential reasons for this difference in magnitude estimation due to differences in sampling:

1 outlier studies concentrate on that part of the population distribution where there is the most explicable variance; and
2 outlier studies are more likely to include process variables due to the smaller sample size of the design, and these process variables are better and more powerful school level factors.

Several studies and reviews have demonstrated that school effects are more evident at the upper and lower ranges of a population distribution in which schools are arrayed by effectiveness status (e.g. Bosker and Witziers, 1996; Brookover et al., 1979; Gray, 1981; Klitgaard and Hall, 1974; Mortimore et al., 1988; Purkey and Smith, 1983; Rutter, 1983a, 1983b; Scheerens, 1992; Stringfield, 1994b; Teddlie and

Stringfield, 1993; Smith and Tomlinson, 1989). These outlier studies typically compare the upper and lower 20 per cent (or 15 per cent or 25 per cent) of schools, to the exclusion of the middle 60 per cent (or 50 per cent or 70 per cent).

It is probable that the range in effectiveness of the middle 60 per cent of schools is truncated relative to the rest of the distribution, as is the case with normally distributed populations. If this is the case, then there is much more variance in the tails of the distribution (more effective and less effective schools) and, therefore, more potential variance that could be explained by school effects, as opposed to family background and other factors.

Outlier studies not only have more variance that is potentially explicable by school factors, but they also are more likely to employ school process variables that are potentially strong predictors of student achievement. These powerful school level factors were described earlier and they are very difficult to assess using archived databases due to cost and time factors.

The potential importance of the continued study of outliers is exemplified by the number of schools that are either studied in this research, or that could potentially be affected by the results from these studies. If we study the upper and lower 20 per cent of schools, then 40 per cent of the total sample are directly included in the research base. Furthermore, the middle 60 per cent of schools can benefit from information gained about becoming more effective, or avoiding becoming less effective.

It is important to note that the 'average' or 'typical' school may have important uses at the level of educational policies that make its presence within sampling frames of considerable importance. In any attempts at transmitting good practice between schools, if there were to be a very large gap between the levels of effectiveness of the schools involved, then it might be difficult for the more ineffective to pick up the knowledge on offer, and the more effective school site may get little beneficial professional development out of the exercise, since it would be required to teach the other school at a level considerably below its own competence. Using average schools to help less effective institutions, and linking the average schools with the more effective ones, may be a more effective network of knowledge transmission than that which would be produced by utilizing only two categories of schools.

Alternative Measures of the Magnitude of School Effects

As we completed this review, other difficulties became apparent with the use of 'variance accounted for by schooling' as the measure of the magnitude of school effects. A major problem was the lack of comparability across the studies reviewed due to differences in types of analyses reported and in choice of variables used. Scheerens (1992) came to the same conclusion in an earlier review concluding that his 'attempt at synthesis was a sobering experience'.

Similarly, Sammons et al. (1996a) concluded:

> It is difficult to compare the *relative* size of school effects in different school effectiveness studies because they are often reported in different ways.
>
> (Sammons et al., 1996a, p.15)

Therefore, there is a growing consensus that 'variance explained' estimates of school effects are not adequate (e.g. Bosker and Scheerens, 1997; Bosker and Witziers, 1996; Jencks et al., 1972; Rutter, 1983a, 1983b; Sammons et al., 1996a, 1996b; Scheerens, 1992; Willms, 1992).

Alternative estimates of 'effect sizes' will be presented in this section. These effect sizes often express the effect of school in terms of percentages of standard deviations, since that measure is well understood among researchers. Several authors have presented their results in ways intended to highlight the importance of school effects, regardless of how small they were in terms of variance explained. Consider the following examples:

- Purkey and Smith (1983) estimated that the difference in achievement level between the least effective schools (lowest 20 per cent of schools) and the most effective schools (top 20 per cent of schools) would amount to 'two-thirds of a standard deviation, or roughly one full grade level of achievement' (p.428). They based these estimates of the size of school effects on their 1983 review of extant SER.

- As noted above, Rutter (1983a) summarized results from his study of 12 secondary schools in London (Rutter et al., 1979) as indicating that children at the most successful secondary school got an average of four times as many exam passes as children at the least successful school after adjusting for intake characteristics.

- The Brookover et al. (1979) study yielded results that indicated that after matching for intake, students in the most successful white elementary schools obtained academic achievement scores an average of about one standard deviation (equivalent to about 15 IQ points) above those in unsuccessful white elementary schools. According to the investigators, these differences was even greater for black elementary schools.

- As noted above, Mortimore et al. (1988) illustrated the importance of the longitudinal study of school effects by reporting the relative importance of school and home influences on student *progress over a three year period*. Their analyses indicated: that the school was roughly four times more important in accounting for differences in pupil progress in reading than were background factors (p.186), and that the school was roughly ten times more important in accounting for differences in pupil progress in mathematics than were background factors (p.188).

- Smith and Tomlinson illustrated the effect of school from their study of multiracial comprehensive secondary schools in the UK as follows:

  > The results of the present study show that there are very important differences between urban comprehensive schools. . . . For certain groups, the variation in exam results between individuals in different schools is as much as one-quarter of the total variation between individuals. . . . Given that individual differences are very large and strongly tend to persist, these findings show that differences in performance between schools are very substantial.
  >
  > (Smith and Tomlinson, 1989, p.301)

- Scheerens (1992) built upon the previous review of SER by Purkey and Smith (1983) to develop an index of the size of school effects:

Thus, in a school effectiveness study we can compare the average score of the least effective 20 per cent of schools with the average score of the most effective 20 per cent and express the difference in proportion to one standard deviation. Differences between 0.2 and 0.5 standard deviations are regarded as small, those between 0.5 and 0.8 are average and above 0.8 as large (Cohen, J., 1977).

(Scheerens, 1992, p.71)

Using the 0.67 standard deviation result from the Purkey and Smith (1983) review of SER, Scheerens concluded that this was an effect of average size. As noted above, this also equates to an entire school year's difference between an average student in the most effective school (top 20 per cent) and one in the least effective school (bottom 20 per cent). Scheerens concluded that an effect of this size had *practical significance* and referred to the work of Rosenthal and Rubin (1982) from educational psychology that had demonstrated that:

. . . effects which in terms of explained variance on the output variable were relatively small still signified a considerable difference in scale points on the dependent variable.

(Scheerens, 1992, p.71)

- Willms expressed the magnitude of school effects as effect sizes associated with *individual schools* again using standard deviation units:

These are estimates of the effects of each school measured as a fraction of a standard deviation of the outcome measure. For example, an effect size of 0.1 means that the estimated attainment score of a pupil with average background characteristics was 10 per cent of a standard deviation higher in that school than the national average attainment score. In terms of percentiles, an effect size of 0.1 places a child at the 54th percentile, instead of the 50th percentile.

(Willms, 1992, p.43)

- Bosker and Witziers (1996) concluded that in the Netherlands, the difference between the top 10 per cent of the schools and the bottom 10 per cent of the schools, after adjusting for intake, is as large as 0.65 of a standard deviation on the original test scale. They estimate that given the structure of secondary education in that country, it would take a student from a highly ineffective primary school two years longer to attain the same achievement certificate at the end of secondary school as an equally talented student from a highly effective school.

It should be remembered that most of the effect sizes reported in this section have been based on schools that are outliers, that is schools at the extremes of the achievement range (e.g. Klitgaard and Hall, 1974; Stringfield, 1994b). Nevertheless, these comparisons afford us some insight into the practical significance of school effects (Scheerens, 1992).

There is a continued need for a standard 'effect size' measure that would be recognized internationally. The work summarized in this section, especially that of the Dutch researchers (Scheerens, 1992; Bosker and Witziers, 1996) points the field in a direction that may eventually lead to such a standard 'effect size' measure.

Emerging Issues Related to Multilevel Modelling

AN OVERVIEW OF THE ISSUES

Throughout this volume, and especially in this chapter and Chapter 6, proper allegiance is paid to the current statistical orthodoxy of employing random coefficient (RC) multilevel models, also referred to as hierarchical linear models (or HLM) in the USA, in the study of the scientific properties of school effects. Multilevel models simply describe more accurately the properties of school effects, as we now envision them, than do traditional techniques such as OLS regression analysis, and school effectiveness researchers of all ilks (scientists, pragmatists, humanists) should acknowledge this. DeLeeuw and Kreft (1995a), answering questions posed by the USA National Center for Educational Statistics regarding the use of multilevel models, addressed the overall acceptance of the use of these models in SER as follows:

> If the question is interpreted as 'Should we take the hierarchical nature of the data into account in our models?', then the answer is yes. We should because it is important prior information that can be used to increase the power and precision of our techniques, and also because it reflects the way the sample is collected.
>
> (DeLeeuw and Kreft, 1995a, p.178)

There is, however, an expanding body of literature that is critical of some aspects of the use of multilevel modelling in SER, and the following section briefly summarizes this work. It has been over a decade since Aitkin and Longford's (1986) milestone article on the use of multilevel modelling in SER, and criticisms are just now beginning to gain some momentum. In some respects, this criticism was predictable, and, if anything, has been somewhat delayed in coming. This delay was due to the initial, and continuing, enthusiasm associated with the discovery of statistical techniques that apparently could deal with the thorny 'unit of analysis' problems that had dogged SER since the Coleman Report.

Mason colourfully and accurately describes the continuing evolution of the use of multilevel models in SER as follows:

> From the sociology of knowledge perspective, the intellectual history of the introduction of multilevel models appears to be running a predictable course: (1) A new statistical formulation is introduced. (2) The new formulation seems to answer a widely perceived need. (3) It is enthusiastically developed and promulgated as The Answer. (4) In response, journeyman practitioners accord the new methodology high status. Graduate students learn some version of it. So do young professors. Older ones consider how close they are to retirement before deciding how much to invest in it. Then comes the reaction: (5) It is said that the new method is like some other, previously used method in various ways. (6) Critics begin to ask, 'Do we really get different answers (from the way we used to do it, and already understand)?' Typically, for any particular methodology, the answer is in some cases no, and in some, yes. In all instances, though, the new methodology has a generality that previous approaches lacked. Moreover, it provides a new way of thinking about problems. (7) Nevertheless, disaffection begins to set

in. The assumptions are not always met and often seem unjustifiable in the context of a particular problem. . . . (8) By now, the high-water mark has been reached and the tide of enthusiasm begins to ebb. (9) But the ark comes to rest somewhere on the side of the mountain, at an elevation that differs from its former resting place, because, in fact, the new methodology has something genuine to offer. . . .

(Mason, 1995, p.221)

Mason (1995) concluded that we are currently at Stage 7, in which highly knowledgeable critics (e.g. DeLeeuw and Kreft, 1995a, 1995b; Fitz-Gibbon, 1991b, 1995a, 1996; Rogosa and Saner, 1995a, 1995b) have begun to point out problems with multilevel modelling and situations in which OLS regression analyses and other more traditional techniques may be as, or even more, appropriate in analysing school effects data.

For instance, Tymms, in a review of Willms (1992) book on school indicators, pointed out three problems with the use of multilevel models:

The first is that . . . if monitoring is to have an impact it must be acceptable and that, in fact means that it must be comprehensible. Multilevel models, with their 'level two variables', subscripted equations and varying slopes, turn 99 per cent, of those who hear about it, off. The second is that, school effects calculated by the readily understandable Ordinary Least Squares regression analysis are often very little different from those developed from multilevel modelling! Added to this is the unmentioned bias introduced into the data by the 'shrinkage' process, which is a valuable property for the researcher, but a millstone around the neck of a small deprived school doing well and wanting to prove it to the outside world.

(Tymms, 1994, p.395)

In following sections, we will summarize some of the emerging criticisms regarding the use of multilevel modelling in SER:

- less complicated techniques may be preferred in those cases in which multilevel models and more traditional techniques generate the same results, since the traditional techniques involve less intense computation and do not entail a variety of other analytical and interpretation complexities associated with multilevel models (e.g. DeLeeuw and Kreft, 1995a, 1995b);
- the fact that residual values are 'shrunk towards the mean' in multilevel models, which can result in the underestimation of the effectiveness status of schools with small numbers of students;
- practical and political issues related to the comprehensibility of multilevel modelling to the majority of practitioners in the field (i.e. the pragmatists and humanists referred to in Chapter 2); and
- comments on the excessive 'scientism', that has characterized some of the writing associated with multilevel modelling, and how that can be detrimental to the field of SER as a whole.

SIMILARITY OF RESULTS OBTAINED THROUGH MULTILEVEL MODELS AND OLS
REGRESSION TECHNIQUES

It is accurate to say that a major historical division in the study of school effects could be called pre-multilevel modelling (1966–85) and post-multilevel modelling (1986–now). In addition to the fact that the new statistical techniques more accurately model school effects, many statisticians and researchers predicted that the properties of school effects, including the estimation of the size of those effects, would be quite different using multilevel models, rather than regression analyses. There is now significant evidence that there is not much difference in the basic statistical results (e.g. estimates of proportion of variance accounted for, beta weights for specific predictors) associated with multilevel models and OLS regression analyses, especially in the results associated with the level of the school.

There is both empirical and conceptual evidence in support of this point, including the following studies and research articles.

1 Daly's (1991) study

Daly's (1991) study of school effects in secondary schools in Northern Ireland compared the magnitude of school effects using both OLS regression and HLM analyses. Daly concluded that results from four HLM and four OLS regression analyses were 'remarkably similar' (p.315) in terms of variance accounted for by school factors and in terms of beta weights associated with the predictors. The only marked difference between the analyses was due to the shrinkage effect in which the 'HLM programme shrinks the OLS measures towards the centre of the distribution' (p.315).

2 Fitz-Gibbon (1991b, 1995a, 1996)

Fitz-Gibbon (1991b, 1995, 1996) has discussed the similarity of OLS regression and multilevel model results in several research articles and summaries. These comparisons come from her studies of data from the A-level Information System (ALIS), one of which was described in detail earlier in this section (Fitz-Gibbon, 1991b). Fitz-Gibbon did these comparative analyses because she was interested in the accuracy and comprehensibility of results from her indicator system, which are read and used by practitioners within the educational community.

Fitz-Gibbon and her colleagues (e.g. Fitz-Gibbon, 1995a; Trower and Vincent, 1995) compared several OLS regression and multilevel models in their analyses. One method, which she called the 'simple Residual Gain Analysis', is the average of all the students' residuals from an OLS regression analysis. Fitz-Gibbon concluded:

> On the datasets examined here, and in all others of which we are aware, the Value Added indicators produced by the simple method correlate at least as well as 0.94, and usually more strongly, with the Value Added indicators derived from multi-level modelling.

> (Fitz-Gibbon, 1995a, p.17)

Trower and Vincent (1995) further concluded:

> The techniques of Hierarchical Linear modelling and OLS produced estimates of

the school residuals which were very similar although the standard errors of these parameters will be greater under OLS. The choice of technique must be made by consideration of other factors – for example comprehensibility and computing efficiency.

(Trower and Vincent, 1995)

Furthermore, Fitz-Gibbon (1996) concluded that as the size of a unit (e.g. department, school) approaches 30 'the difference between a multilevel residual and the simple regression one will be negligible' (p.131).

3 Kennedy et al. (1991, 1993)
Kennedy and his colleagues used HLM to reanalyse results from the Louisiana School Effectiveness Study Phase II (LSES-II) database (Kennedy et al., 1991, 1993), which had initially been analysed using OLS regression, since computerized multilevel programmes were not available at the time the data were gathered (Teddlie et al., 1984). Analysis of the LSES-II data using HLM resulted in very similar estimates to those obtained using OLS regression. For instance, the HLM analyses yielded essentially the same results in terms of the importance of certain school climate variables and in terms of the amount of the variance that was explicable at the school level (Kennedy et al., 1993).

4 Rogosa and Saner (1995a, 1995b)
In a special issue of the *Journal of Educational and Behavioural Statistics* entitled Hierarchical Linear Models: Problems and Prospects, authors compared the results of traditional regression and more advanced multilevel models both empirically (e.g. Rogosa and Saner, 1995a, 1995b) and conceptually (e.g. DeLeeuw and Kreft, 1995a, 1995b). Rogosa and Saner (1995a, 1995b) analysed three sets of longitudinal panel data using both HLM and simpler approaches, such as OLS regression. One database followed the achievement of a cohort of students from grades one through eight.

Rogosa and Saner (1995a, p.149) stated that a major purpose of these comparisons was 'to demystify these analyses by showing equivalences with simpler approaches'. These authors reported results that were virtually identical using the different techniques, thus demonstrating that under certain circumstances you can get the same results using either multilevel analyses or simpler approaches, such as OLS regression.

5 DeLeeuw and Kreft (1995a, 1995b)
DeLeeuw and Kreft (1995a, 1995b) conceptually compared the properties of multilevel models and simpler techniques, such as weighted and unweighted OLS regression techniques. They concluded that 'while HLMs are an elegant conceptualization, they are not always necessary' (DeLeeuw and Kreft, 1995a, p.171).

In a response to comments made by Raudenbush (1995a), DeLeeuw and Kreft (1995b) further noted that:

The first paragraph of Raudenbush's reply sounds like a sales pitch . . . Strong characterisations such as 'mismatch between reality and statistical power', 'misestimated precision' and 'weak power' are enough to make us deeply ashamed for ever using traditional statistical methods. We think that these strong characterisations are misleading. We already know that from the point of view of the practitioner, the differences between 'traditional' and 'modern' methods are small, often tiny.

(De Leeuw and Kreft, 1995b, p.240)

6 Mason (1995)

Mason (1995) summarized these criticisms of both Rogosa and Saner and of DeLeeuw and Kreft as follows:

Rogosa and Saner demonstrate that under certain circumstances . . . you can get the same answers using the HLM software package and using other kinds of software . . . It would be incorrect to assert that fixed-effect and random effect (covariance component) modelling always yield the same end result, and I do not read Rogosa and Saner to be making that claim. DeLeeuw and Kreft argue that for many purposes, it suffices not to estimate a covariance component model: A fixed effects model will do . . . . They argue against routine acceptance of shrinkage estimates obtained by multilevel programs that employ empirical Bayes computations.

(Mason, 1995, p.222)

7 Gray et al. (1995) and Freeman and Teddlie (1997)

Two recent studies of the stability of school effects yielded very similar estimates despite the fact that one (Gray, Jesson, Goldstein, Hedger and Rasbash, 1995) used multilevel models analysing secondary data from England, while the other (Freeman and Teddlie, 1997) used traditional OLS regression analysis of a primary school data-base from the USA. Details regarding the results from these two studies are given later.

The fact that similarities have been demonstrated in the results from multilevel analyses and traditional OLS regression analyses in some studies does not mean that we should return to the use of the more traditional models, which do not model school effects as well as the new techniques. These similarities do, however, seem to indicate the following:

- If researchers or policy makers are interested in simple statistics associated with the effect of the school (e.g. per cent of variance accounted for, beta weights associated with predictor variables), the traditional OLS analyses appear to often yield estimates similar to the more complicated multilevel models.
- Multilevel analyses offer a variety of more advanced statistical results that simpler traditional techniques do not (e.g. within school slopes, cross level analysis). If researchers or policy makers want these more advanced statistics, then they must use multilevel analyses.
- The results from studies conducted before the advent of multilevel models (i.e. before 1986) have been described as relying on 'unsound statistical procedures' (Bosker and Witziers, 1996, p.6) and therefore not included in meta-analyses or excluded from recent literature reviews. The similarity in results between OLS regression and multilevel analyses with regard to basic statistics indicates that to ignore the results from the first twenty years of SER is akin to 'throwing out the baby with the bath wash'.

THE 'SHRINKAGE' ISSUE

A practical issue associated with the use of multilevel models in SER concerns the shrinkage of residual values associated with individual schools (e.g. Daly, 1991; DeLeeuw and Kreft, 1995a; Fitz-Gibbon, 1991b; Tymms, 1994; Willms, 1992).

Willms (1992) describes this shrinkage process as follows:

> Even with complete sample coverage, however, estimates of school effects include measurement error. These errors will also be greater for smaller schools. Estimates based on . . . (HLM) make adjustments for this error by borrowing strength from the data set as a whole. The estimates of school effects are differentially 'shrunk' towards the mean outcome score for the entire sample . . . The shrinkage of estimates for small schools is greater than the shrinkage for large schools.
>
> (Willms, 1992, p.46)

Willms explains that while OLS regression estimates are unbiased, they contain error due to sampling and measurement. On the other hand, HLM (multilevel) estimates are biased (i.e. they include a systematic error due to 'shrinkage'), but they also include an adjustment for sampling and measurement error, therefore presenting 'a more accurate picture of the variation between schools' (Willms, 1992, p.46).

DeLeeuw and Kreft (1995a) discuss the 'frustration of the principal of an excellent school who sees the predictions of success of her students shrunken towards the mean' (p.184). Fitz-Gibbon (1996) describes the 'shrinkage' problem for smaller schools, or classrooms, as follows:

> A final and important reason for caution in using multilevel modelling is that it will take the residuals of the kind we provide (ordinary least squares residuals based on the whole sample) and make adjustments to the data to 'shrink' the estimates towards the average. . . . An inner-city school obtaining a good result will find it shrunk towards zero on the statistical basis that such a result is unreliable. . . . Whilst this shrinkage seems justifiable in statistical terms, for samples, if a teacher had obtained a very good result with a small group of students, he or she would certainly not want the results to be adjusted downward.
>
> (Fitz-Gibbon, 1996, p.130)

Indeed, this shrinkage issue is a good example of the contrast between what is best from a statistical point of view, and what is more important from the point of view of an educational practitioner. The practitioner would prefer the OLS residuals, if they demonstrate that her school or class is performing well. The statistician would question the reliability of the estimate and make adjustments downward. Fitz-Gibbon (1996) argues that this statistical adjustment is less justifiable if entire school and class samples are used, as is the case in many educational indicator systems.

THE COMPREHENSIBILITY OF MULTILEVEL DATA ANALYSIS

The shrinkage issue is but one example of potential conflicts between the views of scientists, on the one hand, and humanists or pragmatists (as defined in Chapter 2), on the other hand, with regard to the use of multilevel models in SER. Probably the most important issue concerns the comprehensibility of multilevel modelling procedures to educational practitioners, who are the primary consumers of the results from educational indicator systems, or from educational research that purports to have practical implications.

As noted above in the quote from Tymms (1994, p.395), statistics associated with multilevel modelling 'turn off' the majority of practitioners, especially when research reports are written with dozens of mathematical formulas interspersed throughout. While 'slopes as outcomes' may more accurately portray the effects of schools than simple residual values, most practitioners have great difficulty interpreting graphs with scores of overlapping slopes.

Fitz-Gibbon (1996) referred to the importance of the 'transparency of the procedures' in indicator systems, or for that matter in any educational research with practical implications.

> Another good reason for not using multilevel modelling, and a very important one, is that it removes the procedures from the understanding of most of the participants in the information system . . . it is very important that the profession can see exactly how the indicators are calculated and be able to make adjustments if justified.
>
> (p.131)

There is an ongoing real life 'experiment' that illustrates difficulties in the practical application of multilevel modelling to indicator systems: the Tennessee Value Added Assessment System (TVAAS). TVAAS was developed by researchers at the University of Tennessee (e.g. Sanders and Horn, 1994) and uses multilevel models (two and three stage) to analyse growth in student achievement. The system attempts to measure district, school, and teacher effects on student achievement on the Tennessee Comprehensive Assessment Program (TCAP), a state-wide testing system for all grades. Bock and Wolfe (1996, p.69) point out that TCAP is 'virtually unique among the states' in that it allows researchers to maintain a continuing record of students' achievement test scores as they move across grades, schools, and counties.

One of the primary criticisms of TVAAS concerns the fact that it is not easily explicable to those who are most affected by it, according to Baker et al. (1995):

> Teachers, principals, and superintendents have all raised questions about the value-added assessment model because they have a great deal of difficulty understanding the process. This is understandable, given the complexity of the statistical techniques, but it makes it difficult to convince those most affected by the evaluation that it is actually an appropriate and reliable means of measuring the impact educators have on student learning.
>
> (Baker et al., 1995, p.19)

While Sanders (1995) agreed that model was not easily explainable, he went on to assert the following:

> Among schools and systems that do not score well on portions of the assessment,

there are two distinct reactions. . . . In the first group, a sincere desire exists to identify areas of weakness, determine the cause, and develop a plan to correct them. . . . In contrast, the second group spends much of its energy in denial. . . . Not surprisingly, they make little effort either to understand the TVAAS process or benefit from the information it provides. To this group, no apology is warranted.

(Sanders, 1995, p.56)

While no apology may be warranted to this second group, they have apparently managed to have a serious impact on the political viability of TVAAS, according to several authors (e.g. Bock and Wolfe, 1996).

Actions by Tennessee legislators include the following:

- a freeze on holding school teachers responsible for test scores at least temporarily and possibly forever;
- a block on sanctions against local officials for poor academic gains;
- a technical review of the value-added system by an independent panel of experts;
- the development of a technique to address the continued confusion over the assessment method by parents and teachers, who are supposed to use the evaluation to guide reform.

Willms and Kerckhoff (1995) addressed this issue of the comprehensibility of statistical techniques in a recent article calling for more complex estimates of school performance (e.g. indicators of the extent of inequality across a school district, indicators of the extent of inequality among subgroups, provision of means for explaining diversity among schools in terms of process variables). These authors concluded that:

The function of statistical techniques is to uncover complexity and help explain it . . . . We cannot presume that parents, teachers, or school administrators are incapable of understanding indicators . . . . If we do, then we must also presume that we are unable to inform them in ways that will improve the schooling system.

(Willms and Kerckhoff, 1995, pp.126–7)

To this end of providing indicator systems with greater comprehensibility, Fitz-Gibbon (1995a) suggested a two stage approach for analysing and reporting data:

A two-stage system, in which a simple, rapid analysis is made available to schools, followed by a second stage of careful investigations of the data and the development of sophisticated modelling, should prove adaptable.

(Fitz-Gibbon, 1995a, p.11)

In this two stage model, results based on simpler procedures (e.g. OLS regression) would first be presented to schools, together with graphs explaining their development and usage. Then, in stage two, multilevel analyses would be used to examine additional, more complex effects that require sophisticated statistical modelling. The fact that OLS regression and multilevel procedures have often been demonstrated to produce similar basic statistics allowed Fitz-Gibbon to propose this two stage process.

COMMENTS ON EXCESSIVE 'SCIENTISM'

As the more sophisticated statistics associated with multilevel modelling (e.g. cross-level effects, slope analysis) have become the standard method for reporting the results of school effects, basic concerns about the statistical conclusion validity of SER have diminished. Nevertheless, some statisticians/researchers are still concerned with the remaining statistical conclusion validity issues associated with these multilevel models. (See Chapter 6 for more details regarding these remaining issues.)

In commenting on an article by Goldstein (1995b), DeLeeuw and Kreft made the following point regarding the increasingly complicated statistical models in SER and the computer applications required to run them:

> Goldstein seems to feel that the route towards solving some of the problems with simple multilevel models is to introduce more complicated ones. . . . For some reason, he refuses to acknowledge that we think that this growing of the model will lead to disaster eventually, and is not necessarily wise if the estimation problems for the simplest possible model are still problematic. The new version of Goldstein's program is called MLn and handles up to 15 levels. We are still not sure if he is really serious, or if this is some kind of Monty Python-type exaggeration.
>
> (DeLeeuw and Kreft, 1995b, p.239)

At a certain point, such complex statistical (and related computer) applications appear quite unrelated to substantive issues regarding school effects. Obsession with these increasingly esoteric considerations leads to the production of 'elite' knowledge, that is simply not accessible to the vast majority of individuals interested in the results from SER. One would hope that we are past the point of needing 25 or more mathematical formulas in order to understand the results from a SER research study, yet DeLeeuw and Kreft (1995a) included 37 such formulas in their recent article on issues regarding the use of multilevel models in educational research. This quite lucid and valuable article was contained in a special issue of an educational statistics journal and was appropriate for that particular context. Nevertheless, when the only people who can understand the nuances of a SER research article are those with a PhD in statistics, then of what practical value are these studies to the pragmatists and humanists in the field?

As noted in Chapter 2 and earlier in this chapter, having individuals with the 'scientific' orientation involved in SER is essential to its long term success, because they are interested in solving the methodological problems that have always plagued the field and that certainly led to its demise in the USA over the past decade. Nevertheless, the answer to methodological problems associated with the accurate estimation of the size of school effects, and of other properties of school effects, cannot be totally statistical in nature.

There has been a tendency to associate all methodological problems in SER with statistical issues associated with the multilevel nature of school effects. While advances in multilevel models have gone a long way toward solving statistical conclusion validity issues, purely statistical solutions cannot, by themselves, solve the other methodological issues defined in Table 3.1: internal validity issues associated with study design and operational definitions of school effects; various types of external validity issues (ecological validity, generalizability across time, generalizability across settings); and various psychometric issues (construct validity, concurrent validity, predictive validity, reliability). A continuing obsession with increasingly esoteric statistical problems detracts from the overall progress that we could, and should, be making toward resolving these other important methodological issues.

ALTERNATIVE DATA ANALYSIS STRATEGIES

Over the past few years, some alternatives to the use of the random coefficient (RC) multilevel models in SER have appeared, including:

- OLS regression under certain circumstances, as described throughout the previous section (e.g. DeLeeuw and Kreft, 1995a; Rogosa and Saner, 1995a);
- both OLS regression and RC multilevel models, as proposed in the two-stage process of Fitz-Gibbon (1995a);
- rapid-fire graphical bootstrapping (RGB), a descriptive technique advocated by Fitz-Gibbon (1991b); and
- path analysis, or structural equation modelling (SEM), which was recently proposed by Hallinger and Heck (1996) as a statistical method for analysing the effect of principal leadership in SER.

Comments from the last section indicate that we do not believe that esoteric statistical discussions will advance the field at this point, but the use of structural equation modelling in future SER may be fruitful, simply because these methods may better model school effects than those currently employed. Hallinger and Heck (1996) presented three general models of principal effects on school effectiveness (direct-effects model, mediated-effects model, reciprocal-effects model) and concluded that SEM is the best way to statistically analyse results from studies employing the reciprocal-effects model. (See Chapter 4 for a further discussion of Hallinger and Heck, 1996).

Several authors (e.g. Creemers and Reezigt, 1996; Hallinger and Heck, 1996) have concluded that school level factors have their largest effects on achievement indirectly through the classroom although the full evidence for such a claim may be lacking. Nevertheless, the relationship between school level factors and student achievement is probably not restricted to indirect effects through intervening classroom factors solely. It is possible that school level factors can also impact student achievement in direct and in reciprocal ways, which is best described using the reciprocal-effects model of Hallinger and Heck. In this model, school factors are linked to student achievement with a causal arrow in both directions, as well as through intervening variables.

These types of relationships are probably best modelled using SEM. Recent statistical advances in this area have resulted in multilevel applications of path models, as described by Kreft (1995):

> Extensions of multilevel modelling to structural equation models can be found in Muthén (1994) and McDonald (1994). These last models are not comparable to RC models, because they allow predictors to be random instead of fixed, and

regression coefficients to be fixed instead of random. Whereas RC models are generalisations of regression models with one dependent variable, these models are generalisations of path models, with or without latent variables, allowing more than one dependent variable.

(Kreft, 1995, p.110)

The Context Specificity of School Effects

The context specificity of school effects will be only briefly described here, since Chapter 5 includes detailed discussion of this issue. In Table 3.1, context effects were associated with the general educational research issue of external validity, particularly ecological validity, which concerns generalizability of results across different environments. It should be reiterated that this generalizability issue is between schools, whereas differential effects (to be discussed later) concern the generalizability of school effects within schools.

Context differences refer to between school differences such as: the SES composition of the student body, the grade phase of schooling, the community type of schools, the governance structure of schools, the country in which schools reside, the size of schools, etc. Several of these between school differences have been shown to have an influence upon the magnitude (and variance) of school effects. Therefore, while the magnitude of between-school effect sizes may be generally estimated at around 8–15 per cent of the individual variance in achievement, they are consistently larger for certain types of schools, and smaller for others. For instance, it may be concluded that effect sizes are larger for elementary (or junior) schools than they are for secondary schools based on studies conducted in both the UK and the USA.

Part of this difference in effect sizes concerns the variance in the context variable under study. For instance, Shavit and Williams (1985) concluded that there needs to be a wide range of variation in the SES contexts of the schools under study in order to detect effects of this contextual factor. Thus, studies that are conducted in settings with little variance in SES of students will be less likely to detect context effects.

The country in which SER occurs certainly has an effect upon the magnitude of school effects as was described earlier. This difference may be due to the methodological orientations of the researchers within those different countries, as well as to actual differences in the influence that schools have on achievement.

A related point concerns the differences in the ways in which researchers from various countries have conceptualized and studied 'context' variables. Chapter 5 contains an extended comparison of the differences in the manner in which researchers in three countries (the UK, the USA, the Netherlands) have studied context effects and the effect that this may have had on their results.

The following context effects are discussed throughout this volume:

- socio economic status of student body;
- grade phase of schooling;
- community type in which school resides;
- governance structure of school; and
- country in which school resides.

The Consistency of School Effects

The next two sections of this chapter concern the issues of the consistency of school effects across multiple indicators at one point in time and the stability of school effects across time. Distinctions between these two issues have been drawn since the mid 1980s (e.g. Crone et al, 1994a, 1994b, 1995; Mandeville, 1988; Mandeville and Anderson, 1987). Despite these distinctions, the two issues are interrelated, since inconsistency in initial classification will later lead to greater instability in school effectiveness indices (SEIs). Results regarding consistency/stability have varied depending upon the country context and the methodology employed. These differences will be explored further in this chapter and in Chapter 5.

General Considerations Regarding the Consistency of School Effects and Concurrent Validity

The consistency of school effects can be defined as the congruence of SEIs at one point in time when different dependent measures of those effects are utilized (Crone et al., 1994a, 1994b). Researchers in the US have usually confined these dependent measures to academic achievement with some exceptions (e.g. Kochan, Tashakkori, and Teddlie, 1996; Teddlie and Stringfield, 1993), while researchers in the UK have been more likely to consider other types of outcomes.

For instance, Sammons et al. (1993a, 1996a) in a review of literature primarily from the UK referred to several different types of outcomes: academic attainment, Boards of the same examination, measures of attendance, measures of attitudes, measures of behaviour, and measures of self-concept. This emphasis on different outcomes is consistent with the conclusion from numerous reviewers that school effects should be measured by outcomes other than academic achievement (e.g. Good and Brophy, 1986; Levine and Lezotte, 1990; Purkey and Smith, 1983; Rowan et al., 1983).

The psychometric issues of concurrent validity refers to the degree to which results from a newly developed instrument correlates with results obtained with a previously validated instrument (Anastasi, 1982). This psychometric concept is expanded in the current discussion of the consistency of school effects to include correlations between any measures of effectiveness, whether they are validated or not, whether they are achievement oriented or not.

In some respects, this concept of the consistency of school effects is akin to the triangulation techniques described in the qualitative research and mixed methods literature (e.g. Denzin, 1978; Patton, 1990). With triangulation techniques, a researcher validates the results from one source of data with that from another source of data. As noted by several authors (e.g. Cook and Campbell, 1979; Willms, 1992), the measurement of any construct should be improved if one collects multiple measures of that construct. For instance, it is more likely that schools will be accurately classified if both quantitative and qualitative data are utilized in making the determination of effectiveness status, as Stringfield and Teddlie (1990) did in their longitudinal case studies of differentially effective schools in Louisiana.

If the results from different measures of school effectiveness are consistent, then the researcher may conclude that the school is effective (or ineffective) with some confidence. On the other hand, if the school appears to be effective with regard to its students' scores on a science test, but not effective with regard to its students' scores on a language arts test, then the researcher faces a dilemma in interpretation of the overall effectiveness status of the school.

In this section, we will review research aimed at determining how consistent SEIs are in general terms. First, we will review studies examining the consistency of school effects across different achievement measures; then we will examine the consistency of school effects among different indicators that measure outcomes other than achievement scores.

Evidence Regarding the Consistency of School Effects across Different Achievement Measures

There are three types of consistency issues regarding SEI classification based on achievement scores at one point in time (Levine and Lezotte, 1990; Lang et al., 1992) : consistency across subject areas, consistency across grade levels, and consistency of alternative test modes (e.g. norm-referenced tests or NRTs versus criterion tests or CRTs). Most studies have focused on consistency across subject areas, although some researchers have studied consistency across grade level (e.g. Mandeville and Anderson, 1987) or alternative test modes (e.g. Lang et al., 1992).

Consistency across Measures of Achievement from Different Subject Areas

Evidence from the US, the UK and the Netherlands indicate a moderate level of consistency of school effects across measures of achievement from different subject areas, which typically involve assessment of basic skills (e.g. mathematics, reading, writing). Most of the studies utilize correlations between schools' effects (operationalized as residuals) on different subjects or grade levels, while some use split samples of students taking the same examinations. Some researchers also generate kappa coefficients, which control for chance agreement among the indices (e.g. Crone et al, 1994, 1995b; Lang, 1991, Lang et al., 1992; Mandeville and Anderson, 1987).

Mandeville and Anderson (1987) and Mandeville (1988) reported moderately strong, positive correlations between same grade mathematics and reading SEIs (r's in the 0.60 to 0.70 range), using an elementary schools database generated by the South Carolina Department of Education. On the other hand, kappa coefficients generated in this study were lower (0.33 to 0.52), as were the correlations reported across grade levels, which were quite low (0.02 to 0.17). This study followed up on a line of research in the US concerning the consistency/stability of school effects that had started in the 1960s (e.g. Dyer et al., 1969; Hilton and Patrick, 1970; Marco, 1974; O'Connor, E., 1972; Rowan et al., 1983). Recently, Yelton et al. (1994) conducted a study of consistency in school effects for a small sample of elementary schools in the US and reported a moderate level of consistency across reading and maths achievement.

Evidence from the Netherlands confirms the general results found in the Mandeville studies. Bosker and Scheerens (1989) summarized research (Bosker, 1989) conducted at the elementary level in the Netherlands that indicated moderately strong, positive correlations ($r = 0.72$).

Mandeville and Anderson (1987) were pessimistic in their conclusions regarding the consistency of school effects across grade levels, where the correlations averaged around 0.10. This is an area that has not been adequately researched. Other evidence from the Netherlands (Bosker, 1989; Bosker et al., 1988; Bosker and Scheerens, 1989) indicated much higher correlations: rank correlations between grades of 0.40–0.80 (Bosker, 1989) and intra-school correlations between grades of 0.47–0.50 (Bosker et al., 1988). Bosker and Scheerens urged caution in interpreting these results, however, since they may be inflated due to the dependency in observations (p. 748).

In the UK, Mortimore et al. (1988) reported modest positive correlations between schools' effects on mathematics and writing ($r = 0.28$) and mathematics and reading ($r = 0.41$) in their study of primary schools in London. Later re-analyses of the data set using a more complex mathematical model yielded somewhat higher correlations between schools' effects on mathematics and reading ($r = 0.61$) (Sammons et al., 1993b). Thomas and Nuttall (1993) generated correlations between schools' effects at Key Stage 1 (age 7 years) that ranged from 0.42 for English and technology to 0.68 for mathematics and English. These primary school results from the UK are in basic agreement with those reported in the US by Mandeville and Anderson (1987) and in the Netherlands by Bosker and Scheerens (1989): correlations across different subject areas are moderately strong and positive.

Sammons et al. (1993a, 1996a) summarized results from several studies of the consistency of school effects across different subject areas at the secondary level from databases generated in the UK (e.g. Cuttance, 1987; Fitz-Gibbon, 1991b; Nuttall et al., 1992; Smith and Tomlinson, 1989; Thomas and Nuttall, 1993; Thomas et al., 1993; Willms and Raudenbush, 1989). These studies yielded positive correlations for school effects across different subject areas, but these results were somewhat smaller (r's in the 0.40 to 0.50 range as summarized by Sammons et al., 1993a, 1996a).

Similarly recent analysis of Key Stage 3 (age 14) data in the UK indicated that there was an $r = 0.49$ between school residuals for mathematics and English (Trower and Vincent, 1995). Correlations between total score and specific tests were higher: total and mathematics ($r = 0.66$) and total and English ($r = 0.73$). On the basis of these and other data, Fitz-Gibbon concluded that:

> In both the secondary and primary datasets Value Added results from different subjects were only moderately correlated, thus suggesting a need to provide data separately, subject by subject.
>
> (Fitz-Gibbon, 1995a, p.3)

Luyten (1994c) came to similar conclusions after analysing data conducted at the secondary level in the Netherlands. While he found evidence for the existence of school effects, a larger percentage of the school-level variance in student achievement at the secondary level was due to subject (e.g. mathematics, history) differences.

Sammons et al. (1996a) summarized these results as follows:

> Given the differences between secondary and primary schools (the greater use of subject specialist teachers and departmental organisation) it might be anticipated that the concept of overall effectiveness would be less applicable than of departmental effectiveness and Luyten's (1994c) analysis supports this view. However,

many studies of the process side of school effectiveness have pointed to the importance of particular school-level factors (e.g. headteacher's leadership) at the secondary level in particular. The extent of consistency in departmental/secondary school effects on different academic outcomes is an area that requires further investigation.

(Sammons, Mortimore and Thomas, 1996, p.8)

Consistency across Measures of Achievement from the Same Subject Areas and from Composite Scores

While there is evidence of inconsistencies in SEIs derived from different subject areas, researchers have reported that SEIs derived from the same subject area yield more consistent SEIs (e.g. Mandeville and Anderson, 1987; Crone et al., 1994a, 1994b, 1995). These studies utilize split samples and compare residuals from the same subject area. There is evidence for greater consistency across split samples of mathematics SEIs: Mandeville and Anderson (1987) reported $r = 0.86$ for mathematics as compared to $r = 0.78$ for reading; Crone et al., 1994b reported $r = 0.80$ (kappa coefficient $= 0.55$) for mathematics as compared to $r = 0.65$ (kappa coefficient $= 0.35$) for language arts; and Crone et al., 1995 reported $r = 0.87$ (kappa coefficient $= 0.54$) for mathematics as compared to $r = 0.76$ (kappa coefficient $= 0.41$) for reading. Mandeville and Anderson (1987) have noted that mathematics is an area in which students acquire most of their knowledge at school, as opposed to reading or language arts, which can be influenced more by home and other factors external to the school. Therefore, the effects of school on mathematics will tend to be more consistent than that for reading or language arts, since there are fewer external influences affecting mathematics outcomes. (More information on the differences in the magnitude of school effects on mathematics and other subject areas will be discussed in a later section of this chapter on differential school effects.)

Crone et al. (1994b, 1995) have presented strong evidence that composite scores generate more consistent SEIs than sub-composite, subject area, or grade level scores. She and her colleagues generated these composite scores in order to address the concerns of reviewers (e.g. Purkey and Smith, 1983) who felt that using only one subject area or one grade level as an SEI gave a very limited view of a school's effectiveness. Witte and Walsh (1990) demonstrated that different predictor variables were required to explain the variance in different subject areas such as mathematics and reading. Also, the literature reviewed in the previous section indicates that SEIs based on tests from different subject areas may not be very consistent. Crone and her colleagues hoped that composite SEI scores would combine these different indicators into a more consistent measure. The composite scores in these secondary level studies conducted in the US were combinations of CRTs and NRTs, generated by converting individual test scores to standardised scores, and then combining the standardised scores. Both NRTs and CRTs were included because previous research (Lang, 1991; Lang et al., 1992) indicated that each yields somewhat different information on the effectiveness levels of schools.

The Crone et al. studies presented evidence that composite SEIs generated greater consistency across split samples of schools than any of the other subcomposite, CRT, NRT, subject area, or grade level scores. In the Crone et al. 1994 study, the composite

SEI generated a $r = 0.82$ across subsamples, with a kappa coefficient of 0.59; in the Crone et al., 1995 study, the composite SEI generated a $r = 0.84$ across subsamples, with a kappa coefficient of 0.53.

Also, the Crone et al. 1994b study demonstrated that the overall composite SEI scores correlated more highly with the other SEI scores than they did with themselves. For instance, the correlation between the composite SEI and the language arts SEI was 0.81, while the correlation between the composite SEI and maths SEI was 0.74. On the other hand, the correlation between the maths and language SEIs was only 0.62, and correlations among other components were even lower (e.g. between science and language arts SEIs ($r = 0.50$); between social studies and maths SEIs ($r = 0.50$)).

The significance of these results can be best understood by recalling the correlations among SEIs reported in the previous section. These correlations ranged from 0.60– 0.70 for elementary school SEIs and from 0.40–0.50 for secondary school SEIs. The Crone et al. (1994a, 1994b) study generated correlations between the composite SEI and component scores (maths and language arts) of 0.74–0.81. If such composite scores are available, then they may suffice as a consistent, overall measure of school effectiveness status. It should be noted that these composite scores consisted of both NRTs and CRTs, and were available in a variety of subject areas (e.g. language arts, mathematics, science, social studies, and writing).

Conclusions Regarding Consistency of SEIs across Multiple Measures of Achievement

The following conclusions may be made based on evidence presented throughout this section:

1   School effectiveness indices across different subject areas are more consistent for elementary than for secondary schools.
2   There is little consistency in SEIs across grade levels, although the empirical work in this area is very limited.
3   Several authors conclude that the degree of inconsistency reported in SEIs for secondary schools makes it necessary to report SEIs for different departments within those schools (e.g. Fitz-Gibbon, 1996).
4   Composite SEIs generate much more consistent SEIs at the secondary level than do component SEIs (e.g. for mathematics, reading, language arts, etc.).
5   An extensive testing programme, including NRTs and CRTs, is required to yield the type of school composite SEIs reported in the literature (e.g. Crone et al., 1994a, 1994b, 1995).
6   As achievement measures become increasingly dissimilar, they yield SEIs with lower inter-correlations, or consistencies. Lower consistency ratings will be generated if some of the achievement measures are highly specialized, or include authentic assessments (e.g. Shavelson et al., 1991), or if academic departments or sub-units function autonomously.

Evidence Regarding the Consistency of School Effects across Different Indicators

A considerable body of evidence that schools can vary in their effectiveness in promoting students' academic achievement has accumulated. Much less evidence exists concerning schools' effects on other important aspects of student development (e.g. behaviour, attendance, attitudes, self-concept). The majority of studies have focused on only one or two measures of academic attainment, most commonly basic skills (reading/mathematics) at primary and total examination scores at secondary level. Only a minority of researchers have attempted to examine consistency in schools' effects on a range of different educational outcomes including social/affective and academic outcomes (examples of studies which have paid some attention to this issue include Brandsma and Knuver, 1989; Cuttance, 1987; Gray et al., 1983; Knuver and Brandsma, 1993; Mandeville and Anderson, 1986; Mortimore et al., 1988; Reynolds, 1976; Rutter et al., 1979).

Early influential British secondary school studies by Reynolds (1976) and Rutter et al. (1979) found fairly strong inter-correlations between schools' academic effectiveness and their social effectiveness (using attendance and delinquency rates). The Rutter et al. (1979) study concluded 'On the whole, schools which have high levels of attendance and good behaviour also tend to have high levels of exam success' (p.92). Substantial rank correlations were reported for delinquency and attendance (0.77); for delinquency and academic outcome (0.68); for delinquency and behaviour (0.72). However, later work by Gray et al. (1983) suggested that outcomes such as liking school and attendance were partially independent of schools' academic outcomes.

Fitz-Gibbon (1991b) reported significant but modest positive correlations (ranging between $r = 0.26$ and $r = 0.53$) between attitude to school, attitudes to subject and aspirations and effects on A-level subject performance for chemistry and mathematics.

For primary schools, although Mortimore et al. (1988) found some significant positive associations (and no negative ones) between particular cognitive and affective outcomes (e.g. attitude to mathematics and self-concept with effects on mathematics progress), it was concluded that the two dimensions of school effects upon cognitive and upon non-cognitive areas were independent. Nonetheless, it was also noted that a number of schools had positive effects upon outcomes in both areas (14 out of 47 schools) whereas very few recorded positive effects for cognitive outcomes but were ineffective in non-cognitive outcomes (3) and six were broadly effective in promoting non-cognitive outcomes but were unsuccessful in most cognitive areas.

In the Netherlands, Knuver and Brandsma (1993) studied the relationships between schools' effects on a variety of affective measures (attitudes to language and arithmetic, achievement motivation, academic self-concept and school well being) and on language and arithmetic attainment. The correlations were very small but never negative. This study also found that 'the strongest relationship between cognitive and affective outcomes can be found when subject specific affective measures are under study' (Knuver and Brandsma, p.201). In line with Mortimore et al.'s (1988) work, it was concluded that the two domains are relatively independent at the school level, but 'not in any way contradictory to one another' (Knuver and Brandsma, 1993, p.201).

Evidence on the extent of consistency of schools' effects on different kinds of educational outcomes appears to be mixed. At both secondary and primary level significant and positive, though far from perfect, correlations between schools' effects on different kinds of academic outcomes have been reported. However, few studies have examined both cognitive and academic/social outcomes. Of those that have, primary studies suggest that schools' effects on the two domains are weakly positively related and may be independent. At the secondary level results suggest that effects on academic and certain affective/social outcomes may be more closely linked, particularly for examination results and attendance and behaviour (e.g. Kochan, et al. 1996). Further research is needed to investigate the issue of consistency in schools' effects on different kinds of outcomes in greater depth and in a wider range of contexts before any firm conclusions can be drawn.

Stability of SEIs across Time (School as Unit of Analysis)

General Considerations Regarding the Stability of School Effects, Reliability, and Generalizability across Time (with School as Unit of Analysis)

Good and Brophy (1986) stated that it would be disturbing if effective schools did not have stable influences on schools over consecutive years, yet there has been considerable debate regarding the stability of school effects. In general, it can be concluded that early estimates of the stability of school effects were relatively low, while more recent studies, with more advanced methodologies, have yielded higher estimates. This evolution in these research results, and in the methodological study of stability, will be discussed in this section of the chapter.

The stability of school effects relates to two different psychometric and design issues in educational research:

1   the psychometric issue of the reliability of SEIs across time, which is analogous to test–retest reliability; and
2   the generalizability of school effects across time, which is a type of external validity issue (Cook and Campbell, 1979).

The first issue relates primarily to the technology of the assessment of school effects; that is, do we have appropriate methods, including instrumentation, to properly assess the stability of school effects? As will be elaborated upon below, we are developing an increasingly sophisticated methodology to assess the stability of school effects. Advances in this area have included:

1   The development of composite SEIs, synthesized from several component indices, that have yielded higher consistency and stability ratings than single component indices alone (e.g. Crone et al., 1995; Kochan et al., 1996).
2   The utilization of multilevel models that more adequately model the longitudinal effects of schools (e.g. Hill and Rowe, 1996; Raudenbush, 1989; Raudenbush and Bryk, 1988a, 1988b).
3   The use of mixed methods to determine more accurately the effectiveness status of schools at a single point in time and longitudinally (e.g. Stringfield and Teddlie, 1990; Teddlie and Stringfield, 1993). Improving the accuracy of SEIs through

triangulation techniques, including both qualitative and quantitative techniques, should enhance the accuracy of stability estimates. The second issue concerns the substantive nature of the generalizability of school effects across time. The issue of whether or not school effects actually persist is empirical, rather than methodological. Once we are sure that our methodologies produce reliable SEIs, then we must empirically determine if schools do indeed stay more effective (or less effective) over a period of years using longitudinal research designs. The following section summarizes our current knowledge regarding that question.

The Longitudinal Nature of Studies Regarding the Stability of School Effects

The issue of the generalizability of school effects across time necessarily involves the longitudinal study of schools. Longitudinal research designs allow for the study of the stability of school effects, since SEIs can be calculated at each data collection point. The most sophisticated school effectiveness research is longitudinal in nature, and the field has an increasing number of such studies for two reasons:

1 Researchers are beginning to understand that the impact of school may be under-estimated in cross-sectional design, where it may be unobserved, under-estimated, or partialled out (e.g. Hill and Rowe, 1996; Stringfield, 1994a).
2 Researchers are beginning to understand that school effectiveness and improvement processes cannot be studied properly in cross-sectional designs, because these processes are constantly changing (e.g. Rosenholtz, 1989; Slater and Teddlie, 1992; Stoll, 1996).

Historical Evidence Regarding the Stability of School Effects

Bosker and Scheerens (1989) reviewed evidence concerning two aspects of stability over time. They make the assumption that 'since we might expect that organizational characteristics of schools are more or less stable over time, we must know if the rank order of schools on output remains the same no matter when we measure the effect' (Bosker and Scheerens, p.747). The extent to which schools' organizational characteristics do remain stable over time is, of course, debatable. Evidence from Mortimore et al. (1988) has demonstrated that many inner city primary schools were subject to substantial change during a three year period. In the UK the implementation of the 1988 Education Reform Act has led to many far-reaching changes in curriculum, funding and organization. Rather similar market driven reforms are now affecting schools in countries such as Australia and New Zealand.

The evidence on whether the effects of schools vary over time is mixed. Early British secondary studies (Reynolds, 1976; Rutter et al., 1979) examined students' examination outcomes for different years and found in general consistency over time (rank correlations of 0.69 to 0.82 for the Rutter study). Work by Willms (1987) and Goldstein (1987a) in the UK reveals correlations ranging from 0.60 to 0.80. In the Netherlands figures ranging from 0.75 to 0.96 (Bosker and Scheerens, 1989) have been reported.

However, Nuttall et al.'s (1989) research in inner London pointed to the existence of lack of stability in secondary schools' effects on student total examination scores over a three year period, although no indication was given of the correlation between years in the estimates of individual schools' effects. They concluded 'This analysis nevertheless gives rise to a note of caution about any study of school effectiveness that relies on measures of outcome in just a single year, or of just a single cohort of students' (Nuttall et al., 1989, p.775). In her A-level work, Fitz-Gibbon (1991b) also drew attention to the need to examine departmental residuals over several years.

Like Nuttall et al. (1989), Raudenbush (1989) also drew attention to the importance of longitudinal models for estimating the stability of school effects. Summarizing results from a study of school effects over two time points covering four years (1980, 1984) in Scotland, it was concluded that the estimated true score correlation was 0.87. In the original analyses Willms and Raudenbush (1989) also looked at English and arithmetic results separately in addition to overall examination results and found that school effects on examination results in specific subjects were less stable than those on an overall attainment measure.

Research on stability in examination results for secondary schools by Sime and Gray (1991) also found considerable stability in schools' effects on students' mean examination results over a period of three years in one LEA and over two years in another (correlations ranging from 0.86 to 0.94).

In the Netherlands (Luyten, 1994c) examined the stability of school effects in secondary education over a period of five years for 17 subjects, and the interaction effect of instability, across years and subjects. Unfortunately, because no measures of prior attainment were available it is possible that, with more adequate control for intake, the results might differ. Nonetheless, it was concluded that 'schools produce fairly stable results per subject across years' (Luyten, 1994c, p.20). It was further noted that *'the interaction effect of subject by year is substantial'* and *'the general year effect turns out to be very modest'* (Luyten, 1994c, p.21).

The results of a study of departmental differences in effectiveness in inner London utilized three level models to examine the percentage of total variance in student scores attributable to fluctuations in results over time using an overall measure of examination attainment and results in individual subjects over a three year period (1990–2). Table 3.2 (after Thomas, Sammons and Mortimore, 1995) shows that the percentage of variance due to school was higher than that due to year for all subjects and that the year effect is smallest for total GCSE performance score.

In addition to the three level models, two level models were used to calculate a separate intercept for each year at the school level and estimate the 'true' correlations between the school effects across the three years for each outcome measure (see Table 3.3).

The correlations over two years are all significant and positive and, as would be expected, are higher than those over three years. It is notable that the correlations for the overall measure of performance (T-score) are higher than those for separate subjects, particularly over three years. This indicates that departmental effects are less stable over time and is in line with Smith and Tomlinson's (1989) analysis of English, mathematics and overall examination performance score. Gray et al. (1995) and Freeman and Teddlie (1996) also recently concluded that school effects in terms of an overall measure of academic outcomes are fairly stable.

In addition to calculating correlations between schools' effects on a range of out-

Table 3.2 Percentage of variance in students' total GCSE performance and subject performance due to school and year

	Percentage Variance	
	due to school 1990–92*	due to year 1990–92*
Total GCSE performance score	6.2	1.1
English	4.1	1.8
English Literature	6.9	3.4
Mathematics	5.9	3.6
Science	6.1	4.7
French	7.8	7.8
History	15.3	3.6

Note
3-level model using 1990–92 data (1: candidate, 2: year, 3: school)
N schools = 94; N students = 17,850.

Source: After Thomas, Sammons and Mortimore, 1995a.

Table 3.3 Correlations between estimates of secondary schools' effects on different outcomes at GCSE over three years

	1990 vs 1991 Final Model	1990 vs 1992 Final Model	1991 vs 1992 Final Model
T-Score	0.88	0.82	0.85
English	0.86	0.40	0.77
Mathematics	0.59	0.56	0.83
Science	0.52	0.41	0.59
History	0.92	0.71	0.83
English Literature	0.84	0.38	0.71
French	0.48	0.38	0.57

Note: N Students 17,850; N Schools = 94; N Years = 3.

Source: After Thomas, Sammons and Mortimore, 1995a.

comes across years, the extent to which results were significantly better or worse than predicted on the basis of intake measures across three years was examined. Thomas et al. (1995) found that, out of a sample of 69 schools for which data were available for each year, only three were consistently classified as broadly more effective in each year and three as less effective. Four schools consistently demonstrated mixed effects (significant positive effects in some subjects and significant negative effects in others). By analysing schools' effects for both consistency and stability over time simultaneously it was possible to identify a small group of ten outlier schools which could be clearly differentiated (as either positive, negative or mixed) in terms of stringent effectiveness criteria.

Less attention has been paid to the stability of school effects at the primary than the secondary level, although Mandeville (1988) reports correlations in the USA ranging from 0.34 to 0.66. However, Bosker and Scheerens (1989) point out that these figures may be 'deflated' because of the inadequacy of the statistical model used.

Although no correlations were reported, another example of USA research (the Louisiana School Effectiveness Study) examined selected schools which were consistent outliers (either negative or positive terms) on the state basic skills test (which focused on reading). Stringfield et al. (1992) concluded in their study of 16 outliers 'most schools appear to have remained stable outliers, either positive or negative, for at least 7 years' (Stringfield et al., 1992, p.394).

Two recent studies of elementary schools in the USA have also pointed to the existence of substantial stability in school effects over time. Crone, Lang and Franklin (1994) investigated the issues of stability and consistency in classifications of schools as effective/ineffective at one point in time. They report correlations of residuals over the two years ranging between 0.49 and 0.78. It was concluded that stability was greater for composite measures of achievement and for mathematics than for reading or language. Unfortunately, the study utilized aggregate school level data in regression analyses, no prior-attainment measures were available and the intake data available for control was limited. This is likely to have had a substantial impact upon the estimate of schools residuals obtained and thus the results should be treated with caution.

Research by Yelton et al. (1994) likewise investigated the stability of school effectiveness for 55 elementary schools. Like the Crone et al. (1994a, 1994b) study, the research used aggregated data, no prior attainment data were included and the control for other intake characteristics was limited. It was found that of the 14 reading achievement outliers (defined as plus or minus 1 sd) identified for each year, nine were outliers in both years. For maths achievement 15 outliers were identified over two years with eight being outliers in both years. However, only three schools were identified as outliers in both cognitive areas and in each of the two years.

This review of the issue of stability in school effectiveness research suggests that there is a fair degree of stability in secondary schools' effects on overall measures of academic achievement (e.g. total examination performance scores) over time (correlations are fairly strong and all positive). The same trend is evident for basic skill areas in the primary sector, though correlations are lower. There is rather less evidence concerning stability for specific subjects at the secondary level, or concerning social/affective (non-cognitive) outcomes of education for any age groups.

On the basis of existing research it is apparent that estimates of schools' effectiveness based on one or two measures of students' educational outcomes in a single year are of limited value. Ideally, data for several years (three being the minimum to identify any trends over time) and several outcomes are needed. Further research which examines both stability and consistency simultaneously is required for a wider range of outcomes and in different sectors.

Differential Effects (Within Schools)

General Considerations Regarding Differential Effects and the Generalizability of Effects Within Schools

Reynolds et al. (1995) noted two types of differential school effects : (1) upon students with different characteristics and (2) upon different academic units within schools. Differential school effects upon students with different characteristics is considered to be an equity issue in the USA (Levine and Lezotte, 1990) and is tied in with the decisions regarding aggregation of data at the school level; that is, the decision about whether data should be reported for the school as a whole, or broken down by student subgroups. This issue is sometimes referred to as mean masking in the USA (e.g. Teddlie et al., 1995).

Differential school effects upon different academic units within a school could be considered a consistency issue, but it will be discussed in this section since it concerns the relative magnitude of SEIs, rather than correlations among SEIs. This issue concerns the research findings that the magnitude of school effects varies by type of curriculum that is assessed (e.g. mathematics versus reading). Differential school effects will be discussed for both the elementary and secondary levels in this section; of course, the academic unit at the elementary level is not as well defined as it is at the secondary level.

The research design issue associated with differential school effects concerns the generalizability of school effects *within schools*. Are schools differentially effective for groups of students within schools? Is there *a* school effect, or multiple school effects? This issue concerns external validity, specifically population validity (Cook and Campbell, 1979).

Evidence Regarding Differential Effects across Students with Different Characteristics

To what extent are schools differentially effective for different groups of students? As noted in the first part of the chapter, the importance of controlling for prior attainment in studies of school effectiveness so that the value-added by the school can be estimated is now widely recognized as standard practice. Nonetheless, there is evidence that a number of pupil-level characteristics remain of statistical and theoretical importance (see Nuttall et al., 1989; Sammons et al., 1993a, 1993b, 1994a, 1994b). Willms (1992) argues that, of such factors, measures of socio-economic status are particularly important.

In considering whether schools perform consistently across differing school memberships it is important to distinguish contextual or compositional effects as they are sometimes labelled, from differential effects. Contextual effects are related to the overall composition of the student body (e.g. the percentage of high ability or of high SES students in a given year group or in the school's intake as a whole) and can be identified by between school analyses across a sample of schools. Such research has been a feature of UK studies of secondary schools in the main and has suggested that contextual effects related to concentrations of low SES, low ability and ethnic minority pupils can be important (e.g. Nuttall, 1990; Sammons et al., 1994a, 1994b; Willms, 1986; Willms and Raudenbush, 1989).

Differential school effects are different and concern the existence of systematic differences in attainment between schools for different pupil groups (those with different levels of prior attainment or different background characteristics), once the *average* differences between these groups have been accounted for.

Prior Attainment

Although the study by Rutter et al. (1979) did not utilize multilevel techniques it did examine schools' examination results for the most and least able children and compared the results for children of different levels of prior ability (using a three category measure at intake – VR band). It was found that 'the pattern of results for each school was broadly similar in all three bands' (Rutter et al., 1979, p.86). However, this study was based on a very small sample of 12 schools.

Smith and Tomlinson's (1989) study of multi-racial comprehensives produced some evidence of differential effectiveness for students with different levels of prior attainment (measured by second year reading test). In particular, differences in English exam results between schools were found to be greater for students with above-average than for students with below-average second year reading schools. The authors conclude that this is 'largely because the exams are such that even the best school cannot achieve a result with a pupil having a below-average reading score' (p.273). However, Smith and Tomlinson found little evidence that the slopes of schools' individual effects on examination results cross over. The same schools are most successful with more *and* less able students, 'but a more able pupil gains a greater advantage than a less able one from going to a good school' (Smith and Tomlinson, 1989, p.273). The findings for mathematics were similar to those for English.

Nuttall et al.'s (1989) and Nuttall's (1990) secondary school analyses report evidence that schools' performance varies differentially, with some schools narrowing the gap between students of high and low attainment on entry. The results suggest that variability in high ability students between schools is much larger than that of low ability students. These studies were limited, however, by inadequate statistical adjustment because the only prior attainment data available was the crude categorization of three VR bands.

In the Scottish context, Willms and Raudenbush (1989) also report some evidence of differential school effectiveness for students of different prior attainment (VRQ) levels. However, in an earlier study of Scottish Secondary Schools Willms (1986) concluded 'the within school relationships between outcomes and pupil characteristics did not vary much across schools' (Willms, 1986, p.239).

Jesson and Gray (1991) investigated the issue of differential school effectiveness for students with different levels of prior achievement at the secondary level. These authors suggested that there is no conclusive evidence for the existence of differential slopes, 'Pupils of different prior attainment levels did slightly better in some schools than in others . . . schools which were more effective for one group of pupils were generally speaking more effective for other groups as well' (Jesson and Gray, 1991, p.246). This conclusion is broadly in line with that of Smith and Tomlinson (1989). Jesson and Gray (1991) suggested a number of possible reasons for the difference between Nuttall et al.'s (1989) and their own results. They drew particular attention to the high degree of social differentiation in inner city areas and to the crude measure of prior attainment in Nuttall et al.'s (1989) research. They concluded that the use of a crude grouped measure rather than a finely differentiated measure of prior attainment may affect findings about the nature and extent of differential school effectiveness.

Most of the evidence concerning differential school effectiveness and prior attainment has been conducted at the secondary level. The original analyses for the *School Matters* (Mortimore et al., 1988) study did not re-examine differential effectiveness for students with different levels of prior attainment. The subsequent re-analysis by Sammons et al. (1993) found some evidence of differential school effectiveness for students with different levels of prior attainment, although this was less notable for reading than for mathematics. Nonetheless, the general conclusion was that although significant, differential effects were fairly modest and that schools which were effective for low attaining students also tended to be effective for those with high prior attainment.

Research in the Netherlands by Brandsma and Knuver (1989) at the primary level also investigated the extent of differential effectiveness in language and arithmetic progress. No evidence of equity differences, as these authors entitle such effects, were found in relation to pre-test scores for mathematics. However, for language 'the effect of language pre-test on post-test differs slightly between schools' but 'these differences are very small' (Brandsma and Knuver, 1989, p.787).

Gender

A few studies have pointed to the existence of differential school effects related to pupil gender (after taking account of the impact of gender at the individual level). For example, Nuttall et al.'s (1989) study of examination results over three years in inner London points to the existence of such differential effects in terms of total examination scores, 'some schools narrowing the gap between boys and girls . . . and some widening the gap, relatively speaking' (p.774). However, in the Scottish context Willms and Raudenbush (1989) who noted differential effects for prior attainment did not identify any differential effects for other background characteristics, including gender.

At the primary level the study by Mortimore et al. (1988) produced no evidence of differential school effectiveness related to gender for reading or mathematics progress and the more detailed reanalysis supports the earlier conclusions (Sammons et al., 1993b).

In the Netherlands, Brandsma and Knuver (1989) found no evidence of differential school effects related to gender for mathematics and only very small equity differences for the Dutch language. 'The influence of gender, (overall positive for girls), does differ somewhat between schools' (Brandsma and Knuver, 1989, p.787) but the authors note that these differences are very small and cannot be explained by the school or classroom factors investigated in their study.

Ethnicity

Several studies at the secondary level point to the existence of differential school effects for students of different ethnic backgrounds. Nuttall et al. (1989) reported within school Caribbean, English, Scottish, Welsh (ESW) differences in effectiveness and comment that other ethnic differences vary across schools even more than the Caribbean-ESW differences: 'the Pakistani-ESW differences has a standard deviation of some 3 score points across schools' (Nuttall et al., 1989, p.775). However, the authors draw attention to the lack of individual-level data about the socio-economic level of students' families which could confound ethnic differences with socio-economic differences.

Elsewhere in the UK, Smith and Tomlinson's (1989) study also produced evidence of differential school effectiveness for children of different ethnic groups although these differences were found to be 'small compared with differences in overall performance between schools' (p.268). The authors make a general conclusion about schools in their sample: 'the ones that are good for White people tend to be about equally good for Black people' (Smith and Tomlinson, 1989, p.305).

At the primary level neither the original Mortimore et al. (1988) analyses nor the re-analysis by Sammons et al. (1993b) found evidence of significant differential school effectiveness for specific ethnic groups. Brandsma and Knuver (1989) likewise found no indications of the existence of differential school effectiveness according to ethnic groups in their study of Dutch primary schools.

Socio-economic Indicators

The importance of taking into account relevant socio-economic factors in studies of school effectiveness has been noted earlier. In addition to effects at the level of the individual pupil, compositional or contextual effects related to the proportion of students from particular social class groups or of low family income have been identified in some studies (see the discussion of contextual effects in Chapter 5). Few studies have examined the extent of within-school differential effects related to socio-economic factors. Willms and Raudenbush (1989) report compositional effects related to SES, but no within-school differences related to such characteristics.

At the primary level Mortimore et al.'s (1988) study found no evidence of differential effectiveness related to non-manual versus manual social class background. Sammons et al.'s (1993b) re-analysis confirmed this earlier conclusion. These authors also tested for differential effects related to low family income (using the eligibility for free school meals indicator) but found no evidence to support their existence. Interestingly, the Mortimore et al. (1988) research found no case in their sample of schools where students from manual backgrounds performed markedly better on average than those from non-manual groups. Schools were unable to overcome the powerful effects of social class. However, it was found that students from manual groups in the most effective schools on average outperformed those from non-manual groups in the least effective schools. The school was the unit of change rather than the social class group within it. The Mortimore et al. (1988) sample was fairly small (just over 1100 students and 49 schools) and it would be of interest to establish whether, with a larger sample, the negative findings concerning differential effects at primary level would be maintained.

The need to examine evidence for differential effectiveness using more complex models which focus on data for more than one year has been noted by Thomas, Sammons, Mortimore, and Smees (1995). In a simultaneous analysis of differential effects as part of the study of departmental differences in secondary school effectiveness reported earlier, Thomas et al. (1995) examined schools' effectiveness for different groups of students in different subject areas and in terms of total GCSE score over a three-year period. This work illustrated the complex nature of differential effectiveness at the secondary level. Evidence of significant differential effects was identified both for total GCSE score and separate subjects. It was most notable for students of different levels of prior attainment at intake, and those of different ethnic backgrounds. Some evidence of differential effects was also found for socio-economic disadvantage and gender (see Thomas et al., 1995). Nonetheless overall all students in more effective schools and departments were likely to perform relatively well at GCSE, but some groups (those not socio-economically disadvantaged) performed especially well. In contrast, all students in ineffective schools tended to perform badly at GCSE but disadvantaged groups were relatively less adversely affected. Their results provided no evidence that more effective schools closed the gap in achievement between different student groups – they did not compensate for society. However, whilst disadvantaged groups did better in more effective than in less effective schools, the gap in achievement increased within the more effective schools. Sammons et al. (1996b) highlight 'the complex nature of the equity implications of our findings'.

Overall, it appears that, at the secondary level, there is some evidence of important contextual effects related to schools' pupil composition in terms of SES, ethnicity and ability or prior attainment in UK and Scottish studies, but less evidence for such effects in studies of younger age groups. For differential school effects (within school differences) again, secondary studies suggest that gender, ethnicity and prior attainment may all be relevant. However, for prior attainment, it is important that the control measure adopted is adequate (finely differentiated). Less evidence for differential effects exists at the primary stage. These inconclusive results point to the need for further research into differential school effectiveness using large data sets which contain adequate individual-level socio-economic as well as ethnic data. Exploration of the possible reasons for the apparent primary–secondary school differences in differential effectiveness are also called for.

Continuity of School Effects

In contrast to the attention increasingly paid to the issues of stability and consistency in schools' effectiveness and the question of differential effects in multilevel school effectiveness studies, scant attention has been given to the continuity of school effects measured at different stages of a student's school career. In other words, what long term effects (if any) does previous institutional membership (e.g. primary school attended) have on later performance at secondary school?

Typically, models of secondary school effects utilize measures of students' prior attainment and background characteristics at intake (commonly at secondary transfer at age 11 in UK studies) in analyses of performance at a later date (e.g. in GCSE examinations taken at age 16, the end of compulsory schooling in the UK). Recent developments in UK school effectiveness research suggest that such models may be seriously mis-specified.

Sammons et al. (1995b) provided an example of the first attempt to address the issue of continuity in school effects using multilevel approaches. Their results suggested that primary schools exert a long term effect upon student performance, even after controlling for student attainment at secondary transfer. Their study was based on a nine year follow-up of the *School Matters* (Mortimore et al., 1988) junior school cohort at secondary school. However, it was limited because it did not model junior and secondary school effects simultaneously by considering the full cross classification of individual students in terms of their secondary by junior school attendance using recently available techniques (Goldstein, 1995a). A recent re-analysis of this data set by Goldstein and Sammons (1995) using such techniques provided a more detailed investigation estimating the joint contributions of primary and secondary schools. The total school (level 2) variance is the sum of a between-junior and a between-secondary variance. Table 3.4 provides details of the results of fitting three different multilevel models with total GCSE performance score as the explanatory variable.

The figures in Table 3.4 demonstrate that the variance in total GCSE performance scores attributable to junior school is much larger for Model C (no control for attainment measures at the end of junior education) than in Model A (control for attainment at secondary transfer and random variation at level 1). However, the junior school variance is larger in all cases. Further analyses were conducted controlling for English and mathematics attainment at entry to junior school (age 7 plus) but these made little difference to the results (and were not significant at the 0.05 level).

Goldstein and Sammons (1995) argued that the standard secondary school effectiveness model (where only secondary school attended is fitted at level 2) considerably over-estimates the secondary school effect. They concluded 'the usual quantitative procedures for estimating school effectiveness need to be augmented with careful measurements of all relevant prior performances, including institutional membership. This applies to studies of value added at A level (age 18 plus) where, in principle we can study the variation from primary, secondary and tertiary institution simultaneously' (Goldstein and Sammons, 1995, p.10).

The data set analysed by Goldstein and Sammons (1995) was relatively small (due to loss of sample over time), being based on only 758 students with 48 junior and 116

Table 3.4 Variance components cross-classified model for total GCSE examination performance score as response

	A	B	C
Fixed			
Intercept	0.51	0.50	0.25
Males	−0.21 (0.06)	−0.19 (0.06)	−0.34 (0.07)
Free school meal	−0.22 (0.06)	−0.23 (0.06)	−0.37 (0.08)
VR2 band	−0.39 (0.08)	−0.38 (0.08)	
VR3 band	−0.71 (0.13)	−0.71 (0.13)	
LRT score	0.31 (0.04)	0.32 (0.04)	
Random			
Level (School)			
(Junior variance) σ^2_{u1}	0.025 (0.013)	0.036 (0.017)	0.054 (0.024)
(Secondary variance) σ^2_{u2}	0.016 (0.014)	0.014 (0.014)	0.019 (0.02)
Level 1 (Student)			
σ^2_{e0}	0.50 (0.06)	0.554 (0.06)	0.74 (0.05)
σ^2_{r01}	0.092 (0.03)	0.064 (0.03)	0.10 (0.05)
σ^2_{e02}	0.093 (0.018)		
σ^2_{e2}	0.033 (0.022)		
−2Log likelihood	1848.8	1884.2	2130.3

Note: *N* Junior Schools = 48; *N* Secondary Schools = 116; *N* Students = 785.

Source: After Goldstein and Sammons, 1995.

secondary schools included. Given the small sample size, caution should be exercised in interpreting the findings. Nonetheless, Goldstein (1995a) has produced results broadly in line with those identified here in a larger study (but with less detailed background data) of Scottish schools.

Given the development of cross-classified techniques, there is a clear need for further investigations of the long term effects of schools using detailed longitudinal samples incorporating prior institutional membership and involving larger samples of schools drawn from a range of different socio-economic and geographical contexts. The need for collaborative research concerning the generalizability of multilevel educational effectiveness models across countries is becoming increasingly recognized (Scheerens and Bosker, 1997).

Conclusion

We have ranged extensively across the knowledge bases of school effectiveness from a number of countries in this chapter. Whilst there are some differences between the findings of the individual studies, and some differences in such areas as the amount of variance explained by the school level in different countries, what is most noticeable about our findings is the presence of a considerable degree of agreement across studies and across countries as to their results. In areas as diverse as the consistency of school effects across different outcomes (only moderate), their stability over time (moderate), and the extent of differential effectiveness in school effects upon different kinds of children (limited) we have replicable findings across studies and countries. We now move on in Chapter 4 to the next logical area where we search for any agreement across studies, namely the processes within schools that are responsible for their effects.

4 The Processes of School Effectiveness

David Reynolds and Charles Teddlie

Introduction

The establishment of those factors within schools that are associated with their effectiveness status has been virtually the 'Holy Grail' of SER in many countries of the world since the inception of the discipline in the 1970s. In the USA, Edmonds (1979a, 1979b) and others explicitly hoped to discover what it was that some schools possessed – the 'validity' – to routinely spread into the schools of black and disadvantaged children – the 'reliability'. In the United Kingdom, part of the reason for the ready acceptance of the SER paradigm across the contemporary political spectrum has been its promise that 'good practice' could be discerned, within a system that continues to exhibit considerable variability in school and teacher quality (see Reynolds and Farrell, 1996 for a review of this evidence and Creemers et al. (1996) for empirical data on the United Kingdom).

What we aim to do in this chapter is to establish what are the confirmed findings as to effective schools 'processes', and also which areas have exhibited more mixed patterns of results, with the issues of the context specificity of findings being dealt with in greater depth in Chapters 5 and 8.

To give a flavour of the intellectual attempt of the SER paradigm, we begin this chapter by outlining the findings on effective processes of six major studies conducted in the field over the last twenty years, two from the United States, three from the United Kingdom and one from Australia. We can call these 'classic studies'.

Two Classic Studies from the United States

The Brookover et al. (1978, 1979) study of Michigan elementary schools has already been mentioned in Chapter 1, with regard to its methodological contributions, and in Chapter 3, with regard to its evidence concerning the magnitude of school effects.

The authors complemented their statistical analysis of 68 elementary schools with case studies of four low-SES schools: one high achieving primarily white school, one high achieving primarily black school, one low achieving primarily white school, and one low achieving primarily black school. The researchers used classroom observations and interviews with participants as their primary data sources, but details regarding the specific methodology employed were sketchy, making it 'very difficult to assess these data and their implications' (Good and Brophy, 1986, p.575). The researchers spent between three weeks and three months in each school.

The cases were selected using the following criteria : all schools had similar SES levels that were considerably below the average level for the study sample; schools within each matched pair had similar racial compositions; one school in each matched pair had achievement scores above the sample mean, while the other had achievement scores below the sample mean; and all schools were located within urban areas. The researchers summarized their findings in eight different areas, as indicated below (Brookover et al., 1979; Good and Brophy, 1986):

1   *Time* – More time was allocated and spent on instruction in the high achieving schools than in the low achieving schools. Time in the high achieving schools more often involved active learning with teachers involved in direct instruction, while the students in low achieving schools more often worked on their own, as teachers attended to administrative duties. Academic interactions between teachers and students occurred more frequently in the high achieving white school than in the high achieving black school.

2   *Write-off (per cent of students not expected to master curriculum)* – Large differences existed between the high and low achieving schools, with the former having few cases of students who appeared to be destined to fail, while the latter had many such cases. In the low achieving black school, in particular, teachers appeared to write off large numbers of students.

3   *Teacher expectations* – At the high achieving white school, all students were expected to work at grade level, while at the high achieving black school, at least 75 per cent of the students were expected to master assigned work. Expectations were very low in the low achieving schools, especially for slow reading students.

4   *Reinforcement practices* – Reinforcement practices were appropriate at the high achieving schools. At the low achieving white school, they were inconsistent, with some teachers using appropriate practices and others using confusing and inappropriate practices. Many teachers at the low achieving black school used inappropriate techniques, often positively reinforcing students when they had *not* done well.

5   *Grouping procedures* – There was considerable range on this variable, with no homogeneous grouping after third grade in the high achieving white school, compared to extensive grouping and regrouping of students at the low achieving black school. The grouping at the low achieving black school appeared to be primarily a management tool and was disruptive to the learning process. At the high achieving black school, there was grouping on the basis of pre-test reading and maths tests, with the teachers appearing to advance students to higher groups as soon as possible. At the low achieving white school, there were two reading groups per grade and there appeared to be little mobility between the groups.

6   *Teaching games* – Higher achieving schools were more likely to use academic games that emphasized team, rather than individual, learning.

7   *Principal's role* – The principal at the high achieving white school was heavily involved in academic matters and visited often in the classrooms. The principal at the high achieving black school emphasized administrative duties, although he did observe classrooms periodically; the previous principal at this school had been a more active instructional leader. At the low achieving schools, the principals

appeared to be primarily administrators and disciplinarians, who very seldom visited classrooms.

8   *Commitment of teaching and administrative staff* – There was high commitment at the high achieving schools, as demonstrated by affirmative statements and warmth toward students. Commitment was not discussed at the low achieving white school, and teachers at the low achieving black school seemed resigned to the belief that there was little that they could do about student achievement.

The Louisiana School Effectiveness Studies of Teddlie and Stringfield (1993) and colleagues (1984, 1989a, 1989b) were originally conceived in 1980, continued through final data collection in the spring of 1996, and are ongoing in terms of the analysis and reporting of data from LSES-V. During that time, the study has progressed through five phases of data collection, interspersed with periods of analysis and report writing. The study was designed to explore school effectiveness using methodologies different from those employed in the extant SER literature, including:

- studying 'context differences' in schools varying by SES of student body (LSES-II) or in terms of community type (LSES-III through V) (see Chapter 5 for these results);
- embedding a teacher effectiveness study, with considerable classroom observation, within a SER design (LSES-III through V);
- employing socio metric measures to better understand the interpersonal relations among faculty in differentially effective schools (LSES-IV and V) (see Chapters 11 and 12);
- studying schools in an extended case study longitudinal design (LSES-III through V);
- using a variety of indicators to determine the effectiveness of a school (LSES-IV); and
- studying the processes of ineffective schooling, as well as effective schooling (LSES II through V) (see Chapter 12).

In LSES-II, 76 schools were divided along two dimensions: school effectiveness status (effective, typical, ineffective) and student body SES (middle, low SES). Researchers were able to compare among the six 'types' of schools generated by the design. This section details process differences among four of the school types generated by this design, eliminating average or typical schools. These results were based primarily on survey responses from students, teachers, and principals (Teddlie and Stringfield, 1985, 1993).

Middle SES, Effective School

Teachers were in frequent contact with parents and perceived them to be highly concerned with quality education. Teachers reported having high present and future academic expectations for students. They accepted responsibility for students' outcomes and actively worked with students to realize high expectations. This attitude was reflected in students' reports noting that teachers cared about them and pushed them to achieve academically.

Students apparently internalized the high expectations expressed by teachers and parents. They had higher expectations for themselves than did their peers in equally affluent schools with lower achievement. The general climate from the effective, middle SES school was one of concern for excellence from all the major participants – principals, faculty, students and parents.

Middle SES, Ineffective Schools

Teachers had unrealistically high perceptions of their students' current level of achievement, expecting them to have high achievement when it was only average. Teachers appeared to base their perceptions on intrinsic student characteristics such as student SES. Students' future academic expectations were not as high as those of other middle SES students. The principals' academic expectations were lower than those of the teachers.

The principals stated that several aspects of student development (enhancing social skills, personal growth and development, education/occupational aspirations) were as important at their school as teaching of academic skills. The principals may have been expending too much of the school's resources in non-academic endeavours in these schools. Principals' actions did not appear to result in changes in these schools.

Low SES, Effective Schools

While principals and teachers had modest long-term expectations for their students' achievement, they held firm academic expectations for their students while at their school. Teachers reported spending more time on reading and maths, and assigning more homework than either of the other two low SES groups. Students perceived teachers as pushing them academically. They also reported receiving more help from their teachers than did students in less successful, low SES schools.

Teachers reported that principals visited their classrooms frequently. The teachers in this group were the youngest, least experienced of the low SES groups. The teachers in this group were the most likely of all the teachers to have teacher's aides. Principals were the most likely to say that they had the major input in hiring their teachers: 23 per cent of the principals said that they hired their own teachers. No other group of schools had higher than 9 per cent of its principals report this power.

These less affluent, successful schools had principals who motivated teachers who, in turn, motivated students. The ability to instil in students a belief that they could learn was critical to the success of these low SES, effective schools.

Low SES, Ineffective Schools

These schools had an overall negative academic climate that contributed to low achievement. Of all the groups, teachers had the lowest expectations for students and rated them the lowest academically; the teachers accepted little responsibility for and perceived having little influence on outcomes; they also appeared less satisfied with teaching and perceived themselves as largely unsuccessful. Principals, teachers, and pupils all perceived the lack of achievement within the schools. It should be remembered that students in this group were at the same SES level as those in effective, low SES schools.

When compared with students in other low SES groups, these students perceived their teachers as less praising, less caring, less helpful, and more critical. Of all the groups, these students reported that their teachers felt learning was the least important. A higher percentage (21 per cent) of teachers in these schools would rather teach elsewhere than any other group. In contrast, only 12 per cent of teachers in effective, low SES schools wanted to teach elsewhere. Teachers in low SES ineffective schools were absent an average of 3.5 days in the fall semester of LSES-II, while teachers in low SES, effective schools were absent an average of only 2 days.

These contrasts between 'types' of schools are shown in summary form in Table 4.1, in which the effective low SES 'John F. Kennedy' school is compared with the ineffective low SES 'Calvin Coolidge' school on a wide range of dimensions. At principal level

Table 4.1 Contrasts between Kennedy and Coolidge elementary schools

John F. Kennedy Elementary	*Calvin Coolidge Elementary*
Principal	
1 Stable, appropriate leadership	1 Unstable, generally inappropriate leadership
2 Appropriate, informal organizational structure	2 Inappropriate, informal organizational structure
3 Shared academic leadership with faculty	3 Nonshared academic leadership
4 Resistant to external change	4 Accepting of external change
5 Close relationship among administrators	5 Strained relationship among administrators
6 Good use of academic support staff	6 Unimaginative use of academic support staff
Faculty	
7 Faculty is warm, friendly	7 Faculty is cold, guarded
8 Strong faculty cohesiveness	8 Lack of faculty cohesiveness
9 No obvious personality conflicts among faculty	9 Open bickering among faculty
10 Integration of support staff into faculty	10 Inappropriate integration of support staff into faculty
11 Cooperative efforts to enhance teaching	11 Top–down effects to enhance teaching
12 High faculty stability	12 Moderate to low faculty stability
13 High time-on-task/positive classroom climate	13 Low time-on-task/evidence of negative climate
14 Fairly uniform teaching across classes	14 Large variances in teaching across classes
15 Assistance freely given to new faculty members	15 Little assistance given to new faculty members
Students	
16 Excellent discipline and understanding of rules	16 Poor discipline and understanding of rules
17 Students involved in running of school	17 Little or no student involvement in running of school
18 Little use of corporal punishment	18 Excessive use of corporal punishment
19 Student-oriented climate	19 Adult-oriented climate
20 Consistently high student achievement	20 Consistently low student achievement

Source: Teddlie and Stringfield, 1993; p.132, based on data from LSES-III and IV.

(combining pressure and support), at staff level (stable staffing and consistent practice) and at student level (pro-social and committed to achievement), the effective school is clearly orientated towards high outcomes. The ineffective school has by contrast a principal (exhibiting inappropriate leadership and presiding over poor relationships), a staff group (fractured by cliques and exhibiting inconsistency across members) and a student group (uninvolved and unaware of school rules) who are clearly predisposed towards poor levels of school 'value added'.

These LSES-II results built upon the results reported by Brookover et al. (1979). This study again demonstrated that schools with very similar inputs or resources can generate very different school climates, but did so with two design improvements: the context variable used was student body SES, which is a more generalizable and powerful context variable than ethnicity; and a typical school level was included, as well as the effective and ineffective levels, as suggested by several critics (e.g. Klitgaard and Hall, 1974; Purkey and Smith, 1983; Stringfield, 1994a).

Three Classic Studies from the United Kingdom

The early Reynolds et al. (1976a, 1976b, 1979) studies used detailed descriptions of schools and school–pupil interaction to attempt to paint rich, sociologically inspired portraits of schools with differing levels of effectiveness, with effectiveness status being based upon simple analysis of a range of pupil intake data related to achievement and family background, and outcome data being on academic achievement, attendance and delinquency.

The studies revealed a number of factors within schools associated with effectiveness including:

- high levels of pupil involvement in authority positions;
- low levels of institutional control of pupils by the school management;
- positive expectations of what students should be able to achieve;
- high levels of involvement of teachers in the running of the school;
- 'truces' on the imposition of rules regarding 'dress, manners and morals' ;
- high level of student involvement in clubs, societies and the like.

The Rutter et al. (1979) study in London also revealed a wealth of data on effective school processes, which were argued to be:

- the system of rewards and punishments, with ample use of rewards, praise and appreciation;
- the school environment, with good working conditions and good care and decoration of buildings;
- high levels of pupils in responsibility positions;
- academic press, involving use of homework, setting clear academic goals and having high expectations;
- good models of behaviour provided by teachers;
- effective classroom management, involving preparing of lessons, unobtrusive discipline, the rewarding of good behaviour and minimizing of disruption;
- a combination of firm leadership and teacher involvement.

Moving to the first study, Mortimore's research was based upon fifty randomly selected London primary schools. Over a period of four years, the academic and social progress of 2000 children were traced. Mortimore and his colleagues identified a number of schools which were effective in both academic and social areas. These schools possessed the following characteristics (Mortimore et al., 1988):

- Purposeful leadership of the staff by the head teacher – This occurred where the head understood the school's needs, was actively involved in the school, but was also good at sharing power with the staff. He or she did not exert total control over teachers but consulted them, especially in decision-making such as spending plans and curriculum guidelines.
- The involvement of the deputy head – Where the deputy was usually involved in policy decisions, pupil progress increased.
- The involvement of teachers – In successful schools, the teachers were involved in curriculum planning and played a major role in developing their own curriculum guidelines. As with the deputy head, teacher involvement in decisions concerning which classes they were to teach was important. Similarly, consultation with teachers about decisions on spending was important.
- Consistency among teachers – Continuity of staffing had positive effects, but pupils also performed better when the approach to teaching was consistent.
- Structured sessions – Children performed better when their school day was structured in some way. In effective schools, students' work was organized by the teacher, who ensured there was plenty for them to do yet allowed them some freedom within the structure. Negative effects were noted when children were given unlimited responsibility for a long list of tasks.
- Intellectually challenging teaching – Not surprisingly, student progress was greater where teachers were stimulating and enthusiastic. The incidence of higher order questions and statements, and teachers frequently making children use powers of problem-solving, was seen to be vital.
- Work-centred environment – This was characterized by a high level of student industry, with children enjoying their work and being eager to start new tasks. The noise level was low, and movement around the class was usually work-related and not excessive.
- Limited focus within sessions – Children progressed when teachers devoted their energies to one particular subject area and sometimes two. Student progress was marred when three or more subjects were running concurrently in the classroom.
- Maximum communication between teachers and students – Children performed better the more communication they had with their teacher about the content of their work. Most teachers devoted most of their time to individuals, so each child could expect only a small number of contacts a day. Teachers who used opportunities to talk to the whole class, for example by reading a story or asking a question, were more effective.
- Record-keeping – The value of monitoring student progress was important in the head's role, but it was also an important aspect of teachers' planning and assessment.
- Parental involvement – Schools with an informal open-door policy, which encouraged parents to get involved in reading at home, helping in the classroom and on educational visits, tended to be more effective.

- Positive climate – An effective school had a positive ethos. Overall, the atmosphere was more pleasant in the effective schools.

The Processes of Effective Schooling

Recent years have seen a number of reviews that attempt to codify what we have learnt from the studies above and from others as to the processes within effective schools (e.g. Purkey and Smith, 1983; Rutter, 1983a, 1983b; Scheerens, 1992; Reynolds and Cuttance, 1992; Reynolds et al., 1994a; Reid et al., 1987; Hopkins, 1994; Mortimore, 1991b, 1993; Scheerens and Bosker, 1997). Two recent reviews have been particularly comprehensive and up to date in their focus, that of Levine and Lezotte (1990) conducted on behalf of the National Center for Effective Schools and that of Sammons, Hillman and Mortimore (1995) conducted on behalf of the British schools inspectorate OFSTED.

These two reviews each refer to several hundred studies of effective schools characteristics, and each concentrate upon rather different knowledge bases, upon the American almost exclusively in the case of Levine and Lezotte, and upon the British (heavily) and the American and the Dutch (less heavily) in the case of Sammons and colleagues. Indeed, only approximately 4 per cent of references out of the total cited by both reviews are the same, indicating the considerable difference in source material.

Nevertheless, if one puts the findings concerning processes together, as in Table 4.2, it is clear that there is a considerable overlap of findings (we have italicized common emphases). Table 4.3 shows our distillation of the Levine and Lezotte 'correlates' and the Sammons 'factors' into ten process areas, which we will now spend the rest of this chapter exploring.

Effective Leadership

We do not know of a study that has not shown that leadership is important within effective schools, with that leadership nearly always being provided by the headteacher. Indeed, 'leadership' is now centrally synonymous with school effectiveness for many, including many operating within the school improvement paradigm also (US Department of Education, 1994; Hopkins et al., 1994).

'Firm and purposeful' leadership has been frequently cited as the first requirement of effective leadership, noted in the Rutter et al. (1979) study, the Mortimore et al. (1988) study, the Louisiana studies (Teddlie and Stringfield, 1993) and the recent work of Sammons et al. (1997). Within the school improvement literature, the role of the Headteacher in being strong and firm enough to buffer and broker external and rapidly occurring change to the staff (Hopkins et al. 1994; Stoll and Fink, 1992, 1994) is stressed, as is the utility sometimes of a 'maverick' orientation (Levine and Lezotte, 1990).

Case studies of improved schools, in both Britain and the United States, show the importance of individual leaders with 'mission' (Louis and Miles, 1992; National Commission on Education, 1995) and there is now a considerable literature concerning those persons who can be regarded as transformational leaders who build school organizations characterized by simultaneous 'top down-ness' and 'bottom up-ness' (Murphy and Louis, 1994).

Table 4.2 Effective schools' characteristics identified in two recent reviews

Levine and Lezotte (1990) Characteristics	*Sammons, Hillman and Mortimore (1995) Factors*

1 Outstanding *Leadership*
  a Superior Instructional Leadership
  b Support for Teachers
  c High Expenditure of Time and Energy for School Improvement
  d Vigorous Selection and Replacement of Teachers
  e 'Maverick' Orientation and Buffering
  f Frequent, Personal Monitoring of School Activities and Sense-making
  g Acquisition of Resources
  h Availability and Effective Utilization of Instructional Support Personnel
	1 Professional *Leadership*
	  a The Leading Professional
	  b A Participative Approach
	  c Firm and Purposeful

2 Effective Instructional Arrangements and Implementation
  a *Effective Teaching*
  b Successful Grouping and Related Organizational Arrangements
  c Classroom Adaptation
  d Active/enriched learning
  e Emphasis on HOTs* in Assessing Instructional Outcomes
  f Coordination in Curriculum and Instruction
  g Easy Availability of Instructional Materials
  h Stealing Time for Reading, Language, Maths
	2 *Purposeful Teaching*
	
	  a Efficient Organization
	  b Structured Lessons
	  c Adaptive Practice
	  d Clarity of practice

3 *Focus on* Student Acquisition of Central *Learning* Skills
  a Maximum Availability and Use of Time for Learning
  b Emphasis on Mastery of Central Learning Skills
	3 *Concentration on* Teaching and *Learning*
	
	  a Maximization of Learning Time
	  b Academic Emphasis
	  c Focus on Achievement

4 *Productive* School Climate and *Culture*
  a *Orderly Environment*
  b Faculty Commitment to a *Shared* and Articulated *Mission* Focused on Achievement
  c Faculty Cohesion and Collegiality
  d Schoolwide Emphasis on *Recognizing Positive Performance*
  e Problem Solving Orientation
  f Faculty Input Into Decision Making
	4 Learning Environment
	  a An *Orderly Environment*
	  b An Attractive Working Environment
	
	5 *Shared Vision* and Goals
	  a Unity of Purpose
	  b Consistency of Practice
	  c Collegiality and Cooperation
	
	6 *Positive Reinforcement*
	  a Clear and Fair Discipline
	  b Feedback

Table 4.2 Continued

Levine and Lezotte (1990) Characteristics	*Sammons, Hillman and Mortimore (1995) Factors*

5 *High* Operationalized *Expectations* and *Requirements for Students*	7 *High Expectations*
	  a High Expectations all Around
	  b Communicating Expectations
	  c Providing Intellectual Challenge

	8 *Pupil* Rights and *Expectations*
	  a Raising Pupil Self-esteem
	  b Positions of Responsibility
	  c Control of Work

6 Appropriate *Monitoring* of Student *Progress*	9 *Monitoring Progress*
	  a Monitoring Pupil Progress
	  b Evaluating School Performance

7 Practice Oriented *Staff Development* at the *School Site*	10 A Learning Organization (*School Based Staff Development*)
8 Salient *Parental Involvement*	11 Home–school Partnership (*Parental Involvement*)

9 Others
  a Student Sense of Efficacy/Futility
  b Multicultural Instruction and Sensitivity
  c Personal Development of Students
  d Rigorous and Equitable Student Promotion Policies and Practices	

Note: The order and assigned numbers of characteristics and factors in this table have been changed from the original to facilitate comparisons.

* HOTs refers to Higher Order Thinking Skills. Levine and Lezotte (1990) noted that their 'other' characteristics were found in a smaller proportion of the studies that they reviewed.

Sources: Levine and Lezotte, 1990; Sammons et al., 1995b.

A second characteristic of effective leadership has been noted as ensuring that others are related in the process, or a participative approach. Mortimore et al. (1988) noted the importance of involving the deputy headteacher in the life of the school and in the taking of decisions. Rutter et al. (1979) noted the importance of ensuring that all teachers felt represented and that their views had been taken into account. Of particular importance is likely to be the headteacher's motivation and use of a senior management team, and work with departmental heads, whose role as middle managers is of crucial importance in determining school outcomes (Sammons et al., 1997). Sharing of academic leadership with faculty in a school was also the characteristic of the effective principals in the Louisiana studies (Teddlie and Stringfield, 1993).

A third characteristic of effective leadership is the exhibiting of *instructional* leadership. In part, this is related to the belief of the headteacher that instruction is the purpose of the school (Levine and Lezotte, 1990).

Murphy's (1990a) review gives detail on four major areas of this instructional leadership:

Table 4.3 The processes of effective schools

Process	Components of the Process
1 The Processes of Effective Leadership	a Being Firm and Purposeful b Involving Others in the Process c Exhibiting Instructional Leadership d Frequent, Personal Monitoring e Selecting and Replacing Staff
2 The Processes of Effective Teaching	a Maximizing Classtime b Successful Grouping and Organization c Exhibiting Best Teaching Practices d Adapting Practice to Particulars of Classroom
3 Developing and Maintaining a Pervasive Focus on Learning	a Focusing on Academics b Maximizing School Learning Time
4 Producing a Positive School Culture	a Creating a Shared Vision b Creating an Orderly Environment c Emphasizing Positive Reinforcement
5 Creating High (and Appropriate) Expectations for All	a For Students b For Staff
6 Emphasizing Student Responsibilities and Rights	a Responsibilities b Rights
7 Monitoring Progress at All Levels	a At the School Level b At the Classroom Level c At the Student Level
8 Developing Staff Skills at the School Site	a Site Based b Integrated with Ongoing Professional Development
9 Involving Parents in Productive and Appropriate Ways	a Buffering Negative Influences b Encouraging Productive Interactions with Parents

- developing a limited number of well-defined goals and communicating them to all school constituencies;
- managing the educational production function through supervising instruction, allocating and protecting instructional time, coordinating the curriculum and monitoring student progress;
- promoting an academic learning climate involving positive expectations for students, maintaining high personal visibility, providing incentives for teachers and students, and of promoting professional development of teachers;
- developing a supportive work environment, involving the creation of a safe and orderly environment, providing opportunities for meaningful student involvement, developing staff collaboration, securing outside resources to support the school and the forging of links between the home and the school.

The fourth and fifth components of effective leadership consist of two direct involvements in school life – the frequent, personal monitoring of staff performance and the proactive selection and replacement of staff. The personal monitoring has, as Levine and Lezotte (1990) note, 'emerged in virtually every study where it has been included as a variable' (e.g. Armor et al., 1976; Brookover et al., 1979; Mortimore et al., 1988; Teddlie et al., 1989a; Austin and Holowenzak, 1985). It is usually characterized by popping in and out of classrooms, conversing informally with staff in routine 'sense making' operations, being on the spot to give advice or help in decision taking, and more generally 'management by Wandering Around' (Peters and Waterman, 1982). Deal and Peterson (1990) note that this is the way in which principals can actually shape school culture.

The selection and replacement of teachers has also been picked out in many studies (Austin and Holowenzak, 1985; Wimpelberg, 1987; Stringfield and Teddlie, 1987, 1988; Teddlie et al., 1987), involving the head hunting of good recruits, and the pressuring of less competent staff to either improve or move on to another school. Bridges (1988) provided detailed information on how to manage, and then dismiss if necessary, incompetent teachers.

Teddlie and Stringfield (1993) provide an interesting case study of how effective schools can be created by manipulation of some of the factors described above. Their study of Herbert Hoover Elementary shows the new principal, Mr Jameson, generating leadership in four areas:

1   The method for selection and replacement of teachers – Mr Jameson had personally recruited nine new faculty members in his short four year tenure at Hoover. He took great pains to recruit the best teachers possible, especially since his school had a negative reputation in the community. He recruited largely by word-of-mouth and carefully perused the files of all respective teachers at the central office.
2   The type of classroom monitoring and feedback provided by the administration – Mr Jameson intuitively followed the procedure advocated by Deal and Peterson (1990): frequent and short visits to the classrooms on an unscheduled basis. Consequently, he could describe in detail the strengths and weaknesses of his teachers, something his predecessor was incapable of doing.
3   The type of support for individual teacher improvement provided by the administration – Knowledge of each teacher's weaknesses enabled Mr Jameson to focus personal assistance and professional inservice to redressing those specific problems. For instance, he had identified questioning skills as an area of weakness for the entire faculty. As a result of this, he had read extensively about strategies for enhancing questioning skills and had designed workshops for the teachers around those strategies.
4   The overall instructional leadership provided by the administration, including allocating and protecting academic time – Mr Jameson exhibited overall instructional leadership by actively managing the educational production function. He had recaptured valuable academic time by rigorously enforcing the stated academic schedule and by personally monitoring lunch and recess breaks. As a result of this, the overall time on task at Hoover had dramatically increased from 52 per cent in LSES-III to 85 per cent in LSES-IV, with an increase from 32 per cent to 62 per cent in interactive time on task.

Teacher and Teaching Effectiveness

The generation of effective classroom learning environments is a particular feature of effective schools, particularly since it is clear that the learning level or classroom level is more important in determining the quality of school outcomes than the level of the school itself (Creemers, 1994). Those factors that are most 'proximal' to the student, such as the teacher, are likely to be more important than those that are more distant from him or her such as the school or the District (Stringfield, 1994a, 1994b).

Crucial in determining the effectiveness of teaching is firstly the management of time. Ensuring that lessons start and finish on time is crucial (Rutter et al., 1979), as is minimizing the amount of time that is lost in routine administrative matters, disciplinary interventions or lesson transitions from one topic/subject/activity to another (Brookover et al., 1984; Mortimore et al., 1988; Alexander, 1992; Slavin, 1996). Maximizing the proportion of time that is spent interacting with pupils may be particularly important (Rutter et al., 1979; Alexander, R., 1992).

Secondly, effective teaching is characterized by effective classroom organization. Of particular importance here is the importance of preparing lessons in advance (Rutter et al., 1979) and of clarity both in explaining the purpose of the lesson and in the actual curricular and content material that is used. The structuring of lessons is also important, which Scheerens (1992) interprets as making clear to students what has to be done, splitting curricular material into manageable units to aid learning, and ensuring a firm structure together with basic skill acquisition.

Thirdly, effective learning at classroom level involves the use of effective teaching practices. There is not space here to cover these extensively (see review in Brophy and Good, 1986 for further evidence) but it is clear that teacher behaviours are particularly important in the following areas:

- questioning both in terms of the frequency of questions and their appropriateness for diverse children;
- having a limited focus in lessons since work on several different curriculum areas is likely to lower levels of work related teacher–child interaction and maximize routine administrative time wasting;
- maintaining task orientation in the classroom;
- rapid lesson pace;
- ensuring that classroom routines and rules are well understood, thus reducing the need for students to seek out their teachers for guidance;
- having a warm and accepting classroom climate in which students feel able to ask for help, particularly important in some formulations for students from lower SES backgrounds.

Interesting ideas have been also in discussion about the potential potency of forms of 'whole class interactive' teaching as practised within the elementary schools of Pacific Rim societies (Reynolds and Farrell, 1996; Alexander, 1996b), although the extent to which this is effective only within certain cultural contexts is unclear. This has led to a recent attempt both with Pacific Rim societies and the United Kingdom to create a 'balance' or 'blend' of methods involving whole class interactive teaching, groupwork and individual work (Reynolds, 1997).

Fourthly, adaptation of practice to the particular characteristics of the learners is the final component of effective teaching. Sizemore et al. (1983) noted that effective teachers were active in adapting their core texts, and Armor and associates (1976) noted that it was effective to allow teachers to adapt or modify reading programmes. Effective schools clearly possess teachers whose driving force is student needs, rather than who exhibit a control by the mechanics of the school management system.

Focusing on Learning

Focusing upon the importance of academic goals and processes and an academic emphasis have been shown to be core correlates of effective schools. This can be seen in such factors as:

- high entry rate for public examinations in the United Kingdom (Reynolds, 1976; Reynolds and Sullivan, 1979; Smith and Tomlinson, 1989; Sammons et al., 1994);
- use of homework with regular checks by senior management to see that this has occurred (Rutter et al., 1979; Sammons et al., 1995b);
- the possession of a student culture or school ethos in which 'academic emulation' is encouraged (McDill and Rigsby, 1973);
- a commitment to the mastery of central learning skills, in some cases involving a formal mastery learning approach utilizing a sequence of teaching, testing and re-teaching as necessary (Levine and Lezotte, 1990);
- high curriculum coverage or opportunity to learn, since both Bennett (1992) and Tizard et al. (1988) show wide variations in children's exposure to curriculum areas within and between subject areas.

Also, maximizing available learning time at school level (as well as at classroom level that was noted above) is important, particularly since the school level practices will set an example to teachers of what is considered to be appropriate. Protecting learning time from leakage has been the characteristic of effective schools in many studies (Anderson, C., 1982; Teddlie and Stringfield, 1993; Teddlie, Kirby and Stringfield, 1989).

Generating a Positive School Culture

Research shows effective schools as possessing a vision or 'mission' that is shared by staff. Hopkins et al. (1994) note the importance of a sense of community that is related to cooperation between colleagues, good communication between staff and widely agreed upon goals. Numerous other studies suggest that agreement upon school goals is associated with 'effectiveness' status (e.g. Rutter et al., 1979; Lightfoot, 1983; Stoll and Fink, 1994; Edmonds, 1979a, 1979b).

Consistency in practice is also important, and Mortimore et al. (1988) noted that where teachers adopt a consistent approach to school curriculum this was associated with a positive impact upon pupil progress. Rutter et al. (1979) noted that consistency in the applications of rules and in disciplinary sanctions was present in more effective schools.

Collegiality and collaboration between staff is also important and we have noted above the evidence on the positive effects of involvement of teachers in the school decision making process. Indeed, the importance of 'ownership' of staff of the school is mentioned within many school improvement literature reviews (e.g. Fullan, 1991; Hopkins et al., 1994). The generation of a learning community amongst staff in which all members share good practice, act as critical friends and engage in a process of mutual education and re-education is clearly essential in the continuation of a positive school culture over time, as well as in its creation.

Order within the school is also important in the creation of a positive climate. Indeed, some of the earliest 'five factor' theories of how to generate effective schools concentrated upon creating order as one of the key factors, since without order, discipline and social control at school level it would be very difficult for staff to attain high levels of student attention and engagement within classrooms (Edmonds, 1979a; Lezotte, 1989). A large number of the so called 'safe school' studies also identify pupil control as a pre-requisite for learning.

Within the school also, a positive climate for pupils is essential. We noted above the Reynolds and Sullivan (1979) studies and their notions of the generation of a hostile pupil culture through use of harsh punishments, overly strict control and a resulting tense and negative pupil attitude towards their teachers. Such findings have been extensively replicated (Mortimore et al., 1988; Rutter et al., 1979).

The rewarding of good behaviour, achievement, effort and attributes is by contrast highly likely to be more productive, and of course can be through instrumental routines (finishing class early or an extra school trip) or expressive ones (a verbal statement of 'well done' or a smile). Reviews of teacher effectiveness noted above suggest that effective rewards policies should be:

- quick in time after the behaviour or achievement they are design to reinforce;
- fairly applied in terms of eliminating variation between individuals in their treatment;
- specific;
- varied.

High Expectations of Achievement and Behaviour

High expectations of students has been one of the most consistent of findings in the literature, together with the communication of such expectations so that students know them, being shown in the original effective schools literature (Weber, 1971; Brookover et al., 1979; Edmonds, 1979a, 1979b, 1981; Venezky and Winfield, 1979) as well as in more recent American research (Teddlie and Stringfield, 1993; Stringfield and Teddlie, 1991b) and in the major British empirical studies (e.g. Rutter et al., 1979; Mortimore et al., 1988; Reynolds and Sullivan, 1979; Tizard et al., 1988). Virtually every review on the topic mentions the importance of this factor, whether British (e.g. Reynolds and Cuttance, 1992; Reynolds et al., 1994a; Sammons et al., 1995b), Dutch (Scheerens, 1992; Creemers, 1992) or American (Levine and Lezotte, 1990; US Department of Education, 1987).

It is highly likely that high expectations need to be communicated to students by the behaviours and the verbal reinforcement of teachers, rather than remaining as within teacher states, to have positive effects. Additionally, it is likely that high expectations are closely related to a number of the other correlates mentioned in this chapter – to time management, to principal leadership and to a positive school climate for example. It may also be that high expectations is a surrogate for other teacher variables such as activism, a sense of internal locus of control and a belief that schools can outweigh the effects of coming from disadvantaged family backgrounds.

It is also highly likely that high expectations for students are associated with a staff group who have themselves high expectations of what it is possible for them to achieve from the principal or headteacher.

The latter's expectations of staff are likely to show in such areas as:

- expecting staff to work at understanding the school before they arrive and in specially designed induction procedures;
- expecting high levels of involvement in staff development activity;
- expecting considerable attention to detail in the areas of monitoring, homework etc.;
- expecting staff to prioritize academic achievement as a goal;
- expecting staff to manage their time well, without 'leaking' time.

Teddlie et al. (1989a) note that effective principals 'guard the integrity of the classroom'. Ensuring that all staff expect the very highest levels of attainment and behaviour from pupils is clearly part of that guarding, in effective schools.

Emphasizing Student Responsibilities and Rights

There are suggestions in some studies (Reynolds, 1976a 1976b; Reynolds and Murgatroyd, 1977; Rutter et al., 1979) that the involvement of pupils in school clubs, societies and representative or leadership systems is present in more effective schools. Such positions involve students having a stake in the school and participating in the formal school organization, which should increase the chance of them acquiring school values and a commitment to school goals. The exercise of responsibility may also make students more 'pro-social'.

There are also hints that giving pupils responsibility for their own work and more control over their learning situation may be associated with positive outcomes, as in the junior school study of Mortimore et al. (1988) where pupils in more effective schools were encouraged to manage their work independently of the teacher over short periods of time.

Monitoring Progress at All Levels

The monitoring of student progress is a factor found in some school effectiveness studies – indeed, frequent monitoring of student progress was one of the original five correlates within the Edmonds (1979a and b) five factor model. The positive effects may be due to:

- the availability of data to assess programme impact and programme quality;
- positive effects on students' sense of self worth and motivation, because it shows the students that teachers are interested in their progress;

- it helps focus schools upon the 'core' goals that are being evaluated;
- it can be used to identify those who need remedial instruction and re-teaching;
- it can be used to analyse students' progress, as in the study of Mortimore et al. (1988), where more effective schools kept and used records to analyse progress and as shown in the study of van der Werf (1995), where evaluation of progress was associated with student gain in language (but not in mathematics interestingly).

There are some hints, however, that monitoring needs to be central, and ongoing, but that some manifestations of over frequent monitoring may be counterproductive, as with the negative effect of frequent testing found in the Mortimore et al. (1988) study.

Using monitoring and evaluation systems at the school level to manage school institutions better is also a characteristic of effective schools, and is now more often mentioned within the school improvement literature as necessary for school development (Hopkins et al., 1994). The innovative High Reliability School programme (Stringfield, 1995; Reynolds and Stringfield, 1996) also makes use of 'data richness' of its schools to encourage reflection and adoption of good practice (see this and other studies in Chapter 8).

Murphy's (1990a) review of literature on effective instructional leadership concluded aptly that such persons practise a wide variety of monitoring behaviour, including:

- testing programmes;
- feeding back data on pupil performance to staff, departments and the whole school;
- evaluation of the school's success in achieving its goals.

Staff Development

Descriptions of effective schools often mention school site based staff development of quality as one of their important characteristics (e.g. Austin and Holowenzak, 1985; Hallinger and Murphy, 1985; Mortimore et al., 1988).

It seems to be important that such development is practical, an integral part of school activities rather than an 'add on' and that it is school site based, with Mortimore et al. (1988) noting that staff attending inservice courses indiscriminately and unrelated to the core mission of the school is associated with ineffectiveness. One-off presentations by outside experts or consultants used as 'hired guns' are likely to be counterproductive (Levine and Lezotte, 1990). Clearly a close synchronization of school developmental priorities with the site based developmental activities, and the generation of a staff culture which involves mutual learning, monitoring and commitment to collaboration are all likely to be important.

Parental Involvement

Research generally supports the belief that parental involvement is productive of effective schools (Armor et al., 1976; Levine and Lezotte, 1990), but some studies have failed to find such a relationship, with effective schools in some specific contexts having less parental involvement (Brookover and Lezotte, 1979; Hallinger and Murphy, 1985, 1986, 1987; Teddlie and Stringfield, 1993).

Clearly the precise type of involvement is important in explaining this pattern, with Mortimore et al. (1988) noting that there were positive benefits to parents helping in the classroom, or with school trips or being allowed into the school as an 'open door' policy, but with negative effects being shown by the presence of Parent Teacher Associations, possibly because of the likelihood that such organizations could develop 'cliques' with destructive effects. Literature from North America indicates that parents' direct involvement in school work has particularly beneficial effects, while involvement in extracurricular activities had little effect (see review in Sammons et al., 1995b).

The potential utility of parental involvement is likely to lie in such areas as:

- synchronizing school and home demands on students;
- reducing class size as taught by acting as unpaid teacher assistants;
- raising resources for the school;
- assisting with homework for school students;
- feeding back information on pupil progress and problems to the school;
- liaising with their children's individual teachers.

It is clear that parental involvement in such areas as criticism of the school or visits to the school to complain are likely to generate ineffectiveness at school level (which is why 'buffering' the school from parents may be important in low SES communities). On the other hand, there is too much evidence of the positive effects of parental involvement, particularly from some of the recent intervention studies in the field of literacy development and basic skills acquisition (Slavin, 1996), for its importance to be denied. It is also worth noting that many accounts of rapid school improvement show principals 'pulling the lever' of enhanced parental involvement to generate momentum and change (National Commission on Education, 1995), which might of course be particularly potent in those low SES communities that have not exhibited much of this factor, rather than in those middle class communities where such involvements are routine.

Future Research on School Effectiveness Processes

The body of knowledge reviewed above is a remarkably robust one, given the contextual differences between the various societies that have generated it. However, there have been in recent years numerous calls for a reconceptualization and re-orientation of work at the school level (Reynolds and Packer, 1992; Mortimore, 1991b) to further develop the study of school level processes. The situation for research at the school level is currently as follows:

- The school variables that do explain variation do not seem to travel as well as the instructional variables, in terms of explanatory power cross-culturally. It may even be that *different* school organizational arrangements are necessary in different national cultures to generate effective classroom learning environments which have the same characteristics cross-culturally (see speculations in Reynolds and Teddlie, 1995).

- The rapid changes in the organization of schools internationally (for example, the decentralization of power to school level and the increased volume and importance of routine assessment of student progress) have generated a need for new measures of school organizational functioning appropriate to the changed nature of the organization's role.

- The widespread use of development planning, now virtually universal within all cultures, is not matched by use of variables related to these activities as school level variables, perhaps because of the historical separation of school improvement (and its insights) from school effectiveness (see Chapter 7).

- The use of multilevel methodologies and analyses of various kinds has been rightly regarded as revolutionizing the study of educational effects, but researchers have been unwilling or unable to appreciate the revolution in data gathering needs at school level that is now necessary. The exposure of within school variation in effectiveness by class, by pupil ability group, by social class, by ethnicity and by subject department that is revealed for the first time in multiple level studies needs to be matched by the introduction of 'interface' level variables concerned with how this variation is maximized or minimized within different types of 'effective' or 'ineffective' schools.

- The link between the school level and the other levels outside the school, such as the local educational advisory structure, has not been adequately explored to date, even though there are hints that these other levels are important in generating differential educational outcomes. Researchers, with the exception of some in Canada and the Netherlands, have been notably unwilling to relate schools to their educational local contexts.

- Understanding has also been hindered by the almost universal practice of measuring different factors at classroom and at school level, thus hindering our explanatory power because we do not know whether the low proportion of variance explained by the school level variables used might be improved by the adoption at school level of some of the variables used at classroom level (e.g. 'expectations' of student progress).

- Aside from the point above, the absence of any 'running through' of the same variables at classroom, school and school/educational community levels reduces our explanatory power. The variables measured at the two levels tend to be very different, and although there is no reason why certain school level variables may have effects upon other different class variables, in the present state of our knowledge the 'opening up' of the interface between the school and the classroom is more likely to take place if the *same* variables are studied at school and within school level, with the difference or lack of difference between the two levels on the same variables being used to open up the management of the school/class interface.

- Where studies have utilized multiple measures of outcome by the adoption of 'social' or 'affective' outcomes, it is noticeable that the numbers of school level variables that are associated with variation in outcomes are notably less for the social outcomes as compared to the academic outcomes, suggesting that we are not at the moment tapping the school variables (climate? emotional tone? relationships?) necessary (see speculations about relational patterns in Chapter 12).

- The power of the instructional level as a determinant of outcomes has not been matched by the necessary reconceptualization of the nature of the school level. Rather than having strong direct influences upon development, the school is now more usefully seen as facilitating or hindering the classroom level to potentiate student learning. Adoption of this reconceptualization would lead to a different focus on somewhat different variables at school level (and probably to a focus upon the interface and the interaction between school organizational arrangements and the classroom level) (see Scheerens and Bosker, 1997).

- The conceptualizations and measurement of variables at school level has been inadequately sensitive to the range of possible factors that may have effects. Most studies have used formal organizational factors but few of these, and few in total, have used the 'culture' of schooling in terms of teachers' attitudes, perceptions, goals etc. The third dimension of school life is that of the psychological or psycho-social which is concerned with the relationships between individuals, and the 'psycho-history' of the patterns of relationships found. The use of sociometric techniques to explore this third dimension of schooling, and the adoption of a 'micropolitical' perspective, have been much neglected within school effectiveness research (we turn to this in more detail in Chapter 12).

- Changes within the educational systems of many societies make the adoption of new school factors vitally important. The role of the headteacher in British schools, for example, has changed considerably in the last decade, with this person now being responsible for a range of new responsibilities (organizing school finances, determining school inservice budgets etc.). It would be utterly inadequate to proceed to measure the role of the headteacher in British schools, for example, without developing new instruments to measure what the new role features are.

- The changed nature of schools, and the changed relationship between schools and other socializing agencies, also makes new approaches to the study of the school important. In the United States, the large number of 'add on' programmes is a noticeable educational feature: the consistency, cohesion and 'coordination' of the educational enterprise may now be even more important concepts to operationalize and measure. Also, the increased value of heterogeneity within societies, and the increased absence of power within the socializing agencies of the family and the community, combine to potentially elevate the consistency of the *school's* socialization process to an importance it would not formerly have had. We return to these issues of 'range' and its possible importance in Chapter 12.

The Interaction of School and Teacher Processes

We have so far reviewed material mostly on the school level determinants of effective student outcomes. However, it is clear that school factors have a complex relationship with outcomes in which the following possibilities exist:

- school factors can have direct effects upon outcomes (as in the case of principals' behaviours to individual students);
- school factors can have indirect effects upon outcomes, through setting a context for the development of classroom level factors.

153

Whilst we are unable to go into detail on the literature that exists upon teacher effectiveness (see references in Chapter 11), it is clear that there are important differences between effective and ineffective schools in the nature of their classroom practices and teacher behaviours.

The Louisiana School Effectiveness studies, already noted earlier in this chapter, were perhaps the most ambitious attempt to 'nest' classrooms in schools and to chart the nature of the instructional processes in effective and ineffective schools.

As part of LSES-III, a comparison was made between schools designated as effective and ineffective during the 1984–5 school years. The report on these two case studies (Stringfield, Teddlie and Suarez, 1985) preceded a later report on the complete set of 16 schools from LSES-III. The district in which this pair of schools resided had a highly centralized elementary curriculum with four tracks: advanced work for gifted students, a curriculum for students scoring in the top 23 per cent on standardized tests, the 'regular' curriculum for students scoring between the 23rd and 77th percentiles, and a slower, remedial track for students scoring in the bottom 23 percentiles.

In spite of this standard curriculum, classroom observations confirm that better teaching was occurring at the effective school (Adams Elementary) than at the ineffective school (Fillmore Elementary). No interactive teaching pattern by a Fillmore third grade teacher reached the lowest percentage of interactive teaching time achieved by an Adams third grade teacher. Moreover, the mean percent of interactive third grade teaching at Adams (45 per cent) nearly doubled the 24 per cent mean from Fillmore. Adams teachers were also rated higher than Fillmore teachers on presentation of new content, teacher expectations, and discipline.

In comparing these two schools, the researchers first noted their similarity : both were public and served middle SES children; both had highly stable staffs and relatively strong parental involvement; and discipline was not a major problem at either school. Both schools had focused major staff development efforts on attending meetings and implementing strategies from Madeline Hunter seminars. The two schools appeared to receive equal district support. Beneath the superficial similarity, however, there were at least four major schoolwide differences in processes that could have had an impact on classroom teaching.

First, the expectation level for student performance was clearly higher at Adams. While Fillmore had by design no students in the highest academic track, Adams had a sizeable portion of its students in that track. Additionally, Adams' students were not allowed in the lowest academic track, while some at Fillmore were placed in this track. The Adams' teachers knew that the school administration expected the highest performance from all students, and this message was apparently translated into higher expectations by teachers in the classrooms.

A second schoolwide difference had to do with a clearer focus on present academic expectations at Adams than at Fillmore. At Fillmore, these expectations tended to take the form of a belief that the students will go to college; on the other hand, at Adams it was expressed as a conviction that *all* students can, and *will*, learn their third grade materials *this* year, starting *now*. The emphasis on the here-and-now apparently had been translated into superior current classroom teaching.

A third difference involved an active programme at Adams for removing teachers who were not performing up to a certain standard. This had resulted in the removal of at least two teachers at Adams, while no such dismissals had occurred at Fillmore. The Adams' administration apparently would not tolerate the low interactive time on task recorded by some teachers at Fillmore.

A fourth difference at the two schools was related to the third one. The Adams' administration had more active, direct monitoring and inservicing of their teachers than did the Fillmore administration. The Adams' principal indicated that 'there are many things we can teach teachers', while the Fillmore principal emphasized the friendly, family atmosphere at her school. At Adams the administration was more aware of deficiencies in particular teachers' techniques and were more willing to try to personally remedy those weaknesses than was the Fillmore administration.

The Teddlie et al. (1989a) study built on the two case studies just described by presenting data from all eight pairs of schools in the LSES-III sample. Results from the study indicated that teachers in effective schools consistently outscored those from ineffective schools on all indices of effective teaching. They were consistently more successful in keeping students on task, spent more time presenting new material, provided more independent practice, demonstrated higher expectations for student success, provided more positive reinforcement, and so forth than did their peers in matched ineffective schools.

Some interesting differences in patterns of variation among teachers were also found. For instance, the standard deviations reported for teaching behaviours were consistently smaller in effective as opposed to ineffective schools. These results imply that some formal or informal socialization process was ongoing at the effective schools resulting in more uniform teaching behaviour. The effective school in one pair (Roosevelt Elementary) was a good example of an appropriate socialization experience for teachers, while the ineffective school of that pair (Coolidge Elementary) provided a good illustration of poor school socialization.

It was concluded that the effective school principals in this study were the central figures 'who guarded the integrity of the classroom' (Teddlie et al., 1989a, p.234). This guarding of academic integrity resulted in a truncation of the lower end of the range of teaching behaviours through a more organized class day and a greater emphasis on interactive teaching. This emphasis resulted in less variance in time on task, classroom instruction and classroom climate scores, since the lower end of the range of teacher behaviours was not tolerated by the principal.

At least five major differences between Roosevelt and Coolidge elementary schools were directly related to the interaction between school and teacher effects:

1   shared academic leadership versus non-shared academic leadership;
2   strong faculty cohesiveness versus lack of faculty cohesiveness;
3   cooperative efforts to enhance teaching versus top-down efforts to enhance teaching;
4   fairly uniform teaching behaviours across classes versus large variances in teaching behaviours across classes; and
5   assistance freely given new faculty members versus little assistance given new faculty members.

The study by Virgilio et al. (1991) sought to replicate the LSES-III findings related to teachers' behaviour, while involving more types of schools. This study examined teacher behaviours in typical as well as effective and ineffective schools and included junior high schools as well as elementary schools.

Results indicated that teachers from the different levels of school effectiveness behaved quite distinctively. Teachers from effective schools demonstrated better teaching skills than those from typical schools, who performed better than those from ineffective schools. This school effect was more pronounced at the elementary school level, but still persisted at the junior high level on high inference indicators of teacher behaviour measuring classroom management, classroom instruction, and classroom climate. These results constituted a strong replication of those reported from LSES-III, with the addition of consistent results on a third level of effectiveness (the typical school).

This study also replicated and extended the findings regarding different patterns of variance that were reported from LSES-III. There was less variance in teaching behaviour at the effective school level than at the typical school level, which in turn had less variance in teaching behaviour than that at the ineffective school level. For instance, the range for time on task across teachers in effective elementary schools was only 19 per cent, while for teachers in ineffective elementary schools it was 71 per cent. The lowest time on task for any teacher in a more effective elementary school was a very respectable 81 per cent. The lower end of the range of effective teaching behaviour in more effective elementary schools was truncated on both the teaching effectiveness indicators.

Virgilio et al. (1991) speculated on the relative importance of selection and socialization factors at work in the truncation of the range of teacher behaviours in effective schools. Stringfield and Teddlie (1989) had contended that an emphasis on the selection and removal of teachers probably has its greatest impact as a school is headed toward effectiveness. During that time, the principal can radically change the school's overall scores on time on task, classroom climate, etc., by encouraging the removal of poor teachers and carefully selecting teachers to replace them. Once weaker teachers have been replaced by stronger ones, the faculty will become more stable and the internal socialization process becomes more important.

Virgilio et al. then discussed three areas in which different school level socialization experiences could have an impact on teacher behaviour once the faculty has been recruited:

1 the type of classroom monitoring and feedback provided by the administration;
2 the type of support for individual teacher improvement provided by the administration;
3 the overall instructional leadership provided by the administration.

Results from LSES-IV (Teddlie and Stringfield, 1993) with regard to teaching behaviours in historically effective/ineffective schools further expanded understanding of teaching effects within school effects. The eight pairs of schools studied in LSES-IV were the same schools that had been described in the Teddlie et al. (1989a, 1989b) LSES-III study. It was more appropriate to refer to these schools as historically effective/ineffective in the 1993 report since the criteria for their initial selection were 6–7 years old when LSES-IV occurred.

There was evidence for the persistence of more positive teaching behaviours within historically effective schools (HESs), as opposed to historically ineffective schools

(HISs), on the high-inference teaching indices. Overall, teachers in HESs outperformed those from HISs on classroom management, presentation and questioning skills, instructional strategies skills and classroom social psychological climate. Furthermore, looking at individual pairs of schools, there was evidence for the persistence of differential teaching effects in five of the seven pairs, excluding one pair that did not have an appropriately selected positive outlier.

In fact, there was greater evidence for the persistence of teacher effects than for school effects. In two of the pairs of schools, the schools' effectiveness status changed while their teachers' effectiveness status did not change. In one pair, the HES became less effective on indices of student achievement, but its teachers continued to outperform those from its matched school. In another pair, even though the HIS improved dramatically on student achievement, its teachers were still outperformed by those from its matched school. The greater instability of school effects may be attributable to the high turnover rate among principals. Fifty per cent of the principalships changed from LSES-III to IV.

Future Research on the Interaction between School Effects and Teacher Effects

As noted above, and elsewhere in this volume (e.g. Chapters 1, 3 and 5), theorists are now calling for the inclusive study of teacher and school effectiveness variables under the name of educational effectiveness research. The clearest statement of this position is the article by Creemers and Reezigt (1996), which calls for three-level studies (school, class, student) to test a theoretical model in which school factors have an impact on student achievement indirectly through classroom level factors. These authors state:

> When quality of instruction, time for learning and opportunity to learn are defined as the essential classroom level factors for student achievement, school level factors should be defined according to the same criteria. This implies that school factors are only supposed to enhance student achievement when it is possible to relate them conceptually to quality, time and opportunity. The selection of school factors along these lines does not result in a totally new set of correlates, but in a conceptual re-ordering of factors. It is expected that the school factors, selected and re-ordered in this way, will better be able to explain differences in student achievement, because of their clear relationship with classroom level factors.
>
> (Creemers and Reezigt, 1996, p.222–3)

Creemers and Reezigt cite some examples of this three-level approach:

- theoretical work by Scheerens (1992), Stringfield and Slavin (1992), and Slater and Teddlie (1992);
- a handful of empirical studies (Bosker, Kremers and Lugthart, 1990; Bosker, 1991; Bosker and Scheerens, 1994; Luyten, 1994a; Scheerens, Vermeulen and Pelgrum, 1989; Stringfield and Teddlie, 1989; Teddlie and Stringfield, 1993; Van der Tuin, 1993).

The recent work of Hill and Rowe (1996) on school and teacher effectiveness in Victoria, Australia should also be added to this list of three-level studies, as well as the ILEA Junior School Project (Mortimore et al., 1988), ISERP (e.g. Creemers, Reynolds, Stringfield and Teddlie, 1996) and dissertation research done in the USA (e.g. Arceneaux, 1993; Crone, 1992). Tymms (1993) also conducted a three-level study, with student, class, and subject department as the levels.

Thus, there is a growing momentum to more thoroughly integrate research that was previously artificially divided into SER and TER. While we applaud these efforts and see them as the wave of the future for SER, there are some cautions that should be taken into consideration:

- Studies and research reviews comparing the effects of school and classroom variables indicate that classroom factors predict more variance than school factors (e.g. Hill and Rowe, 1996; Luyten, 1994a, 1994b, 1994c; Scheerens et al., 1989; Wang, Haertel and Walberg, 1993). As noted by Hill and Rowe (1996, pp.27–8), however, school effects are cumulative and may be 'unobserved, underestimated, or partialled out' in cross-sectional studies, or longitudinal studies that are short term in nature, a point that was also made by Stringfield (1994a). Unless educational effectiveness studies are done longitudinally, school effects are likely to be underestimated.

- The issue of whether schools can have direct and reciprocal, as well as indirect, effects on student achievement is not yet resolved, even though the Creemers and Reezigt (1996) model specifies only an indirect effect through classroom factors. Hallinger and Heck (1996) have recently compared three models (adapted from Pitner, 1988) for assessing the impact of principal leadership (a school level factor) on student achievement: the direct-effects model (with and without antecedent variables), the mediated-effects model (with and without antecedent variables), and the reciprocal-effects model. Hallinger and Heck agree with Creemers and Reezigt that the direct-effects model is not adequate for assessing the impact of principal leadership on student achievement. The mediated-effects model is better, they argue, because it more realistically describes the manner in which principal leadership most often affects student achievement (i.e. through intervening variables).

Nevertheless, the relationship between school level factors and student achievement is probably *not* restricted to indirect effects through intervening classroom factors solely. It is possible that school level factors can also impact student achievement in direct and in reciprocal ways, which is best described using the reciprocal-effects model of Hallinger and Heck. In this model, school factors are linked to student achievement with a causal arrow in both directions, as well as through intervening variables.

An example of the direct effect that a school factor can have on student achievement might involve the establishment of a set of rules intended to lead to an orderly environment (i.e. a school free of disruption, violence, drugs) throughout the school's common areas (e.g. the hallways, the playground, the cafeteria, the auditorium, the bus stops). If such an orderly environment were accomplished, then students should come to classes more willing and able to achieve, independent of anything that then happens in the classrooms.

Also, the intervening variables between school factors and student achievement do not always have to be classroom factors. For instance, another intervening variable could be parental involvement, in cases where school policy directly affects parents, such as mandated parental participation in homework.

Conclusions

It is clear that the interrelation between school factors, classroom factors, student achievement, and other variables is very complex, and we currently do not know how to model it precisely. Specifying only an indirect link between school factors and student achievement through classroom factors will probably underestimate school effects yet again.

The classroom variables specified by Creemers and Reezigt (1996) must be properly measured in order to adequately estimate the influence of the class on student achievement. While time for learning and opportunity to learn may be assessed through survey methods, quality of instruction must be observed directly. Using surveys, or other proxy measures, to assess quality of instruction is likely to result in socially desirable responses, or responses with little meaningful variance. Even direct observation is problematic if the instruments are not specifically designed for the country in which they are administered, or if observers are not properly trained in this use. SER has been chronically plagued with underspecification of causal models due to inadequate operationalization of variables; the study of educational effectiveness will have similar problems if adequate measures of quality of instruction are not utilized.

Nevertheless, the emerging educational (school plus teacher) effectiveness paradigm has great promise in elucidating relationships between variables at different levels, and in enhancing our understanding of the relationship between processes and student outcomes. Children learn in classrooms that are situated in buildings that are called schools – research design needs to in future appreciate that simple fact.

5 Context Issues within School Effectiveness Research

*Charles Teddlie, Sam Stringfield and
David Reynolds*

Introduction

For much of the history of SER, the varied contexts within which schooling occurs have been ignored. In fact, the lack of studies concerning the context of school effects was an area that Good and Brophy listed as a major limitation of extant SER in the mid-1980s (Good and Brophy, 1986). This limitation has been addressed to a significant degree over the past decade, with the publication of a number of both research and theoretical articles on context issues within SER. (Table 5.1 shows some of the significant studies in this area, together with details on their methodology and analytic procedures.)

The study of context in SER has had a profound impact on many areas within the field:

- Contextually sensitive studies have yielded differential results depending on the 'levels' of the context variable that is being studied (e.g. elementary versus secondary phases of schooling; rural versus suburban versus urban community types; primarily low SES versus primarily middle SES student bodies).
- The consideration of context in SER has led to an increased sophistication in theory development which has been greatly needed (see Chapter 10).
- Contextually 'sensitive' models for school improvement have begun to emerge as studies have demonstrated that appropriate improvement processes can vary to a large degree according to context factors (see Chapter 7).

In this chapter, we will first present five definitions of context as it applies to SER. We will then briefly discuss differences that exist between countries in the ways in which SER researchers have studied context. Results from studies including context variables in their design will then be summarized in four areas:

- the socio economic status (SES) of students attending schools;
- the community type of school;
- the grade phases of schooling;
- the governance structure of schools.

Finally, there will be a brief summary of some of the major conclusions drawn from the literature review, plus a few comments concerning useful directions for future research.

Table 5.1 Comparison of methodologies used in seven school effects studies with context variables

Study	Levels of Effectiveness	Context Variable	Operationalization of Context Variable	Sampling Procedure	Data Analysis Procedure
Hallinger and Murphy (1986)	One	SES of student body	Four levels, determined by state department data on parental occupation status and percent of students receiving AFDC[1]	Purposive sample of eight effective schools from a total of 3,100 elementary schools in California	Case studies using qualitative data sources, supplemented by surveys
Teddlie, Stringfield and colleagues (1985, 1989)	Three	SES of student body	Two levels determined by state department data on parental occupation status and educational level	A representative sample of 76 schools from 795 elementary schools in Louisiana, split along SES and effectiveness dimensions	MANOVA[2], with effectiveness status and SES as independent variables (IVs)
Evans and Teddlie (1995)	Two	SES of student body	Two levels determined by state department data on percent of student receiving AFDC	Stratified sample of 53 elementary schools in 19 Louisiana districts	MANOVA[2], with effectiveness status and SES as IVs
Virgilio et al. (1991)	Three	Grade level configuration	Designation by school system as elementary or junior high school	Fifteen elementary and junior high schools from one large urban school district	MANOVA[2], with effectiveness status and grade level as IVs
Heck (1992)	Two	Grade level configuration	Designation by school system as elementary or secondary	Sample of 40 schools with consistent performance over a three year period from all public schools in California	Canonical correlations
Stringfield and Teddlie (1991)	Two	Community type	Researcher designation as rural, urban, or suburban confirmed by principal response to questionnaire items	Two rural, two suburban, two urban outlier schools	Qualitative and quantitative comparisons of pairs of schools
Buttram and Carlson (1982)	One	Community type	Researcher designation as a rural school	One school chosen purposively	Case study

Notes:
1 AFDC refers to Aid to Families with Dependent Children, a government assistance programme in the USA.
2 MANOVA refers to Multivariate Analysis of Variance.

Five Definitions of Context

The following section presents five different definitions of context, as related to SER, that have been used over the past decade. These definitions have come from authors working in three countries (the Netherlands, the UK, the USA): Willms (1985a, 1985b, 1985c, 1986, 1992); Wimpelberg et al. (1989); Scheerens (1992, 1993); Slater and Teddlie (1992). This section concludes with the definition that we will use throughout this volume.

Willms (1985a, 1985b, 1985c, 1986) was among the first researchers to study the impact of student body SES in his research conducted in the UK in the early to mid 1980s. Within that country, the impact of student body SES has been known as the 'compositional' effect, or the 'balance' effect. Willms (1992) defined this 'compositional' effect as follows:

> The composition of a school's intake can have a substantial effect on pupils' outcomes over and beyond the effects associated with pupils' individual ability and social class. Schools with high social class or high ability intakes have some advantages associated with their context.
>
> (Willms, 1992, p.41)

Willms' definition of context (and that of others working within the UK throughout the 1980s) was, therefore, confined to one variable: the SES of the school's student body. Also, the impact of that variable was measured solely in terms of student achievement.

Wimpelberg, Teddlie and Stringfield (1989) expanded the definition considerably in a theoretical article in which they contended that 'the introduction of context variables into the critique and revision of effective schools research designs' altered the history of that research in the USA.

Wimpelberg et al. (1989) stated that:

> 'Context' can include such socio-political facets as the socio-economic background of the students, governance structures that determine the fiscal and operational decision making, grade levels (age of students and curricular program) of the school, and more.
>
> (Wimpelberg et al., 1989, p.82)

Wimpelberg, and others (e.g. Hallinger and Murphy, 1986; Teddlie and Stringfield, 1985; Teddlie et al., 1989b) working within the USA in the mid to late 1980s, not only expanded the definition of context to other variables, but also included the study of process as well as product in their 'contextually sensitive' SER studies.

In his integrated model of school effectiveness, Scheerens (1990, 1992) listed the following variables as being contextual in nature:

- 'covariables', such as school size, student-body composition, school category, urban/rural;
- achievement stimulants from higher administrative levels;
- development of educational consumerism.

Scheerens and other European scholars (e.g. Creemers and Scheerens, 1994; Hofman, 1995; Olthof and Lugthart, 1992; Scheerens, 1992, 1993; Scheerens and Creemers, 1990; Scheerens and Bosker, 1997) have utilized contingency theory (e.g. Fiedler, 1967; Hoy and Miskel, 1991; Mintzberg, 1979) as a framework in which to interpret results from contextually sensitive SER. As Scheerens (1993) noted:

> The central thesis of contingency theory is that in contrast to the assumptions of classic organisational theories, there is no one best way to organise. The effectiveness of organisational structures depends upon situational or contingency factors.
> (Scheerens, 1993, p.29)

In the terminology of SER, these situational or contingency factors are school context factors (e.g. student body composition, community type of school, grade phase, governance structure of school, school size, etc.).

Slater and Teddlie (1992) developed a different theoretical position (the Theory of School Effectiveness and Leadership or TSEL) that explicitly incorporated both contextual and process considerations. (In the TSEL, 'process' indicated that schools are continually going through stages in which they are either improving or declining.)

The TSEL consisted of three elements or 'levels': management and leadership (at the school level), faculty preparedness (at the classroom level), and student learning readiness (at the individual school level). For these authors, 'context' meant the interaction between any two or more of these three elements.

Within the current volume, we will present our own definition of context, which follows from the discussion of methodological issues found in Chapter 3. In that chapter, context effects were related to the methodological issue of the *generalizability* of school effects across different settings or 'contexts'.

The definition of context that we will use throughout this chapter is as follows:

> The study of context in SER refers to the differential effects associated with certain variables (specifically SES of student body, community type, grade phase of schooling, and governance structure) upon the scientific properties of school effects, the characteristics of effective schools, and the school improvement process.

This definition consists of three parts:

1   The term 'differential' indicates that the generalizability of the effect of certain variables depends upon the particular value(s) for that variable employed in the study. For instance, the effect of student body SES on achievement depends upon the particular mixture of middle and low SES students in the schools under study (e.g. predominantly middle or predominantly low SES). Or, the effect of community type upon student retention depends upon whether or not we are studying rural, suburban, or urban schools.

2   The restriction of the definition of context variables to the four noted above is an attempt to avoid further 'Balkanization' of the field, which might lead to the study of a proliferation of context variables, many of which are highly intercorrelated and theoretically entangled with one another. Such a 'Balkanization' of SER

would make it increasingly difficult to discuss the generalizability of results beyond the immediate context of the study being conducted. This point will be discussed more thoroughly later in this chapter.

3 The effect of context variables will be examined within all three strands of SER discussed in Chapter 1: school effects studies (involving the study of the scientific properties of these effects), effective schools research, and school improvement studies.

Different Country Traditions in the Study of Context

It is important to note that different countries have distinct traditions with regard to the study of context variables in SER. Specifically, the study of context has been distinct among the three countries with the longest and richest traditions of studying SER: the USA, the UK and the Netherlands.

It was argued in Chapter 1 that the explicit study of context, beginning in the early to mid 1980s, has been the major catalyst for many of recent advances that have been made in all three strands of SER in the USA (Wimpelberg et al., 1989). Within that country, however, the primary emphasis in contextually sensitive SER has been on the study of the differential processes of *effective schooling* that are found in schools from varied contexts (e.g. Hallinger and Murphy, 1986; Teddlie and Stringfield, 1985, 1993). This emphasis on process differences has led the field to advance beyond static correlate driven models of *school improvement* (e.g. Levine and Lezotte, 1990) and also led to more dynamic formulations of SER theory (e.g. Slater and Teddlie, 1992; Wimpelberg, 1993).

Within the UK, studies of what we now call context also began appearing in the mid 1980s, but they were called 'compositional' or 'balance' studies in that country (e.g. Cuttance, 1992; Rutter et al., 1979; Willms, 1985b, 1986). Emphasis was placed on the impact of different contexts on the *scientific properties of school effects*, especially differential effect sizes. Early work in both the UK and the USA concentrated on SES of student body as the context factor of interest.

It is interesting that the study of context had a parallel development in both the USA and the UK, with little or no interaction between the two literatures until the 1990s, when scholars from both countries became aware of one another's work. This is a classic case of the unfortunate situation described in Chapter 2 concerning researchers from different SER orientations not communicating regarding their work, mainly because the UK studies were firmly within the school effects tradition, and the USA studies were more within the effective schools arena.

The Dutch spin on context research is different from that of either the UK or the USA. As noted above, studies of the effect of school context have led scholars there (e.g. Creemers and Scheerens, 1994; Scheerens, 1990, 1992, 1993) to adapt tenets from a broad social science framework, known as contingency theory (e.g. Mintzberg, 1979, 1983), to explain previously obtained results and to predict further findings. Empirical work on context from the Netherlands is just now surfacing (e.g. Hofman, 1995), and the early emphasis in the Dutch literature is on governance issues (e.g. on school boards).

As other countries produce contextually sensitive SER, it is likely that the variables of interest will differ. For example within developing countries, community type may be the most important context variable, because differences between lesser developed rural areas and more modern urban areas are so great. More discussion of these country differences is found in Chapter 8.

Introduction to the Review of the Research Findings from SER

The next four sections will discuss results from SER studies that have included context variables in their design. Studies using SES as a context variable will be discussed first, followed by those using community type and grade phase. These three types of context studies resulted partially from the criticism that many of the initial 'effective schools' studies were conducted in poor (SES), urban (community type), elementary (grade phase) schools. Studies examining the effects of one other context variable (governance structure) will then be discussed.

As indicated above, discussion in this chapter limits consideration of context to the four variables just noted. Obviously, we could have included other context variables (e.g. size of school, phase of development of school, experience level of principal, experience level of faculty), but elected not to do so. The reason for this is that we want to avoid further 'Balkanization' of the field beyond the major context variables that have been demonstrated to have differential effects upon school processes and outcomes.

At the present time, the four context variables noted above (SES of student body, community type, grade phase of schooling, governance structure), plus size and country, have been studied the most and have yielded the clearest differential results. As noted throughout this chapter, country context effects will be discussed in Chapter 8. Size of school is often confounded either with community type or with grade phase of schooling or with country, and we have chosen to examine these other context variables rather than size.

The Study of Socio Economic Status (SES) of Students as a Context Variable

The inclusion of SES indicators as context variables has occurred within all three strands of SER, illustrating the importance that social scientists have traditionally given to the impact of social class (e.g. Blumberg, 1972; Curtis and Jackson, 1977). In the following section, results from school effects (input–output) studies will be discussed first, followed by research from the 'effective schools' (process–product) studies and school improvement traditions. The study of context variables in the USA has been especially emphasized within the 'effective schools' research strand, where the term 'contextually sensitive' studies of school effectiveness emerged. On the other hand, within the UK, the research has centred around the impact of student body SES on the scientific properties of school effects.

Results from School Effects Studies

The results from studies of the impact of the SES of student bodies on school effects was briefly discussed in Chapter 3, and they will be expanded upon here. There will also be speculation in this section regarding possible reasons for why these differences in achievement exist for schools with students from different SES backgrounds.

Sammons et al. (1996a) referred to these differences due to the SES of student body as inconsistency of effect size 'across different school memberships'. In the UK, these SES context effects have been referred to as 'compositional' effects (since they take into account the SES composition of the student body) or 'balance' effects (since they concern the balance of students from a particular SES class in a school).

Several studies have demonstrated that the composition of a school's 'intake' (i.e. the SES backgrounds of *all the students* attending a school) can have an effect on students' achievement beyond the effects associated with students' *individual* social class and/or ability (e.g. Brookover et al., 1978, 1979; Henderson, Mieszkowski and Sauvageau, 1978; McDill et al., 1969; Rutter et al., 1979; Shavit and Williams, 1985; Summers and Wolfe, 1977; Willms, 1985b, 1986; Willms and Raudenbush, 1989). For instance, Blakey and Heath (1992) concluded that when explaining a student's performance, 'we need to take account both of his or her own social class background and the background of the other children in the school' (p.127). Willms and Raudenbush (1989) demonstrated that these compositional effects can change over time.

In a study using Scottish secondary level data, Willms (1986) demonstrated that such contextual effects were more strongly related to the proportion of higher SES students in a school than to the proportion of lower SES students, a phenomenon that he labelled the 'balance' effect. Willms also concluded that these school SES context effects were 'equally strong for pupils of high and low ability alike' (p.224). This implies that students from all ability levels tend to benefit in terms of academic achievement from attending higher SES schools.

In an earlier review of the USA literature on this issue, Murnane (1981) similarly concluded that the higher the average SES or academic ability of the student body, the more positive was the effect on individual students, although the effect seemed to be more pronounced for lower SES students. The USA research into this issue through the mid-1980s was labelled 'peer group research' (e.g. Hanushek, 1972; Henderson, Mieszkowski and Sauvageau, 1978; Murnane, 1975; Summers and Wolfe, 1977; Winkler, 1975). Murnane (1981) concluded from this research that:

> Thus, it appears that children disadvantaged by low initial achievement or low SES benefited from attending schools with more fortunate students, while the cost to the more fortunate students in these schools in terms of decreased achievement was small.
>
> (Murnane, 1981, p.23)

Some authors have contended that this SES contextual effect may be the result of peer group influences (e.g. Blakey and Heath, 1992; Clifford and Heath, 1984; Erbing and Young, 1979), but other factors may also be at work (Willms, 1986). Willms (1992) has suggested several other advantages that schools with higher SES student bodies may have over those with lower SES students:

- they have greater support from parents;
- they have fewer disciplinary problems;
- they have atmospheres that are more conducive to learning; and
- they are more likely to attract and retain excellent teachers.

(This final point is related to the 'Additive Effect', which is discussed in more detail in Chapter 12.)

While these speculations seem well founded, the precise social psychological processes through which they work are as yet unspecified. Willms and Raudenbush (1989) addressed this issue as follows:

> Researchers have not specified precisely the mechanisms through which contextual effects arise . . . but to some extent they are associated with factors that lie outside teachers' control, such as peer influence or the effects of local community deprivation.
>
> (Willms and Raudenbush, 1989, p.213)

Willms and Raudenbush (1989) calculated the impact of SES as a context variable in a study of Scottish secondary schools. They concluded that an increase of one standard deviation in school mean SES is associated with a gain of 29 per cent of a standard deviation in overall attainment.

Other studies have failed to find evidence of such SES contextual effects (e.g. Alexander, K. and Eckland, 1975; Alwin and Otto, 1976; Bondi, 1991; Hauser, 1970, 1971; Hauser et al., 1976; Mortimore et al., 1988; Trower and Vincent, 1995). For example, Mortimore et al. (1988) found no evidence of the contextual effect in their study of junior schools, a result that was supported by later reanalyses. Hauser (1970, 1971) contended that some contextual effects may, in fact, be a statistical artefact; that is, they may be the result of underspecified mathematical models.

Despite these contradictory results, the overall pattern of data from the UK, the USA, and other countries (e.g. the Shavit and Williams, 1985 results from Israel) indicate that there is, in fact, a compositional effect. It is probable that there are circumstances that make the detection of the compositional effect more or less likely. Willms (1986) concluded that there were two essential ingredients for the detection of these SES contextual effects in input–output studies: a well specified mathematical model and outcome measures that are sensitive to the effects of the school curriculum. Shavit and Williams (1985) suggested a third characteristic required for the detection of such contextual effects: diversity in school contexts. In other words, there needs to be a wide range of variation in the SES contexts of the schools under study to detect effects of this contextual factor.

Thus, if studies are conducted in settings with little variance in SES of students (e.g. as is the situation for many of the schools in the Netherlands or Norway), it is less likely that a compositional effect will be found. Also, if researchers elect to study schools from one particular SES context (e.g. as USA researchers from the Effective Schools tradition did in the 1970s), then it is unlikely that a compositional effect will be found.

Results from Effective Schools Studies of SES as a Context Variable

In the mid-1980s, a number of researchers in the USA began to explore the processes at work in the relationship between the social context of schools and their effectiveness status (e.g. Andrews, R., et al., 1986; Chubb and Moe, 1985; Hallinger and Murphy, 1986; Rowan and Denk, 1984; Teddlie and Stringfield, 1985). In these studies, as in those in the previous section, social context was typically operationalized as the socio economic status (SES) of the student body of the schools that were being studied. In most of these studies, the samples consisted of middle and low SES schools, but some of these studies also included a sample of affluent schools (Hallinger and Murphy, 1986; Miller and Sayre, 1986).

According to Levine and Lezotte (1990) and Scheerens (1992), there have been two comprehensive process–product studies using SES as a context variable conducted in the USA: one by Hallinger and Murphy (1986) in California and one by Teddlie and Stringfield (1985, 1993) and their colleagues in Louisiana. The most interesting aspect of these two studies was that many of their results were congruent, despite significant differences in methodologies and study populations.

The California study involved case studies of eight elementary schools selected from a population of schools that had scored above prediction for three consecutive years on a standardized achievement test. Two of these schools were low in SES, two were classified as lower-middle, two were in middle income communities and two were upper-middle (Hallinger and Murphy, 1986). The Louisiana study included 76 schools that were divided along two dimensions: effectiveness status (more effective, typical, less effective); and SES of student body (middle-, low-SES). Hallinger and Murphy were able to identify four distinct levels of SES communities for their study in the relatively affluent state of California, while Teddlie and Stringfield used only two levels, because Louisiana has fewer affluent communities.

Results from both studies confirmed that there were some characteristics that distinguished effective from ineffective schools, regardless of the SES of the schools: clear academic mission and focus, orderly environment, high academic engaged time-on-task and frequent monitoring of student progress. These characteristics have been frequently mentioned in SER.

While there were definite similarities between effective middle- and low-SES schools, there were a number of very interesting differences between the two groups of schools. The Teddlie and Stringfield (1985, 1993) research indicated that effective schools had implemented somewhat different strategies, depending on the SES context of the particular school under examination. These differences in characteristics associated with effectiveness in middle- and low-SES schools revolve around six areas:

1   Promotion of educational expectations – Middle-SES schools promoted both high present and future educational expectations, while low-SES schools emphasized present educational expectations only.
2   Principal leadership style – Effective middle-SES principals tended to be good managers, while effective low-SES principals tended to be initiators who wanted to make changes in the schools.
3   The use of external reward structures – Visible external academic rewards were emphasized in low-SES schools, while they were downplayed in middle-SES schools.
4   Emphasis in the school curriculum – Curricular offerings were focused on the basic skills in effective low-SES schools, while effective middle-SES schools had an expanded curriculum.
5   Parental contact with the school – Parental involvement was encouraged in

middle-SES schools, while principals and staff in many low-SES schools created boundaries to buffer the school from negative community influences.

6   Experience level of teachers – Effective middle-SES schools had more experienced teachers, while effective low-SES schools had less experienced teachers.

The study conducted in California (Hallinger and Murphy, 1986) confirmed the differences between schools with students from different SES backgrounds, especially with regard to:

1   Differences in curriculum – Curriculum in low-SES schools was narrow, focusing on basic skills; curriculum in high-SES schools was broad, focusing on a variety of academic skills.
2   Differential student expectations – The source of expectations in low-SES schools was the school itself and tended to be moderate; in high-SES schools, the sources were the home and school and tended to be very high.
3   Differences in principal leadership style – Principal leadership style in effective low-SES schools was high with regard to control of instruction and task orientation; in effective high-SES schools it was low to moderate with regard to control of instruction and moderate with regard to task orientation.
4   Differential parental involvement – Home linkages were weak in effective low-SES schools and strong in effective high-SES schools.

Follow-up studies to the Hallinger and Murphy and the Teddlie and Stringfield studies were conducted by Evans and Teddlie (1988, 1993, 1995) and Hebert (1994). These studies specifically examined leadership behaviour in differentially effective schools serving students from different SES backgrounds.

Based on the previous studies, hypotheses were generated by Evans and Teddlie (1993, 1995) using the terminology of Hall et al. (1984) concerning principals' change facilitator styles: *initiators* (make it happen); *managers* (help it happen); and *responders* (let it happen). Evans and Teddlie predicted:

1   an overall difference in the frequencies of teachers' perceptions of their principals' change facilitator styles across school effectiveness (effective, ineffective) and SES categories (low, middle);
2   that a higher percentage of teachers would perceive their principals as initiators in low-SES, effective schools than in low-SES, ineffective schools; and
3   that a higher percentage of teachers would perceive their principals as managers in middle-SES, effective schools than in middle-SES, ineffective schools.

The study produced strong evidence in support of the first two hypotheses, thus confirming that the SES characteristics of schools are related to the type of change facilitator styles that would be most successful at those schools.

Additionally, Evans and Teddlie concluded that teachers perceived their principals as exhibiting mixed styles (e.g. manager-initiator as primary-secondary styles), rather than one predominant style (e.g. manager). Hebert (1994) followed up on this study, predicting differences in teachers' perceptions of predominant and mixed styles in schools varying by both effectiveness ratings and SES contexts. Her study yielded a few differential results using its entire sample of schools; for instance, teachers perceived their principals as responder-managers more often in ineffective low-SES schools than in effective low-SES schools.

Since some of her hypothesized relationships were not demonstrated using the entire sample, Hebert separated the data into schools which had principals with greater than or less than twelve years of experience. Most of the hypothesized relationships were supported in the schools with the more experienced principals, while none were demonstrated in schools with less experienced principals. It appeared that experience level of principal (another potential school context variable) was interacting with the SES context variable in this sample, such that predicted differences in teachers' perceptions of principal leadership styles occurred only after principals had been at their schools for an extended period of time. Hebert (1994) was also interested in determining if teachers' sense of autonomy (Forsyth and Dansiewicz, 1985) differed across SES contexts. She hypothesized and found that teachers in middle-SES schools perceived themselves as having significantly more autonomy than teachers in low-SES schools. This difference in perceived teacher autonomy is apparently related to the differences in principal leadership style found in earlier studies (e.g. Hallinger and Murphy, 1986; Teddlie and Stringfield, 1985). For instance, it may be that effective middle-SES principals are perceived by their relatively autonomous faculty as managers (i.e. they help improvement occur), while effective low-SES principals are perceived by their less autonomous faculty as initiators (i.e. they make improvement occur).

Results from School Improvement Studies

Chrispeels (1992) studied the creation of cultures for improvement in eight schools undergoing restructuring programmes in southern California. This study allowed for multiple (eclectic) approaches to school change, depending on the particular context of the school, and one of the major considerations of the Chrispeels' case studies concerned the impact of the social context of the school community on the form and the success of the restructuring efforts.

The two least successful school restructuring programmes in the Chrispeels' study were at Sierra and Tahoe Elementary Schools (all names are pseudonyms), both of which were located in low-SES communities that appeared to exert great influence on their schools' improvement programmes. In both of these schools, parents were blamed for the failures of the improvement efforts. At Tahoe Elementary, for instance, the principal lamented that if his school were a magnet school, it could be labelled 'the School for Dysfunctional Families' (Chrispeels, 1992, pp.82–3). Similarly, the staff at Sierra Elementary saw parents and their lack of concern as one of the major barriers to improvement. At two other relatively more affluent schools (Yosemite Elementary and Whitney Elementary), the principals and staff did not scapegoat the parents for any difficulties that might have been occurring in the restructuring efforts at their schools.

These results from Chrispeels are similar to those reported by Lightfoot (1983) in her more impressionistic 'portraits' of urban, suburban and elite schools. Her portrait of George Washington Carver School (pseudonym for a low-SES, urban school in Atlanta) describes an improved, tightly administered school, but one that did not appear to have a vision for instructional excellence. Similarly, Teddlie and Stringfield's (1993) description of Theodore Roosevelt Elementary (pseudonym for a low-SES, rural school in Louisiana) presented the image of an improving school that was being driven by a new principal intent on correcting disciplinary problems and creating a very public reward structure for academic achievement in his school, yet who did not have a clear idea of the long-term academic goals for the school.

A common thread runs through the results from all these studies of low-SES schools on the road to improvement: the staffs at low-SES schools typically have to spend more time creating certain components of school success (e.g. high expectation levels, reward structures for academic success, safe and orderly climates) than do middle-SES schools, where the community has often already generated these components, at least in nascent form. Thus, fundamental elements in school improvement programmes often differ between schools located in middle- and low-SES communities, with schools in the low-SES communities making considerable efforts to create certain baseline conditions that may already exist in more affluent communities. The effort required to create these baseline components of successful schooling in low-SES communities necessarily detracts (at least in the short term) from other aspects of school improvement, such as the generation of an excellent instructional system and of long term academic goals.

This analysis of the differences between schools in low-SES and middle-SES contexts implies that the creation of effective schools in the former environments often calls for an initial *compensatory* model in which deficit community resources are made up at the school, sometimes working in conjunction with the home in what Chrispeels (1992) calls HSR (home–school relations). Wimpelberg et al. (1989) used an economic term 'cumulative resource effects' to account for, among other factors, the effects of student body SES upon the ability of schools to accumulate resources, which then often 'pay off' in achievement gain. In low-SES communities, more time and effort has to be expended by the school staff, perhaps in conjunction with concerned parents and community leaders, in generating these cumulative resources than is the case in more affluent communities.

In low-SES schools, then, it appears that change occurs in two phases, often blended together: a compensatory phase, where certain baseline conditions are met (e.g. safe, orderly environment; high expectations from students, parents, staff members; tangible reward structures for the reinforcement of academic success; the creation of academic 'press' at the school); and a long term phase, emphasizsing systemic process change at both the school and teacher levels. In middle-SES schools, where these baseline conditions are often already met, resources can be marshalled with regard to the long term process change phase almost from the beginning.

If this analysis is correct, then different types of principals are needed to improve a school (as opposed to maintaining improvement), as suggested by Good and Brophy (1986). This may especially be the case at low-SES schools, which need an initiator (or initiator-manager in terms of mixed styles) to make improvement happen and a manager (or manager-initiator) to maintain it. Thus, principal tenure at school probably interacts with SES context in predicting what type of leadership style is most successful in creating or maintaining effectiveness, as suggested by the Hebert (1994) study.

In some circumstances, the same principal may play different leadership roles within the same school over time. Teddlie and Stringfield (1993) described such a principal at Kennedy Elementary School (pseudonym for an effective low-SES school in a Louisiana suburban area). This school remained effective over a seven-year period of time, despite the fact that the SES level of the student body was declining due to the loss of middle class industrial jobs in the catchment area. Wimpelberg (1993) summarized the 'stable adaptability' exemplified by the principal at Kennedy Elementary over the period of time that her school was studied:

> . . . between 1984 and 1989, nearly one-third of the middle class students in the school was lost due to economic deterioration in the neighbourhood. The new student body seemed to alter the *conditions* of her work, as the principal defined it, but not its *purpose*.
>
> (Wimpelberg, 1993, p.183, my italics)

'Special strategies' for school improvement in the USA (Stringfield et al., 1994a, 1997) have begun using 'context analysis' in their programmes. For instance, Hopfenberg, Levin et al. (1993) described 'Taking Stock' of the strengths and weaknesses of a school site as a major step in the Accelerated School process (e.g. Accelerated Schools Project, 1991). (See Chapter 7 for more details.)

The Study of Community Type as a Context Variable

There have been fewer studies that have explicitly examined community type as a context factor in SER. Three research studies summarized here have closely examined the effect of multiple levels of community type: Cuttance's (1988) study of the impact of community type (and other geographical factors) on variation in achievement among Scottish secondary schools; Witte and Walsh's (1990) comparison of Milwaukee city and suburban schools; and the Hannaway and Talbert (1993) study of the High School and Beyond (HS&B) database. All three of these studies found significant community influences on the effectiveness of schools.

Cuttance (1988) studied variation in achievement among Scottish schools that was associated with three typologies: type of school (seven types of comprehensive and selective); type of community (city, large burgh, small burgh, rural, new town); and educational authority (17 local educational agencies or LEAs). Cuttance employed multilevel modelling in this study, looking specifically at sector effects for the three typologies noted above. While there were complex interactions across the three typologies, Cuttance concluded that community type had some discernible effects:

> . . . in comparison with the less urbanised sectors, there was considerably greater variation in adjusted attainment among city schools. Overall there is evidence that the range of variation in effectiveness within community types decreases as they become less urban. The city and urban sectors had lower median levels of adjusted attainment among their schools than the burgh and new town sectors.
>
> (Cuttance, 1988, p.212)

These differential community type effects are particularly interesting considering the fact that there was great *similarity* in the SES of the students attending the various types of schools. According to Cuttance, between 67–77 per cent of the students in all five community types have fathers who are employed in a manual occupation.

Why, then, do students in burgh and new town schools appear on the average to do better than those from rural and urban areas in Scotland? Also, why is there more variance in effectiveness within more urban schools than within less urban schools? Cuttance speculated that differences in student achievement between schools from different community types (and different LEAs) may be partially due to other factors such as denominational status of school or the period in which the school was established. These context factors have been examined in other Scottish studies (Cuttance, 1988; McPherson and Willms, 1986) and will be discussed later in this chapter.

A recent study by Freeman and Teddlie (1997) partially replicated the Cuttance results in the USA. These authors found a greater incidence of 'naturally occurring' school improvement in elementary schools located in small city/suburban areas than was found in either urban areas or in rural/town areas. 'Naturally occurring' school improvement happens when schools score higher on achievement tests over a period of time, without any externally mandated school improvement programme being put into place at the school site (Stringfield and Teddlie, 1990). Freeman and Teddlie (1997) speculated that small city/suburban areas have greater community resources, both human and fiscal, than is found in many urban and rural areas in the USA.

Employing regression analyses, Witte and Walsh conducted what they called 'a systematic test of the effective schools model' using data from elementary, middle and high schools. After examining the data broken down by community type, the authors concluded that:

> The Milwaukee metropolitan setting, which we suspect is very similar to a number of other cities, by itself is difficult to understand because there are *two very separate educational worlds – one in the city and one in the suburbs*. In statistical terms, the variables describing the different components of the educational system and educational achievement form two distinct clusters. . . .
>
> (Witte and Walsh, 1990, pp.192–3)

The authors used various statistical adjustments to control for the high intercorrelations among many of their indices, such as community type and the SES of student bodies.

The authors described these two distinct 'educational worlds' as follows: in the city schools, students came from poor, often African-American or Hispanic families; in the suburbs, the students were almost all white and most came from middle-class or higher SES backgrounds. On all achievement indices, the suburban schools performed higher than the city schools. Furthermore, the city schools were larger and had fewer teachers with Master's degrees than the suburban schools. The teachers in the two community types described their schools quite differently, with the city teachers perceiving a much more negative school environment.

Witte and Walsh concluded that student characteristics were very important in determining a school's effectiveness in their study, and that the effect of these characteristics were compounded by the class and racial segregation that exists between Milwaukee city and suburban schools. The community type context differences that they described in their study mirror the SES context differences described in the previous section of this chapter. It is likely that the differences in school processes and routes toward school improvement that were described for low- and middle-SES schools are relevant to the city and suburban schools described by Witte and Walsh.

Two studies from the USA (Hannaway and Talbert, 1993; Purkey and Rutter, 1987) examined schools from different community types using the HS&B database. This type of database, composed of archived data with community type encoded, may be convenient for those researchers lacking the resources to gather their own site based process data (i.e. observations and interviews) across a wide range of community type levels. Results from these two studies tend to support the Witte and Walsh conclusions.

For instance, Hannaway and Talbert (1993) examined the relationship between three levels of community type (urban, suburban, rural) and two dimensions of what they called 'effective school process' (strong principal leadership, teacher community) using HS&B survey datasets. They reported several differences due to community type, including the following:

1 school size had a positive effect on teacher community and principal leadership in suburban schools and a negative effect on those two variables in urban suburban schools;
2 principals in urban high schools had far less autonomy in matters of school policy, personnel decisions, and resource allocation than did principals from other community types;
3 the reported influence of teacher unions was greater in urban high schools than in other community types;
4 the clientele of suburban schools were more wealthy and better educated than the clientele for urban schools; and
5 there was a lack of school size effects for rural schools.

In an earlier study that also employed the extant HS&B database, Purkey and Rutter (1987) compared teachers in urban and suburban high schools. They concluded that the teachers perceived that both they and their students had more difficult tasks and less positive environments in urban than in suburban schools.

In addition to the community type context effects reported in their study, the Hannaway and Talbert (1993) data point out an interesting interaction between size and community type of school: size of school is directly related to school effectiveness indicators in suburban schools and inversely related to those variables in urban schools. This interaction between context variables (in this case community type and size) is repeated in several of the studies reported in this chapter. Such interactions make it difficult to 'tease out' the independent effects of context variables.

In a study involving the comparison of rural and urban schools, Rowan, Raudenbush and Kang (1991) concluded that urban schools were more advantaged, and rural schools more disadvantaged, with regard to the organizational design features associated with teacher morale and commitment. This direct comparison of urban and rural high schools is unusual in studies from the USA.

As noted by DeYoung (1987), the history of American education has been primarily an urban history. Certainly, the study of SER in the USA has been primarily a study of urban schools. The handful of American studies that have looked at rural school effectiveness (e.g. Buttram and Carlson, 1983; Conklin and Olson, 1988; Hord et al., 1992; Lomotey and Swanson, 1990; Stringfield and Teddlie, 1991b) have identified two interesting areas of differentiation between effective rural and urban schools:

resource allocation and cohesiveness. Rural schools are, in general, characterized by scarcer resources than urban schools (Buttram and Carlson, 1983; Stringfield and Teddlie, 1991b). Similarly, rural schools typically have smaller faculties and student bodies that are more culturally homogeneous and, therefore, more likely to be cohesive (Conklin and Olson, 1988; Lomotey and Swanson, 1990).

These differences have obvious implications for producing effective schools in rural as opposed to urban areas. For example, Stringfield and Teddlie (1991b) described how the principal of an effective rural school developed innovative strategies to cope with scarce resources. This principal had set up a programme in which his students regularly visited the library in the local small community. His students had access to a greater number of books through this programme, and the community library, which had been threatened with closure, was better able to justify its existence.

With regard to the smaller size and greater homogeneity of rural schools, Conklin and Olson (1988) have argued that this may have beneficial results. It should be easier, for example, to develop consensual faculty goals in such settings. Also, it may be easier for the principal and faculty members in such schools to work with community members and to solicit greater parental involvement.

Hord, Jolly and Mendez-Morse (1992) examined superintendents' leadership behaviour in five rural school districts in which school improvement efforts were ongoing. These authors concluded that there was aspects of the rural district context that influenced these superintendents' abilities to provide school improvement leadership. Given the small sizes of these districts' central office staffs and their often long distances from other districts, these rural superintendents often spoke of isolation. There was not many 'peer level opportunities' for professional growth and development (Hord et al., 1992). These superintendents suffered from a lack of exposure to leadership ideas, a lack of implementation assistance and a lack of varying role models.

Teddlie (1994b) presented information on contextual differences suggested from the Louisiana School Effectiveness case studies (Teddlie and Stringfield, 1993) of two rural, two suburban, and two urban schools. Each pair of these schools had initially consisted of an effective and an ineffective school, and the pairs were examined in 1984–5 and again in 1989–90. Teddlie presented four major areas of contextual differences (community and district office, leadership, faculty and instructional organization, curriculum and professional development), each of which in turn involved four characteristics that could distinguish among rural, suburban and urban schools (see Table 5.2). These proposed distinctions could be explored in greater detail in future studies crossing effectiveness status by community type.

There is an interesting interaction that also appears to be occurring between country and community type across some of the studies from the USA and the UK studies. Community type appears to not play as significant a role in the UK as it does in the USA, primarily because there is less variance in the UK on this variable. Studying rural schools separately in the UK is probably not as important an issue as it is in the USA, because rural schools in the UK are generally closer geographically and culturally to urban areas and are, therefore, not as isolated as their counterparts in the USA. The importance of certain context variables often depends on other salient context variables in the environment, and country often plays an important role in mediating the effect of other variables.

Table 5.2 Contextual differences in elementary schools due to urbanicity

Urban Elementary Schools	Suburban Elementary Schools	Rural Elementary Schools
	Community and District Office	
Adequate resources, but often inefficient delivery system	Adequate resources and delivery system	Typically inadequate resources
Typically weak community involvement, requiring strong leadership to develop	Intermediate-level community involvement	Strong community involvement
Community from which students are drawn may change radically, or may stay very stable	Community from which students are drawn may change due to rezoning, restructuring, etc.	Stable community
School may buffer itself from negative community influences	Typically no buffer to community influences	No buffer to community influences
	Leadership	
Strong instructional leadership required for success	Managerial style of leadership often successful	Personalized leadership style, intermediate between manager and initiator
Discipline typically a problem requiring principal intervention and monitoring	Discipline varies depending on community, faculty, and principal characteristics	Discipline generally good
Leadership has moderate ties to district office	Leadership has moderate ties to district office	Typically close ties to central office
More participation by faculty in roles such as grade-level lead teacher, due to larger school size	Moderate involvement by faculty in leadership roles such as assistant principal, counsellor (acting as administrator), and grade-level lead teacher	Less participation by faculty in roles such as grade-level lead teacher, due to typically smaller school size

Faculty and Instructional Organization

Most likely to be departmentalized	May be departmentalized	Less likely to be departmentalized, due to smaller number of teachers per grade
Faculty recruitment easy or hard depending on school's reputation; appropriate substitutes moderately easy to find	Faculty easier to recruit; appropriate substitutes typically easier to find	Faculty hard to recruit; qualified substitutes hard to find
Variable student expectations, with present expectations pushed first and future expectations later	Some focus on future expectations for students, as well as present expectations	Focus on present expectations
Large variance in faculty stability, with some schools having greater instability	Moderately stable faculties	Stable faculties

Curriculum and Professional Development

Variable curricula, some emphasizing basic skills and others a broader curriculum	Typically broader curriculum beyond basic skills	Limited curriculum, usually emphasizing basic skills
Moderate to high technology in classrooms	Moderate to high technology in classrooms	Low to moderate technology in classrooms
Adequate opportunities for inservice	Adequate opportunities for inservice	Fewer opportunities for inservice
Curriculum innovation highly varied	Curriculum innovation at moderate to high level	Curriculum innovation at low to moderate level

Source: Adapted from Teddlie and Stringfield, 1993.

The Study of Grade Phase of School as a Context Variable

Differential Effect Sizes across Grade Phase of School

As noted in Chapter 3, the impact of school may be felt more at the elementary (or junior) level than at the secondary level. This general result may be complicated by the fact that studies of school effects have not been equally divided across phases of schooling across different countries.

For instance, the preponderance of school effects studies in the USA have involved elementary schools, while the majority of these studies in the UK have explored secondary schools. There have been very few studies that have examined school effects at both the elementary and secondary levels simultaneously, and part of the reason for this is researchers' focus on particular phases of schooling in particular countries.

Within the USA, the two major studies of school effectiveness both involved elementary schools: Brookover et al. (1979) explored school effects in a sample of Michigan schools focusing on the fourth grade; Teddlie and Stringfield (1993) studied a sample of Louisiana schools focusing on the third grade. Both of these studies found strong evidence for school effects (using Definition 3 of school effects found in Chapter 3). There have been no secondary studies of the scale of these studies conducted to date in the USA.

Sammons (1996) reviewed studies from the UK that examined school effects from different phases of schooling. Their review studied the consistency of the size of school effects across studies that had examined:

- infant schools (e.g. Tizard et al., 1988; Thomas and Nuttall, 1993);
- junior schools (e.g. Mortimore et al., 1988);
- secondary schools (e.g. Cuttance, 1987; Fitz-Gibbon, 1991b; Jesson and Gray, 1991; Nuttall et al., 1989; Reynolds et al., 1987; Rutter et al., 1979; Willms and Raudenbush, 1989);
- post-secondary schools (e.g. Thomas, Nuttall and Goldstein, 1992, 1993).

While all of these studies revealed some school effects, the size of the effects was larger for junior schools than for secondary schools. Studies of school effects conducted at the infant level (ages 5–7) in the UK (e.g. Thomas and Nuttall, 1993; Tymms et al., 1997) indicate that the size of the school effect may be even larger there than at the junior (elementary) level.

Tymms (1992) further explored the relative effectiveness of post-16 institutions in the UK (i.e. comprehensive schools, Catholic schools, sixth form schools, further examination colleges, and Assisted Places Scheme schools) on pre-university exams. Some significant effects were found between the different institutions attended, but the effect sizes were small and varied across outcome and curriculum areas.

It makes sense that schooling should have a greater effect on younger students since there are fewer competing factors (or inputs) that could have affected achievement for those students. Sammons et al. summarized this difference as follows:

> Overall there is considerable evidence that significant school effects can be identified for all phases of schooling. There is some indication that they may be larger

for younger than for older age groups. Further exploration of differences in the relative importance of school effects for different phases of schooling is required to examine this issue.

(Sammons et al., 1996a, p.25)

Further speculation regarding this difference in the magnitude of school effects across grade phases of schooling is found in Chapter 3.

Differences in Processes across Grade Phase of School

We also need studies that examine differences in the processes ongoing in elementary (junior) and secondary schools simultaneously. Most of the extensive studies of process in schooling come from the USA, with the notable exceptions of the UK studies conducted by Reynolds (1976), Rutter et al. (1979) and Mortimore et al. (1988). These UK studies were reviewed extensively in Chapter 4.

Most school process studies in the USA have examined elementary schools exclusively, but there are some that have examined secondary levels (e.g. Firestone and Herriott, 1982a; Firestone and Wilson, 1989; Hallinger and Murphy, 1987; Heck, 1992; Levine and Eubanks, 1989a, 1989b; Levine et al., 1984; Rutter et al., 1979; Virgilio et al., 1991). Most of these studies have investigated secondary levels exclusively and have made comparisons with previously reported research from elementary levels. Other studies, such as Heck (1992) and Virgilio et al. (1991), have included samples of both elementary and secondary schools.

Secondary schools differ from elementary schools on a number of important dimensions (Virgilio et al., 1991) such as:

1   there is a shift in emphasis from child-centred to knowledge-centred curriculum;
2   the content of course materials is more sophisticated;
3   teachers can be different from one another in terms of their teacher preparation programmes and certificates;
4   students are adolescents, making the clientele quite different from elementary school students; and
5   there are multiple academic leaders (principals, assistant principals, department chairs) at the secondary level, as opposed to a single academic leader at the elementary level.

Inasmuch as secondary schools are more complex and perhaps more difficult to improve than elementary schools, it has been speculated that secondary SER studies would yield somewhat different findings than did elementary school studies. As was the case with SES studies, however, many results concerning the basic characteristics of effective schools have been replicated in secondary schools. On the other hand, there are also important differences in the secondary school studies revolving around the curriculum, special types of learning arrangements and school goals.

The curriculum at especially effective secondary schools has been described as enriched and highly relevant to student needs by researchers (Firestone and Wilson, 1989; Hallinger and Murphy, 1987). Firestone and Herriott (1982a) concluded that effective secondary schools differed from effective elementary schools in that they had a broader mission of excelling in all subjects, while effective elementary schools emphasized basic skills. Hallinger and Murphy indicated that effective secondary schools have a 'core of standards,' similar to those found in elementary schools, but that the curriculum is very broad, including courses relevant to a variety of students. Firestone and Wilson (1989) reiterated this theme of relevance, indicating that specialized career programmes and quality counselling were major components of secondary schools nominated for inclusion in their study.

Levine and Eubanks (1989a, 1989b) described the provision of 'alternative types of learning arrangements and experiences' as a characteristic of effective secondary schools. These arrangements can be either within or distinct from the regular secondary curriculum, providing educational opportunities for marginal (low achieving or disaffected) students (e.g. Wehlage, 1983; Wehlage et al., 1987). While the goals of effective elementary schools are primarily academic (Brookover et al., 1979; Teddlie and Stringfield, 1985), effective secondary schools stress students' personal as well as educational goals (Levine et al., 1984). Since secondary students will soon be entering the work force or going to post-secondary institutions, there is a greater need for schools to be sensitive to individual students' goals and provide opportunities for their realization.

From a methodological perspective, concurrent studies of both elementary and secondary schools pose some interesting, but thorny problems. For example, the Virgilio et al. (1991) study indicated that low-inference measures of teacher effectiveness (i.e. time-on-task) could successfully differentiate among levels of school effectiveness at the elementary level, but not at the secondary level. Such measures may be inappropriate at the secondary level, where cooperative learning arrangements and classroom situations emphasizing higher order thinking skills may yield low time-on-task scores. Researchers must be careful that the methods employed in cross-grade level studies are sensitive to the peculiarities of each of these settings.

A major area in need of more research is the study of leadership in secondary schools, as opposed to elementary schools (Virgilio et al., 1991). While the large majority of elementary school effectiveness studies in the USA currently identify the principal as the most important leader in determining school effectiveness, the situation may be quite different at secondary levels. For example, two of the attributes noted by Levine and Lezotte (1990) as being characteristic of effective schools principals are frequent monitoring of school activities and superior instructional leadership. It may be difficult for secondary school principals to personally monitor all school activities, inasmuch as these activities are so much more diverse than those at elementary schools.

Similarly, it is probably impossible for a secondary principal to be an expert in all instructional areas covered by a secondary curriculum; thus, this instructional leadership role will be shared with the department chairs. Future research needs to specify how this leadership is shared and to derive implications for school effectiveness, based on greater participation by the faculty. Of particular importance here is the study of consensual goal development at effective secondary schools.

Fitz-Gibbon (1991a, 1991b) contends that at the secondary school level, the effect of department (e.g. mathematics, English, science) is more important than the effect of schools. To further complicate the matter, she reports that almost all schools contain both effective and ineffective departments and that departments often change in effectiveness status from year to year (Fitz-Gibbon, 1996).

Rowan et al. (1991) found differences in perceived school climate from teachers in a sample of 358 schools from the HS&B database. These authors found that:

> . . . the set of teachers teaching mainly math, science, and English exhibited significantly more negative perceptions of climate than did other teachers (nonacademic and social studies teachers). In the cases of principal leadership and teacher control, more than 60 percent of the variation among the five specialisations was accounted for by this single contrast.
>
> (Rowan et al., 1991, p.259)

Furthermore, Rowan et al. (1991) concluded that:

> The important point here is that hypotheses about the development of school organisation and climate posed at a single level of analysis are inadequate, especially in the study of secondary schools. . . . Specifically, different academic departments or tracks within schools may be characterised by different working conditions, with the result that individuals within these departments might have differential opportunities and predispositions to engage in co-operative interaction or to receive support from administrators.
>
> (Rowan et al., 1991, p.243)

A study by Heck (1992) specifically examined differences in instructional leadership in effective and ineffective elementary and secondary schools. His study concluded that principals in effective elementary schools devoted substantially more time to the implementation of instructional leadership activities than principals from three other school groups (effective secondary, ineffective secondary, ineffective elementary) Secondary school principals, regardless of their schools' effectiveness status, did not allocate the same amount of time to instructional leadership tasks as did effective elementary school principals. These results are consistent with those reported by Virgilio and her colleagues (1991), who indicated that secondary school principals had neither the expertise nor the time to be a strong instructional leader in the manner described by Edmonds (1979a, 1979b).

Many authors (e.g. Pink, 1987; Virgilio et al., 1991) have pointed out the large differences between elementary and secondary schools in terms of size, complexity, populations served, leadership, etc. Since it is hard to match elementary and secondary schools across these variables, almost all studies of elementary or secondary schools have been done within only one level. For instance, the two major SER studies from Great Britain are the Rutter et al. (1979) study of secondary schools and the Mortimore et al. (1988) study of primary schools sponsored by the now defunct Inner London Educational Authority. These studies were conceptualized as two independent projects from their outstart, and probably neither set of researchers would have wanted to tackle the simultaneous study of both levels of schooling in the UK.

Hopefully, the completion of more multiple level studies of community type and of grade level (e.g. Heck, 1992; Virgilio et al., 1991) will encourage other researchers to simultaneously study two or more levels of the same context variable. Without such studies, only speculative comparisons across single level context studies can be made.

The Study of Governance Structure of School as a Context Variable

In general, school effect sizes tend to be larger in school systems that have governance structures that allow individual schools more control of their academic operations. This result from 'contextually sensitive' SER is an excellent rationale for reform initiatives which call for greater faculty voice in the governance of schools, such as the ongoing restructuring movement in the USA.

Governance of school is a context issue that has been studied by both North American and European scholars. As a context variable, there can be little doubt that there are differences in the ways in which private or public schools are governed, or in the ways in which different school boards administer their schools. The issue at question in these context studies concerns whether or not these different governance structures have any effect on their students while in the schools or in their later lives. The following section will divide governance structure issues into three general areas: public versus private schools; the effect of different types of church schools; and the effect of different LEAs and school boards.

Private versus Public Schools

Studies by Coleman and his colleagues (Coleman, J. et al., 1981, 1982a, 1982b; Coleman and Hoffer, 1987) examined the differential effects that public and private high schools in the USA had on their students. Using data from the HS&B Study, they concluded that private school students had a significantly larger sophomore-senior gain than public school students. Coleman and his colleagues attributed these results to factors related to the disciplinary climate and the instructional quality of private schools. For instance, they contended that Catholic schools in the USA do better because they maintain better discipline, demand more homework, and require more advanced courses.

Coleman and Hoffer (1987) further concluded that students from private schools were more successful than those from public schools in college. They attribute this differential success to stronger parental-school ties in Catholic schools and to the 'intergenerational community' that surrounds the Catholic school. They concluded that students from Catholic schools leave their schools with more 'social capital' than do students from public schools.

These results have been questioned by critics who claim that private schools attract students with greater academic potential than public schools, either through the schools' selection procedures or self-selection. Coleman and Hoffer (1987) acknowledged that even though they had controlled for parental background of the students in their study, there might have been other unmeasured factors in the self selection into private schools that are associated with higher achievement. It is important in this regard that the Coleman series of studies do not use any pupil achievements measure as an intake control.

As Rowan, Raudenbush, and Kang (1991) note, Catholic schools may be more likely to have supportive administrative leadership, participative school decision making, and high levels of staff cooperation, because of the things in common that religiosity variable generates, but more research is needed to understand exactly why Catholic schools show a greater tendency toward organic patterns of management. One further possibility is that Catholic schools are more able to develop a unified sense of mission than public schools, in part because they are less subject than public schools to diverse regulations and multiple goals (see Fuller and Izu, 1986). Willms (1985a) also utilized the extant HS&B database in a longitudinal design and found no evidence for the pervasive private schooling effects that Coleman and his colleagues had reported. His study included data on student ability prior to entering high school, information that had not been available for use by Coleman et al. (1982a). Another study conducted by McPherson and Willms (1986), utilizing secondary school data from Scotland, indicated that Catholic schools produced somewhat better achievement scores than non-denominational schools after controlling for student intake variables.

The Effect of Different Types of Church Schools

Van Cuyck-Remijssen and Dronkers (1990) conducted a study in the Netherlands examining the influence that sector of secondary education (Catholic, Protestant, public) had on the success of their pupils in higher education and on the labour market. This study was designed to replicate portions of the Coleman and Hoffer (1987) study of private and public schools that had been conducted in the United States. Some differences were found between the success of students who had attended private (Catholic, Protestant) and public schools: students from public secondary schools entered universities more often than private school students; Catholic students entered vocational education institutions more often than Protestant or public school students; and Protestant school students had different job orientations concerning 'attractive jobs' than did students from Catholic or public schools.

In general, however, Van Cuyck-Remijssen and Dronkers concluded that, unlike the Coleman and Hoffer study, differences in success in higher education and the labour market in the Netherlands were not systematically in favour of the private school students. They found little evidence of the role of churches as 'intergenerational communities' in their country. Differences in these studies from the Netherlands and the USA can probably be attributed, at least partially, to differences in the ways in which private and public high schools operate in the two countries. More details about these international context differences will be forthcoming in this chapter and in Chapter 9.

Francis and Lankshear (1991) examined the effect that Church of England schools had on 'urban church life' in England and Wales. After controlling for several important variables, this study concluded that the presence of church schools increases the urban church's contact with students and increases the number of confirmations. While this study does not examine students' academic or career success, it provides further evidence that the different governance structures of different types of church schools can have differential reverberating effects throughout the communities that the schools serve.

The Effect of Different LEAs and School Boards

Evidence from Scotland (Cuttance, 1988; Willms, 1987) indicates that there are significant, but rather small, differences in the adjusted achievement of students from different local educational authorities. These Scottish studies were primarily quantitative in nature, emphasizing the impact of LEAs on the attainment of schools and students. The Willms (1987) study demonstrated that the compositional effect varied by Scottish school district.

Such studies of LEAs in the USA have been more qualitative in nature, examining what superintendents in effective districts do to provide leadership and guidance for school improvement in their districts (e.g. Chrispeels and Pollack, 1989; Coleman and Laroque, 1988; Hord, 1990; Murphy et al., 1985; Pollack et al., 1988). Some of these studies (e.g. Hord et al., 1992) have documented instances of central offices supporting school improvement. It should be noted that other researchers in the USA (e.g. Teddlie and Stringfield, 1993) have failed to find much evidence of district effects.

A recent study conducted in the Netherlands (Hofman, 1995) asks a related context question: do characteristics of school boards and their administrative control have differential effects on the schools that are within their domains? Hofman concluded that characteristics of school boards in the Netherlands do explain a small percentage of the variance in cognitive achievement, and he explained this in terms of school boards differentially involving school teams and parents in their decision making process. Hofman (1995) concluded that only a few extant studies have examined the influence of the amount and quality of this level of administrative control on the effectiveness of schools. He further concluded that qualitative case studies of school boards could bring more understanding of the processes whereby school community members influence their boards' decision making process.

Conclusions

The preceding review has synthesized results from SER studies that examined four major context variables and how they have affected schooling. A number of conclusions can be drawn from this review:

- Context variables have been demonstrated to have an effect upon research results from all three strands of SER: school effects studies (involving the study of the scientific properties of these effects), effective schools research, and school improvement studies.
- The context variable that has been studied the most is the socioeconomic status of the student bodies that attend schools. Labelled the compositional variable in the UK, the SES makeup of a school has a substantial effect upon student outcomes beyond the effects associated with students' individual ability and social class.
- Contextually sensitive effective schools research has demonstrated that effective schools have implemented somewhat different strategies for success, depending on the SES context of the particular school under examination.
- The context variables of community type, grade phase, and governance structure have also been demonstrated to have an effect upon the scientific properties of school effects and upon the characteristics of effective schools.
- The community type variable demonstrates somewhat the same context differences that were found for low- and middle-SES schools, with urban schools having characteristics similar to low-SES schools and suburban schools having characteristics similar to middle-SES schools. The study of rural schools has yielded a more mixed picture. It is apparent that the impact of community type is

mediated by other context variables, such as SES status of student body, size of school, and country in which the study occurred.

- There have been few comparative studies across grade phases of schooling. The impact of school appears to be more pronounced in the early grades (elementary or junior levels) than at the secondary level. SER at the secondary level must take into account multiple leaders (i.e. departmental chairs) and a more complex curriculum, among other context differences.
- Several governance structures have been studied as context variables: public versus private schools; different types of church schools; and different LEAs and school boards. One generalization from this literature is that school effect sizes tend to be larger in schools that have governance structures that allow more control of their academic operations. This conclusion is complicated by the fact that other context factors (e.g. SES of student body) are inextricably related to governance structures, making simple conclusions regarding the effect of these structures difficult.

Clearly there needs to be more comparative studies of schools from different grade phases and from different community types. While such comparative studies present researchers with difficult methodological issues, comparisons across the levels of these context variables will only be speculative until the levels are studied simultaneously. There also need to be more qualitative case studies of schools from different contexts. This is especially the case for grade phase and governance structure research. Several of the context variables are associated with one another, and it is often difficult to disentangle the effects of these variables. Future research should be especially sensitive to the interaction of context variables, illustrated by the Hannaway and Talbert (1993) study that reported an interaction between the effects of size of school and community type. Due to these interactions among context variables, it is probably better to limit the study of context in SER to a small number of factors and to consider other correlated variables to be mediators of these primary context effects.

It is likely that contingency theory, which takes into account context or situational factors when predicting school effects and the effectiveness of school structures and processes, appears to be the heuristic theory that can enable SER theorists and researchers to analyse empirical results in ways that enable us to explain processes and causal paths. Chapter 10 tackles these issues of theoretical modelling further.

Section 3

The Cutting Edge Issues of School Effectiveness Research

6 Some Methodological Issues in School Effectiveness Research

Eugene Kennedy and Garrett Mandeville

Introduction

Cronbach et al. wrote:

> The majority of studies of educational effects – whether classroom experiments, or evaluations of programs, or surveys – have collected and analysed data in ways that conceal more than they reveal.
>
> (Cronbach et al., 1976, p.1)

This conclusion was based on the fact that studies of school effects, for the most part, had not adequately addressed the hierarchical or multilevel nature of schooling data (see also Burstein, 1980a, 1980b). In a large part this has been due to the fact that statistical methods for handling multilevel data typical of school effects studies have only recently become available. According to Raudenbush and Bryk (1986),

> Research on school effects has been plagued by both methodological and conceptual problems. In our view the two are closely related . . . there is a natural hesitancy to form a judgement when it remains unclear how to test the fruits of that conceptualisation.
>
> (Raudenbush and Bryk, 1986, p.15)

In this chapter we review various statistical models that have been proposed to deal with the multilevel nature of school effects. We begin with a review of analysis strategies which ignore the multilevel nature of schooling data (see Aitkin and Longford, 1986). This is followed by a discussion of the basic multilevel model (MM) and estimation of its parameters. The discussion then turns to applications and extensions of the basic MM. Finally, we review computer software currently available for conducting multilevel analyses.

Statistical Models That Ignore Multilevel Data

Statistical models capable of addressing cross-level inference problems (i.e. how factors at one level of schooling impact outcomes and processes at lower levels) and other issues in quantitative analyses of multilevel data are recent in origin (for a historical perspective, see Raudenbush, 1988). Early techniques either required investigators to ignore the multilevel nature of school data or to incorporate multiple levels in ways that were technically questionable. For example, the so-called single-level regression technique required the investigator to either use student level data and thus ignore school and classroom variables, or to suppress within-school variation by aggregating student data to the building level. Either strategy is fraught with problems. First, neither provides any means of investigating cross-level inferences. Second, the student-level analysis will imply a level of precision in parameter estimates that is misleading, while the school level analysis will generally produce problems of multicollinearity and unstable indices of school effects. And finally, both strategies force unproductive choices of a 'unit of analysis' and both experience problems associated with aggregation bias (see Aitkin and Longford, 1986).

Another solution to dealing with the multilevel aspects of school effects research has been the approach called contextual analysis (see Burstein, 1980a, 1980b). Essentially, these models include a macro or group level variable as a predictor in a model which has student or individual level factors as outputs. While this approach has much greater appeal from a conceptual stance, the methodological problems which are entailed are substantial. For example, typically multiple regression has been used with a group level characteristic included in a model of student outcomes. One of the central problems with this strategy is that standard ordinary least squares (OLS) regression requires the assumption of fixed predictors. To include predictors from the school level requires that all variation in parameters at the lower levels be explained by school level factors. When this is not the case, misestimated precision occurs, meaning that the estimated standard errors are likely to be too small (Raudenbush and Bryk, 1986, 1989).

A number of alternatives to OLS regression have been proposed which have had varying levels of success. One obvious strategy involves two stage estimation. In this approach, the researcher estimates the model for the units within the grouping factor (the within model) and the model with the group level only factors (the between model) separately or in sequence – using one set of parameter estimates to adjust for the other. An example of this approach is presented by Keesling and Wiley (1974). In their formulation the authors propose first predicting a group mean from the regression of the criterion on the within group variables. This mean is then entered as a term in a regression of group means on group level variables. Unfortunately, this procedure requires the assumption of homogeneous regression slopes, a condition which is rarely met in practice.

Because of the limitations of single-level and contextual strategies, a number of researchers have adopted a two-step approach to the estimation of school effects. In the first step, separate regression equations based on student level data are obtained for each school in a data set. In the second step, the slopes from these analyses serve as the dependent variables in the model using school level predictors. Proponents of this strategy have argued that within school slopes are useful indicators of within school processes. Whereas school means might reflect average trends, slopes reflect relationships and treating heterogeneity of slopes as an outcome is a way of attempting to explain relationships within schools by school level characteristics (see Burstein, 1980a, 1980b; Jesson and Gray, 1991).

Slopes as outcomes, despite the theoretical appeal, has a number of statistical limitations. First, within unit sample sizes are typically small. This will generally lead to significant sampling error for within unit slope estimates. Second, estimated regression slopes consist of real differences and differences due to sampling error. If slopes are to be treated as outcomes then this difference should be addressed. Finally, meaningful within unit models usually involve more than one slope of interest. Adequate modelling requires that the covariance structure of the within-unit slopes be considered at the between group level. These and other limitations have, for some time, limited the use of slopes as outcomes in school effects research (Raudenbush and Bryk, 1986).

The Multilevel Model

In contrast to the within-unit and between-unit single level models described above, the multilevel model attempts to more realistically reflect the nested or hierarchical nature of data encountered in school effects studies. Following the notation of Raudenbush and Bryk (1986), let Y_{ij} be the outcome (e.g. achievement score) of student i (i = 1, . . . ,n_j) in school j (j = 1, . . . ,J). The within school regression model for predicting Y from, say, social class (X), is given by,

$$Y_{ij} = \beta_{j0} + \beta_{j1}X_{ij} + e_{ij} \tag{1}$$

where β_{j0} is the intercept of the regression, β_{j1} is the slope and e_{ij} is an error term. The model in Equation 1 allows for the possibility that the regression parameters β_{j0} and β_{j1} vary across schools. If this variability is manifest, it could be due to differences in school policies, practices, or organization. A second model, the between-model, might attempt to predict this variability (parenthetically, if it exists) on the basis of these or other school level attributes. If P represents an attribute of interest, then,

$$\beta_{jk} = \Phi_{0k} + \Phi_{1k}P_{jk} + a_{jk} \tag{2}$$

where k=0, 1 for the model in Equation 2. If Equation 2 is substituted into Equation 1 the result is,

$$Y_{ij} = \Phi_{00} + \Phi_{10}P_{j0} + \Phi_{01}X_{ij} + \Phi_{11}P_{j1}X_{ij}$$
$$+ (e_{ij} + a_{j0} + a_{j1}X_{ij}) \tag{3}$$

This is a general model for multilevel data with one within and one between level variable. Its generality is such that a number of more familiar models are obtained by restricting certain parameters. For example, one approach to multilevel data has been to include school level indicators in OLS regression models with student level data. As noted above, this strategy is appropriate only if all of the variability in within-school regression parameters is attributable to school level or macro indicators included in the model. This implies that the error terms in Equations 3, a_{j0} and a_{j1}, are both zero. In this event the problem becomes a standard fixed-effects regression problem with an interaction term for the variables P and X.

Alternatively, if all the coefficients of P and X were set to zero we obtain the familiar random effects ANOVA model,

$$Y_{ij} = \Phi_{00} + a_{j0} + e_{ij} \tag{4}$$

where Φ_{00} is the overall mean on the outcome Y, a_{j0} is the random effect associated with school j, and e_{ij} is the random error associated with subjects. Of course, this model does not include any predictors at the student or school level.

Mason, Wong and Entwistle (1984) describe how the general model in Equation 3 relates to a number of more restrictive models that could be used to study school effects. Any of the possibilities they discuss may be appropriate in a given situation, but because of its flexibility the general case has been the focus of much recent study in school effects literature (see Hox and Kreft, 1994).

Hierarchical Linear Models

A statistical foundation for the model presented in Equation 3, which we shall hereafter refer to as the multilevel model (MM), was described more than 20 years ago in a paper by Lindley and Smith (1972). Using a Bayesian framework, Lindley and Smith describe a model in which the parameters β_{j0} and β_{j1} in Equation 1 themselves have a prior distribution as is reflected in Equation 2 above. Following the Bayesian argument and with appropriate assumptions, they show that a conditional posterior distribution of β_{j0} and β_{j1} provides the estimates needed for study of the general model in Equation 4.

Raudenbush and Bryk (1986) presented a simplified version of Lindley and Smith's result for the case where the Level-1 data have been centred so that the intercept term, β_{j0}, is zero, and further, there is no between unit predictor in the Level-2 model. Equation 2 then becomes

$$\beta_{j1} = \Phi_{01} + a_{j1} \tag{5}$$

Following their discussion, we first assume that the subject level errors, e_{ij}, are normally distributed with mean zero and a known and constant variance across schools (while we focus our discussion on schools, the results apply to any aggregates of interest). The error a_{j1} is also assumed to have a normal distribution with zero mean and a known variance, θ. Finally, the errors e_{ij} and a_{j1} are assumed to be uncorrelated.

The model in Equation 5 is termed the unconditional model because it specifies that a school's slope is only a function of the overall slope among the population of schools and a component unique to each, (i.e. the slope is not 'conditioned' for other factors). The variance of a_{j1}, θ, represents true slope variability among the population of schools. Of course, only estimates of unit slopes are available. If OLS is used to form the within-school estimates, each school's estimate will have an element of sampling error which depends largely on the amount of data available within each setting. This familiar error estimate is given by,

$$V_j = \sigma^2 / \Sigma X^2 \tag{6}$$

The total variance of the observed within school slopes then has a component due to true parameter variability and a component due to sampling error. If these two components, V_j and θ, are assumed known, then empirical Bayes yields minimum mean squared error point estimates for β_{j1} (B_{j1}) and Φ_{01} (M_{01}). These estimates are,

$$B_{j1} = c_j * \text{OLS}(\beta_{j1}) + (1 - c_j) * M_{01} \tag{7}$$

$$M_{01} = \Sigma(c_j * \text{OLS}(\beta_{j1})) / \Sigma(c_j) \tag{8}$$

where

$$c_j = \theta / (\theta + V_j) \tag{9}$$

and $\text{OLS}(\beta_{j1})$ is the ordinary least squares estimator of β_{j1}.

The c_j weighting factor is considered a reliability coefficient. If there is little error variance, the empirical Bayes estimate will be close to the OLS estimate. Alternatively, if the variability associated with a given slope is largely error variability, then the empirical Bayes estimate moves toward the overall or macro slope estimate.

Estimation

While Lindley and Smith's results have been known for some time, the assumption that V and θ were known has limited applicability. Only recently have developments in statistical theory and computation made these results practical for researchers. The basic problem has been the absence of techniques for dealing with fixed and random coefficients in unbalanced nested designs (Raudenbush, 1988). Recently, however, the EM algorithm (Dempster et al., 1977, 1981; Laird, Lange and Stram, 1987) has been shown to yield satisfactory results for estimating these parameters. As noted by Raudenbush and Bryk (1986), the EM algorithm yields maximum likelihood estimates which are asymptotically unbiased, consistent, efficient, and normally distributed. Other procedures recently used to estimate these parameters include iterative generalized least squares (Goldstein, 1986; 1987), Fisher scoring (Longford, 1987; 1988; 1992), and Markov-chain Monte Carlo methods (Seltzer, 1993; Smith and Roberts, 1993).

The results presented above extend easily to the multivariate case where there are multiple within-school and multiple between-school variables. Any given problem may include both random and fixed predictors and the between-unit predictors need not be the same for each within-unit parameter. Also, in theory, any number of levels of aggregation (e.g. student within class, class within school, school within district, etc.) can be studied and the assumption of homogeneity associated with the variance components can be relaxed.

Applications in School Effects Research

The MM, as described above, has several desirable features:

1 It is possible to decompose relationships into within- and between-group components.
2 Multivariate between-group formulations can be studied.
3 Multiple within-group slopes can be handled in a single analysis.
4 Slope estimates are relatively robust with respect to data quality.

These characteristics have motivated researchers to extend and employ the MM methodology in a variety of education related contexts (see Rubin, 1989; Burstein et al., 1989; Raudenbush and Willms, 1991; Bryk and Frank, 1991). We focus on two common objectives in school effects research: the identification of unusual schools, and the identification of school characteristics that lead to differential student outcomes. Admittedly, there is considerable overlap in the issues related to these two research objectives.

With respect to the identification of unusually effective or ineffective schools, the typical strategy has involved the analysis of residuals from a student-level or school-level regression wherein current achievement was regressed onto previous achievement and some index of social class (Dyer et al., 1969). The limitations of this strategy have led many investigators to consider the usefulness of MM for this problem (e.g. Raudenbush and Willms, 1995; Sanders and Horn, 1994; Tate, 1988). Referring to Equation 2, the error terms a_{j0} and a_{j1} represent, respectively, the deviation of school j from the overall intercept and the overall slope of schools in the population. Once substituted into the student level model as in Equation 3, the sum of a_{j0} and $a_{j1} X_{ij}$, which will be referred to as π_{ij}, represents the difference between an actual student outcome in school j and the prediction of that outcome based on the school level variable P. The variable π_{ij} can then be interpreted as an index of school effectiveness for student i which, given the presence of X_{ij}, may vary among students within a given school.

Many recent studies employing the MM methodology have focused on the identification of school level attributes which are correlated with student outcomes (Lee, V. and Bryk, 1989; Rowe et al., 1994a; 1995). MM is particularly well suited to this task because it allows for the partition of total variation of within-unit parameter estimates (intercept and slopes) into parameter and sampling error components. Typically, an investigator will first estimate an unconditional model as in Equation 5. From this the proportion of total variation that is parameter variation can be estimated. The investigator can then formulate conditional models, that is, add macro variables, and determine the degree to which they account for true parameter variability.

Several investigators have applied the above strategy to the Catholic school/public school data of Coleman and colleagues (see Coleman, J., et al., 1982a; Willms, 1984; 1985a). Raudenbush and Bryk (1988), for example, reported several significant findings. First, school social class was strongly related to school level achievement. They reported that a one unit increase in social class predicts a 0.82 unit increase in math achievement. After controlling for this factor they found that the Catholic school effect on math achievement seemed to disappear. Second, they reported that the relationship of social class to achievement was stronger in high SES schools than in low SES schools. Third, the Catholic school effect on the student social class/achievement relationship remained after considering school social class and homework. Employing this same methodology, V. Lee (1986) attempted to determine those factors which produce the Catholic school effect. She reported that a positive disciplinary climate, a positive academic climate, and course offerings could account for much of the sector effects on achievement (see Bryk and Raudenbush, 1988). (See Chapter 5 for a further discussion of the substantive findings from this research.)

Issues and Recent Developments in School Effects Applications of MM

In this section of the chapter we consider a number of issues that confront the analyst interested in applying the MM methodology to problems of estimating school effects. We consider first the problems associated with the identification of unusual schools. We then consider issues associated with model development. Finally, we review a number of recent extensions of MM.

Identification of Unusual Schools

Raudenbush and Willms (1995) discussed school effects in terms of a structural model of student achievement:

$$(\text{Student Achievement})_{ij} = \text{Grand Mean} + (\text{Student Background})_{ij}$$
$$+ (\text{School Context})_{ij} + (\text{School Process})_{ij}$$
$$+ (\text{Random Error})_{ij}$$

or

$$SA_{ij} = m + SB_{ij} + SC_{ij} + SP_{ij} + RE_{ij} \tag{10}$$

According to this model, the achievement of student i in school j (SA_{ij}) is a function of student background (SB_{ij}), school process (SP_{ij}), school context (SC_{ij}), and random error (RE_{ij}). Student background might include academic ability, the socioeconomic status of a student's family, etc. School processes refer to the organizational, management, and climate aspects of schools such as pupil/teacher ratios, academic press from teachers, etc. School context refers to those aspects of schools that are exogenous or beyond the influence of school officials, but impact within-school processes. These include average SES of the student body, average academic achievement, etc.

Based on this formulation, unusual schools are conceptualized in terms of their unique impact on students beyond the influence of student background factors. Willms and Raudenbush (1989), Willms (1992), and Raudenbush and Willms (1995) distinguish two types of school effects. Type A effects reflect the overall impact, both context and process influences, of attendance at a given school whereas Type B effects reflect the impact of a school on student performance that is solely attributable to school process variables. Type A effects are likely of interest to parents who simply want the greatest boost to their child's performance irrespective of whether the increase stems from school context or process. Type B effects are of most interest to administrators and persons interested in such issues as staff effectiveness, etc. These two types of effects pose different problems for researchers. (See Chapter 3 for a further discussion of Type A and Type B effects.)

Selection Bias

Ideally, for purposes of drawing causal inferences about school effects, students would be randomly assigned to schools and schools would be randomly assigned to context and process conditions. In this instance, estimation of Type A and Type B effects could proceed without difficulty. Unfortunately, the study of school effects is best characterized as a quasi-experiment in which the assignment of subjects to treatment conditions is decidedly non-random. The allocation of students to schools is based on variables that are also related to student outcomes. Thus, students from high SES backgrounds attend schools with other students from high SES backgrounds. School segregation by race, student ability and a host of other factors is common. These complexities pose problems for estimation of Type A effects. Estimation of Type B effects are further complicated in that the allocation of instructional opportunities within schools tends to be related to extraneous variables, and further, there is generally a correlation between school context and school processes.

In the absence of randomization, unbiased estimation of school effects can occur if school assignment is at least 'strongly ignorable', that is, school outcomes and school of attendance are conditionally independent (Rosenbaum and Rubin, 1983). For Type A effects this implies that the researcher identify and include in the model student level covariates that are related to both enrolment in a given school and school outcomes. For Type B effects, the researcher faces the requirement that school assignment to process be also 'strongly ignorable.' The difficulties of specifying process make this unlikely in practice.

Model Specification and Measurement: Type A Effects

According to Raudenbush and Willms (1995), analysts interested in estimating Type A effects have, relatively speaking, few challenges. As noted, what is required is that student background be specified with such a degree of accuracy that treatment or school assignment is 'strongly ignorable.' This requires that variables that are related to school attendance and school success be specified in the model. These include measures of SES background, academic aptitude, race, gender, community, etc. While the list of factors is perhaps endless, research has shown that measures of aptitude or prior achievement and SES background will capture the bulk of the variation in assignment (Willms, 1992).

Model Specification and Measurement: Type B Effects

Type B effects present significant measurement difficulties for the analyst (Raudenbush and Willms, 1995). Assuming that school context and process are correlated, the analyst must specify each in the model. The greatest difficulties occur with the specification of school process. That is, the analyst must identify those management, climate, instructional and other attributes that lead to differential effectiveness of schools. Issues of construct validity, reliability and levels of measurement complicate this process. For example, while research has shown that within-school organization impacts student outcomes, specification of this component of school process requires that the analyst know which variables to include in the model (e.g. classroom, department, etc.) and be able to obtain reliable and valid indicators. When either of these conditions is not met, problems associated with misspecification may occur.

In addition to substantive considerations, several researchers have questioned the utility of π for estimating school effects (e.g. Goldstein, 1991a). Focusing on the empirical Bayes (EB) estimates associated with multilevel modelling, they have questioned the utility of these procedures for identifying unusual schools. Many of these concerns are based on the shrinkage phenomenon associated with the EB estimates wherein within-unit parameters are shrunken toward a conditional mean in proportion to their sampling error. Because sampling error tends to be a function of the number of observations within units, as Seltzer (1987) notes, if unusual schools tend also to be small, it is unlikely that EB procedures would ever recognize them as unusual, (i.e. their effects would be shrunken toward the conditional mean). Also, Goldstein (1991a) argues that the p residuals have relatively large sampling errors and should not be used as exact estimates of a school's unique impact. Further, he points out that the residuals depend on the model fitted and the schools or aggregate units that happen to be in the study (see also Goldstein and Thomas, 1996). (This issue is also discussed in Chapter 3.)

Model Development

Including appropriate process and context variables in a MM, as noted above, is essential if the analyst seeks to isolate Type B effects. It is also true that failure to adequately specify a MM can lead to significantly distorted results for the analyst interested in predicting or explaining variation within and across schools. This is true because the researcher must not only specify the within-school or level-1 model, but also must specify a level-2 model for each parameter of the level-1 model considered random. These estimates are interrelated and poor specification in one instance can affect the results in another (for a complete discussion, see Bryk and Raudenbush, 1992, Chapter 9).

In addition to model specification, several other issues warrant special consideration in the development and use of MMs. These include number of levels, centring and sample size.

Number of Levels

How many levels should be included in studies of school effects? In theory, any number of levels could be included in an analysis. However, it is likely that as the number of levels increases, the stability of the results will decrease (Morris, 1995). Conversely, if important levels of a hierarchy are omitted, the results of the analyses may be misleading. For example, in a study of Australian schools, Hill and Rowe (1996) report that the proportion of variance in students' 'intake-adjusted' achievement scores due to schools shrinks from around 8 to 10 per cent to a modest 0 to 3.4 per cent when classroom is taken into account. In contrast, the proportion of variation due to classes ranged from 28 to 46 per cent. They go on to add that both two-level (students nested within schools) and three-level (students nested within classes within schools) analyses are important. One gives an estimate of the overall impact of schools, and the other helps identify the unique effect of classes, once schools have been taken into account. Finally, Hill and Rowe (1996) argue that school effectiveness research requires at least four level MMs: multiple observations nested within students; students nested within classes; classes nested within programmes or departments and classes nested within schools.

While a number of other studies have addressed the question of number of levels in a multilevel analysis (e.g. Tymms, 1993), Hill and Rowe (1996) point out that this literature is often contradictory and open to multiple interpretations. They identify several design related issues that researchers should address: samples should be sufficiently large to permit simultaneous estimation at each level of the hierarchy studied; a variety of achievement measures (e.g. multiple choice, performance assessments, etc.) should be used and analysts should give careful consideration to the consistency between the student outcome measures used and the focus of instruction provided in various settings; and analysts should use a variety of statistical adjustments (e.g. social background, prior achievement, etc.) that address selection bias problems.

Centring

Because parameter estimates at one level of a MM may be considered outcome variables for a higher level of the study, it is important that these estimates be substantively interpretable. The intercept, for example, is traditionally interpreted as the value of the dependent variable when the predictor in a regression model is zero. In a MM, in which the intercept may become an outcome variable, such an interpretation may be inappropriate. To address this issue, the predictors in the level-1 model can be centred around their respective school means. In this so called group mean centring, the intercept can be interpreted as the school mean on the dependent variable. For researchers interested in predicting variation in group averages on some criterion of interest, for example, mean achievement, group mean centring is a reasonable analytic approach (see Bryk and Raudenbush, 1992).

Another centring possibility is grand mean centring. In this instance, the predictor is centred around the mean for the entire sample. The intercept can then be interpreted as an adjusted mean as is the case in ANCOVA. Also, if the predictor is a dummy variable, say with values of 0 and 1, grand mean centring yields a group mean adjusted for the proportion of 1s in each group.

In addition to substantive implications, centring predictors has several other advantages. These include the following: the inflated correlation among the slope and intercept in the raw metric is eliminated; the level-1 model is not impacted by poor specification problems at the higher levels; centring is needed when predictors have widely different scales; and it is recommended when sample sizes are small (see Kreft et al., 1995).

Sample Size

One of the advantages of the MM methodology is that it can provide estimates of parameters when data are sparse. This is often a problem in school effects studies wherein some aggregate units will have few if any observations at some levels of a studied hierarchy. The consequences of this depend on the degree to which the data are balanced (equal number of observations at various levels, etc.), the estimation procedure used, the magnitude of the variance and covariance parameters in the model, and the types of inferences drawn (Bryk and Raudenbush, 1992; Snijders and Bosker, 1993).

When interest is in the level-1 parameters, several problems emerge from having a small number of observations. First, point estimates of within-unit slopes for aggregates will be shrunken more if sample sizes are small. If interest is in estimating the distance of these slopes from the relevant sample average, this presents a problem (Kreft and de Leeuw, 1991). Second, estimates of V_j depend on the number of observations in unit j. If V_j is considered constant, then the total number of observations in a data set is used in forming an estimate. If it is considered to vary across aggregates, then the number of units in each aggregate is used. In this latter instance, the number of units within each aggregate should be large. Third, the accuracy of inferences about empirical Bayes point estimates of the within-unit slopes will not reflect uncertainty in estimates of the variance components, and will be affected by the estimation procedure used and the number of aggregate units in the study.

If interest is in drawing inferences about level-2 parameters, several problems emerge (Seltzer, 1993). First, when data are sparse, the θ parameter cannot be estimated with any degree of accuracy using traditional procedures. Second, the regression parameters at level-2, while unbiased, are a type of least squares estimate and as such they are susceptible to outlying or unusual observations, particularly if the sample sizes are small. Third, in the conventional MM analysis, point estimates of the level-2 fixed effects depend on the quality of the estimates of the variance components, and vice versa. Fourth, the standard errors of the level-2 regression estimates will be negatively biased or too small. As noted by Seltzer (1987), they will not reflect uncertainty in the estimates of the variance components.

Since limiting MMs to balanced designs and/or large samples is extremely restrictive, several researchers have investigated procedures for addressing the problem of sample size. In particular, Seltzer and others (Seltzer, 1993; Seltzer, Wong and Bryk, 1996) have described a fully Bayesian procedure that permits inferences about the level-2 fixed effects independent of the variance components and provides relatively robust estimates of other model parameters.

Extensions of the Multilevel Model

Longitudinal Models

It has been observed that cross-sectional studies of school effects are largely responsible for pointing to aspects of the schooling experience which produce important differences in student achievement. However, Willms and Raudenbush (1989) argue that cross-sectional designs are open to a number of criticisms. First, it can be argued that differences in school effects based on cross-sectional designs are a product of differences in student inputs and not other school related variables. Second, these designs have limited utility because they do not reflect the fact that schools are constantly changing. That is, not only are different cohorts of students moving through schools, but personnel and programmatic changes act to alter the instructional setting. And finally, cross-sectional studies, by nature are not sensitive to trends or time related changes in school effects. This is especially significant in that the effects of schools are widely believed to be cumulative and thus the most significant questions address issues of change over time (see also Chapter 3). As noted by Raudenbush:

> If Dewey was correct, that education is change, educative activities influence

children by changing their developmental paths. A new model for reading instruction is not intended just to add an increment to a child's reading achievement at a single point in time. . . . Rather, the set of activities which constitute the program are implemented over a period of time for the purpose of modifying the growth trajectory of each child. In this view, the essential dependent variable for studies of educational effects on children is a multivariate representation of the individual growth curve.

(Raudenbush, 1989a, p.721)

It follows that it is not only essential for school effects studies to reflect the multi-level nature of schools, but that they should also address questions of changes over time. Raudenbush (1989) notes that in previous research, the dynamic and multilevel nature of schooling have been studied separately because of an absence of appropriate statistical techniques. The recent emergence of MMs, however, has provided researchers with a set of statistical tools that permit more realistic modelling of the dynamic nature of schooling. In this section we review some of these models, their applications to date, and some of the complexities they pose for the potential researcher.

Bryk and Raudenbush (1987) proposed that observations of an individual over time were essentially nested within the individual and could be treated as multilevel nested data. In particular, they propose an MM formulation of the problem of growth curve analysis. At stage 1 of their two-stage formulation, the individual is observed or measured on T different occasions. These observations are considered a function of an individual growth trajectory plus random error. In essence, this becomes the within-subject model. In the second stage the parameters of the individual growth trajectories are seen as functions of individual characteristics or attributes. This becomes the between-subject model. This development allows for:

> . . . examining the reliability of instruments for measuring status and change, investigating correlates of status and change, and testing hypotheses about the effects of background variables and experimental interventions on individual growth.

(Bryk and Raudenbush, 1987, p.148)

Mandeville and Kennedy (1991), arguing that effective school correlates were based on cross-sectional comparisons rather than considerations of differential student growth, proposed an adaptation of this model to the study of growth in the social class/achievement link as a cohort of students moved from grades 1 through 3. However, their formulation was a two-level model and could not adequately model student growth as a function of student characteristics and school characteristics simultaneously.

Raudenbush and Bryk (1989) proposed a three level model which incorporated student changes over time as the first level, student characteristics as the second level, and school characteristics as the third level. This model, which incorporates both dynamic and multilevel aspects of schools, makes it possible to address questions of school effects on students over time, as well as school effects on successive cohorts of students as they pass through schools (see Willms and Raudenbush, 1989). In an application of this model to a sample of students from the Sustaining Effects Study, Raudenbush reported that initial differences among schools in mathematics achievement were around 14 per cent, typical of other efforts. However, with respect to learning rates, he reported that:

> . . . over 80 per cent of the variance in mathematics learning is between schools! These results constitute powerful evidence of school effects that have gone undetected in past research.
>
> (Raudenbush, 1989b, p.732)

Similarly, Gray et al. (1995) report considerable stability in school effectiveness indices using MM. Finally, Goldstein et al. (1994) describe an extension of the basic longitudinal MM to the case where there is an autocorrelation structure at level-1, which can also be embedded within higher crossed and nested structures.

Multivariate Models

Many of the MM models currently under discussion assume that only a single dependent variable is of interest. This is rarely the case in school effects research. In research on school climate, for example, Raudenbush, Rowan and Kang (1991) note that climate measures usually consist of a number of conceptually distinct scales. The typical MM analysis treats these sub-scales separately. Similarly, in research on achievement, the analyst must repeat analyses in separate areas, failing to address relationships among outcomes of interest. This limitation has both statistical as well as substantive implications.

Single level statistical techniques for multivariate analyses (i.e. those that do not attend to multilevel data structures) are available for a variety of problems. These include comparisons between vectors of means, correlational analysis with multiple indicators, and regression analyses with multiple outcomes. Only recently, however, have multilevel multivariate models become available. Raudenbush, Rowan, and Kang (1991) describe a multivariate model wherein the first level involves multiple outcomes for each subject seen as a function of subject level predictors and measurement error. The parameters from this model are seen as random variables to be predicted by measures at higher levels in the hierarchy. Goldstein (1987a, 1991b) showed how the general multivariate linear (and non-linear) model could be formulated as a multilevel model with an extra lowest level which specified the multivariate structure (e.g. Schmidt, 1969; Goldstein and McDonald, 1988; McDonald and Goldstein, 1989; Thum, 1997).

Random Cross-classified Multilevel Models

Until recently, multilevel models assumed a 'pure nesting' of units. For example, if a researcher were interested in a model that involved student, school, and neighbourhood variables, it was assumed that each neighbourhood sent students to only one school. In this event, a three-level model wherein students (level-1) were nested within schools (level-2), and schools were nested within neighbourhoods (level-3) is appropriate. However, court ordered bussing, school choice, and a number of other factors make such 'pure nesting' rare. In the more typical case, children from multiple neighbourhoods will attend the same school. In this case, neighbourhoods are crossed with schools in the sense of a 2 × 2 design and students are nested within cells of the design. Raudenbush (1993) introduced a two-level two-way additive model that could address this data structure. This model is also appropriate for studying student growth over time as students move from one unit (e.g. classroom) to another. The three-level model for studying growth described earlier assumes that there is no movement across group boundaries.

Raudenbush's model was extended by Kang (1993) to include interaction terms. Goldstein and associates (Rasbash and Goldstein, 1994; Goldstein, 1994) extend Raudenbush's model and Kang's extension to *p*-way classifications at any number of levels. This latter development is the most general development to date which can also accommodate multivariate outcomes at level-1.

Non-linear Models

One common assumption of many multilevel models is that errors are normally distributed. Many important issues in schools effects research, however, involve variables that are decidedly not normal in distributional form. These include studies of grade retention (retained–not retained), dropout (dropout–not dropout), curriculum (academic–non academic) and many more. In addition to non-normality, studies that involve dichotomous dependent variables, present problems of heteroscedasticity, non-linearity, etc.

For single level analyses, these difficulties can be accommodated with the generalized linear model (McCullagh and Nelder, 1983). Extensions of the generalized linear model for multilevel problems are described by Goldstein (1991b; 1995a) and Wong and Mason (1985). The Wong and Mason (1985) model differs from Equation 1 in that the logistic regression model is fitted in each aggregate. The parameters of this model, which are considered to vary from group to group, are then modelled as a function of group characteristics. Goldstein's formulation describes an iterative generalized least squares estimation procedure.

Structural Equation Models

Structural equation modelling (SEM) has gained widespread popularity among educational researchers. Recent applications in school effects research have addressed differences in effects of public and Catholic schools on student achievement using a multigroup approach to testing for differences in means of latent constructs (Marsh and Grayson, 1990). The advantages of this approach include

- explicit tests of factor structures and their invariance over groups;
- explicit incorporation of unique and correlated measurement errors in analyses;
- comparisons of means of latent constructs, not observed variables contaminated by measurement error, and
- provisions for a systematic approach to hypothesis testing.

Despite the advantages SEM offers over traditional study of causal structures, most applications make the assumption that there is no hierarchical ordering of observations in the populations studied. While this may not be problematic in many instances, it is questionable for school effects research. For example, the Marsh and Grayson (1990) study cited above ignored the possibility of correlated errors among students within specific schools; that is, the students may share a common source of error variance. This is a significant omission with implications for the accuracy of inferences drawn from the results.

Recent developments in structural equation modelling have begun to address the multilevel nature of school effects research (McDonald and Goldstein, 1989; Longford and Muthén, 1992; McDonald, 1994). Muthén (1991) describes a multilevel factor model and demonstrates its application to a study of mathematics achievement. The conventional factor model specifies a decomposition of a variance–covariance matrix into common and unique factors. Muthén's model decomposes this matrix into within and between common factors and within and between unique factors. The within factor is interpreted in terms of underlying traits of individuals. The between factor is concerned with correlations among group-level variables and may reflect differences in policies, composition, etc. With this model, it is possible to study the within-reliability and the between-reliability, as well as intra-class correlations of various measures.

The multilevel factor analysis model, while more appropriate for naturally nested observations as are found in schools, is concerned with intercepts and variances, but certainly not with slopes. However, extensions of the multilevel factor analysis model to a multilevel structural equation model permits study of the influence of group membership on structural relations among latent variables, random variation of latent means and variances, and random variation in measurement properties of observed variables. This latter consequence is especially important in that traditional MM procedures assume that predictors at all levels are measured without error (e.g. Muthén, 1989; Muthén and Satorra, 1989; Lee, S.-Y., 1990; Lee, S.-Y. and Poon, 1992; Muthén, 1994; Raudenbush, 1995a, 1995b).

Computer Software

A significant aspect to the recent popularity of MM is that a variety of computer programs have become commercially available. Included among those most widely used are VARCL (Longford, 1990), MLn (Rasbash et al., 1995; Woodhouse, B., 1996), and HLM 4 (Bryk et al., 1986a). These programs differ in their computational algorithms, their versatility with respect to the types of models that can be fitted, the types of diagnostic and summary statistics produced and the statistical sophistication required of the user.

Comparisons of earlier versions of these three and other less well known MM programs have been reported by Kreft and others (see Kreft et al., 1990, 1994). In general, the results of these studies indicate that the various programs, despite their differences, yield similar results when data sets are relatively large and conform reasonably well to the assumptions of the models tested. The most recent editions of the most widely known programs, HLM 4 and MLn, have not been systematically compared as of this writing. However, both programs have substantially increased flexibility in terms of the types of models that can be fitted, and, reportedly, improved computational algorithms.

Conclusions

Schools are indeed complex organizations that present a challenge for potential researchers. In this chapter we have emphasized the formal and informal structural hierarchies that characterize contemporary schooling. We have considered how this structure and other issues complicate the study of school effects. We concluded that statistical models ought, to the extent possible, mirror the instructional and social experiences of students as they exist in schools (e.g. students nested within classrooms, ability groups, cliques, etc.); that studies ought to be longitudinal, examining cohorts of students over extended periods of time, prior to, and following, entrance into a given setting; and that studies ought to utilize valid and reliable measures that are responsive to school-based experiences.

As noted above, multilevel models hold significant promise for researchers interested in school effects: questions can be addressed that could not be asked before; estimates have better sampling properties; and models are becoming ever more responsive to the schooling experiences of students. However, there are many issues that deserve further exploration:

1   De Leeuw and Kreft (1995b), in 'questioning' MMs, argue that they are elegant but not always necessary; that traditional techniques work well when samples are large, intra-class correlations are small, and interest is primarily in level-2 fixed effects. The question of when to use multilevel modelling techniques is an important one and as the models and the available software grow in sophistication, it is likely that practitioners will seek more familiar and simpler alternatives.

2   A variety of computational algorithms are currently available. These procedures, as noted by several authors (e.g. Draper, 1995) have yet to be fully explored with respect to their performance under conditions frequently found in practice.

3   As multilevel modelling techniques grow in their complexity, there should be a simultaneous growth in diagnostic procedures and procedures for checking the adequacy and appropriateness of fitted models. Without these developments, theoretical advances may fail to yield fruitful advances for addressing practical problems.

4   Hierarchies exist not only with respect to formal organizational arrangements or research sampling plans, but informally as well. Practitioners must have ways to detect important hierarchies when they exist in a given dataset (see Draper, 1995). Related to this, there is a need for additional work on the implications of mis-specification for multilevel models. This is particularly true of more complicated models.

5   Bidwell and Kasarda (1980) argue that schools have much of their impact on children indirectly through teachers. Multilevel structural equation modelling techniques allow for explicit study of this and other hypotheses related to direct and indirect effects. However, few large scale studies which utilize this methodology can be found in the literature. This is an area that warrants attention.

6   An issue not often addressed is that the majority of the current literature on school effects has not involved actual observations of processes occurring in schools. Typically, surveys, archival and test data are utilized. Future studies ought to

incorporate more of a qualitative component that reflects the experiences of students, teachers, etc.

7 Despite several books geared to applications and the proliferation of software programs, published research utilizing multilevel modelling is relatively rare in leading journals. Most published research is largely theoretical and largely beyond the reach of most practitioners. Additional work must focus on making these tools available to a broader audience of users.

Finally, as noted by several authors, (e.g. Draper, 1995; Morris, 1995) multilevel models do not relieve researchers of the responsibility of carefully studying the quality of their data and the appropriateness of the models they specify.

7 Linking School Effectiveness and School Improvement

David Reynolds and Charles Teddlie
with David Hopkins and Sam
Stringfield

Introduction

So far in this handbook we have outlined in considerable detail the literature on school effectiveness from across the world, and attempted to relate that literature to various themes or topics within the field. It would be logical to expect a close relationship between this research base in school effectiveness and the programmes of school improvement and school development that are now in existence in virtually every industrialized country across the world, for a number of reasons:

1   The 'founding fathers' of effective schools research in the United States, Edmonds (1979a, 1979b) and Brookover et al. (1979b), had an explicit commitment to the work being utilized to improve schools. The United States has shown, then, a considerable volume of 'school effectiveness' projects where the research knowledge is explicitly used to improve practice. The Rutter et al. (1979) study in the United Kingdom has also been utilized to provide findings for the improvement of schools, although the eventual results were somewhat disappointing. (Ouston et al., 1991; Maughan et al., 1990.)
2   There are clear interests involved in maximizing the relationships between effectiveness and improvement, since effectiveness research can provide the knowledge base concerning what to do, and the improvement community the vehicle within which the knowledge base sits.
3   In many societies there are links made between school effectiveness knowledge and educational policy as a matter of mandate. In the United States the Hawkins/Stafford amendment has led to up to half of school districts to directly utilize school effectiveness knowledge and concepts. In the United Kingdom, central government funding is made available from the Standards Fund for schools to receive training in schools and effectiveness activities.

The much needed relationship between school effectiveness and school improvement that one might expect is, however, not what one would find in most countries of the world. This chapter outlines the reasons for this state of affairs, traces its origins and goes on to outline contemporary developments which suggest the emergence of the much needed relationship.

The Field Surveyed

In North America, particularly within the United States, there exists perhaps the closest of the international relationships between school effectiveness and school improvement. Over half of all American school districts have run improvement programmes based upon, or linked to, the effective schools knowledge base (General Accounting Office, 1989; Taylor, B., 1990). It must be noted however that the knowledge base within the improvement programme is likely to be of the earlier simplistic variety of 'five factor' theories developed by Edmonds (1979a, 1979b) and popularized by Lezotte (1989), rather than that more recently developed from a considerably more advanced research base by researchers like Stringfield and Teddlie (Wimpelberg et al., 1989). In addition, there are in the United States the well known demonstration projects which have involved the direct, controlled transfer of research knowledge into school improvement programmes with built in evaluation of outcomes, which have demonstrated enhanced school effectiveness (e.g. McCormack-Larkin, 1985). In Canada likewise there are programmes which involve the utilization of school effectiveness knowledge within school improvement programmes (Stoll and Fink, 1989, 1992), and the school effectiveness knowledge base has also penetrated many other ongoing improvement projects (see reviews in Sackney, 1985, 1989).

In spite of this evident relationship between the two bodies of knowledge at the level of practice, at the intellectual level there is much less of a relationship or communality of perspective between the scholars who contribute to their respective knowledge bases. In part this may be because school improvement scholars have reacted against the simplistic nature of past North American school effectiveness literature. Whatever the precise reasons, school improvement scholars such as Fullan, Hall and Miles rarely base their school improvement strategies upon the work of school effectiveness researchers. Fullan (1991) for example refers to only half a dozen school effectiveness studies from the United States, only two from United Kingdom and to none from any of the other societies like Australia, the Netherlands or New Zealand in which major school effectiveness projects have been carried out. Were we to take Fullan and the other improvement writers noted above, a survey of their bibliographies suggests that only about 2 or 3 per cent of their total references are from writers commonly regarded as writing within the school effectiveness research paradigm. Were we also to take the American school effectiveness research community and look at the nature of their references, probably only about 1 per cent of total references would relate to writers conventionally located within the paradigm of school improvement.

The situation of two separate, discrete bodies of knowledge and two separate research communities that exists in North America has been in evidence in most other parts of the world; indeed in certain parts of the world the separation is even more in evidence. In the United Kingdom, there has, until the last two or three years, been little collaboration between those working within the school effectiveness and school improvement paradigms, little practitioner take up of the knowledge base of school effectiveness (Mortimore, 1998; Reynolds, 1991a), little use of the research in school improvement or school development programmes (Reid et al., 1987), and little appreciation or referencing of school effectiveness material in the works of 'school improvers' (and vice versa). Indeed, the British Economic and Social Research Council funded from 1993–4 a programme of symposia and seminars for leading persons in the two fields of effectiveness and improvement explicitly to make links (Gray et al., 1996b).

In other parts of the world the situation is similar to that in Britain. New Zealand, for example, was the site of pioneering school effectiveness research (Ramsay et al., 1982), but there are no current signs of engagement of this knowledge base by those working within the 'school improvement through decentralization' paradigm that has existed since the Picot Report in the late 1980s. The Netherlands now has perhaps the world's most extensive research base within the field of school effectiveness (see Scheerens and Bosker, 1997), but there is little evidence of school effectiveness based school improvement programmes, nor of any penetration of school effectiveness research knowledge into schools through the development planning which is now mandatory within Dutch schools. Australia too has a small school effectiveness research base (see Chapter 1), and indeed some of this knowledge has been linked to school improvement through the school self management approach of Caldwell and Spinks (1988). But again, more developmentally orientated material from Australia shows only limited take up of, or reliance on, school effectiveness literature. Indeed, the Australian school improvement tradition relates primarily to the literature on educational management and administration, itself notable for the absence of linkages with the school effectiveness research base. Israel by contrast has seen systematic application of school effectiveness findings in school improvement programmes (Bashi and Sass, 1990).

It is clear from any reading of the international literature on school improvement and school effectiveness that the two areas have historically been very different in their core conceptualizations, beliefs and proposed strategies of furthering school change. We now turn to examine the values, and practices of the 'school improvement paradigm' and the 'school effectiveness paradigm' in turn, before turning to further examine the new, 'merged' or 'blended' paradigm that is gaining intellectual and practical ground.

School Improvement

The disciplinary area of school improvement has gone through a number of phases. The first phase, which dates from the mid 1960s, was the emphasis on the *adoption of curriculum materials*. On both sides of the Atlantic, the curriculum reform movement was intended to have a major impact on student achievement through the production and dissemination of exemplary curriculum materials. Although the materials were often of high quality, being produced by teams of academics and psychologists, in the main they failed to have an impact on teaching. The reason in hindsight is obvious; teachers were not included in the production process and the inservice that accompanied the new curricula was often perfunctory and rudimentary. Teachers simply took what they thought was of use from the new materials and integrated it into their own teaching. The curriculum innovation, however, was consequently subverted.

The second phase – covering most of the 1970s – was essentially one of *documenting failure*, the failure of the curriculum reform movement to affect practice. It became increasingly apparent from this work that 'top down' models of change did not work, that teachers required inservice training to acquire new knowledge and skills, and that implementation did not occur spontaneously as a result of legislative fiat. It was clear that implementation is an extremely complex and lengthy process that required a sensitive combination of strategic planning and individual learning and commitment to succeed. Much was learned about implementation during this period that was to lay the basis for future work.

The third phase, roughly from the late 1970s to mid 1980s, was a period of *success*. It was during this time that the first studies of school effectiveness were published in Britain (Rutter et al., 1979; Reynolds, 1976), and that a consensus was established in the United States as to the characteristics of effective schools (Purkey and Smith, 1983; Wilson and Corcoran, 1988). This is not meant to imply however that this line of enquiry has been unproblematic; there is still much more work to be done, as this handbook constantly argues. It was also during this period that some major large scale studies of school improvement projects were conducted (Crandall, D. et al., 1982, 1986; Huberman and Miles, 1984; Hargreaves, 1984; Rosenholtz, 1989; Louis and Miles, 1990). Much was consequently learned about the dynamics of the change process. As can be seen later, the OECD International School Improvement Study (ISIP) was also at work at this time, producing case studies of, and developing strategies for, school improvement (for an overview see van Velzen et al., 1985; Hopkins, 1987). A number of syntheses of the work during this period also appeared, of which the contributions of Fullan (1985) and Joyce and his colleagues (1983) are very important.

Although this creative period produced knowledge of increasing specificity about the change process and the factors influencing effective schooling, this was a necessary but not sufficient condition to improve the quality of education. As Fullan (1991) points out, clear descriptions of success are not tantamount to solving the problem of the management of change towards that success.

Managing Change, the fourth phase which has been recently entered, will prove to be the most difficult and hopefully productive of all, as researchers and practitioners struggle to relate their strategies and their research knowledge to the realities of schools in a pragmatic, systematic and sensitive way. There is indeed now a move away from the study of change as a phenomenon to actually participating in school development and the best of the current work on educational change is coming from people who are actually studying change as they are engaged in bringing it about (e.g. Hopkins, 1995). Research knowledge and 'change theory' is being refined through action (Fullan, 1993).

Across these four historical phases there have been numerous studies of importance. The 'Rand' study of McLaughlin was originally undertaken in the USA in the mid to late 1970s and concluded that:

> A general finding of the Change Agent study that has become almost a truism is that it is exceedingly difficult for policy to change practice, especially across levels of government. Contrary to the one-to-one relationship assumed to exist between policy and practice, the Change Agent study demonstrated that the nature, amount, and pace of change at the local level was a product of local factors that were largely beyond the control of higher-level policymakers.
>
> (McLaughlin, 1990, p.12)

According to McLaughlin (1990) this general observation has four specific implications:

- policy cannot mandate what matters;
- implementation dominates outcomes;
- local variability is the rule;
- uniformity is the exception.

The 'Rand' study also looked at the strategies that promoted educational improvement (McLaughlin, 1990). Strategies that were generally effective, especially when used together, were:

- concrete, teacher-specific and extended training;
- classroom assistance from local staff;
- teacher observation of similar projects in other classrooms, schools, or districts;
- regular project meetings that focused on practical issues;
- teacher participation in project decisions;
- local development of project materials;
- principals' participation in training.

According to this analysis, the relationship between 'macro-level policies and micro-level behaviour' is paramount. Although policies set directions and provide a framework, they do not and cannot determine outcomes. It is implementation, rather than the decision to adopt a new policy, that determines student achievement. What is needed is an 'implementation friendly' strategy for educational change. A definition of such a strategy, school improvement, is the focus of the following section.

Defining School Improvement

School improvement approaches to educational change embody the long term goal of moving towards the ideal type of the self renewing school. This obviously implies a very different way of thinking about change than the ubiquitous 'top-down' approach discussed earlier. When the school is regarded as the 'centre' of change, then strategies for change need to take this new perspective into account. This approach that centres on the school is exemplified in the work of the OECD sponsored International School Improvement Project (ISIP) and in the knowledge that emanated from it (van Velzen et al., 1985; Hopkins, 1987, 1990). School Improvement was defined in the ISIP as:

> a systematic, sustained effort aimed at change in learning conditions and other related internal conditions in one or more schools, with the ultimate aim of accomplishing educational goals more effectively.
>
> (van Velzen et al., 1985)

School improvement as an approach to educational change therefore rests on a number of assumptions (van Velzen et al., 1985; Hopkins, 1987, 1990):

- The school is the centre of change – This means that external reforms need to be sensitive to the situation in individual schools, rather than assuming that all schools are the same. It also implies that school improvement efforts need to adopt a 'classroom-exceeding' perspective, without ignoring the classroom.

- A systematic approach to change – School improvement is a carefully planned and managed process that takes place over a period of several years.
- A key focus for change are the 'internal conditions' of schools – These include not only the teaching–learning activities in the school, but also the schools' procedures, role allocations and resource uses that support the teaching and learning process.
- Accomplishing educational goals more effectively – Educational goals reflect the particular mission of a school, and represent what the school itself regards as desirable. This suggests a broader definition of outcomes than student scores on achievement tests, even though for some schools these may be pre-eminent. Schools also serve the more general developmental needs of students, the professional development needs of teachers and the needs of its community.
- A multi-level perspective – Although the school is the centre of change it does not act alone. The school is embedded in an educational system that has to work collaboratively if the highest degrees of quality are to be achieved. This means that the roles of teachers, headteachers, governors, parents, support staff (advisers, higher education consultants), and local authorities should be defined, harnessed and committed to the process of school improvement.
- Integrated implementation strategies – This implies a linkage between 'top down' and 'bottom up', remembering of course that both approaches can apply at a number of different levels in the system. Ideally 'top down' policy provides policy aims, an overall strategy, and operational plans; this is complemented by a 'bottom up' response involving diagnosis, priority goal setting, and implementation. The former provides the framework, resources, and a menu of alternatives; the latter, the energy and the school based implementation.
- The drive towards institutionalization – Change is only successful when it has become part of the natural behaviour of teachers in the school. Implementation by itself is not enough.

It is this philosophy and these approaches that underpinned the International School Improvement Project and laid the basis for further thinking and action.

A more recent and succinct definition of school improvement is an 'approach to educational change that enhances student outcomes as well as strengthening the school's capacity for managing change' (Hopkins et al., 1994, p.3). Unfortunately, the history of educational innovation is littered with the skeletons of innovations and changes whose implementers failed to recognize this key idea. School improvement in this idea is concerned not so much about school improvement, but about the process of improving, and indeed part of the problem of centralized educational reform is the preoccupation with outcomes at the expense of the process that leads to such outcomes.

Although the term 'school improvement' is now in common usage, the complexities of the approach as an alternative means of educational change have not necessarily been fully explored. The more rigorous recent definition above implies a broader and more sophisticated view of the concept, in which school improvement can be regarded (Hopkins et al., 1994):

- as a vehicle for planned educational change (but also realizing that educational change is necessary for school improvement);

- as particularly appropriate during times of centralized initiatives and innovation overload when there are competing reforms to implement;
- as usually necessitating some form of external support;
- as having an emphasis on strategies for strengthening the school's capacity for managing change;
- as concerned with raising student achievement (broadly defined).

The Process of Change and School Improvement

The literature on planned school change is crucial to the way in which contemporary school improvement strategies have been formulated. There is now solid, research based evidence about how the change process unfolds over time. As Miles (1986) and Fullan (1991) have demonstrated, the change process is not linear, but consists of a series of three stages that can merge into each other. Although these phases often co-exist in practice, there are some advantages in describing them separately; particularly in terms of what happens during them, and in terms of what behaviours within each phase make for success. The process is generally considered to consist of three overlapping phases – initiation, implementation, and institutionalization.

Although implementation has received the most attention historically, this has most probably been disadvantageous to the understanding of the process as a whole. Emphasizing initiation and implementation at the expense of institutionalization leads to a very short term view of innovation. Consequently, it is probably more helpful to think of the three phases as a series of overlapping phases, rather than as a straight line.

The initiation phase is about deciding to embark on innovation, and about developing commitment towards the process. The key activities in the initiation phase are the decision to start the innovation, and a review of the school's current state as regards the particular innovation. There are however a number of factors associated with initiation that will influence whether the change gets started in the first place. These are issues such as the existence of, and access to, innovations, pressures from within and without the school, the availability of resources and consultancy support, and the quality of the school's internal conditions and organization. Fullan (1991) describes them in detail and emphasizes that it is not simply the existence of these factors but their combination that is important. He concluded that the following factors are of importance in determining the quality of the initiation phase:

1 the existence and quality of innovations;
2 access to innovations;
3 advocacy from central administration;
4 teacher advocacy;
5 presence of external change agents;
6 community factors (pressure, support, apathy);
7 new policy-funds (federal/state/local);
8 problem-solving capacities within the school.

Miles (1986) also made an analysis of the factors that make for successful initiation:

- the innovation should be tied to a local agenda and high profile local need;
- a clear, well-structured approach to change should be present;
- there should be an active champion who understands the innovation and supports it;
- there should be active initiation to start the innovation ('top down' initiation can be acceptable under certain conditions);
- the innovation should be of good quality.

Implementation is the phase of the process which has received the most attention. This is the phase of the attempted use of the innovation. Factors influencing implementation are the characteristics of the change, the internal conditions of the school and the pressure and support from the outside. It is during this phase that skills and understanding are being acquired, some success may be being achieved, and in which responsibility is delegated to working groups of teachers. It is often helpful to regard implementation as being of two types: pre-implementation and implementation. Many innovations founder at the pre-implementation stage because not enough initial support has been generated.

The key activities occurring during implementation are the carrying out of action plans, the development and sustaining of commitment, the checking of progress and the overcoming of problems.

Institutionalization is the phase when innovation and change stop being regarded as something new and become part of the school's 'usual' way of doing things, yet until recently it was assumed to happen automatically, despite the evidence that innovations associated with many centralized initiatives tend to fade away after the initial wave of enthusiasm, or after a key actor leaves, or when the funding ceases. The move from implementation to institutionalization, however, often involves the transformation of a pilot project to a school wide initiative, often without the advantage of the previously available funding. It is change of a new order and in these cases there tends to be widespread use of the change by staff, its impact is seen on classroom practice, and the whole process is no longer regarded as being unusual. As the researchers who worked on the DESSI study remarked (Huberman and Crandall quoted in Miles, 1983):

> In the chronicle of research on dissemination and use of educational practices, we first put our chips on adoption, then on implementation. It turns out that these investments are lost without deliberate attention to the institutional steps that lock an innovation into the local setting. New practices that get built into the training, regulatory, staffing and budgetary cycle survive; others don't. Innovations are highly perishable goods. Taking institutionalisation for granted – assuming somewhat magically that it will happen by itself, or will necessarily result from a technically mastered, demonstrably effective project – is naive and usually self-defeating.
>
> (Miles, 1983, p.14)

Key activities to ensure success at this stage according to Miles (1986) are:

- an emphasis on 'embedding' the change within the school's structures, its organization and resources;

- the elimination of competing or contradictory practices;
- strong and purposeful links to other change efforts, to the curriculum and to classroom teaching;
- widespread take-up in the school and in the local area;
- an adequate 'bank' of local facilitators and/or advisory teachers for skills training.

The School Improvement Paradigm

Approaches to school improvement have, over the past 30 years, been characterized by the following sets of assumptions, as seen in Table 7.1.

In the 1960s and 1970s school improvement in the United States, the United Kingdom and internationally displayed a number of paradigmatic characteristics associated with the empirical–analytic tradition. It was linked as an enterprise to a technological view of school improvement, in which innovations were brought to schools from outside of them and then introduced 'top down'. The innovations were based upon knowledge produced by persons outside the school, the focus was on the school's formal organization and curriculum, the outcomes were taken as given, and the innovation was targeted at the school more than the individual practitioner. The whole improvement edifice was based upon a positivistic, quantitative evaluation of effects. The worldwide failures of this model of school improvement to generate more than very partial take up by schools of the curricula or organizational innovations became an established finding within the educational discourse of the 1970s, explained widely as due to a lack of teacher 'ownership'.

Out of the recognition of this failure came the new improvement paradigm of the 1980s, which is still reflected in some of the writing on school improvement that is current and in evidence today. This new movement celebrated a 'bottom up' approach to school improvement, in which the improvement attempts are 'owned' by those at the school level, although outside school consultants or experts can put their knowledge forward for possible utilization. This new approach tended to celebrate the

Table 7.1 Characteristics of two school improvement paradigms

	1960s	*1980s*
Orientation	'top down'	'bottom up'
Knowledge Base	elite knowledge	practitioner knowledge
Target	organization or curriculum based	process based
Outcomes	pupil outcome orientated	school process orientated
Goals	outcomes as given	outcomes problematic
Focus	school	teacher
Methodology of Evaluation	quantitative	qualitative
Site	outside school	within school
Focus	part of school	whole school

Source: Reynolds et al., 1993.

'folk-lore' or practical knowledge of practitioners rather than the knowledge base of researchers, and focused on changes to educational processes rather than to school management, or organizational features, which were regarded as reified constructs. It wanted the outcomes or goals of school improvement programmes to be debated and discussed, rather than accepted as given. Those working within this paradigm also tended to operate at the level of the practitioner rather than at the level of the school, with a qualitative and naturalistically orientated evaluation of the enterprise being preferred to quantitative measurement. The improvement attempt was 'whole school' orientated and school based, rather than outside school or course based (see Reynolds, 1988).

The School Effectiveness Paradigm

The school effectiveness research paradigm has, of course, a very different intellectual history and has exhibited a very different set of core beliefs concerning operationalization, conceptualization and measurement by comparison with the changing approaches of the school improvers, as will have been clear from Chapters 1, 2 and 3. It has been strongly committed to the use of quantitative methods, since many researchers were concerned to refute the 'schools make no difference' hypothesis advanced by Coleman et al. (1966) and Jencks et al. (1971) by utilizing the same conventional methods of empirical research as their perceived opponents had utilized. Many researchers have also believed that teachers, especially North American ones, would pay more attention to work conducted within the quantitative paradigm.

School effectiveness researchers have also been primarily concerned with pupil academic and social outcomes, which is not surprising given the political history of effective schools research in the United States, where it has grown and built on the beliefs of Ron Edmonds and his associates that 'all children can learn'. Processes within schools only have an importance within the school effectiveness paradigm to the extent that they affect outcomes – indeed, one 'back maps' with the paradigm from outcomes to process. The school effectiveness paradigm furthermore regards pupil and school outcomes as fundamentally unproblematic and as given. School effectiveness researchers indeed often talk of a 'good' or 'excellent' school as if that were unproblematic.

The school effectiveness paradigm is also organizationally rather than process based in terms of its analytic and descriptive orientation, preferring to restrict itself to the more easily quantifiable or measurable. As an example, Fullan's (1985) process factors such as 'a feel for the process of leadership' or 'a guiding value system', or 'intense interaction and communication' are largely eschewed in favour of organizationally and behaviourally orientated process variables such as 'clear goals and high expectations' and/or 'parental involvement and support'. Additionally, the focus within the school improvement paradigm on the attitudinal, and on personal and group 'inner states', is replaced within school effectiveness research by a focus on the more easily measured behaviour of persons.

A last couple of differences are also clear. School effectiveness research has customarily celebrated the importance of a very limited range of outcomes, mostly academic and mostly concerned with the acquisition of basic skills. Indeed, virtually all the early American work focused upon academic achievement virtually exclusively (see review in Reynolds et al., 1994b).

School improvement research by contrast has often conceptualized outcomes more broadly. Often indeed in the British tradition the improvement attempt or project was to debate the 'possible' goals of education, as against the limited 'official' goals, as part of the process of securing improvement. In most accounts of their processes (e.g. Hopkins, 1987), it seems that multiple goals form the intellectual base of school improvement.

Lastly, school effectiveness differs from school improvement in that it is concerned to celebrate the 'end state' of describing what it is that schools which are effective are actually 'like', whereas school improvement has been more concerned to discover what it is that has been done to bring schools to that state. The orientation of school effectiveness has been a 'static' one concerned with the 'steady state' of effectiveness; the orientation of school improvement has been a 'dynamic' one, focusing upon 'change over time'.

New Wave Projects and New Wave Thinking

In the last few years, as we noted in Chapter 2, the voices calling for links between school effectiveness and school improvement have reached something of a chorus. Stoll (1996) argues that 'if practitioners can see and make links between school effectiveness and school improvement, surely it is time for researchers studying the two areas to do the same and to work with schools to develop a deeper and more meaningful understanding of the research and its implications for practice'. Hopkins (1996) argues that 'one of the most encouraging recent developments in the area of school effectiveness and school improvement is the seriousness with which the confluence of these two streams of enquiry is being taken'.

In these years, there have emerged in a number of countries intervention projects which are not *either* effectiveness based *or* school improvement orientated, as defined by the limits of the old disciplines. Much of this 'convergence' or 'synergy' between the two paradigms has in fact resulted from practitioners and local authority/district policy makers borrowing from both traditions because they do not share the ideological commitment to the ways of working of researchers in the fields, whilst some has arisen through the efforts of the International Congress for School Effectiveness and Improvement in breaking down disciplinary as well as geographical boundaries.

Sometimes the adoption of ideas from research has been somewhat uncritical; for example, the numerous attempts to apply findings from one specific context to another entirely different context when research has increasingly demonstrated significant contextual differences (Hallinger and Murphy, 1985; Teddlie et al., 1989b). Sometimes it is clear that projects are partial in their adoption of material from both paradigms – some projects have an understanding of what makes schools effective but an absence of any 'action plan' about how to get to the 'effectiveness' destination, whilst other projects have celebrated the 'core' school improvement cultural ideas of ownership, collegiality and laterality without acknowledgment of the key importance of school process and organization.

Nevertheless, there are a number of projects in action that represent no less than a 'new wave' of thinking about how we improve school quality. A number will now be outlined, but before outlining them in detail it is important to note their general characteristics by comparison with the traditional type of school improvement programmes that we described earlier. In these novel programmes:

- Pupil outcomes in academic (and often social) areas are regarded as the key 'success criteria', rather than the measures to do with teacher perception of the innovations which were used historically.
- These outcomes are increasingly assessed by use of 'hard' quantitative data, that is regarded as necessary to build commitment and confidence amongst those taking part and to measure the success or failure of the project initiative.
- Bodies of knowledge from school effectiveness, school improvement and school development are all used to resource programmes, with a problem centred orientation being used in which philosophical judgments about the nature of appropriate strategies are suspended in favour of a 'what works' approach that is distinctly non-denominational.
- The learning level, the instructional behaviour of teachers and the classroom level are increasingly being targeted for explicit programme attention as well as the school level, a marked contrast again with work from the 1980s where 'the school' was often the sole focus.

It is easy to understand why the 'lever' of the school level had been historically pulled so frequently, since of course school improvement persons and school effectiveness persons have had close relationships with senior school level personnel. Senior school level personnel have gone on the courses run by school effectiveness and school improvement persons. The policy discourse in most societies has concerned the school level, not the classroom level. In some societies such as the United Kingdom, there is indeed no recent knowledge base or literature about teacher effectiveness or on practices at classroom level which can potentiate student achievement which would lead to a balance with the past obsession with the school level.

It is clear though that the historic neglect of coherent focus upon classrooms has been very costly indeed. Firstly, it is clear that the greatest variation is within schools by individual department, rather than between schools. Put simply, the classroom learning level has maybe two or three times the influence on student achievement than the school level does (Creemers, 1994).

Additionally, the reluctance to focus upon classrooms directly or turn round interventions at school level 'downwards' in schools until they impact on classrooms has hindered the development of programmes, because teacher focal concerns within all schools are much more related to those variables that are located at the classroom level, such as teaching, pedagogy and curriculum, than they are related to activities at the school level, like management and organization. This is probably particularly the case in ineffective schools, where there may exist a majority of staff who define the role of the teacher very narrowly as being related to curriculum and instruction, rather than being more broadly related to school level management and organizational factors. It is clear that the neglect of the classroom level and the celebration of the school level may have historically cost us valuable teacher commitment.

- Multiple 'levers' are pulled to encourage school and teacher development, with the focus upon only the school 'owning' the process of change from the 1980s being replaced by a concern to utilize all reinforcers and initiators of change from outside the school (the local education authority or district) and indeed the national policy agenda to stimulate and provoke change.

- It has been clear that improvement programmes historically have not been necessarily organizationally 'tight'. Because of the fact that most of the programmes have been voluntaristic since they are linked to existing ongoing school level and individual level continuing professional development, it is clear that there may have been a huge differential within schools in the extent to which the programmes have been taken up. Reading between the lines, it is clear that there has been a likely tendency for programmes to impact most on the competent 'leading edge' of teachers, whilst it is also clear that a more or less significant 'trailing edge' may not have participated in the programmes, or at least may not have participated very fully. It is highly likely that there has been within schools participating in the programmes, therefore, a substantial variation in the extent to which they have permeated within schools and the extent to which organizational innovations have moved through to implementation from the initiation phase, and ultimately to the institutionalization phase. Given there is increasing evidence within school effectiveness of the importance of organizational cohesion, consistency and constancy, a situation in which there is greater variation between members of staff in a school because of differential take-up of improvement activities could have been adversely affecting the quality of student outcomes. The new range of programmes below share commitments to enhanced 'fidelity' of implementation, and to enhanced organizational *reliability* in the take up of the various programme characteristics.

We proceed now to look at some of the new 'second wave' projects of the 1990s themselves.

Halton's Effective Schools Project in Canada

The Effective Schools Project in the Halton Board of Education in Ontario (Stoll and Fink, 1992, 1994) started, in 1986, as an attempt to bring the results of school effectiveness research carried out within Britain (Mortimore et al., 1988) into the schooling practices of Canada, but it soon became clear that potential difficulties involved in the project's implementation could only be resolved by the adoption at school and system level of organizational and planning arrangements from the school improvement literature. Essentially, 'top down' mandates to schools did not address the issues of ownership and commitment, nor did they pay attention to the process and impact of the changes upon those who worked to implement the policy mandates.

At the beginning of the project, a search of the international effectiveness literature was carried out by members of a taskforce, and a model of the characteristics of effectiveness produced. Visits were undertaken to school districts where change was known to have occurred successfully, and meetings with the school improvement specialist Michael Fullan convinced taskforce members that improvement was more likely to occur if the school was seen as the focal point of change. A school growth planning process was developed, largely based on British models (McMahon et al.,

1984; ILEA, 1986) and similar to the school development plan that is now a feature of many countries, states and territories.

Where do the effective schools characteristics fit in? Within the assessment, or audit, phase, when the school is trying to get a picture of its current successes and areas for improvement, the staff examines Halton's model of characteristics as it relates to its own context. Questionnaires for teachers, students and parents focus on where respondents think the school is in relation to a set of indicators, and how important each indicator is in order to create a more effective school. Through analysing the gap between where the school is and where it should be, the school can identify areas of need. Furthermore, the information from the three sources provides triangulation. Clearly, this is not the only information schools examine during the assessment phase; they also look at current curricula and instructional practices, at initiatives coming out of the school board and the Ontario Ministry of Education, and also at a variety of information related to their students' progress and development. In line with the emphasis on equity in school effectiveness research, schools are encouraged to disaggregate student data, that is to look for any differences in achievement, progress or development between sub-sets of the population.

Further understandings about school improvement have been gained during the project. The school growth planning process that has been adopted is very different from traditional forms of educational planning in Halton. Increased staff development in decision-making has necessitated greater understanding on the part of principals of the processes involved in working with groups. In the more successful schools, attention has been paid early on to the development of clear decision-making structures and organizational processes that will reduce later problems. In short, in these schools a climate has been built within which a more dynamic and ongoing planning process can occur. More importantly, time has been spent building a collaborative culture within the schools, in which teachers continue to learn and feel valued, and risk-taking is encouraged. Finally, teachers are encouraged to articulate their values and beliefs such that a shared vision for the school's future can be developed. In essence, the school growth planning process has shown that the creation of an effective school depends on more than the knowledge of what has been successful and effective elsewhere, although that can be a useful starting point.

Further important characteristics of this project have been the importance of the school district's role in the process. Halton created a strategic plan that emphasized three key directions. One of these was the growth planning process itself. The second, through a link with *The Learning Consortium* (Fullan et al., 1990), was a focus on instruction, in recognition of the central role in the determination of school outcomes of what actually goes on in the classroom, the teaching and learning process.

Improving the Quality of Education for All

The project, which began with only nine schools in 1991, has grown each year, and currently involves 40 schools in several areas of the country. A contract is agreed between school staff, the Local Education Authority and the project team. All staff of a school have to agree that the school will participate, and at least 40 per cent receive release time to engage in specific project-related activities in their own and each other's classrooms, although all staff participate in certain IQEA-focused staff development events. At least two staff members are designated as coordinators and attend 10 days of training and support meetings, for which accreditation is offered. The school selects its own priorities for development and its own methods to achieve these priorities. It also participates in the evaluation of the project and has to commit itself to share findings with other participants in the project.

The original conceptualization of the project was based on the experience that effective changes strategies focus not only on the implementation of centralized policies or chosen initiatives, but also on creating the conditions within schools that can sustain the teaching–learning process. From their work on the IQEA project, there were identified a series of conditions that underpinned the work of these successful schools (Ainscow et al., 1994). Broadly stated the conditions are:

- staff development;
- involvement;
- leadership;
- coordination;
- enquiry and reflection;
- collaborative planning.

As work continued with IQEA schools on the building of 'capacity' in these areas, the project personnel began to observe a number of factors influencing how particular conditions can best contribute to a 'moving school' ethos (Rosenholtz, 1989). As a consequence they began to develop a series of propositions about the relationship between the way a school approaches a particular condition and the impact of that condition on the school's capacity to hold the key to the establishing of a school culture which can meaningfully empower all teachers within the school community (Hopkins and West, 1994). The propositions are summarized in Table 7.2.

These six conditions and the related propositions were the focus of early work with the IQEA project schools. Subsequently the project began to focus some of its research energies onto what was originally thought to be a parallel set of conditions which related to the notion of capacity at the classroom level. These conditions were connected to teacher development, much in the same way as the original set of conditions were to school development. As such they were supposed to be transferable across classrooms and between teachers and related to a variety of teaching/learning initiatives designed to enhance the achievement of students. At this stage the project team adapted a 'Framework for School Improvement' (Hopkins et al., 1994) to express the relationship as the team then saw it, between school and classroom conditions, and the process of development in schools.

The resulting conceptualization looked something like the illustration in Figure 7.1.

The first 'cut' of the classroom conditions was developed through discussion amongst the IQEA team at Cambridge and a series of day conferences with project schools. About 25 schools and 100 teachers had an input into these initial discussions. This is the initial list of classroom conditions which emerged from the deliberations:

- authentic relationships – being the quality, openness and congruence of relationships existing in the classroom;

Table 7.2 A framework for school improvement: some propositions

- *Proposition One*
  Schools will not improve unless teachers, individually and collectively, develop. Whilst teachers can often develop their practice on an individual basis, if the whole school is to develop then there need to be many *staff development* opportunities for teachers to learn together.

- *Proposition Two*
  Successful schools seem to have ways of working that encourage feelings of *involvement* from a number of stake-holder groups, especially students.

- *Proposition Three*
  Schools that are successful at development establish a clear vision for themselves and regard *leadership* as a function to which many staff contribute, rather than a set of responsibilities vested in a single individual.

- *Proposition Four*
  The *coordination* of activities is an important way of keeping people involved, particularly when changes of policy are being introduced. Communication within the school is an important aspect of coordination, as are the informal interactions that arise between teachers.

- *Proposition Five*
  Those schools which recognize that *enquiry and reflection* are important processes in school improvement find it easier to gain clarity and establish shared meanings around identified development priorities, and are better placed to monitor the extent to which policies actually deliver the intended outcomes for pupils.

- *Proposition Six*
  Through the *process of planning for development* the school is able to link its educational aspirations to identifiable priorities, sequence those priorities over time and maintain a focus on classroom practice.

Source: Hopkins and Ainscow, 1993.

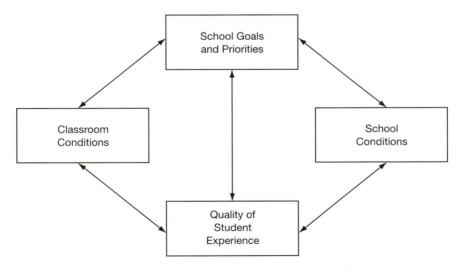

Figure 7.1 The relationship between school and classroom conditions
Source: Hopkins and Ainscow, 1993.

- rules and boundaries – being the pattern of expectations set by the teacher and school of student performance and behaviour within the classroom;
- teacher's repertoire – being the range of teaching styles and models internalized and available to a teacher dependent on student, context, curriculum and desired outcome;
- reflection on teaching – being the capacity of the individual teachers to reflect on their own practice and to put to the test of practice specifications of teaching from other sources;
- resources and preparation – being the access of teachers to a range of pertinent teaching materials and the ability to plan and differentiate these materials for a range of students;
- pedagogic partnerships – being the ability of teachers to form professional relationships within the classroom that focus on the study and improvement of practice.

The IQEA project personnel believe that these conditions are the key to facilitating effective teaching and high quality outcomes at the classroom or learning levels, in just the same way that the other conditions potentiate high quality outcomes at the school level.

The Barclay–Calvert Project in the United States

Our discussion here about this project, and especially about the relationship between school effectiveness and school improvement, is based on a four-year evaluation (Stringfield et al., 1995). In this project the curricular and instructional package of Calvert school, a private school in Baltimore (USA), is being implemented in an inner city public school (Barclay) in the same city. The Calvert school offers a Kindergarten to Grade Six day school programme to a predominantly highly affluent clientele in Baltimore. Since early this century, the school has also offered a highly structured, certified home study curriculum. Procedures for the teachers' provision of lessons, parent/school contact, and evaluation standards for each unit of the curriculum are all unusually specific. Each grade's curriculum and instructional programme is provided in a level of detail that often approximates to scripting. Moreover, the entire programme places an unusually high emphasis on student-generated products. Students generate 'folders' of work that are regularly reviewed by their teacher, their parents, and the school's administrators. According to the evaluation team, the curriculum itself is not revolutionary but reflects decades of high and academically traditional demands, blended with an emphasis on the importance of classwork and homework and an intensive writing programme. All the work undertaken by students reflects the characteristics of effective teaching linked together with a high achievement level of the intakes. It is thus easy to understand why the results on norm-referenced achievement tests are very good. Virtually every grade of the select population of Calvert students score above the 90th percentile when compared to public, elite suburban and private school norms.

By contrast Barclay school is a kindergarten through eighth grade public school in Baltimore. The population served by Barclay is 94 per cent minority. Nearly 80 per cent of the students attending Barclay school receive free or reduced price lunch. The neighbourhood is one of old factories and terraced houses. The school serves some families led by drug dealers, prostitutes, or impoverished graduate students at Johns Hopkins University; however, the great majority of students are the children of working class or unemployed African-Americans, often single-parent families. In the late 1980s it became clear that the school's achievement scores were poor, as well as the attendance rate and levels of student discipline in the classrooms and school halls. So, Barclay could be seen as having the typical problems of an inner-city American school.

The principal at Barclay became interested in the Calvert school programme and the two schools developed a proposal to implement the entire Calvert programme at Barclay school. The programme was to be implemented by the Barclay staff. The staff would receive training in the Calvert philosophy, materials, and instructional system. Ongoing staff development would be provided by a facilitator who had both public school and Calvert teaching experience.

Implementation began in the fall of 1990 in kindergarten at first grade. Each year one additional grade has been added. For two weeks each summer the Barclay/Calvert facilitator trains the next grade's Barclay teachers in the Calvert philosophy, curriculum and methods. The facilitator spends the school year working with each succeeding group of teachers in an effort to maximize the chance of full programme implementation.

The key factors making for the project's success are argued to be:

1 Having funding

The funding of the programme by a private foundation made it possible to appoint a full-time coordinator who acted as the project facilitator. It should be noted, however, that the entire four-year grant has supplied less money than is the annual difference in total funding between a disadvantaged Baltimore City and a suburban Baltimore County school. One of the benefits of this was that everything needed for instruction was there on time in a sufficient quantity (one of the major disadvantages of Barclay school in the past).

2 Having non-fiscal support

The funding foundation was involved in the programme, not only in fiscal decisions, but also in regular staff meetings and in efforts to anticipate and solve problems. The principal was highly talented and very determined to make the programme a success. She visited classes, attended meetings and was very active in involving parents. Furthermore, the Calvert coordinator at Barclay was very supportive with respect to the implementation and brought high levels of knowledge, competence and enthusiasm to the programme implementation. Another source of support was Calvert school itself. The headteacher remained a supporter of the project; he assisted Barclay school, visited classrooms and repeatedly made himself available for consultations. Finally, the parents of Barclay were very actively involved at every stage of the project.

3 Having an achievable plan

The Barclay/Calvert project was very methodical. Barclay did not attempt to implement the whole Calvert curriculum and instructional programme all at once, but gradually, grade level by grade level. In this way it was possible to prepare teachers for the next grade level utilizing a cascade model.

4 Having a high quality curriculum

The curriculum itself involves five processes that are extremely important for its success.

- Students read a lot (that means increasing opportunity to learn).
- All students produce a lot of work.
- Teachers check students' work and also correct all their own work.
- Student folders are read by the coordinator, the principal or the Calvert administrator every month. Therefore, student monitoring is very strong.
- The student folders are sent home every month, which increases parent involvement in what students do and also in checking homework.

5 Having positive teacher attitudes

It is striking in Calvert school that teachers are highly confident that Calvert students can excel academically. It was one of the major changes of the implementation of the Calvert programme in Barclay that the teacher attitudes changed also at Barclay. They were convinced that the Calvert programme was helping them to teach more, teach better, and to help more children perform at higher levels. These are not of course unrealistic expectations, since the teachers have good grounds for their optimistic beliefs, because they have received meaningful, ongoing support and because they were observing enhanced results.

6 Emphasizing classroom instruction

Little changes in students' academic achievement unless something changes between the student, the curriculum and instruction. The Calvert programme is reaching towards the student, for which there are several reasons.

First, the curriculum has been put in place. The curriculum demands high fidelity implementation. Second, a high quality instructional system is also in place. Almost all the teachers have made significant changes in their teaching and have become more effective. In classroom observation it turned out that the student 'on-task' rates in the Calvert/Barclay classes were often very high and that teachers reported that given high quality instruction and instructional support, the Barclay students were responding well to the raised demands. In summary, the Calvert programme has enjoyed a far better chance of achieving full implementation than most novel programmes in school systems.

In the evaluation of the programme, student testing was also included. The data from norm-referenced achievement testing programmes indicate that students in the programme are achieving academically at a rate significantly above their pre-programme Barclay school peers. This finding is consistent across reading, writing, and mathematics, and is particularly striking in writing. The Barclay students are also making progress not only in specific areas of academic content, but also in the ability to integrate new material and absorb new knowledge. Additional data indicate that the Barclay/Calvert project has reduced student absences, reduced student transfers from the school, greatly reduced the number of students requiring Chapter 1 services, reduced referrals to and diagnosis of 'learning disablement', eliminated disciplinary removals and increased the number of students found eligible for the Gifted and Talented Education (GATE) programme. Taken collectively, the diverse measures indicate a very successful school improvement project, which above all has been reliably implemented.

The Dutch National School Improvement Project

The National School Improvement Project (NSIP) was carried out in the Netherlands, started in 1991–2 and went on for three years. Preliminary results have been reported in 1995 (Houtveen and Osinga, 1995).

A major goal of the National School Improvement Project was to prevent and reduce educational disadvantage, especially in reading. The background of the study was that there are clear differences between schools in effectiveness, especially with respect to student performance in the basic skills of language and reading. The school improvement project makes use of the knowledge base of school effectiveness research, especially the insights given by school effectiveness research into the factors that correlate with student performance. Special attention has also been given to instructional and management factors at the classroom level and to the conditional and contingent factors of management and organization at the school level.

The project also made use of the knowledge base developed in other Dutch school improvement projects, of which some were based on effectiveness research. This is especially important, because these type of projects in the Netherlands have been shown to be less effective in the past. Maybe the goals of these past projects have been too ambitious. Another reason for their failure could be the lack of attention to the quality of instruction and management at the classroom level. The Dutch National Improvement Project aimed to learn from these past projects and particularly to ensure that support given by external agencies should be directed to the factors at the classroom and school levels that contribute to student outcomes.

An external evaluation of the project was necessary, but these researchers have also provided information that is useful for focusing and monitoring of the project itself. The goals of the project can be divided into the classroom or teacher level and the school level. At the classroom level the following objectives were included:

1   improving teachers' skills in the field of direct instruction;
2   improving teachers' skills in the field of group management, generating an efficient use of time by the pupils;
3   promotion of teachers' expertise concerning rigorous and methodical working;
4   using effective principles of instruction, with regard to technical reading.

At the school level the following targets were aimed at:

1   to realize a 'results-oriented' school management in which concrete targets concerning basic skills at school and group levels are determined in advance;
2   increasing the evaluation capacity of the school, in connection with point 1, by:

- regular and reliable evaluation of individual pupils' achievements with the help of a pupil 'tracking' system;
- making a valid analysis of the teaching activities and the organizational characteristics of the school with the help of a school diagnosis instrument.

The key features of the project were obviously closely related to the goals of the project:

1 The main focus of the project was on the improvement of education at the classroom level to increase the level of effective instruction. But effective instruction at the classroom level depends on management at the classroom level and upon the different factors and characteristics at the school and the above school levels. So, the first concern of the project was ensuring that the school policy at the different levels is achievement-oriented. This holds for the classroom, school and board or governor level that includes parents.
2 The project reflected the belief that the prevention of reading failure can be achieved by improving the instructional behaviour of teachers.
3 The project believed that support, internal and external, should be directed towards enhancing the practice-oriented professionalism of teachers and school management. This meant that it was not only aimed at knowledge-transfer but also at coaching and putting improvement into practice, which was also given attention in the project. This meant that the project goals are clear, that it had a pre-determined time-span and that it also had a pre-determined set of activities.

The programme itself had specific features that are based on the findings of educational research:

1 Methodical working, which means that all pupils were regularly tested. In this way a database on groups of students, and individual students in the classroom, is available, on which decisions with respect to the entire group, or to individual students, could be made. Also the monitoring of students' progress was rigorous in this programme. The management of the school played an initiating, coordinating and supervising role.
2 Direct instruction as a basic principle of teaching (with the following important phases : evaluation on a daily basis, a clear presentation of the new content or skills, supervised exercise and individual application of knowledge).
3 Structured courses inculcating methods for initial reading.
4 Increasing instructional and effective learning time (connected with the emphasis upon direct instruction).
5 Teaching climate, which was to be made positive for students and included the generation of experiences of success, of positive expectations of teachers towards learning and students' possibilities, and of teachers' confidence in their own possibilities of influence on student results.

The support strategy in the project consisted of a combination of multiple elements, like informing the school board, consultation with principals, guidance at the level of the team of teachers, and coaching of teachers in the classroom.

In the project evaluation, two main questions with respect to the National School Improvement Project were answered:

1 Does the guidance programme result in an increase in effective teaching, more

direct instruction, an increase in the use of the effective methods for teaching reading and an increase in methodical working?

2   Do their teaching behaviours result in an improvement of pupil results in technical reading?

In the evaluation study 29 schools were included, 16 belonging to the 'experimental' group and 13 to the 'control' group. With respect to task-oriented learning and instruction time, direct instruction, methodical working and teaching reading according to effective methods, it can be concluded that the strategy used in this project has been successful, since there is a considerable growth in the experimental group over a period of two and a half years.

In the student achievement study, in the experimental group 319 students were involved and 137 in the control group. These groups were tested in March 1993, (some months before the school year 1993–4) and in June 1994. There was a correction for intake for individual pupil characteristics like initial ability, socio economic background and attitudes towards reading. After correction for the pre-test and student characteristics, there was a significant effect in favour of the experimental group upon student achievement in reading.

It can be concluded that the improvement strategy used in the National School Improvement Project, which was based on a knowledge base with respect to school effectiveness and successful school improvement projects, and the programme content itself, based on a knowledge base with respect to educational effectiveness and instructional effectiveness (especially in the area of initial reading), turns out to be effective. The planned change strategy leads to changes in teaching behaviour, and the students in the experimental group outperformed students in the control group.

Towards Third Wave Programmes

We noted earlier that 'second wave' projects of the 1990s we have outlined above had several differences by comparison with 'first wave' projects of the 1980s. They have:

- focused more closely on classrooms and have been more prepared to utilize teacher effectiveness literature;
- borrowed both from school effectiveness and from school improvement literature and insights;
- been concerned to 'pull all relevant levers' by operating with the outside school, school and classroom levels simultaneously;
- been concerned to address 'reliability' issues as well as validity ones by ensuring that innovations are reliably spread throughout project schools, to ensure cohesion and consistency;
- been concerned to relate programmes very closely to the findings of the existing research base, both in being conceptually rigorous in use of that material and in being sure that there is 'fidelity' in the implementation of the programmes and the research literature;
- focused more closely upon outcomes in academic (and often social) areas as 'success criteria', rather than process factors which were the historic focus;
- attempted to evaluate the success of the innovations using quantitative data, or in

many cases multiple methods of a quantitative and qualitative kind (the Sammons, Taggart and Thomas (1998) evaluation of the Making Belfast Work Study is an example of this).

New issues of 'context specificity' of the improvement attempt are now beginning to characterize 'third wave' efforts.

Drawing largely from the results of a longitudinal study of schools with different SES contexts, Teddlie and Stringfield (1993) recently concluded that results from contextually sensitive SER should lead school improvers to perform two major tasks:

- perform a thorough context analysis of the school before attempting to change it;
- develop a school improvement plan *unique* to the school itself, drawing from generic procedures but also emphasizing information gleaned from contextually sensitive studies.

Similarly, the Halton model (Stoll and Fink, 1989) for school improvement called for examining extensively the particular context of the school during the assessment phase of an improvement project. Also, the Accelerated Schools Project (1991) explicitly calls for 'taking stock' of every facet of the school under study, including all strengths and weaknesses, before planning the school improvement process. This 'taking stock' involves an 'intensive self examination of the school' by the school community.

This approach to school improvement is also similar to Owens' (1987) approach to studying school organizations. Owens proposed three underlying assumptions when using the contingency approach in studying school organizations:

1 There is no one best way to organize and administer school districts and/or schools.
2 Not all ways of organizing and administering are equally effective in a given situation; effectiveness is contingent upon appropriateness of the design or the style to the situation;
3 The selection of organizational design and administrative style should be based upon careful analysis of significant contingencies in the situation (1987, p.82).

Teddlie and Stringfield (1993) further indicate that the context analysis, undertaken long before a school improvement model has been developed, should include answers to the following questions:

- What are the SES backgrounds of parents of the children? Are these backgrounds mixed or homogenous?
- Is the school equally effective for all students, or are some students adequately served while others are not? If inequities exist, how can they be rectified?
- What is the school's geographic context and how might it affect the improvement plan?
- Is the district poor relative to others in the state, and, if so, what can be done to creatively merge community and school resources? Is the school located in a

neighbourhood with many negative influences, and, if so, what kind of buffers can be created to shield the students?

- What is the grade configuration of the school? Does departmentalization exist? Are there different academic tracks? Is the institution maximally organized for learning at the school, class, and student levels? If not, what changes can be made to maximize learning?
- What are the major sociological and historical factors that have led to less than optimal performance at the school? Are these factors still at work and, if so, how can they be eradicated? On the other hand, what positive sociological and historical factors exists, and how can variations in these factors be exploited? (Teddlie and Stringfield, 1993, p.224).

Answers to these, and other, school context questions should have a large influence on the particular school improvement plan adopted by either internal or external school change agents. Reynolds and Packer (1992) concluded that school improvement in the 1990s 'must take into account the interaction between the body of improvement knowledge and the collective psyche of the school (p.80)'. For instance, the SES characteristics of a school's student body should be taken into consideration if a new principal, or secondary change agent, is introduced into the school. As several studies have confirmed (e.g. Evans, R., 1988; Hallinger and Murphy, 1986; Teddlie and Stringfield, 1985), an initiator should be much more successful at improving an ineffective, low-SES elementary school than a manager or responder (Hall et al., 1984). Such a leader, on the other hand, may be inappropriate for a middle-SES school that is not succeeding; in fact, the initiator style may lead to further problems at such a school.

The recognition that change agents, be they internal or external or both, need to develop a unique plan for each school derives from context-sensitive SER. As long as school improvers were interested only in low-SES, urban, elementary schools, then a generic model was not inappropriate. When the contexts of schools changed in SER, so did the models to improve schools. Simply crossing SES level (low, middle) by urbanicity level (rural, suburban, urban) by grade level configuration (elementary, secondary) results in 12 separate plans for school improvement. These plans would obviously have some overlapping goals (e.g. clear academic mission and focus, orderly environment, high academic engaged time-on-task, frequent monitoring of student progress, etc.), but the methods to obtain those common goals, and the methods to obtain goals specific to that particular school context, might be quite different across different contexts.

Thus each school requires an improvement plan (based on 'top down' change, or 'bottom up' change, or preferably a combination thereof) with three types of inputs:

1   Components and procedures taken from generic SER and school improvement literature emphasizing common features that are known to 'work' across contexts.
2   Components and procedures taken from contextually sensitive SER and school improvement research emphasizing the attainment of specific goals which may be of crucial importance in certain settings (i.e. within certain SES contexts, urbanicity contexts, grade level contexts).

3   Components and procedures that seem appropriate to counteract the disturbed interpersonal relations and negative school climate based on the unique psycho-history of the school under study.

These 'ghosts' or 'shadows' have rarely been considered by school improvers (Reynolds et al., 1993), yet they have a profound effect on the success of the change model within that particular school. Uncovering these weaknesses, and also the accompanying strengths of a particular school, is a necessary step in accomplishing 'the internal transformation of culture' that Fullan (1991) and other reformers believe is necessary for school improvement to occur.

From all this we can conclude that what is needed to develop schools are *combinations* of improvement and effectiveness practices and strategies appropriate to the nature of individual schools. Hopkins (1996) has distinguished between three possible different 'types' of strategies, for schools to focus upon in different contexts:

1   Type 1 strategies are those that assist failing schools become moderately effective. They need to involve a high level of external support, since failing schools cannot improve themselves. These strategies have to involve a clear and direct focus on a limited number of basic curriculum and organizational issues in order to build the confidence and competence to continue. Two examples of this directive, externally initiated, approach to school improvement would be the IBIS scheme developed by Hargreaves in the then ILEA (Hargreaves, 1990), or the Schenley High School experiment in school improvement in Pittsburgh (Hopkins et al., 1994).

2   Type 11 strategies are those that assist moderately effective schools become effective. These schools need to refine their developmental priorities to focus on specific teaching and learning issues and to build the capacity within the school to support this work. These strategies usually involve a certain level of external support, but it is theoretically possible for schools in this category to 'improve' by themselves. It may therefore be more helpful to differentiate between 'Type 11a' and 'Type 11b' strategies. Type 11a strategies are characterized by a strategic focus on innovations in teaching and learning that are informed and supported by external knowledge and support. Examples of such school improvement strategies would be Joyce's *Models of Teaching* approach (Joyce et al., 1992, 1993). Type 11b strategies rely less on external support and tend to be more school initiated. Strategic school improvement programmes such as the 'Improving the Quality of Education for All' (IQEA) project outlined earlier (Hopkins et al., 1994), and the 'improvement through planning' approach described by the school inspectors in England and Wales (OFSTED, 1994), are pertinent examples.

3   Type 111 strategies are those that assist effective schools to remain so. In these instances external support, although often welcomed, is not necessary as the school searches out and creates its own support networks. Exposure to new ideas and practices, collaboration through consortia or 'pairing' type arrangements seem to be common in these situations. Examples of these types of school improvement strategies would be those described by Myers and Stoll (1993) in England, and school improvement projects such as the *League of Professional Schools (*Glickman, 1990) or the *Coalition of Essential Schools* (Sizer, 1992) in the USA. Of particular use to this group of schools might be the performance

indicator systems outlined by Fitz-Gibbon (1996) and noted in Chapter 9 of this handbook.

It is worth noting, then, that 'third wave' contextually specific improvement programmes that blend together aspects of SER and of school improvement research in ways appropriate to the context, effectiveness level, culture, capacity for improvement and personal characteristics of the staff employed at each school are likely to provide the way forward both for the generation of programmes which are 'potent' in affecting student outcomes, and for blends in practice of the two 'effectiveness' and 'improvement' paradigms that have formerly been separate but which will in future potentiate our understanding of both school effects and school change. Further speculations on 'context specific improvement' are in Hopkins and Harris (1997).

Conclusions

From a situation of considerable difference in paradigms, school effectiveness and school improvement have recently converged in their interests. The second wave of practice drew from both traditions and in turn moved beyond them, in its emphasis upon the need for reliability in implementation, its use of teacher effectiveness material and a learning level orientation, its concern to pragmatically pull all relevant levers and its concern with 'hard' outcomes data. More recently, the desire for school improvement to be context specific, with specific tailoring of interventions to the specific characteristics of the context, background and ecology of individual schools has further developed the 'second wave' of strategies into a 'third wave'.

One further possible development in the field is also beginning to impact upon the 'third wave' paradigm, which is the potential utility for improvement of 'off the shelf' models of improvement which do not require school invention or elaboration. The United States shows numbers of these such as those featured in the Special Strategies evaluation of Stringfield and colleagues (Stringfield et al., 1994a), including Slavin's *Success for All* initiative, the *Coalition of Essential Schools*, the *Comer Programme* and the *Paidea Programme*. Interestingly, there is evidence from the evaluation of the programmes that there is a more marked change in student outcomes from those programmes that have a strong pre-ordained 'technology' of programme 'levers' and interventions, than from those that expect schools to supply the content of the change (the Slavin programme would be an example of the former and the Coalition of Essential Schools would be an example of the latter). Whilst it is clear that the provision of strong technologies of intervention needs to respect the context specificity of individual schools that is a strong feature of 'third wave thinking' in this field, the potential re-conceptualizing of staff professional development activities towards the provision of foundational material may well be likely to replace the more 'do it yourself' discovery orientation that has characterized school improvement even in its second phase. It seems highly likely, then, that there is even more creative work in prospect with the arrival of 'third phase' school improvement.

8 School Effectiveness: The International Dimension

David Reynolds

Introduction

In these early stages of its development, school effectiveness research has shown heavily ethnocentric tendencies. Literatures referred to within books and articles have been usually almost exclusively based upon scholars and researchers within the country of origin of the writer (see Good and Brophy, 1986 for an American example, and Mortimore et al., 1988 for one from Great Britain). Although there has often been acknowledgment of the seminal American studies of Edmonds (1979a, 1979b), Brookover et al. (1979) and Coleman (1966) and of the British studies of Rutter et al. (1979) and Mortimore et al. (1988) in virtually all school effectiveness publications from all countries, there has clearly been no science of school effectiveness *across* countries as there has customarily been an international reach in the case of medicine, in most branches of psychology and in all of the 'applied' and 'pure' sciences.

The situation within which school effectiveness has been located is even more surprising, given that the sister discipline of school improvement/school development that we reviewed in Chapter 7 shows considerable evidence of a historic internationally established community. The review of the literature by Fullan (1991) for example shows awareness of developments in school improvement practice and theory in probably a dozen societies outside North America, and the review of improvement literature from Great Britain by Hopkins and colleagues shows considerable awareness of American, Canadian, Dutch, Norwegian, Australian and Swedish developments (Hopkins et al., 1994).

Part of the explanation for this 'ethnocentric' state of affairs within school effectiveness has probably been the absence of the specific institutional networks and professional associations/organizations that have made it possible for other disciplines to link internationally and to create context free normal science, with the agreed set of orientations, procedures and methodologies that exist across context. In the case of school improvement, the existence in the early to mid 1980s of the International School Effectiveness Research Project (ISIP) of Bollen and Hopkins (1987) probably explains the more international character of the field, in comparison with the absence of any such enterprises in the sister discipline of school effectiveness. Indeed, school effectiveness did not have until the early 1990s any professional association, professional journal or cross-national networks to integrate research and researchers from different countries. Only now do the International Congress for School Effectiveness and Improvement, the journal *School Effectiveness and School Improvement* and such networks as the Special Interest Group on School Effectiveness of the American Educational Research Association provide the institutional mechanisms to permit international normal science.

One of the features of the historic absence of cross-national communication within the field is the absence of recognition of what the existing internationally based educational effectiveness studies can contribute to our understanding (for speculations on this theme see Reynolds et al., 1994b). The cross national studies of the International Association for the Evaluation of Educational Achievement (IEA) and of the International Assessment of Educational Progress (IAEP) all have fascinating descriptions of cross national variation on achievement scores, together with limited though useful descriptions of classroom and school level processes that appear associated with the national differences (IEA examples are Anderson, L., et al., 1989; Postlethwaite and Wiley, 1992; Robitaille and Garden, 1989; IAEP examples are Keys and Foxman, 1989 and Lapointe et al., 1989).

However, these studies are rarely referenced or their insights used within the *national* research enterprises of the dozen or so countries where significant school effectiveness research is now in progress. Indeed, whilst there is synergy between school effectiveness research and such areas as educational policy, educational assessment and instructional concerns *within* most countries, there is no evidence within any country of engagement between school effectiveness and the comparative educational discipline or even with its concerns. Comparative education itself of course has a number of features that may make it less useful than it might be to the wider educational research community, including the presence of theories drawn up without apparent empirical reference, the absence of 'hard' outcome measures and the very widespread assumption that policy interventions on the educational policies of societies have corresponding effects on the nature of educational process and educational outcomes, a kind of 'for outcomes see policies' approach that is of very dubious intellectual validity (Altbach, 1991).

The Benefits of a Cross National Perspective

The absence of cross national perspectives and relationships between school effectiveness researchers, the neglect of internationally based research on educational achievement and the lack of interaction within societies with the comparative education discipline are all features of the present state of the school effectiveness discipline that must be seen as increasingly proving intellectually costly.

Firstly, the educational debates that are currently in evidence in many societies concerning the appropriate means of improving educational standards (in the United Kingdom, United States, Germany and Sweden to name but a few of the locations) are often based upon simplistic 'transplants' of knowledge from one culture to another, without any detailed acknowledgment in the political or educational policy debate as to the possible context specificity of the apparently 'effective' policies in the original societies utilizing them. Examples of this have been the proposed transplant into the United Kingdom of German schools' links with industry and their organizational commitment to vocational education, which are assumed to be effective and functional within the British context even though Britain has progressively eradicated the apprenticeship system and has historically given very low status to 'applied' knowledge to industrial employment (see Smithers and Robinson, 1991; Prais and Wagner, 1965).

A further example would be the proposed lengthening of the school day and the proposed shortening of school holidays discussed in some American states, because of the popularity of explanations of Japan's educational effectiveness that point to high 'time to learn' as the explanation (e.g. *Business Week*, 14 September 1992).

A final example of simple translation of findings from one culture to another is the current British enthusiasm for whole class direct instruction at Key Stage Two (ages 7–11) in British primary schools, clearly based upon an enthusiasm for the educational practices of the Pacific Rim and the making of an association between their high levels of achievement and their classroom practices (Lynn, 1988). The same enthusiasm has also been clear in the United States (Stevenson and Stigler, 1992).

Simply, in an era when educational policy prescriptions are travelling internationally with increasing frequency, it is unfortunate that school effectiveness researchers still seem locked into a mind set that can handle only the patterns of intakes, processes and outcomes of their own cultures.

The second reason for the importance of internationally based perspectives in school effectiveness is that we need to understand much more about why some utilized variables 'travel' in explaining effectiveness across countries, whilst others do not. Assertive principal instructional leadership is perhaps one of the most well supported of all the American 'correlates' that lie within the range of the 'five factor' theory originally formulated by Edmonds (1979a, 1979b) and subsequently developed into the 'seven factor' theory by Lezotte (1989), yet in spite of the massive empirical support for the importance of this factor in the United States (e.g. Levine and Lezotte, 1990), Dutch researchers have been generally unable to validate its importance within the differing Dutch educational and social climate (apparently Dutch principals are often promoted out of the existing school staff and have a much more facilitative, group based and perhaps 'democratic' attitude to their colleagues). (For a review of Dutch findings see Table 8.1 and the confirmatory empirical study of van de Grift, 1990, which was conducted after the review was published in Creemers and Scheerens, 1989, p.695.)

Other examples are numerous. From the area of research upon developing societies, Lockheed and Komenar (1989) report on the relationship between various instructional variables and student achievement outcomes in the two societies of Swaziland and Nigeria. The two countries exhibit very similar test scores for their samples of students, generated by very similar exposure to schooling (188 and 193 days respectively). However, the precise instructional factors associated with the two countries similar scores are very different, with the Nigerian classes exhibiting a greater concentration upon routine administration/keeping order, direct instruction in both previously covered and new material, testing and grading, and lesser concentration upon student seatwork or blackboard based time.

What explains how similar test scores can be generated by *different* instructional factors in different contexts? Only an appreciation of different contexts and the interaction between instructional (and school) factors and varying contexts is likely to tell us (see Table 8.2 for further details).

A re-analysis of the IEA's Second International Mathematics study by Scheerens et

Table 8.1 An overview of recent Dutch school effectiveness studies

Indicator Author	General Measure of School Climate	Educational Leadership	Orderly Climate	Basic Skills	High Expecta-tions	Frequent Evaluation	Private/ Public Distinction	Direct Instruction	Achievement Orientation
Meijnen, 1985	+								
Marwijk-Kooy, 1985*			+		+	+	+	+	
Hoeven van Doornum Jungbluth, 1987							+		
Stoel, 1986*			+			+			
Bosker Hofman, 1987									+
Brandsma Stoel, 1987		+				+			
Vermeulen, 1987			+						
Tesser, 1985*									
Van der Wolf, 1985								+	
Brandsma Knuver, 1988							+		
Van der Werf Tesser, 1989					+	+			+
De Jong, 1988									+

Note: *Secondary schools: unmarked: Primary schools; + means significant positive relationship with effectiveness indicator.

Source: Scheerens et al., 1989c.

Table 8.2 Variable names, descriptions, means and standard deviations for Nigeria and Swaziland

Variable	Description	Nigeria (N = 700)	Swaziland (N = 587)
SCORE	Student's core test score	14.36 (5.80)	12.92 (6.94)
Background			
YSEX	Student's sex (0 = male; 1 = female)	0.24 (0.43)	0.58 (0.49)
YAGE	Student's age in months	196.20 (20.84)	185.83 (20.30)
YPROF	1 = Father has professional occupation	(0.21) (0.41)	0.13 (0.34)
YPERCEV	Student's self-perception of mathematics ability	3.18 (1.19)	3.91 (1.30)
YMOREED	Years more education expected	3.64 (1.00)	3.26
YMOTIV	Motivation to work hard and do well in mathematics	n.a.	4.18 (1.52)
YPARSUP	Perceived parental support	3.66 (1.53)	n.a.
RURAL	1 = School in rural area	0.22 (0.41)	0.31 (0.46)
School			
ISENROL	School size (no. of students enrolled in the school)	1054.2 (354.5)	374.23 (139.86)
ISDAYSYR	Length of school year in days	188.03 (14.04)	191.02 (0.72)
SINGMALE	1 = All male school	0.41 (0.49)	0.03 (0.18)
SINGFEM	1 = All female school	0.10 (0.30)	0.14 (0.35)
Teacher/Class			
TNSTUDS	Class size (no. of students enrolled in class)	34.92 (15.05)	38.15 (6.73)
TEXPTCH	Teacher's experience (in years)	8.04 (9.10)	4.78 (4.73)
TEDMATH	Semesters post-secondary mathematics education	3.61 (1.44)	2.97 (2.75)
AVYFPROF	% of professional fathers in each class	0.21 (0.17)	0.12 (0.12)
Teaching Process			
TADMNTASK	Weekly minutes for routine adminitration and maintaining order	70.46 (63.68)	30.60 (28.15)
TINSTASK	Weekly minutes for explaining new material and reviewing old material	117.22 (106.36)	28.38 (45.19)
TMONEVAT	Weekly minutes for testing and grading	162.04 (115.22)	138.21 (39.14)
TLISTL	Weekly minutes students spent listening to whole class lectures	37.70 (33.60)	36.17 (27.47)
TSEATL	Weekly minutes students spent at seat or blackboard	42.28 (38.03)	57.79 (44.59)
TPERSMAT	Use of personally produced teaching materials	5.51 (0.84)	4.55 (1.14)

Table 8.2 Continued

Variable	Description	Nigeria (N = 700)	Swaziland (N = 587)
TPUBMAT	Use of commercially published teaching material	8.76 (1.66)	9.57 (1.68)
OTL	Opportunity to learn (number of test questions covered by teacher during current academic year)	11.40 (10.95)	10.41 (5.38)

Source: Lockheed and Komenan 1989.

al. (1989) also suggests interestingly different problems of relationships between school process variables and mathematics achievement within different societies. Table 8.3 shows, for example that the giving of homework is negatively associated with achievement within the Netherlands but not in most other countries. Similarly, class size is positively associated with achievement in the French speaking part of Belgium but negatively associated within the Flemish speaking portion of the country. Scotland has only three significant associations of process variables with achievement – Sweden has nine.

Indeed, it is a review of 'what travels' and 'what does not travel', in terms of types of school and types of instructional factors has generated what is one of the most interesting and provocative new ideas within school effectiveness, since it is apparently the *instructional* variables such as time on task, opportunity to learn, structured teaching and high expectations that apply in explaining variance across countries much more than do the standard *school* factors customarily used (see Scheerens et al., 1989 for further information on this). The fascinating possibility that one needs *different* types of school regimes within different countries to generate *the same* effective classroom processes is a potentially devastatingly important insight. Again, one does not get advanced thinking of this kind from the restricted variation of one's own national research base.

A further example of the potential of these international studies to further our educational speculations in interesting ways is the Meuret and Scheerens (1995) classification of educational systems according to the proportion of decisions in which the school was involved, which generated New Zealand (>70 per cent) and Switzerland (20 per cent) as the two 'extreme' countries, yet both countries generated the very highest reading test scores in the OECD/CERI *Education at a Glance* publication (1993).

It is clear that these interesting patterns of differing relationships between processes and outcomes within different countries can add considerably to our stock of knowledge if they are used to generate a search for their explanation. This variation in 'what works' is likely to in its turn generate a need for more sensitive theoretical explanations than those at present on offer, since the variation by national context that clearly exists in the nature of the 'causal' effectiveness factors literally forces the development of more sensitive, context specific explanations than the present 'streampress' associations that are generated within countries by their nationally based research groups.

The third reason for the importance of an internationally based perspective is that only international studies can tap the full range of variation in school and classroom quality, and therefore in potential school and classroom effects. *Within* any country

Table 8.3 Factors associated with effectiveness in different countries

Predictor Variable*	Belgium (FL)	Belgium (Fr)	Canada (BC)	Canada (Ont)	Finland	France	Hong Kong	Hungary	Israel	Japan	Luxembourg
	15	16	22	25	39	40	43	44	50	54	59
Father's occupation	m	m		p	p	p		p	m		
Father's education									p		
Level of expected further education	p	p	p	p	p	p	p	m	p	p	p
Homework			n				p	p	p	p	
Teacher experience					p	p					p
Time spent keeping order			n		n	n					
Time spent on teaching	p						p				
Teacher expectations			p	p	p	p	p	p	p		p
Use of published tests		p			p			p			
Use of own tests								n			
Opportunity to learn	p	m		p			p	m		p	p
Class size	n	p			p	p					
Urbanization		p						m	p		
Number of female teachers	p										n
Number of male teachers	p								p		
Number of meetings											

* Predictor Variables with significant Positive (p) or Negative (n) Associations with Mathematics Achievement.

Note: School and classroom variables are corrected for father's occupation or father's education—when a predictor variable was not measured in a country this is indicated by the letter m.

Source: Scheerens et al., 1989c.

the range in school factors in terms of 'quantity' variables (such as size, financial resources, quality of buildings etc.) and in terms of 'quality' factors (such as teacher experience, school press for achievement etc.) is likely to be much smaller than when the *between* country variation is added by means of either analysing countries together by aggregating existing national studies in forms of meta-analysis (with re-coding maybe) or if countries are surveyed using identical measures in unique studies, as is the case with the IEA studies.

Put simply, it is likely that the existing estimates we have concerning the size of educational influences (schools and classrooms together) upon students (which have settled into a range of from 8 per cent to 14 per cent of variance explained in virtually all of the recent empirical studies, see Chapter 3) are potentially merely artefacts of the studies' lack of school and classroom variation. The true power of school and classroom variables are, if this reasoning is correct, only likely to be shown by cross cultural and comparative work on international samples (see Chapter 12 for further discussion).

The fourth reason why educational researchers could gain considerable benefits if there was an internationalization of the field is that international study is likely to generate more sensitive theoretical explanations than those at present on offer. The present day situation within school effectiveness displays an absence of theoretical explanations of even a middle range variety and the reason why an international perspective may generate both intellectually interesting *and* practical middle range theories is connected with the ways in which school and classroom factors travel cross culturally to a very varied degree, as noted in the previous point. Why is it that 'assertive principal instructional leadership' does not predict effective school status in the Netherlands – what is it in the local, regional or national ecology that might explain this finding? Answering this question inevitably involves the generation of more complex theoretical explanations that operate on a number of 'levels' of the educational system/society interaction and is likely to be generative of more complex, sensitive and multilayered explanations than those generated by the simple *within* country research findings.

The Contribution from Developing Society Studies

To the potentially useful insights into the conceptualization, operationalization and measurement problems of our discipline in Britain come also the contributions of the large number of studies done on Third World, or developing, societies. Reviews of this literature are available in Fuller (1987), Avalos (1980), Fuller and Heynemann (1989), Walberg (1991) and Lockheed and Verspoor (1990), and the empirical database now consists of over 60 studies (those of importance include Lockheed and Longford, 1989 and Riddell, 1989).

It must be admitted that the validity and utility of the knowledge is severely limited by a number of faults in the design of the studies:

- Only two of the total number utilize multilevel methodologies (those of Riddell, 1989, in Zimbabwe and by Lockheed and Longford, 1989, in Thailand).
- Very few of the studies have prior controls for student achievement (or even basic student ability) to add to the parental SES measures that are usually employed, which magnifies the potential unsuitability of the data.
- The issue of constrained variance is important, particularly in studies undertaken at secondary school level, since in many developing societies only a small fraction of the student cohort enters these schools at all, with the high selectivity generating highly restricted variance in the background of the pupil samples, restricting the power of the home background.
- The body of knowledge is almost exclusively derived from cross-sectional studies, rather than from cohort studies in which the *same* pupils are studied over time.

Fuller (1987) summarizes the findings of these studies, flawed as they are, in Table 8.4.

However, in spite of their methodological problems, the developing country findings are interesting in two respects for the British school effectiveness community. Firstly, the effects of educational processes upon student achievement are very much larger in these studies than in other studies. Heynemann and Loxley (1983) looked at 16 'developing' and 13 'developed' societies, in terms of the relative influence of family background and school/classroom factors on science achievement. In developing societies, the block of school factor variables (covering such factors as textbook availability, teachers' own educational achievement and the length of the instructional

Table 8.4 Factors affecting achievement in developing societies

School Quality Indicator	Expected Direction of Relationship	Total no. of Analyses	No. of Analyses Confirming Effect
School Expenditures			
1 Expenditures per pupil	+	11	6
2 Total school expenditures	+	5	2
Specific Material Inputs			
3 Class size	−	21	5
4 School size	+	9	4
5 Instructional material			
Texts and reading materials	+	24	16
Desk	+	3	3
6 Instructional media (radio)	+	3	3
7 School building quality	+	3	2
8 Library size and activity	+	18	15
9 Science laboratories	+	11	4
10 Nutrition and feeding programmes	+	6	5
Teacher Quality			
11 Teacher's length of schooling			
Total years of teacher's schooling	+	26	12
Years of tertiary and teacher training	+	31	22
12 Inservice teacher training	+	6	5
13 Teacher's length of experience	+	23	10
14 Teacher's verbal proficiency	+	2	1
15 Teacher's salary level	+	14	5
16 Teacher's social class background	+	10	7
17 School's percentage of full-time teachers	+	2	1
18 Teacher's punctuality and (low) absenteeism	+	2	0
Teaching Practices/Classroom Organization			
19 Length of instructional programme	+	14	12
20 Homework frequency	+	8	6
21 Active learning by students	+	3	1
22 Teacher's expectations of pupil performance	+	3	3
23 Teacher's time spent on class preparation	+	5	4
School Management			
24 Quality of principal	+	7	4
25 Multiple shifts of classes each day	−	3	1
26 Student boarding	+	4	3
27 Student repetition of grade	+	5	1

Source: Fuller, 1987.

programme) explained 27 per cent of the variance in achievement in east India and 25 per cent in Thailand (compared to the family background variables' contribution of 3 per cent and 6 per cent respectively). For the 29 countries analysed together, the correlation between GNP per capita and the proportion of student variance explained by school factors was 0.66.

Secondly, the factors themselves that are associated with student achievement in developing societies are interestingly different to those which have been conventionally used within the western research paradigm. Walberg (1991) concludes that the factors promoting science achievement are: (the percentage is of the number of total studies reviewed):

Length of Instructional Programmes	86%
Pupil Feeding	83%
School Library Activity	83%
Years of Teacher Training	71%
Textbook and Instructional Materials	67%

Low effectiveness generating factors are:

Science Laboratories	36%
Teacher Salaries	36%
Reduced Class Size	24%
Pupil Grade Repetition	20%

What are the implications of this research base for the school effectiveness community? Firstly, the developing society studies suggest a need to measure more resource based variables such as financial resources, availability of textbooks, equipment and the like, particularly since Britain now may evidence as much variation in the quantity and quality of these resources as some developing societies (the variation in per capita expenditure per head in the United States is also now estimated to be across States up to a factor of 9). Also, for many resource variables it is possible that provision in some advanced industrial societies like that in developing societies is now *below* the threshold above which resource variables did not formerly have effects (because of the relative abundance of resources in all schools).

Secondly, the importance of teacher quality variables in developing society settings where there are huge variations in training, competencies and initial ability levels of teachers in the different strands of training may be interesting in those societies, like the United Kingdom, in which governments are introducing differentiated 'routes' into teaching.

The Contribution of Cross National Studies

The third and final set of international school effectiveness studies that we consider in this paper are the cross national studies conducted by the International Association for the Education of Evaluation Achievement (IEA), and those conducted by the Educational Testing Services and entitled the International Assessment of Educational Progress (IAEP). The studies themselves are of course numerous, as are commentaries, critiques and reviews of them – indeed, one of the more surprising strands running through the assessments of their studies made by members of the IEA teams is their evident pleasure at the impact that their studies have had as measured by media interest, articles on the work in popular magazines and the like (see for example Noah, 1987). Briefly, the IEA has conducted the *First and Second Science Studies* (Comber and Keeves (1973); Rosier and Keeves (1991); Postlethwaite and Wiley (1992); Keeves (1992), the *First and Second Mathematics Studies* (Husen 1967; Travers and Westbury, (1989); Robitaille and Garden (1989), the *Study of Written Composition* (Purves, 1992) and the *Classroom Environment Study* mentioned earlier (Anderson, L., et al., 1989). Recent projects include the major TIMSS study (the Third International Mathematics and Science Study). The IAEP has conducted a first study of science and mathematics achievement cross culturally (Lapointe et al., 1989; Keys and Foxman, 1989), and the IEA has published the findings of the *First Literacy Study* (Elley, 1992; Postlethwaite and Ross, 1992).

From this vast number of studies, what general conclusions can we make about the utility and usefulness of the findings for use in the school effectiveness community?

Firstly, the general picture shown by the studies is of large variations between countries on their mathematics and science achievement, as shown in the Tables 8.5 and 8.6 from the IAEP studies of mathematics and science.

A full outline of all IEA and IAEP studies is available in Table 8.7.

We will consider the usefulness of the studies in furthering our knowledge, though, after we have assessed the numerous technical and methodological problems that are evident from the structure, design and analyses of the studies themselves.

All studies in this field have two basic problems – societies must be compared in their performance on the *same* skills, bodies of knowledge or tests, and attempts must be made to ensure that the *educational* causes of any differences must be isolated from any other possible causes of country differences.

The majority of the studies referred to in this chapter have attempted to solve the first of the above two problems by using achievement tests of bodies of school knowledge, mathematics and science tests, where there are the same definitions of what is the 'right' answer cross culturally.

Turning to the other problem, one way to 'control out' non-educational influences has been to use a 'cohort' design. Cross-sectional studies of the kind that generated Tables 8.5 and 8.6 below obtain measurements *at a point in time*, and then have to disentangle the various educational, social, economic and cultural influences that were responsible over historic time. By contrast, cohort studies that look at children *over time* can study the relative gains children make, after allowing for the various different starting points in different countries. The 'true' effect of education can then be calculated by 'controlling out' the background factors that are non-educational, leaving the 'true' educational effectiveness of different systems compared. The expense and complicated nature of these 'cohort' studies means, though, that they have been rarely used. The Third International Mathematics and Science Study (TIMMS) had planned such a design as well as a cross-sectional methodology, without English participation, in the attempt to discern the true 'added value' generated by our educational provision. Given the problems involved in the longitudinal element of the Second International Mathematics study (SIMS) (Garden, 1987), including limited participation, limited objectives and use of a very short time period, one can see why this did not occur.

That educational systems and their operation are implicated in the patterns of results shown by the various studies is highly likely however. On the patterns of results obtained from one of the IEA studies of Science (Postlethwaite and Wiley, 1992), England performs quite poorly by comparison with other countries at ages 10 and 14, but then performs very well comparatively with students in their final year of school-

Table 8.5 Percentage correct items for various countries IAEP Maths

	Mathematics	
	Age 9	Age 13
Western Europe		
England	59	61
France	—	64
Ireland	60	61
Italy (Emilia Romagna)	68	64
Portugal	55	48
Scotland	66	61
Spain	62	55
Switzerland	—	71
Eastern Europe		
Hungary	68	68
Slovenia	56	57
Soviet Union	66	70
North America		
Canada	60	62
United States	58	55
South America		
Brazil (Sao Paulo and Fortaleza)	—	35
Middle East		
Israel	64	63
Jordan	—	40
Far East		
China	—	80
Korea	75	73
Taiwan	68	73
Africa		
Mozambique (Maputo and Beira)	—	28
IAEP Average	63	58

Source: Foxman, 1992.

ing. No family 'sleeper' effect could be responsible for an overall rank of seventeenth out of 19 countries at age 14, but fourth out of 12 countries at age 18. No cultural factors have yet been determined that could amount for this pattern. What it is likely to reflect is an English system of education which is highly selective and with a low retention rate.

Although the two problems noted above place limitations on the capacity of existing international surveys of achievement to definitively address the issue, 'Which countries are more effective educationally and what is the educational contribution?' it is important to note that there are further limitations upon the IEA and IAEP achievement studies of the last 20 years (see for further discussion Goldstein, 1989, 1993; and Reynolds et al., 1994b).

There are of course the problems in these surveys that are present in all cross-national research – of accurate translation of material, of ensuring reliability in the

Table 8.6 Overall average percentage correct of all participants
IAEP Science

	Age 9	Age 13
Western Europe		
England	63	69
France	—	69
Ireland	57	63
Italy (Emilia Romagna)	67	70
Portugal	55	63
Scotland	62	68
Spain	62	68
Switzerland	—	74
Eastern Europe		
Hungary	63	73
Slovenia	58	70
Soviet Union	62	71
North America		
Canada	63	69
United States	65	67
South America		
Brazil (Sao Paulo and Fortaleza)	—	50
Middle East		
Israel	61	70
Jordan	—	57
Far East		
China	—	67
Korea	68	78
Taiwan	67	76
Africa		
Mozambique (Maputo and Beira)	—	—
IAEP Average	62	67

Source: Foxman, 1992.

'meaning' of questionnaire items (such as social class or status indicators for example), of problems caused by southern hemisphere countries having their school years begin in January and of problems caused because of retrospective information being required from teachers and principals.

In certain curriculum areas, the cross national validity of the tests themselves gives cause for grave concern, especially since the IEA study of written composition failed in its attempt to compare the rated performance of groups of students in different national systems that used different languages. The latter study concluded that 'The construct that we call written composition must be seen in a cultural context and not considered a general cognitive capacity or activity' (Purves, 1992, p.199). Even the basic administration of an achievement test in the varying cultural contexts of different countries may pose problems, particularly in the case of England where the 'test mode' in which closed questions are asked in an examination style format under

Table 8.7 The IEA and IAEP international studies of educational achievement

Year of Data Collection	Sponsor	Ages of Pupils	Curriculum Topics (number of countries/systems)	Countries
1964	IEA FIMS	13 +final yr.	*Mathematics* (12)	Australia, Belgium, *England*, Finland, France, Germany, Israel, Japan, Netherlands, Scotland, Sweden, United States
1970–2	IEA FISS	10, 13 +final yr.	*Science*(19), *Reading Comprehension* (15), *Literature* (10), and English Foreign Languages (18), Civic Education (10)	Australia, Belgium (Flemish), Belgium (French), Chile, *England and Wales*, Federal Republic of Germany, Finland, France, Hungary, India, Iran, Ireland, Israel, Italy, Japan, Netherlands, New Zealand, Romania, Scotland, Sweden, United States
1980–2	IEA	10–14	Classroom Environment (Mathematics, Science, History) (10)	Australia, Canada, Federal Republic of Germany, Hungary, Israel, Korea, Netherlands, Nigeria, Thailand
1982–3	IEA SIMS	13 +final yr.	*Mathematics* (20)	Belgium (Flemish), Belgium (French), British Columbia, *England and Wales*, Finland, France, Hong Kong, Hungary, Israel, Japan, Luxembourg, Netherlands, New Zealand, Nigeria, Ontario, Scotland, Swaziland, Sweden, Thailand, United States
1984	IEA SISS	10, 14 +final yr.	*Science* (24)	Australia, Canada (English speaking), Canada (French speaking), China, *England*, Finland, Ghana, Hong Kong, Hungary, Israel, Italy, Japan, Korea, Mexico, Netherlands, Nigeria, Norway, Papua New Guinea, Philippines, Poland, Singapore, Sweden, Tanzania, Thailand, United States, Zimbabwe
1984–5	IEA	10, 14–16 +final yr.	*Written Composition* (14)	Chile, *England*, Federal Republic of Germany, Finland, Hungary, Indonesia, Italy, Netherlands, New Zealand, Nigeria, Sweden, Thailand, United States, Wales
1988	IAEP IAEPM 1 IAEPS 1	13	Mathematics (6), Science (6)	Canada, Ireland, Korea, Spain, *United Kingdom*, United States
1988–92	IEA	10, 13	Computers in Education (21)	Austria, Belgium (Flemish), Belgium (French), Canada, China, France, Federal Republic of

Table 8.7 Continued

Year of Data Collection	Sponsor	Ages of Pupils	Curriculum Topics (number of countries/systems)	Countries
				Germany, Greece, Hungary, India, Israel, Italy, Japan, Luxembourg, Netherlands, New Zealand, Poland, Portugal, Slovenia, Switzerland, United States
1988–95	IEA	4	Pre-primary (14) Education	Belgium (French), Germany, Finland, Hong Kong, Hungary, Italy, Kenya, Nigeria, The Peoples Republic of China, Philippines, Portugal, Spain, Thailand, US
1990	IAEP IAEPM 2 IAEPS 2	9, 13	Mathematics (20), Science (20)	Brazil, Canada, China, *England*, France, Hungary, Ireland, Israel, Italy, Jordan, Korea, Mozambique, Portugal, Scotland, Slovenia, Soviet Union, Spain, Switzerland, Taiwan, United States
1991	IEA	9, 14	Reading Literacy (31)	Belgium (French), Botswana, Canada (BC), Cyprus, Denmark, Finland, France, Germany (E), Germany (W), Greece, Hong Kong, Hungary, Iceland, Indonesia, Ireland, Italy, Netherlands, New Zealand, Nigeria, Norway, Philippines, Portugal, Singapore, Slovenia, Spain, Sweden, Switzerland, Thailand, Trinidad/Tobago, US, Venezuela, Zimbabwe
1993/94 1996/97	TIMSS	9, 13, 17	Mathematics and Science (41)	Austria, Australia, Belgium (Flemish), Belgium (French), Botswana, Bulgaria, Canada, Chile, Cyprus, Czech Rep., Slovakia, Denmark, *England*, France, Germany, Greece, Hong Kong, Hungary, Iceland, Indonesia, Ireland, Israel, Italy, Japan, Korea, Luxembourg, Netherlands, New Zealand, Norway, Poland, Portugal, Romania, Singapore, Spain, Sweden, Switzerland, Thailand, United States, USSR, Yugoslavia

Note: Final school year (FY) generally assumes pre-university year—in the case of England this would be the second year of an A-Level course. Obviously the age of this sample varies between countries.

Source: Reynolds and Farrell, 1996.

time pressure may not approximate to students' experience of school. By contrast, the use of this test mode within a society such as Taiwan, where these assessment methods are frequently experienced, may inflate Taiwanese scores, just as it may depress English achievement levels below their 'real' levels.

In addition to these basic problems that affect all large scale international comparative research, there are specific problems concerning the IEA and IAEP studies:

Research Design

- The basic design of the IEA studies, which are concerned to explain country against country variation, may itself have been responsible for problems. Generally a small number of schools each possessing a large number of students are selected, which makes it difficult to make valid comparisons between schools once factors such as school type, socio economic status of students and catchment areas are taken into account. Statistics may also be unstable because of small numbers.
- Curriculum subjects are studied separately, making an integrated picture of schools in different countries difficult.
- There is considerable difficulty in designing tests which sample the curricula in all countries acceptably.

Sampling

- There are very large variations in the response rates that make interpretation of scores difficult. In the IAEP, for example, school participation rates of those schools originally approached varied from 70 per cent to 100 per cent across countries, and student participation rates varied similarly from 73 per cent to 98 per cent. In the IEA Second Science Study, the student response rate varied from 99.05 per cent (in Japan) to 61.97 per cent (in England). Although all IEA and IAEP studies have been weighted to take account of differential response between strata, and although a comparison of responding and non-responding schools on public examinations showed little difference, the potential biases caused by variation in response rates are a matter of considerable concern.
- Sometimes samples of pupils used are not representative of the country as a whole (e.g. one area of Italy was used as a surrogate for the whole country in one of the IAEP studies).
- Sometimes also there are variations as to when during the school year tests are administered, resulting in pupils of different mean ages in different countries.
- Choice of certain 'grades' or ages for sampling, may not generate similar populations for study from different countries. In the IEA Second Science Study, the mean ages of the country samples for the '14 year old' students ranged from 13.9 to 15.1 years. Given the known relationships between age, length of time in school and achievement, this variation may have been responsible for some of the country differences.
- Policies in different countries concerning 'keeping children down' or 'putting children up a year' may generate difficulties of comparison.
- Variations between countries in the proportion of their children who took part in the studies makes assessment of country differences difficult. Mislevy (1995) notes that whilst 98 per cent of American children were in the sampling frame and

eligible to take part in one study, the restriction of an Israeli sample to Hebrew speaking public schools generated only 71 per cent of total children being in eligible schools.

- Sampling of students is usually restricted to so called 'normal' schools, yet there are considerable variations between societies in the proportion of an age cohort that are not within 'normal' schooling. Some societies such as the Netherlands have perhaps 4 or 5 per cent of children at 'special schools' of various kinds – other societies like Sweden or Norway do not even have the 'special schools'. There remains doubt, therefore, as to whether 'like is being compared with like'.

An Absence of Needed Data

- In many studies there is a lack of information upon the non-school areas of children's lives (family and home environment) that might have explained achievement scores. Surrogates for social class utilized such as 'number of books in the home' are not adequate.
- Outcome data has been collected exclusively on the academic outcomes of schooling yet social outcomes may be equally interesting. It is clear from the Stevenson (1992) studies that the 'superiority' of Japanese students over other societies may extend to areas such as children's perception of their control over their lives (locus of control), yet these 'affective' outcomes have been neglected. The explanation for this is clear (the problems of cross-cultural validity and reliability) but it is not clear why routinely available non-cognitive data (such as that on student attendance for example) has not been used as surrogate measures.
- The factors used to describe schools have often been overly resource-based, (because of the greater perceived chance of obtaining reliability between observers across countries no doubt), in spite of the clearly limited explanatory power of such variables. At classroom level only some studies (including TIMMS) have used student attitude measures.
- Some of the most important educational effects are likely to lie in the areas of the 'moral messages' that the humanities subjects, like history, geography and civics, possess and which are integrated with their curriculum content. These differences, which formed the basis of the fascinating analysis by Bronfenbrenner (1972) of variations between the United States and the former Soviet Union in the propensity of their students to be pro-social or anti-social, would probably repay study, but have not been studied because of the clear difficulties of any investigation.
- Variation within societies at the regional, district, *Länder* or local education authority level is inadequately explored, a consequence of sampling procedure and of the 'nation versus nation' orientation.

An Absence of Needed Analyses

- Only limited attempts have been made to analyse student groups differentially, by achievement say or by social class, with the exception of a limited amount of analysis by gender.
- Neither IEA nor IAEP studies have made much attempt to explain their findings.

The Benefits of International Effectiveness Research

From all these points above, it will be clear that the large scale surveys of achievement of the IAEP and the IEA need to be subject to some caution as to the validity of their findings. Not all studies possess the same design, analysis and methodological problems : no studies possess all the design, analysis and methodological problems in total. Enough studies possess enough of the problems, though, to make one cautious about interpretation.

Given these weighty sets of limitations, it may be seen to be overly optimistic to conclude that the international comparative school effectiveness literature has any use for us at all. Nonetheless, their importance is in alerting us to the possibility of having to confront issues of context specificity, and of having to attend to issues that relate to that.

Take, for example the IEA's *Second International Mathematics Study*. Re-analysis by Scheerens et al. (1989) leads to the following estimates of the variance explained by schools and classes within different countries (see Table 8.8).

In some countries (as for example Sweden) the simultaneous estimation of effects shows that school effects are non-existent when the classroom effect is accounted for. What can explain this – the Swedish system's historically strong control over the organization of schooling or the possible absence of student balance effects because of homogeneous school intakes from administratively defined balanced catchment areas? Whatever the precise explanation, the re-analysis confronts us with findings of differences to explain, and forces us to generate theoretical explanations for those differences which link the schools, the meso level local context and the national macro level of educational policy.

Table 8.8 Variance explained within countries

Country	Classroom Variance Component	School Variance Component
15 Belgium (Flemish)		0.50 (0.48)
16 Belgium (French)		0.64 (0.62)
22 Canada (British Columbia)		0.27 (0.27)
25 Canada (Ontario)	0.18 (0.17)	0.09 (0.09)
39 Finland	0.45 (0.41)	0.002
40 France	0.17 (0.16)	0.06 (0.05)
43 Hong Kong		0.51 (0.50)
44 Hungary		0.30 (0.27)
50 Israel	0.22 (0.21)	0.10 (0.08)
54 Japan		0.08 (0.07)
59 Luxembourg	0.29 (0.29)	0.15 (0.15)
62 Netherlands		0.67 (0.66)
63 New Zealand	0.45 (0.42)	0.01 (0.004)
72 Scotland	0.34 (0.31)	0.12 (0.05)
76 Sweden	0.45 (0.45)	0.00
79 Thailand		0.39 (0.38)
81 USA	0.46 (0.45)	0.10 (0.09)

Note: Estimates of the variance explained by schools and classes.

Source: Scheerens et al., 1989c.

A further example of potentially fruitful data to relate to is that derived from the *Classroom Environment Study* (Anderson, L. et al., 1989). In this study, observed classroom activities and teacher behaviours tend to exert virtually no influence upon student achievement, since successful teaching is affected by a variety of cultural and contextual factors. When the variables of class size, years of teaching experience, teachers' expectations of students' abilities, direct teaching, questioning policy and classroom management were added to student variables, the percentage of variance explained in various countries increased from 0 per cent to 2 per cent (in a range of from 34 to 56 per cent already explained). Again, the analysis of the patterns whereby variables influence scores differently within each country, and why, would make for fascinating study.

A further use of international comparative studies of educational achievement is to give descriptions of 'good practice' that might usefully illuminate directions for the nationally based communities to conduct research. One must beware, of course, that one does not violate the complex interactions between the cultures, societies and educational systems of different countries by proposing transplants from one society of practices that are present in the more 'highly achieving' one.

However, the experience of the still small number of studies that have attempted to do this is that attempted descriptions of the nature of educational processes, the societal cultures and the interactions or transactions between these levels that can be conducted within contextually sensitive international theorizing can be potentially rewarding in enhancing our understanding.

Exemplary Countries

A classic case of this is the presence in international surveys of 'outlier' regions or countries which appear to score highly on the achievement surveys used. These societies appear to be particularly in the Pacific Rim, with Korea, Japan and Taiwan often used as examples, and appear also to exist within Europe, with Germany, Hungary and particularly Switzerland used as examples. What factors appear to be associated with these 'successful' societies?

It is widely agreed that a variety of factors are implicated in the high achievement scores. To take cultural factors first, these have been argued to be (Stevenson and Stigler, 1992; Her Majesty's Inspectorate, 1992; Thomas, R. and Postlethwaite, 1983):

- The high status of teachers within societies that because of religious and cultural traditions place a high value upon learning and education, together with salary levels that are more favourable relative to other professional and non-professional salaries than in Europe and North America.
- The cultural stress reflecting Confucian beliefs about the role of effort, the importance of an individual's striving and working hard, and the use of the educational system as a planned and stably resourced instrument of nation building.
- The high aspirations of parents for their children (Stevenson (1992) reports Taiwanese parents as more dissatisfied with school than Americans!).
- The recruitment of able students to become teachers, with intakes into training that are the equal of other students in terms of average achievement levels. Particularly important is argued to be the route to upward social mobility that

teaching is said to offer clever rural born children, clever girls and boys from low socio economic status homes.

- High levels of commitment from children to doing well at school.

Systemic factors are argued to be as follows:

- High quantities of time, with Korea and Taiwan for example having 222 days in school per year, compared to the English 192 and with school days in the Pacific Rim being longer. Time available is also enhanced by the high proportion of students attending 'cramming' institutions in the evenings and by the use of homework from as young as age 6.
- The prevalent belief that all children are able to acquire certain core skills in core subjects, and that there is no need for a trailing edge of low performing pupils. This is argued to contrast with the belief in western societies in the normal distribution, a belief reflecting the considerable influence of the psychometric paradigm, with its elongated tail and 'built in' failure of 50 per cent of the distribution to acquire more than the average level of skill.
- Concentration upon a small number of attainable goals, mostly of an academic variety or concerned with the individual's relationship to society, rather than spreading effort widely across many academic, social, affective and moral goals.

School factors are argued to be:

- mixed ability classes in the early years of school, where all children receive basic skills in an egalitarian setting, and where children learn to value the importance of the group and of cooperation;
- the use of specialist teachers;
- the possibility of teachers working collaboratively with each other, facilitated by teachers having approximately one third of their time out of the classroom;
- frequent testing of pupils' skills in core subjects, which is likely to enhance student attainment on achievement tests obviously, but is also beneficial in that it creates high quality information upon student, teacher and school functioning. In particular, frequent monitoring makes possible short term operation of feedback loops, with corrective action at the level of the child or teacher being possible much more quickly than in the English system, where monitoring of this kind is much rarer;
- direct quality monitoring by the principal of the work of teachers, by means of random sampling once or twice a term of the homework books of all children in the school in Taiwanese elementary schools for example.

Classroom factors are argued to be:

- mechanisms to ensure that things are taught properly first time around, and that there is no 'trailing edge' of children who have to be returned to (an example from Taiwan is that children have to repeat in their homework books, at the beginning of their next piece of homework, any exercises that they have got wrong in their previous homework);

- high quantities of whole class instruction, in which the teacher attempts to ensure the entire class have grasped the knowledge intended;
- children all use the same textbooks, which permits teachers to channel their energy into classroom instruction and the marking of homework, rather than into the production of worksheets and the like that has been so much a feature of English practice;
- mechanisms to ensure that the range of achievement is kept small, such as the practice of children finishing work if they have fallen behind in lesson breaks, at break times and potentially after school that is evident in Taiwanese classrooms for example;
- a well ordered rhythm to the school day, involving in elementary school the use of 40 minute lessons that permit children frequent breaks to 'let off steam', combined with well managed lesson transitions that do not 'leak' time.

Discussion has also centred on the possible systemic features responsible for the high achievement levels of certain European societies. In Germany and Holland (Smithers and Robinson, 1991; Prais and Wagner, 1965; Bierhoff, 1996), these are argued to be:

1   There are close links between school leaving awards and future job opportunities, with particularly the apprenticeships that are the gateway to skilled working class employment being dependent upon good performance in school.
2   Final marks in leaving certificates are averaged across subjects, so students cannot give up on a subject (e.g. mathematics) if they do not like it.
3   Teaching groups are more homogeneous, partly related to the fact that the school system is selective (for most German states), thus 'reducing the range' and making teaching less difficult.
4   Students can be 'kept down' in a grade, until they have acquired the levels of achievement necessary for the next grade up (this affected 10 per cent of the age cohort in the Burghes and Blum (1995) study for example).
5   The use of textbooks as a resource prevents teachers from 're-inventing the wheel' and diverting their energies into work sheet preparation.

In Switzerland high mean scores of pupils, and the low range of scores in mathematics and science, are argued to be produced by (Bierhoff, 1996; Bierhoff and Prais, 1995):

1   High proportions of lesson time (50–70 per cent) being utilized for whole class teaching, not simply of the 'lecture to the class' variety but high quality *interactive* teaching in which the teacher starts with a problem and develops solutions and concepts through a series of graded questions addressed to the whole class. Pupils working on their own in groups are correspondingly much rarer than in England.
2   The use of textbooks which are drafted by groups of experienced teachers to cover the prescribed curriculum of their Canton. There is a textbook for each level of schooling and they are notable in that they contain little self instruction material (the content of English textbooks) but mostly exercises. The textbooks come with substantial teachers manuals, which provide suggestions for teaching each page and master copies for OHP transparencies and the like.

3   Associated with 2 above, work is coherently planned, with clarity of purpose on the part of teachers who know how much material should have been covered at various different time points.

4   The primary school experience of Swiss children is of concentration upon basic number work, use of textbooks with clear goals which provide exercises appropriate for each learning step, use of teacher suggested methods of calculation in number work and the introduction of calculators at a later age than in England for fear of damaging students' capacity to do 'mental arithmetic' and calculation (Bierhoff, 1996).

In Hungary, systemic factors are argued to be (Burghes, 1995):

1   Classroom teaching is, like many European societies, more 'formal', with more teacher direction, more whole class interactive instruction and more open discussion of students' mistakes.

2   Students entering teacher training for primary teaching have high qualifications, the equivalent of 'A' level mathematics.

3   Expectations of what children can achieve are very high, with high lesson 'pace' (itself aided by teacher control) and national guidelines that expect teachers to move to advanced topics quickly.

4   Selective systems of education at secondary age reduce the range of achievement teachers have in school, and enable clear, distinct and different sets of goals to be drawn for children of different achievement levels.

A final example of the use of international comparative research for the school effectiveness community comes from the findings of the International School Effectiveness Research Project (ISERP) (Reynolds et al., 1994a; Reynolds and Teddlie, 1995). The focus of the study has been the extent to which what are 'effective' practices at school or at classroom level are the same or are different in different countries, using a cohort of children passing through schools at ages 7 to 9 in the countries of the United States, Australia, Hong Kong, Taiwan, the Netherlands, Canada, Ireland, Norway and the United Kingdom. Using mathematics achievement tests to furnish data upon the effectiveness levels of schools and national systems, it is clear that the same superiority of Pacific Rim societies in educational achievement is shown in ISERP as in the other studies mentioned earlier.

To explore the reasons for these differences ISERP researchers completed questionnaires concerning the importance of 12 case study dimensions that were utilized in the study. These twelve dimensions were as follows:

1   School Characteristics
2   Child's Experience of Instruction
3   Instructional Style of Teachers
4   Curriculum
5   Parental Influence
6   Principal
7   Expectations of Children
8   School Goals

9   Inter-staff Relations
10   Resources
11   Relationships with Local Authorities/Districts
12   School Image

A questionnaire asked them to rank order the 12 case study dimensions from 1 (the most important) to 12 (the least important) in differentiating between the schools.

Tables 8.9 and 8.10 contain ratings of the case study dimensions broken down by two types of countries: those where English is the first language (Ireland, UK, USA) and those where another language other than English is the first language (Hong Kong, the Netherlands, Norway). Perusal of the data had indicated that this might be a fruitful comparison due to different emerging patterns of results from the written case studies.

Table 8.9 Average Likert ratings of case study dimensions by country type

Dimension	English Speaking	Non-English Speaking
School Characteristics	3.83*	3.0
Child Experience	4.0	4.5*
Instructional Style	3.83	4.25*
Curriculum	2.5	4.0*
Parental Influence	3.33	3.5*
Principal	4.83*	4.0
Expectations	4.5*	4.0
School Goals	4.33*	3.5
Inter-staff Relations	4.5*	3.25
Resources	3.0*	2.5
Relationship with Local Authority	1.83*	1.75
Image	3.33*	3.0
Overall Average	3.65*	3.43

Note: The scales have 5 points, with 5 indicating extremely important. The '*' means the higher average score on that dimension.

Table 8.10 Average rank orders of case study dimensions by country type

Dimension	English Speaking	Non-English Speaking
School Characteristics	7*	9
Child Experience	5.5	2*
Instructional Style	5.5	1*
Curriculum	11	6.5*
Parental Influence	9	8*
Principal	1*	3.5
Expectations	3*	3.5
School Goals	3*	6.5
Inter-staff Relations	3*	5
Resources	10	10
Relationship with Local Authority	12	12
Image	8*	11

Note: The rank orders are from 1 to 12 with 1 indicating the most important dimension of contrast. The '*' means the higher average rank on that dimension.

The dimensions of contrast that were most important in the non-English countries (in comparison to the English speaking countries) were instructional style, the child's experience, curriculum and parental influence. Thus researchers in non-English speaking countries found it easier to differentiate among their schools in the traditional instructional areas and in the influence of parents.

Researchers in English speaking countries, on the other hand, found it easier to differentiate among schools on issues such as the principal, expectations, school goals, inter-staff relations and school image.

A plausible interpretation of these data is that in English speaking countries it is characteristics of the person that explain which institutions are effective, whereas in non-English speaking societies the system itself is so ordered, strong and well engineered/understood that individual characteristics of the principal and the relationships between the staff do not affect, and indeed are not allowed to affect, the quality of the education provided. In these non-English speaking societies, one might argue that the attention to curriculum, to instruction and to pedagogy means that there will be less of the *range* of educational quality amongst principals and staff that is a characteristic of English speaking countries. For these latter, the system and the technology of schooling is so weak that it requires unusually effective individual principals or unusually good inter-staff relations to generate effective schools.

One might even want to go further and argue finally that, therefore, English speaking societies will have effective schools in proportion to the proportion of their individual principals and staff who can be effective – in proportion therefore to the presumably finite personal characteristics of their personnel. For non-English speaking societies, the limit will be imposed by the presumably more infinite number of persons who can acquire the technology of teaching and of schooling.

Interesting speculations about the 'strength' and 'variability' of the educational systems of the different countries are also generated by the ISERP study. Table 8.11 shows the percentage of variance locatable at the school level in the various societies in the study. Note that Taiwan, with a technology of schooling that is well understood and firmly taught in teacher training, has very little variance located at the level of the school.

Table 8.11 Variance components computation test of ISERP country level data

Computation	No Covariates		Controlled for Covariates	
	Student level (%)	*School level (%)*	*Student level (%)*	*School level (%)*
USA	44.4 (82)	9.9 (18)	40.7 (83)	8.6 (17)
Great Britain	63.1 (81)	14.7 (19)	51.4 (89)	5.9 (11)
Taiwan	52.9 (98)	1.1 (2)	45.7 (99)	0.6 (1)
Norway	44.6 (99)	0.3 (1)	36.7 (99)	0.2 (1)
Hong Kong	62.2 (90)	6.9 (10)	54.1 (90)	5.9 (10)
Canada	46.3 (100)	0 (0)	35.5 (95)	2.0 (5)
Netherlands	33.5 (89)	4.0 (11)	29.1 (96)	1.3 (4)

Conclusions

Our excursion into the area of international effectiveness research in this chapter suggests an area so far relatively undeveloped, for obvious reasons. Doing internationally orientated work is difficult and the tendency has been for the difficulty of such studies to have made them an easy target for criticism. However, the benefits of international studies are potentially very great – in the chance to examine a greater range of educational factors and in the chance to generate middle range theory based upon the analyses generated by seeing which effectiveness factors are important in which country cultural contexts. Furthermore, one could quite legitimately argue that only by looking at a wider range of educational factors can one test out the full explanatory power of the 'school variable'. The difficulties are formidable but one could hypothesize that the systematic variation of content that international research entails can do considerable good to the school effectiveness research community.

9   School Effectiveness and Education Indicators

Carol Fitz-Gibbon and Susan Kochan

Introduction

Though public education has been generally available for centuries through much of the developed world, little empirical information on education was collected prior to the end of World War II. In the United States, for instance, what education statistics were utilized tended to be narrow measures of education production such as the number of students enrolled or the number of diplomas awarded (Murnane, 1987). The shape of education data collection changed, however, in the decades following World War II. With the world once again 'at peace,' government officials became increasingly preoccupied with preserving and advancing their nations' economic competitiveness, and with redressing social inequities at home. Education reform was considered crucial to both agendas, but there was insufficient statistical information to inform policy development.

Research in areas crucial to economic development was made a high priority in the 1950s, as evidenced by the creation of the Organization for Economic Cooperation and Development (OECD), a multinational research and policy organization. The real watershed in social sciences (including education) research came in the 1960s, however, when the advent of high-speed computers gave researchers the tools they needed to expand the depth and breadth of data collection and analysis (Shapiro, 1986). These new resources were put to immediate use. In the United States, for example, two Congressionally mandated data collection efforts were initiated that were unprecedented in scope: the National Assessment of Educational Progress (NAEP) and the Equality of Educational Opportunity Survey (EEOS), whose final report is perhaps best known as the Coleman Report (Coleman et al., 1966). In the UK the Assessment of Performance Unit (APU) was created to study national standards and supplement the already extensive and long-standing system of Examination Boards that tested secondary pupils at ages 16 and 18 years with externally set and marked examinations.

In the United States, ambitious as undertakings such as the NAEP and EEOS were, it was immediately obvious that the data collected were inadequate to their intended task: measuring the adequacy and equity of American public education. In retrospect, as we noted in Chapter 3, data limitations contributed greatly to the Coleman team's finding that schools make a relatively small contribution to student achievement (Coleman et al., 1966). The standardized tests unrelated to any defined curriculum for which schools were accountable were not ideal measures for elucidating the effects of schools on pupils. In fact, the Coleman Report's greatest legacy may be that it whetted policy makers' appetites for more detailed and precise information on education, and spurred the development of two research disciplines dedicated to meeting the perceived research need: school effectiveness and school indicator research. Not surprisingly, some of the earliest challenges to the conclusions of the Coleman report used data from countries such as Ireland with curriculum-embedded examination systems, i.e. tests of what was actually taught, rather than of pupils' generalized academic skills (e.g. Kellaghan and Madaus, 1979).

Over the course of the past 30 years, the disciplines of school effectiveness and school indicator research have emerged. From time to time, researchers in both fields have been distracted from their academic task (describing and explaining the education process) by forays into applied research or action research. For school effectiveness researchers, the distraction has been school improvement; for school indicator research, it has been school accountability.

Despite their common origins and similar aims, the two fields remain largely independent today. As evidence, a bibliographic review of several current and comprehensive books in the two fields revealed little overlap in publications cited (Reynolds et al., 1994a; Willms, 1992 and Fitz-Gibbon, 1996).

This chapter represents an attempt to narrow the gap between these two disciplines. Our aim is to provide a brief introduction to the discipline, its methodological strengths and challenges and its wide adoption in many countries. It also charts future trends in the field of education indicator research, as we move into an era characterized by the pervasive use of performance indicators.

What Is an 'Indicator'?

We live with indices and data every day – unemployment rates, cost of living indices, per cent of dietary fat per gram – but what is meant by the term 'indicator?' There have been several definitions offered. For example, 'an indicator is an item of information collected at regular intervals to track the performance of a system' (Fitz-Gibbon, 1990b, p.1). Ergo, an 'education indicator' is a statistic collected at regular intervals to track the performance of an education system. Shavelson et al. described an education indicator as an 'individual or composite statistic that relates to a basic construct in education and is useful in a policy context' (1989, p.5). To discourage researchers from labelling every bit of archival data collected 'an indicator,' the US Office of Educational Research and Improvement (OERI) went so far as to caution that:

> statistics qualify as indicators only if they serve as gauges; that is, if they tell a great deal about the entire system by reporting the condition of a few particularly significant features. For example, the number of students enrolled in schools is an important fact about the size of the educational system, but it tells little about how well the system is functioning. On the other hand, a statistic that reports the proportion of secondary students who completed advanced study in mathematics provides useful information about the level that students are participating and achieving in that subject . . . and can appropriately be considered an indicator.
>
> (OERI, 1988, p.5)

A number of factors must be taken into consideration if education performance indicators are to provide feedback which can be used to assure and develop quality (see Table 9.1). First, the indicators must provide valid information relevant to accepted goals. Second, if the performance indicators are to be relevant to actions that can be taken or avoided, it follows that the indicators must contain information about features of the system which can be influenced by staff and decision makers. Additionally, we know from our knowledge of the change process that practitioners must accept the indicators as credible if they are to be used in guiding change. Furthermore, for acceptance to be likely, the indicators must be informative, fair and sufficiently useful to warrant the effort and cost expended in their collection. Finally, if change does occur, the indicator must be sufficiently sensitive to reflect that change.

Though many approaches can be taken to indicator research, two are widely accepted and will be pursued here. In the 'system modelling' approach, indicators are selected with the express purpose of describing the performance of the system. Given the complexity of the education process, this can be an ambitious venture, involving the collection and analysis of data on a myriad of variables. An attractive alternative is the 'problem-finding' approach, whose aim is to find indicators which will give early warnings of developing problems. The use of a 'problem finding' rather than a 'system modelling' focus is consistent with many informed views of systems management.

If systems have to be constantly improved by *problem-solving*, this requires *problem-location*. If indicators of a negative kind (e.g. unrest in a school, increasing truancy, heavy staff absences) can signal a developing problem, then they can greatly assist management as long as they meet certain criteria such as those listed in Table 9.1. These criteria are designed to ensure that indicators produce beneficial outcomes and avoid becoming expensive distracters with negative impact.

The system modelling and problem finding approaches will often lead to many of the same indicators in that developing a model of the system will involve the specification of desired outcomes; failure to obtain the desired outcomes locates a problem. However, the problem-finding approach to monitoring might lead to an economical set of indicators when we know enough to choose the vital ones. Unfortunately, much educational research is still exploratory; we have much to learn before we can identify the vital indicators with confidence. In the meantime, we will continue with an emphasis on the system modelling approach in this chapter.

If school systems around the world consist of similar elements, and if there are to be comparisons from one system to another, some coherence in terminology will become essential. In a review considering indicators in simply one aspect of schooling – the curriculum – Pelgrum et al. (1995) found more than 170 indicators in use, many with overlapping or coincident meanings despite different names.

Forewarned by this experience, we feel it wise to start our discussion of indicator system design by developing a logical framework to be used in the description of all indicator systems rather than simply to describe the variables which have, by happenstance, emerged in existing systems. This information may assist in developing further generations of indicator systems.

Table 9.1 Indicator selection criteria

Criteria for the Selection of Indicators

- *Criterion 1. Indicators Need to Refer to Valued Outcomes of Managed Units*
  If organisations have values then it will not be difficult to agree on goals—outcomes cared about enough to bother measuring them. But outcomes cannot be defined without consideration as to what part of each organisation is responsible for particular outcomes. A start has to be made by choosing a unit for which indicators will be prepared, whether it be a department, school, LEA, or nation.

- *Criterion 2. Indicators Relate to Outcomes over Which Staff Can Reasonably Be Expected to Have an Influence*
  There is no accountability without causality. Indicators about aspects which schools feel unable to alter are not fair, though they may be of interest.

- *Criterion 3. The Major Outcome Indicators Are Contextualized*
  Outcome indicators must be contextualized, as otherwise, they are neither fair nor interpretable. This criterion almost always requires that indicators are part of a larger system to provide the variables which enable fair comparisons to be made.

- *Criterion 4. Indicators Are Fed Back to the Units of Management—and They Get Back*
  There may be some differentiation in the amount of information on various levels of the system, but in general, the smallest unit of management should receive all the data relevant to that unit. Indicators which simply remain on file fail to have their informative value used. Feeding indicators back both informs those who need to know and promotes the spirit of open information systems and collaborative enquiry, the kind of climate in which information is used most constructively.

- *Criterion 5. Indicators Are, and Are Perceived to Be, Fair*
  Indicators themselves need face validity—they should relate to goals to which there is widespread agreement. Fairness is not always easy to design and the solution often has to be the use of multiple indicators. For example, it would not be fair to expect lower achievement from students from poor as opposed to rich homes. Fairness to students and all SES groups (i.e., what is called equity in the literature) demands that home factors are ignored in the production of indicators. Yet if home-background factors cannot be overcome by schooling, then it is only fair to schools to take this into account. Monitoring with indicators which take account of home factors, and other indicators which do not, will allow us to check each unit on its 'equity'.

- *Criterion 6. Indicators are Accessible*
  If not understood, indicators may be rejected or ignored. Because it is important that indicators are understood, it may sometimes be better to live with slightly larger errors of estimation than to use complex procedures which present barriers to understanding.

- *Criterion 7. Indicators are Explained*
  Indicators do not need to be instantly understood. Explanations delivered in the course of in-service work lead to a higher level of professionalisation, more sophisticated use of indicators and greater interest in them.

- *Criterion 8. Indicators are Incorruptible*
  There have been instances of data being altered in a variety of ways in order to alter indicators. The greater the extent to which the indicators are used publicly to pressure institutions, the greater the need for incorruptible indicators.

- *Criterion 9. Indicators are Checkable*
  Nothing so secures acceptance as the chance to check up on indicators. There are plenty of errors which can creep into the processing of indicators, so a chance to check your own from the original data is desirable.

Table 9.1 Continued

Criteria for the Selection of Indicators

- *Criterion 10. Indicators Perceptibly Improve if the Unit Improves Its Performance Over Time*
  Indicators are required which retain their interpretation from year to year and which make sensitive, longitudinal comparisons possible. Regression-based indicators generally meet this criterion. At least some of the indicators for each management unit should be able to improve if the unit improves its performance.

- *Criterion 11. Behavioural Implications of the Indicators Are Beneficial*
  The crucial question is whether or not the actions taken in response to the indicator will, in fact, be educationally beneficial. Monitoring might turn out to be beneficial and motivating, or destructive and demotivating.

- *Criterion 12. Indicators Are Cost Effective*
  The only way to assess adequately whether or not the costs are reasonable is to have some assessment of the cost-benefits or cost effectiveness of the system.

Source: Summarized with permission from *Monitoring Education: Indicators, Quality and Effectiveness*, Fitz-Gibbon, 1996.

Categories of Indicators

In order to describe the wealth of available indicators and their varying function, a useful initial classification is determined by a time sequence: intake, process and outcome variables (see Table 9.2).

Since the choice of indicators will be driven primarily by what is valued, we start, however, not with intakes, but with outcomes. Cooley pointed out many years ago that indicators are measured because we care about them (Cooley, 1983). Indeed, yet another definition of indicators, particularly outcome indicators, is simply 'things we care about enough to measure,' chosen to highlight the value-laden decisions inherent in the choice of what to measure. The pre-eminent outcome indicator in education is generally student achievement.

Outcome indicators are the central focus of most accountability initiatives and hence indicator systems. As a result, the collection of outcome data typically precedes the collection of other indicators. For example, outcome data on the number of students enrolled and the number of students earning diplomas have been reported in the United States (US) since the mid-nineteenth century (Murnane, 1987). Such data met the information needs of US policy makers so long as they were content simply to know how many children were becoming educated and to what extent. The collection of intake and process indicator data became necessary only when policy makers attempted to improve the efficiency and equity of the schooling process, and therefore began to ask *why* students were being educated at a certain number, and whether those numbers were appropriate.

In the UK an external examination system was developed by universities to meet the needs of highly competitive selection procedures for university entrance. To meet the needs for political accountability inspectors were sent to examine schools (Hogg, 1990). The examination system served well and is retained to this day not only in the UK but also by many former colonies in the Pacific Rim and Africa. Externally set and

Table 9.2 A classification of types of indicator

Time ⟶ Variables	Intake	Process	Immediate Output	Long-term Outcomes
Flow/production: student numbers and school resources	FI Enrolment Resource basis	FP Attendance Resource allocation	FO Completion rates Cost analyses	FL Destinations: employment, education, prisons etc., cost-benefit analyses
Quality of Life: intrinsic values	QI Well-being Satisfaction Interests	QP Experiences – Breadth – Value	QO Satisfaction measures Responses to courses and to institution	QL Adult-reported quality of life. Freedom from negative outcomes
Affective domain	AI Characteristic attitudes, expectations, values, motivation	AP Support services, counselling, pastoral care Teaching and learning processes	AO Attitudes of concern on the course (e.g. social skills satisfaction measures)	AL Values from course and perceived value of the course in the light of experience
Behavioural domain including Skills	BI Prior skills and behaviours (e.g. health habits, IT skills, numeracy, literacy)	BP Teaching and learning processes aimed at the behavioural outcomes including skills	BO Skills (e.g. core skills such as numeracy, literacy, IT) health practices, fitness	BL Retained skills and behaviours
Cognitive domain: aptitudes and achievements	CI Prior achievements and developed aptitudes Expectations of the course	CP Teaching and learning processes aimed at academic outcomes, knowledge and understanding	CO Raw achievement and 'Value Added' (relative progress)	CL Retained knowledge and understanding

marked examinations, based on published syllabi, provided what has come to be seen as needed in the USA: authentic, curriculum-embedded, high stakes tests.

But how do we move beyond the cognitive to a comprehensive list of important and valued outcomes? In attempting to produce a list of education outcomes, we can take the approach of considering the desired sequence of events in the education of a child, then identify the logical outcomes related to each step in the sequence. The pupil should:

- enrol at the school and then attend;
- achieve;
- develop desirable attitudes;
- develop desirable skills;
- have a good quality of life while in the school; and
- then progress appropriately onwards.

The resultant outcome indicators for this series of events emerge in the following order:

- flow (i.e. the child enrols in school and then attends);
- cognitive outcomes (as measured by student achievement data);
- affective outcomes (student attitudes);
- skills outcomes (the vocational skills that students acquire in preparation for entering the workforce);
- quality of life; and
- long-term outcomes/progression to the next stage.

All are outcomes, yet all measure different ends to be derived from the schooling experience. A distinction can even be made between immediate ends (*outputs*) and longer-term results (*outcomes*).

If all of the above features can be measured, we can monitor the major outcomes of schooling for pupils. All of these indicators are currently used in many systems, with one exception: skills, which are rarely identified as a separate outcome domain. We make this a separate area with the idea that the acquisition of skills in music, plumbing, computing or team work cannot be simply subsumed under achievement without being under-valued.

The consideration of value is an important one in *that one of the aims of indicator systems is to attach value to that which is measured*. By measuring skills, we attach value to them. If, as a value judgment, it is felt that vocational skills 'training' is sometimes less highly regarded than academic 'education' and that this is unfortunate, then it might be a beneficial use of indicators to start to measure skills. In the United States, researchers charged with monitoring progress toward a series of National Education Goals are grappling with the development of indicators that will measure progress toward Goal 6, which includes preparing graduates to succeed in the workplace.

It might be thought that one of the outcome indicators (quality of life) would be better seen as a process variable since it refers to the student's experience whilst in school. However, if 'quality of life' is a valued outcome in its own right, not a means to an end, then it is an outcome. This choice rests on a value judgment that life in the here-and-now should be at least tolerable and its quality should not always be sacrificed to the attainment of distant goals. If that value judgment is rejected, then quality of life indicators should be dropped.

The same argument applies to student attitudes. It is often thought that students perform better in the subjects they like. However, if there is such an effect, it is usually found to be weak. If attitudes are to be measured, it should probably be with an eye to an intrinsic preference that students should like their work rather than hate it. Attitudes are not simply a means to obtain achievement outcomes: they are intrinsically valued outcomes, in and of themselves.

Intake Variables

Co-variates and the Value Added Concept

Many indicator systems are now adopting the concept of 'value added': a measure of the relative gain in achievement made by pupils. The rationale is that a school is not responsible for the absolute level of student achievement so much as for the progress made by pupils in its care. This is reasonable, but further caution is still required. The term 'value added' implies that the progress is entirely attributable to the school – that it is the *value added by the school*. In reality, only *part* of the progress can be so attributed, and that only tentatively in the absence of evidence from controlled interventions. This important point about indicators and causality will be a recurrent theme.

In order to assess value added, we need to know what a reasonable level of achievement is for each pupil, and compare that reasonable prediction with the actual level of achievement attained. The value added is the difference between the actual achievement and the predicted achievement. The prediction of achievement is generally made from the best single predictor, namely prior achievement. Lacking a measure of prior achievement, almost any cognitive measure will predict achievement in most subject areas in the school curriculum. The measures of prior achievement, or the alternative cognitive measures, are 'predictors' or 'co-variates.' (See Chapter 3 for a discussion of the differences between adjusted scores, which consider characteristics of students attending schools – e.g. social class, ethnicity – and value-added scores, which consider prior achievement.)

It would be desirable to have predictors or covariates for the socialization variables such as student attitudes toward school and teachers, commitment to lessons, social relations, self-esteem or self-concept as a learner. Ideally, most outcomes should be measured *in terms of the changes brought about during the period of schooling rather than in terms of absolute levels*. This will require that indicator systems be modular: designed with input and output measures for each phase or stage of education. As we shall see in our discussion of indicator systems that are currently in place, in the US state of Tennessee, each academic year is a module within which value added is computed. In England, a national curriculum with tests for pupils at ages 7, 11, 14 and 16 suggests modules from two to four years in length. Four-year modules are probably too long since there will have been a considerable turnover of students in this time.

Contextual or Moderator Indicators (Inputs)

Contextual or moderator variables (or 'inputs,' as they are known in the US) are givens: features of the conditions under which education is delivered which are beyond the power of the school to alter, but which may affect the outcomes.

Student and School Characteristics

Outcomes may vary according to the *students' socio demographic characteristics*: their age, gender, ethnicity, linguistic status, socio economic status (SES) or religion. They also may vary due to *characteristics of the school itself*: the level of instruction offered (pre-school, reception or kindergarten, primary, secondary, etc.); the school's location in an urban, suburban or rural setting; its geographic location; and/or religious affiliation.

Assessment Characteristics

Because achievement is probably the single most agreed-upon outcome expected from schools, one of the most important contextual variables is the nature of the assessment system itself (e.g. standardized testing, portfolio or authentic assessment). This may be particularly important when comparisons are made from country to country or between academic and vocational qualifications, where the systems of assessment may vary considerably.

Four main issues are important regarding the system of assessment:

1   The potential for bias and/or irregularities in data collection – To what extent is the assessment made by teachers of their own pupils and to what extent is it externally made? To what extent is the achievement subjectively rather than objectively scored? Even when assessment is external, if it is subjective, we need to know whether names are routinely left on papers when they are assessed, since names can indicate gender, ethnicity, and even religion.

2   Whether the assessment is based on work that is likely to have been taught (i.e. is it 'curriculum-embedded') – This is often referred to as the question of 'delivery standards' in the US; emphasis is placed on measuring the 'enacted curriculum' because there is no point assessing outcomes if there has been no delivery. In the UK, this problem is largely avoided by the fact that there are national curricula: there are published syllabi for examinations. Teachers, students, parents and school governors all know the content that is to be covered.

3   The extent to which assessments are 'high stakes' and are therefore taken seriously – The higher the stakes the more likely will be attempts to distort the data by fair means or foul. Yet without consequences, the data may be of indifferent quality due to lack of effort and attention. These are difficult areas in the design of indicator systems. One certainly often-repeated mistake in the UK has been to report the percentage of students reaching a certain achievement level rather than the average level reached. When such information is published as indicators (in the 'School Performance Tables' now published annually in the UK) schools react by concentrating resources and attention on students at the borderline. If the

indicator is the percentage of students obtaining a C grade or better, then D students are targeted at the expense of other students whose performance is unlikely to be alterable enough to affect the indicator. This distortion of behaviour arises purely from the arbitrary choice of the high-stakes, published indicator. When indicators are recorded as 'high-stakes' this signals a need to know a great deal about the security and impact of the system.

4   The extent to which the assessment is authentic – There is increasing concern these days about the authenticity of assessments. Indeed, it would seem to be desirable to describe quite elaborately the methods of assessment used if comparisons are to be made from one state to another, from one country to another or indeed from one school to another. As argued elsewhere (Fitz-Gibbon, 1996), transcripts (records of students' grades) should indicate the methods of assessment used to arrive at each grade.

Important as these features seem to be at the moment, there is insufficient evidence that they are all of practical importance. This situation will frequently plague indicator systems: the knowledge base on which they need to rest is often inadequate. However, by establishing the indicator systems, the knowledge base can be strengthened. The database of indicators can be used to provide evidence of problems. For example, if the proportion of variance in outcomes apparently 'attributable' to teachers or schools (i.e. *rho*, or the intra-class correlation) is unusually high, this may signal a problem in the assessment system such as the use of teacher-given grades.

Financial and Resource Indicators: Context or Process?

As far as the school is concerned, there is another set of contextual variables: those concerned with the financial status and resources available to the school. The total sum a school is given is a *contextual variable for a school*, assuming that the school has no control over the level at which it is funded. However, it may be a *process variable for a local education authority* (LEA) if the LEA has some discretion as to how funding is to be divided among schools. The designation of an indicator as a *given contextual indicator* or as a *decision-relevant process indicator* will depend upon the locus of decision-making.

Compositional Variables

There is a particular kind of contextual variable which can be created from pupil-level data: the average level of various student characteristics. In addition to the average, other distributional statistics might be important, such as the standard deviation or skewness. Thus, in addition to each student's prior achievement, we might consider the effect of the average prior achievement of the class in which the student is taught and the spread of prior achievement in the class. These indicators of the composition of the teaching groups are not only expected to have an effect, but they *do* frequently contribute significantly to the prediction of subsequent achievement. The finding that a high average achievement boosts subsequent achievement is fairly widespread. The complexity of the issue is, however, illustrated by Slavin's detailed work on grouping practices, suggesting that homogeneous teaching groups are only exceptionally effective if the work is differentiated in ways appropriate to the groups (Gutierrez and Slavin, 1992). (See Chapter 5 for a further discussion of compositional effects.)

Compliance Indicators

There is another kind of contextual variable which is to some extent a 'given' in that compliance is required by law. Thus, schools in England and Wales must include religion in the syllabus, must employ adequate supervision of students and follow health and safety regulations. In the USA, the designers of Louisiana's education indicator system created an indicator based on the percentage of teachers who are not certified for the subject or level at which they are teaching. Such variables constitute 'givens' and can be called, following Richards (1988), 'compliance indicators.' They are not *process* variables because they are not options for schools, but obligations. However, for the country as a whole, they are important process variables: they are what the country chooses to require of schools.

Thus it is clear that whether or not a variable is a contextual variable, a compliance indicator, or a process variable depends upon *the unit of analysis* (student, school, LEA, nation) and *the locus of decision-making*. These distinctions are needed to track the performance of a system with some hope of attaining a reasonable model represented by the variables.

Process Variables: Actions/Options

Given outcome variables with appropriate covariates, and given input variables, then we have the essentials of an indicator system. To know whether valued outcomes are being achieved and to have fair comparisons between schools are vital pieces of information. The rest could be left to professional judgment as to how to improve, how to change and how to run the school (though empirical evidence should carry greater weight.) However, the question will always arise as to why one school is doing better than another on a particular outcome. Hence, there is pressure for indicators which might cast light on such questions. Process indicators can provide clues as to which schooling processes appear to predict good progress, and can serve to generate grounded hypotheses (i.e. hypotheses grounded in data). (The need for process indicators in school indicator work is similar to the need for process studies in school effectiveness research. See Chapter 4 for a parallel discussion.)

Two dangers are to be avoided in the selection and consideration of process indicators. First, in the absence of experimental conditions, the relationship between process and outcome indicators is invariably *correlational* rather than *causal*. Secondly, the process indicators may sometimes be seen as ends in themselves. If processes are ends in themselves and, like health and safety, are required, then they should be subject to compliance monitoring. Checking compliance with such indicators may require unannounced visits by inspectors rather than self-reported data.

If we knew exactly what constituted 'best practice' in teaching, then this so-called 'best practice' could be legally required and made the subject of compliance monitoring rather than performance monitoring. It is precisely because the link between process and outcomes is so loosely coupled in the dynamic and ever changing situations of schooling that process indicators should generally be seen only as generating hypotheses. In the absence of well-established causal relationships, they should not be used in judgments on schools.

Now that we have established what process indicators should and should not be, it would be instructive to divide process indicators among two categories: those relating to the *school curriculum*, and those relating to the *school organization*.

Process Indicators: Curriculum Time and Content

'Who is taught what, for how long and how' must be central foci in tracking an education system. Indeed, Preece (1983) questioned whether 'effectiveness' was anywhere near as important as what was taught. The school curriculum needs to be seen in the context pertaining to the assessment system, as already discussed. Within that context, it would be helpful to have measures of content inclusion and emphasis (Walker and Shaffarzik, 1974). This could be obtained by knowing the time and resources devoted to each subject and each topic in each subject: a mammoth task of data collection.

Various techniques have been used to try to get at this concept of curricular delivery. Porter (1991) favours teacher diaries, though self-report information gathered via survey or interview is more prevalent. The question must always be asked, however, as to whether the benefits of this information justify the costs of its collection. The reliability of the collected data also is a matter of concern (Porter, 1991).

Pelgrum et al. (1995) gave a clear account of the difficulties of creating curriculum indicators for use in international comparisons, citing terminology such as 'curriculum intensity,' which probably means much the same as 'time spent on teaching and learning.' 'Implemented content' might be found under such labels as 'coverage,' 'opportunity to learn' or 'test-curriculum overlap.' The list of indicators and sources provided by Pelgrum, Voogt and Plomp (1995) shows clearly the danger of having a proliferation of overlapping indicators with different names for the same measurements. Furthermore, the number of *process indicators* which could be developed are probably not countable.

Those considerations constitute a clear warning to policy makers and researchers to focus on student *outcome indicators* and then on the effects of alterations in policy: the *alterable process variables*. In trying to track the performance of an education system, we have first to recognize that the system is far too complex to be exhaustively monitored. What is needed are hypotheses about possible changes in process variables: indicators which may be altered in such a way that the impact of the alterations can be established. Ideally, the effects of changes must be established by controlled experimentation, but just possibly, some clues can arise from time series designs which arise naturally within the framework of a monitoring system.

Process Indicators: Curriculum Teaching and Learning

Teaching and learning processes have been the subject of fashion and opinion as well as research. Child-centred, activity-based, problem-solving approaches (dubbed trendy) have competed with direct teaching and objectives-based education (dubbed rote-learning). If indicators are to intrude into the classroom how are the classroom processes to be measured? Direct observations of classrooms are time-consuming, complicated and expensive. Teacher diaries are demanding and could be subject to distortion if high stakes were involved or social-desirability influences were strong. Could indicator systems rely on questionnaires to students? Such an approach has proved useful in a monitoring project called the A-Level Information System (ALIS), and there is growing evidence of the validity of students' reports of the frequency of use of a number of defined teaching and learning activities, such as the use of 'dictated notes' or 'researching a topic' or 'class discussion led by the teacher.' In Edwards et al. (1997) the ALIS data have been used to distinguish between the delivery styles on academic and vocational courses. Hardman also was able to show that, contrary to teachers' reports, the teaching styles adopted for teaching English Language were very similar to those adopted for English Literature, a finding borne out by video-records of the lessons. However, these teaching and learning questions were completed by pre-university students, aged 17 and 18 years. Whether the frequency of use of various classroom processes could be as reliably assessed by younger students needs investigation.

Processes: School Organization

Turning to school organization, we must again be concerned with whether decisions are or are not within the purview of the school. Is there, for example, *local financial management* for the school, or is the school financially controlled through the LEA? A major impact on what happens in the school is the selection and retention of teachers. Does the school have control over *the hiring of teachers*? The firing of teachers? The differences here are often very strong from one state to another or one country to another.

In England, for example, teachers typically apply for a particular job in a particular school. In the USA, they generally apply to be taken onto the teaching force of a school district and are then assigned to a school by the school district. These differences allow for different amounts of control by the school management of the school staff. Pupils, too, may be selected in some schools and this is a matter which might be recorded as an indicator, or simply reflected in the measures of prior attainment used to interpret the achievement outcomes.

Expenditures and resources exist to promote the desired outcomes and are limited 'givens.' Their *deployment*, however, is not simply a given, and therefore not a contextual variable. Finances can be deployed in different ways. Whether or not the total quantity of money or the allocation impacts on the outcomes of school is a contentious area (Hanushek, 1989, 1996; Hedges et al., 1994). Whether or not *financial allocation* variables are seen as fixed or alterable will affect whether or not they are seen as contextual variables (givens) or process variables (alterable).

A major feature of both school organizations and the curriculum is the extent *of accountability, evaluation requirements and feedback*. These concepts are inherent in indicator systems and apply at every organizational level. Do students get feedback on their performance and progress? Do staff get feedback on their performance and progress? Does the school get feedback on its performance and progress? Do the LEAs get feedback on their performance and progress, as Willms and Kerckhoff (1995) argued they should? Accountability demands such feedback, and indicator systems are a method of providing such feedback.

Examples of Official Indicator Systems

We have outlined the kinds of variables that might well be included in an indicator or monitoring system. We turn now to examples of official and unofficial indicator systems that are in place in a number of countries. In the context of an ever-changing scene, the set of examples provided here is not exhaustive, but is reasonably representative of the work in progress and illustrates the application of the framework developed so far. We shall start with an official system that uses the largest unit of analysis (the country).

We start with an international effort to provide indicators across 25 countries. This 'official' system has been developed among countries through cooperation among their governmental organizations. The likely audiences are policy makers and those studying economic and educational systems, rather than school staff or even LEA staff. The unit of analysis is the country.

The Organization for Economic Cooperation and Development (OECD), which was formed in 1961, has aims that are explicitly economic. Its development of the 'INES' project on international indicators is therefore a clear signal of the widespread belief that economic prosperity and success depend to a significant degree upon effective educational systems. The third edition of *Education at a Glance* (OECD, 1995) is a collection of indicators from 25 countries (Australia, Austria, Belgium, Canada, Czech Republic, Denmark, Finland, France, Germany, Greece, Hungary, Ireland, Italy, Japan, Netherlands, New Zealand, Norway, Portugal, Russia, Spain, Sweden, Switzerland, Turkey, the United Kingdom and the United States) and continues the focus adopted in the first two editions (1992 and 1993) on various 'issues' in education, such as the relationship between education and the labour market. As shown in Table 9.3, four networks, each with a lead country, were set up to work on indicators of various kinds (OECD, 1995).

Canada

Moving on to look at individual countries, in Canada, as in the USA, education is the responsibility of each province (state), not the central government. There is, however,

Table 9.3 The four OECD networks for indicators

	Lead Nation	*Task*
Network A	United States	Student learning outcomes
Network B	Sweden	Education and labour market destinations
Network C	The Netherlands	Schools and school processes
Network D	United Kingdom (Scotland)	Expectations and attitudes to education of the various stakeholder groups in OECD countries

increasing cooperation among the provinces. The Council of Ministers of Education (CMEC) made a first attempt to obtain agreement on elements of a national assessment in 1989 with the School Achievement Indicators Programme (SAIP), which measured achievement in reading, writing, mathematics, and science at ages 13 and 16. Reports on this system were released in 1993 and 1994. The Canadian Education Statistics Council (CESC) is a partnership between CMEC and StatsCan (Statistics Canada), a government department which produces five-year censuses with integrated social and economics statistics. Together they produced a 'Portrait' of elementary and secondary education in Canada in 1990 and they are developing long-term plans for monitoring.

Eleven of the 12 Canadian provinces are participating in the development of official monitoring systems run by CMEC and StatsCan. The provinces are cooperating to develop student outcome indicators, and have recruited teachers from across Canada to help develop test items that are then reviewed for freedom from cultural and gender bias. The teachers also score open-ended response items on SAIP assessments, and StatsCan conducts the data analysis. In creating data reporting procedures, the provinces balance the provisions of Canada's freedom of information legislation against the need to preserve the confidentiality of individual students. In short, Canada is moving toward a national examination system similar to the kind long established in the UK.

Eleven of the 12 participating provinces measure 'flow' using three indicators (participation, graduation rates and drop-out rates). Eleven also measure affective outcomes (satisfaction and attitudes), and the provinces draw on international studies wherever available.

The developments in Canada are centrally driven. At least one province has engaged 'external consultants' to collect and analyse questionnaire data, feeling that this 'third party' involvement enhances the credibility of what is essentially a public opinion survey, (i.e. 'stakeholder' views about schools).

Portugal

In contrast to the 'top down' approach to indicator development that is favoured in Canada, Portugal has adopted an explicit 'bottom up' approach (Climaco, 1995). Climaco noted the need for schools to become aware of data and to learn from it:

> Schools are not used to mobilizing for their own benefit all the information which they usually collect and send to the central services to produce National Statistics. The only thing derived from the numbers they collect is the boredom and bureaucracy of the task. When asked about specific information to characterize their schools, teachers either do not know, or only have a 'global image.'
>
> (Climaco, 1995, p.149)

Portugal's approach to indicator system development was focused on developing indicators which would be used in schools. This involved school-based development, working closely with 12 schools and involving teachers at every stage. An initial set of 50 indicators were derived from the literature; this list was then reduced to 32 in the light of their feasibility and usefulness within schools. Attention was paid to presentation of the data (e.g. Jones, B., and Mitchell, 1990). After the first round of feedback to schools, the perspective shifted from a managerial one to self-evaluation in the school and in the school's reports to its community. Data were specially collected by questionnaires from students, parents, and teachers.

Unfortunately, the cognitive outcomes were assessed only by failure rates and drop-out rates. 'Failure' was indicated by retention in earlier grades, a practice which appears to be widespread since only 27 per cent of students were found to have completed nine years of basic education in nine years. Thirty-five per cent of students were found to be one or two grades behind, 14 per cent were still further behind and 24 per cent were found to have dropped out of school. According to Climaco, 'teachers considered this way of viewing the quality of the education system as rather brutal' (p.161). The use of indicators for both improvement efforts and accountability was stressed, with accountability being seen as 'the other face of the granting of autonomy.'

France

For 12,000 secondary institutions in France, the French Ministry of Education has been introducing a set of performance indicators designed primarily as 'an instrument for use by the head of the school and his or her team to diagnose the situation and operation of the school, to assess its policy, and the results thereof' (Emin, 1995, p.201). Indicators have become a legal necessity since the 1989 Education Act in France, and are related to considerable school autonomy, linked to a need for public accountability.

Indicators were tested during the 1993–4 school year in 600 schools and made available to all colleges (secondary schools) in 1995. Special tests were developed for assessing pupils at the beginning of the third year of primary school, at entry to the high school (lycée) and at entry to college. Teachers, meanwhile, have been provided banks of items referenced to the curriculum.

France already had the advantage of a common exit examination, the Bacca-laureate. However, the Baccalaureate results are reported not in terms of grades achieved but in terms of the proportion of students passing. Exactly how standards of marking are maintained throughout France is not clear.

Given the new tests which are coming 'on stream,' it will soon be possible for French schools to have measures of value added calculated against prior attainment. Previously, they have relied on proxy methods of measuring entry levels by measuring SES and the proportions of pupils who have had to repeat years (i.e. have been held back for lack of attainment).

School indicators are published on the basis of tests administered at the beginning of the school year so that teachers have the remainder of the school year to respond to the strengths and weaknesses identified by the indicators. There is a clear and constant insistence that the data are for the school's use in management and to support a dialogue between schools, children and parents. A number of indicators reflect the resources available to students; these include measures of support services in terms of advisors, medical and paramedical staff, welfare assistants and of 'quality of life' (e.g. student participation in clubs and other extracurricular activities). Other indicators monitor the use of time, including time lost due to teacher absences for either training, school building closures or personal reasons. These time indicators are aimed at calculating the 'proportion of teaching hours actually guaranteed a pupil.' During school year 1993–4, time lost from teaching was reported as 8 per cent for colleges, 12 per cent for lycées and 15 per cent for vocational lycées.

The indicators have been received positively, with some reservations. One weakness is identified as a lack of data analysis expertise in the schools. This problem was estimated by inspectors to be widespread, with only 15 per cent of schools integrating evaluative data into their planning. There was a general appreciation by headteachers of ready analysed data provided by the central system.

France has a rapidly expanding school indicator system. Though not particularly standardized on the achievement indicators, it has produced superbly presented graphical output in books such as *Géographie de L'Ecole* (3rd edition, 1995). Published by the Ministry, the book contains comparative aggregated indicators regarding input, resources, and results for 22 regions of the country.

The United Kingdom: DFEE School Performance Tables

The UK has long had externally set and marked 'public examinations' for students aged 16 and 18. The results were available, but formerly were not published in a standard format, school by school, and LEA by LEA. Data for the School Performance Tables are now processed by a private firm at a cost of approximately £1 million per year and are reprinted in both local and national newspapers, usually as rank-ordered lists of schools.

The tables, which have come to be known informally as the 'League Tables,' provide percentage pass rates for 16-year-olds and a points system for providing the examination results of 18-year-olds. Externally marked tests have been extended to three additional cohorts: 7, 11 and 14-year-olds. These tests, which are based on the recently developed National Curriculum in five subject areas (mathematics, English, science, design and technology and a foreign language), were the subject of a massive boycott by teachers. Though the quality of the English tests in particular has been severely attacked, there are now plans to publish results school by school.

The only non-cognitive outcome regularly reported in the School Performance Tables is a flow variable: truancy. Again, as with percentages of pupils obtaining C grades rather than D grades, the glare of publicity presents problems with this particular indicator. The requirement that truancy figures had to be published led immediately to considerable drops in recorded truancy, since there is a fine line between excused and unexcused absences and the reputation of schools was at stake. Consequently, rather than leading to better information on truancy, the publication has resulted in less reliable information. Plans call for value added scores to be included in the School Performance Tables if these are found to be sufficiently reliable and valid (Department for Education and Employment, 1995).

Australia

As in the USA and Canada, different provinces have different educational systems, but there is a general and vigorous movement, largely led by state administration units, towards providing schools with a data-rich environment within which school self-evaluation can be rigorous and informative. For example, the state of Victoria produces the publication *Guidelines for School Self-assessment* (Department of Education, Victoria, 1996), which advises on an accountability framework consisting of three key elements:

- each school's 'Charter' (consisting of the school's chosen goals);
- the school's 'annual report' (consisting of indicators related to the Charter); and
- a triennial school review.

Computer-based information systems are being developed to manage many of the indicators, and extensive advice is provided on the analysis and presentation of the data. The range of indicators suggested may be among the broadest we have encountered in official systems. Within each school, indicators are collected on time allocation, accident rates, enrolment, exit and destination data, as well as student achievement. In addition, there are annual surveys of parents and, bravely, surveys of school staff to assess morale and their satisfaction with the leadership and management in the school. Financial accounts also form part of annual reports. The achievement data is supported by a 'Board of Studies' (seemingly equivalent to a mixture of examination boards and national assessment organizations). In a forward to *Curriculum and Standards Framework* (Board of Studies, Victoria, 1995) Kelly and Ball reported extensive consultation with teachers and an Australia-wide initiative on 'National Statements and Profiles,' these being attempts to create largely criterion-referenced curricula: efforts that have had an unhappy history elsewhere (Sanders and Horn, 1995a; Black, 1994). The New South Wales Department of School Education has similarly ambitious indicator systems under development. A notable feature of the Australian developments seems to be the commitment to careful measurement evidenced by the skills of the personnel working on school accountability in the state offices. Those developing the systems are using Item Response Theory, Causal Modelling and Effect Sizes to bring a sense of proportion and magnitude to statistics, going beyond the arbitrary and overworked tests of statistical significance.

The United States

National Education Indicators

The US Constitution guarantees every American the right to life, liberty, and the pursuit of happiness, but not a free public education. The authors of the US Constitution reserved that authority and responsibility for education to the states, creating a tradition of local control over education that persists today. That tradition has in fact remained so strong that the federal government did not develop its first national indicators of education performance until the 1960s, and has yet to implement a comprehensive national system.

Though the US Department of Education (USDE) has collected education production statistics since the end of the Civil War, the first national indicators of what American school children learn were the Equality of Educational Opportunity Survey (EEOS) and the National Assessment of Educational Progress (NAEP), both of which date to the Vietnam era (Murnane, 1987). The EEOS, whose final report is more widely known as the *Coleman Report* (Coleman et al., 1966), was mandated by Section 402 of the US Civil Rights Act of 1964. Its purpose: to document the availability of equal educational opportunities (EEO) for all Americans, regardless of race, colour, religion or national origin (Coleman et al., 1966). Though its specific EEO findings are seldom cited today, the Coleman study is recognized as a landmark in the history of American educational research, for two reasons. As noted by then-Commissioner of Education Harold Howe II, it was the first 'comprehensive collection of data gathered on consistent specifications throughout the whole nation' (Coleman et al., 1966, p.1) and therefore can be considered as America's first national indicator of education performance. Perhaps more importantly, its resounding conclusion that schools have comparatively little effect on student learning triggered the establishment of two parallel disciplines within education research, the fields of school effectiveness and education performance indicators.

Though the EEOS was impressive in scope for the time, the resultant study was hampered by data limitations. The Report's release in 1966 and subsequent reanalyses of its data therefore lent momentum to the development of a second indicator project already underway: the National Assessment of Educational Progress (NAEP).

The purpose of NAEP (which was established by the USA Office of Education, with support from the Carnegie and Ford Foundations) was to 'report on the condition and progress of American education.' Unlike the *Coleman Report*, which focused on the *schooling* outcomes of American children, the NAEP was originally intended to assess knowledge and skills acquired both within *and outside* of school. Toward that end, the study sample consisted of USA residents aged 9, 13 and 17. 'Young adults' in the 25–35 age range also were sampled. Public, private, and out-of-school populations were all represented.

The test design, as initially conceived, was state-of-the-art. The testing programme covered 10 subject areas ranging from reading, writing, and math to art, citizenship and career/occupational development. One or more subjects were covered each test cycle, and each test included equal numbers of 'easy,' 'moderate' and 'difficult' items. In a deliberate departure from more traditional standardized testing, NAEP emphasized short-answer questions and performance tasks completed by individuals or groups. Finally, special accommodations were built into test administration procedures to ensure that even poor readers could demonstrate their subject area knowledge (Jones, L., 1996).

The NAEP was first administered in 1969–70, with follow-up tests scheduled at four-year intervals thereafter. Over time, budgetary constraints have forced compromises to reduce the programme's high sampling and administration costs; for example, young adults and out-of-school 17-year-olds were dropped from the sampling scheme in the mid-1970s. Substantial modifications also have been made to the test design itself, so that the later assessments more closely resemble traditional standardized achievement tests. Despite the compromises made in the overall programme, there has been a concerted effort over the years to maintain special 'bridge samples' whose testing conditions are comparable to the earlier assessments. As a result, NAEP has been able – compromises notwithstanding – to issue valid long-term trend reports. For example, sub-group analysis of bridge sample data has demonstrated that, despite a general increase in the percentage of minority and low-income children tested, USA achievement in math and reading was as high (or higher) in the early 1990s as it was 20 years before (Mullis et al., 1994).

Though NAEP is now in its third decade, the USA has yet to develop a full-blown national indicator system that combines outcome data with information on schooling inputs and processes. Several models for such a system have been recommended (National Study Panel on Education Indicators, 1991; Oakes, 1989; Porter, 1991); however, there are many problems inherent in the implementation of these models, not the least of which is the cost and effort required to collect process data that accurately reflect the condition of education. Much of the research conducted to date in the development of process indicators of instruction has been funded by the National Science Foundation (NSF); hence, research into instructional delivery in those subjects far outstrips work in measuring curriculum and instruction in other valued subject areas.

Frequently, researchers and policy makers find themselves at odds over the utilization of education indicator data. Many leading researchers argue that using indicator data for accountability purposes can have unintended and undesirable consequences (Oakes, 1989). For example, school staff may feel compelled to 'teach to the test,' or focus their efforts on selected sub-groups of students, all in the interest of maximizing mean test scores. Unlike researchers, policy makers tend to favour increasing school accountability by offering financial incentives for improving and/or effective schools, but sanctions for declining or stable ineffective schools. Even the USDE has warned that 'when high stakes consequences such as large cash awards or district consolidations are linked to performance, incentives exist for deception or manipulation of data in order for a school to look good'. This constitutes explicit recognition from the USDE that indicators can be 'corrupting.' Designers of indicator systems have to take into account Deming's warning that 'whenever there is fear we get the wrong figures' (Deming, 1982, p.266).

Such warnings apparently have had little impression upon some policy makers. *Measuring Up: Questions and Answers About State Roles in Educational Accountability* (USDE, 1988), reported that in 25 states performance triggered rewards, sanctions or other consequences; 22 states reported no such contingencies; and four states gave no response. As far as public reports were concerned, 25 reported that the level of reporting was the school, 37 the school district and 43 at the level of the state. An updated discussion of accountability reports and indicator systems (CCSSO cited in Fitz-Gibbon 1996) reveals that 45 states have at least one annual accountability indicator report, 41 publish at least one report providing statistics at the district level, and 35 report statistics at the school level. In 37 states, there was a state law or mandate requiring a public education report.

State Indicators

Both the EEOS and NAEP were designed to assess the performance of American education, utilizing samples designed in such a way as to provide national statistics for a national audience. The Coleman Report presented regional comparison data (e.g. north, south, midwest, west), but did not have state-representative samples. In fact, the publication of state-by-state comparison data on education was long opposed by the Council of Chief State School Officers (CCSSO), a highly influential professional organization made up of the senior education administrator in each USA state and territory. Admittedly, the CCSSO's opposition to state comparison data was not frivolous. In a nation as large and diverse as the United States, there are tremendous regional differences in the populations served by schools, the resources available for education and the data collection methods used by the various states.

The very socio demographic differences that make education performance so variable across US states nonetheless argue for the development of individualized educational reforms and for the collection of statistics appropriate to monitoring their impact. Pressure for state comparison data on education mounted throughout the decade of the 1980s, bolstered by the publication of *A Nation at Risk* (National Commission on Excellence in Education, 1983). Shortly thereafter, the USDE initiated the annual *Condition of Education* and began publishing its now (in)famous 'Wall Chart,' a collection of state-by-state comparison statistics most notable for the *in*comparability of the data.

In 1985, the CCSSO dropped its opposition to state comparison statistics and lent its full support to the development of a comprehensive system of education indicators that would report valid and reliable comparison statistics at both the state and national levels. Two years later, Congress enacted the 1987 Hawkins-Stafford Amendments, which mandated the creation of a national education indicator study panel and also authorized NAEP Trial State Assessments (TSAs) to begin in 1990. To date, four waves of state-level assessments have been conducted (1990, 1992, 1994, and 1996) involving 33 of 50 states.

As mentioned previously, the majority of states have education indicators that predate the NAEP Trial State Assessments and many have full-blown systems that combine outcome indicators of student achievement with input and process measures.

Virginia

Virginia has adopted a 'stakeholder approach' in the development of indicator systems. The stakeholders were seen as teachers, school superintendents, school board members, and education group representatives. The authors of a report on this activity (Henry, Dickey and Areson, 1991) reported 'teachers, who might be expected to resist a performance monitoring system, were the most positive about the efficacy of the process and the most committed to the system.'

Tennessee

In 1992, the Tennessee General Assembly mandated the creation of the Tennessee Value-Added Assessment System (TVAAS), which is based on a series of nationally normed tests administered annually to students in grades 2–8 inclusive (ages 7 through 13 years). Students are tested in five subjects (mathematics, science, reading, language and social studies), using 'freshly developed' items that are trialed and tested each year using Item Response Theory. The general fashion for criterion-referencing and 'performance assessment' is robustly questioned by Sanders and Horn (1995a).

The entire TVAAS system combines the value added approach with hierarchical linear modelling (HLM) to analyse the effects of districts, schools, and teachers on student learning. Thus, performance data on districts, schools, and teachers are based on the *improvement* students make, rather than on 'absolute levels of achievement' (Baker et al., 1995). By state law, the TVAAS data are used in combination with other performance indicators (attendance, drop-out, and promotion rates) to determine whether schools and districts will receive rewards or sanctions. Individual schools must earn a cumulative value-added score equal to or greater than 100 per cent of the national norm gain in each of the five subject areas and are rewarded if they meet or exceed their specified goals. Districts must achieve at least a 95 per cent cumulative gain average over all five subjects, with a minimum cumulative gain of 90 per cent in each subject. Districts that fall short must demonstrate that they are making statistically significant progress toward reaching their target performance or become subject to sanctions.

TVAAS data may not be used for individual teacher evaluations until three years of data are available. To date, the teacher effects (which Dr William Sanders, the TVAAS developer identifies as a large source of variation) – have been reported only to the teacher, school administrators, and school board members. The system also has been plagued by unexplained variability in national norm gains across grade levels, some of which may be attributable to problems with the test instrument itself (Baker et al., 1995).

Generally speaking, the TVAAS is a highly sophisticated statistical system of large proportion with a potential of generating pupil-level records in the millions. (Every child is tracked as long as he or she remains in or returns to schools in Tennessee.) Sanders has developed highly efficient storage, retrieval and analysis procedures. It is a remarkable system, the results from which are awaited with interest.

Louisiana

Like many other indicator programmes created in the 1980s, Louisiana's 'Progress Profiles Programme' was the result of a gubernatorial promise to increase educational quality through greater school accountability (Children First Act, 1988). From the programme's inception, the Louisiana Department of Education (LDE) has been required to provide all public school parents an individualized '*School Report Card*' on the school(s) their children attend. In addition to distributing roughly 800,000 parent reports each year, the LDE Bureau of School Accountability produces annual *District Composite Reports* containing six years of longitudinal data aggregated to the school, LEA and state levels, and an annual *Progress Profiles State Report*, offering LEA and state summary statistics.

Roughly a dozen indicators are reported each year, including school input measures (e.g. the percentage of faculty with advanced degrees and the percentage of classes taught within specified class size ranges), student achievement measures (criterion- and norm-referenced test results, average scores on the American College Test and Scholastic Assessment Test) and selected student behavioural outcomes (i.e. data on student attendance, suspensions/expulsions and drop-outs). Statistics are also presented on the percentage of high school graduates who require remediation in college as first-time freshmen.

The Profiles were initially beset by the same data comparability problems that plagued the USDE's 'Wall Chart,' triggering a long and hard-fought campaign to standardize data definitions and collection procedures statewide. In 1996, the Profiles Programme made the transition to a new statewide, student-level database (the Student Information System, or 'SIS') which tracks student behavioural performance from kindergarten through high school completion. The improvements in data accuracy and comparability have been accompanied by sweeping changes in the format and content of the Profiles' reports, particularly those produced for parent consumption. With parent, teacher and school district feedback to guide them, the LDE staff have streamlined and clarified the Profiles so that the information they contain is accessible to even poorly educated readers. In fact, one of the more startling findings from the programme's ongoing evaluation has been the large number of parents and school staff who are intimidated by data presented in either tabular or graphic form (Kochan et al., 1994).

The 1988 legislation which established the Profiles Programme also created a statewide School Incentive Programme (SIP), designed to recognize schools with higher than expected mean achievement. School performance was measured, using a school-level composite indicator of student achievement (SIPscore) that was created by standardizing, combining and then averaging student scores on state-administered criterion- and norm-referenced tests (Crone et al., 1994b). Though Incentive Awards were offered only one year, school effectiveness researchers have used the SIPscore methodology to calculate composite indicators of elementary school effectiveness (Teddlie and Stringfield, 1993).

More recently, Louisiana researchers have used Profiles data to construct a composite behavioural indicator of secondary school effectiveness, based on school-level measures of student attendance, retention and discipline (Kochan et al., 1996). The researchers are using the behavioural indicator in tandem with a traditional achievement-based index in order to determine the extent to which high schools strike a balance between promoting academic achievement and keeping all of their students actively engaged in schooling. The team recently calculated effectiveness indices for 310 secondary schools over a three-year period, and found a moderate correlation (r = .65) between the achievement and behavioural indicators. Though most schools were consistently classified on the two effectiveness indices, some were 'effective' on one indicator, but 'ineffective' on the other. Site-based qualitative research is underway in four representative cases (one consistently effective, one consistently ineffective, and two differentially effective) in order to verify and document the conditions in the schools.

Examples of Unofficial Indicator Systems

Early innovation often takes place, very appropriately, in universities. Such work might then be followed by the adoption of safe indicators into a national official system. We draw attention to one informal system which may have led to the development of the first valued added system on a national scale: The Value Added National Project (VANP) in the UK. Due to the existence of the examination system in the UK, there was a framework available in which many school effectiveness studies could be undertaken with data from authentic, curriculum embedded tests that were 'high-stakes' for students since examination passes meant university places (fully funded until recently) and jobs. Policy initiatives such as the Technical and Vocational

Education Initiative were evaluated by methods that would come to be called 'value added' (Fitz-Gibbon et al., 1988; Tymms et al., 1990; Fitz-Gibbon, 1990a). Substantial studies of the effects of schools benefited from credible outcome data from examinations and became classics (Rutter et al., 1979; Smith and Tomlinson, 1989; Gray et al., 1983 and Mortimore, Sammons, Stoll, Lewis and Ecob, 1988). Work related to the analysis of examination data was supported by LEAs, notably the Inner London Education Authority (Nuttall et al., 1989) and also by the Scottish Office Educational Department and Scottish LEAs (McPherson and Willms, 1986). Impressive work on multilevel modelling (e.g. Rasbash et al., 1989) was taken up enthusiastically by many researchers (Gray et al., 1986; Fitz-Gibbon, 1991b; Tymms and Fitz-Gibbon, 1991, 1992, 1995; Donoghue et al., 1996; Sammons, 1995; Daly, 1991, 1995a, 1995b). It may have diverted the efforts of a few educational researchers into statistical details that were attended to at the expense of getting the underlying systems working. Multilevel analyses of small samples of data were conducted with no feedback to school departments, no disaggregation by school subject and so elaborately modelled as to remove the information from the appreciation of most teachers. Such research, though academically interesting, was of no major practical import, and was sometimes over interpreted (Preece, 1989).

A system that has worked with schools is the A-Level Information System (ALIS) started in 1983 (Fitz-Gibbon, 1985). The extraordinary result of this research is that a value-added system will be adopted nationally after years of development paid for not by central government but largely by schools and teachers' organizations with some support from LEAs. In other words, the English value-added system will have been largely a 'bottom up' rather than 'top down' development.

Sampling in the ALIS project is 100 per cent population data, and each school subject is considered separately to provide departmental rather than school effectiveness. Datasets from questionnaires to students regarding their attitudes, aspirations and the teaching and learning processes they have experienced have been added to examination data for ages 16 and 18 years. After six years as a single-researcher project, the central government's Department of Education and Science (DES) lent a small amount of financial support (about £14,000 over two years, or about half a very modest one year salary). When invited to conduct a controlled trial to see if the impact of monitoring on schools was beneficial, the DES declined to do so. Sustaining support has come from some LEAs followed by individual schools and colleges and all the professional associations of headteachers. Smaller projects providing feedback largely on examination results in context were developed by the National Foundation for Educational Research and the London Institute of Education. By 1995 the projects from the Curriculum Evaluation and Management Centre (CEM), home of the ALIS project, were providing value-added measures and other indicators throughout primary and secondary schooling, working with between a quarter and a third of secondary schools in England, Wales and Northern Ireland. By the time the government became seriously interested in value added, it was largely up and running, funded by the profession.

In 1995 the CEM Centre was successful in responding to a tender for a 'Value Added National Project' from the School Curriculum and Assessment Authority. The interim reports in December 1995 used statistical trialling with actual data with the following results:

- Against many expectations, the national curriculum tests showed the kind of predictive validity found throughout school effectiveness studies (correlations of about 0.7, explaining about 50 per cent of the variance in outcomes).
- Simple residual gain analyses yielded school effectiveness indicators that were for all practical purposes almost identical with those from multilevel modelling (correlations generally higher than 0.98, with the lowest being 0.94). Thus the simple analyses were quite adequate.

It is likely that value added will become a routine feature of UK secondary schools by about 1998, and of primary schools shortly thereafter.

Although schools are often portrayed as antagonistic to accountability, such a view is not consistent with the willingness of schools not only to look at their own effectiveness but also to commit the funds necessary to do so, a point made forcefully by Slavin (1996) and certainly illustrated in the UK. Whilst the influence of external pressures, such as the publication of raw results (the League tables) cannot be entirely discounted, the ALIS project nevertheless started *before* accountability pressures were strong, *before* the School Performance Tables were introduced, *before* a fairly benign inspection system mutated to malignant (Fitz-Gibbon, 1995a, 1995b) and *before* school governors were given strong powers.

In summary, an informal, research-based, voluntary and school-funded project laid a foundation for a national system. In this 'bottom up' development schools led the way not only with participation but also funds. However, this could only happen in a framework of information provided by adequate testing.

The commitment of schools to improvement efforts in which they have confidence suggests the importance of

1 entrusting schools with financial power (UK schools have benefited from 'Local Financial Management' initiatives, devolving about 85 per cent of school district budgets to schools); and
2 involving schools in research that has credibility and meets their needs.

One of these needs is probably for indicators of some richness and detail. This chapter has shown that such efforts are now in place in many countries. Another need is to create evidence-based policies, validated by adequate experimentation and evaluation.

Conclusions

Monitoring education is *not* like monitoring a power station or landing an aeroplane (Stringfield, 1995). In power stations and aeroplanes, a finite number of definable and measurable variables are in operation, each governed by laws of physics that are quite well measured. In education, countless numbers of ill-defined variables, both contextual and procedural, are interacting in an ever-changing, dynamic system with feedback loops which almost certainly make the system fundamentally unpredictable (Waldrop, 1993; Glass, 1979; Tymms, 1996a; Fitz-Gibbon, 1996). Monitoring may be able to do little more than alert us to the occasional outbreak of a problem: 'fire-fighting,' as Glass (1979) argued years ago with great prescience.

If indicators are presumed to track the 'performance' of a system, the implication is that the system is in some way responsible for the particular process or outcome reflected by the indicator. One of the most important types of information that will eventually arise from indicator systems will be *a sense of the extent to which schools have an impact on various outcomes*. Such information, however, will not be simple to acquire. Value-added indicators show considerable instability from year to year, as would be expected since the errors on gain scores have long been known to be greater than those on single scores (Harris, C., 1967). Without randomized controlled trials it is extremely difficult to derive strong causal inferences.

For example, researchers should have taken heed of the unfortunate events following Wiley and Harnischfeger's (1974) insistence that allocated time was a powerful variable for policy. Based on analyses which failed to differentiate between inner city schools and suburban schools, they hypothesized that longer school days would increase student learning. Though Karweit (1985) pointed out inadequacies in their analyses very promptly, it was too late to prevent policy makers from seizing on a clearly alterable variable: the length of the school day. (Not only had Wiley and Harnischfeger interpreted correlation as causation, they had failed to take account of the fact that their data contained urban schools with short school days and suburban schools with long school days. In datasets without this confound, Karweit showed that the relationship of allocated time-in-school and achievement was not present.) Throughout the USA, teachers were presented with lengthened teaching days. The expected increase in reading achievement did not follow, and Wiley can hardly defend the policy now. The cost to teachers in terms of extended teaching time was, it seems, never considered.

There is an important lesson to be learned from this. It is highly important, both scientifically and ethically, to *ensure that policy recommendations for costly actions be based on controlled, well-evaluated interventions*, not on correlational data that can so easily be misinterpreted.

Research methods courses often consist of 'measurement, design and statistics'. Now that researchers have brought politicians to the point of collecting good *measurements* in indicator systems, perhaps they can move on to educate policy makers about *design*. As for the application of *statistics*, that is the least of the problems.

10 Theory Development in School Effectiveness Research

Bert Creemers, Jaap Scheerens and David Reynolds

Introduction

There are several reasons to produce a model. First, a model serves to explain previous research parsimoniously. It maps a series of avenues for future research which may serve to alert policymakers that investment in the field would be rewarding, and thus potentially stimulates the funding of further research. A model may provide a useful 'road map' for practitioners, and indeed there are hints that it has been partially an absence of school effectiveness theory that has hindered the take up of effectiveness knowledge by practitioners in schools. Arguments from Scheerens and Creemers (1989b) also concern the need for a model to generate both a more theoretical orientation, a secure foundation for research and a guide to the field to prevent new entrants from re-inventing the wheel by conducting already existing research.

With respect to educational effectiveness, a model can therefore explain differences in student learning results by specifying the relationships between the components in the model and student outcomes. Based upon earlier research, it can be understood that such a model should include several levels, such as the student level, the classroom level, the school level and the contextual (above school) level. Higher levels should be seen as providing conditions for what takes place at lower levels.

The Carroll Model

In the immediate past, various different models for educational effectiveness were designed, for example the model of elementary school effects by Stringfield and Slavin (1992) which was based on Slavin's earlier QAIT model, and the models of Scheerens (1992) and Creemers (1991). These models all have in common that they take as their point of departure the learning of students, and all models are based upon Carroll's earlier model of student learning (Carroll, J., 1963) in which learning rate is considered as a function of five elements: aptitude, ability to understand instruction, perseverance, opportunity, and the quality of instruction.

Virtually all multilevel school effectiveness models refer to the model of Carroll (1963), which offers a set of relevant factors at the student and the classroom level (Creemers, 1991; Scheerens, 1992; Stringfield and Slavin, 1992; Walberg, 1984). This model was originally developed to predict the success of foreign language training.

Carroll (1963) defines student achievement, the degree of learning, as a function of the time actually spent divided by the time actually needed by a student. The time needed is influenced by factors at the student level: aptitude (task-specific skills) and ability to understand instruction (general intelligence) and by a factor at the classroom level: quality of instruction, defined as telling students what they have to do and the way they have to do it. The time spent is also influenced by a factor at the student level: the time the student is willing to spend on learning (perseverance or motivation) and a factor at the classroom level: the time allowed for learning by the teacher. Essentially, the degree of learning is predicted by the main constructs described above.

The Carroll model is not the first model for learning and it will not be the last one. Probably the model was so influential in the further development of instruction and research, because it was directed very precisely to what happens in schools. Other learning theories and models are much more concerned with the learner and internal processes of learning than with the relationship with what goes on in schools. For example, although the model of Gage (1963) is also directed to learning in schools, it mainly explains how intellectual skills can be acquired and stages can be discerned. It does not provide guidelines nor is it connected with what is happening in ordinary schools.

The different components of the Carroll model were developed further by other authors. The concept of time, one of the basic constructs of the Carroll model, was developed by Harnischfeger and Wiley (1976). The concept of perseverance or motivation was developed by Keller (1983), who was criticizing the attention to effectiveness and efficiency of instruction in the instructional design. The ARCS-model (Attention, Relevance, Confidence and Satisfaction) can be considered as a further elaboration of motivation and perseverance in the Carroll model.

The Carroll model generated several research traditions of which the research on mastery learning, time spent (learning time and time allowed) and opportunity to learn were most influential. Mastery learning (Bloom, 1976) aims at equalizing time allowed by teachers and time needed by students. To reach this aim teachers should set goals, check students for mastery of these goals, and offer corrective measures when mastery is not attained. These activities constitute high quality of instruction. Eventually, differences in time needed might even disappear according to Bloom and his associates. The effectiveness of mastery learning is supported by some authors (Block and Burns, 1976; Guskey and Pigott, 1988; Kulik et al., 1990), but questioned by others (Weeda, 1982; Arlin, 1984; Slavin, 1987). On the whole, it seems justified to conclude that mastery learning when implemented accurately can have positive effects. However, there is not much evidence on the disappearance of differences in time needed.

Carroll (1985, 1989) states that mastery learning research paid too little attention to differences in aptitude and ability to understand instruction as relatively stable predictors of time needed along with quality of instruction. Research on time spent and student achievement rather consistently yielded positive relations (Karweit, 1985) and this also holds for the related concept of time allowed (often defined as classroom management) to time spent. Carroll factors at the student level influencing time spent were seldom incorporated in research (Karweit, 1985) although their relative impact may be large (Karweit and Slavin, 1989) and account for a major proportion of variance in achievement (Creemers, 1991). The time allowed by teachers, often described as allocated time (Creemers, 1994) started to encompass the concept of opportunity to learn, defined as the curriculum content a teacher covers in his lessons. Research on opportunity to learn in general focuses on a direct relationship with achievement and does not incorporate time spent as an intermediate factor (Pelgrum, 1989) nor quality of instruction as another determining factor of achievement. Carroll has defined opportunity to learn as time allowed by the teacher. Husen (1967) has shown that it is not only time that counts but also the way the time is used. Therefore Husen and later on the IEA studies defined opportunity to learn as content covered. In many studies opportunity to learn seems to be one of the most powerful predictors of achievement as measured in terms of content covered or, more specifically, the pages of the curriculum covered or the percentage of test items taught (Brophy and Good, 1986).

Although the Carroll model has been very important for educational research and theories, it has some drawbacks too. The narrow definition of a learning task is one of them. A learning task is defined as going from incapability of performing an act to mastering it. So learning tasks are activities to be undertaken in order to acquire predetermined knowledge and skills. The model applies only to one learning task at a time. The task should be unequivocally described and there should be means for making a valid judgment as to when the learner has accomplished the task, i.e. has achieved the learning goal that has been set for him (Carroll, J., 1963). The Carroll model also does not pay much attention to the definition of factors at the classroom level. Bloom (1976) elaborated some notions on quality of instruction in his theory on mastery learning. Also, the concept of content covered can be seen as a useful elaboration of time allowed.

Further Models

At the second level, the classroom level, factors that can be related to the learning of students are discerned. Stringfield and Slavin (1992) summarize these factors as QAIT: Quality, Appropriateness, use of Incentives, and Time for instruction at the classroom level. At the school level, they distinguish five important factors: *meaningful* and universally understood goals, *attention* to daily academic functioning, *coordination* among programmes and between schools and parents over time, development of all staff and the *removal* of unsuccessful teachers from the school, and the *organization* of the school to support universal student learning. These five school level factors are abbreviated as MACRO. The level above that of the school includes the community, the school district, and the state and federal government, but the model does not specify the interaction with these further factors at these levels in detail.

In their recent development of the basic model developed earlier (Scheerens and Creemers, 1995), Scheerens has put special emphasis on the school level and Creemers has emphasized the importance of the classroom level (Scheerens, 1992; Creemers, 1994).

The educational effectiveness model of Creemers (1994) distinguishes between school curriculum variables and 'other' variables. Connected with this idea of a formal relationship between what goes on in classrooms, between classrooms and between the class and the school level, are the concepts of consistency, cohesion, constancy and control. Basic variables at the student level in addition to students' aptitude and motivation are the time spent on learning and the opportunity they need to attain their goals. Education at classroom level provides time and the opportunity for learning. The quality of instruction contributes to the effectiveness of education, but is mediated by time and opportunity. At the school level and the contextual level, above the classroom level, variables related to time, opportunity and the quality of teaching are conditions for instructional effectiveness. In this way, all levels are synchronized and it is hoped that this may clarify the way they influence each other and ultimately contribute to student achievement. There is empirical evidence, either strong or moderate, for the influence of most of the factors mentioned at the classroom level in the model on student achievement (Creemers, 1994). At the school level, the empirical evidence for the selected factors (a selection of correlates provided by empirical, mostly correlational studies) is also sufficient (Scheerens, 1992; Levine and Lezotte, 1990). The formal characteristics have been under study (Creemers and Reezigt, 1996; Weide, 1995), although it is accepted that all factors need more empirical support through experimental studies. The importance of the factors at the contextual level as yet have little empirical support from educational effectiveness studies, and to study these factors properly, internationally comparative research is needed. Their significance is plausible, however, based on case study data from the International School Effectiveness Research Study (Reynolds et al., 1994).

Student Level

The students' background, their motivation and their aptitudes strongly determine their achievement. Time on task is the time students are willing to spend on school learning and on educational tasks. Time on task is not only determined by the motivation of students, but also by factors at the school and the classroom level. Time on task is the time students are actually involved in learning, but this time has to be filled by opportunities to learn. These opportunities concern the supply of learning materials, experiences and exercises by which students can acquire knowledge and skills. In fact, learning opportunities are the instructional operationalization of the objectives of education, whereas tests are the evaluative operationalization of the same objectives. In this respect one can speak about the content coverage of the curriculum. A distinction is made between opportunities offered in the instructional process and students' actual use of the offered experiences. It is expected that the latter can explain learning outcomes better than the learning opportunities provided by the curriculum of the teacher.

Classroom Level

In addition to the variables of time and opportunity, the quality of instruction determines the outcomes of education. Based on theoretical notions and empirical research, it is possible to select characteristics of the three components of quality of classroom instruction, curriculum, grouping procedures and teacher behaviours.

The *curriculum* refers to the documents like textbooks and the other material used by the teacher, which means that the effects of material are influenced by the way teachers use them. The characteristics that contribute to the quality of instruction are:

- explicitness and ordering of goals and content;
- structure and clarity of content;
- use of advance organizers;
- use of material for evaluation of student outcomes, feedback and corrective instruction.

The research into *grouping procedures* is mostly comparative, trying to prove that a specific procedure is better than others. The results show that the success of grouping is highly determined by the availability of proper instructional material and by teacher behaviours. The following procedures turn out to be effective:

- mastery learning;
- ability grouping;
- cooperative learning.

but the results are highly dependent on use of:

- differentiated material;
- material for evaluation, feedback and corrective instruction.

Teacher behaviour is not only a determinant of the success and failure of the curriculum and grouping procedures, but also has an independent contribution to effectiveness. Teachers set the time framework (for lessons as well as for homework), organize the instructional environment and provide, initiate, and continue the instructional process. The effective characteristics are the following:

- effective class management/an orderly and quiet atmosphere;
- use of homework;
- high expectations;
- clear goal setting;
  - a restricted set of goals
  - an emphasis on basic skills
  - an emphasis on cognitive learning and transfer
- structuring the curriculum content;
  - ordering of goals and content
  - use of advance organizers
  - use of prior knowledge of students
- clarity of presentation;
- frequent questioning;
- use of an immediate exercise after presentation of new content;
- use of evaluation, feedback and corrective instruction.

It is obvious in the model that teachers are the central component in the instruction at the classroom level. They make use of curricular materials and they actually set out grouping procedures in their classrooms.

In addition to these characteristics, the more formal characteristic of consistency can also be noted at the classroom level. Consistency points to the need for the characteristics of the components to be synchronized with each other.

School Level

Looking at the lists of effective school factors (Levine and Lezotte, 1990; Scheerens, 1992), it becomes clear that most of these factors, such as 'an orderly climate in the school' and 'the evaluation of student achievement', are in fact reflections of the indicators of quality of instruction, time and opportunity to learn that operate at the classroom level. Because of a lack of research studies that analyse school and classroom levels simultaneously in one design, it is hard to say what the separate contribution of these factors might be in accounting for student level variance when controlling for their effects as classroom level factors. In any case, many school level factors are rather meaningless when they are not clearly linked to classroom factors. Even if they do have an independent effect on pupil achievement, it is still not clear how these effects come about and therefore how they should be interpreted in policy terms. In the current model, therefore, all school level factors are defined as conditions for classroom level factors. This definition restricts the selection of school level factors only to those factors conditional for, and directly related to, quality of instruction, time or opportunity to learn.

We distinguish conditions for the *quality of instruction* with respect to the *educational* aspects:

- rules and agreements about all aspects of classroom instruction, especially curricular materials, grouping procedures and teacher behaviour, and the consistency between them;
- an evaluation policy and a system at the school level to check student achievement, to present learning problems or to correct problems at an early stage. This includes regular testing, remedial teaching, student counselling, and homework assistance.

With respect to the *organizational* aspects at the school level, important conditions for the *quality of instruction* are:

- a school policy on coordination and supervision of teachers, departmental heads and school principals (educational leadership), and a school policy to correct and further professionalize teachers who do not live up to the school standards;
- a school culture inducing and supporting effectiveness.

Conditions for *time* at the school level are:

- the development and provision of a time schedule for subjects and topics;
- rules and agreements about time use, including the school policy on homework, pupil absenteeism and cancellation of lessons;
- the maintenance of an orderly and quiet atmosphere in the school.

Conditions for *opportunity to learn* at the school level are:

- the development and availability of a curriculum plan or school working plan;
- a consensus about the mission of the school;
- rules and agreements about how to proceed and how to follow the curriculum, especially with respect to transition from one class to another or from one grade to another.

At the school level, consistency between the components, which are synchronized with each other, is an important condition for instruction. All members of the school team should take care of this, thereby creating cohesion. Schools should not change rules and policies frequently, generating the constancy principle. The control principle not only refers to the fact that student achievement should be evaluated, but also to a quiet atmosphere in the school. Control also refers to teachers holding themselves and others responsible for effectiveness. In these factors, like consistency, constancy and cohesion, one can see the importance of some of the concerns of persons in school improvement to generate 'ownership' (Fullan, 1991) or 'collegiality' (Rosenholtz, 1989).

Context Level

The same components as were mentioned before (quality, time and opportunity to learn) can also be distinguished at the context level.

Quality at this level concerns the following conditions:

- a national policy that focuses on the effectiveness of education;
- the availability of an indicator system and/or a national policy on evaluation/a national testing system;
- training and support which promotes effective schools and instruction;
- the funding of schools based on outcomes.

Time refers to:

- national guidelines with respect to the time schedules of schools;
- supervision of the maintenance of schedules.

Opportunity to learn refers to:

- national guidelines and rules with respect to the development of the curriculum, the school working plan and the activity plan at the school level, for example through a national curriculum.

It is clear that, at the different levels, and especially at the context level, resources are also important, but resources should be operationalized as such things as the availability of materials, teachers and other components supporting education in schools and classrooms (Hanushek, 1989; Gray, 1990; Hedges et al., 1994), rather than as a more general, global level of financial resources.

At the context level, consistency, constancy and control are again important formal characteristics which can be utilized, emphasizing the importance of the same characteristics over time and of mechanisms to ensure synchronicity at a point in time.

Relating School Effectiveness to Meta Theories

Public choice theory provides the diagnosis of instances of organizational ineffectiveness, such as goal displacement, over-production of services, purposefully counter-productive behaviour, 'make work' (i.e. officials creating work for each other), hidden agendas and time and energy consuming schisms between sub-units. When discretional leeway of subordinate units goes together with unclear technology this too adds to the overall nourishing ground for inefficient organizational functioning; see Cohen, March and Olsen's famous garbage can model of organizational decision-making (Cohen, M., et al., 1972). Not only government departments but also universities are usually mentioned as examples of types of organizations where these phenomena are likely to occur.

Theoretically the remedy against these sources of organizational malfunctioning would be a close alignment, and ideally even a complete union, of individual, sub-unit and organizational goals. The practical approach to go about this offered by public choice theory is to create external conditions that will force, at least part, of the inefficient divergency of individual level and organizational rationality out of the system. The level that is recommended to be used is the creation of market-mechanisms replacing administrative control. The competition resulting from these market-conditions will be an important incentive to make public sector organizations more efficient. The essence of *choice* as an alternative to the bureaucratic controls that result from the way representative democracy works is that a completely different, more 'local' type of democracy is called for in which most authority is vested directly in the schools, parents and students (Chubb and Moe, 1990, p.218). In their 'proposal for reform' these authors draw a picture of an educational system where there is a lot of liberty to found schools, a funding system that is largely dependent on the success of schools in free competition for students, freedom of choice for parents and freedom for schools to have their own admission policies.

It should be noted that the leverage-point of 'choice' differs from that of synoptic planning and bureaucracy as an alternative mechanism that might explain educational effectiveness phenomena. Whereas the former applies to the design of the primary process and supportive managerial conditions in the areas of supervision and coordination, the latter (choice) points at external, school environmental conditions. This means that, perhaps surprisingly, both mechanisms could theoretically be employed simultaneously. Although internal bureaucratic functioning (in the sense described in the previous section) will most likely be seen as being embedded in the larger central or state bureaucracy there is no necessity that this is indeed the case.

Notes of criticism that have been made with respect to the propagation of choice are that parents' choices of schools are based on other than performance criteria (Scheerens, 1997), that 'choice' might stimulate inequalities in education (Scheerens and Bosker, 1997) and that completely autonomous primary and secondary schools create problems in offering a common educational level for further education (Leune, 1994).

Scheerens (1992, pp.17–18) mentions the following three instances in which deductions from public choice theory are in line with the results of empirical school effectiveness research:

1   To the extent that public choice theory draws attention to overemphasizing general managerial and maintenance functions at the cost of investment in the organization's primary process, the results of USA and British studies showing that instructional leadership is associated with relatively high performance are in line with this observation.

2   Second, the construct of 'opportunity costs', which draws attention to the phenomenon that functionaries in public sector organizations have opportunities to be active in non-task related activities, can be seen as indicative of the general finding that more 'time on task' and thus 'less foregone teaching and learning', leads to better educational achievement (examples of foregone teaching and learning are lessons not taught, truancy and time required to maintain discipline).

3   Third, public choice theory offers a general explanation for the results of comparisons between private and public schools. Generally in developed countries, private schools appear to be more effective, even in countries where both private and public schools are financed by the state, as is the case in the Netherlands (Creemers and Osinga, 1995).

Explanations for the alleged superiority of private schools are that

- parents who send their children to these schools are more active educational consumers and make specific demands on the educational philosophy of schools; and
- a greater internal democracy of private schools (the latter conclusion was drawn on the basis of an empirical study of Hofman (1995)).

The evidence that schools that are more autonomous are more effective (regardless of religious denomination or private/public status) is not very strong, however. Although Chubb and Moe (1990) claim to have shown the superiority of autonomous schools their results have been criticized on methodological grounds (Witte and Walsh, 1990). At the macro level, there is no evidence whatsoever that national educational systems where there is more autonomy for schools perform better in the area of basic competencies (Meuret and Scheerens, 1995).

The political image of organizational functioning and public choice theory rightly challenge the assumption of synoptic rationality and bureaucracy that all units and individuals jointly pursue the organization's goal. The arguments and evidence concerning the *diagnosis* (inefficiency caused by a failing alignment between individual level and organizational level rationality) are more convincing than the *cure* (privatization, choice) as far as the effectiveness of schools is concerned. The critical factor appears to be that market forces (e.g. parents' choice of a school) may not be guided by considerations concerning school performance, so that schools may be 'rewarded' for other than efficient goal-oriented performance.

It should be emphasized again that our perspective is the internal or instrumental interpretation of school effectiveness (see the introduction) and that the evaluation of the merits of choice may be quite different when the *responsiveness* of schools is seen as the central issue, particularly for higher educational levels (e.g. vocational schools, higher education) as compared to primary and general secondary schools.

Although in many industrialized countries there are tendencies towards decentralization and increased autonomy of schools, for primary and secondary education these tendencies are stronger in the domains of finance and school management than in the domain of the curriculum (Meuret and Scheerens, 1995). The United Kingdom is a case in point, where local management of schools is combined with a national curriculum and a national assessment programme. Also in case studies of 'restructuring' programmes in the USA and Canada (Leithwood, 1995) increased school autonomy is concentrated in (school-based) management and 'teacher empowerment' whilst curriculum requirements and standards are maintained or even further articulated at an above-school level.

Stringfield (1995, p.70) notes that several states in the USA have created new curriculum standards, and new, more demanding and more performance-based tests.

What remains then as a possible fruitful direction for future school effectiveness research as a result of this analysis of the 'political' image of organizational functioning? The market-metaphor appears to be only useful in a limited sense for primary and secondary education, because governments will generally see the need for a certain standardization in key-areas of the curriculum to provide a common base for further education. At the same time 'choice'-behaviour of the consumers of education may diverge from stimulating schools to raise their performance, and undesired side-effects (more inequalities) cannot be ruled out. The critical factor appears to be that schools experience external pressures and incentives to enhance performance in key-areas of the curriculum. Consumers of education, if properly informed, may well be one source for creating these conditions, but not the only source. From this perspective, contrary to the strong adherents of 'choice', consumerism could well be seen as compatible with accountability requirements from higher educational levels. These different external conditions that may stimulate school performance have not been the object of many empirical studies (exceptions are, Kyle, 1985; Coleman and Laroque, 1991; Hofman, 1995) and deserve to be further investigated, also in an international comparative context. As a second area for further research the statements about 'bad' internal organizational functioning of public sector organizational deducted from public choice theory might be used as guidelines in studying unusually *in*effective schools.

Contingency Theory

'Contingency' is described as a 'thing dependent on an uncertain event' and 'contingent' as 'true only under certain conditions' (Concise Oxford Dictionary). In organizational science 'contingency theory', also referred to as the 'situational approach' or contingency approach, is taken as the perspective in which the optimal structure of an organization is seen as dependent on a number of 'other' factors or conditions. These other factors are mostly referred to as 'contingency factors' (Mintzberg, 1979). Contingency factors are a rather heterogeneous set of conditions, both internal and external to the organization: age and size of the organization, the complexity of the organization's environment and the technology of the organization's primary process (see Scheerens (1997), from which the next sections are drawn).

Some well-known general hypotheses about effective combinations of contingency factors and structural configurations are:

- the older the organization, the more formalized its behaviour;
- the larger the organization, the more elaborate its structure, that is, the more specialized its tasks, the more differentiated its units, and the more developed its administrative components;
- the more sophisticated the technical system, the more elaborated the administrative structure, specifically the larger and more professional the support staff, the greater the selective decentralization (to that staff), and the greater the use of liaison devices (to coordinate the work of that staff);
- the more dynamic the environment, the more organic the structure (Mintzberg, 1979, ch.12).

The terms in which organizational structure is described are organizational dimensions like the division of work ('specialization') and authority or vertical 'decentralization', the use of prestructured arrangements ('standardization') and the use of written regulations or formalization, the level of skills to carry out tasks or 'professionalization' and the interdependence of units ('coordination requirements'). Frequently a distinction is made between mechanistic and organic structure. A mechanistic structure is characterized by high levels of standardization and supervisory discretion and low levels of specialization, intra-unit interdependence, and external communication. An organic design, in its turn, is characterized by low levels of standardization and supervisory discretion and high levels of specialization, interdependence and external communication and is less prone to information saturation (Gresov, 1989, p.432). Mechanistic structure is likely to be efficient when tasks are simple and repetitive and environmental uncertainty is low. When tasks are uncertain and interdependence is high and the environment is dynamic the organic structure would be more 'fitting'.

The central and global thesis from contingency theory which says that organizational effectiveness results from a fit between situation and structure has been interpreted in various ways.

The 'congruence thesis' states that effective structure requires a close fit between the contingency factors and the design parameters (Mintzberg, 1979, p.217). Drazin and Van de Ven (1985) specify *congruence* as theories that just hypothesized fit between contingency factors and structure, without examining whether this context–structure relationship actually affected performance. They preserve the term 'contingency hypothesis' for analyses that look into the joint influence of context and structure on performance.

The 'contingency thesis' is focused at the internal consistency of structural characteristics, whereas the 'extended configuration hypothesis' states that effective structure requires a consistency among the structural characteristics *and* the contingency factors. These four different hypotheses call for four different research designs that are progressively more complicated.

1   Configuration is technically the least demanding since it could just look at structural parameters and their supposed harmonious fit, for instance by computing simple correlations.

At the same time interpretation would be quite circumscribed since no claims about context-structure fit nor of organizational effectiveness in terms of performance are involved.

2   Congruence (in Drazin and Van de Ven's more limited sense) would likewise call for simple correlations, this time between structural characteristics and contingency-factors. In fact much of the early empirical literature on contingency theory in organizational science went no further than testing congruence relationships (see for example Kieser and Kubicek, 1977).

3   Testing 'real' *contingency hypotheses* would involve some kind of configuration of three types of variables: contingency factors, organizational structure-variables and an operational effectiveness criterion, (e.g. profit, goal achievement, performance). Kickert (1979) has shown that at least three different interpretations of this configuration are possible.

4   'The extended configuration hypothesis' in its simplest form would investigate configurations of at least one contingency factor, a pattern of structural variables and performance. More realistically there would also be more than one contingency factor involved. The problem of multiple contingencies could be that one contingency factor would 'pull' structure in one direction, whereas another contingency factor could exercise influence in the opposite direction. For example in a situation where the task environment would become simplified as less interdependent whereas, at the same time, the external environment would become less predictable and dynamic, there would be opposing forces towards mechanistic and organic structure respectively. Gresov (1989) offers three ways for acting managers or organizational advisors to resolve problems of multiple and opposing contingencies. Two of these imply changing or redesigning the organization or the organizational context.

For researchers only the third approach appears to be realistic, namely to presuppose a dominance ordering of contingency factors, e.g. if technology and environment exercise opposing demands on structure then the influence of technology is the most important. There is, however, no common understanding about a universal importance ranking of contingency factors. If a solution would be sought in statements like: the predominance of one contingency factor over the other depends on certain situational characteristics one would presuppose a 'second degree' contingency theory, which looks like ending up with an infinite regress.

There are still more problematic aspects of contingency theory, at least from a researcher's perspective. The concept of 'equifinality' recognizes the possibility that different patterns of context–structure relationship may be equally effective. In a situation like that effectiveness researchers might come up with outcomes like the identification of ranges of effective and ineffective context–structure interrelationships. Probing deeper would inevitably lead up again to hypothetical 'second order' contingency factors, namely those background factors that would interact with different context–structure patterns to produce equal performance.

Next, contingency theory is sometimes criticized for its static nature, while at the same time it is recognized that organizations (i.e. management) may not only adapt structural characteristics of the organization but may also actively shape their environment (for instance through co-optation and marketing).

A third questionable area is the specificity of application of contingency theory. In organizational science it has frequently been used to compare broad categories of organizations, like when industries using craft, batch, mass, or continuous process production are compared. The question could be raised how useful contingency theory could be in comparing the effectiveness of context–structure relationship for a particular type of organization, in our case educational organizations. Here one should be more demanding than applying contingency hypotheses to explain differences between primary, secondary and tertiary (i.e. universities) educational organizations. For this example a general hypothesis could be that, given an average position of educational organization on the dimension mechanistic-organic, lower education levels would tend to the mechanistic and higher education levels to the organic pole.

For our purposes, theory development on educational effectiveness, contingency theory should be able to predict results of what has been termed as 'contextual effectiveness', the idea that different performance-enhancing conditions of educational organizations work in different contexts. Drawing on Teddlie's review on 'context in school effects research' (Teddlie, 1994b), it becomes clear that contextual effectiveness is indeed a viable part of educational effectiveness research. The most frequently studied context variables are: average socio economic status of students, urbanicity and educational level (i.e. primary versus secondary schools). A relatively new type of contextual analysis is the comparison of performance enhancing educational conditions across nations (Scheerens et al., 1989; Postlethwaite and Ross, 1992; Creemers et al., 1996).

Some illustrative results from contextual effectiveness studies are the following:

- a more short term orientation towards educational expectations in effective low SES schools as compared to middle SES schools (Teddlie et al., 1989b);
- more pronounced external reward structure in effective low SES schools as compared to high SES schools (ibid.);
- invitational versus a more careful (sometimes even 'buffering) attitude of middle SES schools as compared to effective low SES schools (ibid.);
- controlling educational leadership with respect to instruction and task orientation in effective low SES schools as compared to low or moderate controlling leadership in these areas in effective high SES schools (Hallinger and Murphy, 1986);
- primarily academic goals in effective elementary schools as compared to both personal as well as educational goals in secondary schools (various authors, cited by Teddlie, 1994b);
- strong instructional leadership required for success in urban elementary schools, whereas a managerial leadership style proved often successful in suburban elementary schools and an 'intermediate' between manager and initiator worked best in rural elementary schools (Teddlie and Stringfield, 1993).

It appears that the research results on contextual effectiveness, as is almost always the case with educational effectiveness research, have mostly been induced from exploratory correlational analysis, rather than being the result of the testing of hypothesis deduced from theory. Making a lot of sense as they do, the outcomes of contextual effectiveness studies are only vaguely related to contingency hypotheses from the general organization science literature. Perhaps the more controlling leadership in effective urban, low SES schools as compared to suburban, middle SES elementary and secondary schools, could be connected to the general contingency hypothesis that relatively simple, rather unconnected tasks in a generally stable environment call for a more mechanistic type of organization structure.

The question should be raised as to what can be expected of contingency theory when it comes to giving a more theoretical turn to educational effectiveness research. Can we deduce substantive hypotheses from contingency theory that could further research into contextual effectiveness? It is my impression that a careful study of the general organization literature on contingency, particularly the empirical research literature, can indeed yield interesting hypotheses.

In this sense the promising areas appear to be:

- hypotheses concerning changes in the technology of the primary process of learning and instruction;
- hypotheses concerning increased environmental uncertainty for educational organizations.

There is sufficient variety in the technology of learning and instruction to expect concrete implications for the structuring of educational organizations. If one compares, for instance, very structured approaches as the Calvert-Barclay programme, described by Stringfield (1995), with educational practice inspired by constructivism this variation is evident, even within a certain educational level (elementary education in this case). In the first instance, structural patterns would be expected to be in line with a mechanistic type of organization (little interdependence between units, standardization and direct control) whereas in the second instance a more organic type of organizing would be expected (horizontal decentralization, much interdependence between units, less standardization).

These overall patterns are more or less confirmed in publications describing the organizational context of the two polar types of educational technology, see Stringfield's description of 'high reliability organizations' and Murphy's analysis of the managerial context of constructivist teaching (Murphy, 1992) (also see Scheerens, (1994)). Barley's reference to role theory, already referred to in an earlier section (Barley, 1990), could be used as a guideline to study the more minute ways in which these task characteristics have an impact on organizational structures.

The second type of hypothesis could be applied to the variation in patterns of school autonomy versus dependency that arises from the current restructuring of educational governance in many countries. Policies of functional and territorial decentralization (see Meuret and Scheerens, 1995) as well as deregulation, paired to ideas about 'school-based management' and 'teacher empowerment' as well as the stimulation of market mechanisms, all make for a less stable and predictable school environment and would therefore be expected to force educational organizations to more organic structure, in order to remain effective. Since these configurations of centralization/decentralization differ strongly between countries, international comparative educational effectiveness studies could be used to test this type of hypothesis.

Finally, it should be noted that the logic of the contingency approach is very close to substantive and formal methodological interpretations of multilevel school effectiveness models, which were referred to in the introduction. The general idea of higher level facilitation of lower level conditions can be seen as an instance of the configuration thesis. Moreover, some of the intricacies of formalizing across level relationships (e.g. interactive, additive, non-recursive) in multilevel school effectiveness models are also present in the alternative formal specifications of contingency-hypotheses.

In making up the balance, in spite of all methodological problems, contingency theory appears to have more 'in it' than has currently been used in educational effectiveness research. In this way it offers certain possibilities to improve the theoretical basis of educational effectiveness in that research could become driven by specific hypotheses deduced from theory:

- a heightened attention to endogenous developments within the organizations, an active attitude towards influencing environmental conditions;
- a focus on feedback and learning functions;
- a increased tolerance for intuition, political vision and ethos in management style.

To the extent that schools' environments can be seen as turbulent, these three managerial factors could, likewise, be seen as relevant to enhancing school effectiveness and thus as relevant 'process features' or effectiveness enhancing conditions. However, here the same reservations are in place as were made in the section on the learning organization: schools' environments generally may not be turbulent, after all.

Conclusions and Implications for School Effectiveness Research

In their analysis of alternative models of school effectiveness Bosker and Scheerens (1994) conclude that 'the actual problem might in fact be that the most likely model might be indirect, non-recursive, contextual, synergetic, and interactive at the same time'. All of these characteristics imply increased complexity as opposed to simpler (direct, recursive, additive) versions. This means that state-of-the-art multilevel and structural modelling techniques based upon the general linear model could fall short of dealing with the complexity inherent in conceptual school effectiveness models.

Another basis for concern about the current state of the art of school effectiveness research are doubts about the progress that is being made in building a well-established knowledge-base and even – to a lesser degree – whether school effectiveness can be studied as a relatively stable phenomenon.

Doubts about the solidity of the current knowledge-base on school effectiveness are expressed by Tymms (1996a) who in fact presents a first attempt to apply chaos-theoretical reasoning to school effectiveness by means of a simulation study, and by Scheerens (1993). As progress is being made in properly adjusting outcome data for prior achievement and other relevant background variables at the student level the proportion of the total student variation that can be attributed by attending a particular school appears to drop to values of 5–7 per cent (see Bosker and Witziers, 1996; Hill et al., 1995). If roughly half of this proportion of variance can be accounted for by a set of effectiveness enhancing process conditions of schooling, it is clear that it is extremely difficult to accumulate evidence on a stable set of malleable correlates of 'net'-achievement. Scheerens and Creemers (1995) demonstrate this lack of consistency among relevant process characteristics in a quantitative review of about 40 Dutch educational effectiveness studies (see Chapter 2).

In the area of stability of school effects the authors of recent studies conclude that 'there is a substantial amount of instability across years' (Luyten, 1994a, p.56) and 'that there is a significant degree of change over time' (Thomas, S., et al., 1995, p.15). Correlations of effects across years vary according to subjects roughly from 0.40–0.90. These authors found that only at the extremes (either effective or non-effective) consistent (across subjects) and stable (across years) positioning patterns were found.

Considering these areas of unexplained variation (both with respect to process correlates of net school effects and (in)stability over time) two approaches can be considered:

- continue using the current linear analysis techniques, but preferably with larger samples, more reliable measures and controlled (quasi-experimental) research designs;
- employ the more complex systems dynamics modelling techniques that are associated with the general label of chaos theory.

Preferably both approaches should be followed. There appears to be insufficient ground (in terms of lack of consistency and stability) to abandon the more traditional methods. On the other hand it seems worthwhile to further explore the possibilities of dynamic systems theory approaches to try and discover patterns in the so far 'unexplained regions' in our knowledge on what causes schools to be effective. In a more practical sense this approach could have the following implications for school effectiveness research:

- efforts in examining the long term effects of differences in entrance-conditions (achievement of students, contextual effects of grouping of students, matching of teachers and groups of pupils);
- efforts in creating longitudinal data-files on outcomes, student background and process characteristics per school;
- perhaps a new source of inspiration to carry out qualitative studies of school-specific measures that might explain the improvement or deterioration of a school's functioning and increased effort to try and reach some type of accumulation and synthesis from numbers of qualitative studies.

Section 4

The Future of School Effectiveness Research

11 School Effectiveness Research and the Social and Behavioural Sciences

Charles Teddlie and David Reynolds

Introduction

The academic specialization known as School Effectiveness Research (SER) has occasionally been treated as a sub-field within larger, longer established fields of study such as Educational Administration (e.g. Bossert, 1988; Hoy and Miskel, 1991), or as a complementary 'adjunct' to areas such as teacher effectiveness or teacher research (e.g. Wittrock, 1986). In this handbook, we have treated SER as an independent field of study, which is within the general discipline of education, and which has now generated its own sub-fields of inquiry (see Chapter 2).

While SER resides in general within the discipline of education, it has 'roots' and evolving 'branches' throughout the entirety of the social sciences. In this chapter, we will first discuss the 'roots' of the area within disciplines such as economics, psychology, sociology, and criminology; then, we will discuss its future in terms of new extensions into areas as diverse as social network analysis and psychiatry.

Specific Contributions from the Historical 'Roots' of SER

The Economics of Education

The economists' educational production function (EPF) has been used extensively in education to investigate school productivity and efficiency (e.g. Benson, Medrich, and Buckley, 1980; Bowles, 1970; Coleman et al., 1966; Geske and Teddlie, 1990; Glasman and Binianimov, 1981; Hanushek, 1971, 1972, 1979, 1981, 1986, 1987; Henderson et al., 1978; Katzman, 1971; Lau, 1979; Monk, 1989, 1992; Murnane, 1975, 1981; Murnane and Nelson, 1984; Summers and Wolfe, 1977). The assumption in these EPF studies is that inequities in easily measurable, financially related inputs (e.g. teacher salaries, student teacher ratio, number of volumes in the library, size of science labs, age of buildings, years of faculty experience) were related to student achievement.

The economists' orientation is highly rational, perhaps even mechanistic, and is based on the traditional hypothetico-deductive model:

> For purposes of school productivity research, efficiency is typically defined as the potential for achieving increases in outputs of schooling without incurring increases in the physical qualities or quantities of the resources used. . . . The economist's production function is typically used in education to examine the

effects of different factors on students' school performance. The educational production function is based on the assumption that there is some systematic relationship between school inputs and educational outputs that influence student achievement.

(Geske and Teddlie, 1990, pp.192–3)

Coleman's 1966 Report was based on the assumption that financially defined inputs could predict student achievement, and his failure to find the expected relationships not only served as a catalyst for the development of SER, but also presaged the frustrating search for consistent relationships between those variables. Hanushek (1986) conducted an extensive review of the field and concluded:

> The results are startlingly consistent in finding no strong evidence that teacher–student ratios, teacher education, or teacher experience have an expected positive effect on student achievement. According to the available evidence one cannot be confident that hiring more educated teachers or having smaller classes will improve student performance. Teacher experience appears only marginally stronger. . . . *There appears to be no strong or systematic relationship between school expenditures and student performance.*
>
> (Hanushek, 1986, p.1162)

Despite these overall negative findings, some studies have demonstrated that school resources affect different students in different ways, but few school resources consistently benefit all students (Geske and Teddlie, 1990). Two of the most outstanding studies in this tradition are Summers and Wolfe (1977) and Murnane (1975), both of which painstakingly tied specific school resource data to individual student achievement (see Chapters 1 and 3 for more details).

The most discerning criticisms aimed at the Coleman Report and later EPF studies concerned the underspecification of the economists' models; specifically, this criticism charged that important input variables were not included. Many economists did not consider attitudinal variables, such as school climate, or measures of classroom behaviour appropriate for their models. These economists (e.g. Murnane and Nelson, 1984) stressed an orthodox position that assumed that:

> . . . production inputs and techniques are well articulated and fully detailed and that the manufacturing process becomes highly standardised, with little tolerance for variation.
>
> (Geske and Teddlie, 1990, p.199)

Within this orthodox, economic orientation, variables such as teaching skills were too varied and idiosyncratic to be included in the EPF. As Murnane and Nelson (1984) stated:

> Variation in educational practice is unavoidable and in fact is crucial to effective teaching. . . . In other words, effective teaching requires intensive problem solving activity, and creative and personalised response to frequent unpredicted circumstances. . . . Many details have to be worked out by the individual teacher, and

what one teacher does in applying a particular broadly defined method will diverge, often considerably, from what another teacher does.

(Murnane and Nelson, 1984, pp.362–3)

It could be argued that the exclusion of behavioural variables (e.g. teacher classroom performance) and attitudinal variables (e.g. school climate) from traditional EPF studies doomed that area from making further advances in explaining variance in student performance. Indeed, it will be argued in this chapter that advances coming from social psychology, in terms of the measurement of attitudes, and from teacher effectiveness research, in terms of the measurement of classroom behaviour, led to great improvement in the proper specification of mathematical models predicting student achievement in SER.

Despite this, the EPF, in greatly modified and expanded form, is still an essential part of SER today. The multilevel models described in Chapter 6 are the successors to the regression driven EPF models of the 1960s and 1970s. Researchers using these modern multilevel models incorporate attitudinal and behavioural predictors that orthodox EPF theorists would eschew, but the basic hypothetico-deductive mathematical model (student performance = a function of controllable and uncontrollable predictors) is the same as that employed by Coleman and his colleagues in the mid-1960s.

The Sociology of Education

Another strong influence on the development of SER came from the American and British branches of the sociology of education. Numerous early studies were conducted within the USA in the structural-functional paradigm, specifically within the status attainment literature, that sought to relate adolescent educational achievement and, in some cases, adult occupational status/income to a variety of 'background' variables including those relating to school attended (e.g. Alexander, K. and McDill, 1976; Alexander, K. et al., 1978, 1981, 1985; Bidwell and Kasarda, 1975; Brookover and Erickson, 1975; Erbing and Young, 1979; Enthwistle and Hayduk, 1988; Hannan et al., 1976; Hauser, 1971; Hauser et al., 1976; Heynemann and Loxley, 1983; Heyns, 1974; Hoffer et al., 1985; Lee, V., and Bryk, 1989; McDill et al., 1967, 1969; Raudenbush and Bryk, 1986; Sewell et al., 1969; Shavit and Williams, 1985). Chapters 1 and 3 contain brief reviews of this literature.

In the United Kingdom, developments in the sociology of education from a concern with the influence of family background (e.g. Davie et al., 1972; Douglas, 1964, 1968) towards an acknowledgment of the importance of the school had an important influence on the development of school effectiveness. Hargreaves (1967) and Lacey (1970) published interesting material that looked at the impact of school academic differentiation upon student outcomes, arguing for the importance of 'streaming by ability' in generating low academic achievement and delinquency outside the school. Byrne and Williamson (1971) also argued for the importance of resource factors in different geographical areas being associated with differing regional levels of academic achievement. Other useful contributions were made from the field of classroom studies which, although they were not undertaken with the same observational vigour as those in the USA noted later in this chapter, generated an enhanced interest in the factors within the educational system that were worthy of future study.

Social Psychology

The contributions of social psychology to SER are primarily within the area of instrument development related to the input side of the EPF. The inability of the economic and sociological input variables to adequately capture school and classroom process factors led educational researchers to borrow conceptual variables from social psychology including the following:

- student internal-external locus of control scales;
- expectation levels for student performance;
- academic self-esteem scales; and
- school educational 'climate' scales.

The remainder of this section will trace the development of these social psychological scales and their deployment in SER. This development was briefly described in Chapter 1 in the section on the history of SER in the USA.

Internal/External Locus of Control (Student Sense of Academic Futility)

The social psychological concept of internal/external locus of control was popularized by Rotter (1966). If individuals have an internal locus of control, then they believe that their own actions can have an efficacious impact upon their environment; conversely, if individuals have an external locus of control, then they believe that their own actions do not have much of an impact upon their environment.

This construct was entered into the SER literature by Coleman et al. (1966), who asked students to agree or disagree with statements such as:

> People like me don't have much of a chance to be successful.
> Good luck is more important than hard work for success.
> Every time I try to get ahead, something or somebody stops me.

Results from the Coleman Report indicated that student 'sense of control of the environment' was the most important student attitudinal variable measured in terms of its relationship to student achievement. Coleman and his colleagues concluded that:

> It may well be, then, that one of the keys toward success for minorities which have experienced disadvantage and a particularly unresponsive environment – either in the home or the larger society – is a change in that conception.
>
> (Coleman et al., 1966, p.321)

Brookover et al. (1978, 1979) adapted this 'student sense of control over the environment' into a scale measuring what they called 'student sense of academic futility'. This scale was the most important predictor of student achievement in the Brookover study, explaining over one-half of the variance in student achievement. Brookover's adaptation of the sense of control variable made it into a construct that could be directly affected by the particular school environment in which students exist: the school should be able to affect their students' sense of the degree to which they can be successful in that particular environment, if not in the society as a whole. Teddlie and Stringfield (1993) replicated the results of the Brookover study using both the student 'sense of futility scale' and scales measuring both students' and faculty's sense of external *and* internal locus of control in an academic environment (Crandall, V. et al., 1965; Taylor, R. et al., 1981).

Teacher and Student Expectation Levels

The evolution of the concepts of teacher and student expectation levels started in animal studies in psychology in the 1960s and has extended through contextually sensitive SER in the 1990s.

Rosenthal's work on experimenter bias effects (Rosenthal, 1968, 1976) first documented the effect on laboratory animals. Rosenthal and Fode (1963) discovered that albino rats trained by experimenters who thought that their rats were 'maze bright' earned significantly higher scores than rats trained by experimenters who thought that their rats were 'maze dull'. Actually, the albino rats were assigned to experimental condition (bright or dull) randomly.

Rosenthal and Jacobsen (1968) extended the experimenter bias effect results to the classroom in their famous formulation of the self fulfilling prophecy described in *Pygmalion in the Classroom*. In this research, randomly chosen students were classified as 'bloomers' to the faculty in a school. Later retesting showed that the IQ of these 'bloomers' went up significantly more than the remainder of the class. This research has been controversial, with replications of the self fulfilling prophecy occurring in some studies, but not in others.

The self fulfilling prophecy research in turn led Brookover and others (e.g. Brophy and Good, 1974; Cooper and Good, 1982; Crano and Mellon, 1978; Persell, 1977) to study how teacher expectancies account for between school variations in student achievement. Brookover and his colleagues (1978, 1979) expanded the scales to include student and principal expectations (as well as those of teachers) and further differentiated between current and future expectations. The results from SER using these scales led to the inclusion of 'high expectations for student achievement' as one of the original correlates of effective schooling (e.g. Brookover and Lezotte, 1979; Edmonds, 1979a, 1979b, 1981; Lezotte, 1990; Lezotte and Bancroft, 1985).

Context differences in expectations associated with the SES of students attending the schools were reported by both Hallinger and Murphy (1986) and Teddlie and Stringfield (1985, 1993). Hallinger and Murphy concluded that the source of expectations in low-SES schools was the school itself and tended to be moderate; in high-SES schools, the sources were the home and school and tended to be very high. Teddlie and Stringfield concluded that middle-SES schools promoted both high present and future educational expectations, while low-SES schools emphasized present educational expectations only. (See Chapter 5 for more details regarding these context differences.)

Academic Self Concept or Self Esteem

The pioneering and popularizing work in the area of self concept or self esteem came from Rosenberg (1963, 1965) and Coopersmith (1967). Put simply, self concept is a

person's personal beliefs about himself or herself, and is the product of multiple interactions with significant others, such as people in the family and school (Stoll and Fink,
1996). Rosenberg's early work involved the influence of parents on the self concepts
of their children. Work over the past thirty years has determined that self concept, or
self esteem, is a multidimensional construct and that it varies greatly by factors such as
culture, ethnicity, and sex (e.g. Stoll and Fink, 1996; Tashakkori and Kennedy, 1993).

Scales specifically measuring academic self concept, which is a particular type of
self esteem related solely to academic matters, have been developed (e.g. Brookover et
al., 1978; Michael and Smith, 1976). Brookover and his colleagues did much of the
early work with regard to conceptualizing and measuring academic self esteem (e.g.
Brookover et al., 1962; Brookover and Schneider, 1975). Miller (1983) summarized
Brookover's work in this area:

> In sum, self concept of ability functions as an intervening variable between signifi-
> cant other expectations and evaluations of students on one side and student
> achievement on the other. The construct also functions as a threshold variable, i.e.
> a necessary but not sufficient factor in high achievement.
>
> (Miller, 1983, p.26)

While academic sense of futility, teacher expectations, and school climate have
generally been used as predictors of achievement in SER, academic self concept has
been conceptualized several ways:

- as an intervening variable between expectations/evaluations and achievement (e.g.
  Brookover and Schneider, 1975; Miller, 1983);
- as a criterion variable; that is, as a product of the schooling experience (e.g.
  Brookover et al., 1978; Mortimore et al., 1988);
- as a predictor variable related to student achievement (e.g. Teddlie and Stringfield,
  1993).

Criminology

Criminological research in general, and particularly that on juvenile delinquency,
has made a significant contribution to SER in both the USA and the United Kingdom
(for a review see Reynolds and Jones, 1978). In the USA, the emergence of theories
concerning the generation of delinquency that gave a central position to the role of the
school was notable in the early 1960s, with one version proposing that the school
encouraged delinquency because of its blocks upon goal attainment in academic
spheres by low social class male youth (Cloward and Ohlin, 1964) and the other
version arguing that the school generated delinquency through a 'reaction formation'
generated by its alien, middle class values impacting upon lower class youth who
possessed a different value system (Cohen, 1965). By the late 1960s, the education/
delinquency interaction was very well established with a paradigm that related low
educational achievement and high levels of 'officially recorded' or 'self reported'
delinquency (see Reynolds and Jones, 1978).

The Report of the *President's Commission on Youth Crime* (1967) indeed gave an
official seal of approval to the thesis of 'school effects', and summarized a great deal of

the knowledge then available on the 'school factors' responsible for generating 'at risk' youth, amongst them:

- negative labelling by teachers, particularly of youths from low SES homes;
- a non-relevant curriculum, unrelated to the world that lower SES youth inhabited or to their occupational destinations;
- streaming or 'tracking' that acted to depress expectations;
- a 'youth culture' within many schools that celebrated different ways of obtaining status to those of the official school procedures.

Further interesting development of the 'school effect' thesis came from Hirschi (1969) with his notion of the importance of the 'social bond' that linked young people to the wider society.

Within the United Kingdom, the very first findings of substantial school differences came from delinquency research in the seminal work of Power and associates (1967, 1972) that showed twenty-fold differences in delinquency rates of outwardly similar schools in a homogenous working class community. British research explicitly maintained this link with criminology by keeping individual and school delinquency rates as a dependent variable, as in such studies as Reynolds et al. (1976); Rutter et al. (1979); Clegg and Megson (1968) who discovered an interesting link between schools' propensity for corporal punishment and their delinquency rates.

The United Kingdom interface and interaction between school effectiveness and criminology has been maintained by the continued focus within British sociology of education upon 'problem' or antisocial or marginal youth (e.g. Willis, 1976) and by a continued view of the school child as a victim of poor schooling (Hammersley and Woods, 1976). Reviews of this literature (e.g. Hargreaves, 1982), have often ended up 'adopting' a 'control' orientation to the school/student relationship in a similar vein to that of Hirschi (1969) in the United States described above. Some of the classic British studies of the school as a social organization have also been explicitly concerned with the role of the school in the generation of delinquent careers, as in the classic study of 'Lumley' secondary modern school by Hargreaves (1967) in which school streaming or tracking systems, the reaction of the organization to student rule breaking and the consequent counter reaction of the student sub-culture all interacted to generate a 'delinquescent' sub-culture of low achieving students.

Educational Administration

The field of educational administration has also contributed significantly to SER, especially in terms of research and theory exploring the relationship between the leadership of principals and superintendents on the one hand and school effectiveness and improvement on the other. Examples include the following:

- Within mainstream academic educational administration, a number of articles have appeared on SER in journals such as *Educational Administration Quarterly* over the past 10–15 years (e.g. Clark, D., et al., 1984; Firestone and Wilson, 1985; Hallinger and Heck, 1996; Hannaway and Talbert, 1993; Sirotnik, 1985; Wimpelberg et al., 1989).

- Within practitioner oriented educational administration, articles concerning effective schools and school improvement were especially numerous from the late 1970s through the mid- to late 1980s. For example, there were several articles on effective schools and school improvement published in the journal *Educational Leadership* during this period (e.g. Andrews, R. and Soder, 1987; Brandt, 1989; Deal and Kennedy, 1983; Dwyer, 1984; Edmonds, 1979a; Firestone and Herriott, 1982a; Hall et al., 1984; Levine and Eubanks, 1989a, 1989b; Lezotte and Bancroft, 1985; McCormack-Larkin, 1985; McCormack-Larkin and Kritek, 1982; Mortimore and Sammons, 1987; Murphy et al., 1985; Purkey and Smith, 1982; Stringfield and Teddlie, 1988; Sweeney, 1982).
- Within the mainstream SER literature, leadership and administrative processes are often the topics of journal articles. (See Chapter 4 for a discussion of the processes of effective leadership.) For instance, numerous articles have appeared in *School Effectiveness and School Improvement* on various aspects of principal and superintendent leadership over the past seven years (e.g. Anderson, S., 1991; Bamburg and Andrews, 1991; Cheng, 1994, 1996; Corbett and Wilson, 1992; Crowson and Morris, 1992; Dimmock and Hattie, 1996; Dimmock and Wildy, 1992; Goldring and Pasternack, 1994; Hallinger and Edwards, 1992; Hallinger and Leithwood, 1994; Heck et al., 1991; Hord et al., 1992; Leithwood, 1992a, 1992b; Leithwood and Jantzi, 1990; Leitner, 1994; Silins, 1994; van de Grift, 1990; van de Grift and Houtveen, 1991; VanderStoep et al., 1994).

The following section of this chapter will discuss the contribution of the field of educational administration to SER in three general areas:

1 leadership theory and research;
2 other educational administration constructs, such as organizational effectiveness, organizational culture or climate, and loose and tight coupling; and
3 contributions to instrument development.

Leadership Theory and Research

Theory and research on leadership occurs within many disciplines (e.g. business administration, education, social psychology), so SER has a rich literature from which to draw. Over the past 60 years, the study of leadership particularly relevant to educational settings in the USA has gradually shifted from social psychology to educational administration, although both fields continue to make contributions. Many of the classic studies from social psychology (e.g. Cartwright and Zander, 1968; Fiedler, 1967, 1973; French and Raven, 1968; Lewin et al., 1939; Lippitt and White, 1952) have been incorporated into mainstream educational administration literature (e.g. Hoy and Miskel, 1991).

Lewin, Lippitt and White (1939) conducted a classic study to determine which leadership style (i.e. authoritarian, democratic, *laissez-faire*) worked best in after-school clubs. While the democratic style generated more positive affective responses and independent behaviour, the authoritarian style led to higher production of masks, which was the goal of the clubs (Lippitt and White, 1952). This early work on leadership styles has had a continuing influence on the study of leadership in SER. For instance, Hall et al. (1984) described three different 'change facilitator styles' (i.e. initiators, managers, responders) that principals exhibit in school improvement situations. Later SER has interpreted research results on the leadership styles of these three types of change facilitators (e.g. Evans, L., and Teddlie, 1995, Teddlie and Stringfield, 1993).

Fiedler (1967, 1973) conducted extensive research related to the contingency theory of leadership, which asserts that there is not one best style of leadership, but rather the effectiveness of leadership depends upon situational or contingency factors (e.g. Mintzberg, 1979, 1983; Scheerens, 1993). Contingency theory remains one of the major theoretical frameworks in both educational administration and SER. Contextually sensitive SER (e.g. Hallinger and Murphy, 1986; Teddlie and Stringfield, 1985, 1993) has confirmed predictions from contingency theory: for instance, effective schools with students from different SES contexts (i.e. lower or middle SES) have principals that differ according to their leadership styles (i.e. initiators or managers). (This research is discussed further in Chapter 5.)

Hoy and Miskel (1991), in a standard text on educational administration, discussed several frameworks that could be used in studying leadership in schools, including the following:

- typologies of different power bases (e.g. referent, expert, legitimate, reward, coercive) that educational administrators can use (e.g. Etzioni, 1975; French and Raven, 1968; Mintzberg, 1983; Yukl, 1981);
- trait theory, or the great man theory (e.g. Immegart, 1988; Stogdill, 1981; Yukl, 1981);
- situational theory (Hersey and Blanchard, 1982); and
- three types of contingency theories: the path-goal theory (House, 1971; House and Baetz, 1979); Fiedler's (1967) contingency theory; and Fiedler and Garcia's (1987) cognitive resource theory.

Comprehensive, integrated reviews of leadership in schools (e.g. Hallinger and Heck, 1996; Murphy, 1990a) from the field of educational administration offer researchers studying school effectiveness a variety of theories, together with research literatures, with which to study educational leadership in schools varying in terms of effectiveness. These theoretical perspectives are often useful in planning studies or interpreting results from SER.

For instance, Wimpelberg (1987, 1993) utilized both Bolman and Deal's (1984, 1991) 'managerial frames' and Mitchell's (1990) cultural theory of the principalship to explain the leadership behaviour of principals in differentially effective schools (i.e. stable effective, improving, declining, stable ineffective) from the Louisiana School Effectiveness Study.

Other Educational Administration Constructs

Other educational administration constructs of interest to researchers in SER are: the organizational effectiveness of schools, organizational culture or climate, school climate, the climate continuum, open and closed climates, and loose and tight coupling. The definition of the organizational effectiveness of schools is a controversial topic in educational administration, with no widely accepted formulation available. Hoy and Miskel (1991, pp.382–3), using a framework provided by Parsons (1960), referred to four organizational effectiveness dimensions, together with multiple indicators:

1　adaptation – adaptability, innovation, growth, development;
2　goal attainment – achievement, quality, resource acquisition, efficiency;
3　integration – satisfaction, climate, communication, conflict;
4　latency – loyalty, central life interests, motivation, identity.

Of course, school effectiveness is typically defined in terms of achievement alone, although many critics have stated that multiple criteria should be used in defining it. (See Chapter 3 for more discussion of the definition of school effectiveness.) SER theorists and researchers could benefit from considering the other indicators noted by Hoy and Miskel (1991), such as:

1　innovation and growth as indicators of school improvement;
2　quality and efficiency as complementary components of effectiveness;
3　climate as an outcome of schooling, rather than an input into the prediction of achievement;
4　satisfaction and identity as alternative definitions of school effectiveness, in addition to achievement.

Organizational culture in contemporary educational administration has an anthropological basis that emphasizes 'shared orientations that hold the unit together and give it a distinct identity' (Hoy and Miskel, 1991, p.212). Much of the contemporary focus on organizational culture in education derives from popular theories of distinct corporate cultures from the field of business (e.g. Deal and Kennedy, 1982; Ouchi, 1981; Peters and Waterman, 1982).

Organizational climate, on the other hand, has roots in psychology, as described in a previous section of this chapter. It may be defined as the enduring characteristics of the organization that sets it apart from other organizations (e.g. Gilmer, 1966; Hoy and Miskel, 1991; Litwin and Stringer, 1968; Tagiuri and Litwin, 1968). Furthermore, school climate is defined in the educational administration field as:

> . . . a relatively enduring quality of the school environment that is experienced by participants, affects their behaviour, and is based on their collective perceptions of behaviour in the schools.
>
> (Hoy and Miskel, 1991, p.221)

A distinguishing characteristic of the school climate construct is that it has been tied to specific measurement instruments since its initial formulation. In a previous part of this chapter, school climate was discussed primarily in terms of the social psychological literature, which greatly influenced the development of the Brookover et al., school climate (1978, 1979) scales.

Within the field of educational administration, Halpin and Croft (1962, 1963) developed the Organizational Climate Description Questionnaire (OCDQ) in the early 1960s and used it to develop profiles of elementary schools. The concepts of open and closed school climates emerged from this research. Later research indicated that school climate existed on a continuum, rather than in discrete categories (e.g. Andrews, J., 1965; Brown, R., 1965; Watkins, 1968). (Information on the further development of the OCDQ is found in the next section of this chapter.)

The constructs of loose and tight coupling have also been usefully applied to schools within the fields of educational administration and SER. Weick (1976) and Orton and Weick (1990) describe loose coupling as a situation in which elements of a system are responsive, but retain elements of separateness and identity.

Weick (1976) and Bidwell (1974) analysed structural looseness in schools and concluded that schools are loosely coupled systems. For instance, there is loose control in schools over how well the work (e.g. classroom teaching) is done, partially due to professional norms of autonomy (e.g. Forsyth and Dansiewicz, 1985). Some research (e.g. Abramowitz and Tenenbaum, 1978; Deal and Celotti, 1980; Firestone, 1985; Meyer, 1978) has confirmed Weick's concept of schools as loosely coupled. On the other hand, Hoy and his colleagues (Hoy, Blazovsky, and Newland, 1980, 1983; Hoy et al., 1977) described schools from their research as highly centralized and formalized (i.e. tightly coupled).

Work by Firestone and his colleagues indicate that different types of schools may be loosely or tightly coupled (e.g. Firestone and Herriott, 1981, 1982b; Firestone and Wilson, 1985; Herriott and Firestone, 1984). For instance, their work indicates that secondary schools are more likely to be loosely coupled, while elementary schools are more likely to be tightly coupled.

These concepts of loose and tight coupling have been applied within SER. Hallinger and Murphy (1986) described effective, low-SES schools as having a tightly coupled, narrow curriculum emphasizing basic skills and having a high degree of control of instruction by strong instructional leaders. Control of instruction at effective, high-SES schools, on the other hand, was low to moderate. Teddlie and Stringfield (1985, 1993) reported essentially the same results, indicating that effective, low-SES schools may be characterized as tightly coupled, while effective, middle- and high-SES schools have characteristics of both tight and loose coupling.

Murphy (1992) summarized differential linkages in effective and ineffective schools as follows:

> One of the most powerful and enduring lessons from all the research on effective schools is that the better schools are more tightly linked – structurally, symbolically, and culturally – than the less effective ones. They operate more as an organic whole and less as a loose collection of disparate subsystems. There is a great deal of consistency within and across the major components of the organization, especially those of the production function – the teaching–learning process.
>
> (Murphy, 1992, p.96)

Creemers and Reezigt (1996), summarizing the work of several scholars (e.g. Creemers, 1994; Reynolds and Creemers, 1992; Reynolds, 1993; Stringfield, 1994b; Stringfield and Slavin, 1992), referred to four 'formal criteria' for effectiveness at the school level: consistency, cohesion, constancy, and control. All of these criteria of effective schools reflect tightly coupled organizations.

Contributions to Instrument Development

Several of the instruments developed in the field of educational administration, and their various adaptations, have been used in SER. These instruments have the characteristics of being conceptually based within a particular theoretical orientation and of having well defined psychometric properties. As with all previously developed instruments, they are not appropriate for use in SER projects in which the theoretical constructs do not match those that are assessed by the instruments.

Instruments from educational administration that have been used in original or modified form in SER include the following.

- *OCDQ* (Organizational Climate Description Questionnaire), *OCDQ-RE* (OCDQ revised for elementary schools), *OCDQ-RS* (OCDQ revised for secondary schools). As noted above, this measure of climate was originally developed by Halpin and Croft (1962, 1963). Due to numerous criticisms that evolved over the first 20 years of its use, the instrument was revised extensively, resulting in an elementary education version (Hoy and Clover, 1986) and a secondary education version (Kottkamp et al., 1987) toward students.
- *LBDQ* (Leadership Behaviour Description Questionnaire). This questionnaire was developed at Ohio State University in the 1940s. It measures two dimensions of leadership: initiating structure and consideration (e.g. Halpin, 1966; Hoy and Miskel, 1991). Several theoretically interesting constructs, such as professional zone of acceptance (e.g. Kunz and Hoy, 1976) have been examined in research using the LBDQ.
- *IPOE* (Index of Perceived Organizational Effectiveness). This instrument was developed to assess several dimensions of organizational effectiveness (Miskel et al., 1979, 1980; Mott, 1972). Research by Hoy and Ferguson (1985) indicate that the instrument is a valid measure of organizational effectiveness.
- *OHI* (Organizational Health Inventory), *OHI-E* (OHI for elementary schools). This instrument measures seven specific interaction patterns in schools (e.g. Hoy and Feldman, 1987; Hoy et al., 1990). A form was also developed specifically for elementary schools (Hoy et al., 1991).
- *PCI* (Pupil Control Ideology form). This instrument measures the degree to which a school has a custodial (traditional) orientation or a humanistic orientation (Willower et al., 1967).

Other instruments developed within the area of educational administration may be of interest to SER researchers including the Central Life Interests Questionnaire (Miskel et al., 1975) and questionnaires measuring educators' job satisfaction (e.g. Miskel and Gerhardt, 1974).

The Ongoing Linking of SER with Other Disciplines

Teacher Effectiveness Research

Creemers and his colleagues (e.g. Creemers and Reezigt, 1996; Creemers and Scheerens, 1994) have recently called for the study of 'educational effectiveness' to replace the separate fields of school effectiveness and teacher effectiveness (or teacher effects) (e.g. Brophy and Good, 1986). They have proposed an integrated model that combines variables that have been traditionally associated with either school or teacher effectiveness. Their call echoes an earlier sentiment expressed by Good (1989):

> Now that researchers have clarified that schools and teachers make a difference, it is important to explain more completely how processes at both levels operate and how they can be combined. Researchers should not only examine school practices (e.g. school rules) or classroom assignments (e.g. the extent to which instruction emphasises rote learning or meaningful learning) but should also study how the effects of one teacher can be combined with the effects of other teachers in ways that do not threaten teacher autonomy yet make schooling more coordinated and effective for all concerned.
>
> (Good, 1989, p.36)

In this section, we will:

- describe how this sentiment for merging the two fields of school and teacher effectiveness evolved from the situation a decade ago when the two literatures were essentially non-overlapping;
- briefly review some of the results from the field of teacher effectiveness research (TER) that are particularly relevant to SER;
- describe constructs and instruments from TER that are already being used in SER; and
- briefly speculate on how SER and TER can be effectively integrated with regard to programmes for school improvement and other issues.

The Separate Emergence of SER and TER and the Initial Integration of the Two Approaches in SER

Teddlie (1994a) described the separate evolution of SER and TER as follows:

> Simply put, most teacher effectiveness studies have been concerned only with processes that occur within the classrooms to the exclusion of anything going on schoolwide. Similarly, most school effectiveness studies have involved phenomena that occur throughout the school, with little emphasis on particular teaching behaviours within individual classrooms. This segregation of the two literatures has occurred in spite of the logical link between the two fields.
>
> (Teddlie, 1994a, p.111)

There were a number of reasons for this separate development of the two fields, including the following:

- The researchers in the two fields came from different academic and intellectual backgrounds, with those in SER more likely coming from educational administration and sociology of education, while those in TER were more likely to have come from educational psychology.

- Researchers from SER were interested in molar behaviour that consistently varied across schools, while researchers from SER were interested in molecular behaviour that varied across classrooms.
- There were differences in the designs used by the two groups, with researchers in TER conducting experimental and survey studies, while those in SER typically utilized survey and archival research.
- There were differences in the instruments used by the two groups, with researchers in TER more often using behavioural measures, while those in SER more often used attitudinal measures.
- The two groups of researchers had different agendas regarding educational improvement, with those in SER emphasizing school improvement and those in TER emphasizing teacher improvement.

The segregation of the two literatures was maintained through the mid-1980s. Two review pieces written at that time concerning SER (Good and Brophy, 1986) and TER (Brophy and Good, 1986) listed a combined total of 328 references. Of these references, only nine overlapped between the two articles, representing less than 3 per cent of the total.

Researchers conducting more sophisticated SER (e.g. Brookover et al., 1979; Mortimore et al., 1988; Rutter et al., 1979; Teddlie et al., 1984) began exploring the processes of schooling more closely in the late 1970s and 1980s, due to their dissatisfaction with the explanatory power of the economic and sociological models described in previous sections of this chapter. Survey data that included proxies for classroom observations (e.g. survey items regarding the social psychological climates of classes and schools) gradually became a part of SER, as did informal observation of classroom and schoolwide behaviour. For example, the four case studies presented by Brookover et al. (1978, 1979) included extensive information on the proportion of classtime spent on instruction, the use of competitive groups as opposed to individual learning in classrooms and the use of positive reinforcement in classrooms based on survey data and informal classroom observations.

Researchers using these variables were rewarded as they were able to explain aspects of the schooling process that had not been explored in SER heretofore. Starting in the mid-1980s, researchers working within the SER paradigm began explicitly including classroom observations (and consequently teacher effectiveness variables) in their research (e.g. Creemers et al., 1996; Crone and Teddlie, 1995; Stringfield, Teddlie and Suarez, 1985; Teddlie et al., 1989a; Teddlie and Stringfield, 1993; Virgilio et al., 1991). The commonality for these investigations was their study of teacher effects data within the context of school effectiveness research studies. These studies revealed consistent mean and standard deviation differences between schools classified as effective or ineffective. (See Chapter 4 for a review of these studies.)

Relevant Research from the Teacher Effectiveness Literature

Some researchers working within the EPF tradition in the 1970s and 1980s concluded that classroom variables (or constructs) should *not* be added to their models because teaching was characterized by techniques that are basically tacit and idiosyncratic (e.g. Murnane and Nelson, 1984). As noted above, these researchers doubted that consistent relationships could be demonstrated between teacher classroom behaviours and student achievement.

Teacher Effectiveness Research demonstrated this point of view was ill informed, as significant relationships were reported between measurable teacher classroom behaviours and student achievement (e.g. Brophy and Good, 1986; Gage, 1978, 1983). The teacher effectiveness field progressed from a series of correlational studies (e.g. Brophy and Evertson, 1974; Evertson et al., 1980; Fisher et al., 1980: Stallings and Kaskowitz, 1974) through a series of quasi-experiments in which the alteration of classroom processes produced mean gains in student achievement (e.g. Anderson, L. et al., 1979; Good and Grouws, 1979; Stallings, 1980; Tobin, 1980; Tobin and Capie, 1982).

The area of TER was very active from the early 1970s through the mid-1980s, when a substantial body of literature concerning the characteristics of effective teaching was fully developed (e.g. Brophy, 1979; Fraser et al., 1987; Good, 1979; Good and Brophy, 1986; Good and Grouws, 1979; Rosenshine, 1983; Rosenshine and Stevens, 1986; Walberg, 1984). Reviews of effective teaching characteristics, based on this extensive body of research, include the following topics (e.g. Brophy and Good, 1986): quantity and pacing of instruction, opportunity to learn, time allocation, classroom management, active teaching, whole-class versus small group versus individualized instruction, redundancy/sequencing, clarity, proper use of praise, pacing/wait-time; questioning skills, social-psychological climate of the classroom, etc. These classroom behaviour variables are now as much a part of SER as the attitudinal variables and financial input variables described in previous sections of this report.

These TER studies also yielded a plethora of classroom observational systems; Brophy and Good reported that there were more than 100 of these systems by 1970, and many more have been added over the past 25 years. Some of these observational systems have already been used in SER, as summarized by Schaffer, Nesselrodt, and Stringfield (1994). Among the classroom observational systems are:

- Flanders' Interaction Analysis Categories (FIAC) – one of the earliest classroom observation systems developed by Flanders (1970) to measure indirect and direct teacher behaviour.
- Stallings' (1980) Classroom Snapshot (CS) – a low-inference measure of time-on-task and interactive teaching, that has been used in evaluation studies, studies of early childhood education, studies of student learning and SER (Stallings and Freiberg, 1991).
- Classroom Activity Record (CAR) (Evertson and Burry, 1989) – the CAR systematically collects data on classroom behaviour related to instruction, management and context.
- The IEA Classroom Environment Study instruments (Anderson, L. et al., 1989) – low-inference, quantitative observation instruments used in the IEA studies.
- The Virgilio Teacher Behaviour Inventory (VTBI) – a closed-ended 38 item instrument used in the Louisiana School Effectiveness Study (LSES), other SER studies (e.g. Virgilio, Teddlie and Oescher, 1991), and the International School Effectiveness Research Programme (ISERP) (Creemers et al., 1996); this instrument was validated in a study conducted in the USA schools and measures

classroom management, instruction presentation skills, questioning skills, and social-psychological climate of classroom (Teddlie, Virgilio and Oescher, 1990).

- The Classroom Observation Instrument (COI) – an instrument designed for the LSES (Teddlie and Stringfield, 1993) to provide high-inference classroom data in the form of field notes regarding 15 general indicators of teacher effectiveness gleaned from the TER reviews of Rosenshine (1983) and Rosenshine and Stevens (1986); these field note data were later converted to numeric data through the quantitizing methodology described by Miles and Huberman (1994).
- Special Strategies Observation System (SSOS) (Schaffer and Nesselrodt, 1992) – adapted from the CAR by researchers in a study of special school improvement strategies conducted in the USA.
- International Classroom Observation Survey (ICOS) (Schaffer, Nesselrodt, and Stringfield, 1994) – researchers created an instrument by adapting the SSOS and adding rating scales related to Quality of Instruction, Appropriateness of Instruction, Incentives for Students, and Time Usage (QAIT) (Slavin, 1987); this instrument was also used in ISERP.

Future Links Between SER and TER

There are at least three areas in which SER and TER may be linked in the immediate future:

- international studies embedding teacher effects variables within the context of SER; such studies require instruments that are valid cross-culturally;
- national studies (outside the USA) studying teacher effects within the context of SER; such studies require instruments that are valid for the country that is being studied, and few countries have such instruments at this time;
- school improvement efforts that utilize teacher effectiveness indicators, as well as school effectiveness indicators.

Schaffer et al. (1994) discussed the issues involved in developing classroom observation instruments that could be used in international studies:

> The challenges of developing and/or choosing classroom observation instruments designed for international studies begin with insuring that the researchers involved can gather accurate and complete data in diverse settings. The instrument must yield data that permit international . . . comparisons. If instruments are designed to be used by researchers from various countries, attention must be paid to the development of appropriate methods of data analysis consistent with each country's research questions and policy interests.
>
> (Schaffer et al., 1994, p.137)

Lessons learned from ISERP are particularly relevant to this issue (e.g. Creemers, Reynolds, Stringfield and Teddlie, 1996). Some of the items on the VTBI, which was validated for use in the USA, did not make sense or were irrelevant to researchers from other countries in the study. There were two empirical results related to this: a factor analysis of the ISERP data yielded only one dimension (Creemers et al., 1996), while earlier factor analytic work done from the USA sample alone had yielded five interpretable factors (Teddlie et al., 1990); and there was no variance on certain items in certain countries.

Schaffer et al., (1994, pp.140–1) concluded that instruments used for classroom observation in future international studies must have three characteristics:

1   include variables from TER that are 'basic, generic, and replicable' in a variety of settings that can serve as the basis for cross-country comparisons;
2   include variables from instruments that represent the questions of interest of *all* researchers in the study 'regardless of their own specialization or cultural orientation';
3   allow for the emergence of other variables that become evident from the gathering of qualitative data in the classrooms during the study.

As of the mid-1990s, the USA was the only country to have extensively utilized classroom observations to generate teacher effects data within the context of SER. ISERP demonstrated that countries such as the Netherlands, the UK and Taiwan did not have valid classroom observation systems for conducting this type of intra-country research. Countries wishing to conduct TER and SER simultaneously must develop classroom instruments valid for their own particular context, and the development of such instruments will be a major contribution to the future development of SER cross-culturally.

In the future, there should be an increased emphasis on the utilization of classroom observation data in the development of school improvement plans. Brookover et al. (1984) were prescient in their inclusion of three modules on classroom teaching (effective instruction, academic engaged time, classroom management) as part of their school improvement inservice programme *Creating Effective Schools*, which was developed in the early 1980s.

Slavin's school change model (e.g. Slavin et al., 1996), *Success for All*, emphasizes that change has to occur at the intersection of the student, the teacher, and the curriculum. His strategy for classroom improvement emphasizes active learning and cooperative learning (Slavin et al., 1996; Stringfield et al., 1994a). (See Chapters 4 and 8 for more information on the processes of teacher effectiveness and school improvement.)

Recently, Teddlie and Meza (1996) have examined two schools that had been involved in the Accelerated Schools improvement process (e.g. Hopfenberg et al., 1993; Levin, 1996) for five years with regard to the teaching effectiveness of their respective faculties. Using baseline data from a number of studies of TER/SER conducted over the past 10 years, Teddlie and Meza (1996, 1999) discovered that one school had effective teaching ongoing in its classrooms, while the other school's classrooms were characterized as having ineffective teaching. Furthermore, the classroom behaviours in these schools varied considerably by grade level. The authors made specific recommendations for staff development aimed at particular grade level teaching weaknesses at the school in which poor teaching was occurring. This study is an example of the use of TER in developing school improvement programmes for schools with particular teaching weaknesses.

Social Network Analysis

Two recent studies (Durland, 1996; Durland and Teddlie, 1996; Teddlie and Kochan, 1991) have utilized Social Network Analysis to analyse communication patterns found in elementary and secondary schools. These studies found interesting differences in the communication networks of differentially effective schools and utilized sociograms to illustrate these differences. Before describing the results from these studies in more detail, a brief review of the evolution of the field of Social Network Analysis will be presented.

Social Network Analysis evolved from work done by the sociologist Moreno (1934), the developer of sociometry, which concerns 'the measurement of interpersonal relationships in small groups' (Wasserman and Faust, 1994, p.11). Moreno's sociometric questions and resultant matrices and sociograms allow 'the study of positive and negative affective relations . . . among a set of people' (Wasserman and Faust, 1994, p.77). Sociometric questions are typically very simple; for example, they may ask students to indicate all the individuals that they talked to in their classroom over the past week, or they may ask faculty members to indicate the three individual teachers with whom they talked the most in the past month.

From these simple questions Moreno and his contemporaries (e.g. Festinger, 1949; Forsyth and Katz, 1946; Katz, 1947; Luce and Perry, 1949; Moreno, 1946; Moreno and Jennings, 1938; Northway, 1940) developed both sociomatrices (numeric indices) and sociograms (two dimensional drawings of relationships among social units). Moreno preferred sociograms to sociomatrices, placing a greater emphasis on the visual displays that one could generate from sociometric data.

Sociomatrices were preferred by methodologists more interested in the power of mathematics to explain the differences in social networks. Sociomatrices are relational data presented in two-way matrices, with the rows representing the sending actors and the columns representing the receiving matrices. Katz and others (e.g. Festinger, 1949; Forsyth and Katz, 1946; Katz, 1947; Harary et al., 1965; Luce and Perry, 1949) preferred the application of mathematics to sociomatrices, as described by Wasserman and Faust (1994):

> Even with the growing interest in figures such as sociograms, researchers were unhappy that different investigators using the same data could produce as many different sociograms (in appearance) as there were investigators . . . Consequently, the use of the sociomatrix to denote social network data increased. . . . Sociograms waned in importance as sociomatrices became more popular and as more mathematical and statistical indices were invented that used sociomatrices, much to the dismay of Moreno. . . .
>
> (Wasserman and Faust, 1994, pp.78–9)

By the mid-1950s, many of the basic sociometric concepts of cliques, centrality, density, and isolates had been identified (e.g. Lindzey and Borgatta, 1954). A 20-year 'incubation' period (Durland, 1996) ensued, during which researchers working in different fields made further methodological contributions, often in isolation from researchers in other fields. By the mid-1970s, the advent of computer based analysis techniques (e.g. Breiger, 1976; Burt, 1978; Freeman, L., 1977, 1979) led to advances in sociomatrix analysis, while further innovations in computing led to renewed interest in graphical representations (e.g. Klovdahl, 1986). The journal *Social Networks*, devoted primarily to Social Network Analysis, was established in 1978.

Social Network Analysis has involved researchers from a wide variety of the social and behavioural sciences, as well as mathematics, computer technology, and statistics. As Wasserman and Faust (1994) noted:

> Social network analysis is inherently an interdisciplinary endeavor. The concepts of social network analysis developed out of a propitious meeting of social theory and application, with formal mathematical, statistical, and computing methodology. . . . Further, and more importantly, the central concepts of relation, network, and structure arose almost independently in several social and behavioral disciplines.

(Wasserman and Faust, 1994, p.10)

While sociometry evolved primarily from the fields of sociology, psychology and education, recent work in Social Network Analysis has been concentrated more on applications in business, political science and urban studies. The current study in SER of relationship patterns within differentially effective schools began with an evaluation of a highly ineffective high school (Teddlie and Kochan, 1991).

In analysing this school, the evaluators used sociometric techniques to study the interaction patterns that existed among staff members. The results indicated that there were four distinct cliques in this faculty of 20 individuals, two primarily composed of white members and two consisting primarily of African-American members. Over 80 per cent of the interactions in the school were within racial groups; only 18 per cent of the interactions involved Whites and African-Americans. The African-American principal appeared to be an isolate in the group, interacting with only a couple of African-American teachers.

The sociometric results from this evaluation study of a single ineffective school led Durland and Teddlie (1996) to attempt to apply Social Network Analysis methodology to the study of leadership and communication in a set of differentially effective schools. Durland (1996) developed a model, the Centrality-Cohesiveness Model of School Effectiveness, that predicted the types of sociogram patterns she expected from schools varying in terms of school effectiveness index (SEI, effective or ineffective) and SES of student body (middle or low). These predictions were based on SER theory and research regarding the types of leaders and communication patterns that one might expect to find in such schools. This study (Durland, 1996; Durland and Teddlie, 1996) utilized the most advanced computer programs to calculate the sociomatrices and the sociograms: UCINET IV (Borgatti et al., 1992) to produce the numeric indices and KrackPlot (Krackhardt et al., 1993) to generate the sociograms.

Results indicated that there were differences between effective and ineffective schools in terms of the centrality of the principals in the schools and the cohesiveness of the faculties. In terms of numeric data, the results indicated that effective schools had principals with higher 'centrality' scores than ineffective schools, and that effective schools had higher network density, a measure of connectedness or cohesiveness, than did ineffective schools. While these results were found in general, there was considerable variance within the effective and the ineffective schools on the numeric indices. Sociogram analysis indicated that effective schools were more likely to be 'well webbed', while ineffective schools were more 'stringy' in appearance.

Conclusions: Further Potentially Fruitful Interactions

The above list of areas where there have been useful interactions between SER and other cognate disciplines is not, of course an exhaustive one and other potentially useful areas suggest themselves such as 'Political theory', 'Psychiatric theory', 'Organizational theory' and Chaos theory'.

One area to consider is political theory, since the accounts of school improvement that appear in the literature often stress the need to 'coalition build', get the micropolitics of school organizations right, and 'horse trade' and/or 'cut deals' to generate school improvement (see examples in National Commission on Education, 1995).

A second area is psychiatric theory and practice, since there are hints that ineffective schools particularly may have numerous characteristics that at an organizational level parallel those of individuals. Suggestions about these (Reynolds, 1996; Stoll, Myers and Myers, 1996; Stoll and Myers, 1997) include:

- projections of teachers' own personal failing onto their pupils and catchment areas;
- fear of failure generating a reluctance to risk;
- poor inter-personal relationships, with cliques etc., restricting the opportunity for interaction and professional communication;
- strong defences, in which apparent certainty hides considerable professional and personal insecurity.

A third area is organizational theory, since there appears to be similarities between schools and other organizations involved in people processing, particularly those in service industries that form the focus of the Peters and Waterman (1982) theses. Of particular interest is the applicability to schools of notions such as:

- simultaneous loose/tight organizational properties;
- laterality combined with vertical pressure in the generation of mission;
- 'sticking with the knitting', in terms of focusing on the organizations' core mission or goals;
- short term feedback loops that ensure organizations have information on their outcomes and/or consumer reactions very quickly.

Of particular interest is the possibility of modelling schools upon the particular organizational characteristics of High Reliability Organizations (Stringfield, 1995; Reynolds and Stringfield, 1996), such as air traffic control, nuclear power plants, chemical processing etc. These 'failure free' organizations have developed distinctive organizational patterns because of the widespread agreement that any failure would be a calamity, and evidence the following organizational characteristics:

- a focus upon a small number of goals or 'sense of primary mission';
- the use of a strong technology of education, involving standard operating procedures (SOPs) that prescribe organizational patterns;

- 'data richness' involving use of indicator systems, performance assessment and serialization to understand and improve organizational functioning;
- a concern to benchmark against organizational 'best practice';
- pro-active recruitment and high quality training;
- a combination of hierarchical, vertical organization with an ability to 'go lateral' at moments of peak load, stress or crisis;
- a concern with legislating for organizational detail and fine print, since the organizations are concerned with avoiding of 'cascading errors' that occur when minor malfunctioning leads to progressively more serious organizational failure.

A fourth area is chaos theory (Tymms, 1996a; Bosker and Scheerens, 1997) in which systems such as schools are viewed as an inherently unstable state within educational systems and societies that are similarly in states of 'dynamic disequilibrium'. Attempts to understand and generate 'good practice' in education are seen from this perspective as misplaced, since the school is subject to so many constantly changing pressures that 'what works' at one stage may not 'work' at another.

Chaos perspectives lead to a desire to give schools information above all, to improve their powers for organizational decision making, and for speedy analysis and re-analysis within a constantly shifting set of parameters.

12 The Future Agenda for School Effectiveness Research

David Reynolds and Charles Teddlie

Introduction

Several authors have speculated upon the future of school effectiveness research (e.g. Good and Brophy, 1986; Mortimore, 1991b; Reynolds, 1992a, 1992b; Scheerens and Bosker, 1997; Teddlie and Stringfield, 1993) over the past decade. However due to rapid developments in the field, both in terms of methodology and substantive findings, the areas identified in need of further research 10 years ago or even five years ago are either no longer relevant, or have been significantly reconceptualized.

The following Chapter contains a summary of 11 issues that we have identified as being on the 'cutting edge' of school effectiveness research as we approach the twenty-first century. These issues emerged as we reviewed the substantial body of the world's research findings presented in the previous eleven chapters of this handbook. Some of these issues are simply embodiments of repetitive themes in the literature (e.g. the need for multiple outcome measures to judge school effects and the importance of context issues), while others have only emerged in the past one or two years (e.g. the study of the relational aspects of schooling and the study of the possibly additive effects of school and family).

Before examining each of these issues, we will briefly review some of criticisms of SER and speculate on the general health of the field.

The Current Criticisms of SER

It has been somewhat fashionable in certain educational circles to criticize SER, with assaults being launched on the earliest work (e.g. Acton, 1980; Cuttance, 1982; Goldstein, 1980; Musgrove, 1981; Ralph and Fennessey, 1983; Rowan, 1984; Rowan, Bossert and Dwyer, 1983) and through to the present (e.g. Elliott, 1996). Part of the reasons for these criticisms have been political, part methodological and part theoretical.

SER will always be politically controversial, since it concerns 'the nature and purposes of schooling' (e.g. Elliott, 1996), but it is interesting that SER has been criticized politically on contradictory grounds. For instance, much of the scathing early criticism of effective schools research in the USA (e.g. Ralph and Fennessey, 1983; Rowan, 1984) concerned the researchers' embrace of well defined political goals (i.e. equity in schooling outcomes for the disadvantaged and ethnic minorities), which critics believed blocked the researchers' use of appropriate scientific research methods.

Critics believed that these effective schools' researchers were liberal reformers more interested in improving the lot of the children of the poor than in conducting good science.

In the UK, on the other hand, much recent criticism (e.g. Elliott, 1996) of SER has come from 'progressive' educators. These critics portray SER as being underpinned by an ideology of social control and SER researchers as having an overly 'mechanistic' view of the organization of educational processes. Critics from the UK perceive SER as giving credence and legitimization to a conservative ideology. As Elliott stated:

> The findings of school effectiveness research have indeed been music in the ears of politicians and government officials. Currently, for example, they are being used to politically justify a refusal to respond to teachers' anxieties about the increasing size of the classes that they teach, the use of traditional teaching methods, such as whole class instruction, and a tendency to blame headteachers for 'failing schools' on the grounds that they lack a capacity for strong leadership.
>
> (Elliot, 1996, p.199)

Political criticism is probably always going to be a part of the literature associated with SER. It seems safe to conclude that as long as the researchers in the field are accused at the same time of supporting *both* conservative *and* liberal causes, these criticisms can be accepted as simply an unwarranted part of the territory in which we work.

Methodological criticisms have been a part of SER since the original Coleman and Plowden Reports. Much of the history of SER, as outlined in Chapter 1, has been a reaction to these methodological criticisms. With the advent of the methodological advances described in Chapter 3, many of these criticisms have now become muted. In fact, a sign of the health of the field is that we now have a set of generally agreed prescriptions for conducting methodologically correct studies, including the following:

- School effects studies should be designed to tap sufficient 'natural variance' in school and classroom characteristics.
- School effects studies should have units of analysis (child, class, school) that allow for data analysis with sufficient discriminative power.
- School effects studies should use adequate operationalization and measures of the school and classroom process variables, preferably including direct observations of process variables, and a mixture of quantitative and qualitative approaches.
- School effects studies should use adequate techniques for data analysis, which involves multilevel models in most cases.
- School effects studies should use longitudinal cohort based data, collected on individual children.
- School effects studies should adequately adjust outcome measures for any intake differences between schools.

Not only do we now know how to design methodologically correct studies, we also know how to conduct the kind of studies that will be more likely to demonstrate relatively larger school effects. Based on our review of the literature from Chapters 3, 4 and 5, we can conclude, in general, that school effects will be *larger* in SER studies:

- that involve a variety of SES contexts, rather than a sample of schools with homogeneous student SES backgrounds;
- that examine the elementary (or junior) school level;
- that examine schools from a wide variety of community types and in which types of community truly vary among themselves;
- that examine schools that have more control of their academic operations;
- from a country that has more variance in its educational system processes;
- that use mathematics as the dependent variable; and
- that involve the gathering of process variables that relate to measures of teachers' behaviour rather than their other attributes.

Similarly we can conclude that school effects will be *smaller* in studies of schools:

- that have similar SES contexts;
- that examine the secondary level;
- that examine community types that are homogeneous in terms of economics, economic structure and culture;
- that have less control of their academic operations;
- from a country that has less variance in its educational system factors;
- that use reading as the dependent variable, and
- that do not involve the gathering of process variables such as in-class measures of teacher behaviour.

SER has also been criticized as having little or no theoretical basis. This criticism still has some validity, but evidence presented in Chapter 10 indicates that researchers and theoreticians are busily working to address this perennial problem and appear to be making some headway, at least in terms of the development of heuristic midrange theories, and in the illumination of some of the possible theoretical explanations between various school and classroom factors by interrogating existing studies with the predictions of 'meta' or 'grand' theories such as contingency theory or public choice theory (e.g. Scheerens and Bosker, 1997).

We now move beyond issues of criticism, and responses to our 11 'cutting edge' areas where the future of the discipline lies:

- the need for multiple outcome measures in SER;
- the need for the study of the third relational dimension of schooling (relationship patterns);
- the need to expand the study of context variables;
- the need to analyse range within schools and classrooms;
- the need to study the possibly additive nature of school and family;
- the need to explore the interface between levels in schooling;
- the need to study naturally occurring experiments;
- the need to expand variation at the school level;
- the need to study school failure/dysfunctionality;

- the need to gain the benefits of multilevel path structural equation modelling;
- the need to recognize the salience of issues to do with curriculum and assessment.

The Need for Multiple Outcomes Measures in SER

This issue has been discussed by many since the 1970s (e.g. Good and Brophy, 1986; Levine and Lezotte, 1990; Rutter, 1983a, 1983b; Rutter et al., 1979; Sammons et al., 1996a), with most commenting that multiple criteria for school effectiveness are needed. Critics have noted that schools may *not* have consistent effects across different criteria, and that to use one criterion (typically academic achievement) is not adequate for ascertaining the true effectiveness status of a school. This issue was discussed in Chapter 3 under the scientific properties of consistency and differential effectiveness. It is also now widely recognized that multiple outcomes force the development of more sensitive explorations than are likely with restricted measures, since the pattern of why school and teacher factors are associated with some outcomes but not others (as in Mortimore et al., 1988 for example) is exactly the kind of scientific dissonance that is needed for creative theorizing.

Within the past decade, researchers have been making progress in this area as follows:

1 More sophisticated studies of consistency across different achievement scores have emerged, especially from the USA (e.g. Crone et al., 1994a, 1994b, 1995; Lang, 1991; Lang et al., 1992; Teddlie et al., 1995). These studies have utilized more statistically appropriate measures of consistency across achievement scores (e.g. kappa coefficients), have compared consistency ratings generated by composite and by component scores and have compared consistency ratings across very different types of academic achievement tests (e.g. criterion-referenced tests versus norm-referenced tests, or different public examination boards in the United Kingdom).

2 Studies from the UK have continued to compare different criteria for school effectiveness beyond academic achievement scores. These comparisons have included academic versus affective/social, different measures of attitudes, different measures of behaviour and different measures of self-concept (Sammons et al., 1996).

3 Recent research utilizing composite academic achievement scores have yielded higher estimates of consistency, thus indicating the value of constructing such scores (e.g. Crone et al., 1994a, 1994b, 1995). Additionally, Kochan et al. (1996) have explored the use of composite scores measuring student participation rates (including student attendance, dropout and suspension data) at the high school level in the USA. Results from a comparison of two composite school effectiveness indices from this study (one based on academic achievement scores and the other on student participation rates) indicated moderate agreement between them (Kochan et al., 1996).

4 Teddlie and Stringfield (1993, pp.84–5) utilized a matrix approach to classifying schools in a longitudinal study of school effects. In this study, seven different indicators of school effectiveness (two concerning academic achievement, four behavioural and one attitudinal) were compared to determine the current

effectiveness status of matched pairs of schools that were being studied longitudinally. The resulting classification of school effectiveness status was multidimensional, involving achievement, behavioural and attitudinal SEIs.

These results studies point the way toward designing SER that utilizes multiple criteria in the determination of school effectiveness status. Guidelines as to 'good practice' include the following:

1 Use varied measures of the effectiveness of schooling, including academic achievement, attitudes (toward self, and toward others), and behaviour.
2 Use measures that are sensitive to the mission of schools in the twenty-first century. For instance, measures of perceived racism may be important indicators of the effectiveness of schooling in some contexts (e.g. Fitz-Gibbon, 1996). Equal opportunities concerns are important in schools in many countries, yet equal opportunities orientated behaviours and attitudes are rarely used to assess school effectiveness. 'Learning to learn' or 'knowledge acquisition' skills are widely argued to be essential in the information age, yet achievement tests utilized continue to emphasize student ability to recapitulate existing knowledge.
3 Use composite variables where possible, since they present a better overall picture of a school's effectiveness.
4 Use where possible multidimensional matrices to assess the effectiveness of schools.
5 Use measures of student behaviour wherever possible, since it is behaviours that are likely to be crucial in determining the nature of the future society that young people inhabit.

The Need for Study of the Third Dimension of Schooling (Relationship Patterns)

A new area of study has emerged in SER over the past few years : the study of the relationship patterns that exist within staff and within student groups. This relational component constitutes the third dimension of schooling, joining the more frequently studied organizational and cultural components (Reynolds, 1992b). There are three reasons why the relational component of schooling has *not* been featured much in SER until now:

1 The relational patterns of faculties and teachers of students is difficult to measure, since questionnaires and interviews regarding school relationships may constitute 'reactive' instruments susceptible to socially desirable responses (e.g. Webb et al., 1981). By contrast, sociograms are relatively non-reactive instruments designed to measure the social structure of a group and to assess the social status of each individual in the group (e.g. Borg and Gall, 1989; Moreno, 1953). The study of Teddlie and Kochan (1991) was the first within SER to use sociograms to assess the types of relationships that exist among faculty members, although of course, many researchers have used sociograms to measure student peer relationships in classes and schools (e.g. Asher and Dodge, 1986; Tyne and Geary, 1980), including individuals working within the SER paradigm (e.g. Reynolds, 1976; Reynolds

et al., 1976b, 1987). It is also important to note that in many cultures (such as probably the Netherlands, Scandinavia and the countries of the Pacific Rim) it would be regarded as an unwarranted intrusion into aspects of teachers' lives to even ask them the sorts of questions that are needed to evoke analysable data (e.g. 'Which three of your colleagues would you approach for help if you had a professional problem?').

2   The interpersonal relations of teachers and of students has been difficult to conceptualize and analyse due to the complexity of interactions within such social groups. The analytic technique that has been used in the handful of studies in the area is network analysis, utilizing data gleaned from the administration of sociograms to staff members.

Social network analysis is a relatively new field, begun in the late 1970s and early 1980s (e.g. Rogers and Kincaid, 1980; the first issue of *Social Networks* appeared in 1979), that appears to provide the requisite analytical and modelling tools for analysing school generated sociograms. The recent work of Durland (e.g. Durland, 1996; Durland and Teddlie, 1996) is the first in SER to utilize network analysis to model and analyse data from sociograms administered to faculty members in schools.

3   There is a common perception that interpersonal relations within a school, especially among staff members, are very difficult to change, so researchers in the school improvement area have not been particularly interested in studying these patterns of relationships until recently.

The recent realization of the importance of the relational dimension, especially in the case of interpersonal relations among staff members (Reynolds, 1991b; Reynolds and Packer, 1992; Reynolds, 1996), has been due to three factors:

- Empirical work in the USA noted above (e.g. Durland, 1996; Durland and Teddlie, 1996; Teddlie and Kochan, 1991) that has successfully linked the effectiveness levels of schools with their different patterns of interpersonal relations among staff members.
- More speculative work done both in the school effectiveness and school improvement traditions in the UK and the USA that has linked ineffective schools with the presence of dysfunctional relations among staff members (e.g. Reynolds and Packer, 1992; Myers, 1995; Stoll, 1995; Stoll et al., 1996; Stoll and Fink, 1996; Teddlie and Stringfield, 1993). Reynolds (1996) has characterized these 'grossly dysfunctional relationships' in such schools as follows:

> The presence of numerous personality clashes, feuds, personal agendas and fractured interpersonal relationships within the staff group, which operate . . . to make rational decision-making a very difficult process.
>
> (Reynolds, 1996, p.154)

These dysfunctional relationships arise through the unique social-psychological history of the school (Teddlie and Stringfield, 1993) and have a tendency to continue unless drastic changes (planned or not) occur. Often these relationships manifest themselves in the generation of sharply delineated sub-cultures (Stoll and Fink, 1996) or cliques within the school.

- Some of those in the school improvement tradition have found that the existence of relational 'shadows' or 'ghosts' of the past have had a considerable influence in affecting the progress of attempts at staff professional development (Hopkins et al., 1994).

Recent interesting work in this field has been done by Durland and Teddlie (1996), who posit the Centrality-Cohesiveness Model of Differentially Effective Schools, which was briefly described in Chapter 11. This model postulates that differentially effective schools can be distinguished by how cohesive the faculty is (measured in network analysis as network density) and how central the principal (or surrogate) is within the organization (measured by group centralization, or betweenness centralization in network analysis terminology).

Sociograms generated by network analysis can be utilized to detect the presence of cliques, such as those that occur in dysfunctional schools. Durland and Teddlie (1996) have presented some suggestive preliminary results utilizing network analysis to analyse the differences between effective (described as 'well webbed') and ineffective (characterized by cliques and/or 'stringy' structures) schools, but this area of research is obviously still in its infancy (see Figure 12.1 for an effective school).

If relational patterns do relate to effectiveness levels, then clearly they require more intensive study, particularly since school improvement is likely to have to

Effective school: Sample principal not ranked but linked
to first ranked individual based on top three choices

No isolates in network

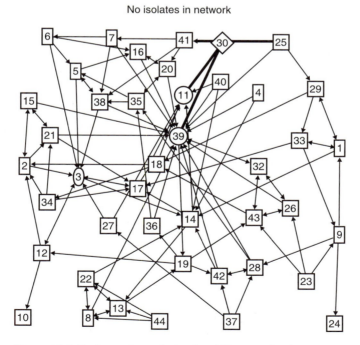

Figure 12.1 Sociometric analysis of an effective school

influence these factors as well as school organization and culture if schools are to be changed.

Further research in this area could develop in several ways:

1   More work needs to be done on more refined descriptions of effective and ineffective schools in terms of sociometric indices and sociograms. Hopefully, this work will lead us to sets of prototypical sociometric indices and sociograms for differentially effective schools.
2   Longitudinal studies of sociometric indices and sociograms should prove useful in describing how social relations change over time (e.g. setting the sociograms in 'motion' over time) and whether or not those changes are associated with changes in effectiveness status.
3   Sociometric indices and sociograms should also be developed for students within classrooms. These data may be considered as additional school effectiveness indicators, if one assumes that effective schools should be fostering positive relationships among students. It may also be that there are different *student* relational patterns in more effective classes and schools than in less effective.

The Need to Expand the Study of Context Variables

The introduction of context variables into SER has had a large impact on all three strands within the field (school effects, effective schools, school improvement), as described earlier in Chapter 5. The consideration of contextual variation in SER has also led to increased sophistication in theory development (e.g. Creemers and Scheerens, 1994; Scheerens, 1992, 1993; Scheerens and Creemers, 1989a, 1989b; Slater and Teddlie, 1992; Wimpelberg et al., 1989) as theorists have explicitly taken into account the impact that different levels of a context variable can have on school effects and processes associated with them. These contextually 'sensitive' theories of school effectiveness have incorporated tenets of contingency theory (e.g. Mintzberg, 1979; Owens, 1987) as a framework from which to interpret results from SER.

Contingency theory purports to explain why certain school effectiveness variables 'travel' across levels of context, while others do not. For instance, the failure of the well known principal leadership effect on student achievement in the Netherlands (e.g. van de Grift, 1989, 1990) is a good illustration of a school effectiveness variable that did not 'travel' from one country to another due to the differences in country contexts.

The study of context in SER is also beginning to have an impact on theories of school improvement, because school improvers realize now that there aren't 'silver bullets' that always lead to school improvement. Instead, as we noted in Chapter 7, contextually sensitive models for school improvement with 'multiple levers' have emerged as studies have demonstrated that what works to change processes can vary to a large degree by context factors such as SES of catchment area, school effectiveness level or schools improvement 'trend line'.

Our review in Chapter 5 indicates that several context variables (i.e. SES of student body, community type, grade phase, and governance structure) have a 'main effect' upon school effects and the processes that accompany them. Perhaps even more interesting, however, are the 'interactions' between context variables that have emerged periodically in the literature, including the following:

1   Community type by school size – Hannaway and Talbert (1993) reported that school size had a positive effect on teacher community in suburban schools and a negative effect on teacher community in urban schools: as the size of school increased in suburban schools, so did indicators of a positive teacher community, whereas when size of school increased in urban schools indicators of a positive teacher community decreased.

2   Community type by country – An interaction also appears to be occurring between country and community type across some of the USA and UK studies. Community type does not play as significant a contextual role in the UK as it does in the USA, primarily because there is less variance in the UK on this variable. Rural schools in the UK are generally closer geographically and culturally to urban areas than they are in the USA, and this mitigates the effect of the community type variable in the UK.

While the impact of context variables in SER is now well established, there are several research areas where additional work would be useful:

1   The variation in context should be expanded by the enhanced use of 'nation' as a context variable. However, the enhanced range of educational factors and cultural contexts that this produces may be potentially damaging if study leads to the simplistic, direct import of 'what works' without analysis of cultural differences. The study of the interaction between context variables is clearly of considerable importance.

2   Researchers should enhance the variation in context factors where possible. Considering international studies, it would be very beneficial to have more developing societies in comparative studies of SER. It would be interesting to determine the magnitude of school effects for these countries compared to first world countries using a common methodology, and it would be also interesting to expand further our knowledge of the 'context specificity' of effectiveness factors that was mentioned in Chapter 1.

3   Other, new context variables should be added to SER designs. For instance, the region of a country could have a large impact in some countries. In the USA, for instance, it could be argued that school effects and the processes associated with them may be quite different in the Northeast, the Midwest, the South, and the West. In the UK, there are considerable historical differences and cultural differences between regions (Reynolds, 1998), such as the tradition of sons following their fathers into mining or industrial employment in the Northeast, compared with the Welsh tradition of encouraging the 'escape' of children from the prospects of such employment, both of which differential contextual responses to disadvantage could be argued to have considerable implications for 'what works' within schools. Another example concerns grade level : pre-school and college could be added as additional levels of this context variable.

4   In general, as the study of context in SER matures, there should be more levels of the context variables and more range across the variables.

The Need to Analyse Range within Schools and Classrooms

There are some interesting hints in the recent literature that the *range* or variation in school and teacher factors may be important determinants of outcomes and effectiveness additionally to the *average* levels scored on the factors themselves. The Louisiana School Effectiveness Studies mentioned earlier in this handbook noted the reduced range evident in effective schools and in their teachers within lesson behaviours (Teddlie and Stringfield, 1993), as did the study of Crone and Teddlie (1995) (see Table 12.1).

The International School Effectiveness Research Project (ISERP) of Creemers et al. (1996) also found both that successful and educationally effective countries possessed a more homogeneous set of teachers and schools, and that effective schools in all of the nine countries participating evidenced predictability and consistency in their organizational processes both over time and between organizational members at a point in time. Interesting speculations about consistency, constancy and cohesion, and the power of these factors to socially control young people, have been offered by Creemers (1994) and Reynolds (1996). In a similar way, Murphy (1992) has talked about the symbolic, cultural and organizational 'tightness' of effective school organizations and, by implication, the looseness and range of ineffective organizations.

Table 12.1 Comparison of variance in scores on teacher behaviour for effective versus ineffective schools

Variable	Teachers in Effective Schools (n = 25)			
	Lowest Score	*Highest Score*	*Range*	*Coefficient of Variation*
Time-on-task (interactive)	0.15	0.85	0.71	31.22
Time-on-task (overall)	0.55	0.90	0.36	10.39
Management	2.37	5.00	2.64	11.78
Instruction 1	2.74	4.61	1.88	12.28
Instruction 2	2.75	4.88	2.14	12.42
Climate 1	2.60	4.90	2.31	12.71
Climate 2	2.33	5.00	2.68	17.88

Variable	Teachers in Ineffective Schools (n = 30)			
	Lowest Score	*Highest Score*	*Range*	*Coefficient of Variation*
Time-on-task (interactive)	0.08	0.75	0.68	34.45
Time-on-task (overall)	0.48	0.96	0.49	19.01
Management	2.10	4.60	2.51	18.86
Instruction 1	1.28	4.30	3.03	23.74
Instruction 2	1.38	4.38	3.01	22.04
Climate 1	2.30	4.80	2.51	16.97
Climate 2	1.50	4.67	3.18	22.07

Note: The coefficient of variation is computed by dividing the standard deviation by the mean and multiplying by 100.

Source: Crone and Teddlie, 1995.

And from school improvement, as we noted in Chapter 7, has come a recognition that reliability or fidelity of implementation (i.e. lack of range) is necessary to ensure improved educational outcomes from school improvement programmes. Indeed, the growing recognition that school improvement can generate enhanced range (and lower its potential effectiveness) because the educational ceiling of competent persons/ schools improves much faster than the floor of less competent persons/schools, seems to be a powerful face valid exploration for the consistently disappointing effects of school improvement that has been unconcerned with 'range', viewing it as a necessary part of teacher professional development.

Such ideas are not surprising – the literature upon family socialization has always indicated parental consistency in rule enforcement as of crucial importance to healthy child development, and erratic and inconsistent discipline, role enforcement and goal setting has long been seen as a cause of disturbed and dysfunctional individual behaviour.

It is arguable, though, that the influence of the range of school and teacher factors may have become more important of late, since many of the more historically consistent influences upon child development such as the family, the community, the mass media and the wider society have all become more heterogeneous and varied. The past possibility that inconsistent schooling, with a wide range in goals and means, might have been outweighed in any possible negative influences by consistency emanating from non-educational sources seems to have been reduced by social changes of the last 30 years.

All this suggests that we need further research to establish the importance of 'range', 'variance' and variation in such areas as:

- teacher behaviours in lessons, looking at differences between teachers at a point in time, and at individual teacher consistency over time;
- the goals of education as perceived and practised by school members;
- consistency in the relationship between classroom factors, school factors, district level factors and societal factors.

Ensuring that SER always presents the standard deviations for all variables (and other measures of variation), as well as the more conventionally used means, would seem to be axiomatic if these speculations are to be further developed.

The Need to Study the Possibly Additive Nature of School and Family

There are now a number of datasets across a variety of national contexts which suggest that family background and school quality may be related, with consequent considerable importance both for children affected and for educational policy in general. Work in London by Mortimore and Byford (1981), in Sweden by Grosin (1993) and in the United States by Teddlie (1996) shows that even after one has controlled out the effects of individual pupil background factors and/or achievement levels, there is a tendency for schools in low SES areas to do worse than one would have predicted and for schools in middle class areas to do better. Particularly marked is the existence of a group of schools 'below the regression line' in disadvantaged communities, even though such schools have often been the source of additional financial resources to help them improve and even though they have often attracted considerable attention from educational reformers. Figures 12.2 and 12.3 show this situation for the schools of an English local education authority, and Figures 12.4 and 12.5 for a group of American high schools.

What may be happening, then, is that school and home have additive effects, a possibility also suggested by an intriguing study of male delinquency by Farrington (1980), in which schools acted to increase the levels of delinquency when the prediction was already for a high rate, and to lower it below prediction when that prediction was for a low rate. From within recent writing on dysfunctional schools noted earlier (Reynolds, 1991b, 1996; Stoll et al., 1996) has also come an appreciation of the depth of problems that schools in this category can face, an appreciation now increasingly shared by those school improvers who are attempting to unravel the complexities of such schools (Hopkins, 1996).

The 'additive' idea is an important one, since it might explain that most persistent finding of all post-war educational reform attempts – that social class inequality in access to educational qualifications has been largely unchanged by educational 'improvement' on both quantity and quality dimensions. It also integrates the two literatures which have appeared to be at cross purposes, much to the detriment of the mutual understanding of the scholars working in the two fields – that from the sociology of education which stresses the influence of social structure, and that from school effectiveness which stresses the independent effects of schools. Schools do make a difference in this formulation, but that difference acts to reinforce pre-existing differences in the structure of society.

We still need to know, of course, why there is this tendency for the more effective schools to be in more advantaged areas. Differential quality in schools' teacher supply may be a factor, given the likelihood of a greater number of applications for jobs going to schools in advantaged areas. The 'drift' of good people to more socially advantaged settings, offering expanding job prospects because of population growth and a less stressful environment, may also be a factor, as may the tendency for high stress situations such as the education of the disadvantaged to find 'flaws' and 'weaknesses' in organizational arrangements and personnel that would not occur in the absence of the 'stressors' that are associated with disadvantage.

The Need to Explore the Interface between Levels in Schooling

The recent popularity of multilevel methodology has clearly created a need for reconceptualization of the process data that has historically been collected, since the use of the individual, class, school and potentially outside school factors (such as district or even possibly country) has clearly created multiple levels where formerly in the early years of SER there was only one (a group of pupils generating a school mean).

At present, we have very little understanding of the 'interactions' or 'transactions' between levels, either at the more commonly used focus of classrooms nested in schools (class/school) or the more rarely used schools nested in districts (school/district), although Scheerens and Bosker (1997) have begun to explore this issue. The growing recognition of the importance of 'range' or variation noted above propels us

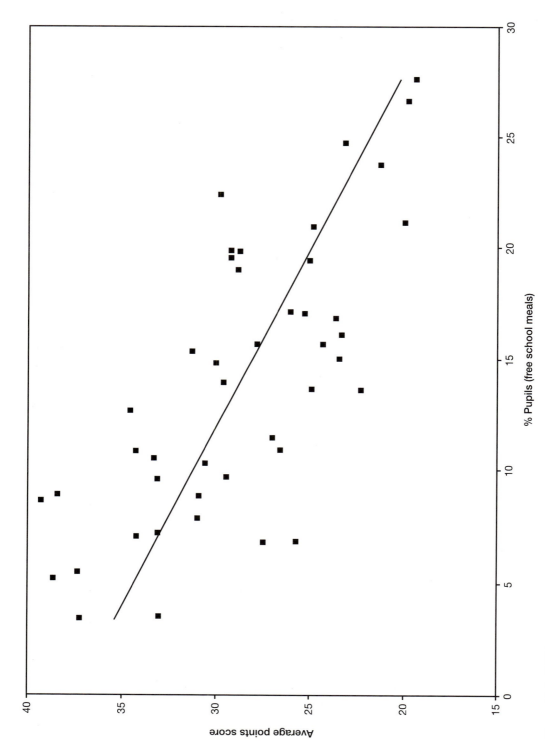

Figure 12.2 GCSE average points score versus per cent of pupils entitled to FSM (1992)

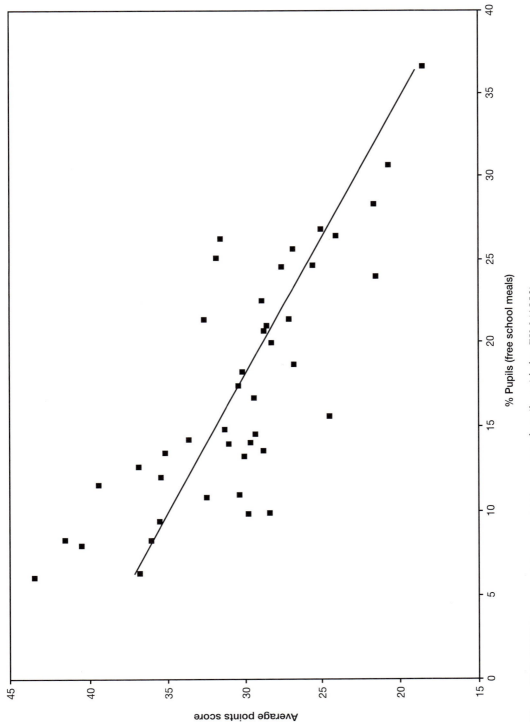

Figure 12.3 GCSE average points score versus per cent of pupils entitled to FSM (1993)

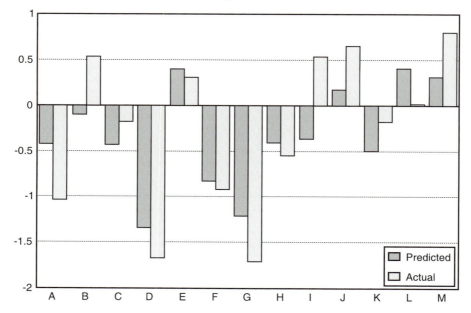

Figure 12.4 High school achievement: Spring 1993
Source: Based on 1993 GEE scores.

urgently in this direction also, given that the management interface between school and classroom generates enormous variation in classroom effectiveness in some settings, but not in others (e.g. Teddlie and Stringfield, 1993).

What might the focus of investigation be for, example, of the classroom/school interface? Possible areas of interest might include:

- the selection of teachers;
- monitoring of the teachers' performance by the principal (at the school level);
- the schools' use of mechanisms to ensure homogeneity of teachers' goal orientation;
- the use made of performance data to detect 'unusual' or 'outlier' teacher performance;
- the constancy of personnel at the two levels, and the relational patterns between them.

Other interactions take place at other levels, with perhaps the interaction between the school and the district level being of considerable importance. Areas of interest here include:

- school variation in what is evoked from district level advisers, inspectors and personnel;
- district differential allocation of staff to different schools (in the case of schools in the USA where this is a possibility).

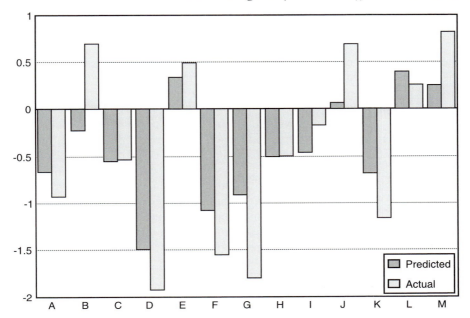

Figure 12.5 High school achievement: Spring 1994

Source: Based on 1994 GEE scores.

The pupil/class interface would also be an interesting one to explore further, with interesting areas here including:

- the extent to which there are well managed transitions between teachers across grades/years;
- the coordination of various distinctive pupil level programmes for children with special needs perhaps, or for children of high ability.

The Need to Study Naturally Occurring Experiments

All societies, and perhaps especially Anglo-Saxon ones, currently show considerable experimentation with their educational systems, involving both national macro level policy changes and more micro level classroom and school changes in organization, curriculum, governance, assessment and much else.

Experimental studies have, of course, considerable advantages for the study of school effectiveness, with the methodological 'gold standard' (Fitz-Gibbon, 1996) being the random allocation of some educational factor to a 'treatment' group of children and the use of other children as an untouched 'control'. However, various considerations have greatly held back the utilization of experiments, namely:

- ethical problems concerning the difficulty of denying any control group the factors that were being given to some children in the 'treatment' group;
- contamination between the experimental and the control groups if the random

allocation is within a school, or if the schools being used are geographically close together in a district.

The use then of experiments of nature could be of considerable potential use within the field since this involves the utilization of *already existing* experiments to generate knowledge, with schools or classes or children that are being given educational factors being studied by contrast with those similar schools or classes or children that are not being given the educational novelties. If the groups compared are similar in the background factors that may affect educational outcomes, then any differences in educational outcomes can be attributed to the effects of educational factors.

This method has the benefit of avoiding (by the separating out of home and school effects) the problems of multicollinearity that we noted in Chapter 3 have bedevilled the field since its inception, given the well researched tendency for more able children to be educated in more highly performing schools. Inevitably the study of experiments of nature is likely to involve a long term and often cohort based design, given the tendency of the experiments to be long term themselves.

However, the problems involved in utilization of this methodology of educational research cannot be overlooked either – experiments of nature are sometimes themselves changed over time, and are sometimes taking place where *multiple* factors are changing, as is the case currently with educational reform in Britain that involves teacher training, school organization, school curriculum and teaching methods. Attempting to unravel the effects of some of the component parts of the 'experiment' from the general effects of the experiments may be difficult, and in the long term the problem of multicollinearity may return, given that the already advantaged students from already advantaged homes often seem able to find the schools that are showing the most promise in their utilization of new programmes.

However, the considerable advantages offered by experiments of nature to generate a more rigorous and robust knowledge base in SER seem to heavily outweigh any disadvantages. We would hope that SER researchers would be increasingly drawn to the 'quasi experiment', particularly since virtually all countries are conducting multiple experiments of nature at the present time and are thereby providing multiple opportunities for study (e.g. Cook and Campbell, 1979).

The Need to Expand Variation at the School Level

Everything that we have read in our field is strongly suggestive of the view that the 'class' level or 'learning level' is a more powerful influence over children's levels of development and their rate of development than the 'school' level, which is in turn a more powerful level than that of the district or local education authority (see Chapter 3). Until the development of various forms of multilevel methodology, variance at the classroom level was 'hidden', by the exclusive use of school level 'averages'. Now the classroom variance within schools is clearly exposed. As Stringfield (1994b) rather nicely puts it, 'Children don't learn at the Principal's knee – they learn in classrooms', although if one examined SER historically one would see much greater concentration upon the principal's knee than the classroom context. The teacher and classroom are the 'proximal variables'.

We have been insistent throughout this handbook, however, on the need to continue and develop the study of the school. The school and its processes is the unit of policy analysis and of policy intervention, as discussed in Chapter 4. Schools have their own effects separate from those of classrooms or departments. School influence at the level of 'culture' or 'ethos' is more than the influence of the summation of their component parts, as Rutter et al. (1979) originally noted.

Part of the reason for the inability of researchers to show much 'strength' or 'power' at school level has been that they have been operating with highly constricted variance in the 'school' factor itself, since samples have been taken from within countries and cultures that already possess schools that are quite similar because of the influence of national traditions. As an example, British schools for the primary age range vary from the smallest of perhaps 15 pupils to the largest of perhaps 750 pupils, so within Britain sampling will generate a range. However, in Taiwan the smallest schools (in the rural areas) are of restricted size perhaps 60, whilst the largest is perhaps of 8000 pupils. Sampling cross culturally and across national boundaries would therefore be likely to generate much greater variation than sampling within country.

Classroom variation is unlikely to increase as much as school variation if sampling were to be cross national. To take size as a factor, class sizes within the United Kingdom perhaps range from 17/18 up to a maximum 40. Sampling across the globe would only increase the variation probably to 12/13 at the lower end and perhaps 60/70 in some developing societies at the top end.

The hugely enhanced range, and likely enhanced explanatory power of the school, if one deliberately seeks to maximize its range rather than minimize it by within nation sampling, is also likely to be found in terms of school *quality* factors, not just *quantity* factors. As an example, within Britain there would be a degree of variation in the leadership styles of headteachers, ranging from the moderately lateral or involving/participatory, to the moderately centralized and dominating. Looking outside the United Kingdom context, one could see apparently totally autocratic, non-participatory leadership in Pacific Rim societies such as Taiwan, and also apparently virtually totally 'lateral' decision making within the primary schools of Denmark, where school policy is generated by teachers.

We would argue, then, that our existing estimates as to the size of school effects noted in Chapter 3 and reflected throughout this handbook are an artefact of researchers' unwillingness to explore the full range of variation on the 'school variable'. Cross national research would expand variation on the school level by much more than on the classroom level – since classrooms are more alike internationally than are schools – and is essential if a more valid picture of school/classroom influence is to be generated.

The Need to Study School Failure/Dysfunctionality

SER has historically taken a very different disciplinary route to that of many other 'applied' disciplines such as medicine and dentistry, in that it has studied schools that are 'well' or effective, rather than those that are 'sick' or ineffective. Indeed, with notable exceptions in SER (Reynolds, 1996; Stoll and Myers, 1997) and in school improvement (Sarason, 1981), the dominant paradigm has been to study those already effective or well and to simply propose the adoption of the characteristics of the former organizations as the goal for the less effective.

In medicine by contrast, research and study focuses upon the sick person and on their symptoms, the causes of their sickness and on the needed interventions that may be appropriate to generate health. The study of medicine does not attempt to combat illness through the study of good health, as does school effectiveness: it studies illness to combat illness.

It is, of course, easy to see why school effectiveness has studied the already 'well' or effective schools. The failure of the experiments of social engineering in the 1970s (Reynolds et al., 1987), combined with the research and advocacy that suggested that schools make no difference (Coleman et al., 1966; Jencks et al., 1971; Bernstein, 1968), led to a defensiveness within the field of school effectiveness and to an unwillingness to explore the 'trailing edge' of 'sick' schools for fear of giving the educational system an even poorer public image. Access to sick schools additionally has always been more difficult than to well or effective schools, given the well known tendency of such ineffective schools to want to isolate themselves from potential sources of criticism from the world outside. The routine involvements of professional life in education have also tended to be between the good schools and the researchers who tend to prefer to involve themselves in the successful schools, rather than to put up with the toxicity, problems and organizational trauma that is the day to day life of the ineffective school.

The problems for SER because it has concentrated upon the effective rather than the ineffective schools are numerous. Because the effective schools have already become effective, we do not know what factors *made* them effective over time. There may be whole areas of schooling which are central to educational life in non-effective schools that simply cannot be seen in effective schools, such as staff groups that possess 'cliques' or interpersonal conflict between staff members for example. Dropping into the context of the ineffective school these factors that exist in the effective school may be to generate simply unreachable goals for the ineffective school, since the distance between the practice of one setting from the practice of the other may be too great to be easily eradicated.

If SER were to re-orientate itself towards the study of the sick, then a number of likely events would follow. Given that these schools are likely to increasingly be the site for numerous interventions to improve them, then there will be naturally occurring experiments going on that are much more rare in the 'steady state' effective schools. The study of sickness usually necessitates a clinical audit to see which aspects of the patient are abnormal – an educational audit can perform the same function, which of course is not necessary in an effective school because there is no concern about organizational functioning.

We believe that SER has been fundamentally misguided in its belief that the way to understand and combat sickness is through the study of the already well. The sooner that the discipline re-orientates itself to the study of sickness, ineffectiveness, dysfunctionality and failure the better.

Curriculum and Assessment

It will be obvious that the study of curricular variation within and between schools has not been a focus at all over the last three decades of SER. The explanations for this are simple:

- The orientation of researchers has been towards a behavioural, technicist approach in which the vessel of the school is studied rather than the contents.
- SER has often possessed a conservative political orientation in which schooling was seen as a 'good' which SER was to encourage more children to take up. In such a formulation any evaluation of the 'most effective curriculum' in terms of desired knowledge produced was superfluous, and less important than cascading existing knowledge at more children.
- SER was in many ways a reaction against those educationalists who generated a discourse within educational research that concentrated upon discussion of value judgments about what ought to be, and what ought to be the goals of education. SER therefore accepted existing goals, accepted the pattern of existing curricular knowledge that existed to orientate children towards those goals and concentrated upon discussion as to the most appropriate school organizational means that were appropriate to achieving them.
- SER has been well aware of the immense difficulties involved in measuring the variable 'curriculum'. Time allocated to curricular knowledge in general has not been difficult to measure, likewise the time allocation to different subject groups (see for example the results of international surveys reported in Reynolds and Farrell, 1996). However, attempts to move further and develop typologies of curriculum content and organization, along continua such as 'open–closed', 'traditional–new', or 'culturally relevant–culturally elitist' have resulted in the expenditure of considerable effort for very little reward! Indeed, perhaps the best known attempt to organize and analyse curriculum as *knowledge*, that of Bernstein (1968), was systematically destroyed by the work of King (1983) who noted that there were in practice only perhaps a tenth of relationships between curricular variables that were in the direction predicted by Bernstein's theory of classification and framing.

Whilst the neglect of curricular issues is not surprising, there is now the possibility that such neglect may be damaging the field. Partly this is because the reluctance to think about curricular issues cuts the field off from the very widespread discussions now in progress about the most appropriate bodies of knowledge that should be in the schools of a 'post modern age' or an 'information economy and society'. (Also, the reluctance to discuss curriculum matters and participate in the debates about whether 'new' bodies of knowledge may be more effective than the 'old' ones encourages the discipline to continue with what can only be labelled as a strikingly traditional range of outcomes, rather than diversify towards new and more broadly conceptualized ones.)

As an example, meta-cognitive skills are currently receiving a considerable amount of attention, in which learning is seen as an active process in which students construct knowledge and skills by working with the content (Resnick et al., 1992). The new meta-cognitive theories differ considerably from the traditional views that are on offer historically within SER, in which teacher instruction generates the possibility of a student mastering the task, with the knowledge being mainly declarative (how it works) and procedural (how to do it). With meta-cognitive theorizing the focus is more upon conditional knowledge (how to decide what to do and when to do it). The old model of instruction that SER represents aims mainly at the direct transfer and the reproduction of the existing knowledge as it is defined by schools and teachers in curricula, while the new model of instruction takes the learning of strategies by students as the centre of attention. These new models see a consequent need to change the role of the teacher, since the students being responsible for their own learning means that the teacher is no longer the person who instructs but who now teaches the techniques and strategies that students need to use to construct their own knowledge.

SER and its conservative curricular and outcome orientation is, therefore, not engaging with, and learning from, the new paradigms in the field of learning and instruction. Additionally, it is not learning from or debating with those who argue for a new range of social or affective outcomes to be introduced relevant to the highly stressed, fast moving world of the 1990s, except through some of the interesting speculations of Stoll and Fink (1996).

The SER of the present may, because of its reluctance to debate issues of values that are incorporated in discussions of the curriculum, and because of its reluctance to countenance new outcomes measures that are appropriate to the future rather than to the past, be in danger of being left behind by those who are actively exploring these issues. Will the new outcomes that an information age requires such as 'students' capacity to handle and access and construct information' be generated by the schools that are 'effective' that we have characterized in this book? Will the schools successful in generating conventional academic, and occasionally social, excellence through their predictability, cohesion, consistency and structure be the schools to generate the new social outcomes of 'coping' and 'psychosocial resilience' that are needed for today's youth?

We fear the answers to both these questions are 'no'.

Multilevel Structural Equation Modelling

The great success of multilevel modelling has been largely due to the fact that such models more adequately depict the process of schooling, as we currently envision it, than does regression analysis. It is possible that multilevel structural equation modelling (SEM) will eclipse multilevel modelling in the future for the same reason.

Several authors (e.g. Hallinger and Heck, 1996; Scheerens and Bosker, 1997) have speculated that the effect of the school on the student is indirect, largely through the mediating level of the class. Recent advances in multilevel SEM, discussed in Chapter 6 make it possible to model statistically the indirect effects of school variables on student achievement using the multilevel approach. Given the tremendous enthusiasm that has been associated with multilevel modelling among the 'scientists' studying SER, the emergence of multilevel SEM is likely to generate much high quality theoretical and statistical work over the next few years.

Conclusions: Understanding the Research Base

Over the twelve chapters of this handbook we have ranged broadly over the field of SER, and into the related fields of school improvement, indicator research and comparative education. We have found a remarkable degree of consistency across cultures in our findings in such areas as the processes associated with school effectiveness, the size of school effects and their scientific properties. We have also found evidence of the importance of national and local context in determining the knowledge base, as we have made clear in numerous areas above.

It is clear that some of these differences between contexts reflect differences in the methodological structure of the research enterprise in different countries, such as the tendency of research in the USA to not use prior achievement measures as input variables, and the commonplace use of these measures in European research. Likewise, the choice of elementary schools for the research sites of SER in the USA by comparison with the customary choice of secondary schools in the United Kingdom (reflecting the availability of routine assessment data in the case of the USA and secondary school examinations in the case of the UK) may also have influenced the pattern of results. In our opinion, after having undertaken this compendious review, it is absolutely essential that researchers make themselves far more aware than hitherto as to the methodological strategies employed in different national contexts to avoid the possibility of methodological variation passing itself off as substantive variation in knowledge.

Notes on Contributors

Bert Creemers Professor of Education, GION, University of Groningen, The Netherlands.

Carol Fitz-Gibbon Professor of Education, University of Durham, UK.

David Hopkins Professor of Education, University of Nottingham, UK.

Eugene Kennedy Associate Professor of Education, Louisiana State University, Baton Rouge, USA.

Susan Kochan Office of State Education, Baton Rouge, USA.

Garrett Mandeville Professor of Education, University of South Carolina, USA.

Sharon Pol Educational Consultant, Louisiana, USA.

David Reynolds Professor of Education, University of Newcastle upon Tyne, Newcastle upon Tyne, UK.

Pam Sammons Reader in Education, Institute of Education, London, UK.

Jaap Scheerens Professor of Education, University of Twente, Twente, The Netherlands.

Sam Stringfield Principal Research Scientist, Johns Hopkins University, Baltimore, USA.

Charles Teddlie Professor of Education, Louisiana State University, Baton Rouge, USA.

Tony Townsend Associate Professor of Education, Monash University, Victoria, Australia.

References

Abbott, R. et al. (1988) *GRIDS School Handbooks* (2nd edition, Primary and Secondary versions) York: Longman for the SCDC.

Abramowitz, S. and Tenenbaum, E. (1978) *High school '77* Washington, DC: National Institute for Education.

Accelerated Schools Project (1991) 'Getting started', *Accelerated Schools*, **1**, 2, pp.12–16.

Acton, T. A. (1980) 'Educational criteria of success: Some problems in the work of Rutter, Maughan, Mortimore and Ouston', *Educational Researcher*, **22**, 3, pp.163–73.

Ainscow, M., Hargreaves, D. H. and Hopkins, D. (1995) 'Mapping the process of change in schools', *Evaluation and Research in Education*, **9**, 2, pp.75–90.

Ainscow, M., Hopkins, D., Southworth, G. and West, M. (1994) *Creating the Conditions for School Improvement*, London: David Fulton Publishers.

Ainsworth, M. and Batten, E. (1974) *The Effects of Environmental Factors on Secondary Educational Attainment in Manchester: A Plowden Follow Up*, London: Macmillan.

Aitkin, M. and Longford, N. (1986) 'Statistical modeling issues in school effectiveness studies', *Journal of the Royal Statistical Society, Series A*, **149**, 1, pp.1–43.

Aitkin, M. and Zuzovsky, R. (1994) 'A response to Raudenbush's comment', *School Effectiveness and School Improvement*, **5**, 2, pp.199–201.

Aitkin, M. and Zuzovsky, R. (1994) 'Multilevel interaction models and their use in the analysis of large-scale school effectiveness studies', *School Effectiveness and School Improvement*, **5**, 1, pp.45–74.

Aitkin, M., Anderson, D. and Hinde, J. (1981) 'Statistical modeling of data on teaching styles', *Journal of the Royal Statistical Society, Series A*, **144**, 4, pp.419–61.

Alexander, K. L. and Eckland, B. K. (1975) 'Contextual effects in the high school attainment process', *American Sociological Review*, **4**, pp.402–16.

Alexander, K. L. and McDill, E. L. (1976) 'Selection and allocation within schools: Some causes and consequences of curriculum placement', *American Sociological Review*, **41**, pp.963–80.

Alexander, K. L., Cook, M. and McDill, E. L. (1978) 'Curriculum tracking and educational stratification: Some further evidence', *American Sociological Review*, **43**, pp.47–66.

Alexander, K. L., Natriello, G. and Pallas, A. (1985) 'For whom the bell tolls: The impact of dropping out on cognitive performance', *American Sociological Review*, **50**, pp.409–20.

Alexander, K. L., Pallas, A. M. and Cook, M. A. (1981) 'Measure for measure: On the use of endogeneous ability data in school-process research', *American Sociological Review*, **46**, pp.619–31.

Alexander, R. (1992) *Policy and Practice in Primary Education*, London: Routledge.

Alexander, R. (1996a) *Versions of Primary Education*, London: Routledge.

Alexander, R. (1996b) *Other Primary Schools and Ours: Hazards of International Comparison*, Warwick: Centre for Research in Elementary and Primary Education, University of Warwick.

References

Altbach, P. (1991) 'Trends in comparative education', *Comparative Education Review*, August, pp. 491–507.

Alwin, D. F. and Otto, L. B. (1976) 'High school context effects on aspirations', *Sociology of Education*, **49**, pp.294–303.

Anastasi, A. (1982) *Psychological Testing*, (5th edition), New York: Macmillan.

Anderson, C. S. (1982) 'The search for school climate: A review of the research', *Review of Educational Research*, **52**, pp.368–420.

Anderson, L., Evertson, C. and Brophy, J. (1979) 'An experimental study of effective teaching in first-grade reading groups', *Elementary School Journal*, **79**, pp.198–223.

Anderson, L. W., Ryan, D. W. and Shapiro, B. J. (1989) *The IEA Classroom Environment Study*, Oxford: Pergamon Press.

Anderson, S. (1991) 'Principal's management style and patterns of teacher implementation across multiple innovations', *School Effectiveness and School Improvement*, **2**, 4, pp.286–304.

Andrews, J. H. M. (1965) 'School organisational climate: Some validity studies', *Canadian Education and Research Digest*, **5**, pp.317–34.

Andrews, R. L. and Soder, R. (1987) 'Principal leadership and student achievement', *Educational Leadership*, **44**, 3, pp.9–11.

Andrews, R. L., Soder, R. and Jacoby, D. (1986) 'Principal roles, other in-school variables, and academic achievement by ethnicity and SES', Paper presented at the annual meeting of the American Educational Research Association, San Francisco, CA.

Angus, L. B. (1986a) *Schooling, the School Effectiveness Movement and Educational Reform*, Geelong: Deakin University Press.

Angus, L. B. (1986b) 'The risk of school effectiveness: A comment on recent education reports', *The Australian Administrator*, **7**, pp.1–4.

Arceneaux, L. S. (1993) 'The influence of teacher behavior on the distribution of achievement in the classroom: An application of the hierarchical linear model', unpublished doctoral dissertation, Louisiana State University, Baton Rouge, LA.

Arlin, M. (1984) 'Time, equality, and mastery learning', *Review of Educational Research*, **54**, 1, pp.65–86.

Armor, D., Conry-Oseguera, P., Cox, M., King, N., McDonnell, L., Pascal, A., Pauly, E. and Zellman, G. (1976) *Analysis of the School Preferred Reading Program in Selected Los Angeles Minority Schools*, Santa Monica, CA: The Rand Corporation.

Ashenden, D. (1987) 'An odd couple? Social justice: Performance Indicators', Public lecture sponsored by the Victorian State Board of Education. Melbourne: Australia.

Asher, S. R. and Dodge, K. A. (1986) 'Identifying children who are rejected by their peers', *Developmental Psychology*, **22**, 4, pp.444–9.

Aspin, D., Chapman, J. and Wilkinson, V. (1994) *Quality schooling*. London: Cassell.

Austin, G. (1989) 'School effectiveness and improvement in the United States', in Reynolds, D., Creemers, B. P. M. and Peters, T. (eds) *School Effectiveness and Improvement, Proceedings of the First International Congress*, Cardiff, University of Wales College at Cardiff.

Austin, G. and Holowenzak, S. P. (1985) 'An examination of 10 years of research on exemplary schools', in Austin, G. and Garber, H. (eds) *Research on Exemplary Schools*, Orlando FL: Academic Press.

Avalos, B. (1980) 'Teacher effectiveness: research in the Third World, highlights of a review', *Comparative Education*, **16**, 1, pp.45–54.

Averch, H. A., Carroll, S. J., Donaldson, T. S., Kiesling, H. J. and Pincus, J. (1971) *How Effective Is Schooling? A Critical Review and Synthesis of Research Findings*, Santa Monica, CA: Rand Corporation.

Baker, A. P., Xu, Dengke and Detch, E. (1995) *The Measure of Education: A review of the Tennessee Value Added Assessment System*, Office of Education Accountability, Tennessee Department of Education, Nashville, TN: Comptroller of the Treasury.

346

Bamburg, J. (1990) 'Review of unusually effective schools: A review and analysis of research and practice', *School Effectiveness and School Improvement*, 1, 3, pp.221–4.

Bamburg, J. and Andrews, R. (1991) 'School goals, principals and achievement', *School Effectiveness and School Improvement*, 2, 3, pp.175–91.

Banks, D. (1988) 'Effective schools research and educational policy making in Australia', Paper presented at the First International Congress for School Effectiveness, London: England.

Banks, D. (1992) 'Effective schools research: A multilevel analysis of the conceptual framework', unpublished doctoral thesis, Melbourne University.

Barber, M. (1994) *Urban Education Initiatives: The National Pattern*, A Report for the Office of Standards in Education, University of Keele.

Barber, M. (1995) 'Shedding light on the dark side of the moon', *Times Educational Supplement*, 12th May, pp.3–4.

Barber, M., Denning, T., Gough, G. and Johnson, M. (1996) 'Urban education initiatives: The national pattern', in Barber, M. and Dann, R. (eds) *Raising Educational Standards in the Inner Cities: Practical Initiatives in Action*, London: Cassell.

Barker, R. G. and Gump, P. V. (1964) *Big School, Small School*, Stanford, California: Stanford University Press.

Barley, S. R. (1990) 'The alignment of technology and structure through roles and networks', *Administrative Science Quarterly*, 35, pp.61–103.

Bashi, J. (1995) 'Key national assignments for advancing and improving the Israeli education system during the 1990's', in Creemers, B. P. M. and Osinga, N. (eds) *ICSEI Country Reports*, Leeuwarden: GCO.

Bashi, J. and Sass, Z. (1990) *School Effectiveness and School Improvement*, Proceedings of the Third International Congress, Jerusalem: Magnes Press.

Beaton, A. E. (1974) 'Multivariate commonality analysis', in Mayeske, G.W., Beaton, A.E., Wisler, C.E., Okada, T. and Cohen, W.M. *Technical Supplement to 'A Study of the Achievement of Our Nation's Students'*, Washington, DC: US Department of Health, Education, and Welfare.

Bennett, N. (1992) *Managing Learning in the Primary Classroom*, Stoke: Trentham Books for the ASPE.

Benson, C. S., Medrich, E. A. and Buckley, S. (1980) 'A new view of school efficiency: Household contributions to school achievement', in Guthrie, J. W. (ed.) *School Finance Policies and Practices*, Cambridge, MA: Ballinger, pp.169–204.

Berghout, A. M. and Draper, D. C. (1984) 'The relationship among peer acceptance, social impact, and academic achievement in middle childhood', *American Educational Research Journal*, 21, 3, pp.597–604.

Bernstein, B. (1968) 'Education cannot compensate for society', *New Society*, 387, pp.344–7.

Bidwell, C. E. (1974) 'The school as a formal organisation', in March, J. G. (ed.) *Handbook of Organisation*, Chicago, IL: Rand McNally, pp.972–1022.

Bidwell, C. E. and Kasarda, J. D. (1975) 'School district organisation and student achievement', *American Sociological Review*, 40, pp.55–70.

Bidwell, C. E. and Kasarda, J. D. (1980) 'Conceptualising and measuring the effects of school and schooling', *American Journal of Education*, 88, 4, pp.401–30.

Bierhoff, H. (1996) *Laying the Foundation of Numeracy: A Comparison of Primary School Textbooks in Britain, Germany and Switzerland*, London: National Institute for Economic and Social Research.

Bierhoff, H. J. and Prais, S. J. (1995) *Schooling as Preparation for Life and Work in Switzerland and Britain*, London: National Institute for Economic and Social Research.

Black, P. J. (1994) 'Performance assessment and accountability: the experience in England and Wales', *Educational Evaluation and Policy Analysis*, 16, 2, pp.191–203.

References

Blackman, B. (1991) *Qualpro User's Manual: Version 4*, Tallahassee, FL: Impulse Development Co.

Blakey, L. S. and Heath, A. F. (1992) 'Differences between comprehensive schools: Some preliminary findings', in Reynolds, D. and Cuttance, P. (eds) *School Effectiveness: Research, Policy and Practice*, London: Cassell.

Blank, R. K. (1993) 'Developing a system of education indicators: Selecting, implementing, and reporting indicators', *Educational Evaluation and Policy Analysis*, 15, 1, pp.65–80.

Blau, P. and Duncan, O. D. (1967) *The American Occupational Structure*, New York: Wiley and Sons.

Block, J. H. and Burns, R. B. (1976) 'Mastery learning', in Shulman, L. (ed.) *Review of Research in Education*, 4, Ithaca: Peacock, pp.3–39.

Blok, H. and Hoeksma, J. B. (1993) 'The stability of school effects over time: An analysis based on the final test of primary education', *Tijdschrift voor Onderwijsresearch*, 18, 6, pp.331–42.

Bloom, B. S. (1976) *Human Characteristics and School Learning*, New York: McGraw-Hill.

Blumberg, P. (ed.) (1972) *The Impact of Social Class*, New York: Thomas Y. Cromwell Co.

Board of Studies, Victoria (1995) *Curriculum and Standards Framework*, Victorian Board of Studies.

Bock, R. D. and Wolfe, R. (1996) *Audit and Review of the Tennessee Value-Added Assessment System (TVAAS): Final Report*, Chicago, IL: University of Chicago.

Bollen, R. and Hopkins, D. (1987) *School Based Review: Towards a Praxis*, Leuven, Belgium: ACCO.

Bolman, L. G. and Deal, T. E. (1984) *Modern Approaches to Understanding and Managing Organisations*, San Francisco: Jossey-Bass.

Bolman, L. G. and Deal, T. E. (1991) *Reframing Organisations: Artistry, Choice, and Leadership*, San Francisco: Jossey-Bass.

Bondi, L. (1991) 'Attainment in primary schools', *British Educational Research Journal*, 17, 3, pp.203–17.

Borg, M. and Gall, W. (1989) *Educational Research* (Fifth Edition), New York: Longman.

Borgatti, S. P., Everett, M. G. and Freeman, L. C. (1992) *UCINET IV, Version 1.0*, Columbia, SC: Analytic Technology.

Borger, J. B., Lo, C., Oh, S. and Walberg, H. J. (1985) 'Effective schools: A quantitative synthesis of constructs', *Journal of Classroom Interaction*, 20, pp.12–17.

Bosker, R. J. (1989) 'Theory development in school effectiveness research: In search for stability of effects', Paper presented at the multi-level conference, Nijmegen.

Bosker, R. J. (1990) 'Extra kansen dankzij de school?: het differentieel effect van schoolkenmerken op loopbanen in het voortgezet onderwijs voor lager versus hoger milieu leerlingen en jongens versus meisjes' [Does the school provide more chances?], Nijmegen: Institut voor Toegepaste Sociale Wetenschappen.

Bosker, R. J. (1991) 'The consistency of school effects in primary education', *Tijdschrift voor Onderwijsresearch*, 16, pp.206–18.

Bosker, R. and Dekkers, H. (1994) 'School differences in producing gender-related subject choices', *School Effectiveness and School Improvement*, 5, 2, pp.178–95.

Bosker, R. J. and Guldemond, H. (1991) 'Interdependency of performance indicators: An empirical study in a categorical school system', in Raudenbush, S. W. and Willms, J. D. (eds) *Schools, Classrooms, and Pupils: International Studies of Schooling from a Multilevel Perspective*, San Diego: Academic Press.

Bosker, R. J. and Scheerens, J. (1989) 'Issues in the interpretation of the results of school effectiveness research', in Creemers, B. P. M. and Scheerens, J. (eds) *Developments in school effectiveness research*, Special issue of *International Journal of Educational Research*, 13, 7, pp.741–51.

Bosker, R. J. and Scheerens, J. (1994) 'Alternative models of school effectiveness put to the test', *International Journal of Educational Research*, **21**, pp.159–81.

Bosker, R. J. and Witziers, B. (1996) 'The magnitude of school effects, or: Does it really matter which school a student attends?', Paper presented at the annual meeting of the American Educational Research Association, New York, NY.

Bosker, R. J., Guldemond, H., Hofman, R. H. and Hofman, W. H. A. (1988) *Kwaliteit in Her Voortgezet Onderwijs*, Groningen: RION.

Bosker, R. J., Kremers, E. and Lugthart, E. (1990) 'School and instruction effects on mathematics achievement', *School Effectiveness and School Improvement*, **1**, 4, pp.233–48.

Bossert, S. T. (1988) 'School effects', in Boyan, N. J. (ed.) *Handbook of Research on Educational Administration*, New York: Longman, pp.341–52.

Bossert, S. T., Dwyer, D. C., Rowan, B. and Lee, G. (1982) 'The instructional management role of the principal', *Educational Administration Quarterly*, **18**, pp.34–64.

Bowles, S. (1970) 'Towards an educational production function', in Hansen, W. L. (ed.) *Education, Income, and Human Capital*, New York: Columbia University Press, pp.11–61.

Bowles, S. and Gintis, H. (1976) *Schooling in Capitalist America*, London: Routledge and Kegan Paul.

Bowles, S. S. and Levin, H. M. (1968) 'The determinants of scholastic achievement – An appraisal of some recent evidence', *Journal of Human Resources*, **3**, pp.3–24.

Brandsma, H. P. (1993) *Basisschoolkenmerken en de Kwaliteit van Het Onderwijs* [*Characteristics of primary schools and the quality of education*], Groningen: RION.

Brandsma, H. P. and Knuver, A. W. M. (1989) 'Effects of school classroom characteristics on pupil progress in language and arithmetic', in Creemers, B. P. M. and Scheerens, J. (eds) *Developments in School Effectiveness Research*, Special issue of *International Journal of Educational Research*, **13**, 7, pp.777–88.

Brandsma, H. P., Edelenbos, P. and Bosker, R. J. (1995) *Effecten van Trainingen voor Docenten en Schoolleiders* [*The effects of training programmes for teachers and school leaders*], Groningen/Enschede: GION/OCTO.

Brandt, R. S. (1989) *Readings from Educational Leadership: Effective Schools and School Improvement*, Alexandria, VA: Association for Supervision and Curriculum Development.

Breiger, R. L. (1976) 'Career attributes and network structure: A blockmodel study of a biomedical research speciality', *American Sociological Review*, **41**, pp.117–35.

Brewer, J. and Hunter, A. (1989) *Multimethod Research: A Synthesis of Styles*, Newbury Park, CA: Sage.

Bridge, R. G., Judd, C. M. and Moock, P. R. (1979) *The Determinants of Educational Outcomes – The Impact of Families, Peers, Teachers, and Schools*, Cambridge, MA: Ballinger Publishing Co.

Bridges, E. (1988) *The Incompetent Teacher*, Lewes: Falmer Press.

Brimer, A., Madaus, G. F., Chapman, B., Kellaghan, T. and Woodrof, R. (1978) *Differences in School Achievement*, Slough: NFER-Nelson.

Bronfenbrenner, U. (1972) 'Another world of children', *New Society*, 10 February, pp.278–86.

Bronfenbrenner, U. (1979) *The Ecology of Human Development*, Cambridge, MA: Harvard University Press.

Brookover, W. B. (1985) 'Can we make schools effective for minority students?' *The Journal of Negro Education*, **54**, 3, pp.257–68.

Brookover, W. B. and Erickson, E. (1975) *Sociology of Education*. Homewood, IL: Dorsey Press.

Brookover, W. B. and Lezotte, L. W. (1979) *Changes in School Characteristics Coincident with Changes in Student Achievement*, East Lansing: Institute for Research on Teaching, College of Education, Michigan State University.

Brookover, W. B. and Schneider, J. M. (1975) 'Academic environments and elementary school achievement', *Journal of Research and Development in Education*, **9**, pp.82–91.

References

Brookover, W. B., Beady, C., Flood, P., Schweitzer, J. and Wisenbaker, J. (1979) *Schools, Social Systems and Student Achievement: Schools Can Make a Difference*, New York: Praeger.

Brookover, W. B., Beamer, L., Efthim, H., Hathaway, D., Lezotte, L., Miller, S. Passalacqua, J. and Tornatzky, L. (1984) *Creating Effective Schools: An In-service Program for Enhancing School Learning Climate and Environment*. Holmes Beach, FL: Learning Publications, Inc.

Brookover, W. B., Paterson, A. and Thomas, S. (1962) *Self-concept of Ability and School Achievement*, East Lansing: College of Education, Michigan State University.

Brookover, W. B., Schweitzer, J. G., Schneider, J. M., Beady, C. H., Flood, P. K. and Wisenbaker, J. M. (1978) 'Elementary school social climate and school achievement', *American Educational Research Journal*, **15**, pp.301–18.

Brophy, J. E. (1979) 'Advances in teacher research', *The Journal of Classroom Interaction*, **15**, pp.1–7.

Brophy, J. E. and Evertson, C. (1974) *Process–Product Correlations in the Texas Teacher Effectiveness Study: Final Report*, Research Report No. 74–4, Austin, Texas: Research and Development Center for Teacher Education, University of Texas (ERIC Document Reproduction Service No. ED 091 094).

Brophy, J. E. and Good, T. L. (1974) *Teacher-Student Relationships: Causes and Consequences*, New York: Holt, Rinehart, and Winston.

Brophy, J. E. and Good, T. L. (1986) 'Teacher behavior and student achievement', in Wittrock, M. (ed.) *Third Handbook of Research on Teaching*, New York: Macmillan, pp.328–75.

Brotherhood of St Laurence (1996) 'What is happening to free public education? Low income families experiences of primary and secondary education', *Changing Pressures Bulletin*, No. 3, Melbourne: Brotherhood of St Laurence.

Brown (1954) *The Board of Education of Topeka, Kansas*, 347 US 483.

Brown, R. J. (1965) 'Organizational climate of elementary schools', Research Monograph No. 2, Minneapolis, MN: Educational Research and Development Council.

Brown, S., Duffield, J. and Riddell, S. (1995) 'School effectiveness research: The policymakers tool for school improvement?', *European Educational Research Assocation Bulletin*, **1**, 1, pp.6–15.

Brown, S., Riddell, S. and Duffield, J. (1996) 'Possibilities and problems of small-scale studies to unpack the findings of large-scale studies of school effectiveness', in Gray, J., Reynolds, D., Fitz-Gibbon, C. and Jesson, D. (eds) *Merging Traditions: The Future of Research on School Effectiveness and School Improvement*, London: Cassell, pp.93–120.

Bryk, A. S. and Frank, K. (1991) 'The specialization of teachers' work: An initial exploration', in Raudenbush, S. W. and Willms, J. D. (eds) *Schools, Classrooms and Pupils: International Studies of Schooling from a Multilevel Perspective*, San Diego, CA: Academic Press, pp.185–201.

Bryk, A. S. and Raudenbush, S. W. (1987) 'Application of hierarchical linear models to assessing change', *Psychological Bulletin*, **10**, 1, pp.147–58.

Bryk, A. S. and Raudenbush, S. (1988) 'Toward a more appropriate conceptualisation of research on school effects: A three-level hierarchical linear model', in Bock, R. D. (ed.) *Multilevel Analysis of Educational Data*, pp.159–204.

Bryk, A. S. and Raudenbush, S. W. (1992) *Hierarchical Linear Models: Applications and Data Analysis Methods*, Newbury Park, CA: Sage.

Bryk, A. S. and Thum, Y. M. (1989) 'The effects of high school on dropping out: An exploratory investigation', *American Educational Research Journal*, **26**, pp.353–84.

Bryk, A. S., Raudenbush, S. W. and Congdon, R. T. (1986a) *MM4: Hierarchical Linear and Nonlinear Modeling with the MM/2L and MM/3L Programs*, Chicago, IL: Scientific Software Internation.

Bryk, A. S., Raudenbush, S. W., Seltzer, M. and Congdon, R. T. (1986b) *An Introduction to MM: Computer Program and Users' Guide*, University of Chicago, Department of Education.

Burghes, D. (1995) 'Britain gets a minus in maths', *Sunday Times*, 14 May, p.11.

Burghes, D. and Blum, W. (1995) 'The Exeter Kassel comparative project: A review of Year 1 and Year 2 results', in Gatsby Foundation, *Proceedings of A Seminar on Mathematics Education*, London: Gatsby.

Burstein, L. (1980a) 'The analysis of multi-level data in educational research and evaluation', in Berliner, D. C. (ed.) *Review of Research in Education*, 8, pp.158–233.

Burstein, L. (1980b) 'The role of levels of analysis in the specification of education effects', in Dreeban, R. and Thomas, J. A. (eds) *The Analysis of Educational Productivity*, vol.1, *Issues in microanalysis*, Cambridge, MA: Ballinger, pp.119–90.

Burstein, L. (1980c) 'The use of within-group slopes as indices of group outcomes', Paper presented at the annual meeting of the American Educational Research Association, Washington DC.

Burstein, L. and Knapp, T. (1975) *The Unit of Analysis in Educational Research*, Technical report no. 4, Consortium on Methodology for Aggregating Data in Educational Research, Milwaukee, WI; Vasquez Associates.

Burstein, L. and Miller, M. D. (1979) 'The use of within-group slopes as indices of group outcomes', Paper presented at the annual meeting of the American Educational Research Association.

Burstein, L., Kim, K.S. and Delandshere, G. (1989) 'Multilevel investigations of systematically varying slopes: Issues, alternatives and consequences', in Bock, R. D. (ed.) *Multilevel Analysis of Educational Data*, San Diego, CA: Academic Press, pp.233–76.

Burt, R. S. (1978) 'Applied network analysis: An overview', *Sociological Methods and Research*, 7, pp.123–212.

Buttram, J. L. and Carlson, R. V. (1983) 'Effective schools research: Will it play in the country?', *Research in Rural Education*, 2, 2, pp.73–8.

Byrne, D. and Williamson, B. (1971) *The Poverty of Education*, London: Martin Robertson.

Cain, G. C. and Watts, H. W. (1970) 'Problems in making policy inferences from the Coleman report', *American Sociological Review*, 35, pp.228–42.

Caldwell, B. (1995) 'The provision of education and the allocation of resources', in Evers, C. and Chapman, J. (eds) *Educational Administration: An Australian Perspective*, Sydney: Allen and Unwin.

Caldwell, B. J. (1997) 'The future of public education: A policy framework for lasting reform', *Educational Management and Administration*, 25, 4, pp.357–71.

Caldwell, B. J. and Hayward, D. K. (1998) *The Future of Schools: Lessons from the Reform of Public Publication*, London: Falmer Press.

Caldwell, B. and Hill, P. W. (1996) *Funding Models for Locally Managed Schools: The Case of Schools of the Future in Victoria*, MBA seminars, University of Lincolnshire and Humberside, London, October.

Caldwell, B. and Misko, J. (1983) *The Report of the Effective Resource Allocation in Schools Project*, Hobart: Centre for Education, University of Tasmania.

Caldwell, B. and Spinks, J. (1986) *Policy Making and Planning for School Effectiveness*, Hobart: Department of Education.

Caldwell, B. and Spinks, J. (1988) *The Self Managing School*, Lewes, Sussex: Falmer Press.

Caldwell, B. and Spinks, J. (1992) *Leading the Self Managing School*, Lewes, Sussex: Falmer Press.

Caldwell, B. J. and Spinks, J. M. (1998) *Beyond the Self Managing School*, London: Falmer Press.

Caldwell, B., Hill, P. W., Hind, I., Marshall, G. and Odden, A. (1995) *The School Global Budget in Victoria: Matching Resources to Student Learning Needs*, Interim Report of the Education Committee, Melbourne: Directorate of School Education.

Caldwell, B., Lawrence, A., Peck, F. and Thomas, F. (1994) 'Leading Victoria's schools of the future: Baseline survey in 1993', Paper presented at the 7th Annual Conference of the International Congress for School Effectiveness and Improvement, Melbourne, Australia.

Cambridge University (1994) *Mapping Change in Schools – The Cambridge Manual of Research Techniques*, Cambridge: University of Cambridge Institute of Education, June.

Campbell, D. T. and Stanley, J. (1966) *Experimental and Quasi-experimental Design for Research*, Chicago: Rand McNally.

Campo, C. (1993) *Collaborative School Cultures: How Principles Can Make a Difference*, San Francisco: Jossey-Bass.

Carroll, H. (1992) 'School effectiveness and school attendance', *School Effectiveness and School Improvement*, **3**, 4, pp.258–71.

Carroll, J. B. (1963) 'A model of school learning', *Teachers College Record*, **64**, 8, pp.723–33.

Carroll, J. B. (1985) 'The model of school learning: Progress of an idea'. in Fisher, C. W. and Berliner, D. W. (eds) *Perspectives on Instructional Time*, New York: Longman, pp.29–59.

Carroll, J. B. (1989) 'The Carroll Model, a 25-year retrospective and prospective view', *Educational Researcher*, **18**, pp.26–31.

Carter, L. F. (1984) 'The sustaining effects study of compensatory and elementary education', *Educational Researcher*, **13**, 8, pp.4–13.

Cartwright, D. and Zander, A. (1968) *Group Dynamics: Research and Theory*, 3rd edn, New York: Harper and Row.

Carver, R. P. (1975) 'The Coleman Report: Using inappropriately designed achievement tests', *American Educational Research Journal*, **12**, 1, pp.77–86.

Chapman, J. D. (1985) *Victorian Primary School Principal: The Way Forward*, Melbourne: Globe Press.

Chapman, J. D. (1991a) 'The role of school leadership in enhancing the effectiveness of schools and developing a capacity to innovate and experiment', Paper presented to OECD, Paris.

Chapman, J. D. (1991b) 'The effectiveness of schooling and of educational resource management', Paper presented to the OECD, Paris.

Chapman, J. D. (1992) 'Decentralisation and school improvement', Paper presented to OECD, Paris.

Chapman, J. (1993) 'Leadership, school based decision making and school effectiveness', in Dimmock, C. (ed.) *School Based Management and School Effectiveness*, London: Routledge.

Chapman, J. and Aspin, D. (1997) 'Autonomy and mutuality: Quality education and self-managing schools', in Townsend, T. (ed.) *Restructuring and Quality: Issues for Tomorrow's Schools*, London: Routledge.

Chapman, J. and Stevens, S. (1989) 'Australia', in Reynolds, D., Creemers, B.P.M. and Peters, T. (eds) *School Effectiveness and Improvement*, Groningen: RION.

Cheng, Y. C. (1993) 'Profiles of organisational culture and effective schools', *School Effectiveness and School Improvement*, **4**, 2, pp.85–110.

Cheng, Y. C. (1993) 'The theory of the characteristics of school-based management', *International Journal of Educational Management*, **7**, 6, pp.6–17.

Cheng, Y. C. (1994) Principals' leadership as a critical factor for school performance: Evidence from multi-levels of primary schools', *School Effectiveness and School Improvement*, **5**, 3, pp.299–317.

Cheng, Y. C. (1996) 'A school-based management mechanism for school effectiveness and development', *School Effectiveness and School Improvement*, **7**, 1, pp.35–61.

Cheung, J. (1992) 'An exploration of the relationships between teaching approaches and cognitive demand of the physics curriculum at the sixth form level in Hong Kong', *School Effectiveness and School Improvement*, **3**, 1, pp.2–18.

Cheung, K. (1993) 'The learning environment and its effect on learning: Product and process modelling for science achievement at the sixth form level in Hong Kong', *School Effectiveness and School Improvement*, **4**, 4, pp.242–64.

Children First Act (1988) *La. R.S.17:3911–12*, Louisiana Revised Statues.

Chrispeels, J. H. (1992) *Purposeful Restructuring: Creating a Culture for Learning and Achievement in Elementary Schools*, London: Falmer Press.

Chrispeels, J. H. and Pollack, S. (1989) 'Equity schools and equity districts', in Creemers, B., Peters, T. and Reynolds, D. (eds) *School Effectiveness and School Improvement*, Amsterdam, Netherlands: Swets and Zeitlinger, pp.295–308.

Chubb, J. E. and Moe, T. M. (1985) 'Politics, markets, and the organization of schools', Paper presented at the annual meeting of the American Political Science Association, New Orleans, LA.

Chubb, J. E. and Moe, T. M. (1990) *Politics, Markets and America's Schools*, Washington DC: The Brookings Institution.

Clark, D. L., Lotto, L. B. and Astuto, T. A. (1984) 'Effective schools and school improvement: A comparative analysis of two lines of inquiry', *Educational Administration Quarterly*, 20, 3, pp.41–68.

Clark, M. L. (1991) 'Social identity, peer relations, and academic competence of African-American adolescents', *Education and Urban Society*, 24, 1, pp.41–52.

Clark, T. A. and McCarthy, D. P. (1983) 'School improvement in New York City: The evolution of a project', *Educational Researcher*, 12, 4, pp.17–24.

Clegg, A. and Megson, B. (1968) *Children in Distress*, Harmondsworth: Penguin.

Clifford, P. and Heath, A. (1984) 'Selection does make a difference', *Oxford Review of Education*, 10, pp.85–97.

Clift, P. et al. (1987) *Studies in School Self Evaluation*, Lewes, Sussex: Falmer Press.

Climaco, C. (1995) 'The use of performance indicators in school improvement and in accountability', in OECD (ed.) *Measuring the Quality of Schools*, Paris: OECD, pp.145–77.

Cloward, D. and Ohlin, B. (1964) *Delinquency and Opportunity*, London: Routledge and Kegan Paul.

Clune, W. H. (1993) 'The best path to systemic educational policy: Standard/centralised or differentiated/decentralised?', *Educational Evaluation and Policy Analysis*, 15, pp.233–54.

Cohen, J. (1969) *Statistical Power Analysis for the Behavioural Sciences (2nd ed.)*, Hillsdale, NJ: Lawrence Erlbaum Associates.

Cohen, J. (1977) *Statistical Power Analysis for the Behavioural Sciences*, New York: Academic Press.

Cohen, M. (1982) 'Effective schools: Accumulating research findings', *American Education*, Jan–Feb, pp.13–16.

Cohen, M. D., March, J. G. and Olsen, J. P. (1972) 'A garbage can model of organisational choice', *Administrative Science Quarterly*, 17, 1, pp.1–25.

Cohen, N. (1965) *Delinquent Gangs*, Glencoe: The Free Press.

Coleman, J. S. and Hoffer, T. (1987) *Public and Private High Schools: The Impact of Communities*, New York: Basic Books.

Coleman, J. S., Campbell, E., Hobson, C., McPartland, J., Mood, A., Weinfeld, R. and York, R. (1966) *Equality of Educational Opportunity*, Washington, DC: Government Printing Office.

Coleman, J. S., Hoffer, T. and Kilgore (1981) *Public and Private Schools: A Report to the National Center of Education Statistics by the National Opinion Research Center*, Chicago, IL: University of Chicago.

Coleman, J. S., Hoffer, T. and Kilgore, S. (1982a) *High School Achievement*, New York: Basic Books.

Coleman, J.S., Hoffer, T. and Kilgore, S. (1982b) 'Cognitive outcomes in public and private schools', *Sociology of Education*, 55, pp.65–76.

Coleman, P. and Collinge, J. (1991) 'In the web, internal and external influences affecting school improvement', *School Effectiveness and School Improvement*, 2, 4, pp.262–85.

Coleman, P. and LaRoque, L. (1988) *Reaching Out: Instructional Leadership in School*

Districts, Simon Fraser University and the Social Sciences and Humanities Research Council of Canada.

Coleman, P. and Laroque, L. (1991) *Striving to be Good Enough*, Lewes: Falmer Press.

Coleman, P., Collinge, J. and Seifert, T. (1993) 'Seeking the levers of change: Participant attitudes and school improvement', *School Effectiveness and School Improvement*, 4, 1, pp.59–83.

Comber, L. C. and Keeves, P. (1973) *Science Education in Nineteen Countries*, London: John Wiley.

Conklin, N. F. and Olson, T. A. (1988) *Toward More Effective Education for Poor, Minority Students in Rural Areas: What the Research Suggests*, Portland, OR: Northwest Regional Educational Laboratory.

Cook, T. D. and Campbell, D. T. (1979) *Quasiexperimentation: Design and Analysis Issues for Field Settings*, Boston: Houghton Mifflin Company.

Cooley, W. W. (1983) 'Improving the performance of an educational system', *Educational Researcher*, 12, 6, pp.4–12 .

Cooper, H. and Good, T. (1982) *Pygmalion Grows Up: Studies in the Expectation Communication Process*, New York: Longman.

Coopersmith, S. (1967) *Antecedents of Self Esteem*, San Francisco, CA: W.H. Freeman.

Corbett, H. and Wilson, B. (1992) 'The central office role in instructional improvement', *School Effectiveness and School Improvement*, 3, 1, pp.45–68.

Cotton, K. (1995) *Effective School Practices: A Research Synthesis (1995 Update)*, Portland, Oregon, Northwest Regional Educational Laboratory.

Crandall, D. et al. (1982) *People, Policies and Practice: Examining the Chain of School Improvement*, (Vols 1–10), Andover, MA: The Network.

Crandall, D., Eiseman, J. and Louis, K. S. (1986) 'Strategic planning issues that bear on the success of school improvement efforts', *Educational Administration Quarterly*, 22, 2, pp.21–53.

Crandall, V. C., Katkovsky, W. and Crandall, V. J. (1965) 'Children's beliefs in their own control of reinforcements in intellectual-academic situations', *Child Development*, 36, pp.91–109.

Crano, W. D. and Mellon, P. M. (1978) 'Causal influence of teachers' expectations on children's academic performance: A cross-lagged panel analysis', *Journal of Educational Psychology*, 70, 1, pp.39–49.

Creemers, B. P. M. (1991) 'Review of Effective teaching: Current research', *School Effectiveness and School Improvement*, 2, 3, pp.256–60.

Creemers, B. P. M. (1992) 'School effectiveness and effective instruction – The need for a further relationship', in Bashi, J. and Sass, Z. (eds) *School Effectiveness and Improvement*, Jerusalem: Hebrew University Press.

Creemers, B. P. M. (1994) *The Effective Classroom*, London: Cassell.

Creemers, B. P. M. and Knuver, A. W. M. (1989) The Netherlands, in Creemers, B. P. M., Peters, T. and Reynolds, D. (eds) *School Effectiveness and School Improvement. Proceedings of the Second International Congress, Rotterdam*, Lisse: Swets and Zeitlinger, pp. 70–82.

Creemers, B. P. M. and Osinga, N. (eds) (1995) *ICSEI Country Reports*, Leeuwarden, Netherlands: ICSEI Secretariat.

Creemers, B. P. M. and Reezigt, G. J. (1991) *Evaluation of Educational Effectiveness*, Groningen: ICO.

Creemers, B. P. M. and Reezigt, G. J. (1996) 'School level conditions affecting the effectiveness of instruction', *School Effectiveness and School Improvement*, 7, 3, pp.197–228.

Creemers, B. P. M. and Reynolds, D. (1990) 'School effectiveness and school improvement: A mission statement', *School Effectiveness and School Improvement*, 1, 1, pp.1–3.

Creemers, B. P. M. and Scheerens, J. (eds) (1989) 'Developments in school effectiveness research', A special issue of *International Journal of Educational Research*, 13, 7, pp.685–825.

Creemers, B. P. M. and Scheerens, J. (1994) 'Developments in the educational effectiveness research programme', in Bosker, R. J., Creemers, B. M. P. and Scheerens, J. (eds) *Conceptual and Methodological Advances in Educational Effectiveness Research*, Special issue of *International Journal of Educational Research*, **21**, 2, pp.125–40.

Creemers, B. P. M., Reynolds, D., Stringfield, S. and Teddlie, C. (1996) *World Class Schools: Some Further Findings*, Paper presented at the annual meeting of the American Educational Research Association, New York.

Creswell, J. W. (1994) *Research Design: Qualitative and Quantitative Approaches*, Thousand Oaks, CA: Sage Publications.

Crévola, A. M. and Hill, P. W. (1997) 'A whole school approach to prevention and intervention in early literacy', *Journal of Education for Students Placed at Risk*.

Cronbach, L. J. (1982) *Designing Evaluations of Educational and Social Programs*, San Francisco: Jossey-Bass.

Cronbach, L. and Furby, L. (1970) 'How we should measure "change" – or should we?', *Psychological Bulletin*, **74**, pp.66–80.

Cronbach, L. J., Deken, J. E. and Webb, N. (1976) 'Research on classrooms and schools: Formulation of questions, designs, and analysis', Occasional Paper of the Stanford Evaluation Consortium, Palo Alto, CA: Stanford University.

Crone, L. J. (1992) 'The methodological issues of variance in teacher behavior and student achievement: The relationship of variance to teacher and school effectiveness', unpublished doctoral dissertation, Louisiana State University.

Crone, L. J. and Teddlie, C. (1995) 'Further examination of teacher behavior in differentially effective schools: Selection and socialisation processes', *Journal of Classroom Interaction*, **30**, 1, pp.1–9.

Crone, L. J., Lang, M. and Franklin, B. J. (1994a) 'Achievement measures of school effectiveness: Comparison of consistency across years', Paper presented at the Annual Meeting of the American Educational Research Association, 4–8 April, New Orleans.

Crone, L. J., Lang, M., Franklin, B. and Halbrook, A. (1994b) 'Composite versus component scores: Consistency of school effectiveness classification', *Applied Measurement in Education*, **7**, 4, pp.303–21.

Crone, L. J., Lang, M. H., Teddlie, C., and Franklin, B. (1995) 'Achievement measures of school effectiveness: Comparison of model stability across years', *Applied Measurement in Education*, **8**, 4, pp.365–77.

Crow, G. (1993) 'Reconceptualising the school administrator's role: Socialisation at mid-career', *School Effectiveness and School Improvement*, **4**, 2, pp.131–52.

Crowson, R. and Morris, V. (1992) 'The superintendency and school effectiveness: an organisational hierarchy perspective', *School Effectiveness and School Improvement*, **3**, 1, pp.69–88.

Cuban, L. (1983) 'Effective schools: A friendly but cautionary note', *Phi Delta Kappan*, **64**, pp.695–6.

Cuban, L. (1984) 'Transforming the frog into a prince: Effective schools research, policy, and practice at the district level', *Harvard Educational Review*, **54**, pp.129–51.

Cuban, L. (1993) 'Preface', in Teddlie, C. and Stringfield, S. (eds) *Schools Make a Difference: Lessons Learned from a 10-year Study of School Effects*, New York: Teachers College Press.

Curtis, R. and Jackson, E. (1977) *Inequality in American Communities*, New York: Academic Press.

Cuttance, P. (1982) 'Reflections on the Rutter ethos: The professional researchers' response to *Fifteen thousand hours: Secondary schools and their effects on children*', *Urban Education*, **16**, 4, pp.483–92.

Cuttance, P. (1985) 'Frameworks for research on the effects of schooling', in Reynolds, D. (ed.) *Studying School Effectiveness*, Lewes: Falmer Press.

Cuttance, P. (1987) *Modelling Variation in the Effectiveness of Schooling*, Edinburgh: CES.

References

Cuttance, P. (1988) 'Intra system variation in the effectiveness of schooling', *Research Papers in Education*, 3, 2, pp.183–219.

Cuttance, P. (1992) 'Evaluating the effectiveness of schools', in Reynolds, D. and Cuttance, P. (eds) *School Effectiveness: Research, Policy and Practice*, London: Cassell, pp.71–95.

Cuttance, P. (1994) 'Monitoring educational quality through performance indicators for school practice', *School Effectiveness and School Improvement*, 5, 2, pp.101–26.

Daly, P. (1991) 'How large are secondary school effects in Northern Ireland?', *School Effectiveness and School Improvement*, 2, 4, pp.305–23.

Daly, P. (1995a) 'Public accountability and the academic effectiveness of grant-aided catholic schools', *School Effectiveness and School Improvement*, 6, 4, pp.367–79.

Daly, P. (1995b) 'Science course participation and science achievement in single-sex and co-educational schools', *Evaluation and Research in Education*, 9, 2.

Darling-Hammond, L. (1994) 'Performance-based assessment and educational equity', *Harvard Educational Review*, 64, 1, pp.5–29.

David, J. (1989) 'Synthesis of learning on school based management', *Educational Leadership*, 48, 8, pp.45–53.

Davie, R. et al. (1972) *From Birth to Seven*, London: Longman.

Davis, E. and Caust, M. (1994) 'How effective are South Australian schools? Development of and results from effective practice instruments', Paper presented at the 7th Annual Conference of the International Congress for School Effectiveness and Improvement, Melbourne, Australia.

Davis, G. A. and Thomas, M. A. (1989) *Effective Schools and Effective Teachers*, Boston, MA: Allyn and Bacon.

de Haan, D. M. (1992) *Measuring Test-curriculum Overlap*, Enschede: Universiteit Twente.

de Leeuw, J. and Kreft, I. (1986) 'Random coefficient models for multilevel analysis', *Journal of Educational Statistics*, 11, 1, pp.57–85.

de Leeuw, J. and Kreft, I. G. G. (1995a) 'Questioning multilevel models', in Kreft, I. G. G. (Guest Editor) 'Hierarchical linear models: Problems and prospects', Special issue of *Journal of Educational and Behavioural Statistics*, 20, 2, pp.171–89.

de Leeuw, J. and Kreft, I. G. G. (1995b) 'Not much disagreement, it seems', in Kreft, I. G. G. (Guest Editor) 'Hierarchical linear models: Problems and prospects', *Journal of Educational and Behavioural Statistics*, 20, 2, pp.239–40.

Deal, T. E. and Celotti, L. D. (1980) 'How much effects do (and can) educational administrators have on classrooms?' *Phi Delta Kappan*, 61, pp.471–3.

Deal, T. E. and Kennedy, A. A. (1982) *Corporate Cultures*, Reading, MA: Addison-Wesley.

Deal, T. E. and Kennedy, A. A. (1983) 'Culture and school performance', *Educational Leadership*, 40, 2, pp.14–15.

Deal, T. E. and Peterson, K. D. (1990) *The Principal's Role in Shaping School Cultures*, Washington, DC: US Department of Education.

Deming, W. E. (1982) *Out of the Crisis: Quality Productivity and Competitive Position*, Cambridge: Cambridge University Press.

Dempster, A. P., Laird, N. M. and Rubin, D. B. (1977) 'Maximum likelihood from incomplete data via the EM algorithm', *Journal of the Royal Statistical Society, Series B*, 39, pp.1–8.

Dempster, A. P., Rubin, D. B. and Tsutakawa, R. K. (1981) 'Estimation in convariance components models', *Journal of the American Statistical Association*, 76, pp.341–53.

Denzin, N. K. (1978) 'The logic of naturalistic inquiry', in Denzin, N. K. (ed.) *Sociological Methods: A Sourcebook*, New York: McGraw-Hill.

Department for Education and Employment (1995) *Value Added*, London: Department for Education.

Department for Education, Victoria (1996) *Guidelines for School Assessment*, Melbourne: State of Victoria.

Department of Education and Science (1967) *Children and Their Schools* (The Plowden Report), London: HMSO.

Department of Education and Science (1983) *School Standards and Spending: Statistical Analysis*, London: DES.

Department of Education and Science (1984) *School Standards and Spending: Statistical Analysis: A Further Appreciation*, London: DES.

DeYoung, A. (1987) 'The status of American rural education research: An integrated review and commentary', *Review of Educational Research*, **57**, 2, pp.123–48.

Dimmock, C. (ed.) (1993) *School Based Management and School Effectiveness*, London: Routledge.

Dimmock, C. and Hattie, J. (1996) 'School principal's efficacy and its measurement in a context of restructuring', *School Effectiveness and School Improvement*, **7**, 1, pp.62–75.

Dimmock, C. and Wildy, H. (1992) 'The district superintendency and school improvement: A western Australian perspective', *School Effectiveness and School Improvement*, **3**, 2, pp.150–72.

Donoghue, M., Thomas, S., Goldstein, H. and Knight, T. (1996) *DfEE Study of Value Added for 16–18 Year Olds in England*.

Doolaard, S. (1995) 'Stabiliteit van schoolkenmerken in het basisonderwijs [Stability of school characteristics in primary education]', Paper presented at the Onderwijs-researchdagen, June 19–21, Groningen, The Netherlands.

Dougherty, K. (1981) 'After the fall: Research on school effects since the Coleman report', *Harvard Educational Review*, **51**, pp.301–8.

Douglas, J. W. B. (1964) *The Home and the School*, London: Panther.

Douglas, J. W. B. (1968) *All Our Future*, London: Panther.

Doyle, W. (1986) 'Classroom organization and management', in Wittrock, M. C. (ed.) *Handbook of Research on Teaching*, New York: Macmillan, pp.392–431.

Draper, D. (1995) 'Inference and hierarchical modelling in the social sciences', *Journal of Educational and Behavioural Statistics*, **20**, 2, pp.115–47.

Drazin, R. and Ven, A. H. van de (1985) 'Alternative forms of fit in contingency theory', *Administative Science Quarterly*, **30**, 514–39.

Dreeban, R, (1973) 'The school as a workplace', in Travers, R. M. W. (ed.) *Second Handbook of Research on Teaching*, Chicago, IL: Rand McNally College Publishing.

Durland, M.M. (1996) 'The application of network analysis to the study of differentially effective schools', unpublished doctoral dissertation, Louisiana State University, Baton Rouge, LA.

Durland, M. and Teddlie, C. (1996) 'A network analysis of the structural dimensions of principal leadership in differentially effective schools', Paper presented at the annual meeting of the American Educational Research Association, New York.

Dwyer, D.C. (1984) 'The search for instructional leadership routines and subtleties in the principal's role', *Educational Leadership*, **41**, 2, pp.32–7.

Dwyer, D.C., Lee, G.V., Rowan, B. and Bossert, S.T. (1982) *The Principal's Role in Instructional Management: Five Participant Observation Studies of Principals in Action*, San Francisco, CA: Far West Laboratory for Educational Research and Development.

Dyer, H. S. (1970) 'Toward objective criteria of professional accountability in the schools of New York City', *Phi Delta Kappan*, **52**, pp.206–11.

Dyer, H. S., Linn, R. L., and Patton, M. J. (1969) 'A comparison of four methods of obtaining discrepancy measures based on observed and predicted school system means on achievement tests', *American Educational Research Journal*, **6**, pp.591–606.

Edmonds, R. R. (1978) 'A discussion of the literature and issues related to effective schooling', Paper prepared for the National Conference on Urban Education, St Louis, MO.

Edmonds, R. R. (1979a) 'Effective schools for the urban poor', *Educational Leadership*, **37**, 10, pp.15–24.

References

Edmonds, R. R. (1979b) 'Some schools work and more can', *Social Policy*, 9, 2, pp.28–32.

Edmonds, R. R. (1981) 'Making public schools effective', *Social Policy*, 12, pp.56–60.

Education Committee (1996) *Consultation Paper: The Stages of Schooling in Core Funding*, Melbourne: Directorate of School Education.

Education Victoria (1996) *Guide to the 1997 School Global Budget*, Melbourne: Department of Education.

Edwards, A. D., Fitz-Gibbon, C. T., Hardman, F., Haywood, R. and Meagher, N. (1997) *Separate but Equal?: Academic v. Vocational Education post-16*, London: Routledge.

Ellett, C. D., Wren, C. Y., Callendar, K. E., Loup, K. S. and Liu, X. (1996) 'Looking backwards with the Personal Evaluation Standards: An analysis of the development and implementation of a statewide teacher assessment system', *Studies in Educational Evaluation*, 22, 1, pp.79–113.

Elley, W. B. (1992) *How in the World Do Students Read?*, Newark, DE: IEA.

Elliott, J. (1996) 'School effectiveness research and its critics: Alternative visions of schooling', *Cambridge Journal of Education*, 26, 2, pp.199–224.

Elmore, R. (1990) *Restructuring Schools*, Oakland, CA: Jossey-Bass.

Emin, J. C. (1995) 'Implementation of a system of indicators for the Steering of French Secondary School', in *Measuring the Quality of Schools*, Paris: OECD.

Emmer, E. T. (1987) 'Classroom management', in Dunkin, M. J. (ed.) *The International Encyclopaedia of Teaching and Teacher Education*, Oxford: Pergamon Press, pp.437–46.

Enthwistle, D. R. and Hayduk, L. A. (1988) 'Lasting effects of elementary school', *Sociology of Education*, 61, pp.147–59.

Erbing, L. and Young, A. A. (1979) 'Individuals and social structure: Contextual effects as endogenous feedback', *Sociological Methods and Research*, 7, pp.396–430.

Etzioni, A. (1975) *A Comparative Analysis of Complex Organizations*, New York: Free Press.

Evans, R. L. (1988) 'Teachers' perceptions of principals' change facilitator styles in schools that differ according to effectiveness and socioeconomic context', unpublished doctoral dissertation, University of New Orleans.

Evans, R. L. and Teddlie, C. (1993) 'Principals' change facilitator styles in schools that differ in effectiveness and SES', Paper presented at the annual meeting of the American Educational Research Association, Atlanta, Georgia.

Evans, R. L. and Teddlie, C. (1995) 'Facilitating change in schools: Is there one best style?', *School Effectiveness and School Improvement*, 6, 1, pp.1–22.

Evertson, C. and Burry, J. (1989) 'Capturing classroom context: The observation system as lens for assessment', *Journal of Personnel Evaluation in Education*, 2, pp.297–320.

Evertson, C. M. and Green, J. L. (1986) 'Observation as inquiry and method', in Wittrock, M. C. (ed.) *Handbook of Research on Teaching*, New York: Macmillan.

Evertson, C. M., Anderson, C. S. and Brophy, J. (1978) 'Process-outcome relationships in the Texas junior high school study: Compendium', Paper presented at the Annual Meeting of the American Educational Research Association, Toronto, Canada.

Evertson, C., Anderson, C., Anderson, L. and Brophy, J. E. (1980) 'Relationships between classroom and student outcomes in junior high mathematics and English classes', *American Educational Research Journal*, 17, pp.43–60.

Farrington, D. (1980) 'Truancy, delinquency, the home and the school', in Hersou, L. and Berg, I. (eds) *Out of School*, Chichester: John Wiley.

Festinger, L. (1949) 'The analysis of sociograms using matrix algebra', *Human Relations*, 2, pp.153–8.

Fiedler, F. (1967) *A Theory of Leadership Effectiveness*, New York: McGraw-Hill.

Fiedler, F. E. (1973) 'The contingency model and the dynamics of the leadership process', *Advances in Experimental Social Psychology*, 11, pp.60–112.

Fiedler, F. E. and Garcia, J. E. (1987) *New Approaches to Effective Leadership: Cognitive Resources and Organizational Performance*, New York: Wiley.

Firestone, W. A. (1985) 'The study of loose coupling: Problems, progress, and prospects', *Research in the Sociology of Education and Socialisation*, 5, pp.3–30.

Firestone, W. A. and Herriott, R. (1981) 'Images of organisation and the promotion of change', *Research in the Sociology of Education and Socialisation*, 2, pp.221–60.

Firestone, W. A. and Herriott, R. (1982a) 'Prescriptions for effective elementary schools don't fit secondary schools', *Educational Leadership*, 40, 12, pp.51–2.

Firestone, W. A. and Herriott, R. (1982b) 'Two images of schools as organisations: An explication and illustrative empirical test', *Educational Administration Quarterly*, 18, pp.39–60.

Firestone, W. A. and Wilson, B. (1985) 'Using bureaucratic and cultural linkages to improve instruction: The principal's contribution', *Educational Administration Quarterly*, 21, pp.7–30.

Firestone, W. A. and Wilson, B. (1989) 'Using bureaucratic and cultural linkages to improve instruction: The principal's contribution', in Burdin, J. L. (ed.) *School Leadership*, Beverly Hills, CA: Sage, pp.275–96.

Fisher, C., Berliner, D., Filby, N., Marliave, R., Cahen, L. and Dishaw, M. (1980) 'Teacher behaviors, academic learning time and student achievement: An overview', in Denham, C. and Lieberman, A. (eds) *Time to Learn*, Washington, DC: National Institute of Education.

Fitz-Gibbon, C. T. (1985) 'A-level results in comprehensive schools: The Combse project, year 1', *Oxford Review of Education*, 11, 1, pp.43–58.

Fitz-Gibbon, C. T. (1990a) 'Learning from unwelcome data: Lessons from the TVEI examination results', in Hopkins, D. (ed.) *TVEI at the Change of Life*, Clevedon, Avon: Multilingual Matters.

Fitz-Gibbon, C. T. (1990b) *Performance Indicators: A BERA Dialogue*, Clevedon, Avon, Multilingual Matters.

Fitz-Gibbon, C. T. (1991a) *Evaluation of School Performance in Public Examinations*, a report for the Scottish Office Education Department, Newcastle upon Tyne: Curriculum Evaluation and Management Centre.

Fitz-Gibbon, C. T. (1991b) 'Multi-level modeling in an indicator system', in Raudenbush, S. W. and Willms, J. D. (eds) *Schools, Classrooms, and Pupils: International Studies of Schooling from a Multilevel Perspective*, San Diego: Academic Press, pp.67–84.

Fitz-Gibbon, C. T. (1992) 'School effects at A-level – Genesis of an information system', in Reynolds, D. and Cuttance, P. (eds) *School Effectiveness: Research, Policy and Practice*, London: Cassell.

Fitz-Gibbon, C. T. (1995a) *The Value Added National Project General Report: Issues to be Considered in the Design of a National Value Added System*, London: The School Curriculum and Assessment Authority.

Fitz-Gibbon, C. T. (1995b) 'Ofsted, schmofsted', in Brighouse, T. and Moon, B. *School Inspection*, London: Pitman Publishing.

Fitz-Gibbon, C. T. (1996) *Monitoring Education: Indicators, Quality and Effectiveness*, London, New York: Cassell.

Fitz-Gibbon, C. T. (1997) *The Value Added National Project Final Report*, London: SCAA.

Fitz-Gibbon, C. T. and Tymms, P. B. (1996) *The Value Added National Project: First Report*, London: School Curriculum and Assessment Authority.

Fitz-Gibbon, C. T., Hazelwood, R. D., Tymms, P. B. and McCabe, J. J. C. (1988) 'Performance indicators and the TVEI pilot', *Evaluation and Research in Education*, 2, 3, pp.49–60.

Fitz-Gibbon, C. T., Tymms, P. B. and Hazlewood, R. D. (1989) 'Performance indicators and information systems', in Reynolds, D., Creemers, B. P. M. and Peters, T. (eds) *School Effectiveness and Improvement: Selected Proceedings of the First International Congress for School Effectiveness*, Groningen, Netherlands: RION, pp.141–52.

References

Flanders, N. (1970) *Analyzing Teacher Behavior*, Reading, MA: Addison-Wesley.

Forsyth, E. and Katz, L. (1946) 'A matrix approach to the analysis of sociometric data: Preliminary report', *Sociometry*, 9, pp.340–7.

Forsythe, R. A. (1973) 'Some empirical results related to the stability of performance indicators in Dyer's student change model of an educational system', *Journal of Educational Measurement*, 10, pp.7–12.

Forsyth, P. B. and Dansiewicz, T. J. (1985) 'Toward a theory of professionalism', *Work and Occupations*, 12, 1, pp.59–76.

Foshay, A. W. (1962) *Educational Achievements of Thirteen Year Olds in Twelve Countries*, Hamburg: UNESCO.

Foxman, D. (1992) *Learning Mathematics and Science (The Second International Assessment of Educational Progress in England)*, Slough: National Foundation for Educational Research.

Francis, L. and Lankshear, D. (1991) 'The impact of church schools on urban church life', *School Effectiveness and School Improvement*, 2, 4, pp.324–35.

Fraser, B. J., Walberg, H. J., Welch, W. W. and Hattie, J. A. (eds) (1987) 'Synthesis of educational productivity research', *International Journal of Educational Research*, 11, 2.

Freeman, J. and Teddlie, C. (1997) 'A phenomenological examination of "naturally occurring" school improvement: Implications for democratization of schools', Paper presented at the annual meeting of the American Educational Research Association, New York.

Freeman, L. C. (1977) 'A set of measures of centrality based on betweeness', *Sociometry*, 40, pp.35–41.

Freeman, L. C. (1979) 'Centrality in social networks: I. Conceptual clarification', *Social Networks*, 1, pp.215–39.

Freibel, A. J. J. M. (1994) *Planning van Onderwijs en Het Gebruik van Planningsdocumenten: Doet dat ertoe?* [*Planning of education and the implementation of planning documents*], dissertation, Oldenzaal: Dinkeldruk.

Freiberg, H., Prokosch, N., Treister, E. and Stein, T. (1990) 'Turning around five at-risk schools', *School Effectiveness and School Improvement*, 1, 1, pp.5–25.

French, J. R. P. and Raven, B. H. (1968) 'Bases of social power', in Cartwright, D. and Zander, A. *Group Dynamics: Research and Theory*, New York: Harper and Row, pp.259–70.

Fresko, B., Robinson, N., Friedlander, A., Albert, J. and Argaman, N. (1990) 'Improving mathematics instruction and learning in the junior high school: An Israeli example', *School Effectiveness and School Improvement*, 1, 3, pp.170–87.

Fullan, M. G. (1985) 'Change processes and strategies at the local level', *Elementary School Journal*, 85, 13, pp.391–421.

Fullan, M. G. (1991) *The New Meaning of Educational Change*, London: Cassell.

Fullan, M. G. (1992) 'Visions that blind', *Educational Leadership*, 49, 5, pp.19–20.

Fullan, M. G. (1992) *Successful School Improvement*, Buckingham/ Philadelphia: Open University Press.

Fullan, M. G. (1993) *Change Forces. Probing the Depths of Educational Reform*, London/New York/Philadelphia: Falmer Press.

Fullan, M. G. and Hargreaves, A. (1991) *What's Worth Fighting For: Working Together for Your School*, Toronto, Ontario Public School Teachers Association.

Fullan, M. G., Bennett, B. and Rolheiser Bennett, C. (1990) 'Linking classroom and school improvement', *Educational Leadership*, 47, 8, pp.13–19.

Fuller, B. (1987) 'School effects in the Third World', *Review of Educational Research*, 57, 3, pp.255–92.

Fuller, B. and Clark, P. (1994) 'Raising school effects while ignoring culture? Local conditions and the influence of classroom tools, rules and pedagogy', *Review of Educational Research*, 64, pp.119–57.

Fuller, B. and Heynemann, S. P. (1989) 'Third World school quality: Current collapse, future potential' in *Educational Researcher*, **18**, 2, pp.12–19.

Fuller, B. and Izu, J. (1986) 'Explaining school cohesion: What shapes the organizational beliefs of teachers?' *American Journal of Education*, **94**, pp. 501–35.

Gage, N. L. (ed.) (1963) *Handbook of Research on Teaching*, Chicago: Rand McNally.

Gage, N. L. (1966) 'Research on cognitive aspects on teaching', in Association for Supervision and Curriculum Development, Seminar on Teaching, *The Way Teaching Is*, Washington, DC: National Education Association.

Gage, N. L. (1978) *The Scientific Basis of the Art of Teaching*, New York: Teachers College Press, Columbia University.

Gage, N. L. (1983) 'When does research on teaching yield implications for practice?' *Elementary School Journal*, **83**, pp.492–6.

Gage, N. L. (1985) *Hard Gains in the Soft Sciences*, Bloomington, IN: Phi Delta Kappan.

Gage, N. L. and Needels, M. C. (1989) 'Process–product research on teaching: A review of criticisms', *The Elementary School Journal*, **89**, pp.253–300.

Galloway, D. (1983) 'Disruptive pupils and effective pastoral care', *School Organisation*, **13**, pp.245–54.

Galton, M. and Simon, B. (1980) *Progress and Performance in the Primary Classroom*, London: Routledge and Kegan Paul.

Garden, R. A. (1987) 'The Second IEA Mathematics Study', *Comparative Education Review*, **31**, 1, pp.47–68.

Gath, D. (1977) *Child Guidance and Delinquency in a London Borough*, London: Oxford University Press.

General Accounting Office (1989) *Effective Schools Programs – Their Extent and Characteristics*, Gaithersberg, MD: General Accounting Office.

Gennip, J. van (1991) *Veranderingscapaciteiten van Basisscholen*, Nijmegen: ITS.

Geske, T. G. and Teddlie, C. (1990) 'Organizational productivity of schools', in Reyes, P. (ed.) *Teachers and Their Workplace: Commitment, Performance, and Productivity*, Berkeley, CA: McCutchan Publishing, pp.191–221.

Gifford, B. R. and O'Connor, M. C. (eds) (1992) *Changing Assessment: Alternative Views of Aptitude, Achievement and Instruction*, Boston, MA: Kluwer Academic Publishers.

Gilmer, B. von Haller (1966) *Industrial Psychology* (2nd edn), New York: McGraw-Hill.

Glasman, N. S. and Biniaminov, I. (1981) 'Input–output analysis of schools', *Review of Educational Research*, **51**, pp.52–64.

Glass, G.V. (1979) 'Policy for the unpredictable', *Educational Researcher*, **8**, 9, pp.12–14.

Glickman, C. (1990) 'Pushing school reforms to a new edge: The seven ironies of school empowerment', *Phil Delta Kappan*, **72**, 1, pp.68–75.

Goldring, E. and Pasternack, R. (1994) 'Principals' coordinating strategies and school effectiveness', *School Effectiveness and School Improvement*, **5**, 3, pp.239–53.

Goldstein, H. (1980) 'Critical notice – "Fifteen thousand hours"', Rutter et al., *Journal of Child Psychology and Psychiatry*, **21**, 4, pp.364–6.

Goldstein, H. (1986) 'Multilevel mixed linear model analysis using iterative generalised least squares', *Biometrika*, **73**, 1, pp.43–56.

Goldstein, H. (1987a) 'Multilevel covariance component models', *Biometrika*, **74**, pp.430–1.

Goldstein, H. (1987b) *Multilevel Models in Educational and Social Research*, London: Oxford University Press.

Goldstein, H. (1989) 'Multilevel modelling in large scale achievement surveys', Paper presented to the American Educational Research Association, San Francisco, March.

Goldstein, H. (1991a) 'Better ways to compare schools?' *Journal of Educational Statistics*, **16**, 2, pp.89–92.

References

Goldstein, H. (1991b) 'Nonlinear multilevel models, with an application to discrete response data', *Biometrika*, **78**, pp.45–51.

Goldstein, H. (1993) *Interpreting International Comparisons of Student Achievement*, Paris: UNESCO.

Goldstein, H. (1994) 'Multilevel cross-classified models', *Sociological Methods and Research*, **22**, 3, pp.364–75.

Goldstein, H. (1995a) *Multilevel Models in Educational and Social Research: A Revised Edition*, London: Edward Arnold.

Goldstein, H. (1995b) in Kreft, I. G. G. (Guest Editor) 'Hierarchical linear models: Problems and prospects', special issue of *Journal of Educational and Behavioural Statistics*, **20**, 2.

Goldstein, H. (in press) 'The methodology of school effectiveness research', *School Effectiveness and School Improvement*.

Goldstein, H. and McDonald, R. P. (1988) 'A general model for the analysis of multilevel data', *Psychometrika*, **53**, pp.455–67.

Goldstein, H. and Sammons, P. (1995) *The Influence of Secondary and Junior Schools on Sixteen Year Examination Performance: A Cross-classified Multilevel Analysis*, London: ISEIC, Institution of Education.

Goldstein, H. and Thomas, S. (1996) 'Using examination results as indicators of school and college performance', *Journal of the Royal Statistical Society*, Series A 159, pp.149–63.

Goldstein, H., Healy, M. J. R. and Rasbash, J. (1994) 'Multilevel time series models with applications to repeated measures data', *Statistics in Medicine*, **13**, pp.1643–55.

Goldstein, H., Rasbash, J., Yang, M., Woodhouse, G., Pan, H., Nuttall, D. and Thomas, S. (1993) 'A multilevel analysis of school examination results', *Oxford Review of Education*, **19**, 4, pp.425–33.

Good, T. L. (1979) 'Teacher effectiveness in the elementary school', *Journal of Teacher Education*, **30**, 2, pp.52–64.

Good, T. L. (1989) *Classroom and School Research: Investments in Enhancing Schools*, Columbia, MO: Center for Research in Social Behavior.

Good, T. L. and Brophy, J. E. (1986) 'School effects', in Wittrock, M. (ed.), *Third Handbook of Research on Teaching*, New York: Macmillan, pp.570–602.

Good, T. L. and Grouws, D. (1979) 'The Missouri Mathematics Effectiveness Project: An experimental study in fourth grade classrooms', *Journal of Educational Psychology*, **71**, pp.355–62.

Good, T. L. and Weinstein, R. (1986) 'Schools make a difference: Evidence, criticisms, and new directions', *American Psychologist*, **41**, pp.1090–7.

Gray, J. (1981) 'A competitive edge: Examination results and the probable limits of secondary school effectiveness', *Educational Review*, **33**, 1, pp.25–35.

Gray, J. (1982) 'Towards effective schools: Problems and progress in British research', *British Educational Research Journal*, **7**, 1, pp.59–79.

Gray, J. (1989) 'Multilevel models: Issues and problems emerging from their recent application in British studies of school effectiveness', in Bock, D. R. (ed.) *Multi-level Analyses of Educational Data*, University of Chicago Press, pp.127–45.

Gray, J. (1990) 'The quality of schooling: frameworks for judgements', *British Journal of Educational Studies*, **38**, 3, pp.204–33.

Gray, J. and Jesson, D. (1987) 'Exam results and local authority league tables', *Education and Training UK 1987*, pp.33–41.

Gray, J. and Wilcox, B. (1995) *Good School, Bad School*, Buckingham: Open University Press.

Gray, J., Goldstein, H. and Jesson, D. (1996a) 'Changes and improvement in school effectiveness: Trends over five years', *Research Papers in Education*, **11**, 1, pp.35–51.

Gray, J., Hopkins, D., Reynolds, D., Wilcox, B., Farrell, S. and Jesson, D. (1999) *Improving Schools: Performance and Potential*, Buckingham: Open University Press.

Gray, J., Jesson, D. and Jones, B. (1984) 'Predicting differences in examination results between Local Education Authorities: Does school organisation matter?', *Oxford Review of Education*, 6, pp.20–35.

Gray, J., Jesson, D. and Jones, B. (1986) 'The search for a fairer way of comparing schools' examination results', *Research Reports in Education*, 1, 2, pp.91–122.

Gray, J., Jesson, D. and Sime, N. (1990) 'Estimating differences in the examination performance of secondary schools in six LEAs – A multilevel approach to school effectiveness', *Oxford Review of Education*, 16, 2, pp.137–58.

Gray, J., Jesson, D., Goldstein, H., Hedger, K. and Rasbash, J. (1995) 'A multi-level analysis of school improvement: Changes in schools' performance over time', *School Effectiveness and School Improvement*, 6, 2, pp.97–114.

Gray, J., McPherson, A. F. and Raffe, D. (1983) *Reconstructions of Secondary Education: Theory, Myth, and Practice Since the War*, London: Routledge and Kegan Paul.

Gray, J., Reynolds, D., Fitz-Gibbon, C. and Jesson, D. (1996b) *Merging Traditions: The Future of Research on School Effectiveness and School Improvement*, London: Cassell.

Green, R. L., Hofman, L. J., Morse, R. J., Hayes, M. E. and Morgan, R. F. (1964) *The Educational Status of Children in a District Without Public Schools*, East Lansing, MI: Bureau of Educational Research, Michigan State University, Cooperative Research Project No. 2321.

Greenwald, R., Hedges, L. V. and Laine, R. (1994) 'The effect of school resource on student achievement', *Review of Educational Research*, 66, 3, pp.361–96.

Gresov, C. (1989) 'Exploring the fit and misfit with multiple contingencies', *Administrative Science Quarterly*, 34, pp.431–53.

Grosin, L. (1993) 'School effectiveness research as a point of departure for school evaluation', *Scandinavian Journal of Educational Research*, 37, pp.317–30.

Guskey, T. R. and Pigott, T. J. (1988) 'Research on group-based mastery learning programs: A meta-analysis', *Journal of Educational Research*, pp.197–216.

Gutierrez, R. and Slavin, R. E. (1992) 'Achievement effects of the nongraded elementary school: A best evidence synthesis', *Review of Educational Research*, 62, 4, pp.333–76.

Hall, G. E., Rutherford, W. L., Hord, S. M. and Huling, L. L. (1984) 'Effects of three principalship styles on school improvement', *Educational Leadership*, 41, pp.22–9.

Hallinger, P. and Edwards, M. (1992) 'The paradox of superintendent leadership in school restructuring' *School Effectiveness and School Improvement*, 3, 2, pp.131–49.

Hallinger, P. and Heck, R. H. (1996) 'Reassessing the principal's role in school effectiveness: A review of the empirical research, 1980–1995', *Educational Administration Quarterly*, 32, 1, pp.5–44.

Hallinger, P. and Leithwood, K. (1994) 'Introduction: Exploring the impact of principal leadership', *School Effectiveness and School Improvement*, 5, 3, pp.206–18.

Hallinger, P. and Murphy, J. (1985) 'Assessing the instructional leadership behaviour of principals', *The Elementary School Journal*, 86, 2, pp.217–48.

Hallinger, P. and Murphy, J. (1986) 'The social context of effective schools', *American Journal of Education*, 94, pp.328–55.

Hallinger, P. and Murphy, J. (1987) 'Instructional leadership in the school context', in Greenfield, W. (ed.) *Instructional Leadership*, Boston: Allyn and Bacon, pp.179–202.

Halpin, A. W. (1966) *Theory and Research in Administration*, New York: Macmillan.

Halpin, A. W. and Croft, D. B. (1962) *The Organizational Climate of Schools*, US Office of Education, Research Project (Contract #SAE 543–8639).

Halpin, A. W. and Croft, D. B. (1963) *The Organizational Climate of Schools*, Chicago, IL: Midwest Administration Center, University of Chicago.

Hamilton, D. (1996) 'Peddling feel good fictions', *Forum*, 38, 2, pp.54–6.

Hammersley, M. and Woods, P. (1976) *The Process of Schooling*, London: Routledge and Kegan Paul.

References

Hannan, M. T., Freeman, J. H. and Meyer, J. W. (1976) 'Specification of models for organizational effectiveness', *American Sociological Review*, **41**, 1, pp.136–43.

Hannaway, J. and Talbert, J. E. (1993) 'Bringing context into effective schools research: Urban–suburban differences', *Educational Administration Quarterly*, **29**, 2, pp.164–86.

Hanushek, E. A. (1971) 'Teacher characteristics and gains in student achievement: Estimation using micro data'. *The American Economic Review*, **61**, pp.280–8.

Hanushek, E. A. (1972) *Education and Race: An Analysis of the Educational Production Process*, Lexington, MA: D.C. Heath and Company.

Hanushek, E. A. (1979) 'Conceptual and empirical issues in the estimation of educational production functions', *Journal of Human Resources*, **14**, pp.151–88.

Hanushek, E. A. (1981) 'Throwing money at schools', *Journal of Policy Analysis and Management*, **1**, pp.19–41.

Hanushek, E. A. (1986) 'The economics of schooling: Production and efficiency in public schools', *Journal of Economic Literature*, **24**, pp.1141–77.

Hanushek, E. A. (1987) 'Educational production functions', in Psacharopoulous, G. (ed.) *Economics of Education: Research and Studies*, Oxford: Pergamon Press, pp.33–42.

Hanushek, E. A. (1989) 'The impact of differential expenditures on student performance', *Educational Researcher*, **18**, 4, pp.45–51.

Hanushek, E. A. (1996) 'A more complete picture of school resource policies', *Review of Educational Research*, **66**, 3, pp.397–409.

Hanushek, E. A. and Kain, J. F. (1972) 'On the value of equality of educational opportunity as a guide to public policy', in Mosteller, F. and Moynihan, D. P. (eds) *On Equality of Educational Opportunity*, New York: Vintage Books, pp.116–45.

Harary, F., Norman, R. Z. and Cartwright, D. (1965) *Structural Models: An Introduction to the Theory of Directed Graphs*, New York: John Wiley and Sons.

Hargreaves, D. H. (1967) *Social Relations in a Secondary School*, London: Routledge and Kegan Paul.

Hargreaves, D. H. (1982) *The Challenge for the Comprehensive School*, London: Routledge and Kegan Paul.

Hargreaves, D. H. (1984) *Improving Secondary Schools*, London: ILEA.

Hargreaves, D. H. (1990) 'Accountability and school improvement in the work of LEA inspectorates: The rhetoric and beyond', London: ILEA.

Hargreaves, D. H. and Hopkins, D. (1989) *Planning for School Development*, London: DES.

Hargreaves, D. H. and Hopkins, D. (1991) *The Empowered School: The Management and Practice of Developing Planning*, London: Cassell.

Harnischfeger, A. and Wiley, D. T. (1976) 'The teaching learning process in elementary schools: A synoptic view', *Curriculum Inquiry*, **6**, pp.5–43.

Harris, A., Jamieson, I. and Russ, J. (1995) 'A study of effective departments in secondary schools' *School Organisation*, **15**, 3, pp.283–99.

Harris, C. W. (1967) *Problems in Measuring Change*, Milwaukee and London: University of Wisconsin Press.

Harris, R. J. (1985) *A Primer of Multivariate Statistics*, New York: Academic Press.

Hauser, R. M. (1970) 'Context and consex: A cautionary tale', *American Journal of Sociology*, **75**, pp.645–54.

Hauser, R. M. (1971) *Socioeconomic Background and Educational Performance*, Washington, DC: Arnold M. Rose Series, American Sociological Association.

Hauser, R. M., Sewell, W. H. and Alwin, D. F. (1976) 'High school effects on achievement', in Sewell, W. H., Hauser, R. M. and Featherman, D. L. (eds) *Schooling and Achievement in American society*, New York: Academic Press.

Heal, K. (1978) 'Misbehaviour among schoolchildren: The role of the school in strategies for prevention', *Policy and Politics*, **6**, pp.321–33.

Heath, A. and Clifford, P. (1980) 'The seventy thousand hours that Rutter left out', *Oxford Review of Education*, **6**, pp.3–19.

Hebert, C. (1994) *Teachers' perceptions of principal style and sense of autonomy in differentially effective schools*, unpublished doctoral dissertation, Louisiana State University.

Heck, R. H. (1992) 'Principals' instructional leadership and school performance: Implications for policy development', *Educational Evaluation and Policy Analysis*, **14**, 1, pp.21–34.

Heck, R., Marcoulides, G. and Lang, P. (1991) 'Principal instructional leadership and school achievement: The application of discriminant techniques', *School Effectiveness and School Improvement*, **2**, 2, pp.115–35.

Hedges, L. V., Laine, R. and Greenwald, R. (1994) 'Does money matter? A meta-analysis of studies of the effects of differential school inputs on student outcomes', *Educational Researcher*, **23**, 3, pp.5–14.

Henderson, V., Mieszkowski, P., and Sauvageau, Y. (1978) 'Peer group effects and educational production functions', *Journal of Public Economics*, **10**, pp.97–106.

Henkin, A. B. and Wanat, C. L. (1994) 'Problem-solving teams and the improvement of organisational performance in schools', *School Organisation*, **14**, 2, pp.121–39.

Her Majesty's Inspectorate (1992) *Teaching and Learning in Japanese Elementary Schools*, London: HMSO.

Herriott, R. F. and Firestone, W. A. (1984) 'Two images of schools as organisations: A refinement and elaboration', *Educational Administration Quarterly*, **20**, pp.41–58.

Hersey, P. and Blanchard, K. H. (1982) *Management of Organizational Behavior: Utilising Human Resources*, 4th edn, Englewood Cliffs, NJ: Prentice Hall.

Heynemann, S. P. and Loxley, W. A. (1983) 'The effect of primary school quality on academic achievement across twenty-nine high and low income countries', *American Journal of Sociology*, **88**, 6, pp.1162–94.

Heyns, B. (1974) 'Social selection and stratification within schools', *American Journal of Sociology*, **79**, pp.1434–51.

Hill, P. W. (1995) 'School Effectiveness and Improvement: Present realities and future possibilities', *Inaugural Professorial Lecture*, 24 May 1995, Faculty of Education: University of Melbourne.

Hill, P. W. (1996) 'Leadership for effective teaching', Paper presented at the International Principals Institute, USC, Los Angeles, July.

Hill, P. W. (1997a) *Shaking the Foundations: Research Driven School Reform*, plenary address to ICSEI, Memphis.

Hill, P. W. (1997b) *Towards High Standards for All Students: Victorian Research and Experience*, IARTV Seminar Series, No. 61.

Hill, P. W. and Crévola, C. (1997) 'Redesigning schools for improved learning', a paper presented to the Successful Schools Conference, Melbourne, June.

Hill, P. W. and Rowe, K. J. (1996) 'Multilevel modelling in school effectiveness research', *School Effectiveness and School Improvement*, **7**, 1, pp.1–34.

Hill, P. W., Holmes-Smith, P. and Rowe, K. J. (1993) *School and Teacher Effectiveness in Victoria: Key Findings from Phase I of the Victorian Quality Schools Project*, University of Melbourne. ERIC (RIE) EA 025 661.

Hill, P. W., Rowe, K. J. and Holmes-Smith, P. (1995) 'Factors affecting students, educational progress: Multilevel modelling of educational effectiveness', a paper presented at the 8th International Congress for School Effectiveness and Improvement, Leeuwarden, The Netherlands.

Hilton, T. L. and Patrick, C. (1970) 'Cross-sectional versus longitudinal data: An empirical comparison of mean differences in academic growth'. *Journal of Educational Measurement*, **7**, pp.15–24.

Hind, I. W. and Caldwell, B. J. (1995) 'Resource allocation and outcomes in the radical transformation of Victoria's schools of the future', a paper presented at the International Congress for School Effectiveness, Leeuwarden, The Netherlands.

Hirschi, T. (1969) *Causes of Delinquency*, Berkeley: University of California Press.

Hoeben, W. Th.J.G. (1989) 'Educational innovation or school effectiveness: A dilemma', in Creemers, B. P. M., Peters, T. and Reynolds, D. (eds) *School Effectiveness and School Improvement: Selected Proceedings of the Second International Congress for School Effectiveness*, Amsterdam: Swets and Zeitlinger, pp.157–66.

Hoffer, T. A., Greeley, A. M. and Coleman, J. S. (1985) 'Achievement growth in public and Catholic school', *Sociology of Education*, 58, 2, pp.74–97.

Hofman, R. H. (1993) *Effectief Schoolbestuur: Een Studie naar de Bijdrage van Schoolbesturen aan de Effectiveit van Scholen* [*Effective schoolboards*], Groningen: RION.

Hofman, R. H. (1995) 'Contextual influences on school effectiveness: The role of school boards', *School Effectiveness and School Improvement*, 6, 4, pp.308–31.

Hofman, R. H. and Lugthart, E. (1991) *Interne Capaciteiten in Het Voortgezet Onderwijs*, Groningen: RION.

Hofman, W. H. A. (1994) 'School effects on performances of minority pupils', *School Effectiveness and School Improvement*, 5, 1, pp.26–44.

Hogg, G. W. (1990) 'Great performance indicators of the past', in Fitz-Gibbon, C. T. (ed.) *Performance Indicators*, Clevedon, Avon: Multilingual Matters.

Holdaway, E. and Johnson, N. (1993) 'School effectiveness and effectiveness indicators', *School Effectiveness and School Improvement*, 4, 3, pp.165–88.

Holly, P. (1990) 'Catching the wave of the future: Moving beyond school effectiveness by redesigning schools', *School Organisation*, 10, 3, pp.195–212.

Hopfenberg, W. S., Levin, H. M., Bruner, I., Chase, C., Christiansen, S.G., Keller, B., Moore, M., Rodrigues, G. and Soler, P. (1993) *The Accelerated Schools Resource Guide*, San Francisco: Jossey-Bass.

Hopkins, D. (1987) *Improving the Quality of Schooling*, Lewes: Falmer Press.

Hopkins, D. (1988) *Doing School Based Review*, Leuven, Belgium: ACCO.

Hopkins, D. (1990) 'The International School Improvement Project (ISIP) and effective schooling: Towards a synthesis', in *School Organisation*, 10, 3, pp.129–94.

Hopkins, D. (1991) 'Changing school culture through development planning', in Riddell, S. and Brown S. (eds) *School Effectiveness Research: Messages for School Improvement*, Edinburgh: HMSO.

Hopkins, D. (1995) 'Towards effective school improvement', *School Effectiveness and School Improvement*, 6, 3, pp.265–74.

Hopkins, D. (1996) 'Towards a theory for school improvement', in Gray, J., Reynolds, D. and Fitz-Gibbon, C. (eds) *Merging Traditions: The Future of Research on School Effectiveness and School Improvement*, London: Cassell.

Hopkins, D. and Ainscow, M. (1993) 'Making sense of school improvement: An interim account of the IQEA project', Paper presented to the ESRC Seminar Series on School Effectiveness and School Improvement, Sheffield.

Hopkins, D. and Harris, A. (1997) 'Understanding the schools capacity for development: growth states and dialogues', *School Leadership and Management*, 17, 3, pp.401–11.

Hopkins, D. and Reynolds, D. (1999) 'Moving on and moving up: Confronting the complexities of school improvement in "The Improving Schools Project"', *Educational Research and Evaluation*, 4, pp.23–51.

Hopkins, D. and Stern, D. (1996) 'Quality teachers, quality schools: International perspectives and policy implications', *Teacher and Teacher Education*, 12, 5, pp.501–17.

Hopkins, D., Ainscow, M. and West, M. (1994) *School Improvement in an Era of Change*, London: Cassell.

Hopkins, D. et al. (1997) 'A case of the "Improving the Quality of Education for All" school improvement project', in Harris, A. (ed.) (1997) *Organisational Effectiveness and Improvement in Education*, Buckingham: Open University Press.

Hord, S. M. (1990) *Images of Superintendents' Leadership for Learning*, Austin, TX: Southwest Educational Development Laboratory.

Hord, S. M., Jolly, D. V. and Mendez-Morse, S. E. (1992) 'The superintendent's leadership in school improvement: A rural perspective', *School Effectiveness and School Improvement*, 3, 2, pp.110–30.

House, E. R. (1981) 'Three perspectives on innovation: Technological, political and cultural', in Lehming, R. and Kane, M. (eds) (1981) *Improving Schools: Using What We Know*, Beverly Hills: Sage, pp.17–42.

House, R. J. (1971) 'A path-goal theory of leadership effectiveness', *Administrative Science Quarterly*, 16, pp.321–38.

House, R. J. and Baetz, M. L. (1979) 'Leadership: Some empirical generalisations and new research directions', *Research on Organisational Behavior*, 1, pp.341–423.

Houtveen, A. A. M. and Osinga, N. (1995) 'A case of school effectiveness: Organisation, programme, procedure and evaluation results of the Dutch National School Improvement Project', Paper presented to the Eighth International Congress for School Effectiveness and Improvement, Leeuwarden, the Netherlands.

Howe, K. R. (1988) 'Against the quantitative–qualitative incompatibility thesis or dogmas die hard', *Educational Researcher*, 17, pp.10–16.

Hox, J. J. and Kreft, I. G. G. (1994) 'Multilevel analysis methods', *Sociological Methods and Research*, 22, 3, pp.283–99.

Hoy, W. K. and Clover, S. I. R. (1986) 'Elementary school climate: A revision of the OCDQ', *Educational Administration Quarterly*, 22, pp.93–110.

Hoy, W. K. and Feldman, J. A. (1987) 'Organisational health: The concept and its measure', *Journal of Research and Development in Education*, 20, pp.30–8.

Hoy, W. K. and Ferguson, J. (1985) 'A theoretical framework and exploration of organisational effectiveness of schools', *Educational Administration Quarterly*, 21, pp.117–34.

Hoy, W. K. and Miskel, C. G. (1991) *Educational Administration: Theory, Research, and Practice* (4th edn), New York: McGraw-Hill.

Hoy, W. K., Blazovsky, R. and Newland, W. (1980) 'Organisational structure and alienation from work', Paper presented at the annual meeting of the American Educational Research Association, Boston.

Hoy, W. K., Blazovsky, R. and Newland, W. (1983) 'Bureaucracy and alienation: A comparative analysis', *The Journal of Educational Administration*, 21, pp.109–21.

Hoy, W. K., Newland, W. and Blazovsky, R. (1977) 'Subordinate loyalty to superior, esprit and aspects of bureaucratic structure', *Educational Administration Quarterly*, 13, pp.71–85.

Hoy, W. K., Tarter, C. J. and Bliss, J. R. (1990) 'Organisational climate, school health, and effectiveness: A comparative analysis', *Educational Administration Quarterly*, 26, 3, pp.260–79.

Hoy, W. K., Tarter, C. J. and Kottkamp, R. B. (1991) *Open Schools, Healthy Schools*, Newbury Park, CA: Sage.

Huberman, M. (1993) 'Linking the practitioner and researcher communities for school improvement', *School Effectiveness and School Improvement*, 4, 1, pp.1–16.

Huberman, M. and Miles, M. (1984) *Innovation Up Close*, New York: Plemen.

Husen, T. (ed.) (1967) *International Study of Achievements in Mathematics, Volumes One and Two*, Stockholm: Almquist and Wiksell.

Hyde, N. and Werner, T. (1984) *The Context for School Improvement in Western Australian Primary Schools*, Paris: OECD/CERI Report for the International School Improvement Project.

References

ILEA (1986) *Primary School Development Plans: A Support Booklet*, Primary Management Studies, Inner London Education Authority.

Immegart, G. L. (1988) 'Leadership and leader behavior', in Boyan, N. J. (ed.) *Handbook of Research on Educational Administration*, New York: Longman, pp.259–77.

Jaeger, R. M., Johnson, R. and Gorney, B. (1993) *The Nation's Schools Report to the Public: An Analysis of School Report Cards*, Center for Educational Research and Evaluation, University of North Carolina at Greensboro.

Jencks, C. (1972) 'The Coleman report and the conventional wisdom', in Mosteller, F. and Moynihan, D. P. (eds) *On Equality of Educational Opportunity*, New York: Vintage Books, pp.69–115.

Jencks, C. S., Smith, M., Ackland, H., Bane, M. J., Cohen, D., Ginter, H., Heyns, B. and Michelson, S. (1972) *Inequality: A Reassessment of the Effect of the Family and Schooling in America*, New York: Basic Books.

Jenni, R. (1991) 'Application of the school based management process development model', *School Effectiveness and School Improvement*, 2, 2, pp.136–51.

Jesson, D. and Gray, J. (1991) 'Slants on slopes: Using multi-level models to investigate differential school effectiveness and its impact on pupils' examination results', *School Effectiveness and School Improvement*, 2, 3, pp.230–47.

Jones, B. K. and Mitchell, N. (1990) 'Communicating evaluation findings: The use of a chart essay', *Educational Evaluation and Policy Analysis*, 12, 4, pp.449–62.

Jones, Lyle V. (1996) 'A history of the National Assessment of Educational Progress and some questions about its future', *Educational Researcher*, 25, 7, pp.15–22.

Joyce, B. (1991) 'The doors to school improvement', *Educational Leadership*, May, pp.59–62.

Joyce, B. (1992) 'Cooperative learning and staff development research: Teaching the method with the method', *Cooperative Learning*, 12, 21, pp.10–13.

Joyce, B. and Calhoun, E. (1991) 'Review of the New Meaning of Educational Change', *School Effectiveness and School Improvement*, 2, 4, pp.336–43.

Joyce, B. and Showers, B. (1988) *Student Achievement through Staff Development*, New York: Longman.

Joyce, B., Hersh, R. and McKibbin, M. (1983) *The Structure of School Improvement*, New York: Longman.

Joyce, B. et al. (1992) *Models of Teaching* (4th edn), Englewood Cliffs, NJ: Prentice Hall.

Joyce, B. et al. (1993) *The Self Renewing School*, Alexandria, VA: ASCD.

Kang, S. J. (1993) 'A covariance components model with two-way crossed random effects and ML estimation via the EM algorithm', unpublished doctoral dissertation, University of Michigan.

Karweit, N. (1985) 'Time scales, learning events and productive instruction', in Fisher, C. W. and Berliner, D. C. (eds) *Perspectives on Instructional Time*, New York: Longman, pp.169–89.

Katz, L. (1947) 'On the matrix analysis of sociometric data', *Sociometry*, 10, pp.233–41.

Katzman, M. T. (1971) *The Political Economy of Urban Schools*, Cambridge, MA: Harvard University Press.

Keesling, J. W. and Wiley, D. E. (1974) 'Regression models for hierarchical data', Paper presented at the annual meeting of the Psychometric Society, Stanford University, Palo Alto, CA.

Keeves, J. P. (1992) *The IEA Study of Science III: Changes in Science Education and Achievement, 1970 to 1984*, Oxford: Pergamon Press.

Kellaghan, T. and Madaus, G. F. (1979) 'Within school variance in achievement: School effect or error?' *Studies in Educational Evaluation*, 5, pp.101–7.

Keller, I. M. (1983) 'Motivational design of instruction', in Reigeluth, C. (ed.) *Instructional Design and Models*, Hillsdale, NJ: Erlbaum.

Kennedy, E. (in press) 'A study of students' fears of seeking academic help from teachers', *Journal of Classroom Interaction*.

Kennedy, E., Stringfield, S. and Teddlie, C. (1993) 'Schools do make a difference', in Teddlie, C. and Stringfield, S. *Schools Make a Difference: Lessons Learned from a 10-year Study of School Effects*, New York: Teachers College Press, pp.15–26.

Kennedy, E., Teddlie, C. , and Stringfield, S. (1991) 'A multilevel analysis of Phase II of the Louisiana School Effectiveness Study', Paper presented at the fourth annual meeting of the International Congress for School Effectiveness and Improvement, Cardiff, Wales.

Keys, W. and Foxman, D. (1989) *A World of Differences (A United Kingdom Perspective on an International Assessment of Mathematics and Science)*, Slough: National Foundation for Educational Research.

Kickert, W. J. M. (1979) *Organisation of Decision-making: A Systems-Theoretical Approach*, Amsterdam: North-Holland Publishing Company.

Kilgore, S. and Pendleton, W.W. (1986) 'Discussion of paper by Aitkin and Longford', *Journal of the Royal Statistical Society, Series A*, **149**, 1, pp.36–7.

King, R. (1983) *The Sociology of School Organisation*, London: Methuen.

Kirby, P. C. (1993) 'Teacher socialisation in effective and ineffective schools', in Teddlie, C. and Stringfield, S. (eds) *Schools Make a Difference: Lessons Learned from a 10 Year Study of School Effects*, New York: Teachers College Press, pp.202–15.

Kirby, P. C., Stringfield, S., Teddlie, C. and Wimpelberg, R. (1992) 'School effects on teacher socialisation', *School Effectiveness and School Improvement*, **3**, 3, pp.187–203.

Klitgaard, R. E. and Hall, G. R. (1974) 'Are there unusually effective schools?', *Journal of Human Resources*, **74**, pp.90–106.

Klovdahl, A. S. (1986) 'VIEW-NET: A new tool for network analysis', *Social Networks*, **8**, pp.313–42.

Knapp, T. R. (1977) 'The unit-of-analysis problem in applications of simple correlation analysis to educational research', *Journal of Educational Statistics*, **2**, pp.171–86.

Knuver, A. W. M. and Brandsma, H. (1993) 'Cognitive and affective outcomes in school effectiveness research', *School Effectiveness and School Improvement*, **4**, 3, pp.189–204.

Kochan, S., Franklin, B. J., Crone, L. J. and Glascock, C. (1994) 'Improving Louisiana's School Report Cards with input from parents and school staff', Paper presented at the annual meeting of the American Educational Research Association, New Orleans, LA.

Kochan, S. E., Tashakkori, A. and Teddlie, C. (1996) 'You can't judge a high school by test data alone: Constructing an alternative indicator of secondary school effectiveness', Paper presented at the annual meeting of the American Educational Research Association, New York.

Kottkamp, R. B., Mulhern, J. A. and Hoy, W. A. (1987) 'Secondary school climate: A revision of the OCDQ', *Educational Administration Quarterly*, **23**, pp.31–48.

Krackhardt, D., Lundberg, M., and O'Rourke, L. (1993) 'KrackPlot: A picture's worth a thousand words', *Connections*, **16**, pp.37–47.

Kreft, I. G. G. (1995) 'Introduction', Kreft, I. G. G. (Guest Editor) 'Hierarchical linear models: Problems and prospects', special issue of *Journal of Educational and Behavioural Statistics*, **20**, 2, pp.109–13.

Kreft, I. G. G. and de Leeuw, J. (1991) 'Model-based ranking of schools', *International Journal of Educational Research*, **15**, pp.45–61.

Kreft, I. G. G., de Leeuw, J. and Kim, K. S. (1990) *Comparing Four Different Statistical Packages for Hierarchical Linear Regression: GENMOD, MM, ML3, and VARCL* (CSE Tech. Rep. 311), Los Angeles: University of California, Center for Research on Evaluation, Standards, and Student Testing.

Kreft, I. G. G., de Leeuw, J. and van der Leeden, R. (1994) 'Review of five multilevel analysis programs: BMDP-5V, GENMOD, MM, ML3, VARCL', *The American Statistician*, **48**, pp.324–35.

References

Kreft, I. G. G., de Leeuw, J. and Aiken, L. S. (1995) 'The effect of different forms of centering in hierarchical linear models', *Multivariate Behavioral Research*, 30, 1, pp.1–21.

Kruger, M. (1994) *Sekseverschillen in Schoolleiderschap*, Alphen aan de Rijn: Samson H.D. Tjeenk Willink.

Kulik, C. L. C., Kulik, I. A and Bangert Drowns, R. L. (1990) 'Effectiveness of mastery learning programs: A meta analysis', *Review of Educational Research*, 60, 2, pp.265–99.

Kunz, D. and Hoy, W. K. (1976) 'Leader behavior of principals and the professional zone of acceptance of teachers', *Educational Administration Quarterly*, 12, pp.49–64.

Kyle, M. J. (ed.) (1985) *Reaching for Excellence: An Effective Schools Sourcebook*, Washington DC: US Government Printing Office.

Lacey, C. (1970) *Hightown Grammar*, Manchester: Manchester University Press.

Lagerweij, N. A. J. and Haak, E. M. (1994) *Eerst Goed Kijken . . . de Dynamiek van Scholen-in-ontwikkeling*, Leuven/Apeldoorn: Garant.

Lagerweij, N. and Voogt, J. (1990) 'Policy making at the school level: Some issues for the 90's', *School Effectiveness and School Improvement*, 1, 2, pp.98–120.

Laird, N. M and Ware, J. H. (1982) 'Random effects models for longitudinal data', *Biometrics*, 38, pp.963–74.

Laird, N., Lange, N. and Stram, D. (1987) 'Maximum likelihood computation with repeated measures: Application of the EM algorithm', *Journal of the American Statistical Association*, 82, pp.97–105.

Lam, J. F. and Grift, W. J. C. M. van de (1995) 'Het didastisch handelen in het basisonderwijs', [Teaching strategies in primary education], Paper presented at the Onderwijs-researchdagen, June 19–21, Groningen: The Netherlands.

Lang, M. H. (1991) 'Effective school status: A methodological study of classification consistency', unpublished doctoral dissertation, Louisiana State University, Baton Rouge.

Lang, M. H., Teddlie, C. and Oescher, J. (1992) 'The effect that varying the test mode had on school effectiveness ratings', Paper presented at the annual meeting of the American Educational Research Association, San Francisco.

Lapointe, A. E., Mead, N. and Phillips, G. (1989) *A World of Differences: An International Assessment of Mathematics and Science*, Princeton, NJ: Educational Testing Services.

Lau, L. J. (1979) 'Educational production functions', in Windham, D. M. (ed.) *Economic Dimensions of Education*, Washington, DC: National Academy of Education, pp.33–69.

Lee, S. Y. (1990) 'Multilevel analysis of structural equation models', *Biometrika*, 77, 4, pp.763–72.

Lee, S. Y. and Poon, W. Y. (1992) 'Two-level analysis of covariance structures for unbalanced designs with small level-one samples', *British Journal of Mathematical and Statistical Psychology*, 45, pp.109–23.

Lee, V. (1986) 'Multi-level causal models for social class and achievement', Paper presented at the annual meeting of the American Educational Research Association, San Francisco, CA.

Lee, V. and Bryk, A. S. (1989) 'A multilevel model of the social distribution of high school achievement', *Sociology of Education*, 62, pp.172–92.

Leithwood, K. (1992a) 'Guest editor's introduction: Qualitative studies of superintendents' leadership for school improvement', *School Effectiveness and School Improvement*, 3, 1, pp.42–4.

Leithwood, K. (1992b) 'Editor's conclusion: What have we learned and where do we go from here?', *School Effectiveness and School Improvement*, 3, 2, pp.173–84.

Leithwood, K. (1995) 'School restructuring in British Columbia: Summarising the results of a four year study', Paper presented at the annual meeting of the American Educational Research Association, San Francisco, April 1995.

Leithwood, K. and Jantzi, D. (1990) 'Transformational leadership: How principals can help reform school cultures', *School Effectiveness and School Improvement*, 1, 4, pp.249–80.

Leithwood, K. and Steinback, R. (1995) *Expert Problem Solving*, Albany: State University of New York Press.

Leitner, D. (1994) 'Do principals affect student outcomes: An organisational perspective', *School Effectiveness and School Improvement*, 5, 3, pp.219–38.

Leune, J. M. G. (1994) 'Onderwijskwaliteit en de autonomie van scholen' [Quality of education and autonomy of schools], in Creemers, B. P. M. (ed.) *Deregulering en de Kwaliteit van Het Onderwijs*, Groningen: RION, pp.27–59.

Levin, H. M. (1988) 'Cost effectiveness and educational policy', *Educational Evaluation and Policy Analysis*, 10, pp.51–70.

Levin, H. M. (1996) 'Powerful learning in accelerated schools', *Accelerated Schools*, 3, 3, p.2.

Levine, D. U. and Eubanks, E. E. (1989a) 'Instructional and organisational arrangements that improve achievement in inner-city schools', *Educational Leadership*, 40, 3, pp.41–6.

Levine, D. U. and Eubanks, E. E. (1989b) 'Organizational arrangement at effective secondary schools', in Walberg, H. and Lane, J. (eds) *Organizing for Learning*, Reston, VA: National Association of Secondary School Principals, pp. 41–9.

Levine, D. U. and Lezotte, L. W. (1990) *Unusually Effective Schools: A Review and Analysis of Research and Practice*, Madison, WI: National Center for Effective Schools Research and Development.

Levine, D. U. and Ornstein, A. C. (1989) 'Research on classroom and school effectiveness and its implications for improving big city schools', *Urban Review*, 21, pp.81–94.

Levine, D. U., Levine, R. and Eubanks, E. E. (1984) 'Characteristics of effective inner-city intermediate schools', *Phi Delta Kappan*, 65, pp.707–11.

Lewin, K., Lippitt, R. and White, R. K. (1939) 'Patterns of aggressive behavior in experimentally created "social climates"' *The Journal of Social Psychology*, 10, pp.171–99.

Lezotte, L. (1989) 'School improvement based on the effective schools research', *International Journal of Educational Research*, 13, 7, pp.815–25.

Lezotte, L. W. (1990) 'Lessons learned', in Taylor, B. O. (ed.) *Case Studies in Effective Schools Research*, Madison, WI: National Center for Effective Schools Research and Development, pp.195–9.

Lezotte, L. W. and Bancroft, B. (1985) 'Growing use of effective schools model for school improvement', *Educational Leadership*, 42, 3, pp.23–7.

Lightfoot, S. (1983) *Good High Schools: Portraits of Character and Culture*, New York: Basic Books.

Lincoln, Y. and Guba, E. (1985) *Naturalistic Inquiry*, Newbury Park, CA: Sage.

Lindley, D. V. and Smith, A. F. M. (1972) 'Bayes estimates for the linear model', *Journal of the Royal Statistical Society, Series B*, 34, pp.1–41.

Lindzey, G. and Borgatta, E. F. (1954) 'Sociometric measurement', in Lindzey, G. (ed.) *Handbook of Social Psychology*, 1, pp.405–48, Cambridge, MA: Addison-Wesley.

Link, C. R. and Ratledge, E. C. (1979) 'Student perceptions, IQ, and achievement', *The Journal of Human Resources*, 14.

Lippitt, R. and White, R. K. (1952) 'An experimental study of leadership and group life', in Swanson, G. E., Newcomb, T. M. and Hartley, E. L. (eds) *Readings in Social Psychology* (Revised edn), New York: Henry Holt and Company.

Litwin, G. H. and Stringer, R. A., Jr. (1968) *Motivation and Organizational Climate*, Boston, MA: Harvard University Press.

Lockheed, M. E. and Komenan, A. (1989) 'Teaching quality and student achievement in Africa' The case of Nigeria and Swaziland, *Teaching and Teacher Education*, 5, 2, 93–113.

Lockheed, M. E. and Longford, N. T. (1989) *A Multilevel Model of School Effectiveness in a Developing Country* (World Bank Discussion paper no. 69), Washington, DC: World Bank.

References

Lockheed, M. E. and Verspoor, A. M. (1990) *Improving Primary Education in Developing Countries*, Washington DC: World Bank.

Logan, L., Sachs, J., Dempster, N., Distant, G. and Baglioni (1994) 'School development planning: Increasing teachers' control?' Paper presented at the 7th Annual Conference of the International Congress for School Effectivenes and Improvement, Melbourne, Australia.

Lomotey, K. and Swanson, A. (1990) 'Restructuring school governance: Learning from the experiences of urban and rural schools', in Jacobson, S. and Conway, J. (eds) *Educational Leadership in an Age of Reform*, White Plains, NY: Longman.

Longford, N. T. (1986) 'VARCL-Interactive software for variance components analysis', *The Professional Statistician*, 5, pp.28–32.

Longford, N.T. (1987) 'A fast scoring algorithm for maximum likelihood estimation in unbalanced mixed models with nested random effects', *Biometrika*, 74, 4, pp.817–27.

Longford, N. T. (1988) 'Fisher scoring algorithm for variance component analysis of data with multilevel structure', in Bock, R. D. (ed.) *Multilevel Analysis of Educational Data*, Orlando, FL: Academic Press, pp.297–310.

Longford, N. T. (1990) 'VARCL software for variance component analysis of data with nested random effects (maximum likelihood)' [Computer software], Princeton, NJ: Educational Testing Service.

Longford, N. T. (1992) 'Factor analysis for clustered observations', *Psychometrika*, 5, pp.581–97.

Longford, N. T. (1993) *Random Coefficient Models*, Oxford: Oxford University Press.

Longford, N. T. and Muthén, B. (1992) 'Factor analysis for clustered observations', *Psychometrika*, 5, pp.581–97.

Louis, K. (1994) 'Beyond "managed change": Rethinking how schools improve', *School Effectiveness and School Improvement*, 5, 1, pp.2–25.

Louis, K. S. and Kruse, S. D. (1995) *Professionalism and Community*, Thousand Oaks, CA: Corwin Press.

Louis, K. S. and Miles, M. B. (1990) *Improving the Urban High School: What Works and Why*, New York: Teachers College Press.

Louis, K. and Miles, M. (1991) 'Managing reform: Lessons from urban high schools', *School Effectiveness and School Improvement*, 2, 2, pp.75–96.

Louis, K. S. and Miles, M. B. (1992) *Improving the Urban High School*, London: Cassell.

Louis, K. and Smith, B. (1991) 'Restructuring, teacher engagement and school culture: Perspectives on school reform and the improvement of teacher's work', *School Effectiveness and School Improvement*, 2, 1, pp.34–52.

Louisiana Department of Education (1996) *School Report Cards*, Baton Rouge, LA: Author.

Luce, R. D. and Perry, A. D. (1949) 'A method of matrix analysis of group structure', *Psychometrika*, 14, pp.95–116.

Luyten, H. (1994a) *School Effects: Stability and Malleability*, Enschede: University of Twente.

Luyten, H. (1994b) 'Schools size effects on achievement in secondary education: Evidence from the Netherlands, Sweden, and the USA', *School Effectiveness and School Improvement*, 5, 1, pp.75–99.

Luyten, H. (1994c) 'Stability of school effects in Dutch secondary education: The impact of variance across subjects and years', in Bosker, R. J., Creemers, B. P. M. and Scheerens, J. (eds) *Conceptual and Methodological Advances in Educational Effectiveness Research*, Special issue of *International Journal of Educational Research*, 21, 2, pp.197–216.

Lynn, R. (1988) *Educational Achievement in Japan: Lessons for the West*, London: Macmillan/ Social Affairs Unit.

McCormack-Larkin, M. (1985) 'Ingredients of a successful school effectiveness project', in *Educational Leadership*, March, 42, 6, pp.31–7.

McCormack-Larkin, M. and Kritek, W. J. (1982) 'Milwaukee's project RISE', *Educational Leadership*, **40**, 3, pp.16–21.

McCullagh, P. and Nelder, J. A. (1983) *Generalised Linear Models*, London: Chapman and Hall.

McDill, E. L. and Rigsby, L. C. (1973) *Structure and Process in Secondary Schools: The Impact of Educational Climates*, Baltimore, MD: Johns Hopkins Press.

McDill, E. L., Meyers, E. D., Jr. and Rigsby, L. C. (1967) 'Institutional effects on the academic behavior of high school students', *Sociology of Education*, **40**, pp.181–9.

McDill, E. L., Rigsby, L. C. and Meyers, E. D., Jr. (1969) 'Educational climates of high schools: Their effects and sources', *American Journal of Sociology*, **74**, pp.567–86.

McDonald, R. P. (1994) 'The bilevel retricular action model for path analysis with latent variables', *Sociological Methods and Research*, **22**, 3, pp.399–420.

McDonald, R. P. and Goldstein, H. (1989) 'Balanced versus unbalanced designs for linear structural relations in two-level data', *British Journal of Mathematical and Statistical Psychology*, **42**, pp.215–32.

McGaw, B., Piper, J., Banks, D. and Evans, B. (1992) *Making Schools More Effective*, Hawthorn, Victoria: Australian Council for Educational Research.

McIntosh, R. G. (1968) 'Equal educational opportunity' special issue of *Harvard Educational Review*, **38**, 1.

McLaughlin, M. (1990) 'The Rand Change Agent Study Revisited: Macro Perspectives, Micro Realities', *Educational Researcher*, **19**, 9, pp.11–16.

McLean, A. (1987) 'After the belt: School processes in low exclusion schools', *School Organisation*, **7**, 3, pp.303–10.

McLean, R. A., Sanders, W. L. and Stroup, W. W. (1991) 'A unified approach to mixed linear models', *American Statistican*, **45**, pp.54–64.

McMahon, A., Bolam, R., Abbott, R. and Holly, P. (1984) *Guidelines for Review and Internal Development in Schools* (Primary and Secondary School Handbooks), York: Longman/ Schools Council.

McManus, M. (1987) 'Suspension and exclusion from high school – the association with catchment and school variables', *School Organisation*, **7**, 3, pp.261–71.

McPherson, A. (1992) 'Measuring value added in schools', *National Commission on Education, Briefing No. 1*, London: NCE.

McPherson, A. F., and Willms, J. D. (1986) 'Certification, class conflict, religion, and community: A socio-historical explanation of the effectiveness of contemporary schools', in Kerckhoff, A. C. (ed.) *Research in Sociology of Education and Socialization*, **6**, Greenwich, CT: JAI Press, pp.227–302.

McPherson, A. F. and Willms, J. D. (1987) 'Equalisation and improvement: Some effects of comprehensive reorgansiation in Scotland', *Sociology*, **21**, 4, pp.509–39.

Madaus, G. F., Airasian, P. W. and Kellaghan, T. (1980) *School Effectiveness: A Reassessment of the Evidence*, New York: McGraw-Hill.

Madaus, G. F., Kellaghan, T., Rakow, E. A. and King, D. J. (1979) 'The sensitivity of measures of school effectiveness', *Harvard Educational Review*, **49**, pp.207–30.

Madden, N., Slavin, R., Karweit, N., Dolan, L. and Wasik, B. (1991) 'Success for all', *Phi Delta Kappan*, **72**, 8, pp.593–9.

Mandeville, G. K. (1988) 'School effectiveness indices revisited: Cross-year stability', *Journal of Educational Measurement*, **25**, pp.349–65.

Mandeville, G. K. and Anderson, L. W. (1986) 'A study of the stability of school effectiveness measures across grades and subject areas', Paper presented at the Annual Meeting of the American Educational Research Association, San Francisco.

Mandeville, G. K. and Anderson, L. W. (1987) 'The stability of school effectiveness indices across grade levels and subject areas', *Journal of Educational Measurement*, **24**, pp.203–16.

References

Mandeville, G. K. and Kennedy, E. (1991) 'The relationship of effective schools indicators and changes in the social distribution of achievement', *School Effectiveness and School Improvement*, **2**, 1, pp.14–33.

Mann, D. (1992) 'School reform in the United States: A national policy review 1965–91', *School Effectiveness and School Improvement*, **3**, 3, pp.216–30.

Marco, G. (1974) 'A comparison of selected school effectiveness measures based on longitudinal data', *Journal of Educational Measurement*, **1**, 1, pp.225–34.

Marsh, H. W. and Grayson, D. (1990) 'Public/Catholic differences in the high school and beyond data: A multigroup structural equation modeling approach to testing mean differences', *Journal of Educational Statistics*, **15**, 3, pp.199–235.

Marx, E. C. H. (1975) *De Organisatie van Scholengemeenschappoen in Onderwijskundige Optiek*, Groningen: Tjeenk Willink.

Mason, W. M. (1995) 'Comment', in Kreft, I. G. G. (Guest Editor) 'Hierarchical linear models: Problems and prospects', special issue of *Journal of Educational and Behavioural Statistics*, **20**, pp.221–7.

Mason, W. M., Wong, G. M. and Entwistle, B. (1984) 'Contextual analysis through the multilevel l linear model', in Leinhardt, S. (ed.) *Sociological Methodology*, San Francisco: Jossey-Bass, pp.72–103.

Maughan, B. P., Mortimore, P., Ouston, J. and Rutter, M. (1980) '*Fifteen Thousand Hours*: A reply to Heath and Clifford', *Oxford Review of Education*, **6**, pp.289–303.

Maughan, B., Ouston, J. and Rutter, M. (1991) 'Can schools change? II – practice in six London secondary schools', *School Effectiveness and School Improvement*, **2**, 1, pp. 188–210.

Maughan, B., Ouston, J., Pickles, A. and Rutter, M. (1990) 'Can schools change I – Outcomes at six London secondary schools', in *School Effectiveness and Improvement*, **1**, 3, pp.188–210.

Maxcy, S. J. and Maxcy, D. O. (1993) 'Educational reform in Louisiana', *International Journal of Educational Reform*, **2**, 3, pp.236–41.

Maxwell, W. S. (1987) 'Teachers' attitudes towards disruptive behaviour in secondary schools', *Educational Review*, **39**, 3, pp.203–16.

Mayeske, G. W., Wisler, C. E., Beaton, A. E., Jr., Weinfield, F. O., Cohen, W. M., Okada, T., Proshek, J.M. and Taber, K.A. (1972) *A Study of Our Nation's Schools*, Washington, DC: US Department of Health, Education, and Welfare.

Mellor, W. and Chapman, J. (1984) 'Organisational effectiveness in schools', *Educational Administration Review*, **2**, pp.25–36.

Meuret, D. and Scheerens, J. (1995) *An International Comparison of Functional and Territorial Decentralisation of Public Educational Systems*, Twente: University of Twente.

Meyer, M. W. (1978) 'Introduction: Recent developments in organisational research and theory', in Meyer, M. W. (ed.) *Environments and Organizations*, San Francisco: Jossey-Bass, pp.1–19.

Meza, J., Jr. and Teddlie, C. (1996) *An Examination of Differential Teacher Effectiveness in Two Restructuring Schools*, New Orleans, LA: University of New Orleans Accelerated Schools Center.

Michael, W. B. and Smith, R. A. (1976) *Dimensions of Self-Concept, Form E, Grades 4–6* developed for the Los Angeles Unified School District, Programs for the Gifted.

Miles, M. (1983) 'Unravelling the mysteries of institutionalism', *Educational Leadership*, **41**, 3, pp.14–19.

Miles, M. (1986) 'Research findings on the stages of school improvement', Center for Policy Research: New York (mimeo).

Miles, M. B. and Ekholm, M. (1985) 'What is school improvement?', in van Velzen, W., Miles, M. B., Ekholm, M., Hameyer, V. and Robin, D. (eds) *Making School Improvement Work: A Conceptual Guide to Practice*, Leuven: OECD.

Miles, M. B., and Huberman, A. M. (1994) *Qualitative Data Analysis* (2nd edn), Newbury Park, CA: Sage.

Miller, S. K. (1983) *The History of Effective Schools Research: A Critical Overview*, Annual Meeting of the American Educational Research Association, Montreal, Canada. ERIC Document # ED 231818.

Miller, S. K. and Sayre, K. A. (1986) 'Case studies of affluent effective schools', Paper presented at the annual meeting of the American Educational Research Association, San Francisco, CA.

Mintzberg, H. (1979) *The Structuring of Organizations*, Englewood Cliffs, NJ: Prentice Hall.

Mintzberg, H. (1983) *Structures in Fives: Designing Effective Organisations*, Englewood Cliffs, NJ: Prentice Hall.

Mintzberg, H. (1990) *Over Veranderen* (Congresmap), Vlaardingen: Nederlands Studie Centrum.

Mintzberg, H. (1992) *Organisatie Structuren*, Schoonhoven: Academic Service Economie en Bedrijfskunde.

Miskel, C. and Gerhardt, E. (1974) 'Perceived bureaucracy, teacher conflict, central life interests, voluntarism, and job satisfaction', *Journal of Educational Administration*, 12, pp.84–97.

Miskel, C., Bloom, S. and McDonald, D. (1980) *Structural Coupling, Expectancy Climate, and Learning Strategies Intervention Effectiveness: A Pilot Study to Establish the Reliability and Validity Estimates for the Measurement System*, Final report for the Learning Disabilities Institute, University of Kansas.

Miskel, C., Fevurly, R. and Stewart, J. (1979) 'Organisational structures and processes, perceived school effectiveness, loyalty, and job satisfaction', *Educational Administration Quarterly*, 15, pp.97–118.

Miskel, C., Glasnapp, D. and Hatley, R. (1975) 'A test of the inequity theory for job satisfaction using educators' attitudes toward work motivation and work incentives', *Educational Administration Quarterly*, 11, pp.38–54.

Mislevy, R. J. (1995) 'What can we learn from International Assessments?', *Educational Evaluation and Policy Analysis*, 17, 4, pp.419–37.

Mitchell, D. (1990) *Principal Leadership: A Theoretical Framework for Research*, Urbana-Champaign, IL: National Center for School Leadership, University of Illinois at Urbana-Champaign.

Monk, D. H. (1989) 'The education production function: Its evolving role in policy analysis', *Educational Evaluation and Policy Analysis*, 11, pp.31–45.

Monk, D. H. (1992) 'Education productivity research: An update and assessment of its role in education finance reform', *Educational Evaluation and Policy Analysis*, 14, 4, pp.307–22.

Moreno, J. L. (1934) *Who Shall Survive?: Foundations of Sociometry, Group Psychotherapy, and Sociodrama*, Washington, DC: Nervous and Mental Disease Publishing Co. Reprinted in 1953 (2nd edn) and in 1978 (3rd edn) by Beacon House, Beacon, NY.

Moreno, J. L. (1946) 'Sociogram and sociomatrix: A note to the paper by Forsyth and Katz', *Sociometry*, 9, pp.348–9.

Moreno, J. L. (1953) *Who Will Survive?*, New York: Beacon.

Moreno, J. L. and Jennings, H. H. (1938) 'Statistics of social configurations', *Sociometry*, 1, pp.342–74.

Morris, C. N. (1995) 'Hierarchical models for educational data: An overview', *Journal of Educational and Behavioral Statistics*, 20, 2, pp.190–200.

Mortimore, P. (1991a) 'Effective schools from a British perspective: Research and practice', in Bliss, J. and Firestone, W. (eds), *Creating Effective Schools*, London: Prentice Hall.

Mortimore, P. (1991b) 'School effectiveness research: Which way at the crossroads?' *School Effectiveness and School Improvement*, 2, 3, pp.213–29.

Mortimore, P. (1993) 'School effectiveness and the management of effective learning and teaching', *School Effectiveness and School Improvement*, 4, 4, pp.290–310.

References

Mortimore, P. (1998) *The Road to Improvement*, Lisse: Swets and Zeitlinger.

Mortimore, P. and Byford, D. (1981) 'Monitoring examination results within an LEA', in Plewis, I., Gray, J., Fogelman, K., Mortimore, P. and Byford, D. (eds) *Publishing School Examination Results: A Discussion*, London: Institute of Education.

Mortimore, P. and Sammons, P. (1987) 'New evidence on effective elementary schools', *Educational Leadership*, **45**, 2, pp.4–8.

Mortimore, P., Sammons, P., Stoll, L., Lewis, D. and Ecob, R. (1988) *School Matters: The Junior Years*, Somerset, Open Books (Reprinted in 1995 by Paul Chapman: London).

Mortimore, P., Sammons, P., Stoll, L., Lewis, D. and Ecob, R. (1989) 'A study of effective junior schools'. in Creemers, B. P. M. and Scheerens, J. (eds) *Developments in School Effectiveness Research*, Special issue of *International Journal of Educational Research*, **13**, 7, pp.753–68.

Mosteller, F. and Moynihan, D. P. (eds) (1972) *On Equality of Educational Opportunity*, New York: Vintage.

Mott, P. E. (1972) *The Characteristics of Effective Organizations*, New York: Harper and Row.

Mullis, I.V.S., Dossey, J. A., Campbell, J. R., Gentile, C. A., O'Sullivan, C. and Latham, A. S. (1994) *NAEP 1992: Trends in Academic Progress*, Washington, DC: US Government Printing Office.

Murnane, R. J. (1975) *The Impact of School Resources on the Learning of Inner City Children*, Cambridge, MA: Ballinger Publishing Co.

Murnane, R. J. (1981) 'Interpreting the evidence on school effectiveness' *Teachers College Record*, **83**, pp.19–35.

Murnane, R. J. (1987) 'Improving education indicators and economic indicators: The same problems?', *Educational Evaluation and Policy Analysis*, **9**, 2, pp.101–16.

Murnane, R. J. and Nelson, R. R. (1984) 'Production and innovation when techniques are tacit', *Journal of Economic Behavior and Organizations*, **5**, pp.353–73.

Murnane, R. J. and Phillips, B. R. (1981) 'Learning by doing, vintage and selection: Three pieces of the puzzle relating teaching experience and performance', *Economics of Education Review*, **4**, pp.453–65.

Murphy, J. (1988) 'Methodological, measurement, and conceptual problems in the study of instructional leadership', *Educational Evaluation and Policy Analysis*, **10**, 2, pp.117–34.

Murphy, J. (1990) 'Principal instructional leadership', in Thurston, P. and Lotto, L. (eds) *Advances in Educational Leadership*, Greenwich, CT: JAI Press, pp.163–200.

Murphy, J. (1990) 'Review of *The school effect: A study of multi-racial comprehensives*', *School Effectiveness and School Improvement*, **1**, 1, pp.81–6.

Murphy, J. (1992) 'School effectiveness and school restructuring: Contributions to educational improvement', in *School Effectiveness and School Improvement*, **3**, 2, pp.90–109.

Murphy, J. (1993) 'Restructuring schooling: The equity infrastructure', *School Effectiveness and School Improvement*, **4**, 2, pp.111–30.

Murphy, J. and Louis, K. S. (1994) *Reshaping the Principalship: Insights from Transformational Reform Efforts*, Thousand Oaks, CA: Corwen Press.

Murphy, J., Hallinger, P. and Peterson, K. D. (1985) 'Supervising and evaluating principals: Lessons from effective school districts', *Educational Leadership*, **43**, 2, pp.78–82.

Musgrove, F. (1981) *School and the Social Order*, Chichester: Wiley.

Muthén, B. O. (1989) 'Latent variable modelling in heterogeneous populations', *Psychometrika*, **54**, pp.557–85.

Muthén, B. O. (1991) 'Multilevel factor analysis of class and student achievement components', *Journal of Educational Measurement*, **28**, 4, pp.338–54.

Muthén, B. O. (1994) 'Multilevel covariance structure analysis', *Sociological Methods and Research*, **22**, 3, 376–98.

376

Muthén, B. O. and Satorra, A. (1989) 'Multilevel aspects of varying parameters in structural models', in Bock, R. D. (ed.) *Multilevel Analaysis of Educational Data*, San Diego, CA: Academic Press, pp.87–99.

Myers, K. (1995) 'Intensive care for the chronically sick', Paper presented at the European conference on Education Research Association, Bath, UK.

Myers, K. (1995) *School Improvement in Practice: Schools Make a Difference Project*, London: Falmer Press.

Myers, K. and Stoll, L. (1993) 'Mapping the movement', *Education*, **182**, 3, p.51.

National Commission on Education (1995) *Success against the Odds*, London: Routledge and Kegan Paul.

National Commission on Excellence in Education (1983) *A Nation at Risk: The Imperative for Educational Reform*, Washington, DC: US Government Printing Office.

National Education Goals Panel (1991) *Measuring Progress toward the National Education Goals: A Guide to Selecting Indicators*, September 1991 progress report, Washington, DC: Author.

National Study Panel on Educational Indicators (1991) *Education Counts: An Indicator System to Monitor the Nation's Education Health*, Washington, DC: US Department of Education, National Center for Education Statistics.

Nelson-Le Gall, S. and Glor-Scheib, S. (1986) 'Academic help-seeking and peer relations in school', *Contemporary Educational Psychology*, **11**, pp.187–93.

Nisbet, J. (ed.) (1973) *Creativity of the School*, Paris: OECD.

Noah, H. J. (1987) 'Reflections', *Comparative Education Review*, **31**, 1, pp.137–49.

Northway, M. L. (1940) 'A method for depicting social relationships obtained by sociometric testing', *Sociometry*, **3**, pp.144–50.

Nuttall, D. (1990) *Differences in Examination Performance*, RS 1277/90, London: Research and Statistics Branch, ILEA.

Nuttall, D. L., Goldstein, H., Prosser, R. and Rasbash, J. (1989) 'Differential school effectiveness', in Creemers, B. P. M. and Scheerens, J. (eds) *Developments in School Effectiveness Research*, Special issue of *International Journal of Educational Research*, **13**, 7, pp.769–76.

Nuttall, D. L., Sammons, P., Thomas, S. and Mortimore, P. (1992) *Differential School Effectiveness: Departmental Variations in GSCE Attainment*, ESRC award R000234130, London: Institute of Education.

O'Connor, E. F. (1972) 'Extending classical test theory to the measurement of change', *Review of Educational Research*, **42**, pp.73–97.

O'Connor, M. C. (1992) 'Rethinking aptitude, achievement and instruction: Cognitive science research and the framing of assessment policy', in Gifford, B. R. and O'Connor, M.C. (eds) *Changing Assessment: Alternative Views of Aptitude, Achievement and Instruction*, Boston, MA: Kluwer Academic Publishers.

Oakes, J. (1989) 'What educational indicators? The case for assessing the school context', *Educational Evaluation and Policy Analysis*, **11**, 2, pp.181–99.

Odden, A. (1990) 'Educational indicators in the United States: The need for analysis', *Educational Researcher*, **19**, 4, pp.24–9.

OECD (1989) *Decentralisation and School Improvement*, Paris: OECD – CERI.

OECD (1995) *Education at a Glance: OECD Indicators*, Paris: OECD.

OERI (Office of Educational Research and Improvement) (1988) *Creating Responsible and Responsive Accountability Systems*, Washington, DC: US Department of Education.

OFSTED (1994) *Improving Schools*, London: HMSO.

Olthof, A. L. and Lugthart, E. (1992) 'Effectiveness of various types of secondary school organisation: A contingency approach', in Bashi, J. and Sass, Z. (eds) *School Effectiveness and Improvement: Proceedings of the Third International Congress for School Effectiveness*, Jerusalem: Magnes Press, pp.344–69.

References

Orton, J. D. and Weick, K. E. (1990) 'Loosely coupled systems: A reconceptualization', *Academy of Management Review*, **15**, 2, pp.203–23.

Ouchi, W. (1981) *Theory Z*, Reading, MA: Addison-Wesley.

Ouston, J. and Maughan, B. (1991) 'Can schools change?' *School Effectiveness and School Improvement*, **2**, 1, pp.3–13.

Owens, R. G. (1987) *Organizational Behavior in Education* (3rd edn), Englewood Cliffs, NJ: Prentice Hall.

Pallas, A. (1988) 'School climate in American high schools', *Teachers College Record*, **89**, pp.221–38.

Parsons, T. (1960) *Structure and Process in Modern Societies*, Glencoe, IL: Free Press.

Patton, M. Q. (1990) *Qualitative Evaluation and Research Methods*, Newbury Park, CA: Sage.

Pelgrum, W. J. (1989) *Educational Assessment: Monitoring, Evaluation and the Curriculum*, De Lier: Academisch Boeken Centrum.

Pelgrum, W. J., Voogt, J. and Plomp, T. (1995) 'Curriculum indicators in international comparative research', *Measuring the Quality of Schools*, Paris: OECD, pp.83–98.

Persell, C. H. (1977) *Education and Inequality: The Roots and Results of Stratification in America's schools*, New York: Free Press.

Peters, T. J. and Waterman, R. H., Jr. (1982) *In Search of Excellence*, New York: Harper and Row.

Petri, M. (1995) *Samen Vliegeren Methodiek en Resultaten van Interactieve School Diagnose*, Leuven: ACCO.

Pink, W. T. (1987) 'In search of exemplary junior high schools: A case study', in Noblet, G. W. and Pink, W. T. (eds) *Schooling in Context: Qualitative Studies*, Norwood, NJ: Ablex, pp. 218–49.

Pink, W. (1990) 'Staff development for urban school improvement: Lessons learned from two case studies', *School Effectiveness and School Improvement*, **1**, 1, pp.41–60.

Pitner, N. (1988) 'The study of administrator effects and effectiveness', in Boyan, N. (ed.), *Handbook of Research on Educational Administration*, New York: Longman, pp.105–8.

Plowden Committee (1967) *Children and Their Primary Schools*, London: HMSO.

Pollack, S., Chrispeels, J., Watson, D., Brice, R. and McCormick, S. (1988) 'A description of district factors that assist in the development of equity schools', Paper presented at the annual meeting of the American Educational Research Association, New Orleans.

Porter, A. (1991) 'Creating a system of school process indicators', *Educational Evaluation and Policy Analysis*, **13**, 1, pp.12–29.

Postlethwaite, T. N. and Ross, K. (1992) *Effective Schools in Reading: Implications for Educational Planners*, Newark, DE: IEA.

Postlethwaite, T. N. and Wiley, D. E. (1992) *The IEA Study of Science II, Science Achievement in Twenty Three Countries*, Oxford: Pergamon Press.

Power, M. J. (1967) 'Delinquent schools', *New Society*, **10**, pp.542–3.

Power, M. J., Benn, P. T., Morris, J. (1972) 'Neighbourhood, schools and juveniles before the courts', *British Criminology*, **12**, pp.111–32.

Prais, S. J. and Wagner, K. (1965) 'Schooling standards in England and Germany: Some summary comparisons based on economic performance', *Compare*, **16**, pp.5–36.

Preece, P. F. W. (1983) 'The quantitative principle of teaching', *Science Education*, **67**, 1, pp.69–73.

Preece, P. (1989) 'Pitfalls in research on school and teacher effectiveness', *Research Papers in Education*, **4**, 3, pp.47–69.

Report of the President's Commission on Youth Crime (1967), Washington DC: US Government Printing Office.

Pring, R. (1995) 'Educating persons: Putting education back into educational research', *Scottish Educational Review*, **27**, 2, pp.101–12.

Purkey, S. C. and Rutter, R. A. (1987) 'High school teaching: Teacher practices and beliefs in urban and suburban public schools', *Educational Policy*, **1**, pp.375–93.

Purkey, S. C. and Smith, M. S. (1982) 'Too soon to cheer? Synthesis of research on effective schools', *Educational Leadership*, **40**, 12, pp.64–9.

Purkey, S. and Smith, M. (1983) 'Effective schools', *The Elementary School Journal*, **83**, pp.427–52.

Purves, A. C. (1992) *The IEA Study of Written Composition II: Education and Performance in Fourteen Countries*, Oxford: Pergamon Press.

Quinn, R. E. and Rohrbaugh, J. (1983) 'A spatial model of effectiveness criteria: Towards a competing values approach to organisational analysis', *Management Science*, **29**, 3, pp.363–77.

Raffe, D. (1988) 'Making the gift horse jump the hurdles', *British Journal of Education and Work*, **2**, 3.

Ralph, J. H. and Fennessey, J. (1983) 'Science or reform: some questions about the effective schools model', *Phi Delta Kappan*, **64**, 10, pp.689–94.

Ramsay, P. D. K., Sneddon, D. G., Grenfell, J. and Ford, I. (1982) 'Successful vs unsuccessful schools: A South Auckland study', *Australia and New Zealand Journal of Sociology*, **19**, 1.

Rasbash, J. and Goldstein, H. (1994) 'Efficient analysis of mixed hierarchical and cross-classified random structures using a multilevel model', *Journal of Educational Statistics*, **19**, pp.337–50.

Rasbash, J., Goldstein, H. and Woodhouse, G. (1995) *MLn-Software for n-level Analysis (version 1)*, Multilevel Models Project, Institute of Education, University of London.

Rasbash, J., Prosser, R. and Goldstein, H. (1989) *ML3 Software for Three-level Analysis*, Institute of Education, University of London.

Raudenbush, S. W. (1986) 'Educational applications of hierarchical linear models: A review', *Journal of Educational Statistics*, **13**, pp.85–116.

Raudenbush, S. W. (1988) 'Educational applications of hierarchical linear models: A review', *Journal of Educational Statistics*, **13**, 20, pp.85–116.

Raudenbush, S. W. (1989) 'The analysis of longitudinal, multilevel data', in Creemers, B. P. M. and Scheerens, J. (eds) 'Developments in school effectiveness research', Special issue of *International Journal of Educational Research*, **13**, 7, pp.721–39.

Raudenbush, S. W. (1993) 'A crossed random effects model for unbalanced data with applications in cross sectional and longitudinal research', *Journal of Educational Statistics*, **18**, pp.421–49.

Raudenbush, S. (1994) 'Searching for balance between a priori and a post hoc model specification: a "general approach" desirable?' *School Effectiveness and School Improvement*, **5**, 2, pp.196–8.

Raudenbush, S. W. (1995a) 'Maximum likelihood estimation for unbalanced multilevel covariance structure models via the EM algorithm', *British Journal of Mathematical and Statistical Psychology*, **48**, pp.359–70.

Raudenbush, S. W. (1995b) in Kreft, I. G. G. (Guest Editor) 'Hierarchical linear models: Problems and prospects', special issue of *Journal of Educational and Behavioural Statistics*, **20**, 2, pp.221–7.

Raudenbush, S. W. and Bryk, A. S. (1985) 'Empirical Bayes meta-analysis', *Journal of Educational Statistics*, **10**, pp.75–98.

Raudenbush, S. W. and Bryk, A. S. (1986) 'A hierarchical model for studying school effects', *Sociology of Education*, **59**, pp.1–17.

Raudenbush, S. W. and Bryk, A. S. (1987a) 'Quantitative models for estimating teacher and school effectiveness', Paper presented at the Invitation Conference of the Center for Student Testing, Evaluation, and Standards, Princeton, New Jersey.

Raudenbush, S. W. and Bryk, A. S. (1987b) 'Examining correlates of diversity', *Journal of Educational Statistics*, **12**, pp.241–69.

Raudenbush, S. W. and Bryk, A. S. (1988b) 'Quantitative models for estimating teacher and school effectiveness', Paper presented at the Invitation Conference of the Center for Student Testing, Evaluation, and Standards, Princeton, New Jersey.

Raudenbush, S. W. and Bryk, A. S. (1989) 'Methodological advances in analysing the effects of schools and classrooms on student learning', in Ernest Z. Rothkopf (ed.) *Review of Research in Education*, **15**, Washington, DC: America Educational Research Association, pp. 423–75.

Raudenbush, S. W. and Wilms, J. D. (eds) (1991) *Schools, Classrooms, and Pupils: International Studies of Schooling from a Multilevel Perspective*, Orlando, FL: Academic Press.

Raudenbush, S. W. and Willms, J. D. (1996) 'The estimation of school effects', *Journal of Educational and Behavioral Statistics*, **20**, 4, pp.307–35.

Raudenbush, S. W., Rowan, B. and Kang, S. J. (1991) 'A multilevel, multivariate model for school climate with estimation via the EM algorithm and application to US high school data', *Journal of Educational Statistics*, **16**, pp.295–330.

Reezigt, G. J. (1993) *Effecten van Differentiate op de Basisschool* [*Effects of grouping in primary education*], Groningen: RION.

Reichardt, C. S. and Rallis, S. F. (1994) *The Qualitative–Quantitative Debate: New Perspectives*, Number 61 of the series *New Directions for Program Evaluation*, San Francisco, CA: Jossey-Bass Publishers.

Reid, K., Hopkins, D. and Holly, P. (1987) *Towards the Effective School*, Oxford: Blackwell.

Resh, N. and Dar, Y. (1992) 'Learning segregation in junior high schools in Israel: Causes and consequences', *School Effectiveness and School Improvement*, **3**, 4, pp.272–92.

Resnick, L. B. and Resnick, D. P. (1992) 'Assessing the thinking curriculum', in Gifford, B. R. and O'Connor, M.C. (eds) *Changing Assessment: Alternative Views of Aptitude, Achievement and Instruction*, Boston, MA: Kluwer Academic Publishers.

Reynolds, D. (1976) 'The delinquent school', in Woods, P. (ed.) *The Process of Schooling*, London: Routledge and Kegan Paul.

Reynolds, D. (1982) 'The search for effective schools', *School Organisation*, **2**, 3, pp.215–37.

Reynolds, D. (1985) *Studying School Effectiveness*, London: Falmer Press.

Reynolds, D. (1988) 'British school improvement research: The contribution of qualitative studies', *International Journal of Qualitative Studies in Education*, **1**, 2, pp.143–54.

Reynolds, D. (1991a) 'School effectiveness in secondary schools', in Riddell, S. and Brown, S. (eds) *School Effectiveness Research: Messages for School Improvement*, Edinburgh: HMSO.

Reynolds, D. (1991b) 'Changing ineffective schools', in Ainscow, M. (ed.), *Effective Schools for All*, London: David Fulton.

Reynolds, D. (1992a) 'School effectiveness and school improvement', in Bashi, J. and Sass, Z. (eds) *School Effectiveness and Improvement: Selected Proceedings of the Third International Congress*, Jerusalem, Israel: Magnes Press, pp.67–87.

Reynolds, D. (1992b) 'School effectiveness and school improvement: An updated review of the British literature', in Reynolds, D. and Cuttance, P. (eds) *School Effectiveness: Research, Policy and Practice*, London: Cassell, pp.1–24.

Reynolds, D. (1993) 'Linking school effectiveness knowledge and school improvement practice', in Dimmock, C. (ed.) *Leadership, School Based Decision Making and School Effectiveness*, London: Routledge and Kegan Paul, pp.184–200.

Reynolds, D. (1996) 'Turning around ineffective schools: Some evidence and some speculations', in Gray, J., Reynolds, D., Fitz-Gibbon, C. and Jesson, D. (eds) *Merging Traditions: The Future of Research on School Effectiveness and School Improvement*, London: Cassell.

Reynolds, D. (1997) 'The East looks West', *Times Education Supplement*, June 27, p.21.

Reynolds, D. (1998) 'School effectiveness: Retrospect and prospect' (the 1997 SERA Lecture) in *Scottish Educational Review*, **29**, 2, pp.97–113.

Reynolds, D. and Creemers, B. P. M. (1992) *The International School Effectiveness Research Programme: An outline*, Cardiff: University of Wales.

Reynolds, D. and Cuttance, P. (1992) *School Effectiveness: Research, Policy and Practice*, London: Cassell.

Reynolds, D. and Farrell, S. (1996) *Worlds Apart? – A Review of International Studies of Educational Achievement Involving England*, London: HMSO for OFSTED.

Reynolds, D. and Jones, D. (1978) 'Education and the prevention of juvenile delinquency', in Tutt, N. S. (ed.) *Alternative Strategies for Coping with Crime*, Oxford: Basil Blackwell and Martin Robertson.

Reynolds, D. and Murgatroyd, S. (1977) 'The sociology of schooling and the absent pupil: The school as a factor in the generation of truancy', in Carroll, H. C. M. (ed.), *Absenteeism in South Wales: Studies of Pupils, Their Homes, and Their Secondary Schools*, Swansea: Faculty of Education, University of Swansea.

Reynolds, D. and Packer, A. (1992) 'School effectiveness and school improvement in the 1990's', in Reynolds, D. and Cuttance, P. (eds) *School Effectiveness: Research, Policy and Practice*, London: Cassell.

Reynolds, D. and Stringfield, S. (1996) 'Failure free schooling is ready for take off', *Times Education Supplement*, 19 January, **10**.

Reynolds, D. and Sullivan, M. (1979) 'Bringing schools back in', in Barton, L. (ed.) *Schools, Pupils and Deviance*, Driffield: Nafferton.

Reynolds, D. and Sullivan, M. (1981) 'The effects of school: A radical faith re-stated', in Gillham, B. (ed.) *Problem Behaviour in the Secondary School*, London: Croom Helm.

Reynolds, D. and Teddlie, C. (1995) 'World class schools: A review of data from the International School Effectiveness Research Programme', Paper presented at the British Educational Research Association, Bath, UK.

Reynolds, D., Creemers, B. P. M. and Peters, T. (eds) (1989a) *School Effectiveness and Improvement: Proceedings of the First International Congress, London 1988*, Cardiff, University of Wales College of Cardiff and Groningen, RION.

Reynolds, D., Creemers, B. P. M., Bird, J., Farrell, S. and Swint, F. (1994b) 'School effectiveness – The need for an international perspective', in Reynolds, D., Creemers, B. P. M., Nesselrodt, P. S., Schaffer, E. C., Stringfield, S. and Teddlie, C. (eds) *Advances in School Effectiveness Research and Practice*, London: Pergamon Press, pp. pp.217–37.

Reynolds, D., Creemers, B. P. M., Hopkins, D., Stoll, L. and Bollen, R. (1996) *Making Good Schools*, London: Routledge.

Reynolds, D., Creemers, B., Nesselrodt, P., Schaffer, E., Stringfield, S. and Teddlie, C. (eds) (1994a) *Advances in School Effectiveness Research and Practice*, Oxford: Pergamon.

Reynolds, D., Davie, R. and Phillips, D. (1989b) 'The Cardiff programme – An effective school improvement programme based on school effectiveness research', *Developments in School Effectiveness Research. Special Issue of the International Journal of Educational Research*, **13**, 7, pp.800–14.

Reynolds, D., Hopkins, D. and Stoll, L. (1993) 'Linking school effectiveness knowledge and school improvement practice: Towards a synergy', *School Effectiveness and School Improvement*, **4**, 1, pp.37–58.

Reynolds, D., Jones, D. and St. Leger, S. (1976) 'Schools do make a difference', *New Society*, **37**, pp.223–5.

Reynolds, D., Jones, D., St. Leger, S. and Murgatroyd, S. (1980) 'School factors and truancy', in Hersov, L. and Berg, I. (eds) *Out of School: Modern Perspectives in Truancy and School Refusal*, Chichester: Wiley.

Reynolds, D., Sammons, P., Stoll, L., Barber, M. and Hillman, J. (1995) 'School effectiveness and school improvement in the United Kingdom', in Creemers, B. P. M. and Osinga, N. (eds) *ICSEI Country Reports*, Leeuwarden: GCO.

References

Reynolds, D., Sullivan, M. and Murgatroyd, S. J. (1987) *The Comprehensive Experiment*, Lewes: Falmer Press.

Reynolds, D., Teddlie, C., Creemers, B., Cheng, Y.C., Dundas, B., Green, B., Ep, J.R., Hauge, T.E., Schaffer, E. and Stringfield, S. (1994c) 'School effectiveness research: A review of the international literature', in Reynolds, D., Creemers, B., Nesselrodt, P., Schaffer, E., Stringfield, S. and Teddlie, C. *Advances in School Effectiveness Research and Practice*, London: Pergamon Press, pp.9–23.

Richards, C. E. (1988) 'A typology of educational monitoring systems', *Educational Evaluation and Policy Analysis*, **10**, 2, pp.106–16.

Riddell, A. R. (1989) 'An alternative approach to the study of school effectiveness in Third World countries', *Comparative Education Review*, **33**, 2, pp.481–97.

Robitaille, D. F. and Garden, R. A. (1989) *The IEA Study of Mathematics II: Contexts and Outcomes of School Mathematics*, Oxford: Pergamon Press.

Roeleveld, J., de Jong, U. and Koopman, P. (1990) 'Stabiliteit van schooleffecten', *Tijdschrift voor Onderwijsresearch*, **15**, 5, pp.301–16.

Roelofs, E., Raemaekers, J. and Veenman, S. (1991) 'Improving instructional and classroom management skills: Effects of a staff development programme and coaching', *School Effectiveness and School Improvement*, **2**, 3, pp.192–212.

Rogers, E. M. and Kincaid, D. L. (1980) *Communication Networks: Toward a New Paradigm for Research*, New York: Macmillan.

Rogosa, D. and Saner, D. (1995a) 'Longitudinal data analysis examples with random coefficient models', *Journal of Educational and Behavioural Statistics*, **20**, 2, pp.149–70.

Rogosa, D. and Saner, D. (1995b) 'Reply to discussants: Longitudinal data analysis examples with random coefficient models', in Kreft, I. G. G. (Guest Editor) 'Hierarchical linear models: Problems and prospects', special issue of *Journal of Educational and Behavioural Statistics*, **20**, 2, pp.234–8.

Ros, A. A. (1994) *Samenwerking Tussen Leerlingen en Effectief Onderwijs: De Invloed van de Leerkracht* [Collaboration between students and effective education], Groningen: RION.

Rosenbaum, P. R. and Rubin, D. B. (1983) 'The central role of the propensity score in observational studies for causal effects', *Biometrika*, **17**, pp.41–55.

Rosenberg, M. (1963) 'Parental influence in children's self-conceptions', *Sociometry*, **26**, pp.35–49.

Rosenberg, M. (1965) *Society and the Adolescent Self-image*, Princeton, NJ: Princeton University Press.

Rosenholtz, S. (1985) 'Effective schools: Interpreting the evidence', *American Journal of Education*, **93**, pp.353–87.

Rosenholtz, S. J. (1988) 'Workplace conditions that affect teacher quality and commitment: Implications for teacher induction programs', *Elementary School Journal*, **89**, pp.421–39.

Rosenholtz, S. J. (1989) *Teachers' Workplace: The Social Organization of Schools*, New York: Longman.

Rosenshine, B. (1979) 'Content, time and direct instruction', in Peterson, P. L. and Walberg, H. J. (eds) *Research on Teaching*, Berkeley, CA: McCutchan.

Rosenshine, B. (1983) 'Teaching functions in instructional programs', *Elementary School Journal*, **83**, pp.335–51.

Rosenshine, B. and Stevens, R. (1986) 'Teaching functions', in Wittrock, M. (ed.) *Third Handbook of Research on Teaching*, New York: Macmillan.

Rosenthal, R. (1968) 'Self-fulfilling prophecies in behavioral research and everyday life', *Claremont Reading Conference Yearbook*, **32**, pp.15–33.

Rosenthal, R. (1976) *Experimenter Effects in Behavioral Research, Enlarged Edition*, New York: Irvington.

Rosenthal, R. and Fode, K. L. (1963) 'The effect of experimenter bias on the performance of the albino rat', *Behavioral Science*, **8**, pp.183–9.

Rosenthal, R. and Jacobsen, L. (1968) *Pygmalion in the Classroom*, New York: Holt, Rinehart, and Winston.

Rosenthal, R. and Rubin, D. B. (1982) 'A simple, general purpose display of magnitude of experimental effect', *Journal of Educational Psychology*, **74**, pp.166–9.

Rosier, M. J. and Keeves, J. P. (1991) *The IEA Study of Science I – Science Education and Curricula in Twenty Three Countries*, Oxford: Pergamon.

Rotter, J. B. (1966) 'Generalised expectancies for internal versus external control of reinforcement', *Psychological Monographs*, **80** (1, whole No. 609).

Rowan, B. (1984) 'Shamanistic rituals in effective schools', *Issues in Education*, **2**, pp.76–87.

Rowan, B. and Denk, C. E. (1982) *Modelling the Academic Performance of Schools Using Longitudinal Data: An Analysis of School Effectiveness Measures and School and Principal Effects on School-level Achievement*, San Francisco: Far West Laboratory.

Rowan, B. and Denk, C. (1984) 'Management succession, school socioeconomic context and basic skills achievement', *American Educational Research Journal*, **21**, 3, pp.517–37.

Rowan, B., Bossert, S. T. and Dwyer, D. C. (1983) 'Research on effective schools: A cautionary note', *Educational Researcher*, **12**, 4, pp.24–31.

Rowan, B., Raudenbush, S. W. and Kang, S. J. (1991) 'Organizational design in high schools: A multilevel analysis', *American Journal of Education*, **99**, pp.238–66.

Rowe, K. (1991) *Students, Parents, Teachers and Schools Make a Difference: A Summary Report of Major Findings from the 100 Schools Project – Literacy Programs Study*, Melbourne, School Programs Division, Ministry of Education.

Rowe, K. J. and Hill, P. W. (1994) 'Multilevel modelling in school effectiveness research: How many levels?', Paper presented at the seventh International Congress for School Effectiveness and Improvement, World Congress Centre, Melbourne, Australia.

Rowe, K. J. and Rowe, K. S. (1992) 'Impact of antisocial, inattentive and restless behaviours on reading', in Elkins, J. and Izzard, J. (eds) *Student Behaviour Problems: Context Initiatives and Programs*, Hawthorn, Vic: Australian Council for Educational Research.

Rowe, K. J., Hill, P. W. and Holmes-Smith, P. (1994a) 'The Victorian quality schools project: A report on the first stage of a longitudinal study of school and teacher effectiveness', symposium paper presented at the 7th International Congress for School Effectiveness and Improvement, World Congress Center, Melbourne.

Rowe, K., Hill, P. and Holmes-Smith, P. (1994b) 'Assessing, recording and reporting students, educational progress: The case for profiles', Paper presented at the 1994 annual conference of the Australian Association for Research in Education, Newcastle, New South Wales, Nov–Dec, 1994.

Rowe, K. J., Hill, P. W. and Holmes-Smith, P. (1995) 'Methodological issues in educational performance and school effectiveness research: A discussion with worked examples', *Australian Journal of Education*, **39**, pp.217–48.

Rowe, K., Holmes-Smith, P. and Hill, P. (1993) 'The link between school effectiveness research, policy and school improvement', Paper presented at the 1993 annual conference of the Australian Association for Research in Education, Fremantle, Western Australia, November 22–25.

Rubin, D. B. (1989) 'Some applications of multilevel models to educational data', in Bock, R. D. (ed.) *Multilevel Analysis of Educational Data*, San Diego, CA: Academic Press, pp.1–17.

Rutter, M. (1980) *Changing Youth in a Changing Society*, Oxford: Nuffield Provincial Hospitals Trust.

Rutter, M. (1983a) 'School effects on pupil progress – Findings and policy implications', *Child Development*, **54**, 1, pp.1–29.

Rutter, M. (1983b) 'School effects on pupil progress: Research findings and policy implications', in Shulman, L. and Sykes, G. (eds) *Handbook of Teaching and Policy*, New York: Longman, pp.3–41.

Rutter, M., Maughan, B., Mortimore, P. and Ouston, J. with Smith, A. (1979) *Fifteen Thousand Hours: Secondary Schools and Their Effects on Children*, London: Open Books and Boston, MA: Harvard University Press.

Sackney, L. (1985) 'School district imperatives for effective schools' *Canadian School Executive*, **16**, 2, pp.2–13.

Sackney, L. (1989) 'School effectiveness and improvement: The Canadian scene', in Reynolds, D., Creemers, B. and Peters, T. (eds) *School Effectiveness and Improvement*, Groningen: RION.

Sammons, P. (1995) 'Gender, ethnic and socio-economic differences in attainment and progress: A longitudinal analysis of student achievement over 9 years', *British Educational Research Journal*, **21**, 4, pp.465–86.

Sammons, P. (1996) 'Complexities in the judgement of school effectiveness', *Educational Research and Evaluation*, **2**, 2, pp.113–49.

Sammons, P. (1999) *School Effectiveness: Coming of Age in the Twenty-First Century*, Lisse: Swets and Zeitlinger.

Sammons, P. and Reynolds, D. (1997) 'A partison evaluation – John Elliott on school effectiveness', *Cambridge Journal of Education*, **27**, 1, pp.123–6.

Sammons, P., Hillman, J. and Mortimore, P. (1995b) *Key Characteristics of Effective Schools: A Review of School Effectiveness Research*, London, Office for Standards in Education and Institute of Education.

Sammons, P., Mortimore, P. and Thomas, S. (1993a) 'Do schools perform consistently across outcomes and areas?', Paper presented at the annual conference of the British Educational Research Association, Oxford.

Sammons, P., Mortimore, P. and Thomas, S. (1996a) 'Do schools perform consistently across outcomes and areas?', in Gray, J. Reynolds, D., Fitz-Gibbon, C. and Jesson, D. (eds) *Merging Traditions: The Future of Research on School Effectiveness and School Improvement*, London: Cassell, pp.3–29.

Sammons, P., Nuttall, D. and Cuttance, P. (1993b) 'Differential school effectiveness: Results from a re-analysis of the Inner London Education Authority's junior school project data', *British Educational Research Journal*, 19(4), 381–405.

Sammons, P., Nuttall, D., Cuttance, P. and Thomas, S. (1995a) 'Continuity of school effects: A longitudinal analysis of primary and secondary school effects on GCSE performance', *School Effectiveness and School Improvement*, **6**, 4, pp.285–307.

Sammons, P., Taggartt, B. and Thomas, S. (1998) *Making Belfast Work: Raising School Standards – An Evaluation* (A report prepared for the Belfast Education and Library Board), London: Institute of Education.

Sammons, P., Thomas, S. and Mortimore, P. (1996b) 'Differential school effectiveness: Departmental variations in GCSE attainment', Paper presented at the School Effectiveness and Improvement Symposium of the Annual Meeting of the American Educational Research Association, New York.

Sammons, P., Thomas, S. and Mortimore, P. (1997) *Forging Links: Effective Schools and Effective Departments*, London: Paul Chapman.

Sammons, P., Thomas, S., Mortimore, P., Owen, C. and Pennell, H. (1994b) *Assessing School Effectiveness: Developing Measures to Put School Performance in Context*, London: OFSTED.

Sanders, W. L. (1995) *The Measure of Education: A Review of the Tennessee Value Added Assessment System: Appendix G. Response by Dr William Sanders*, Nashville, TN: Tennessee Comptroller of the Treasury.

Sanders, W. L. and Horn, S. (1994) 'The Tennessee value-added assessment (TVAAS): Mixed methodology in educational assessment', *Journal of Personnel Evaluation in Education*, **8**, pp.299–311.

Sanders, W. L. and Horn, S. P. (1995a) 'Educational assessment reassessed: The usefulness of standardized and alternative measures of student achievement as indicators for the assessment of educational outcomes'. *Education Policy Analysis Archives*, **3**, 6.

Sanders, W. L. and Horn, S. P. (1995b) *An Overview of the Tennessee Value-added Assessment System* (TVAAS), Knoxville, TN: University of Tennessee.

Sarason, S. (1981) *The Culture of the School and the Problem of Educational Change*, Allyn & Bacon.

Sashkin, M. and Egermeier, J. (1992) *School Change Models and Processes. A Review and Synthesis of Research and Practice*, Washington: US Department of Education.

Scardamelia, M. and Bereiter, C. (1985) 'Development of dialectical processes in composition', in Olson, D. R., Torrance, N. and Hildyard, A. (eds), *Literacy, Language and Learning*, Cambridge: Cambridge University Press, pp.307–29.

Schaffer, E. C. and Nesselrodt, P. S. (1992) 'The development and testing of the special strategies observation system', Paper presented at the annual meeting of the American Educational Research Association, San Francisco, CA.

Schaffer, E. C., Nesselrodt, P. S. and Stringfield, S. (1994) 'The contributions of classroom observations to school effectiveness research', in Reynolds, D., Creemers, B. P. M., Nesselrodt, P. S., Schaffer, E. C., Stringfield, S. and Teddlie, C. (eds) *Advances in School Effectiveness Research and Practice*, London: Pergamon, pp.133–52.

Scheerens, J. (1990) 'School effectiveness research and the development of process indicators of school functioning', *School Effectiveness and School Improvement*, **1**, 1, pp.61–80.

Scheerens, J. (1992) *Effective Schooling: Research, Theory and Practice*, London: Cassell.

Scheerens, J. (1993) 'Basic school effectiveness research: Items for a research agenda', *School Effectiveness and School Improvement*, **4**, 1, pp.17–36.

Scheerens, J. (1994) 'The school-level context of instructional effectiveness: A comparison between school effectiveness and restructuring models', *Tijdschrift voor Onderwijsresearch*, **19**, 1, pp.26–38.

Scheerens, J. (1997) 'Conceptual models in theory embedded principles on effective schooling', *School Effectiveness and School Improvement*, **8**, 3, pp.269–310.

Scheerens, J. and Bosker, R. (1997) *The Foundations of Educational Effectiveness*, Oxford: Pergamon Press.

Scheerens, J. and Creemers, B. P. M. (1989a) 'Conceptualising school effectiveness', *International Journal of Educational Research*, **13**, pp.689–706.

Scheerens, J. and Creemers, B. (1989b) 'Towards a more comprehensive conceptualisation of school effectiveness', in Creemers, B., Peters, T. and Reynolds, D. (eds) *School Effectiveness and School Improvement: Proceedings of the Second International Congress*, Amsterdam: Swets and Zeitlinger, pp.265–78.

Scheerens, J. and Creemers, B. P. M. (1990) 'Conceptualising school effectiveness', in Creemers, B. P. M. and Scheerens, J. (eds) *Developments in School Effectiveness Research*, Special issue of *International Journal of Educational Research*, **13**, 7, pp.691–706.

Scheerens, J. and Creemers, B. P. M. (1995) 'School effectiveness in the Netherlands: Research, Policy and Practice', in Creemers, B. P. M. and Osinga, N. (eds) *ICSEI Country Reports*, Leeuwarden, Netherlands: ICSEI Secretariat, pp.81–106.

Scheerens, J., Vermeulen, C. J. and Pelgrum, W. J. (1989c) 'Generalisability of school and instructional effectiveness indicators across nations', in Creemers, B. P. M. and Scheerens, J. (eds) *Developments in School Effectiveness Research*, special issue of *International Journal of Educational Research*, **13**, 7, pp.789–99.

Schmidt, W. H. (1969) 'Covariance structure analysis of the multivariate random effects model', unpublished doctoral dissertation, University of Chicago.

References

Schmuck, R. R. and Miles, M. (eds) (1971) *Organisation Development in Schools*, Palo Alto, CA: National Press Books.

Schweitzer, J. H. (1984) 'Characteristics of effective schools', Paper presented at the Annual Meeting of the American Educational Research Association, New Orleans, LA.

Seltzer, M. H. (1987) 'An empirical Bayes approach to the identification of effective schools', Paper presented at the annual meeting of the American Educational Research Association, Washington, DC.

Seltzer, M. H. (1993) 'Sensitivity analysis for fixed effects in the hierarchical model: A Gibbs sampling approach', *Journal of Educational Statistics*, **18**, 3, pp.207–35.

Seltzer, M. H., Wong, W. H. and Bryk, A. S. (1996) 'Bayesian analysis in applications of hierarchical models: Issues and methods', *Journal of Educational and Behavioral Statistics*, **21**, 2, pp.131–68.

Sewell, W. H., Haller, A. O. and Portes, A. (1969) 'The educational and early occupational attainment process', *American Sociological Review*, **34**, pp.82–92.

Shapiro, J. (1986) 'Evaluation research and educational decision-making: A review of the literature', in Smart, J. (ed.) *Higher Education: Handbook of Theory and Research*, **2**, New York: Agathon Press.

Sharp, D., Cole, M. and Lave, C. (1979) 'Education and cognitive development: The evidence from experimental research', *Monographs of the Society for Research in Child Development*, Number 178.

Shavelson, R. J. (Guest Editor) (1994) 'Performance assessment', *International Journal of Educational Research*, **21**, 3, pp.233–350.

Shavelson, R., Baxter, G., Pine, J., Yure, J., Goldman, S. and Smith, B. (1991) 'Alternative technologies for large scale assessment: Instruments of education reform', *School Effectiveness and School Improvement*, **2**, 2, pp.97–114.

Shavelson, R., McDonnel, L., Oakes, J. and Carey, N. (1989) *Indicator Systems for Monitoring Mathematics and Science Education*, Santa Monica, CA: RAND Corporation.

Shavit, Y. and Williams, R. A. (1985) 'Ability grouping and contextual determinants of educational expectations in Israel', *American Sociological Review*, **50**, pp.62–73.

Silins, H. (1994) 'The relationship between transformational and transactional leadership and school improvement outcomes' *School Effectiveness and School Improvement*, **5**, 3, pp.272–98.

Silver, P. and Moyle, C. (1985) 'The impact of school leadership on school effectiveness', *Educational Magazine*, **42**, pp.42–5.

Sime, N. and Gray, J. (1991) 'The stability of school effects over time', Paper presented to the British Educational Research Annual Conference, Nottingham Polytechnic, August.

Sirotnik, K. A. (1985) 'School effectiveness: A bandwagon in search of a tune', *Educational Administration Quarterly*, **21**, 2, pp.135–40.

Sirotnik, K. A. (1987) 'The school as the centre of change', (Occasional Paper No. 5) Seattle WA: Center for Educational Renewal.

Sirotnik, K. A. and Burstein, L. (1985) 'Measurement and statistical issues in multilevel research on schooling', *Educational Administration Quarterly*, **21**, 3, pp.169–85.

Sizemore, B. A., Brossard, C. A. and Harrigan, B. (1983) *An Abashing Anomaly: The High Achieving Predominantly Black Elementary School*, University of Pittsburgh, Abstract NIE-G-80–0006.

Sizer, T. (1992) *Horace's School: Redesigning the American high school*, New York: Houghton Mifflin.

Slater, R. O. and Teddlie, C. (1992) 'Toward a theory of school effectiveness and leadership', *School Effectiveness and School Improvement*, **3**, 4, pp.247–57.

Slavin, R. (1987) 'A theory of school and classroom organisation', *Educational Psychologist*, **22**, pp.89–108.

Slavin, R. E. (1996) *Education for All*, Lisse: Swets and Zeitlinger.

Slavin, R., Madden, N., Dolan, L., Wasik, B., Ross, S., Smith, L., and Dianda, M. (1996) 'Success for all: A Summary of research', *Journal for the Education of Children Placed at Risk*, **1**, 1, pp.44–76.

Slee, R., Weiner, G. and Tomlinson, S. (eds) (1998) *School Effectiveness for Whom? Challenges to the School Effectiveness and School Improvement Movements*, London: Falmer Press.

Sleegers, P. J. C. (1991) *School en Beleidsvoering*, Nijmegen: Universiteitsdrukkerij.

Sleegers, P. J. C., Bergen, Th. C. M. and Giebers, J. H. G. I. (1992) 'School en beleidsvoering', *Pedagogische Studien*, **69**, 3, pp.177–99.

Smith, B. (1990) 'Review of *Spotlight on School Improvement*', *School Effectiveness and School Improvement*, **1**, 1, pp.87–8.

Smith, A. F. M. and Roberts, G. O. (1993) 'Bayesian computation via the Gibbs sampler and related Markov-chair Monte Carlo methods', *Journal of the Royal Statistical Society*, Series B, **55**, pp.3–23.

Smith, D. J. and Tomlinson, S. (1989) *The School Effect. A Study of Multi-racial Comprehensives*, London: Policy Studies Institute.

Smithers, A. and Robinson, P. (1991) *Beyond Compulsory Schooling: A Numerical Picture*, London: Council for Industry and Higher Education.

Smylie, M. A. (1992) 'Teacher participation in school decision making: Assessing willingness to participate', *Educational Evaluation and Policy Analysis*, **14**, 1, pp.53–67.

Smyth, J. (1993) 'Schools of the Future and the Politics of Blame', A Public Lecture sponsored by the Public Sector Management Institute, Melbourne, Monash University, 2 July.

Snijders, T. A. B. and Bosker, R. J. (1993) 'Standard errors and sample sizes for two-level research', *Journal of Educational Statistics*, **18**, 3, pp.237–59.

Spade, J. Z., Vanfossen, B. E. and Jones, E. D. (1985, April) 'Effective schools: Characteristics of schools which predict mathematics and science performance', Paper presented at the Annual Meeting of the American Educational Research Association, New Orleans, LA.

Stallings, J. (1980) 'Allocated academic learning time revisited, or beyond time on task', *Educational Researcher*, **9**, 11, pp.11–16.

Stallings, J. A. and Freiberg, H. J. (1991) 'Observation for improvement of teaching', in Waxman, H. C. and Walberg, H. J. (eds) *Effective teaching: Current research*, Berkeley, CA: McCutchan Publishing, pp.107–34.

Stallings, J. and Kaskowitz, D. (1974) *Follow through Classroom Observation Evaluation (1972–1973)*, Menlo Park, CA: SRI International.

Steedman, J. (1980) *Progress in Secondary Schools*, London: National Children's Bureau.

Steedman, J. (1983) *Examination Results in Selective and Non-Selective Schools*, London: National Children's Bureau.

Stevenson, H. (1992) 'Learning from Asian schools', *Scientific American*, December, pp.32–8.

Stevenson, H. W. and Stigler, J. W. (1992) *The Learning Gap: Why Our Schools Are Failing and What We Can Learn from Japanese and Chinese Education*, New York: Summit Books.

Stevenson, H. W., Parker, T., Wilkinson, A., Bonnevaux, B. and Gonzales, M. (1978) 'Schooling, environment, and cognitive development: A cross-cultural study', *Monographs of the Society for Research in Child Development*, Number 175.

Stogdill, R. M. (1981) 'Traits of leadership: A follow-up to 1970', in Bass, B. M. (ed.) *Stogdill's Handbook of Leadership*, New York: Free Press, pp.73–97.

Stoll, L. (1992) 'Teacher growth in the effective school', in Fullan, M. and Hargreaves, H. (eds) *Teacher Development and Educational Change*, London: Falmer Press.

Stoll, L. (1995) 'The complexity and challenge of ineffective schools', Paper presented at the European Conference on Educational Research Association, Bath, UK.

Stoll, L. (1996) 'Linking school effectiveness and school improvement: Issues and possibilities', in Gray, J., Reynolds, D., Fitz-Gibbon, C., and Jesson, D. (eds) *Merging Traditions: The*

References

Future of Research on School Effectiveness and School Improvement, London: Cassell, pp.51–73.

Stoll, L. and Fink, D. (1989) 'An effective schools project: The Halton Approach', in Reynolds, D., Creemers, B. and Peters T. (eds) *School Effectiveness and Improvement*, Groningen: RION.

Stoll, L. and Fink, D. (1992) 'Effecting school change: The Halton approach', *School Effectiveness and School Improvement*, 3, 1, pp.19–41.

Stoll, L. and Fink, D. (1994) 'School effectiveness and school improvement: Voices from the field', *School Effectiveness and School Improvement*, 5, 2, pp.149–77.

Stoll, L. and Fink, D. (1996) *Changing Our Schools*, Buckingham: Open University Press.

Stoll, L. and Mortimore, P. (1995) *School Effectiveness and School Improvement*, Viewpoint Number 2, London: University of London Institute of Education.

Stoll, L. and Myers, K. (1997) *No Quick Fixes: Perspectives on Schools in Difficulty*, Lewes: Falmer Press.

Stoll, L. and Thomson, M. (1996) 'Moving together: A partnership approach to improvement', in Earley, P., Fidler, B. and Ouston, J. (eds) *Improvement Through Inspection: Complementary Approaches to School Development*, London: David Fulton.

Stoll, L., Myers, K. and Reynolds, D. (1996) 'Understanding ineffectiveness', Paper presented at the annual meeting of the American Educational Research Association, New York.

Stringfield, S. (1994a) 'The analysis of large data bases in school effectiveness research', in Reynolds, D., Creemers, B.P.M., Nesselrodt, P.S., Schaffer, E.C., Stringfield, S. and Teddlie, C. (eds) *Advances in School Effectiveness Research and Practice*, London: Pergamon, pp.55–72.

Stringfield, S. (1994b) 'A model of elementary school effects', in Reynolds, D., Creemers, B.P.M., Nesselrodt, P.S., Schaffer, E.C., Stringfield, S. and Teddlie, C. (eds) *Advances in School Effectiveness Research and Practice*, London: Pergamon, pp.153–88.

Stringfield, S. (1994c) 'Outlier studies of school effectiveness', in Reynolds, D., Creemers, B.P.M., Nesselrodt, P.S., Schaffer, E.C., Stringfield, S. and Teddlie, C. (eds) *Advances in School Effectiveness Research and Practice*, London: Pergamon, pp.73–84.

Stringfield, S. (1995) 'Attempting to enhance students' learning through innovative programs: The case for schools evolving into High Reliability Organisations', *School Effectiveness and School Improvement*, 6, 1, pp.67–96.

Stringfield, S. and Herman, R. (1995) 'Assessment of the state of school effectiveness research in the United States of America', in Creemers, B. P. M. and Osinga, N. (eds) *ICSEI Country Reports*, Leeuwarden, Netherlands: ICSEI Secretariat, pp.107–28.

Stringfield, S. and Herman, R. (1996) 'Assessment of the state of school effectiveness research in the United States of America', *School Effectiveness and School Research*, 7, 2.

Stringfield, S. and Slavin, R. (1991) 'Raising societal demands, high reliability organisations, school effectiveness, success for all and a set of modest proposals', Paper presented at Interuniversitair Centrum Voor Onderwijsevaluie: Twente.

Stringfield, S. C. and Slavin, R. E. (1992) 'A hierarchical longitudinal model for elementary school effects', in Creemers, B. P. M. and Reezigt, G. J. (eds), *Evaluation of Educational Effectiveness*, Groningen: ICO, pp.35–69.

Stringfield, S. and Teddlie, C. (1987) 'A time to summarise: Six years and three phases of the Louisiana School Effectiveness Study', Paper delivered at the Annual Meeting of the American Educational Research Association, Washington DC.

Stringfield, S. and Teddlie, C. (1988) 'A time to summarise: The Louisiana School Effectiveness Study', *Educational Leadership*, 46, 2, 43–9.

Stringfield, S. and Teddlie, C. (1989) 'The first three phases of the Louisiana School Effectiveness Study', in Creemers, B., Peters, T. and Reynolds, D. (eds) *School Effectiveness and School Improvement: Proceedings of the Second International Congress*, Amsterdam, Netherlands: Swets and Zeitlinger, pp.281–94.

Stringfield, S. and Teddlie, C. (1990) 'School improvement efforts: Qualitative and quantitative data from four naturally occurring experiments in Phases III and IV of the Louisiana School Effectiveness Study', *School Effectiveness and School Improvement*, **1**, 2, pp.139–62.

Stringfield, S. and Teddlie, C. (1991a) 'Observers as predictors of schools' effectiveness status', *Elementary School Journal*, **91**, 4, pp.357–76.

Stringfield, S. and Teddlie, C. (1991b) 'School, classroom, and student-level indicators of rural school effectiveness', *Journal of Research in Rural Education*, **7**, 3.

Stringfield, S., Bedinger, S. and Herman, R. (1995) 'Implementing a private school program in an inner-city public school: Processes, effects and implication from a four year evaluation', Paper presented at the ICSEI Congress in Leeuwarden, January.

Stringfield, S., Millsap, M. A. and Herman, R. (1997a) *Urban and Suburban/rural Special Strategies for Educating Disadvantaged Children: Findings and Policy Implications of a Longitudinal Study*, Washington DC: US Department of Education.

Stringfield, S., Ross, S. and Smith, A. (1997b) *Bold Plans for School Restructuring*, New York: Lawrence Erlbaum.

Stringfield, S., Teddlie, C., and Suarez, S. (1985) 'Classroom interaction in effective and ineffective schools: Preliminary results from phase III of the Louisiana school effectiveness study', *Journal of Classroom Interaction*, **20**, 2, pp.31–7.

Stringfield, S., Teddlie, C., Wimpelberg, R. K. and Kirby, P. (1992) 'A five year follow-up of schools in the Louisiana School Effectiveness Study', in Bashi, J. and Sass, Z. (eds), *School Effectiveness and School Improvement: Proceedings of the Third International Congress, Jerusalem*, Jerusalem: Magnes Press.

Stringfield, S., Winfield, L., and Abt Associates (1994a) *Urban and Suburban/rural Special Strategies for Educating Disadvantaged Children: First Year Report*, Washington, D.C.: US Department of Education.

Stringfield, S., Winfield, L., Millsap, M., Puma, M., Gamse, B., and Randall, B. (1994b) *Special Strategies for Educating Disadvantaged Children: First Year Report*, Washington, DC: US Department of Education.

Stufflebeam, D. L. (1971) 'The relevance of the CIPP evaluation model for educational accountability', *Journal of Research and Development in Education*, **5**, pp.19–25.

Stufflebeam, D. L. (1983) 'The CIPP model for program evaluation', in Madaus, G.F., Scriven, M. and Stufflebeam, D.L. (eds) *Evaluation Models*, Boston, MA: Kluver-Nijhoff.

Summers, A. A. and Wolfe, B. L. (1977) 'Do schools make a difference?', *American Economic Review*, **67**, pp.639–52.

Sweeney, J. (1982) 'Research synthesis on effective school leadership', *Educational Leadership*, **39**, pp.346–52.

Szaday, C. (1994) *Trends in School Effectiveness and School Improvement Research: A Survey of Expert Opinion*, Ebikon: ZBS.

Tagiuri, R. and Litwin, G. H. (eds) (1968) *Organizational Climate*, Boston: Harvard Graduate School of Business Administration.

Tashakkori, A. (1993) 'Race, gender, and pre-adolescent self structure: A test of construct-specificity hypothesis', *Journal of Personality and Individual Differences*, **4**, pp.591–8.

Tashakkori, A. and Kennedy, E. (1993) 'Measurement of self-perception in multi-cultural context: Psychometric properties of a Modified Self-Description Questionnaire', *British Journal of Educational Psychology*, **63**, pp.337–48.

Tashakkori, A. and Teddlie, C. (1998) *Mixed Methods: Combining the Qualitative and Quantitative Approaches*, Thousand Oaks, CA: Sage.

Tate, R. L. (1988) *School Comparisons with Hierarchical Linear Models: An Illustration*, Technical report prepared to report activities supported by COFRS grant 5001151648, Florida State University, FL.

Taylor, B. O. (ed.). (1990) *Case Studies in Effective Schools Research*, Madison, WI: National Center for Effective Schools Research and Development.

References

Taylor, R. C., Sadowski, C. J. and Preacher, R. K. (1981) 'Development of a likert-type locus of control scale for teachers', Paper presented at the annual meeting of the Southeastern Psychological Association, Atlanta, Georgia.

Teddlie, C. (1994a) 'Integrating classroom and school data in school effectiveness research', in Reynolds, D. et al., *Advances in School Effectiveness Research and Practice*, Oxford: Pergamon, pp.111–32.

Teddlie, C. (1994b) 'Using context variables in school effectiveness research', in Reynolds, D. et al., *Advances in School Effectiveness Research and Practice*, Oxford: Pergamon, pp.85–110.

Teddlie, C. (1996) *School Effectiveness Indices: East Baton Rouge Parish Public Schools, Academic Years 1991–92, 1992–93, 1993–94*, Baton Rouge, LA: Louisiana State University, College of Education.

Teddlie, C. and Kennedy, G. (1997) *An Overview of the Louisiana School Effectiveness and Assistance Program (SEAP)*, Baton Rouge, LA: Louisiana Department of Education.

Teddlie, C. and Kochan, S. (1991) 'Evaluation of a troubled high school: Methods, results, and implications', Paper presented at the annual meeting of the American Educational Research Association, Chicago, IL.

Teddlie, C. and Meza, J. (1999) 'Using formal and informal measures to create classroom profiles', in J. Freiburg (ed.) *School Climate: Measuring, Improving and Sustaining Healthy Learning Environments*, London: Falmer Press, pp.77–99.

Teddlie, C. and Roberts, S. (1993) 'More clearly defining the field: A survey of topics in school effects research', Paper presented at the Annual Meeting of the American Educational Research Association, Atlanta, Georgia.

Teddlie, C. and Stringfield, S. (1985) 'A differential analysis of effectiveness in middle and lower socioeconomic status schools', *Journal of Classroom Interaction*, **20**, pp.38–44.

Teddlie, C. and Stringfield, S. (1989) 'Ethnics and teachers: Implications of research on effective schools', *Ethics in Education*, **9**, 2, pp.12–14.

Teddlie, C. and Stringfield, S. (1993) *Schools Do Make a Difference: Lessons Learned from a 10-year Study of School Effects*, New York: Teachers College Press.

Teddlie, C., Falkowski, C. Stringfield, S., Desselle, S. and Garvue, R. (1984) *The Louisiana School Effectiveness Study: Phase two, 1982–84*, Baton Rouge: Louisiana Department of Education (ERIC Document Reproduction Service No. ED 250 362).

Teddlie, C., Kirby, P.C. and Stringfield, S. (1989a) 'Effective versus ineffective schools: Observable differences in the classroom', *American Journal of Education*, **97**, 3, pp.221–36.

Teddlie, C., Lang, M. H., and Oescher, J. (1995) 'The masking of the delivery of educational services to lower achieving students', *Urban Education*, **30**, 2, pp.125–49.

Teddlie, C., Stringfield, S. and Desselle, S. (1985) 'Methods, history, selected findings, and recommendations from the Louisiana School Effectiveness Study: 1980–85', *Journal of Classroom Interaction*, **20**, 2, pp.22–30.

Teddlie, C., Stringfield, S., Wimpelberg, R. and Kirby, P. (1987) 'Contextual differences in effective schooling in Louisiana', Paper presented at the annual meeting of the American Educational Research Association, Washington DC.

Teddlie, C., Stringfield, S., Wimpelberg, R. and Kirby, P. (1989b) 'Contextual differences in models for effective schooling in the USA', in Creemers, B. P. M., Peters, T. and Reynolds, D. (eds) *School Effectiveness and School Improvement: Proceedings of the Second International Congress, Rotterdam, 1989*, Amsterdam: Swets and Zeitlinger.

Teddlie, C., Virgilio, I. and Oescher, J. (1990) 'Development and validation of the Virgilio Teacher Behavior Inventory', *Educational and Psychological Measurement*, **50**, 2, pp.421–30.

Thomas, F. (Chair) and others (1993) *Base-line Survey of Principals in 1993* (Co-operative Research Project), Melbourne: Directorate of School Education.

Thomas, F., Beare, H., Bishop, P., Caldwell, B., Lawrence, A., Liddicoat, T., Peck, F. and Wardlaw, C. (1995a) *One Year Later: Co-operative Research Project Leading Victoria's Schools of the Future*, Melbourne: Directorate of School Education.

Thomas, F., Beare, H., Bishop, P., Caldwell, B., Lawrence, A., Liddicoat, T., Peck, F. and Wardlaw, C. (1995b) *Taking Stock: Co-operative Research Project Leading Victoria's Schools of the Future*, Melbourne: Directorate of School Education.

Thomas, F. (Chair) and others (1996) *A Three Year Report Card* (Co-operative Research Project), Melbourne, Directorate of School Education.

Thomas, F. (Chair) and others (1997) *Still More Work to be Done But . . . No Turning Back* (Co-operative Research Project Report), Melbourne: Department of Education.

Thomas, R. and Postlethwaite, N. (1983) *Schooling in East Asia: Forms of Change*, Oxford: Pergamon Press.

Thomas, S. and Nuttall, D. (1993) *An Analysis of 1992 Key Stage 1 Results in Lancashire – Final Report: A Multilevel Analysis of Total Subject Score, English Score and Mathematics Score*, London: Institute of Education.

Thomas, S., Nuttall, D. and Goldstein, H. (1993) 'The Guardian survey' (of A-level examination results), *The Guardian*.

Thomas, S., Sammons, P. and Mortimore (1994) 'Stability in secondary schools: Effects on students GCSE outcomes', Paper presented at the Annual Conference of the British Educational Research Association, Oxford.

Thomas, S., Sammons, P. and Mortimore, P. (1995a) 'Determining what adds value to student achievement', *Educational Leadership International*, **58**, 6, pp.19–22.

Thomas, S., Sammons, P. and Mortimore, P. (1997) 'Stability and consistency in secondary schools' effects on students' GCSE outcomes over 3 years', *School Effectiveness and Improvement*, **8**.

Thomas, S., Sammons, P., Mortimore, P. and Smees, R. (1995b) 'Differential secondary school effectiveness: Examining the size, extent and consistency of school and departmental effects on GCSE outcomes for different groups of students over three years', Paper presented at the ECER/BERA Annual Conference, Bath, September 1995.

Thum, Y. M. (1997) 'Hierarchical linear models for multivariate outcomes', *Journal of Educational and Behavioural Statistics*, **22**, 1, pp.77–108.

Tichy, N. M. (1983) *Managing Strategic Change: Technical, Political and Cultural Dynamics*, New York: Wiley and Sons.

Tickell, G. (1995) *Decentralising the Management of Australia's Schools*, Vol. II, Melbourne: Australia, National Industry Education Forum.

Tizard, B., Blatchford, P., Burke, J., Farquhar, C. and Plewis, I. (1988) *Young Children at School in the Inner City*, Hove: Lawrence Erlbaum.

Tobin, K. (1980) 'The effects of an extended teacher wait-time on student achievement', *Journal of Research in Science Teaching*, **17**, pp.469–75.

Tobin, K. and Capie, W. (1982) 'Relationships between classroom process variables and middle-school achievement', *Journal of Educational Psychology*, **74**, pp.441–54.

Townsend, T. (1994) *Effective Schooling for the Community*, London and New York: Routledge.

Townsend, T. (1994) 'Goals for effective schools: The view from the field', *School Effectiveness and School Improvement*, **5**, 2, pp.127–48.

Townsend, T. (1995a) 'Matching the goals of schools of the future with the demographic characteristics of their local communities', an ongoing research project funded by the Australian Research Council.

Townsend, T. (1995b) 'Community perceptions of the schools of the future', an ongoing research project funded by the Research Committee of the Faculty of Education, Monash University.

References

Townsend, T. (1996a) *School Effectiveness and the Decentralisation of Australia's Schools*, Melbourne, Australia, National Industry Education Forum.

Townsend, T. (1996b) 'The self-managing school: Miracle or myth?', *Leading and Managing*, **2**, 3, pp.171–94.

Townsend, T. (ed.) (1997) *Restructuring and Quality: Issues for Tomorrow's Schools*, London: Routledge.

Townsend, T. (1998a) 'Resource allocation', in Townsend, T. (ed.) *Primary School in Changing Times: The Australian Experience*, London and New York: Routledge.

Townsend, T. (1998b) 'The Primary school of the future: Third World or Third Millenium?', in Townsend, T. (ed.) *Primary School in Changing Times: The Australian Experience*, London and New York: Routledge.

Townsend, T. and Walker, I. (1998) 'Different families: New issues for schools', in Townsend, T. (ed.) *Primary School in Changing Times: The Australian Experience*, London and New York: Routledge.

Travers, K. J. and Westbury, I. (1989) *The IEA Study of Mathematics I: Analysis of Mathematics Curricula*, Oxford: Pergamon Press.

Travers, R. M. W. (ed.) (1973) *Second Handbook of Research on Teaching*, Chicago: Rand McNally.

Trower, P. and Vincent, L. (1995) *The Value Added National Project Technical report: Secondary*, London: School Curriculum and Assessment Authority.

Tymms, P. B. (1992) 'The relative effectiveness of post-16 institutions in England', (including Assisted Places Scheme Schools), *British Educational Research Journal*, **18**, 2, pp.175–92.

Tymms, P. (1993) 'Accountability – Can it be fair?', *Oxford Review of Education*, **19**, 3, pp.291–9.

Tymms, P. (1994) 'Monitoring school performance: A guide for educators' (Review of Monitoring school performance: A guide for educators), *School Effectiveness and School Improvement*, **5**, 4, pp.394–7.

Tymms, P. B. (1995) 'The long-term impact of schooling', *Evaluation and Research in Education*, **9**, 2, pp.99–108.

Tymms, P. (1996a) 'Theories, models and simulations: School effectiveness at an impasse', in Gray, J., Reynolds, D., Fitz-Gibbon, C. and Jesson, D. (eds) *Merging Traditions: The Future of Research on School Effectiveness and School Improvement*, London: Cassell, pp.121–35.

Tymms, P. B. (1996b) *Baseline Assessment and Value Added*, London: School Curriculum and Assessment Authority.

Tymms, P. B. and Fitz-Gibbon, C. T. (1991) 'A comparison of exam boards: "A" levels', *Oxford Review of Education*, **17**, 1, pp.17–31.

Tymms, P. B., Fitz-Gibbon, C. T., Hazelwood, R. D. and McCabe, J. J. C. (1990) 'The effect of a national initiative on exam results', in *School Effectiveness and School Improvement*, **1**, 4, pp.281–98.

Tymms, P, Merrill, C. and Henderson, B. (1997) 'The first year at school: A quantitative investigation of the attainment and progress of pupils', *Educational Research and Evaluation*, **3**, 2, pp.101–18.

Tyne, T. F. and Geary, W. (1980) 'Patterns of acceptance–rejection among male-female elementary school students', *Child Study Journal*, **10**, pp.179–90.

US Department of Education (1987) *What Works*, Washington, DC: Government Printing Office.

US Department of Education (1988) *Measuring Up: Questions and Answers About State Roles in Educational Accountability*, Washington, DC: Government Printing Office.

US Department of Education (1994) *The Goals 2000: Educate America Act*.

van Cuyck-Remijssen, A. and Dronkers, J. (1990) 'Catholic and Protestant schools, a better choice in the Netherlands?' *School Effectiveness and School Improvement*, **1**, 3, pp.211–20.

van de Grift, W. (1989) 'Self perceptions of educational leadership and mean pupil achievements', in Reynolds, D., Creemers, B. P. M. and Peters, T. (eds) *School Effectiveness and Improvement: Selected Proceedings of the First International Congress for School Effectiveness*, Groningen, Netherlands: RION, pp. 227–42.

van de Grift, W. (1990) 'Educational leadership and academic achievement in secondary education', *School Effectiveness and School Improvement*, 1, 1, pp.26–40.

van de Grift, W. and Houtveen, T. (1991) 'Principals and school improvement', *School Effectiveness and School Improvement*, 2, 1, pp.53–70.

van der Tuin, A.C. (1993) *School Characteristics and the Effectiveness of Comprehensive Schools*, Groningen, the Netherlands: Rijksuniversiteit Groningen, Vakgroep Sociologie.

van Velzen, W. (1979) *Autonomy of the School*, 's Hertogenbosch, Netherlands: PKC.

van Velzen, W. (1987) 'The international school improvement project', in Hopkins, D. (ed.) *Improving the Quality of Schooling: Lessons from the OECD International School Improvement Project*, Lewes: Falmer Press.

van Velzen, W., Miles, M., Ekholm, M., Hameyer, U. and Robin, D. (1985) *Making School Improvement Work: A Conceptual Guide to Practice*, Leuven: Belgium, ACCO.

Vandenberghe, R. (1993a) *De Determinaten van Het Professionele Handelen van Leerkrachten Secundair Onderwijs en de Invloed op de Onderwijskwaliteit*, Leuven: Centrum voor Onderwijsbeleid en -vernieuwing.

Vandenberghe, R. (ed.) (1993b) *Scholen en Vernieuwing: een Kans Tot Professionele Groei en Schoolverbetering*, Leuven: Centrum voor Onderwijsbeleid en -vernieuwing.

Vandenberghe, R. and Vegt, R. van der (1992) *Scholen in de Vernieuwingsarena*, Leuven/Apeldoorn: Garant.

VanderStoep, S., Anderman, E. and Midgley, C. (1994) 'The relationship among principal "venturesomeness", a stress on excellence, and the personal engagement of teachers and students', *School Effectiveness and School Improvement*, 5, 3, pp.254–71.

Venezky, R. L. and Winfield, L. F. (1979) *Schools That Succeed Beyond Expectations in Teaching Reading*, Newark, DE: University of Delaware.

Vermeulen, C. J. (1987) 'De effectiviteit van onderwijs bij zeventien Rotterdamse stimuleringsscholen' [Educational effectiveness in seventeen educational priority schools in Rotterdam], *Pedagogische Studien*, 64, pp.49–58.

Virgilio, I. (1987) 'An examination of the relationships among school effectiveness and teacher effectiveness in elementary and junior high schools', unpublished doctoral dissertation, University of New Orleans.

Virgilio, I., Teddlie, C. and Oescher, J. (1991) 'Variance and context differences in teaching at differentially effective schools', *School Effectiveness and School Improvement*, 2, 2, pp.152–68.

Voogt, J. C. (1986) 'Werken aan onderwijs verbetering', in Reints, A. and Voogt, J. C. (eds) *Naar Beter Onderwijs*, Tilburg: Uitgeverij Zwijsen.

Voogt, J. C. (1988) *Systematic Analysis for School Improvement (SAS)*, in Hopkins, D. (ed.) (1988) Doing School Based Review, Leuven, Belgium: ACCO.

Voogt, J. C. (1989) *Scholen Doorgelicht; een Studie over Schooldiagnose*, Academisch proefschrift, De Lier: ABC.

Voogt, J. C. (1994) *Instrument voor Schooldiagnose*, Utrecht: APS.

Walberg, H. J. (1976) 'Psychology of learning environments: Behavioral, structural, or perceptual?', in Shulman, L. S. (ed.) *Review of Research in Education* (Volume 4) Itasca, IL: F.E. Peacock, American Educational Research Association.

Walberg, H. J. (1984) 'Improving the productivity of America's schools', *Educational Leadership*, 41, pp.19–30.

Walberg, H. J. (1991) 'Improving school science in advanced and developing countries', *Review of Educational Research*, 61, 1, pp.25–69.

References

Walberg, H. J., Schille, D. and Haertle, G. (1979) 'The quiet revolution in education research', *Phi Delta Kappan*, **5**, pp.179–83.

Waldrop, M. M. (1993) *Complexity, the Emerging Science at the Edge of Order and Chaos*, London: Viking.

Walker, D. D. (1976) *The IEA Six Subject Survey: An Empirical Study of Education in Twenty One Countries*, New York: John Wiley.

Walker, D. F. and Schaffarzick, J. (1974) 'Comparing curricula', *Review of Educational Research*, **44**, 1, pp.83–112.

Wang, M. C., Haertel, G. D. and Walberg, H. J. (1993) 'Toward a knowledge base for school learning', *Review of Educational Research*, **63**, 3, pp.249–94.

Wasserman, S. and Faust, K. (1994) *Social Network Analysis: Methods and Applications*, Cambridge: Cambridge University Press.

Watkins, J. F. (1968) 'The OCDQ – An application and some implications', *Educational Administration Quarterly*, **4**, pp.46–60.

Webb, E. J., Campbell, D. T., Schwartz, R. D., Sechrest, L. and Grove, J. B. (1981) *Nonreactive Measures in the Social Sciences*, Boston, MA: Houghton Mifflin.

Weber, G. (1971) *Inner City Children Can Be Taught to Read: Four Successful Schools*, Washington, DC: Council for Basic Education.

Weeda, W. C. (1982) 'Beheersingslesen: Her model getoesst in de malitijk' [Mastery Learning: testing of the model in educational practice], Dissertation, Tilburg: University of Tilburg.

Wehlage, G. (1983) *Effective Programs for the Marginal High School Student*, Bloomington, IN: Phi Delta Kappan.

Wehlage, G., Rutter, R. and Turnebaugh, A. (1987) 'A program model for at-risk high school students', *Educational leadership*, **44**, 6, pp.70–3.

Weick, K. E. (1976) 'Educational organisations as loosely coupled systems', *Administrative Science Quarterly*, **21**, pp.1–19.

Weide, M. G. (1995) *Effectif Basisonderwijs voor Allochtone Leerlingen* [Effective elementary education for ethnic minority students], Groningen: RION.

Weiler, H. N. (1990) 'Comparative perspectives on educational decentralisation: an exercise in contradiction?', *Educational Evaluation and Policy Analysis*, **12**, pp.443–8.

Werf, M. P. C. van der (1995) *The Educational Priority Policy in the Netherlands: Content, Implementation and Outcomes*, The Hague: SVO.

Werf, M. P. C. van der, and Tesser, P. (1989) 'The effects of educational prorities on children from lower income and ethnic minorities', in Creemers, B. P. M. and Reynolds, D. (eds) *School Effectiveness and School Improvement*, Cardiff: University of Cardiff.

West, D. J. and Farrington, D. (1973) *Who Becomes Delinquent?*, London: Heinemann.

West, M. D. and Hopkins, D. (1995) 'Re-conceptualising school effectiveness and school improvement', Paper presented to the European Educational Research Association, Bath.

Westbury, I. (1992) 'Comparing American and Japanese achievement: Is the United States really a low achiever?', in *Educational Researcher*, June/July, pp.18–24.

Westerhof, K. (1992) 'On the effectiveness of teaching: Direct versus indirect instruction', *School Effectiveness and School Improvement*, **3**, 3, pp.204–15.

White, J. and Barber, M. (1997) *Perspectives on School Effectiveness and School Improvement*, Bedford Way Papers, London: Institute of Education.

Wiley, D. E. and Harnischferger, A. (1974) 'Quantity of schooling and exposure to instruction, major educational vehicles', *Educational Researcher*, pp.7–12.

Willett, J. B. (1988) 'Questions and answers in the measurement of change', in Rothkopf, E. Z. (ed.) *Review of Research in Education*, **15**, Washington, DC: American Educational Research Association, pp.345–422.

Willis, P. (1976) *Learning to Labour*, Aldershot: Gower Press.

Willms, J. D. (1984) 'School effectiveness within the public and private sectors: An evaluation', *Evaluation Review*, 8, pp.113–35.

Willms, J. D. (1985a) 'Catholic-school effects on academic achievement: New evidence from the high school and beyond follow-up study', *Sociology of Education*, 58, 2, pp.98–114.

Willms, J. D. (1985b) 'The balance thesis: Contextual effects of ability on pupils' O-grade examination results', *Oxford Review of Education*, 11, 1, pp.33–41.

Willms, J. D. (1986) 'Social class segregation and its relationship to pupils' examination results in Scotland', *American Sociological Review*, 51, 2, pp.224–41.

Willms, J. D. (1987) 'Differences between Scottish educational authorities in their educational attainment', *Oxford Review of Education*, 13, 2, pp.211–32.

Willms, J. D. (1992) *Monitoring School Performance: A Guide for Educators*, London: Falmer Press.

Willms, J. D. and Cuttance, P. (1985c) 'School effects in Scottish secondary schools', *British Journal of Sociology of Education*, 6, 3, pp.289–305.

Willms, J. D. and Kerckhoff, A. C. (1995) 'The challenge of developing new educational indicators', *Educational Evaluation and Policy Analysis*, 17, 1, pp.113–31.

Willms, J. D. and Raudenbush, S. W. (1989) 'A longitudinal hierarchical linear model for estimating school effects and their stability', *Journal of Educational Measurement*, 26, 3, pp.209–32.

Willower, D. J., Eidell, T. L. and Hoy, W. A. (1967) 'The school and pupil control ideology', Monograph No. 24, University Park, PA: Pennsylvania State University.

Wilson, B. C. and Corcoran, T. B. (1988) *Successful Secondary Schools*, London: Falmer Press.

Wimpelberg, R. K. (1987) 'Managerial images and school effectiveness', *Administrator's Notebook*, 32, 4, pp.1–4.

Wimpelberg, R. (1993) 'Principals' roles in stable and changing schools', in Teddlie, C. and Stringfield, S. (eds) *Schools Make a Difference: Lessons Learned from a 10-year Study of School Effects*, New York: Teachers College Press, pp.165–86.

Wimpelberg, R., Teddlie, C. and Stringfield, S. (1989) 'Sensitivity to context: The past and future of effective schools research', *Educational Administration Quarterly*, 25, 1, pp.82–107.

Winkler, D. R. (1975) 'Educational achievement and school peer group composition', *Journal of Human Resources*, 10, pp.189–205.

Wisler, C. E. (1974) 'Partitioning the explained variance in a regression analysis', in Mayeske, G. W., Beaton, A. E., Wisler, C. E., Okada, T. and Cohen, W. M. *Technical Supplement to 'A study of the Achievement of Our Nation's Students'*, Washington, DC: US Department of Health, Education, and Welfare.

Witte, J. F. and Walsh, D. J. (1990) 'A systematic test of the effective schools model', *Educational Evaluation and Policy Analysis*, 12, pp.188–212.

Wittrock, M. (ed.) (1986) *Third Handbook of Research on Teaching*, New York: Macmillan.

Witziers, B. (1992) *Coordinatie Binnen Scholen voor Voortgazet Onderwijs*, Academisch proefschrift, Enschede: z.u.

Wolf, R. G. (1977) *Achievement in America*, New York: Teachers College Press.

Wong, G. Y. and Mason, W. M. (1985) 'The hierarchical logistic regression model for multilevel analysis', *Journal of the American Statistical Association*, 80, pp.513–24.

Woodhouse, B. (1996) *Multilevel Modelling Applications: A Guide for Users of MLN*, London: Institute of Education.

Woodhouse, G. and Goldstein, H. (1988) 'Educational performance indicators and LEA league tables', *Oxford Review of Education*, 14, 3, pp.301–20.

Woodhouse, G., Yang, M., Goldstein, H. and Rasbash, J. (1996) 'Adjusting for measurement error in multilevel analysis', *Journal of the Royal Statistical Society*, Series A., 159, 2, pp.201–12.

References

Yelton, B. T., Miller, S. K. and Ruscoe, G. C. (1994) 'The stability of school effects: Comparative path models', Paper presented at the Annual Meeting of the American Educational Research Association, New Orleans, LA.

Young, D. and Fraser, B. (1993) 'Socioeconomic and gender effects on science achievement: An Australian Perspective', *School Effectiveness and School Improvement*, 4, 4, pp.265–89.

Yukl, G. A. (1981) *Leadership in Organizations*, Englewood Cliffs, NJ: Prentice Hall.

Zuzovsky, R. and Aitkin, M. (1990) 'Using a multi-level model and an indicator system in science education to assess the effect of school treatment on student achievement', *School Effectiveness and School Improvement*, 1, 2, pp.121–38.

Index

Note: differing levels of schooling i.e. primary, secondary, elementary, etc. have been omitted due to lack of space and because they also appear throughout.